English game of cricket; comprising a digest of its origin, character, history & progress; together with an expostion of its laws & language

Charles Box

THE

ENGLISH GAME OF CRICKET:

COMPRISING A DIGEST OF ITS

ORIGIN, CHARACTER, HISTORY, AND PROGRESS,

TOGETHER WITH

AN EXPOSITION OF ITS LAWS AND LANGUAGE.

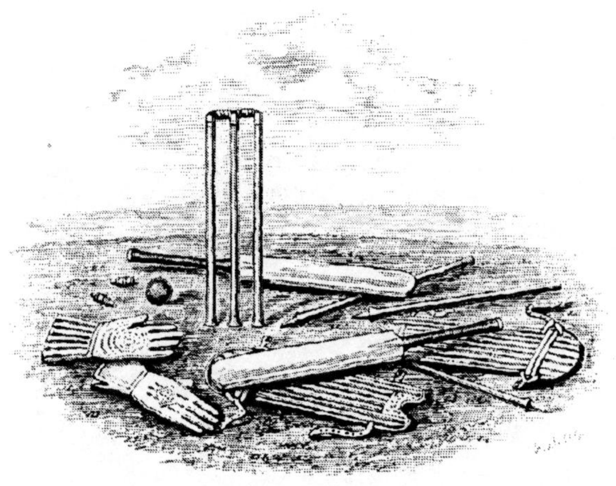

BY CHARLES BOX,

Author of "The Cricketers' Manual," "Reminiscences of Celebrated Players," Essays on the Game, "Songs and Poems," "Theory and Practice of Cricket," &c.

LONDON:
"THE FIELD" OFFICE, 346, STRAND.

1877.

PREFACE.

A DISTINGUISHED writer on rural sports, who flourished in the last century, says "Delectando pariterque monendo" should be the design in sending every book into circulation. It is, however, much to be apprehended or feared that real success in this particular falls to the lot of few. Of late years writers on English pastimes have fully equalled the wants of the public. Hence the increased difficulty in the race of competitors —Who shall be first? Whether it be that more literary men are sportsmen now, or that more sportsmen are literary men than formerly, is a question on which the votaries of sport or letters might probably find plenty of argument to support their respective opinions. With regard to cricket, one thing is certain—that all ranks and conditions of society, either theoretically or practically, participate to some extent in the game—hence the great and increasing diffusion of knowledge developed in one way or another concerning it. Yet, after all, if many things of great importance and interest had not been left unsaid, the contents of this volume would never have found a way into print.

In the compilation hereof one great object has been kept steadily in view —viz., that of proving cricket to be purely of English origin; and in so doing a chapter dealing chiefly in negations became almost a matter of necessity, seeing that in the remote past no positive, or even relative, evidence can be adduced. The process thus adopted is capable of determining once for all that cricket is the invention of the Briton, notwithstanding the learned, as well as the unlearned, attempts to prove the contrary. Obscure, very obscure, are the traces of its origin; and the fragments of information relative to its early growth perplex quite as much as they enlighten. From a few scraps gathered now from this quarter and then from that, a rough idea may be formed how the promoters and patrons of a game—as yet without shape—nourished and brought up the bantling till it attracted notice. Its growth must have been slow; and very few writers who have given attention to the subject have troubled themselves with the task of penetration To acquire knowledge of a country, it is not enough to stand upon the hill top and take a view of the glowing expanse No! To be properly known, it must be explored and surveyed with a care utterly regardless of labour or inconvenience, yea, and if the object sought is below the surface, the choicest faculties of mind and body are indispensable for the purpose, and must therefore be vigorously exercised.

As before intimated, the traces of cricket are very faint and obscure up to the close of the Plantagenet dynasty No attempts at learned writing can therefore succeed with those well versed in the sports of the age to prove that the game under any other name existed. A few cognate facts may be necessary in support of this proposition, but they will be used as sparingly as possible, and condensed into the smallest compass consistent with intelligibility, in order to prevent a ponderous volume. Here and there a lengthy extract has been introduced, chiefly to show what the essential principles of cricket were when the stripling could but just walk alone, and how slightly these have changed up to the present time, when it boasts of a growth as muscular as it is colossal

The drawings are not, as some might suppose, the product of fanciful imaginings, but faithful copies of pictures representing cricket at the time to which they refer The single figures also, of batsmen in various positions or attitudes, are portraits, or intended so to be, of some of the most distinguished players living at the time of this publication Furthermore, it may be well to say that no attempts to relieve the gaunt scores in the early periods of cricket have been made, seeing that their historical character, truth, and interest, would be materially affected by any "touching up."

Errors and imperfections will find their way into print, no matter how the avoidance of such intruders is studied and deprecated, and it is not likely that the volume here submitted has escaped the common lot It is nevertheless hoped they will be few and unimportant, and that the readers who have the sagacity to discover will have the generosity to forgive

If it be asked whether the work is to be regarded as a History of Cricket in the broad sense of the question, the answer is No, and for this simple reason—the bulk of paper necessary for such a purpose would be out of all proportion to the real value of the printed composition Moreover it is far easier to compile a big book, with plenty of materials of a mixed and common order, than to write a compact, readable, and useful one. Chaff is always greater in bulk, though not in density, than the corn it encloses; and something beyond a mere mechanical apparatus is necessary for the seeking out or winnowing. How far these efforts have succeeded in the present attempt to enlarge the circle of cricket literature will be the task of the great arbiter Time to decide.

The plan of the work is a division into twenty-six chapters, most of them independent. Although the number has no mystery about it, like some others that might be named, it was chosen as the number of persons concerned in playing a legitimate match, and also of the weeks usually occupied in the United Kingdom in completing an annual programme. Another convenience is afforded by these divisions: the reader will not have to wade through a quantity of matter foreign to his purpose before arriving at the information sought. It is believed that there is scarcely a point of interest connected with the game left unnoticed, and should the design of the author be accomplished he will feel amply rewarded for the outlay of his time, labour, and research.

CAMBERWELL, Feb. 10th, 1877.

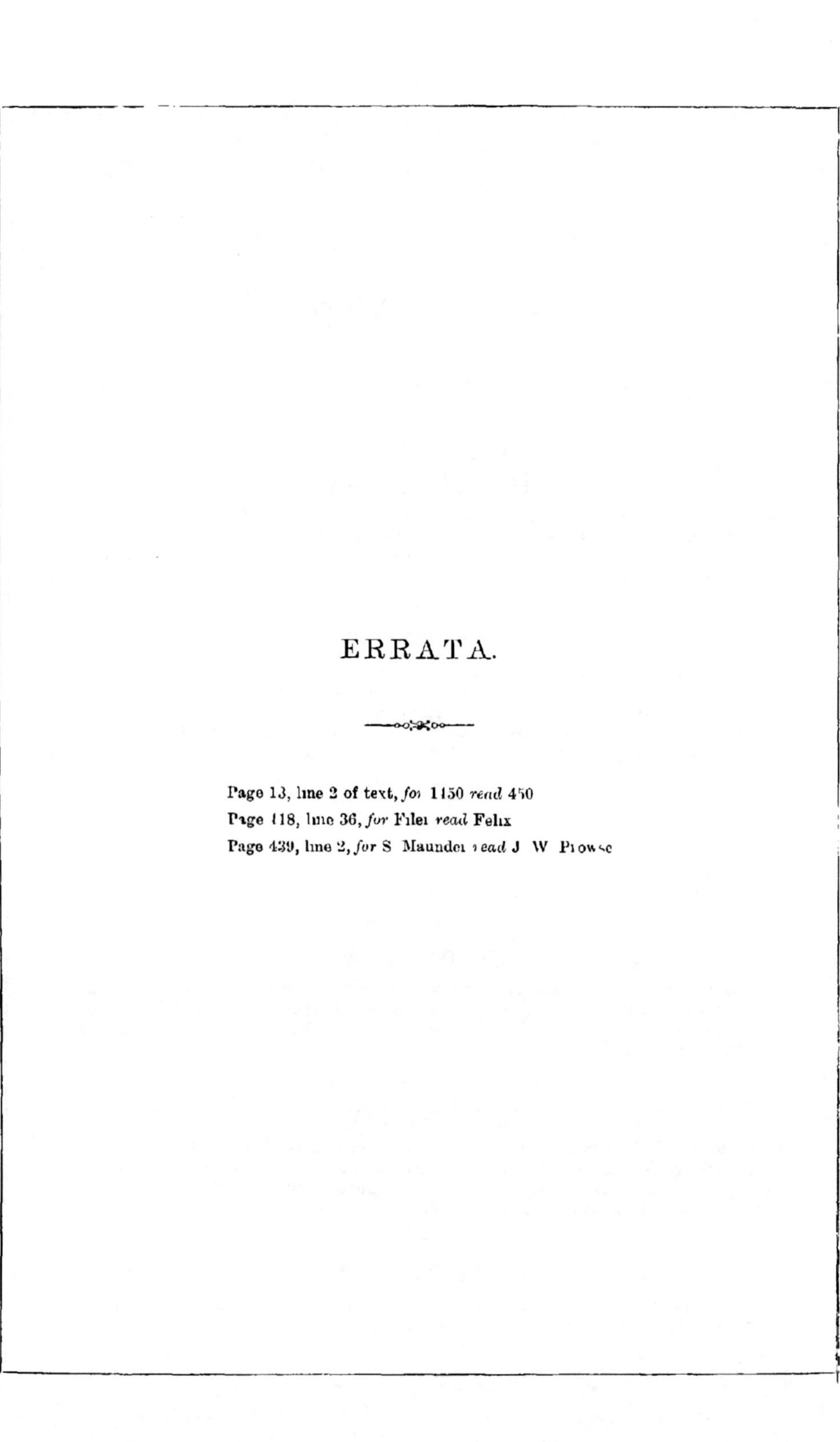

ERRATA.

Page 13, line 2 of text, *for* 1150 *read* 450

Page 418, line 36, *for* Filer *read* Felix

Page 439, line 2, *for* S. Maunder *read* J. W. Prowse

CONTENTS.

CHAPTER I.

INTRODUCTORY.

CHAPTER II.

CHAPTER III

CHAPTER IV.

CHAPTER V

CHAPTER VI.

CHAPTER XX.

INTERCOLONIAL MATCHES (con)

CHAPTER XXI.

SCHOOL AND VILLAGE MATCHES.

CHAPTER XXII.

CURIOSITIES OF CRICKET.

CHAPTER XXIII

CRICKET GROUNDS.

CHAPTER XXIV.

LAWS OF THE GAME.

CHAPTER XXV

POEMS, SONGS, AND BALLADS.

CHAPTER XXVI.

POSTSCRIPT

THE ENGLISH GAME OF CRICKET.

INTRODUCTORY CHAPTER

"Out of monuments, names, wordes, proverbs, traditions, brasses, private records and evidences, fragments of stones, and the like, we doe save and recover somewhat from the deluge of time."—BACON on the "Advancement of Learning," Vol II

ORIGIN OF BALL-PLAY—ITS REMOTE ANTIQUITY—SCARCITY OF INFORMATION ON THE SUBJECT—CLIMATE AND ITS INFLUENCES—INDIAN JUGGLERS AND MOUNTEBANKS—GAMES OF BALL ATTRIBUTED TO THE EGYPTIANS—HEROD THE GREAT, AND THE INTRODUCTION BY HIM OF GREEK AND ROMAN CUSTOMS INTO PALESTINE—NO TRACE OF ANY GAME RESEMBLING CRICKET IN ASSYRIA DURING MR LAYARD'S RESEARCHES—HERODOTUS, XENOPHON, AND CTESIAS SILENT WITH RESPECT TO PERSIA—VARIOUS KINDS OF BALL-PLAY AMONG THE GREEKS—THEIR SACRED GAMES—DISDAIN OF THE ANCIENT GERMANS TO ELABORATE AND SKILFUL PASTIMES—THE SCLAVONIC GROUP FEEBLE IN ATHLETIC GAMES—NATURAL DISPOSITION OF THE CELTS NOT IN HARMONY WITH THE GENIUS OF CRICKET, NOR AS YET THE HIGHLANDERS—PALLONE, THE BALL-PLAY OF THE ITALIANS—ITS POPULARITY—APPARENT TRACES OF EARLY CRICKET IN SPAIN—ORIGIN OF THE GAME REFERRED TO JEU DE MAL BY M DE LA BEDOLLIÈRE—CAUSE OF ITS DEVELOPMENT IN ENGLAND—PROGRESS IN AUSTRALIA, INDIA, AMERICA, AND SOUTH AFRICA—DEVOTION OF THE MODERN GERMANS TO ATHLETIC EXERCISES—THE HUMANIZING AND MANLY CHARACTER OF CRICKET—ENGLAND ITS PARENT THE WORLD ITS FAMILY

THERE are few things more easy to be determined than that cricket is a game entirely and exclusively of English origin, and that there is no game in ancient times or in foreign countries that so closely resembles it as to claim any approach to kindredship Games of ball are of such remote antiquity that they must have existed before the historic period The first child who can enlist another child in sport, say with an acorn, or anything else equally harmless, is an imitator of a game of ball, so that from the earliest times till now there have been millions of antetypes Many fruits when falling ripe from the tree have a rebound, so if the tree stands at a declivity they have a succession of rebounds Here Nature herself is seen playing at ball, and is at once imitated What, also, are the weapons which man, whether in a savage or civilized state spontaneously uses when angry?

His first a stone, then a stick or club Soon as his fierce word is over he takes the stone and plays with it, either by itself or by the aid of the stick, so that both in peace and war the game of ball is in many ways suggested. Round, even rugged, stones would, for a season, satisfy all requirements But after a while artificial balls would take the place of stones, possessing, along with other advantages, the light and charming characteristic of elasticity These few sentences contain the pith of the matter, whatever developments and varieties the game of ball might take

Sources of information touching pastimes are very rare indeed, not only among the Greeks, the Romans, and Orientals, but among all nations and in all countries, and the trustworthy chronicles that can be got at are so lamentably foolish and scant as to defy anything like a fanciful interpretation It is generally admitted that civilization was more ancient in India than in any other land, and that it was from this region of the globe that Egypt was both colonised and civilised Thousands of years ago games of ball, as various as doubtlessly they were ingenious, must have existed in India but they vanished without leaving any historical trace The influence of climate, too, and the moulding of society into castes would gradually rob games of ball, and other games likewise, of the popular character Men, instead of taking part in amusements sat with Oriental indolence to watch the marvellous tricks of professing performers. India has still the most astounding jugglers in the world Delighted by the lascivious songs and dances of the bayaderes and the legerdemain of the magicians, the wealthier natives felt no inclination for active exercise, and the multitude of Druses were too crushed by exhausting toil to find leisure or heart for amusement As cricket is the most scientific of field games, and chess the most scientific of what—for want of a better term—are called table games, and as chess had its birthplace in India—although many credit the Persians with it—it would not be altogether unreasonable to expect to find games in India resembling cricket however barren such expectation might prove. From analogy it is, notwithtanding, probable that such might have at one time existed, but were this conjecture just, it would not affect the independent growth of cricket as a national game in England.

Passing from India to Egypt, a few better materials for forming a judgment come under notice, for the grand monuments of Egypt reveal not only the history of the country, but the whole life of the people The plates in one of the vastest and most famous works on Egypt, that of Sir J Gardner Wilkinson, contain various representations of games of ball which seem to have been special favourites with the ancient Egyptians, but in none of these representations is there any resemblance to the game whose origin has been for ages, and still is, with the public a disputed matter The worthy knight says himself "there is no appearance of anything resembling rackets, nor is the Roman game of striking the ball with the hand represented anywhere in the Egyptian sculptures" No inference, however, can be drawn from this absence, and considering the remote antiquity of these paintings, it is somewhat singular that any should have been preserved to the present period to give an insight into their customs and amusements. Though so much has been well written, and so much yet remains to be written, on ancient Egypt, the pith of the hosts of volumes is, as regards games of ball, contained, doubtlessly, in these passages, which give no glimpse of cricket or of aught having affinity therewith.*

From their long stay in Egypt the Hebrews in all probability adopted some of the games belonging to the country, and among others the games of ball; but neither in the Bible itself nor in the commentators upon it are they presented. The learned Frenchman, Claude Fleury, equally famous as an educator of French princes and as a writer on ecclesiastical history, in his work on the Memoirs of the Israelites, says: "The easy and tranquil life of the Hebrews and the beauty of their country led them into much pleasure, but their enjoyments were simple and unpretending; they consisted almost exclusively of good cheer and music. Their feasts were limited to plain dishes, which they took at home, and their music was still less costly and troublesome, for they could nearly all play an instrument and sing." The aged Barzillai mentions only these two pleasures when declaring he is too old to enjoy life.† In the 32nd chapter of Ecclesiasticus it is said, "A concert of music in a banquet of wine is as a signet of carbuncle set in gold. As a signet of an emerald set in a work of gold, so is the melody of music with pleasant wine." Ulysses, likewise, when coming among the Phœnicians, confessed frankly that he knew no other felicity than a banquet accompanied by music. The same pleasures are alluded to in the reproaches hurled by the Prophet at those by whom these pleasures are abused. But, in addition to excesses at the wine table, crowns of flowers and perfumes, such as were customary among the Greeks, are mentioned. The Hebrews were happiest when taking their repasts in gardens, under trees, and in arbours; for it is natural in hot countries to seek air and the fresh breezes. In accordance with this, their Scripture, when indicating a time of prosperity, says "that everyone ate and drank under his own vine and under his own fig tree"—these being the two fruit trees whose leaves are the largest. There are no traces of games or hunting, which rank among the leading diversions of the present day. As to gaming, the Hebrews appear to have been absolutely ignorant of it, for the very name is not to be found throughout the Scriptures. The chase, whether beasts or birds are concerned, was not altogether unknown among them, but they occupied themselves with the chase less for pleasure than for utility. Either they aimed at enriching their tables, or preserving their cornfields and vineyards from injury. Nets and snares are often spoken of, but dogs or hunting attendants never, even in the case of kings, who would no doubt have rendered themselves odious if they had sported on cultivated ground, or kept animals that caused waste and ruin. Hunting, on a gigantic scale, began in the vast forests and the uncultivated tracks of cold countries.

A worthy Jew, who published an admirable work on Palestine in the French

* See Wilkinson's Manners and Customs of the Ancient Egyptians.

† See 2 Samuel xix. 35.

language not many years ago, says, "that by the traditional law of the Israelites games of chance are strictly forbidden, and that the testimony of those who violated the prohibition could not be received before the tribunals" A few passages from Munk will confirm what Fleury has stated. "The principle pleasures of the ancient Hebrews were feasts and music On festival days the young girls went and danced in the vineyards, and the young men attended their innocent pleasures Often when the labours of the day were over, the Hebrews went and sought recreation on the public spaces situate near the gates of the city There all sorts of affairs were treated of, and there great multitudes always assembled They listened to legal proceedings or to the discourses of prophets and public orators, they conversed on public affairs, or any other subject. Such were the relaxations of persons of ripe age On the other hand, the young gathered themselves together at the gate to play on instruments of music, and to sing According to St Jerome, the prophet Zechariah alludes to a game, or rather a gymnastic exercise, which consisted in a trial of strength to raise to a certain height extremely heavy stones, and the same prophet speaks of boys and girls playing in the streets * A passage in the Book of Job leads to the belief that children were in the habit of playing with tame birds" Compare herewith the poem of Catullus on the sparrow, and "The Captives" of Plautus †

The influence first of Greek, then of Roman civilisation, could not be wholly unfelt in Palestine with regard to games as well as other matters Considerably before the time of Jerome—a well ascertained fact—Herod the Great (great chiefly in wickedness) attempted to introduce Greek and Roman culture and customs But to what extent the habits and thoughts of the people of Palestine were moulded by Greece and Rome history is silent It is evident, however, that if Greek or Roman games of ball found their way into the Holy Land, they could not become transfigured and made more like cricket than those games were in their original form

In the colossal Assyrian monarchy, and others almost as colossal, which sprung up after its overthrow, culture and art attained a remarkable development. The researches of Mr Layard and others summon as it were from the sepulchre of the past, gigantic and fantastic shapes Among these shapes may be such as to impress the mind with the oft-repeated truth, "that amusement is a need of the human heart amid labour, and after sorrow" But even were games of ball as common at Nineveh or at Babylon as at Memphis or Thebes, cricket, or anything bearing the faintest resemblance to it, is most assuredly not one of them

The last of the eight Oriental monarchies was that founded by Cyrus the Great, and destroyed by Alexander, also surnamed the Great, but the history of the celebrated Persian Emperor is wrapt so completely in the mists of fable, that the most searching examiner must grope in vain for solid facts There is no harmonizing Herodotus with Xenophon, nor Xenophon with Ctesias, nor all three with the speculations of compilers such as Rollin, nor with the traditions of the

* Chap VIII, ver 8

† Act V, scenes 4 and 5

modern Persians The work of Xenophon is a moral fiction, a philosophical romance, which has no historical foundation, and has often, very often, led inquirers astray In the narration of Herodotus, though there is plenty of fable, there is still a considerable amount of substantial truth It was, according to Herodotus, when playing at tin games with companions of his own age, and when elected by them king of their pastimes, that Cyrus, by ordering a disobedient playfellow to be beaten, was revealed to Astyages as his grandson Although brought by this incident into the domain of ancient Persian sports, not a ray of light breaks forth, cricket hides its face even here just as obstinately as do the ruins of Persepolis Ancient writers, and especially Herodotus, tell many interesting tales about the Scythians their origin, career, and final disappearance from the historic scene In the Scythian cloud, or chaos, it would, therefore, be as fruitless to try to grasp a cricket bat or ball as it would be the wires of an electric telegraph Of Phœnicia, Palmyra, Numidia, Carthage, and other states which have played a more or less important part in that human drama which never ends, it is hardly necessary to examine farther, for a long array of names could neither infuse life nor light into an absolute blank

On approaching Greece and Rome, a few luminous streaks dart across the dense atmosphere Games of every sort crowd around, those of ball, though not foremost, stand out prominently Among the Greeks few games, except for children, were merely pastimes, they had a moral, religious, and patriotic purpose The Isthmian and other national games were a worship of Beauty, still more than athletic displays, they helped to make more important whatever gave Greece its place apart on the earth As so much has been said on the exalted vocation of the national games of Greece, it is not needful to refer to the subject at any length Their games of ball have been made known by Greek writers, and handed down to the present generation in such works as Smith's valuable dictionaries of Greek and Roman antiquities

The first was the *Ourania*, which derived its name from *Ouranos*, the sky, the heaven, the firmament A clumsy word, but as accurate a translation as possible of *Ourania* would be *skyey* In this game the ball was thrown up into the air, and each of the persons who played strove to catch it before it fell to the ground The second game was called *Epicoinos*, signifying common mixed, promiscuous It was, in fact, football, played much in the same way as at the present time, a great number of persons were divided into two opposing parties It was a great favourite at Sparta The third bore the title *Ephetinda*. The peculiarity of this game consisted in the person who had the ball pretending to throw it to a certain individual, and while the latter was expecting it, suddenly turning round and throwing it to another The fourth was called the *Harpaston*, in Latin *Harpastum*, the *snatching* game, in which, as appears from the etymology of the name, and also from the statement of Galen—a ball was thrown among the players, each of whom endeavoured to get possession of it, the exercise seems to have required a great deal of bodily exertion In another Latin dictionary the word Harpestum is said to mean a ball of cloth or leather stuffed with flocks, which several endeavour to catch at once There is also an allusion to this game as a *dusty* one in Martial The Harpaston, which he calls "pulverulentum," may mean either the ball, or by a poetic licence the game itself

The fifth was the *Aporraxis*, which may be rendered into English, "The throwing off" In this the player threw the ball to the ground with such force that it rebounded, when he struck it down again with the palm of his hand, and so continued to do many times, the number of times being counted. At a game of exactly the same sort every English schoolboy is no doubt familiar There have been other amusements with the ball by boys, for one is mentioned by Plato, in which the conquered was called *ass*, and the conqueror *king* but it is not described Here, again, it is necessary to state that no likeness to cricket in any of the pre-named games can be traced Mr Edwards, in his translation from the Greek of Archias, says

> "Four sacred games illustrious Greece are thine,
> Of human passions two, and two divine
> Jove's mighty hand the Olympic *olive* guides,
> Apollo o'er the Pyrrhic *palm* presides,
> Nemæan *parsley* is Ophite's care,
> And th' Isthmian *pine* Palemon's envied share!"

Whether in imitation of the Greeks, or from native invention and inspiration, a learned writer says —"Among the Romans the game of ball was played in various ways *Pila* was used in a general sense for any kind of ball, but the Roman balls were of three sorts, the *pila*, in its narrower sense, a small ball, the *follis*, a great one filled with air, and the *paganica*, smaller than the *follis* and larger than the *pila* The latter seems to have been chiefly patronized The most popular was that played by three persons standing in the form of a triangle, and hence it was called the *trigon*, or the *pila trigonalis* Skilful players prided themselves upon catching and throwing the ball with the left hand Besides meaning a ball, *follis* also signified a bag, purse, and scrip of leather, and a pair of bellows Hence it was generally used to indicate something of considerable size This is proved by the adverb *follitim*, which is derived from it the literal English equivalent of which is "by the large bag" There is a passage in one of the plays of Plautus, in which *follitim* is contrasted with *peratim*, and the sense is "not to play at small game, not to cheat for pence but pounds Every scholar knows that *pagus* means "a village, a tribe, or division of country and people, a canton, or district" *Paganus*, a country man, a peasant, anyone not a soldier It has been conjectured that the Christians called the Gentiles Pagani, or Pagans, because they did not come under the banner of Christ The word *Paganicus*, taken as an adjective, signifies "of or belonging to the country, pertaining to the peasantry as contra-distinguished from the soldiery" The game of ball, therefore, in which the *Paganica pila* was used may originally have had some foreign rural characteristics, while the others were more of an inborn kind

Trigon, and *trigonalis* derived from the Greek *trigonos*, means a three-sided court for playing as well as the play itself It was in battering that the Romans made use in sport of the *trigonalis pila*, and probably they aimed at warming themselves by exercise after they had taken the battery In Rich's Illustrated Companion to the Latin Dictionary and the Greek Lexicon, under Pila, five sorts of ball are described

The Pila Picta, a painted ball,

„ Vitrum, a glass ball,

„ Mattiaca, a pomade ball, used by the crudus of Rome and by the young men of fashion It was of a light and fair colour It had its name from the town of Mattiacum, where the best was manufactured, and whence it was imported. The Mattiaca Pilæ is sometimes described as soap or washing balls

Finally, Pila is introduced in the form of an effigy or guy, made out of old pieces of cloth and stuffed with hay, employed to try the temper of animals, bulls and buffaloes when baited, or to infuriate them if they appeared tame and impassive—a practice still continued at Molu on certain festival occasions, at which it is not unusual to bait buffaloes in the main street All these definitions and explanations show how immensely diversified the import that Pila assumed, they do not, however, traverse the wide domain of pastimes after all. But the Romans did not merely play at ball, they watched the professional jugglers accomplishing marvels therewith, as may be seen from the following account by Rich of the Palarius —"One who exhibits feats of dexterity with a number of balls, similar to the Indian juggler, by throwing them up with both hands, catching them on and making them rebound from the inner joint of the elbow, the leg, the forehead, and the instep, so that they keep playing in a continuous circle round his person without falling to the ground, as minutely described by Chambers in his "Astronomica," and as exhibited on a diptych in the museum of Verona The player is performing with seven balls in a handsome building, with a number of boys and other persons surrounding him Two figures, in precisely the same attitude and with the same number of balls each, are sculptured in a sepulchral marble in the collection at Mantua In what sense soever Pila is understood, and after what fashions the Romans may have amused themselves with games of ball, it is obvious that the "conquerors of the world" were as unacquainted as the ingenious Greek with any pastime having a similitude to cricket in the slenderest manner or degree

The tribes of ancient Germany are known to all generations by means of Latin authors, especially Tacitus as well as by a prodigious mass of traditions, but their stalwart men were too busy hunting wild beasts in the forest, or rushing to conflict with hostile hosts, to be in the mood for inventing an elaborate and scientific game like cricket—a game which could only be the slow growth of tranquil times Of the ancient Scandinavians, who were cognate in race to the Germans, nearly the same thing may be said from the moment when history first mentions them to the time when, as Norsemen, they were devastators and vanquishers on every coast accessible to their bold exploits * That they were desperate gamblers is a familiar fact, and,

* See Holmberg on the Manners and Customs of the Norsemen

compared with war, the chase, and the like, cricket would not by any means consort with their taste

In the Sclavonic group of nations the Polish and Russian people are the principal members There seems always to have existed a passionate yearning for excitement and amusement, but for athletic games the feeling appears to have been of a very languid character, for many games the climate was not suitable In addition to the gorgeous ceremonies attendant on religion and the village festivals, music, dancing, and drinking were the chief delights, and these had more charm for the multitude than athletic games could present Among the higher classes, gambling held, and still holds, a powerful sway A recent work by "A Patriotic Pole' says "Of all games the most fatal was faro, which was played with the maddest excess towards the close of the last century. Played with French cards, it found entrance everywhere—into family circles, into halls of high society, and even into the royal castle Often the stakes amounted to a hundred thousand florins A single night devoured palaces, estates—yea, whole fortunes All these debts were paid with the utmost exactness, for when the feeling of honour did not suffice, which was rare, the tribunals permitted goods to be seized for obligations contracted at the gaming table' Seeking stimulation of the wildest sort, both within doors and without, the Sclavonic tribes would laugh at cricket as childish or stupid if it had been brought before them, except as a vague tradition from England, which assuredly it never was

The grandest race which migrated from the East to seek a home in Europe was the Celtic, the grandest and the most unfortunate Two of the things which characterised the Celts were intense melancholy and the yearning for tumultuous emotion With neither one nor the other could a steady, solid, prosaic game like cricket harmonize The most remarkable descendants and representatives of the Celts are the Highlanders of Scotland, but the games of the Highlanders, which are probably modified forms of ancient Celtic, are chiefly displays of individual strength and skill, and as such contrast to English games, but not till the present century did cricket cross the Tweed, and it is not yet in Scotland much more than a tolerated intruder

The savage expends whatever ingenuity he may possess on his war instruments and war canoes, and he is indifferent to pastimes not made gloomy by flood nor foul by barbarity Games of ball, therefore, and consequently the wildest pursuit of games of ball, cricket, which requires profound and prolonged calculations, and comprehensive combinations, it would be vain to seek for among the savages of the Pacific, or in fact among any others All men cannot be naturally mathematicians, and yet they are practically so The boomerang of the Australian savage, for instance, is a marvel of mathematical adroitness Between, however, the simple mathematics of the savage and the complex, the gulf is deep and wide, and it is to the complex that cricket in one of its leading characteristics belongs

From this rapid glance at ancient, as well as at modern countries, it will be seen that from the most civilized to the most savage the same silence is preserved with respect to cricket In fact, not the faintest analogy is anywhere encountered

The conclusion of this is irresistibly enforced, that cricket is pre-eminently an English game,—English in its origin, English in its character,—just as the vigorous game of curling is entirely Scottish in its attributes, and just as almost every nation has some pastime or pastimes peculiar to itself though not perhaps national games properly so called

Strutt, in commencing his essay on games of ball, says "I have appropriated this chapter to such of them as are or have been and are practised in the fields and open places The most ancient amusement of this kind is distinguished with us by the name of hand ball, and is—if Homer may be accredited—coeval with the destruction of Troy. Herodotus attributes the invention of the ball to the Lydians, succeeding writers have affirmed that the head of a family of distinction named Anagalla, a native of Corcyra, was the first who made a ball for the purpose of pastime, which she presented to Nausicaa, the daughter of Alcinous, King of Phæacia, and at the same time taught her the use of it This piece of history is partly derived from Homer, who introduces the Princess of Corcyra with her maidens amusing themselves at hand ball

> O'er the green mead the sporting virgins play
> (Their shining veils unbound) along the skies,
> Tost and retost, the ball incessant flies *

Homer has restricted this pastime to the young maidens of Corcyra, at least he has not mentioned the practice of it by men, in times posterior to the poet the game of hand ball was indiscriminately played by both sexes"

After all, this learned talk on the part of the excellent Strutt, must be considered as superlatively small It is ridiculous to regard fables and poetic fancies as a test of historical data Hand ball so naturally arises from the throwing of stones, or other things harmless, that games of ball must have arisen of themselves wherever there were children at play, and wherever one man lifted something to fling at another, either in frolic or in anger This being granted, and the intensely, nay, the exclusively, English character of cricket admitted, it may be asked why the English people possess the only field game of a truly scientific type In the first place the English are fonder than other nations of athletic games More have been practised in England than elsewhere, and with an absolute and joyous oblivion, for the time, of all social distinctions Patricians and plebeians have mingled together, plebeians and patricians played together, thus giving to pastimes of this character a degree of popularity not otherwise easily attainable, and certainly not accompanied by refining influences

The Italians have recently introduced into this country the ball play known as "Pallone." This holds almost as high a position in Italy as cricket does in England Its origin is traceable to high antiquity Plautus mentions it, so also does Martial. The game is played with a large ball, which is struck backwards and forwards on a level floor, similar to tennis; the area or locality in which it

* Pope's "Odyssey," Book 5

takes place strongly resembles our tennis courts. The great claim of pallone to the admiration of Englishmen is its athletic and manly character. In fact, on this score it has been termed "the game of giants." The ball used weighs twelve ounces, and the "bracciale," or wooden instrument with which it is struck, and which is held in one hand, weighs no less than four pounds; the usual distance to which it is struck is from two hundred and fifty to three hundred feet, and from fifty to one hundred feet in height. It is stated by Dr. Fisher, the author of an excellent work on the subject, that the perspiration induced by the exertion is so profuse that each player constantly holds a napkin in his left hand for the purpose of wiping the perspiration from his face.

Not long since a gentleman travelling in Spain became very elate on the supposed discovery, among some old brasses and books, of the real origin of cricket in that country, but on examination—and that a very slight one—neither the engraving, the letterpress revealing its meaning, nor the musty books,* have anything whatever to do with the subject. Unfortunately the taste of Spaniards, as a rule, runs in a contrary direction to that derived from the pursuit of cricket. Their diversions are, in fact, of such a character that Englishmen not only deplore, but execrate. * * * Nor was this the only attempt about the same time made to deprive England of the honour of its nationality. "Cricket," says M. de la Bédollière, "is nothing but a variety of the old French *jeu de mail*." I have often seen varieties of the *jeu de mail* played both in France and Italy, and even in Spain, but somehow or other it never struck me that I was looking on at the origin of cricket." Against this theory a language has to be found—a strong proof that cricket is not of French origin. At present any attempt to write of it in its native idiom would either produce a string of barbarisms, most distasteful to French ears, or else the tamest of paraphrases. Moreover, the French mind at present seems almost hopelessly bewildered in the attempt to distinguish between the sense, sound, and pronunciation of cricket and wicket (both of break-jaw difficulty in utterance to Frenchmen). Probably it may come right in time, and a language will be either framed or familiarized in the best, if not the only, way it can be, viz., by practice and custom.

Usus quem penes arbitrium est.

In the meantime M. de la Bédollière would be conferring a great benefit in provincial towns by the introduction of cricket in place of the eternal *deux billiards* and dominoes, and draw his countrymen to the open ground from the hot and often foul café, and thereby improve both their moral and social condition to a far nobler extent than the *Society d'Encouragement* has the breed of French horses. M. Kervigan, in his work entitled "L'Anglais à Paris" (1866), thus describes cricket:—"Two (or more) players armed with bats like harlequins, but three or four centimètres thick, stand opposite one another at a distance of from fifty to seventy paces, more or less, according to their skill. Behind them are planted two stakes, three feet high. Two little sticks, *appellés wicket,* are placed across the top

* Oviedo, lib. 4, chap. 2; Herrera, lib. 3, chap. 4.

of the stakes. Finally, there is a wooden ball covered with leather about the size of a large orange, and the skill consists in hurling the ball by means of the bat, so that it may strike the stakes of the adversary, which one is assured of having done when one sees the wicket fall."

The scientific development of cricket is referable in a great degree to the countenance and support received at public schools and universities. Classic culture and mathematical knowledge, though not strictly essential, did much in refining the coarse elements which formed part and parcel of the game, and this, too, without losing its popular attributes. While many of the old English games show signs of decadence, cricket every year gains in strength and dominion, not only in the United Kingdom, but wherever the British banner waves. Both commercially and otherwise, Australia is beginning to claim a leading part in the affairs of the world, and New Zealand—or as the natives more beautifully call it, Ingarama—is advancing as rapidly, if not with such brilliant strides, as its neighbour. In the North of America and in the South of Africa, too, England's sons and daughters are creating homes for themselves as happy, if not in some respects happier, than those they left. England's grandest dependency, India, has no reason to be ashamed of a bondage which is too mild to be felt, and if it gives many benefits to the protecting power, it receives more in return. But while England's greatness across oceans and continents is expanding, England's famous national game is sure to be one among the many necessary and indisputable accompaniments. No true Englishman can behold, without deep emotion, this curious and astonishing spectacle. It reminds him of the influence which his country, in its colonisations and its conquests, has since gained as much by its gymnastic exercises as by its genius, its arts, and its arms. The most marvellous of military expeditions was that of Alexander the Great to the East. It brought opposites together and commenced that vast interchange of productions and ideas between East and West which is so momentous. But it was in the representation of Greece in its games, as well as in its valour and glory, that Alexander stamped so profound an impress of himself, and the national became a popular hero down to the middle ages. The games of the Romans, especially the Circensian Games, were even worse, more bloody and monstrous, they excited the execration of mankind, and the plans of barbarians crushed Rome, "the wicked and the proud." Just as the games of Greece extended and established the sway of the kingdom, the games of Rome hastened its downfall. Since the beginning of the present century the Germans have devoted considerable attention to gymnastic exercises, but they possess little good in themselves, and as a training for martial deeds cannot be properly called games. Germans often cut a sorry figure when attempting to amuse themselves. A brief sojourn in Paris or in any French town where the inhabitants have an extravagant fondness for amusements, and any one may see at a glance that there is no resemblance in any of them to the sturdy English games—certainly not to cricket.

Seeing that the world outside the British Isles has been hitherto a stranger to the "manly and noble game," it may not be altogether amiss to inquire in what its lasting greatness consists. It is certainly a charming recreation, though to some excitable and quick temperaments its movements may not seem rapid or varied enough. It is a perfect physical discipline; an admirable moral training. It is food to the patriotic conviction, and fire to the patriotic soul. From its measured character it must be so, taking into account the laws which regulate it. Even down to the minutest point it is in harmony with those conservative tendencies and habits which are as eminently English as the warm love of freedom is English. Two of the things which a nation should be most ambitious of cherishing are manliness and humanity; such as the old Douglases aimed by their motto at being —"Tender and true." It cannot be manly without being humane; nor humane without being manly. Under the manifold relations in which cricket may be met, it must always be regarded as a school of pity as well as of manliness. Let cricket be viewed as a mode of warfare; cricketers the bravest of the brave, magnanimous to offenders, and forgetful of social differences in the feeling that cricket is an English game, and such a game that all others having any claim to nationality must be dimmed in comparison with it, if they do not suffer a total eclipse.

CHAPTER II.

ORIGIN AND PROGRESS.

When yet thou wast a grovelling puling chit,
Thy bones not fashioned and thy joints not knit,
The Roman taught thy stubborn knee to bow,
Though twice a Cæsar could not bend thee now.
* * * * * *
He brought thy land a blessing when he came,
He found thee savage and he left thee tame.—*Cowper.*

CONDITION OF THE BRITON ON THE FINAL DEPARTURE OF THE ROMANS—DARK PART OF ENGLISH HISTORY—AMUSEMENTS OF THE SAXONS AND DANES—CHIEF SPORTS IN THE REIGN OF EDWARD III.—SIR THOMAS ELYOT'S LIST OF GAMES IN THE TIME OF HENRY VIII.—PUNY DIVERSIONS DURING THE LONG REIGN OF ELIZABETH—ROWLAND, THE POLITICAL PAMPHLETEER—EARLY MENTION OF THE WORD "CRICKET"—BOOK OF SPORTS (JAMES I.)—FIRST MENTION OF CRICKET AS A GAME IN ANY DICTIONARY—THE REIGN OF THE STUARTS NOT FAVOURABLE TO IT—BETTER PROSPECTS ON A CHANGE OF DYNASTY—ANOTHER MENTION OF CRICKET—BURTON'S ANATOMY—THEORIES RESPECTING THE BASIS OF THE GAME—A DOCUMENT REVEALING THE PRACTICE OF THE GAME AT GUILDFORD IN THE TIME OF ELIZABETH—REV. THOMAS WILSON AND THE "PROPHANE" TOWN OF MAIDSTONE—NOTICE OF THE GAME IN 1685—ADVANCE IN THE EARLY PART OF THE 18TH CENTURY—SUPPORT GIVEN TO IT BY THE BETTER CLASSES OF SOCIETY—LAWS FRAMED FOR THE GOVERNMENT OF THE GAME—FIRST RECORDED CHALLENGE OF KENT TO PLAY ALL ENGLAND—A LAW SUIT RESULTING THEREFROM—CHARACTER OF CRICKET AND THE BALL REVIEWED IN A LETTER TO ROGER GALE—THE PREVALENCE OF GAMBLING, AND ITS EFFECTS—REBUKES—LOVE'S POEM—OLD ENGRAVINGS—GUTHRIE'S DEFINITION OF CRICKET—THE GAMBLING SPIRIT OF THE AGE AGAIN BROUGHT UNDER NOTICE—FIRST SET OF PRINTED RULES—PRIMITIVE STYLE OF SCORING—POEM RECITED AT MERCHANT TAYLOR'S SCHOOL—VISIT OF GEORGE III. AND HIS QUEEN TO A MATCH, ETC.

ADMITTING the generally accepted account of the departure of the Romans to be strictly true, upwards of 1450 years of the Christian era had now trickled into the ocean of time. All early history of the Briton, and the management of affairs when left to himself, is so imperfectly chronicled that it is next to impossible to draw any satisfactory view of his state and condition. Poets, for prize themes, have often found in him a capital subject for the outflow of a vivid imagination and odd conceits. Still centuries roll on and on without affording the faintest historical equivalent as to the moral and social progress made. Dynastic changes, doubtless, among such an unenlightened community, would check rather than assist the advance of literary intelligence. The invasion of Cerdic, after a century of self rule, and even for

300 years subsequently—i e, up to the time when Alfred assumed the reins of sovereignty—is little better than a blank, and to occupy this dark part of British history with the fictions of romance and the tales of improbabilities would be an affront to common sense It is well known that the natives were reduced to great extremities, soon after the departure of the Romans, by the ravages of the Picts and Scots Moreover, the manners of the Saxons were tinctured with all the ferocity attendant upon a warlike, turbulent, and illiterate nation They were, in fact, entirely unacquainted with the sciences, and ignorant even of the elements of literature; devoid, too, of the slightest knowledge of the polite arts, and far from being conversant with the useful ones But it is not intended to go so far back as the Heptarchy for a starting point to prove either by negation or affirmation the paternity of cricket, seeing that England for century after century figured but dimly on the page of the world's history Equally vain is the search for much needed information in the middle ages, as the dawn of intelligence broke so slowly The amusements of the Anglo-Saxons and Danes were chiefly three· martial exercises, rural sports, and domestic games War being the employment of both Saxons and Danes, the chief of their amusements consisted in athletic exercises, such as running, wrestling, and fighting, all of which tended to improve their bodily strength, and accustom them betimes to warlike pursuits, and also to endure the fatigues attendant upon them Martial exercises and mock fights were so delightful to the Danes that they conceived them to be the chief diversions they should enjoy in a future state, when their souls were received by Odin into his seat of glory These martial games were the origin of the tournaments which were so famous and frequent in succeeding ages In the year 1341 mention is made of a tournament given by Edward III. in honour of the young noblemen of Gascoigne, whom he had trained up in feats of war, on this occasion "the lords and knights exercised themselves in martial feats, and many fair ladies and virgins of prime quality diverted the whole assembly with their songs and dances" The sports and pastimes of the youth partook also of the exercises and usages of chivalry, although after a somewhat coarse fashion They fought with clubs and bucklers, they practised running at the quintain; and when frost set in they would go upon the ice and tilt at one another with poles in imitation of lances in a joust In time chivalry lost its primitive spirit, and many exercises calculated to develop muscular strength were abandoned to the "meaner sort," who, not having the means, nor probably the inclination, to imitate their betters in mental culture, readily aped them in their vices, resorting to games and recreations that promoted idleness, dissipation, and gambling.

The Wars of the Roses also had their influence on the practice of tilts, for real battles afforded little time and less disposition to indulge in the mockery of war, and what had once been regarded as a valuable school of war and of all knightly accomplishments, had now degenerated into a tawdry and unmeaning game Sir Thomas Elyot, in his "Gouvernour," speaking of exercises in the time of Henry VIII for students, recommends deambulations, or moderate walking, labouring with poises made of lead, or rather metal called in Latin *alteres*, lifting or throwing the heavy stone or bar, playing at tennis, and divers semblable exercises Some of these are explained in another part of the book, but there is not the slightest allusion to cricket During the long reign of Elizabeth the instincts of the people for sports manifested themselves in a variety of funny pastimes, not worthy the designation of a game, but which, nevertheless, seem to have adapted themselves to the tastes and mental calibre of the people Records are still extant of the diversions most common *Ex uno disce omnes* That selected for illustration is taken from one of those curious little tracts which the commentators of Shakespeare have occasionally called to their assistance It certainly is an amusing enumeration of the sports prevalent in the reign of the queen just mentioned According to some authorities, the author was Samuel Rowlands, a ' powerful poetical pamphleteer," and who wrote thirty-seven epigrams and satires "The Letting of Humour's Blood in the Head Vaine with a new moused danced by seven satyrs upon the bottome of Diogenes Table, imprinted in London by W White, 1611"

Man, I dare challenge thee to throw the sledge,
To jumpe or leape over ditch or hedge,
To wrestle, play at stooleball, or to runne,
To pitch the cane, or shoot off a gunne,
To play at loggets nine holes, or ten pinnes,
To try it out at footeball by the shinnes
At tick-tacke, Irish noddie, maw and ruffe,
At hot cockles, leap frogge, or blindman buffe
To drink half pots, or deale at the whole can,
To play at base, or pen and inkhorne, Sir Jhan
To daunce the morris, play at barley brake,
At all exploytes a man can think or speake
At shoue-groate, venter point, or cross and pile,
At beshrow him that s last at yonder style
At leaping ore a midsummer bonfire,
Or at the drawing Dan out of the myre
At any of those, or all these presently
Wagge but your finger, I am for you
I scorne that any youngster of our towne
Should for the Bow Bell cockney put me downe

Ritson, in his "Bibliographia Poetica," speaks of an edition of the book—whence the above was sketched—reprinted in 1807, under the title of "Humors Ordinarie," where a man may be verrie merry and exceeding well used for his sixpence

Before parting with Elizabeth, notice must be taken of the introduction of the dissyllable 'cricket" for the first time as a game, and though mentioned without giving the faintest outline or idea of its character, the circumstance is noteworthy, as setting at rest many vague questions respecting a more remote antiquity Not that the word was previously unknown, for instance—

> CHAR And what you'll do when you are seated on
> The throne to win your subjects' love, Philoma?
>
> PHIL I'll stand upon a cricket and then make
> Fluent orations to 'em, call 'em trusty
> And well beloved loyal and true subjects
>
> Cartwright's *Lady Errant*, 1651

A writer in criticising the oft-quoted tale about the wardrobe of Edward II, A D 1300, viz ("Domino Johanni de Leek, Capellano Domini Edwardi fil ad creag et alios ludos par ucis per manus proprias apud Westm 10 die Aprilis 1000") says, "the variation of *creag*, from an old Saxon word signifying a game played with a crooked bat, is not great, nor, considering the lapse of time, can cricket be thought a remarkable corruption" He concludes it probable of the sport of cricket that it was so denominated nearly 500 years ago, and that then it was a favourite pastime of the Prince of Wales Nor is it unlikely but that John de Leek, his highness' chaplain, might be his playfellow The latter supposition has only this idea to back him up, in our more sedentary age, members of John Leek's profession have proved themselves admirable cricketers

Everybody knows that on the accession of James a great change was attempted by that monarch in the sports of the people He endeavoured to ingratiate himself with the public by distasteful means His "Book of Sports" was very unfavourably received by many in authority as tending to subvert the morals of the nation The Lord Mayor of London had the temerity to order the king's carriage to be stopped as he was driving through the city on Sunday during the hours of divine service This threw his Majesty into a great rage, and, saying that he thought there were no more kings in England than himself, directed a warrant to the Lord Mayor compelling him to let him pass This the magistrate was forced to do * The book, which had so long shocked the religious feeling of the nation, was burnt in 1643 by order of Parliament † Full forty years elapsed ere the name of cricket was publicly broached Twenty years later, however, it not only found a place in a book entitled "The New World of English Words," but another in a song. In very few instances does it reappear during the remaining part of the 17th century The troubles of the Stuarts and the puritanical spirit of the age seem to have blotted out the memory of the word, nor

* Allen's "History of London

† See Maitland's "History of London" "The 'Book of Sports,' drawn up under the sanction if not the advice of James in 1617, shows—though a strenuous asserter of ecclesiastical authority—the king to be a latitudinarian in morals Nor by this alone, for in 1620 he gave by grant to one Clement Cotrell a groom porter of his household, leave to licence gaming houses for cards, dice, bowling alleys, and tennis courts The number allowed in London and Westminster, including the suburbs, was twenty-four bowling alleys, fourteen tennis courts, and forty taverns or ordinances for playing at cards and dice The motives expressed in the grant for this indulgence were for the honest and reasonable recreation of all good and civil people, who for their quality and ability may lawfully use the games of bowling, tennis, cards, tables, nineholes, or any other game hereafter to be mentioned " (Anderson's "History of London," vol II, p 5)

does it scarcely find a place in any book that may instruct a fresh generation what the principles of the game were

On the opening of the 18th century the clouds sheer oft, and a sunbeam, which appeared to have lost its way, once more illumined the page of history, although it failed to throw back the faintest gleam upon the long dark night of silence The reason for this may be three-fold In the first place the game had, without doubt, its origin among the lower classes, who, as a rule, were too ignorant either to read or write Then the means of transit from one place to another at a distance were difficult and expensive Thirdly, the game had not as yet received the countenance of the wealthy, who held aloof from it as being unpopular From the date of its first mention the game does not appear to have travelled forty miles taking the metropolis as a centre A great deal of learned talk has already been expended in the attempt to prove a much higher antiquity than Guildford can claim Very odd expedients have been had recourse to at times by enthusiasts to fill up a void which the chain of historical truth has failed to furnish Words of skinny meanings and distorted phrases have been brought into play to prove, if proof were possible, that in the earlier ages cricket was not unknown but practised It is even stated that an antiquary in such matters had discovered a monument on which letters were inscribed to cricket, but unfortunately for his theory the little cherub with his stony trumpet had not been able to blow away the parasites and creepers that ate out and obliterated so many letters in the dates and names, that nothing could be made of the fiasco

Another legend, but of little if any value, has been mentioned by the sticklers for a greater antiquity than is generally allowed In a volume of "Miscellany Poems by the most eminent hands," published by Mr Dryden in 1716, occurs the old ballad of Tom and Will, two brothers, enamoured of one and the same village beauty, which neither succeeded in obtaining, and as a result both became dispirited, in fact melancholic, the poet says

Tom was forlorn and Will was sad,
No huntsman nor no fowler,
Tom was held the properer lad,
But Will the better bowler

Now that the latter can have no allusion to cricket is evident from the close of the poem—

Their nine pins and their bowls they broke,
Their sports were turn'd to tears,
'Tis time for me an end to make—
Let them go shake their ears

It is pretty generally admitted that bards and troubadours are among the earliest heralds of discoveries, and if this be so, how strange the silence observed by the playwrights and poets of that and the preceding century Where are Massinger, Marlowe, Shirley, Shakespeare? Respecting the latter it will be found necessary to devote a chapter in reply to a challenge from an American writer, who stubbornly insists on Shakespeare's frequent reference to the game, both in his serious and lighter productions.

In Burton's Anatomy (Oxford edition, 1632) reference is made to recreations "which be much in use, as ringing, bowling, shooting, which Ascham commends in a just volume, and hath in former times been enjoined by statute as a defensive exercise, and an honour to our land, as well may witness our victories in France. Keelpins, tronks, quoits, pitching of bars, hurling, wrestling, wasters, foils, football, balowne, quintance, and many such, which are the common recreations of the country folk. Riding of great horses, running at ring, tilts and tournaments, horse racing, wild goose chases, which are the disports of greater men, and good in themselves, though many gentlemen by that means gallop quite out of their fortunes." It is evident from this quotation that cricket formed no ingredient in the games or pastimes mentioned by the learned Burton, although the word was in use a century before his time.

At this point it may be well to glance at a few other amusements which are relied upon as forming the basis of cricket. As far back as the 16th century mention is made of "cat and dog," which outlines roughly the game of cricket in its rudest forms. Strutt holds the opinion that club ball is its more likely parent, from the circumstance chiefly that the ball was struck with a straight bat or cudgel. In support of this theory he produces two engravings, one from a genealogical roll of the kings of England up to the time of Henry III, marked "14 B V" in the royal library, the other from a manuscript in the Bodleian, dated 1344. In each of these there are but two players, and no clue whatever is given of the laws by which the game was regulated. Stool ball was frequently alluded to in the 17th century, and D'Urfey wrote a poem respecting it, yet, strange to say, no one appears to have given particulars of its character in the way of definition until Johnson fills up the void by saying it is "a play where balls are driven from stool to stool," in what manner or to what purpose, the learned doctor does not vouchsafe an explanation. Strutt says, in his day there was a pastime called stool ball practised in the northern parts of England, which consisted in simply setting a stool upon the ground, when one of the players takes his place before it while his antagonist, standing at a distance, tosses the ball with the intention of striking the stool, and this it is the business of the former to prevent by beating it away with the hand, reckoning one to the game for every stroke of the ball. If, on the contrary, it should be missed by the hand and strike the stool, the players change places. The conqueror of the game is he who strikes the ball the most times before it touches the stool.

Dr Jamieson, in his Etymological Dictionary, throws more light upon the subject, he says "Three play at this game who are provided with clubs, they cut out two holes each, a foot in diameter, and seven inches in depth. The distance between them is about twenty-six feet. One stands at each hole with a club; these clubs are called dogs. A piece of wood, about four inches long, and one inch in diameter called a cat is thrown from the one hole to the other by a third person. The object is to prevent the cat from getting into the hole. Every time that it enters the hole, he who has the club at that hole loses the club, and he who threw the cat gets possession both of the club and the hole, while the former possessor is obliged to take charge of the cat If the cat be struck, he who strikes it changes places with the person who holds the other club, and as often as these positions are changed one is counted in the game by the two who hold the clubs and are viewed as partners"

Various theories have been propounded for a title, viz the Saxon word "Cricce," signifying a stick or staff, "Creag," a crooked stick, cross wicket, &c , but the most obvious derivation of the word as applied to the sport, is from the stool bowled at, which, as before observed was called a "Crickit" What more likely than the use of a bat instead of the hand—a ball in lieu of a four inch stick—the erection of a stool upon its legs, and then a deepening of the hole a few inches This done, and all the elementary machinery for cricket being at hand, new ideas of a manly game would rapidly thrust themselves into the minds of a rustic population, among whom by slow degrees the game became moulded into shape

A great deal more might be advanced in the way of speculation upon the origin of cricket, but as no useful purpose will be answered thereby, it may be enough to say that no satisfactory proof has ever been adduced to show that it was the offspring of the ancient game of club ball—the pet theory of Strutt and others who have not taken the trouble to search out and analyze the various properties which ancient games possessed in their relation to each other. Many instances are recorded of the support given to tennis by the "Merry Monarch," but scarcely any mention of cricket during the whole Stuart dynasty In fact, from the middle of the sixteenth to the opening of the seventeenth century there is a void mocking all research to fill. The game was either very slow in its development, or wanting in attraction, as up to the close of William III's reign, little advance appears to have been made.

It may be well to summarise its history—such as it is—during the first hundred years A document now in existence at Guildford refers to a piece of land—about an acre and a quarter—in that town A dispute arose respecting its occupation by one John Parrishe, who appropriated this piece of land for the purposes of a timber yard and framing ground The inhabitants claimed the entire right, and maintained by the uses to which the aforesaid John Parrishe applied it, that the 'garden was withheld from the town" One of the witnesses declared that he knew the land in question for fifty years, or more. It lay waste, and was occupied by the inhabitants of Guildford to saw timber on, and for saw pits, and for making of frames of timber for the said inhabitants When he was a scholar of the Free School at Guildford, he and several of his fellows did run and play there at cricket and other plays, and that the same was used for the baiting of bears in the said town until the said John Parrishe did enclose the said parcell of land." This inquiry arose in the fortieth year of Elizabeth's reign *

The reading of the "Book of Sports," previously referred to, by clergymen in their respective churches, gave rise to much disquietude. Several refused to comply with the king's commandment, and lost their livings in consequence. The Rev. Thomas Wilson, the suspended rector of Otham, in Kent, was popular among the

* Russell's "History of Guildford"

inhabitants of the village, and also at the town of Maidstone close by He used frequently to preach in the open street, and invariably attracted large numbers to hear him His biographer states "Maidstone was formerly a very prophane town, insomuch that I have seen morrice dancing, cudgell playing, stoolball, cricketts, and many other sports openly and publickly on the Lord's Day" Seeing that the "Book of Sports" was burnt at Cheapside by the common hangman in 1643, there elapse forty years between the first and second recorded mention of the word

Another forty years roll away with merely a hunt after the existence of cricket The scene of action is then laid at Antioch Here is a wide field for the play of a fervid imagination How did the English game get there? Well, it is said that one Henry Tonge, a chaplain on board his Majesty's ships *Assistance, Bristol,* and *Royal Oak,* indulged in pastimes and sports, such as duck-hunting, fishing, shooting, hand-ball, and *crickitt* Now, it this story be "gospel truth," when and where did he learn the game, and with whom could he recreate himself in the noble pastime? John Timbs, in his "School-days of Eminent Men," says, in 1650, "Thomas Ken, afterwards the well-known Bishop of Bath and Wells, used to wield a cricket bat at Winchester School" This is questionable, for it Ken did not enter the school named till his fifteenth year—as some affirm—being born in Hertfordshire in July, 1637, the story about the bat may be placed in the catalogue of doubts Better evidence is afforded of the progress of the game in 1685, where, in a work entitled the "Mysteries of Love and Eloquence," a bumpkin is made to address his betrothed in these words, "Will you not, when you have me, throw stools at my head and cry, 'Would my eyes had been beat out by a *cricket-ball* the day before I saw thee?'"

With the dawn of the eighteenth century, the reign of silence ended, and "the clouds that loured around the art," such as it was, vanished * Whether the oracle then proclaimed itself, and in what way, is still a mystery, but in a very limited space of time cricket, as a game, became the subject of correspondence, material for law-suits, and a theme for censors It had spread itself into the centre of the kingdom Among many cases that might be cited is that which records a match played at Birmingham during the battle with rebels at Preston.† In an age of poetry, it is somewhat remarkable that the imagination of the muse was not stretched a little in portraying a subject both novel and inviting Here a stanza,‡ and there a line,§ are all the contributions as yet gathered up, none of which throw the least light upon the principles and practices of the game, at this time evidently put into rough shape The humble classes were not the only sections of the community to mature it Laws were framed, and these, though comparatively speaking crude, had in them the elements of order, which implied a design and intelligence not likely to be found among a class of persons devoid of education and social status

About the year 1710, it appears from a legal document the county of Kent had grown into such colossal proportion that it was able to challenge England, and

* "The lower classes divert themselves at football, wrestling, cudgels, nine-pins, shovelboard, *cricket*, snowballs, ringing of bells, quoits, pitching the bar, &c" (Strype's Edition of Stowe's "Survey," 1720)

† See "Warwickshire"

‡ D'Urfey in "Pills to Purge Melancholy"

§ "New World of English Words" (E. Phillips)

considerable sums of money were staked upon the result of the play Differences arose as to the payment of certain stakes deposited, and a law-suit was the result The game had grown by this time into favour, but the element of gambling had so strongly infused itself therein as to call forth a remark from the judge to the effect that, though the game was good enough in itself, the purposes to which it might be appropriated were far otherwise *

A few years later (May 13, 1743), there is a communication between a Mr. Maurice, jun , and Roger Gale, which throws a strong light upon the game The former says, " I must add a notice to you who are universally learned, which may not be perhaps unacceptable , it is entirely new here (Spalding) even to our butchers —from one of whom Dr. Green (my fellow secretary) had brought last meeting to our museum, a wool-ball of a deep dark brown colour, like a globe, but compressed on all sides, or rather a cube as rounded off at angles and corners, of half the size of the hair-balls commonly cut out of the stomach of oxen and cows, as this was cut out of a sheep's stomach—that is about the common size of a handball, and some part of the surface as it were glazed or japanned and shining It is extremely lighter than even the hair balls in proportion to its size You see, sir, how covetous I am in continuing my converse with you to the *scriptus et in tergo*—on discourse of plays, observing that the instrument used thereat generally gives the denomination to the game, and in recollecting all I could of the ball plays used by the Greeks and Romans, and consulting Bullenger (*De Ludis Vet*), Rouse, Goodwyn, and Kennet, I find nothing of cricket there—a very favourite game with our young gentlemen I conceive it a Saxon game called *crice*, a crooked club as the batte is wherewith they strike the ball ; as billiards I take to be a Norman pastime from *billart*, a stick so called with which they do the like thereat " †

As yet no means reveal themselves of understanding what the game really was, or how played although too much is afforded of the ill uses to which it was applied Small rebukes availed nothing and large ones had little or no effect upon the gambling spirit of the age, and cricket found but little favour either as a moral or a noble game Thomas Gray, the accomplished poet, in a letter to Richard West (1742), says " There are, my Lords —— and ——, they are now statesmen , do not you remember them dirty boys playing at cricket ? " A writer in the *Gentleman's Magazine* (1743) says ·

In diversions as well as business things alter mightily, and what in one man may be decent, in another may be ridiculous , what is innocent in one may be quite the contrary in another , neither is it at all impossible that exercise may be strained too far A journeyman shoemaker may play from five o'clock on Saturday until it is dark, at skittles, provided he has worked all the rest of the week Yet I can't say it would shock me but a little if I saw honest Crispin stopping against a member of either House of Parliament All diversions at exercises have certain bounds as to expense, and when they exceed this, it is an evil in itself and justly liable to censure Upon what reasons are all the laws against gaming founded ? Are not these the chief, that they break in upon business, expose people to great dangers, and cherish a spirit of covetousness in a way directly opposed to industry ? The most wholesome exercise and the most innocent diversions may change their natures entirely if people, for the sake of gratifying their humour, keep unfit company I have been led into these reflections, which are certainly just in themselves, by some odd stories I have heard of cricket

* See " Kent "

† Bibliothoca Topog Britannia, No 2, part 3

matches, which I own, however, to be so strange and incredible that if I had not received them from eye-witnesses I could never have yielded to them any belief Is it not a very wild thing to be as serious in making such a match as in the most material occurrences of life? Would it not be extremely odd to see lords and gentlemen, clergymen and lawyers, associating themselves with butchers and cobblers in pursuit of their diversions? or can there be anything more absurd than making such matches for the sake of profit, which is to be shared among so remote in their quality and circumstances? Cricket is certainly a very innocent and wholesome exercise, yet it may be abused if either great or little people make it their business It is grossly abused when it is made the subject of public advertisements, to draw together great crowds of people who ought all of them to be somewhere else Noblemen, gentlemen, and clergymen have certainly a right to divert themselves in what manner they think fit—nor do I dispute their privilege of making butchers, cobblers, or tinkers their companions, provided they are gratified to keep their company, but I very much doubted whether they have any right to invite thousands of people to be spectators of their agility at the expense of their duty and honesty The time of people of fashion may be indeed of very little value, but in a trading country the time of the meanest man ought to be of some worth to himself and the community The diversion of cricket may be proper in holyday-time and in the country, but upon days when men ought to be busy and in the neighbourhood of a great city, it is not only improper but mischievous in a high degree It draws numbers of people from their employments to the ruin of their families It brings together crowds of apprentices and servants whose time is not their own It propagates a spirit of idleness at a juncture when, with the utmost industry, our debts, taxes, and decay of trade will scarce allow us to get bread It is a most notorious breach of the laws, as it gives the most open encouragement to gaming, the advertisements most impudently reciting that great sums are laid, so that some people are so little ashamed of breaking the laws that they had hand in making, that they give public notice of it

This is certainly a gloomy picture of the past, with the dark colours laid on thickly, but from the whole tone of the production its author had little liking for the game, and less for those who promoted or took part in its development It is quite refreshing to turn the eye upon another picture, from the glowing pencil of James Love, comedian, and author of the epilogue "Bucks have at ye all" For the first time in discovered history the manner and quality of the play is sketched in Homeric verse, with the following prelude —

While others, soaring on a lofty wing,
Of dire Bellona's cruel triumphs sing,
Sound the shrill clarion, mount the rapid car,
And rush delighted through the ranks of war
My tender muse, in humbler, milder strains,
Presents a bloodless conquest on the plains,
Where vigorous youth, in life's fresh bloom, resort
For pleasing exercise and healthful sport,
Where emulation fires, where glory draws,
And active sportsmen struggle for applause—
Expert to bowl, to run, to stop, to throw,
Each nerve collected at each mighty blow *

* * * * *

Previous to the two pictures here referred to, there was one of another sort published, that, however, was "done on canvas," and from which several engravings are still in existence This serves to illustrate the manner in which the game was played What is now called a wicket consisted then of two stumps apparently about two feet wide and one foot high, with a stick stretching across

* See entire poem in another chapter

Cricket in the Olden Time.

and beyond the stumps The bat had a long handle, and the extremity of the pod was curved in the form of a volute Between the stumps was a hole which, according to a few memoranda furnished by the late Mr Ward, was deep enough to contain the ball and the butt end of the bat This hole served the purpose of a popping crease From the position of the fielders it may be inferred that a batsman could be disposed of in at least four ways, viz, bowled, caught, run out, and stumped *

Towards the close of the reign of George the Second, Guthrie describes the amusements of English folk in the following fashion —"The customs of the English have since the beginning of this century undergone an almost total alteration Many of the favourite diversions are now disused Those remaining are operas dramatic exhibitions, ridottos, and sometimes masquerades in or near London, but concerts of music, and card, and dancing assemblies are common all over the kingdom. Of stag and fox hunting and horse races all denominations are fond even to infatuation Somewhat may, however, be offered by way of apology for these diversions the intense application which they give to business, their sedentary lives and luxurious diet require exercise; and some think that their excellent breed of horses is increased and improved by such amusements Next to horse racing and hunting, cock fighting, to the reproach of the nation, is a favourite diversion among the great as well as the vulgar The athletic diversion of cricket is still kept up in the southern and western parts of England, and is sometimes practised by people of the highest rank It is performed by a person who, with a clumsy wooden bat, defends a wicket raised by two slender sticks with one across, which is attacked by another person, who endeavours to beat it down with a hard leather ball from a certain stand The farther the distance is to which the ball is driven, the oftener the defender is able to run between the wicket and the stand This is called gaining so many notches, and he who gets the most is the victor Other diversions which are common to other countries, such as tennis, fives, billiards, coursing, and the like, are familiar to the English"

The ill odour of gambling that as yet attended cricket did much to neutralise some of its essential attributes This is not to be wondered at when the rein was thrown upon the "neck of the wild horse" Parents and guardians very naturally regarded with alarm the temptations to which the young might easily fall a prey The danger did not consist so much in the speculation incident to any particular match in course of play as in the association of persons who cared nothing about the attributes of cricket beyond the chances of getting money out of it, and though the names of noblemen figured frequently among others not accredited as safeguards to the public, the principle of playing a match often between their own retainers found but little favour with those who had the well-being of a community at heart

> England, when once of peace and wealth possest,
> Began to think frugality a jest,
> So grew polite, hence all her well-bred heirs
> Gamesters and jockeys turn'd, and cricket players †

* See Engraving

† See Jenyn's Horatii Epistolarum imitated

As time wore on, and the public censor asserted his power, the atmosphere sweetened, and the game, by degrees, grew into favour The adjectives "manly and noble" were applied to it These are proudly retained to this day In a hygienic sense it commanded attention, and as a social pastime it was found to possess many of those requirements which fit man for the battle of life—no matter in what station his lot might be cast.

Information respecting the advance of the game pops out occasionally in printed paragraphs and private correspondence but the glimpses are too few and faint to afford more than an idea—not an actuality In 1756 the *Connoisseur* places a low estimate upon cricket, but a poem of the same date lauds just as much as its contemporary undignifies. It was written as "an exercise at Merchant Taylor's School "

Peace and the arts we sing—her genial power
Can give the breast to pant, the thought to tower—
Thought guiltless, not inglorious, souls inspires,
And boasts less savage, not less noble, fires
Such is her sway, when cricket calls her train,
The sons of labour, to the accustom'd plain,
With all the heroes' passion and desire
They swell, they glow, they envy, and admire
Despair and resolution reign by turns,
Suspense torments, and emulation burns
See, in due rank disposed, intent they stand,
In act to start—the eye, the foot, the hand,
Still active, eager, seem conjoined in one
Though fixed, all moving, and while present, gone
In ancient combat from the Parthian steed
No more winning flew the barbed reed
Than rolls the ball with varied vigour played—
Now levelled—whirring o'er the springing blade,
Now toss'd to rise more fatal from the ground,
Exact and faithful to the appointed bound
Yet vain its speed, yet vain its certain aim,
The wary batsman watches o'er the game
Before his stroke the leathern circle flies—
Now wheels oblique, now mounting threats the skies
Nor yet less vain the wary batsman's blow,
So intercepted by the circling foe
Too soon the nimble arm retorts the ball,
Or ready fingers catch it in its fall
Thus various art with varied fortune strives,
And with each changing chance the sport revives
Emblem of many coloured life—the state,
By cricket rules, discriminates the great,
The outward side, who place and profit want,
Watch to surprise and labour to supplant,
While those who taste the sweets of present winnings,
Labour as healthily to keep their innings.
On either side the whole great game is played—
Untried no shift is left, unsought no aid,

Skill vies with skill, and power contends with power,
And squint eyed prejudice computes the score
In private life, like single-handed players,
We get less notches, but we meet less cares
Full many a lusty effort, which at court—
Would fix the doubtful issue of the sport—
Wide of the mark, or impotent to rise
Ruins the rash, and disappoints the wise
Yet all in public and in private strive
To keep the ball of action still alive,
And just to all when each his ground has run
Death tips the wicket, and the game is done

The *London Magazine* of 1771 refers in favourable language to the Poem by Love, written five and twenty years before, but the reviewer appears to have had but little idea of the game, or of its antiquity *

It is obvious enough to anyone who has studied the subject, that there must have been wholesome laws for playing a game which, by this time had assumed considerable proportions The "fortuitous concourse of atoms" is not design, let philosophers say what they will Whatever the unwritten laws of cricket might have been at a time when noblemen and gentlemen would endanger their fortunes and imperil their reputation is not sufficiently known That they had laws is certain, and one great feature in the history of cricket takes its date from the year 1774, when a committee of noblemen and gentlemen † met at the Star and Garter in Pall Mall, and "settled" them in the form here produced —

The pitching yᵉ first Wicket is to be determined by yᵉ cast of a piece of Money When yᵉ first Wicket is pitched and yᵉ popping Crease Cut which must be exactly 3 Foot 10 Inches from yᵉ Wicket yᵉ Other Wicket is to be pitched directly opposite at 22 yards distance and yᵉ other popping crease cut 3 Foot 10 Inches before it The Bowling Creases must be cut in a direct line from each stump The Stumps must be 22 Inches long and yᵉ Bail 6 Inches The Ball must weigh between 5 and 6 Ounces When yᵉ Wickets are both pitched and all yᵉ Creases Cut The party that wins the toss up may order which side shall go in first at his Option

"LAWS FOR Yᵉ BOWLERS 4 BALLS AND OVER

The Bowler must deliver yᵉ Ball with one foot behind yᵉ Crease even with yᵉ Wicket and When he has Bowled one Ball or more shall Bowl to yᵉ number 4 before he Changes Wickets and he Shall Change but once in yᵉ Same Innings He may order yᵉ Player that is in at his wicket to Stand on which side of it he Pleases at a reasonable distance If he delivers yᵉ Ball with his hinder foot over yᵉ Bowling crease the Umpire Shall Call no Ball though she be struck or yᵉ Player is Bowled out Which he shall do without being asked and no Person shall have any right to ask him

LAWS FOR Yᵉ STRIKERS, OR THOSE THAT ARE IN

"If yᵉ Wicket is Bowled down its out If he Strikes or treads down or falls himself upon yᵉ wicket in Striking [but not in over running] its out A Stroke or Nip over or under his Batt or upon his hands [but not arms] if yᵉ Ball be held before She touches yᵉ Ground though She be hugged to

* "A very decent classical poem, does credit to the taste, spirit and good sense of the author, and may give pleasure to the critical as well as the cricketical reader"

† President Sir William Draper, His Grace the Duke of Dorset, Right Honourable Earl of Tankerville, Sir Horace Mann, Rev Charles Pawlett, Messrs J B Davis, J Cooke, C Coles, P Delancy, H Peckham, F Vincent, W Rich, and — James

the Body its out If in Striking both his feet are over ye popping Crease and his Wicket put down except his Batt is down within its out If he runs out of his Ground to hinder a Catch its out If a Ball is nipped up and he Strikes her again Wilfuly, before she comes to ye Wicket its out If ye Players have crossed each other he that runs for the Wicket that is put down is out If they are not Crossed he that returns is out If in running a Notch ye Wicket is struck down by a Throw before his Foot Hand or Batt is over ye Popping crease or a Stump hit by ye Ball though ye Bail was down its out But if ye Bail is down before he that catches ye Ball must strike a Stump out of ye Ground Ball in Hand then its out If the Striker touches or takes up ye Ball before she is lain quite still unless asked by ye Bowler or Wicket-keeper its out

BATT FOOT OR HAND OVER ye CREASE

When ye Ball has been in Hand by one of ye Keepers or Stopers and ye Player has been at home He may go where he pleases till ye next Ball is bowled If Either of ye Strikers is crossed in his running Ground designedly, which design must be determined by the Umpires NB The Umpires may order that notch to be Scored When ye Ball is hit up either of the Strikers may hinder ye catch in his running Ground or if She is hit directly across ye Wickets ye Other Player may place his Body any where within ye Swing of his Batt so as to hinder ye Bowler from catching her, but he must neither Strike at her nor touch her with his hands If a Striker nips a Ball up just before him he may fall before his Wicket, or pop down his Batt before Shee comes to it to Save it The Bail hanging on one Stump though ye Ball hit ye Wicket is not out

LAWS FOR WICKET KEEPERS

The Wicket Keepers shall stand at a reasonable distance behind ye Wicket and shall not move till ye Ball is out of ye Bowler's Hands and shall not by any noise incommode ye Striker and if his hands knees foot or head be over or before his Wicket though the Ball hit it it shall not be out

LAWS FOR Ye UMPIRES

To allow 2 Minutes for each man to come in when one is out, and 10 Minutes between Each Hand To mark ye Ball that it may not be changed They are sole judges of all outs and inns, of all fair and unfair Play of frivolous delays, of all hurts whether real or pretended and are discretionally to allow what time they think Proper before ye Game goes on again In case of a real hurt to a Striker they are to allow another to come in and the Person hurt to come in again But are not to allow a fresh Man to Play on either side on any Account They are sole judges of all hindrances, crossing ye Players in running and Standing unfair to Strike and in case of hindrance may order a Notch to be Scored They are not to order any man out unless appealed to by one of ye players These Laws are to ye Umpires Jointly Each Umpire is ye Sole Judge of all Nips and Catches Ins and outs good or bad runs at his own Wicket and his determination shall be absolute and he shall not be changed for another Umpire without ye Consent of both Sides When ye 4 Balls are Bowled he is to call over These Laws are separately When both Umpires shall call Play 3 Times 'tis at ye Peril of giving ye Game from them that refuse Play

These foundation laws have undergone such a variety of changes that very few of the present day retain the features which their forefathers impressed upon them Doubtlessly they were adapted to the circumstances of the age, and as improvements marched on, changes in the framework of the constitution needed a change in the construction, which had to be fortified by new laws To go through all these changes would be less interesting than tedious

The reader's attention has by this time probably been arrested by the frequent recurrence of the word "notch," and its plural "notches" These take their rise from the strips of lath which were used to indicate the number of runs obtained by the batsman, every time a run was effected the parties in charge of the piece of wood made a notch on the edge, and upon the accomplishment of ten the notch was cut deeper to facilitate the reckoning of the total Now, as this method lumped the runs, without specifying by whom they were obtained, recourse was in time had to putting down the names of the parties who headed the respective sides, and the remaining ten were represented by figures in the order of going in, thus 1 had his runs marked against it, say 20, and so on to the last man This slight move in the right direction soon gave place to a real name, not an impersonality, and anon the manner in which a batsman was disposed of Still, in the majority of reports, the word notch retained its hold for generations after, and is not quite obsolete in the present day, although common sense decrees its extinction

From the period of "settling" the laws to the close of the 18th century the game made wonderful strides, especially in the home counties and Hampshire * Its principles were beginning to be understood by the public, and its applicability to the needs and means of all classes pretty generally recognised. Its old stigma of a game for idlers and blackguards had worn itself out, and its moral influences upon society obtained credence Occasionally some powerful journal would bring the subject under notice, but these instances were so few in comparison to what they ought to have been that, in 1792, the *Sporting Magazine* was started to make up seeming deficiences, and a most successful experiment it proved to be, even for its promoters, and a most valuable storehouse of information it has ever since been for sportsmen of every kind and degree In the prospectus occurs this passage "It has long excited our astonishment that among the magazines which have hitherto been ushered into the world not one has been expressly calculated for the sportsman" Even up to this period the plan and character of the game lacked an interpreter Strutt then comes forward and disposes of his task in the following way

Cricketing has of late years become exceedingly fashionable, being much countenanced by the nobility and gentlemen of fortune, who frequently join in the diversion This game, which is played with a bat and a ball, consists of a single and a double wicket The former requires five players on each side the latter eleven but the number may be varied on both sides at the pleasure of the parties At single wicket the striker with the bat is the protector of the wicket, the opposing party stand in the field to catch or stop the ball, and the bowler, who is one of them, takes his place by the side of a small baton, or stump, set up for that purpose 22 yards from, and thence delivers the ball with the intention of beating it down If he prove successful, the batsman retires from his play and another of his party succeeds If, on the contrary, the ball is struck by the bat, and driven into the field beyond the reach of those who stand up to stop it, the striker runs to the stump at the bowler's station, which he touches with his bat and then returns to the wicket If this be performed before the ball is thrown up it is called a run, and one notch or score is made upon the tally towards the game If, on the contrary the ball be thrown up, and the wicket beaten down with it by the opposite party before the party is at home, or can ground his bat within 3 feet 10 inches of the wicket, he is declared to be out of his play, and the run is not reckoned, he is also out if he strikes the ball into the air and if he be caught by any of his antagonists before it reaches the ground, and retained long enough to be thrown up again When double wicket is played two batsmen go in at the same time, one at each wicket, there are also two bowlers, who usually bowl four balls in succession alternately Both parties have two innings, and the side which obtains most runs in the double

* ' Bavin of Bays," by Dr William Perfect

contest claims the victory. These are the general outlines of this noble pastime, but there are many other particular rules and regulations by which it is governed, and those rules are subject to varieties according to the joint determination of the players.

This description of the game is merely to be understood as that given by the spectator for the instruction of those who never saw a wicket erected or a match played. The laws of the game, and their alteration from time to time, are, by the general consent of the whole community of cricketers, received from the Marylebone Club, of which a comprehensive history is furnished in another chapter.

Before quitting the 18th century it may not be amiss to note a circumstance recorded in the *Times* of October 3, 1798, with respect to the visit of George III. and his queen to a cricket match. The occasion was the birthday of their majesties' eldest daughter. The Duchess of Wurtemburg, and all the princesses, with a number of the nobility, went to Marden Castle, near Dorchester, to see some sports to be held in honour of that event. First on the list stood the item: "To be played for at Cricket, a round of beef; each man of the winning set to have a *ribband.*" This appears to be the only instance of the kind that has hitherto "turned up," or, at least, has been historically revived. Some go so far as to say that the king was often present at games of cricket, and would, if the playing was good, sit out a double innings with relish and pleasure. He had as great a horror of "duffers" as the smart captain of a modern team has, and bad fielding especially disgusted him. Indifferent bowling and weak batting he could tolerate, but lazy fielding soon caused him to retreat from the field.

CHAPTER III.

PROGRESS AND DEVELOPMENTS

FROM THE COMMENCEMENT OF THE 19TH CENTURY UP TO THE CLOSE OF THE FIRST QUARTER OF THE SAME

As in successive course the seasons roll,
So circling pleasures recreate the soul,
Here blooming health exerts her gentle reign,
And strings the sinews of the industrious swain —*Gay*

THE VALUE OF LEGENDS—ABSENCE OF EARLY DOCUMENTS HOW TO PLAY THE GAME OF CRICKET—STRUTT'S BRIEF HISTORY ON THIS POINT—LAMBERT'S CRICKETER'S GUIDE—THE OBJECT OF THE WORK STATED—FIRST BOOK OF THE KIND RECORDED—DOUBTS RESPECTING AUTHORSHIP—JOHN NYREN'S WORKS—RAPID INCREASE OF IMITATORS—EFFECTS OF THE VARIED KINDS OF WRITING ON THE PUBLIC MIND—NEW CHANNELS OF COMMUNICATION—DEATHS OF LAMBERT AND NYREN—ROUND ARM BOWLING, AND THE CONSEQUENT REVOLUTION IN THE GAME—CLAIMANTS FOR THE DISCOVERY.

LEGENDS are often more substantially true than many received historical facts and analogies, although they prove nothing, not unfrequently tend to develop some important truth Bards and minstrels, too, play a prominent part in the history of their time by one line here and another there, a crooked stanza with a not very smooth melody, and a precept not always in keeping with the recognised rules of a finished composition, Still they serve a purpose and help to furnish materials that can be turned to account by more crafty and experienced dealers in historic ware

But these agencies were for a long time sadly at fault in revealing some of the principles of the game of cricket They could, and did occasionally, rehearse a portion of the laws, and narrate, in humorous strains, the triumphs and defeats of village heroes Nevertheless these afforded very faint glimpses, at the best, of the fundamental principles of the game—scarcely strong enough to give a view of its unshapen form That there were laws for its government was manifest from the words "settled" by the meeting of noblemen and gentlemen at the memorable meeting in 1774 Strange to say, no document bearing on the subject appears to have been published, nor hints given respecting the mode of playing the game beyond what may be inferred from the laws of it The greatest players of the age, and in all probability the best scholars who sanctioned and took part in cricket, do not seem to have penned a line, and this barrenness of information induced others far less competent to assume a task either in a practical or literary sense to explain the thing wanting to be known As few persons in the humbler walks of life were able to discharge such a duty, it occurred that two might perform a task which ought to have been performed by one Strutt, as before observed, says "these are the general outlines, &c"—outlines which certainly needed a considerable amount of filling up before an accurate idea of the game could be entertained by ordinary mortals Strutt, it should be remembered, published his "Sports and Pastimes" in 1801, and his second edition of the same work in 1810—the year in which he died—without the addition of a single line to those already quoted. This suggested the idea of "Lambert's Cricketer's Guide," the joint production of a popular player and a careful scribe. The literary machine once set in motion proved so tempting a speculation, that in the course of a few years these "guides" multiplied surprisingly, but, being obliged to keep a little out of the beaten path often became perplexed—the more so the farther they departed from the "standard"* At all events, notwithstanding a few changes in the elementary principles of the game, the book bearing Lambert's name was *the* guide for at least a quarter of a century A few extracts will show to what extent the principles of the game have changed from the dawn of the present century till now. Upon the issue of the tenth edition, the *Sporting Magazine* (1816) remarks "These instructions and rules for playing the game of cricket, coming from a person so well acquainted with the subject as Mr Lambert, we cannot doubt must be highly acceptable to all who are fond of this manly diversion The object of the work, it is stated, is to reduce cricket-playing to a system with as little variation as possible It is intended as a help to young beginners, and also as a guide to other players who have accustomed themselves to habits inconsistent with good playing Mr Lambert's well known experience in the diversion is, we should imagine, a sufficient guarantee for the correctness of the principles laid down, and, as cricket appears increasing in its attractions, we cannot doubt that the work will be highly acceptable to all its votaries" Lambert had little confidence in his literary attainments, for in his address to the Marylebone Club, he says 'It is with great diffidence that I venture to appear before you and the public in the character of an author on the noble game of cricket, but having, from considerable experience in the various parts of the kingdom, found the want of a familiar introduction to this manly exercise, similar to those which are to be found in almost every other art I have ventured, with the assistance of the publisher,† to arrange and commit to the press the directions contained in the following pages If this attempt should have the effect of assisting the progress of young beginners, or of correcting in older players any improper habits which may have been formed, I shall consider my pains and attention amply rewarded" He then goes on to say "The particulars necessary to be attended to when a game of cricket is to be played are (1) the number of players, (2) the selection of the ground, (3) the choice of umpires, (4) the pitching

* It was called "England's Standard"

† Baxter, Lewes

of the wickets, and (5) the disposition of the players The eleven fieldsmen are distinguished by different names, viz, bowler, wicket-keeper, first short slip, a second short slip (sometimes necessary), point middle wicket off, leg or hip, long stop, long slip to cover the short slip, cover point and middle wicket, long field (off side), long field (on side)" The bowler, who occupies the most important post, is thus instructed "It is best to practise with a ball of full size and weight observing the length the ball should be pitched, and using yourself to one particular distance of running and attitude before delivering the ball A small variation in the distance will materially injure your mode of bowling, and therefore after you have once discovered the proper distance you will do well to make some small mark on the ground as a guide, and to deliver the ball with one foot over, or in the bowling crease, and the other behind it, at which side of the wicket you find most convenient, and which you have the liberty of varying as often as you please Bowling is an important part of the game, and requires great steadiness and composure Bad bowling is often the cause of losing a game, and as some indifferent players are apt to put themselves forward as bowlers when there are others in the eleven much more proper for that place, who are not so assuming, great care ought to be taken in the choice, particularly as it will be to the advantage of all to select, without partiality, the best qualified persons, in whom they can place confidence A bowler should always consider the state of the ground on which he is going to bowl, as very fast bowling on hard rough ground is difficult to the striker But where the ground is in proper condition the following rules may be observed, viz In slow bowling the ball should be delivered so as to ground about 3½yds before the wicket, middling, 4¾yds, and fast bowling, 5yds, but the bowler must use his own judgment in making variations, according to the play of the striker, and such variations often prove very advantageous. When a ball is delivered to the off stump, it will, if hit, frequently cause a catch on the off side, and if directed to the leg of the striker or near stump, it is frequently hit to the hip, when runs may be expected if not caught or stopped If the bowler should not deliver the ball at the most advantageous place to oppose the striker the person at the wicket should, by a secret sign known by the bowler and himself, place his foot occasionally on the spot on which he thinks the bowler may be successful, either to oppose the striker or to cause a catch to be given, but this must be acted upon with judgment

"A bowler should not be too systematic or formal in his mode, but vary faster or slower, according to the peculiarities of the striker If it should be found necessary to change the position of the players by placing them further in the field or nearer the wicket, and if the bowler makes any sign to the others in the field he should do it, if possible so as not to be perceived by the striker, as it will then be the more likely to produce the desired effect Any one plan of bowling continued for a length of time will be hit to advantage by some players, and no certain rule to avoid it can possibly be laid down In the different modes of bowling, we recommend the ball to be held with the seam across, so that the top of the fingers may touch it, but some vary a little in the mode, nor should it be held too firm, but just so as to secure a proper hold, by this means it will keep steady, and leave the hand with more ease Aided by a turn, or motion of the wrist, the ball may be made to cut or twist after it has grounded, and will perplex most strikers, so as to derange their mode of hitting more than the general mode of delivering the ball dead from the hand; at least, it is considered much more deceiving to the striker. It may be prudent with the commencement of a fresh striker to begin slow bowling; strikers are generally cautious at first, which will frequently cause a catch, and if this method should fail, and the striker succeed in getting runs, deliver him occasionally a ball as much faster as you can well do it In both instances take the same space of ground before you deliver the ball, and make use of the same motion and attitude, so that the striker may not be aware of your intended variation till the ball is actually delivered But it is advisable generally to make use of such bowling as you are most master of, the laws of the game allowing but little variation in the method

"A bowler may practice by himself, first measuring the proper distance of twenty-two yards, and having pitched the wicket, sticking up a feather, or some other mark where he intends pitching the ball in a direct line with the wicket, so that when the ball is pitched to such a mark, it will rise to the wicket, but if the bowler should practise the twisting plan, he must then place his mark as far out of the line with the wicket as he may think proper, and in such a manner that the ball, being pitched to the mark, may twist or turn to the wicket, delivering the ball from the hand with the body in an upright position, as before directed.

"When the wickets are placed across a hill rather sloping the ball will, of course, twist or gather to the wicket The young bowler should at all times strive to pitch the ball to a good length, whether straight or twisting, avoiding its touching the ground more than once between himself and the wicket (except some balls which will cut on the ground), and although we have before mentioned the distance, some degree of variation will be necessary with regard to the nature of the ground and the swiftness of the bowling The bowler should be sufficient master of the ball so as to deliver it to any place he may judge proper, and which may be continued by placing a mark as before mentioned It is well to use himself to either side of the wicket, as he may be frequently placed very unfavourably to bowl on one side, and yet advantageously so on the other Let him fix his eyes on the spot where he intends to pitch or deliver the ball, and start gently at first, increasing his pace on coming nearer the bowling crease, and deliver the ball in an upright posture, as the higher the ball is delivered from the bowler's hand, the quicker and higher it will rise from the ground The ball should be delivered with the hand below the elbow, and must neither be thrown nor jerked If the elbow hits the side it is considered a jerk It is not advisable for young beginners to bowl too long at one time, but to practise often, and there will be little doubt of success If you find that the striker is rather partial to receiving the ball from one side of the opposite wicket, vary by bowling from the adverse side—this often meets with success

"A bowler will soon discover the striker's favourite hit, and he will, after delivering the ball, endeavour to place himself in a situation to stop it, but if it should be hit away, he must return to his wicket to take the ball if thrown to him If a batsman goes out of his ground with an intent to run before the ball is delivered, the bowler may put him out The practitioner is advised to make a white mark on the ball, and by tossing it across a room, so as to hit the floor at once, he will discover on its rising whether it twists to the right or to the left, or whether it rolls in a straight line, by this method, and taking notice how the hand was held when the ball was delivered, he will get master of it so as to bias it at pleasure When the ball goes from the hand of the bowler, he may make it twist by holding the back part of the hand towards the ground, and at the instant of delivery bring the thumb, with the aid of the wrist, rather under According to the laws of the game, the arm must not be straight, but the hand below the elbow—the ball must not be delivered with the back part of the hand uppermost By this particular twist, after the ball hits the ground it will roll the same as when it came from the bowler's hand, yet at the same time it must be observed that it will twist or roll from whatever part of the hand or fingers it touches last, therefore a bowler must be uniform in his mode, and judge how it left his hand when he gave a good ball, and follow this plan until he becomes quite master of the art If the ball be exactly straight between where it touches the hand last and the mark at which you mean to pitch it, most probably it will not twist, but when it leaves the hand or fingers a little on one side of the straight line which you mean to pitch at, then it will twist after it leaves the ground The twisting bowling is generally performed straight armed, but the hand must be below the elbow when the ball is delivered The ball may be twisted by the usual mode of under-arm bowling, by observing to deliver the ball when it leaves the hand so that the force of the hand, or a touch with the finger, shall give one side of it a twist or bias

"When runs are got very fast, it is the custom with most players to change the bowler, or bowlers, a consultation first taking place (except where any experienced person has the management), and after a short time to take the former bowler or bowlers again, as probably they were considered the persons best adapted for that purpose. The reason of this is, that when the striker has had sufficient practice with a good bowler, it will be as difficult for him to bowl him out as it would be for another who could not bowl so well, if he had not practised with him Very few bowlers run alike before the delivery of the ball, or deliver it in the same manner, therefore any fresh bowler may materially alter the mode of the striker's hitting, and in such cases it is always advisable to change, though it be for such as are not so well qualified

"The Wicket Keeper is in general the most proper person to see that the fieldsmen are in their places, and any directions given by him should be done by the motion of the hand, without calling any names, as this puts the striker on his guard, and in windy weather it would be difficult for the field to hear Indeed, the avoiding of noise and confusion at the game, contributes much to the enjoyment of both players and spectators. The wicket keeper should pay particular attention to the game, and if the striker should move off his ground with an intention to run, he must then do his best endeavour to put down the wicket, which is called 'stumping out', and if the ball is thrown to him when the strikers are running, he must place himself in the most convenient situation for taking the ball, and putting down the wicket with the utmost dexterity he is master of As the event of a match depends much on the bowlers, the wicket keeper should toss the ball home to them, or so far as to come with a fair bound into their hands, that they may not reach or step after it, as bowling will be quite sufficient for them without labouring after the ball unnecessarily

"The First Short Slip is next the wicket keeper, and should stand so as to reach within about two feet of him This situation being so near the wicket, the ball will go from the bat to him, generally, very swiftly, giving him very little sight of it, and rendering it necessary for him to be continually on the alert He must likewise exert himself by getting behind the wicket keeper when the ball is thrown in, which is called backing up, and if the wicket keeper should go from the wicket after the ball, the first short slip should take his place until he returns, but no player should take the ball before the wicket keeper, providing it is coming straight to him

"Second Short Slip —It has sometimes been found advantageous to have four men placed near the wicket, when the ground is hard particularly in slow, or middle-paced bowling When this is the case, the fieldsman that can be best spared is placed between the first slip and point

"The Point —The person who stands at the point, should place himself in such a line with the popping crease, about seven yards from the striker, and, by observing where the ball will pitch as it comes from the bowler, endeavour to judge whether the striker is about to hit hard, in that case he will do well to draw back a few steps, to obtain a clearer sight of the ball If it should be a well pitched ball, it is probable the striker will not attempt to hit hard, he should then step forward a little In backing up he should take care to give the man at the slip sufficient room

"Middle Wicket Off —This man should stand on the off side, not far from the bowler's wicket, and about twenty-three yards from the striker's wicket, he must be active, and observe at the moment of hitting where the ball will come As this situation is important, it should be kept well, and in throwing the ball to the wicket keeper, he must observe not to do it harder than is necessary, and at about the height of the top of the wickets If the bowler should find it necessary to leave his place to run after the ball, the middle wicket man should take it until his return

"Leg or Hip —The person who takes this place should stand a little back from the straight line of the popping crease, and if it should be thought advisable for him to stand to save a run, it should be within about sixteen yards of the wicket

"Long Stop —This man should stand a proper distance behind the wicket, to save a run, if the ball should not be stopped by the striker, or wicket keeper The person who is placed in this situation, should be one who is not afraid of the ball, when bowled swift, and can throw in well, as it is not only the balls that pass the wicket keeper, but to such as are just tipped with the edge of the bat, both off and on, that he will have to attend He must also be active in backing up

"LONG SLIP.—This man must stand to save a run, about the same distance from the wicket as the long stop, in a line with the striker, between the point and short slip. A ball being hit to the short slip, after grounding, generally twists towards the long slip. When four men are placed near the wicket, this man should stand the same distance, playing between the point and second slip.

"COVER POINT AND MIDDLE WICKET.—This man's place is on the off side, to cover the point and middle wicket men. If the ball should be hit to either of these and missed, then he will be in readiness to receive it.

"LONG FIELD OFF SIDE.—This man should stand on the off side, between the middle wicket man and bowler at a considerable distance in the field, so as to cover them. In throwing the ball to the wicket keeper, he must endeavour to throw it home to his hands. It is desirable to appoint a person in this situation who can throw well and judiciously. It sometimes happens that the ball is struck to so great a distance, or in such a manner, that a second man is necessary to throw it to the wicket keeper, by receiving the ball from the first by a catch; this may be done quicker than by one long throw, unless the second man should miss the ball.

"LONG FIELD-ON SIDE.—This man's place is at some distance wide of the bowler's wicket, so as to prevent a second run. If the striker should hit mostly on the near side, then the man who covers the point and middle wicket man should come over and cover the middle wicket man on this side, and the middle wicket man, off side, will then stand wider from the bowler to assist in filling this place, and will play between the long field and the point at a distance to save a run.

"IN CATCHING OR STOPPING A BALL step well to do it, and receive it into the hand with ease, rather yielding to the force and keeping the eye steadily fixed on it; at the moment of catching the fingers must be extended to receive the ball and shut the instant it is caught. It is likewise necessary in stopping the ball to get before it, so as to meet it in full, and when it is coming with a bound to wait or step in as the case may require; if it be close to the ground and moving with considerable velocity, a proportionate expedition must be used in putting down the hands.

"THE BATSMAN should place himself in an easy position and though strikers vary in their position of standing to hit, yet we recommend young players who are right-handed to stand as follows, viz., the toes of the right foot to be just behind the popping crease, and both toes to incline a little towards the bowler, keeping the feet, toes, &c., clear of the wicket, so that the bowler may have a fair view of it, except that part which may be hidden by the bat, which should be upright when guarding the wicket. If right-handed the right foot should be nine or ten inches from a line drawn from one wicket to the other, the left foot to be ten or twelve inches from the right foot. No person who is a good player will ever stand in such a position as to hinder the play of the ball, except an accident should happen by slipping or otherwise.

"GUARDING THE WICKET being considered a very necessary part to be observed by the batsman, we shall remark that as the bat is only 4¼in. wide and the wicket is 8in., the striker cannot guard all three stumps which compose his wicket; therefore we consider it necessary to guard the middle stump, or that which is most generally hit by the bowler, always guarding the weakest side, and when the bowler is about to deliver the ball, raise the bat at ease until you can judge where the ball will pitch

"It may here be remarked that strikers should early adopt the method of hitting upright By this phrase it is not meant that the bat should be exactly perpendicular, for the handle should be a little inclined to the bowler, but by no means either to the right or to the left, and in this sense the term *hitting upright* must be understood

"There are only three proper modes of striking safely and well while guarding the wicket (1) Supposing the ball to be in a straight line to the wicket, play the bat upright to oppose its progress (2) Suppose the ball to be coming a little wide on the off side, you must be cautious of it, as it may turn to the wicket, but by playing the bat upright you may hit off to advantage. (3) We will suppose the ball coming a little wide on the *near* side—play the bat upright and well out. It must be observed in the above hits that the striker must always suppose that the ball, if missed, would hit the wicket, and then it will avoid danger There are several other advisable strokes to make, provided the direction of the ball be such as to preclude all danger of its hitting the wicket

'Best Method of Stopping a Good Length Ball, that is a ball pitched to its proper distance, according to the directions before given with regard to the art of bowling It may be well in common practice to draw a line or place a mark across the play at a distance of $4\frac{1}{2}$yds from the wicket, and if the ball be dropped on or over the line, let the striker step his left foot forward about 3ft without moving his right foot off the ground, which will enable him to play his bat at the ball 3ft or more before the popping crease, so that he will be enabled to stop or strike the ball before it rises high enough to hit his fingers Another advantage arises from this, that if the bowler twists the ball, it will give but little room to do so, after it hits the ground If a striker cannot play with his bat upright, we recommend him, at practice, in addition to the bowling line or mark given, to draw a line from the middle stump in a straight direction towards the opposite wicket, about $3\frac{1}{4}$ft before the popping crease, or as far as he can pleasantly reach, which will direct him to play forward at the before-mentioned bowling and enable him to see whether the bat is leaning a little forward, in a proper direction to meet the ball In playing with this line he must suppose the ball to be pitched straight and not twisting, as the crease is merely to teach the striker to hit upright and play well forward at the ball, he should, at practice, receive straight bowling It is also necessary for young players in learning to hit upright, to observe that when the bowler is about to deliver the ball the bat must, as usual, be on or near the popping crease, he will then by stepping out the left foot, as before mentioned, carry his bat upright and in a straight line forward, to meet the ball, not varying it above 2in from either side of the crease towards the ball, and which will finally clear the wicket, until he can strike upright, when the line before mentioned may be dispensed with, and he may play at the ball as his judgment directs him

"Very few players can at all times strike upright, as when the balls come quicker than was expected, it will deceive the best of players If the striker is in too great haste to meet the ball, and has had but little practice, he is likely to miss, but by placing the bat nearly close to the ground and keeping the handle forward, when he meets the ball it cannot slip under, nor rise when hit It is too often the case with players, when meeting a ball, that the handle of the bat is leaning backward, particularly the upper edge, which will be disposed to hit up the ball for a catch, the face of the bat should be played square, and not one edge before the other except a wide ball, when hit *off* or *on* When a ball is pitched short of its usual and proper length, and the striker expects it to rise, it frequently happens, on the contrary, that it shoots on the ground, and then the striker is often too late, but if at these kinds of balls he plays back about two feet behind the popping crease in case he can manage so to do without striking the wicket with his bat, it will afford him a little more time to judge how the ball is coming, and to strike with more certainty We consider it good judgment not to strike at those balls which rise five inches or more above the stumps, but rather to let the ball pass without hitting, if it can be done without touching the bat or hand as very little good can be expected if hit, and it is very likely to produce what is called a bad hit, and perhaps the striker may be caught out If a ball should rise so fast that you cannot let it pass without striking, raise your bat perpendicularly, bring the handle forward so as to strike it on the ground before the fieldsman can get near enough to catch, this will save the fingers, and frequently prevent a catch Let nothing take off your attention when about to receive the ball, otherwise it may hit the wicket, or be struck up so as to cause a catch, which might otherwise have been avoided It requires but little motion in stepping in to strike, as a person who stands steady has the best view of the ball It seldom requires both feet to move in striking at a ball that is well pitched, and as bowlers are not confined to pitching the ball at the same length, the striker must judge what kind of ball he is about to receive, and where it will probably pitch according to the space If the ball should come four or five inches on the leg side, the striker should move his right foot back at the moment of hitting, playing the ball between his left leg and the wicket, but if the ball be seven or eight inches wide, or more behind the legs the striker should turn as quickly as possible and strike, which is generally an advantageous stroke, as in addition to the rapidity of the ball from the bowler's hand, the bat adds to the velocity, and the ball will, in all probability, run a considerable distance We must here observe that it should be a practice as much as possible to strike on the top, or over the ball, rather than under it, to prevent it from rising, and keep it to the ground If a ball be tossed higher than the wicket, and on the off side, it should be struck back as far as the straight line of the popping crease If it be tossed within two feet of the popping crease, the striker should move back and strike as hard as possible, and if a straight ball nearly in the same direction The striker should always endeavour to hit the ball on the same side on which it is bowled, and not to draw it across the play, as this is a very dangerous mode of striking, and frequently is the cause of hitting down the wicket

"We shall now consider the proper method of striking well pitched balls If the ball is five inches or more wide on the off side of the wicket, it is difficult, particularly with young beginners, to strike such balls in a proper manner, as there is a necessity of reaching after them, therefore the striker must be careful, as he will strike under the ball, and by that means may probably cause a catch. It is for this reason that experienced bowlers use occasionally wide bowling, which should be directed to the off side of the wicket. If the striker is right-handed, and wishes to play the ball forward, he should step with the left foot foremost, and, supposing the ball not straight to the wicket by five or seven inches to the off side, he will be enabled to play on the ball so as not to rise on the striker. If he is desirous of hitting the ball behind the wicket, provided it be wide enough on the near side, so that there is no fear of its twisting into the wicket, he should step his right foot a little past the line in which the ball is coming, which will enable him to face the ball until it is hit. For all balls that are hit behind a straight line of the popping crease, step the right foot forward and hit the ball well on the top part. Never strive to hit a ball behind the wicket which is in a straight line with it. If a ball should pitch short of its proper length on the off side, and should twist toward the top of the wicket, the striker must be very careful in playing back that he does not hit his own wicket, as is sometimes the case even with the best players. If the ball should be coming high in a direct line towards the bail, and the striker intends to play back, he should step within about seventeen inches of the wicket, playing well on the ball. In hitting a fair ball hard, the striker should keep his hands very near, or close together, that the one may not produce a check to the other, exerting the arms, shoulder, and wrist, and striking the ball five or seven inches from the top of the bat, as it is of little use to hit the ball hard, except it be done with the proper part of the bat playing on it like the lash of a whip, with the arms easy, when the striker will scarcely perceive the ball going from the bat. The striker should be careful and attentive in running both his own and partner's hits, and when his partner is about to strike, it is advisable to stand before the popping crease, toward the wicket, but he must not start to run before the ball is out of the bowler's hand, for in that case he is giving the bowler a chance of putting down his wicket, and he is *out*, the ball being in play though not delivered. When the ball is delivered, the striker may follow it, but should be careful not to run too far, that in case no runs are to be obtained, he may return in time without endangering his wicket.

"Many things may occur at the striker's wicket which he cannot see, particularly by fast bowling, viz., the ball may hit the edge of the bat, the leg or hand of the wicket-keeper, or the long stop may miss it, &c., all of which his partner must attentively observe and act on, as the striker cannot see it so quick as he can. Always run the first time quick, which may enable you to get a second run easy, taking care not to overrun your ground till you observe where the ball is. One batsman should judge for the other, as it sometimes happens that one can run to the most dangerous wicket, where the ball is near, when it would not be safe for the one at the wicket to start, but you had better lose a run than risk a wicket. In running between the wickets keep the bat on the outside of your partner, taking care not to run against him for in so doing you may lose a run and probably a wicket If one striker be left-handed and the other right, they should agree on which side they should pass each other in running"

Some exceedingly astute critics of the present day boldly assert that Lambert had nothing whatever to do with the composition of the Guide in question in consequence of defective education, and that he was, moreover, a bad man Such an argument might be applied in all probability to many books as well as men with equal, if not greater, force if the adjectives were defined One thing is certain, he called his book by a right name, as it has "guided" a troop of imitators to claim authorships of similar works with no practical knowledge whatever of the game of cricket, and with but a slender acquaintance with literature John Nyren is an honourable exception, but *his* "Cricketer's Guide" varies so little in principle from that of Lambert's that quotations are scarcely necessary Nyren was unquestionably a man of good taste, with a fair amount of education, and possessed withal a philanthropic disposition Of his knowledge respecting cricket as it then existed a mean estimate never ought to be entertained In his "Cricketers of my Time"—probably a subsequent production—there is a suitableness of phraseology to the persons and subjects treated of that it would be very difficult to amend even in these times of sensational and pictorial writing Both were celebrated among the principal cricketers of the age Nyren was born in 1764, and died in 1837 Lambert was born in 1779, and died in 1851 Chiefly by the productions of these two heroes, cricket claimed a place in the field of print Individuals who had to write for a living—no matter what the subject—seized upon the facts and theories propounded by Lambert and Nyren to garnish a substantial dish of veritable knowledge with fables and fancies, and thus make what in the esteem of the literary world would be "dry reading" a subject of some interest Strutt was rushed after as one of the hardest used books in the Museum, and among the thumb-worn and greasy pages few appear at the present day to have been more frequently scanned than those relating to cricket But the paucity of information afforded, forced into play a lively imagination, and a great deal of nonsense was the result There was a market for the article, but as truth often lies in a well too deep for the indolent to search out, pretty stories were introduced to save such exercise This, too, at a time when "mental culture" was a sounding theme, and the track of the "schoolmaster abroad" a national boast Specimens of the style frequently adopted might be given in abundance, let one suffice—"A player who flutters and flurries himself had better, when in as a batsman, throw down his club and walk out, for 'twill save time. and perhaps prevent the mischief of his getting out the other player. Had we to pick a side at sight, without personal acquaintance with their qualifications, we should select those called by the doctors sanguine—eschewing the heavy, lymphatic, or dark bilious subject—and taking the man of light complexion, of clear blue eye, and firm elastic step—eschewing all larks except those in the fields of a summer's morning" Thinking people, however, conversant with the full character of the incidents of cricket pay little heed to this chattering order of writers, who if taxed closely would perhaps be found wanting in the important elements of their native tongue, or puzzled to decide off-hand whether a dactyle is longer or shorter than a spondee

Good, bad, and indifferent writing, nevertheless, produced a wonderful effect upon the minds of the sporting community from the earliest issue of Lambert's Guide up to the close of the first quarter of the 19th century The *Sporting Magazine*—hardly adapted to meet the growing wants of the public—confined its columns chiefly to the notice of first-class matches Journalists of a broader sheet then turned their attention to the subject, and as the cricket column increased the popularity of the journal in which it appeared, a better class of men were by degrees introduced among the contributors Gentlemen of birth and education did not scruple to allow their names to be affixed to articles of their own writing, and hence a new field for discussing important theories was open, and it is scarcely a deviation from the truth to say that the literature of a few years by such agencies did more for the advancement of cricket than the efforts of all the pens in the previous century

But a revolution in the whole theory of the game was now at hand, for the plans of attack and defence underwent so material a change that a comparatively speaking simple pastime made an approach to science The round-arm bowling was loudly decried, and protested against by the great majority of players and patrons too Lambert objected strongly, and Nyren prophesied that if permitted to continue it would reduce the noble game to a mere exhibition of rough, coarse horse-play * Bowling received the epithet "scientific," and the bowler was denominated one of the "march of intellect" school Elaborate treatises appeared in quick succession upon the cut, &c, and the principles of scientific batting were ably enunciated by an Oxford scholar Nor was the discovery of the new principle a subject to be passed over in silence In fact, two counties claimed the honour of its introduction Sussex insisted on Broadbridge, and Kent on Wills, the public meanwhile being led to believe that one was neither before nor after the other Persons versed in mathematical history had their memories refreshed by this incident about "The Doctrine of Fluxions," and the difficulty said at the time to exist respecting the discovery Germany claimed it for Leibnitz, and England for Newton The idea might have possessed both of these profound philosophers at the same time, but as Newton was the first to enunciate it, the honour was awarded to him, the analogy between the two cases will be admitted by cricketers only, perhaps—still they are analogous The Sussex player might have entertained the idea of the round-arm delivery at the same time that it possessed the mind of the Kentish yeoman—so might many persons previous to either, but as the latter was the first to give nativity to thought, and to expound it, moreover, to the whole

* "Protest against the modern innovation of Throwing"

community of cricketers, he, for the want of a better word, was recognised as the discoverer. Of course the story of a country lass relieving the dullness of a dreary winter, in a dull district, by bowling to her brother in a barn could hardly fail to attract the attention of romancists, and much truth was diluted through the channels it was doomed to pass. The main facts of this event were, however, so well tested at the time, and the originality of the idea so long undisputed, that they have ever since been bound up in the bundle of "Kentish Legends."

CHAPTER IV.

GREAT AND RAPID EXPANSION

From the Close of the First Quarter of the Century to that of the Second.

"Image of war without its guilt."—*Somerville.*

The Public competent to Judge of the Play and Players—Honest and Timely Criticism Healthy — Effects of the Countenance given to Village Clubs by the Local Gentry—Bat-makers—Influence of the Clergy when taking part in the Game—Pilch, Wenman, Sewell, and Mynn's early Cricket — Village Clubs the Chief Source whence greater are supplied — Institution of I Zingari Club — First Mention of a properly constituted Match—The New Style of Bowling—Its Reception—Exciting Discussions upon its Character and Merits—Introduction of India-rubber Gloves and Leg Guards — First Visit of Prince Albert to a Match—Improvement in the Score Sheet—The All England Eleven—Formation of other Migratory Bands—The Cricketers' Fund—The Canterbury Week—Gentlemen and Players' Match—Public Schools—Resuscitation of the Surrey County Club—The Decline of Kent—Match at Malling—Description of it.

IN the Olympian revels lookers on were considered the most competent judges of the training, skill, prowess, and character of the various contenders, and now the world outside the cricket circle is in the main the best able to form a correct estimate as regards the physical and moral attributes essential to the proper discharge of the duties involved. Admitting that the game was at this period establishing a claim to the terms manly, noble, national, and so forth, the rapid enlargement of its borders gathered within the fold men of every kind—many physically unfit, and as much out of place as a lame dancing master, a purblind or a deaf man where the deficient faculties were most required. Then the sullen or quick temper, which hardly consorts with a pastime requiring amenities corresponding with at least the status of society in which the parties, no matter how humble, move. These observances give a tone and complexion to the whole affair. Few things tend more successfully to agitate wrong dispositions among villagers than the sneer or jest at their performances, either in the vocal choir of the church or instrumental military exercises in the field. So, too, on the village green. But as the latter admits of freer scope for coarse observations, there is the greater danger of carrying jokes too far. Not that honest criticism should be cried down, even if it be conveyed in a somewhat hard and harsh phrase, for it keeps the would-be hero of the bat and ball up to the mark. One of the great spurs to fame was found in the almost certainty of appearing in print, for at this period nearly every local journal reserved a corner for cricket. It is hardly possible to say with any degree of correctness what the material of the village green and the cricket column did at this time towards furthering the game. The countenance of the local gentry and others of position had a beneficial tendency, as it brought to the front many an obscure individual eventually found to possess talents for which he had hitherto received no credit. As the object of the humblest was, as a rule, glory rather than gain, such trophies of victory as a bat and a ball were household gods, receiving no inconsiderable amount of hero worship. The "bone of contention" between two humble parish elevens rarely extended beyond a plain supper, which the losing side agreed to pay—not a serious matter in those days, although most of the guests surrounded the evening table with tolerably strong appetites. Nor was the number of the guests always confined to the combatants alone. Occasionally an *entrepreneur* would catch the attention of the public with the announcement on a flaring bill that the match was to be played for 50*l* a-side, perhaps more, but this stupid device brought little grist to the mill. Everybody immediately connected with the affair knew it to be a sham that must soon defeat itself. The time for making humble and honest men instruments in the hands of gamblers had passed, the press proved a great power in stamping out what little fire might perchance be kindled even among the embers of a defunct generation. Higher motives than fear of transgressing law actuated the contenders during the whole process of the play. A match of cricket in many a rural district was the event of the year, it can therefore be readily imagined how the heart and soul of two well-poised elevens went into the matter, for to them it was as important as if the fate of empires hung upon their individual skill and prowess.

The great changes incident to advancement in higher quarters forced their way by almost insensible degrees into the lower strata of cricketing society. Many rustic customs yielded to the general laws for the successsful prosecution of the game. Bat making, as a special art was hardly known, and either the village carpenter or cooper could shape the instrument to answer general purposes. As time grew on, the bat assumed proportions and finish, and every member of a club with any pretensions to position and importance took care to provide himself with a "willow weapon," of which, if it happened to be the agent in procuring a long score, he was not a little proud.

To enter minutely into, or even speak of the incidents of this quarter of the century, with its anecdotes and stories, its marvels and rapid strides, would require the labour of a Stow, and a volume as compendious as his "Survey," without a corresponding amount of usefulness. The lay and clerical influences were frequently united, not merely by patronising airs, but by taking part in the game itself. This was a great power, and the unsympathising public—that portion of it naturally ascetic—began to discern in such gatherings a tendency to a much wider spread field, of a moral and hygienic character, than they had before contemplated. It must be understood that the remarks thus far made relate almost exclusively to the progress of cricket in rural districts. The colossal strides effected in the meantime by clubs of position and standing, will be found separately chaptered Pilch was a village tailor, Wenman a village carpenter, Sewell a village printer of fabrics, and A Mynn a village yeoman Probably no men were greater ornaments to the cricket world than they were at the period in question Numbers of names might be mentioned which now stand enrolled on the page of history—representatives of men whose school was the village green, and Nature their schoolmaster There is a profundity of truth in the philosophical axiom, "That which hath been is now, and that which is now is the thing that shall be" Yes, many a military hero has been formed of the stuff drawn by the recruiting sergeant at a village festival, and enough remains to supply the gaps which time is yearly, ay, daily making in the ranks of accomplished cricketers, if they be sought out and patronised

That great matches are superb in their way, few will be hardy enough to deny In them the "science" of the game is displayed in its fullest grandeur But of all contests rightly bearing the name of cricket, the pleasantest beyond comparison are those when one eleven drives merrily away for a dozen miles on a country road with all its ups and downs and irregularities to meet a neighbouring club All the fun of a race-day is embodied without its coarseness, the lads laugh, "lark," and sing, while the steadier discourse about the favourite hits of the opponents they are about to encounter, or the sinuous character of such a bowler, and how he twists the ball irresistibly into the leg stump from the "off," &c While these discussions lighten the journey, little blue coils of fragrant smoke curl up among the trees by the roadside Then there is the hearty welcome on the tented field, the amusing incidents attending a manly fight, and as jolly a drive home as man can wish for—all the jollier if, when the match seemed desperate, the captain by pluck and patience "pulled it out of the fire" These visits often required the man who undertook the necessary journey to rise with the morning beams of the sun, and not unfrequently reminded him of the lay of "We won't go home," &c No stiff joints were allowed, though perchance a few aching heads consequent upon excitement, &c, there really might be, yet unfelt because unacknowledged, seeing that

"The labour we delight in physics pain"

Parish matches then will ever be the source whence the great supply of cricketers must come, and on this account too much attention and encouragement can hardly be given Here it is that talent is most easily perceived, for here it is natural, and all the learned talk in the world about science comes to nothing when placed beside the rough and ready faculties of the rustic, who, after leaving his bench, his forge, or his seat, strikes wonder among the gazers by the facility with which he handles either the leather or the willow, and the marvellous precision and exactitude with which he measures the rapidity of the ball on its course, and the return of the same to the properly appointed place

One of the prominent characteristics of this period was the institution of the club denominated I Zingari, one purely of aristocratic origin, and from its birth till now has so remained It is stated, that when at Cambridge, Messrs F Ponsonby, Bolland, C Taylor, and others devoted some of their leisure moments to cricket and theatricals Hence sprang many matches under various names, several private theatrical meetings, and finally the annual Canterbury gatherings Ultimately a club was formed for cricket under the designation of "I Zingari" The starting number of members was twenty-five Rules and regulations, as a matter of course, were drawn up, and have been ever since adhered to with commendable pertinacity No professionals are ever allowed to take part in their matches except in the character of umpire, the object being to cultivate the art of bowling among themselves

The first match played by I Zingari was in August, 1845, against Newport Pagnel, when the wanderers were defeated by 39 runs On this occasion every man of the losing side scored something Mr Charles Taylor made 60 runs in his double innings, Mr Dewing 37, the Hon F. Ponsonby 21, and the Hon Mr Lyon 23 The lowest contribution was four In the double innings they put together 113 and 96—total 209, against 109 and 139, total 248, of the other side It was not likely that such a band of accomplished cricketers should be without a laureate In fact, they possessed writers of varied orders and of more than common excellence The Canterbury week would soon collapse without the presence of I Zingari, both with the sun above the horizon and the sun below it One song by the president of the club (Mr Bolland) runs thus

"We are told England's armies assembled,
When Liberty's cause was in view,
We are told, too, that tyranny trembled
'Neath the folds of the Red, White, and Blue
Yes, the Red, White, and Blue o'er the ocean,
Has floated in conquests of old,
But to night let us pledge our devotion
To the folds of the Red Black, and Gold
Chorus—To the folds, &c

The ball the stout cricketer urges,
Cleaves a pathway of peace o'er the plain,
The weapon he wields leaves no scourges,
No record of carnage or pain,
No, 'tis his to cement man's affection,
Reviving his pastime of old,
In our camp we fear no defection
'Neath the folds of the Red, Black, and Gold
Chorus—'Neath the folds, &c

As the eagle scans desert and mountain,
As the sea-bird the wilds of the deep,
As the water springs free from the fountain,
And dashes unbound down the steep
So our wandering band shuns all warning,
In every soil plants its hold,
Each tract of Old England adorning
With the folds of the Red, Black, and Gold
Chorus—With the folds &c

Then the wine cup, the wine cup bear hither,
Fill high, we sip nought but the brim,
May the germ we have planted ne'er wither,
Nor the star of our birth right grow dim
May the friendships we have formed never sever,
May each link lengthen long and grow old
Then a bumper, "Here's cricket for ever,"
'Neath the folds of the Red, Black, and Gold
Chorus—'Neath the folds &c

Long before the formation of I Zingari Club, the spirit of migration evinced itself in two or three parts of Europe outside the British dominions, and the Italians speak of a match well played at Naples, the combatants being Eton v The World Mention is also made of a match played at Port Munychia (formerly a strong garrison of the Lacedemonians), between the officers of H M frigate the "Portland," then lying at Piræus * It may also be well to take notice here of a match played at Toronto between the St George's Club of New York and the Canadian Club, when the New Yorker's travelled a distance—in round numbers—of 1000 miles to the place appointed for the contest, long before the introduction of railways But a still more remarkable occurrence forces itself into notice "Cricket on the ice" is a sort of dandy pastime in England, and is chiefly commented upon as such To play for hours in "regions of thick ribbed ice" presents a scene of a vastly different character The frozen zone never was adapted for the sports of the temperate, and yet wickets have been pitched in latitudes above 80° In an account of Sir Edward Parry's second voyage in search of a north-west passage it is said "The weather (March 13, 1823) was now so pleasant, and the temperature in the sun so comfortable to the feelings when a shelter could be found from the wind, that we set up various games for the people, (the crews of the Hecla and Fury) such as cricket, football, and quoits, which some of them played for many hours during the day" Capt Lyon made a drawing of the cricketers and the "field," afterwards engraved by Finden, and this forms a frontispiece to the history of the voyage † Before proceeding further with the progress of the period under discussion, it may be well to state as briefly as possible what reception the new style of bowling met with, and in order to make this intelligible, a few extracts from the *Sporting Magazine*, the favoured organ of cricket among the leading classes at the time of its introduction

It was during this period that Mr G Knight, an influential member of the Marylebone Club, adopted the "high delivery," and he, in consequence of the opposition that was raised to its introduction, formally brought the subject before the Committee of that aristocratic body Not succeeding, however, he addressed three letters to the cricketing world through the medium of the magazine in question, in whose pages the point underwent considerable discussion In the first of these letters, the author says·

It is my intention, early in next season, to propose to the Marylebone Club a law, which will afford to bowlers a larger field for the exertion of science than they now enjoy, and as this measure

* See Cochrane's "Wanderings in Greece" † See Parry's second voyage, published 1824

does not appear to be generally known to cricketers, either in its nature, the reasons which have given rise to it, or the benefits anticipated from its adoption, I should be glad to afford an explanation of these points through the medium of your valuable magazine It may not be generally known that, from the earliest time of cricket, down to a very late period, *no law whatever existed to restrain the bowling* From time immemorial the under hand style alone was practised, for the best possible reason, namely, that it was found amply sufficient to meet the batting of those days About twenty four years ago, however, the system of batting suddenly underwent an almost total change and was carried to a degree of perfection never before known Instead of the cautious defence hitherto practised, with one foot always within the crease, the method then introduced was running in at the ball, hard hitting, and a bold forward play, which altogether changed the nature of that part of the game The effect of this was, that the number of runs increased greatly, matches, from requiring more time, and consequently more expense, soon became much less frequent than they had been before, and thus, from the single circumstance of the batting having got the start of the bowling, cricket, in some measure, began to decline The superiority of the batting to the bowling, with the bad effects above mentioned, has been for years a theme of universal complaint, and has never been checked, except when it has been met by the straight-armed bowling (erroneously called throwing), which it is my wish to restore I say restore, because the system is none of mine, nor is it a new one, but, on the contrary, about twenty years ago it prevailed in a considerable degree, especially in the county of Kent About that time, when the leading object of interest amongst cricketers was to devise some method of putting the batting and the bowling more upon a par, the straight-armed delivery was invented, and introduced by an eminent player (Wills) in Kent, and practised by him and a few others so successfully, that their county, not otherwise powerful, was in a short time able to cope with All England, which was then at the zenith of its strength * * * The straight armed bowling being thus introduced, was practised for a period of eight or ten years with perfect success, and without any interruption being offered to it nor is it probable that any would have been (although, from the difficulty of playing it, it had many enemies), if it had been kept within those bounds which at first confined it But this, unfortunately, was not the case other bowlers arose, who quickly adopted the new system, and, observing the effect of delivering the ball with the arm extended horizontally, they thought to become more formidable still, the more they got their hands up, and thus leading each other on, there being no law to restrain them, they raised them higher and higher, till at length, in a grand match at Brighton (in which many members of the Marylebone Club played,) one of the new practitioners raised *his hand so very high above his head* that it was thought quite time for the Club to interpose Instead however, of going deliberately to work, instead of endeavouring to restrain and regulate the new system, by discarding what was bad and retaining what was good, they immediately determined that *all* was evil, and, with that feeling, hastened to pass the law under which cricket has so long suffered, and which it is my object to repeal

I am far from blaming the Marylebone Club for interfering at that time, on the contrary, I think their interposition was loudly called for, but I do blame them for discarding at once, and without trial of the possibility of curbing it, the most effective style of bowling that ever was invented, merely because there being no law to restrain it, it naturally ran into excess A law for that purpose I now mean to propose The line then drawn I wish to relax a little, I desire to restore the straight-armed bowling to what it was when it was first introduced my object, in short, is, to steer a *middle course*, avoiding alike the tameness of the Old School and the extravagance of the New So far am I from approving that extravagance, that, though I shall advocate to the utmost of my power the straight armed bowling, without which, or some equivalent advantage, I am confident that cricket will greatly decline, there is no more determined enemy than myself to throwing at the wicket, as is well known by all those with whom I had the pleasure of playing last year The fear that the introduction of this bowling will lead to throwing, is in truth quite chimerical, and only shows to what length men will sometimes be carried, by, I do not say the spirit of opposition, but rather, I believe, the dread of change, for, so far is it from resembling a throw, that it is diametrically opposite to it Throwing is the most forcible mode of delivering the ball, this is the weakest The arm is never in a position so incapable of exertion as when it is extended horizontally, it is an attitude common enough to a girl about to slap another's face, but the last adopted by a pugilist Of all the four methods of delivery, viz, straight-armed bowling, under hand bowling, jerking, and throwing, the first is by far the most feeble, so much so that straight-armed bowlers are invariably slow bowlers Their balls, indeed, get up fast, but they never come fast to the long stop To call it a throw is quite ridiculous If a man were to attempt throwing a hundred yards for a bet, who would expect to see him deliver the ball with his arm extended horizontally? would not everybody laugh at the idea of that being called throwing? It may, however be said, never mind what is not a throw, but tell us what is define a throw I answer no In the first place, I might possibly not be able to give an accurate definition of it, and if I could I certainly would not, for this reason that it is perfectly well known already, and that, as the object of a definition is to convey accurate knowledge of the thing defined nothing can be more absurd than to attempt to define that which is accurately known already It may do harm, and can do no good If, again, I matched a horse to trot so many miles in an hour, I should not think of defining what a trot was No one probably could do it, no one could so exactly mark the precise elevation of the feet, the tension of the muscles, and the relative position of the limbs, could so minutely define that pace as to make his description apply to it through all the vast variety of horses without the chance of misconstruction Yet everybody knows the pace when he sees it nobody mistakes it for a walk or a canter no one would wish to define it, or suppose, if it could not be defined, that it could not therefore be distinguished So is it with throwing every body knows what a throw is when he sees it, and that is enough for practical purposes That they do know it, is proved (if proof be necessary) by the fact that, though the part of the tenth law, which I seek to repeal, in no way affects *underhand* throwing (a mode as easy to practise, and nearly as forcible and effective as the over handed), *yet it has never been attempted*, and merely because the beginning of that law, *which I retain in mine*, runs thus—' the ball shall be bowled, not thrown nor jerked," the mere words, "shall not be thrown," have for ten years been sufficient to exclude that mode of throwing My proposed law runs thus The ball shall be bowled if it be thrown or jerked, or if any part of the hand or arm be *above* the *shoulder* at the time of delivery the umpire shall call *no ball*" The first part of the old one is thus substantially retained and why, having been effective during time past, it will not be equally so for the time to come, why, having invariably been found adequate to bar one kind of throwing, it will not be equally so to bar another, is a question which I have frequently asked, but have never yet received an answer to, and it is quite out of the reach of my capacity to furnish one The fact is, that the straight-armed bowling has no more to do with throwing than it has with jerking, and its adoption is just as likely to introduce one as the other The proposed law has not a greater tendency than the existing one to promote either the action of a throw is so peculiar, the arm is bent and drawn back in a manner so distinct from any other method of delivery, that, whether under-hand or over-hand, it is always the same, and as easy to be distinguished from any other, as the trot of a horse is from the walk or gallop If, however, there are still some persons who insist on calling the straight-armed bowling *throwing*, I shall make no objection, as it is scarcely worth while to dispute about terms I would rather ask them why, in their opinion, there are any restrictive laws at all as to the delivery of the ball? Why throwing and jerking are especially and alone excluded? I would remind them that there are but two qualities which enter into the character of any mode of delivery, and those are *the force* and *the bound*—these two ingredients make up every species of throwing bowling, and jerking The force is the rough portion, the bound, the scientific, the one should be restrained, the other encouraged, and the only reason why throwing and jerking have been excluded is, because those are by far the two most forcible modes of delivery, as almost every body can throw and jerk with such violence as to set all skill at defiance It is not, therefore, the *action* of throwing or jerking that is objectionable, but only the *force*, and consequently, to find fault with a mode of delivery which approaches one of those actions in appearance, but not at all in effect, is quarrelling with a shadow, and exactly illustrating the old adage of "Give a dog a bad name and hang him" To make balls *twist* and *rise in the bound* is the object Thus, bowling becomes more scientific, and if those qualities of throwing and jerking could be retained, and the *speed* excluded there would be no longer any occasion for restrictive laws at all In viewing the straight-armed bowling therefore, it is not enough to say that it is a throw (which, in fact, to a practised eye it in nowise resembles), but it must be shown that it carries with it something at least approaching to the force of a throw, which is in truth too absurd to insist upon, since it is well known, as I have before observed, to be the most feeble method of delivery Still, however, objections are not wanting, for in small things, as in great, there are those whose dread of change is their ruling passion, and I have often heard it said, "We have a definition now which serves us in some stead, before you wipe it away give us a better"

This revolution in the art of bowling brought together, as a matter of course, a large hostile army Long, loud and angry were the protestations against what was sternly denominated, and with some show of reason, "throwing bowling" The chieftains of the old school were dead against it, and Nyren, with much bitterness, compared the results to mere 'horse play" Several letters appeared in the *Magazine* both in support of Mr Knight's theory and against it These were subsequently collated by Mr W Denison and published in a small octavo volume entitled "Sketches of the Players" As a rule, every aspirant for fame went in for pace rather than exactness, and great danger attended his performances, especially on hard and uneven surfaces To mitigate this, recourse was had to leg guards, indiarubber gloves, and other protectors When first introduced, they assumed a grotesque effect to the eye of the uninitiated observer, but as they became a necessity, and their adoption general, they ceased to attract special notice, except by way of ridicule Rough, absurd, and silly poems occasionally cropped up One specimen—the fragment of a serio-comic—will here suffice

SOLILOQUY BY AN OLD CRICKETER

Gone are the days, the merry days of youth,
When I with others through the island ranged,
But cricket's altered, and the game, forsooth,
Barring the name is altogether changed
Full well I prize the oft repeated truth,
"This is the age for science making way,"
But why at cricket men should be so ruth
I can't make out Farewell! it's had its day

Bless me! how altered since those days of yore
When Bird and Beldham, Budd, and such as they—
Lord Frederick, too, once England's chief and flower—
Astonished all who came to see them play,
When in the field turned out, they looked like men
Fit for great deeds, and by true play were tried.
The ball was bowled no slingy, round stuff then—
'Tis all up now—the game's transmogrified,

Now batsmen try these dangers to elude,
And greave knee deep in buff to check the shocks
Which the red ball, by throwing, visits rude
The understandings, and 'gainst them marks its knocks
Bruises are here,—there cicatrice and scar
It often makes me really shrug and shiver,
Though hands are gloved as if bent on a spar,
Their pins are patched as if with bullock's liver

The change in the style and character of bowling necessitated corresponding changes in other departments. The bat once anything but an elegant weapon of defence, assumed by degrees a much lighter and smarter appearance than hitherto The theories of Lambert and Nyren were at a discount when contrasted with that of Mr Wanostrocht (alias "Felix") The first of these literary instructors in "the art of playing the game of cricket" possessed a vast amount of practical knowledge combined with great proficiency both as a batsman and bowler, but was, so to speak, no orator, the second, though not so renowned as a player, understood the game quite as well, and could describe it with greater force and interest, but the third had the rare gifts of a polished and effective style of batting, great command of his pencil, and could wield his pen with the skill of a scholar Aware of the service rendered to cricket at this stage of its history, the Marylebone Club resolved to play a match "in honour of him" All the choice talent of the community underwent the scrutiny of the club, and a great success was the result For the first time His Royal Highness Prince Albert was attracted to a cricket match The ground was crowded to its utmost capacity, and the Prince could not forbear remarking on the quiet and excellent demeanour of the multitude, composed as it was of every grade of society The sides were headed by Mr Felix and Fuller Pilch respectively; that of the latter won the match by thirty-four runs Mr Felix maintained his celebrity unbroken up to the 20th of May, 1857, when he was seized with paralysis "Felix on the Bat" is, however, a work destined to survive a long shock of time Another feature characteristic of the period was the advance made in scoring, one result of the peripatetic movements of the All England Eleven A reference to almost any old printed score will convey at once an idea of deficiency with regard to details Following closely upon improvements in the score sheet was a table of averages, designed to show in a condensed form the relative merits of the most celebrated batsmen and bowlers At the outset the plan was practicable, and it afforded a tolerably correct notion of the efficiency of the parties concerned It was also easily to be comprehended and understood As the game progressed, and as many persons of questionable merit as players were anxious to see their names in print, abuses crept in, and the valuable element deteriorated in an equal ratio The tables were for years all the go, and watched for eagerly at the close of every season The fever has not yet died out, but the interest in the tables is extremely small among the meditative portion of the cricket community, who repudiate the idea of placing two or three fortunate innings of an indifferent player against the contingencies of three times that number by first class men against foes formidable as themselves in the field A plan, which, though suitable to the vanity of the simple minded, excites the pity of the judicious

The movements of the All England Eleven had a wonderful effect upon the cricket spirit of the age, for it not only introduced the game to places and peoples hitherto but very imperfectly acquainted with it, but served also to widen the sphere of its popularity to an extent not calculated upon Wherever the foot of these chieftains trod they left the mark of cricket behind, and, without an exception, the imprint remains to this day

Nor was this the only migratory band of professional cricketers which distinguished the period in question Great events often spring from trifling causes

Such was the success of Clarke, the chief manager of these matches, that other bands, imitating his example, convinced the world that professional cricket was not a bad vocation, although a danger of relying too much upon sunshine and smiles had to be apprehended, and against which aspirants for fame, especially of this kind, were hardly equal. The advice of good men—such, for instance, as that of Mr. Bass—was often found to be as the evening cloud and morning dew, and the prospects of many a young player of promise were prematurely blighted.

To Mr. Denison may be credited the original idea of "The Cricketers' Fund," formed especially to meet the cases of sudden distress as well as of chronic calamity. When first set on foot, it received a ready response from a large and influential circle of the cricket-loving public, now about thirty years ago. Whether actuated by wise or foolish promptings is not the question to be here debated, but certainly the players, for whose benefit the fund was disinterestedly promoted, appeared to be sadly deficient in gratitude by the proceedings they adopted in rudely persisting for accounts in a public, and at that time a ruling, journal. In self justification Mr. Denison replied: "In consequence of the players having laughed at the idea of having any rules for the guidance and conduct of the benefit society which I had for upwards of two years been endeavouring to establish for their sole benefit, under the title of 'The Cricketers' Fund,' I had abandoned all further intention of carrying out that object, and should therefore return the money I had received to the respective parties. The subscriptions of the players were accordingly returned to them upon one of the days during the match between the Eleven of England and Fourteen of Surrey, at the Oval, with a deduction of one shilling and sixpence in the pound towards the expenses. There are not, therefore, any accounts to be settled between the players and myself. Soon after the announcement in 1846 of my intention to form this benefit society, a committee of the players was named to arrange and complete rules for the management and conduct of the society, which rules I was to obtain the approval of and certificate for from the barrister appointed by the Act of Parliament for that purpose. They would then have to be registered, whereupon the benefit society—'The Cricketers' Fund'—would have been formally established, and its objects could have been at once carried out. The refusal, however, of that committee of players to have any set of rules put an end to all further attempts at the formation of the society, and consequently the 'Cricketers' Fund' which I had proposed has never been established, whilst the conduct of some of the players had induced me to decline any further efforts in their behalf. With regard to the sums which were placed in my hands by several gentlemen to be applied to this benefit society when it should have been finally formed, a considerable portion has been returned, whilst the remainder will be forwarded as the various parties either return to town, or furnish me, as requested in my letter of July, with their present addresses. As I have already stated, I have not any accounts to settle with the players; but, for my own satisfaction, I shall, at the commencement of the next season, submit a statement of them to the Marylebone Club."

So excellent and beneficial a project was not, however, allowed to drop.

Several influential supporters of cricket placed themselves at the head of it, and for several years "The Cricketers' Fund Society" prospered right well. A match occurred annually at Lord's, until a schism arose among the players, which so annoyed the Marylebone Club that the match was scratched from the yearly programme, and in its stead was substituted one for the exclusive benefit of the "Ground," regularly played on Whit-Monday. In course of a short time the fund began to show signs of decay, and some leading members of it suggested the unwise resolve of winding it up. This proved to be a task of no mean difficulty. Certain rules had to be complied with, not by mere talk. The Court of Chancery had a scowling look about it, and, as one of the more sensible portion of the members remarked, "it would be a disastrous step to take, as it would be playing into the hands of lawyers who would get the 'oyster' (money in hand) and leave us the shell only." Upon this the project for dividing the funds at a proposed early meeting was not carried out (1868).

Before the first half of the present century came to its close, the popularity of I Zingari Club had wonderfully increased. In fact the Canterbury Week was nothing without the presence of the "Red, Black, and Gold." Not that the cricket afforded a greater treat to the lovers of the game than the other matches provided for the occasion, but the members composing the team in the field could, and did in the majority, provide an evening entertainment seldom to be met with among amateur performers on the stage. As, however, the subject is treated of at some length in another portion of this work, the passing mention of I Zingari merely as a matter of chronology may suffice.

The annual match between Gentlemen and Players was not kept up with strict regularity till the year 1830 onward. In order at times to equalise the contending forces, some curious devices were had recourse to. During the first twenty years the Players won fourteen matches and the Gentlemen six. The Inter-University matches had not obtained a footing as yet at Lord's, although the Public Schools attracted considerable and a yearly increasing interest.

Another feature of the period was the single wicket match between two of the most celebrated amateurs in the county of Kent, viz., Messrs. Felix and Mynn. As batsmen, both bore a high character in the cricket world—not as bowlers. The disparity between the two as single wicket players was so great that it was no match at all, notwithstanding the expectations formed by the admirers of Mr. Felix. Nearly two thousand persons attended the match, and among this number were persons of almost every grade of society. The event had the stamp of novelty about it. With the exception of two crack single wicket matches between Pilch and Marsden, of Sheffield, and Mynn and Dearman, also of Sheffield, there had not been a game of the kind in Kent for nearly thirty years. Mr. Felix had no chance whatever with his opponent, for although in full catapulta practice, he soon found out his mistake, and was easily vanquished. He scored but four runs in two innings, Mr. Mynn five runs in one innings. In a second trial Mr. Felix one run from the bat in two innings, extras 11, total, 12. Mr. Mynn four and nine not out. A.D. 1846.

The revival of the Surrey County Club about this time excited a great deal of attention So low had Surrey fallen for nearly thirty years, that the mention of being raised again to its former elevation produced ridicule in the minds of the sleepy and short-sighted After a few determined efforts the project was put into shape, and instead of a resort to the Montpelier, the Beehive, and such like, the market garden at the Oval was converted into a ground befitting a county famed in many a past age, and not likely to be blotted out easily in the present one.*

In contradistinction to this, may be noticed the decline of Kent about the period of Surrey's resuscitation More than a century and a half previously, Kent was recognised as one of the few centres of cricket in England, and down to the time referred to—as Lord Macauley would perhaps have said—within the memory of middle aged men now living, they had as fine an eleven as were ever seen engaged in a bat and ball contest It has been repeatedly said that a young amateur from a public school or university would grow inches if he had the honour to be asked to play in a county match, but not the wealth of the Indies, or the interest of both Houses of Parliament put together, would have gained him admission into the county ranks, unless he could pass muster with the experienced hands who had charge of the management It was no joke to miss a ball, much less a catch, with the Kentish yeomen watching and backing their county There was no mistake about it The wealthy and well-to-do found the money and guaranteed each match, and the honour of the county was usually entrusted to Alfred Mynn Felix, Pilch, Wenman, or men of such a stamp. Ever since the tents were struck at Malling, few assemblages like those gathered there have since been witnessed in the county A writer in a local journal was so charmed with the portion of a match, Kent v England, that he advised his friends to haste to Malling and witness its conclusion He says, "When Kent commenced their second innings, a more animated scene it would be difficult to pourtray. Reader, have you ever been at a cricket match? If not, go, and, understand it or not, you will not fail to realize many happy moments! Here all rude and jarring feelings subside Men of all shades congregate, and no alloy creeps in to mar the delightful scene. The Radical finds himself alongside the Conservative, and each recognises his political opponent with that degree of blandness which is reserved for peculiar occasions The laugh of the man who had been 'born a Whig' is as hearty as the man whose political creed has to be formed, and to countenance the exertions of Kent's athletic sons, to crown, in fact, the whole scene with brilliant lustre and joyousness, Kent's fair damsels form a galaxy of unrivalled loveliness and beauty" To estimate this seeming rhapsody at its proper value, it should be stated that its author belonged to the school of what is now designated "advanced political opinions" He had never seen a cricket match in such colossal proportions, comprehending, as it did, a large number of the best players of the day There surely must have been a mysterious influence connected with the sunny month of August, and the scene of the match down "Offham Lane," to have extracted thus much of the acerbity from a man's severe creed, as to

* See "Surrey"

enable him to be so politically charitable in severe times. The writer might have thrown into this picture "Old Topper" Dorrinton, the father of three sound cricketers, and who, though far more expert with scissors and bodkin than pen and ink, was invariably mounted in a primitive looking box to note how the game proceeded. Woe to the pestering inquirer when intent on his scoring—his answer to him was usually as rough as it was ready, and as ready as it was rough. Topper sometimes used really to swear outright, and sometimes in the presence of his superiors. He used to say he couldn't help swearing when the match was running very close, or going on anyhow. Another *habitue* was always to be seen on great occasions. This took the form of a peripatetic pastry cook, neatly dressed, and carrying her wares in a large square basket. As the rustics generally found an increase of appetite on occasions of a cricket match, the stock of pastry soon vanished; the purchases were as frequently made through the process of "heads or tails" as that of buying outright. Then there was the man with a whip, by profession a rat-catcher, not particularly tender towards defiant yokels or mongrel dogs; out of the ring they must go, either from the smack of the whip or the next handy process. A little stir was now and then occasioned among small knots of stockjobbers and backers of opinion, for the season was now at its height.

Yes, truly at its height with Kent as a county. Its decadence may be dated from the peculiarity and triumph of the match in question, even when from untoward circumstances it appeared to be lost. Three among the greatest heroes on the Kent side were bowled in such rapid succession by Redgate of Nottingham, that no time was afforded for acquiring a run. So close was the contest, that Kent claimed the victory by two runs only. This result formed the chief feature of the cricket season generally, and Pilch's benefit, which embraced this and other striking incidents will, doubtlessly, be long remembered in the locality where it occurred, for

> The spinsters, and the knitters in the sun,
> And the free maids who use their thread with bones,
> Do use and chant it.—*Twelfth Night, Act 2, Scene 4.*

So rapid were the advances at this time, that a demand grew for an annual recapitulation of the great matches played, and Mr Denison came to the front with his "Cricketer's Companion." In this work of about sixty pages octavo nearly all the information necessary was reproduced from the files of the most recognized journals appropriated to cricket, He says: "To the old soldier, or the old sailor, the fighting over again 'the battles of the day' has at all times been a source of gratification and delight. But whilst in the instance of a battle the names of the various regiments, or of the ships which were respectively engaged in any particular contest are usually found to be engraven on the remembrance of those who have survived the havoc of the fray—in cricket the relatively same points of information are not so easily borne in mind." The utility of such a work may perhaps be best estimated by the variety of copyists, who probably found it far more profitable, in a financial point of view, than the promoter did. There is not anything wonderful herein, for "one soweth and another reapeth" in this form or that every day.

Nor was the "pen of a ready writer" the only instrument in proclaiming the advance of cricket and the support it was receiving. An engraved plate forty-two inches by thirty-six was published by Mr Mason of Brighton. This contains no less than seventy-two portraits of the most remarkable men of the time, taken by Messrs W Drummond and C J Basebee, and engraved by Mr G H Phillips. It represents a match between Kent and Sussex at Brighton. An artist's proof copy of what was termed a "National picture" to subscribers was charged eight guineas, the lowest price three. The cost of production was estimated at 1500 guineas, and although the work neither lacked sale nor support, Mr Mason, it is said, profited more in fame than purse by its production.

Another example of the countenance given to cricket at the period in question, ought not to be passed over or "willingly let die." A match was played annually in Richmond Park, under the special patronage of Her Royal Highness the Duchess of Gloucester. The parties invited were usually gentlemen residing in the locality, and the East Sheen Club. The Duchess and an illustrious train of visitors honoured the players with their presence. There was also invariably a concentration of what was termed the highly respectable portion of society to be met with. Suitable marquees and tents spotted the park opposite her mansion, and an abundance of creature comforts supplied after the good old English fashion from the storehouse of the royal patron. Nor were the poor unthought of, or uncared for—there was enough, and to spare for them. It was the "cricket event" of the year in that locality, one of unalloyed enjoyment—sufficient, forsooth, to make a Stoic dance, and draw an anchorite "out of his shell." At least so thought, and so said, many of the guests on these annual festivities. They induced three or four local sippers at the poetic fountain to distil their fanciful imaginings, but as the reader is cognizant of the simple history of the match, mention of poet and poem relating thereto may be dispensed with, for, although they were well up to the mark in spirit, they were not quite so in the letter.

For some years the speculation of the All England Eleven previously spoken of proved to be so lucrative, that the monopoly was broken by a second England eleven, scarcely inferior to the first. The practice of uneven sides never found favour with that portion of the cricket public advocating the orthodox number. Others encouraged it on the ground of novelty, and as leading in the end to the advance of the game in many districts inconveniently remote from places where sound cricket was a common affair. In nine cases out of ten the professional visitors left the scene of contest in the character of victors even though their opponents were as a rule, numerically speaking, two to one. Among these there were rarely one-fifth who possessed any real qualification whatsoever. Nowhere with the bat, and anywhere but the right place in the field. Clarke and his party found abundant opportunities for the exercise of their preceptive faculties, and in a few instances they yielded good fruit. Probably at the end of a three day contest, the vanquished were told that they had been rather unfortunate in this, that, or the other particular, and often a cold compliment served to gratify the vanity of some whose local renown had been hitherto somewhat over estimated.

With a rival team in the field the aspect underwent an entire change, for with one side as good as the other the proper order of things became restored. Cricket in its loftier character could be seen nowhere to greater advantage than when the "Two Elevens" were confronted at Lords. On these annual meetings it was frequently difficult to discover on which side victory would rest. So sharp at times was the fighting, and so evenly were the scales poised, that "a moth might turn the balance." For several years this match figured prominently among the coming events of a season. The Cricketer's Fund received large accessions to its exchequer, and the players themselves suffered nothing either in purse or popularity by the fixture. With the gigantic strides now being made, however, in every quarter, neither of these teams kept pace sufficiently. The schoolmaster was abroad, and the effects of his teaching the game on sound principles were visible everywhere. Country gentlemen took up the matter with spirit. Colts' matches were found to be valuable experiments, as they served to bring out talent scarcely known beyond the village or hamlet in which the parties resided. From these matches to county clubs the draft was often very speedy, and should the young aspirant answer expectation and "keep within compass," a bright future was usually spread out before him, independently of the honour of being a county player, which, to say the least, for a professional cricketer is one of which he may be justly proud.

With respect to naval and military cricket it is hardly possible to estimate the advantages resulting therefrom. Though not quite of so recent an origin as some other institutions of the kind, it is carried by warlike agencies into situations which could hardly be pierced by other means. To the mind of the great circumnavigator before alluded to, the idea of amusement out of doors was not deemed impracticable or unimportant while in the pursuit of such an inaccessible spot as the North Pole. Dreary indeed must have been the solitude of himself and companions in that "land of desolation," but for the ennobling thought of adding something to the usefulness and glory of his nation and the world at large. The very same idea pervades both arms of the service now as then. Wherever the duties attendant upon discoveries are required, the right men are found at their places. If the stern realities of war call them abroad, no post is vacated in the hour of need; should the island be threatened by invaders, the watchdogs on the deep would soon be heard to bark. In a double sense our army and navy are pioneers of civilization. How intolerable, however, would the life of either service be but for occasional relaxations out of doors and on shore, such for instance as that which is afforded by the mimic strife of cricket—one which Marlborough in all probability never saw, nor Nelson cast his eye towards, but one that Wellington gazed upon and applauded. Nor he alone; hundreds of illustrious heroes in peaceful times have not only sanctioned military and naval matches by their presence, supported them by their authority, but countenanced them still farther by participating therein.

CHAPTER V.

THE AUGUSTAN OR GOLDEN AGE.

Happy Britannia!
Rich is thy soil and merciful thy clime;
Bold, firm, and graceful are thy generous youth;
Thy SONS OF GLORY many.—*Thomson.*

EPOCHS OF THE GAME—EFFECTS OF THE GREAT EXHIBITION ON CRICKET—PROFESSIONAL PLAYERS AND PUBLIC SCHOOLS—INSUFFIENCY OF PLAYING GROUNDS—WESTMINSTER BOYS AND VINCENT SQUARE—COMMONS AND WASTE LANDS—BATTERSEA AND REGENT'S PARKS—MIGRATORY CLUBS—CRICKET PARLIAMENT—VISITS OF CRICKETERS TO CANADA, AUSTRALIA, ETC.—VIEWS OF CONTINENTAL WRITERS ON THE CHARACTER OF CRICKET—JUTLAND—PROGRESS OF THE GAME IN IRELAND, SCOTLAND, AND WALES—COUNTY QUALIFICATIONS—DUTIES OF SECRETARY AND CAPTAIN—OPENING OF PRINCE'S GROUND—CRICKETERS IN PARLIAMENT—UNIVERSALITY OF CRICKET, ETC.

WITHOUT question there have been periods in the world's history in which these epithets may be traced as relating to some eventful reign or course of circumstances. It is not necessary, however, for the purpose of this paper to "tread the long extent of backward time," or travel out of the dominion of Great Britain and its Dependencies. Some writers have assigned to Elizabeth the Augustan age of literature, and to Anne that of military renown and political achievements. Be it so; but when placed side by side with Victoria, how faded both become—not merely in the array of learning and learned men, in military heroism and heroes, but in the vaster and far more *important* phalanx of conquerors destined to subdue the world by the arts of peace and universal brotherhood. This, too, such as in no wise entered the mind of the philosopher or the imaginings of even a poet. The world never before witnessed a similar advance in the exalted ranks of science. What a magnificent scheme was that propounded by the late Prince Consort, most truly named "Albert the Good," at the commencement of the third quarter of the present century. No one can reflect upon it at this date without being struck with the grandeur of the thought, combined with the skill and judgment with which it was carried out. It brought opposites together, and gave all the families of the earth an opportunity—though in some instances a difficult one—of coming into personal contact with each other Well might the Laureate say of Victoria—

> 'She brought a vast design to pass,
> When Europe and the scattered ends
> Of our fierce world were mix'd as friends
> And brethren in her halls of glass"

Nor were the triumphs of science exhibited under that glittering roof confined to stupendous inventions of art Contrivances of smaller minds were not overlooked if they were of a character calculated to benefit society in the least degree In fact, nothing was considered beneath notice and commendation if degrees of excellence were made apparent The department devoted to the exhibition of instruments of pastime seemed to create no little astonishment among foreigners especially those fashioned for the purposes of cricket Difficult indeed was it for some to comprehend the fun of being bowled or thrown at with a ball—though prettily got up—as mischievous as a shot, and why, if danger attended its use, it could not be made soft and harmless The highly polished "strip of wood" also seemed to mock their comprehension, and, above all, the necessity for pads and gauntlets in an innocent pastime But familiarity with the sight dissipated a great deal of ridiculous terror, and long before the memorable exhibition in Hyde Park closed, the area of cricket widened to an unparallelled extent In some cases the materials for playing the game were purchased, and the use of them acquired afterwards, thus, by degrees, cricket found its way into many lands where it has since taken root, and is not likely to be easily eradicated For cricket, then, the third part of the present age deserves the title of Augustan or Golden, especially if compared with the reigns of the two monarchs previously mentioned Elizabeth was the bead light of the glow-worm, Anne the faint streaks of morning, Victoria the full blaze of a midsummer noon day

The time, albeit, was ripe for introducing cricket as a part and parcel of education in all public schools—so called Professional players of character and ability found profitable and permanent engagements Not many years elapsed before the Eton, Harrow, and Winchester were cognizant of the advances made by other "foundations" in different parts of England Every day something transpired which acted as a spur to exertion New grounds were being constantly set out, and persons to superintend them inquired for Many neglected spots also were got into order. One instance in proof may here suffice The plot of ground left by Queen Elizabeth to St Peter's College, Westminster, when she founded the school, had for a considerable time in the early part of the present century been devoted to sports which often gave rise to misunderstanding, and which were not uncommonly settled by a fistic tournament In consequence, the Dean enclosed the ground with a wooden fence This fell to pieces from the tooth of time and the vagaries of passers-by In 1843 the subject forced itself on the notice of the authorities Eventually an iron rail replaced the wooden one, and the ground, about nine acres in extent, was inclosed Yet for cricket purposes the area was scarcely fit, having too much sand in its composition To remedy this, the

"Westminster Boys" entered into a subscription, and had a large portion of it returfed. Since that time Vincent Square has been enrolled among metropolitan grounds of note. The bannerets of I Zingari and the Marylebone Club may have been seen floating not unfrequently in the season in opposition to the Westminster flag with its initials R S W surrounded by the motto, "In patriam populumque". Such a return to a right condition of things could not be so easily accomplished now. The great difficulty staring newly organised clubs in the face is a good and convenient spot for play, and this difficulty every day increases, owing to the vast number of clubs springing into existence especially around the metropolis. There are not a few of long standing that have been necessitated to shift their quarters owing to the omnivorous demands of the builder. A French traveller fifty years ago remarked that "London was no longer a city, but a province covered with houses". What would he say now, and within what limits define a province? Ever since this utterance, the process of covering with brick and mortar has been carried on to at least a five-fold extent. Every little patch of green or vacant spot is being converted into streets or squares. London is so rapidly expanding into the country, that it effaces the boundaries of suburbs and absorbs the life of villages. Villas shoot up by the once lonely roadside, gas lamps extend along bye lanes, and the gin palace towers over hedgerows. Even our parks, not unaptly termed the lungs of the metropolis, are scarcely free from the danger of invasion. A writer on modern festivals and games* asks whether it would not be wise, both in reference to the bodily and moral health of the people, if in all new inclosures for building provision were legally made for the unrestricted enjoyment of their games and diversions, by leaving large open spaces to be appropriated for that purpose. No doubt, but how is it to be accomplished? The machinery of "the strong arm" has proved generally speaking quite inefficient to protect what some persons call national rights. Through one insidious process or another recreation spaces outside of London are being narrowed, and if continued much longer, it will be difficult to find a convenient and settled spot—at least for cricket—within a dozen miles of its Royal Exchange. Take the locality in which the late Mr. Felix resided for many years—a prettier sight of the kind on a bright summer evening could not be witnessed. Cricket and the voice of merriment was only limited to the capacities of Blackheath itself, a general trysting spot and the "long walk" of the pedestrian. In 1815 Wilson, a famed pedestrian of the time, undertook to walk 1000 miles in 20 days on the Heath. He accomplished 750 in 15 days, and was then stopped by order of the magistrates. Look at it now. Although contiguous to a park, how changed its condition. The gravel digger and turf cutter have sadly marred its once smooth and verdant character. Crown rights, too, are subordinated to the schemes of speculators, and the open space "ribbed in" by masses of brickwork. Nor is Epping Forest treated with a less ruthless hand. The old wood has been assailed root and branch. Everybody knows what a beautiful attractive, expanse of country for the near neighbourhood of a great city that was only a few years since

* Horatio Smith

The whole metropolis has an affection for Hampstead Heath—that breezy and healthy upland, but here again war is making swift advances upon the popular playing ground, though its soil is not exactly suitable for good cricket It is resorted to as being more free and airy than the parks It is nearer than Wimbledon, and has not been degraded like Wandsworth, where gravel pits, muddy ponds, fourfold railway works upon a gigantic scale, and enclosures for charitable institutions, have cramped the space, stopped the walks, changed cricket grounds into morasses, and where mock gipsydom haunts with its larceny and beggary the wretched patches of common apparently uncared for

The case of Plumstead Common is even less agreeable Again and again the commoners protested against the infringement of their rights, until a riot ensued, with very unsatisfactory results, for while an "example" was made of one side, the intruders—as they were designated—were scarcely remonstrated with

'Tis felony in man or woman
To steel a goose from off a common,
But what must be that man's excuse
Who steals the common from the goose?
Rustic Epigram

Now, the popular idea of a "common" is, that it is a kind of NO MAN'S LAND, on which any one may do what he pleases A great mistake A common is as much the subject of property as enclosed land Such an idea might to a great extent have been correct in ages far back when men were few, uncultivated acres many, and money scarcely coined, when, too, men struck their tents and repitched them as convenience or inclination suggested, without let or hindrance In these vastly altered times, however, when one man can scarcely put down his foot without treading upon another man's corns, the idea alluded to is full of error But what is a common? The answer may be legal or topographical The word topographically carries its own description with it Who does not figure to himself an open, breezy spot, dotted here and there with stunted bushes, and heaths leading off into the dim distance, hedgerows of old timber, the virgin covering of tender grass cropped closely by sheep and cattle What odours and invigorating exhalations of vital oxygen? The freedom felt suggests the idea of personal right But to whom does this fine tract of land belong, and why is it called a common? A common, then, is neither more nor less than the waste or unappropriated part of a manor. It is hardly necessary to say that manors were created by the action of some great man who, from force of character or circumstances, had either become a king, or superior over his fellows—and as those who had helped him looked for reward, tracts of land under certain conditions were given to them In the absence of what is now called capital, these new owners had no means of rendering their possession of the land profitable, and they in their turn granted portions of the same land to others These grantees and sub-grantees held on condition of rendering certain services, and held at the will of their superiors, which was literally the case for many years, but the capricious exercise of such will gradually abated by customs which grew up in each manor The lords, either through fewness of people, or love of the chase, did not grant certain portions of the land, which were called "the lord's wastes," and these, in the course of time, came to be called commons, for the following reasons —The tenants of the manor who, of course, lived in the neighbourhood of the waste lands, gradually acquired right over them, *i e*, of feeding cattle, cutting turf and firewood, digging clay, &c, and these rights were enjoyed in *common* with each other and with their lord A common, therefore, in popular language, may be said to be the property of the lord and the copyholders, or tenants of the manor One cannot infringe on the rights of the other, but together they can do what they please with the land Thus Lord Spencer and the copyholders of the manor of Wimbledon have the *right* to enclose Wimbledon common Should such an attempt, however, be made, the Guildhall of the City of London would, doubtless, soon be at the service of any beneficent leader of the people, and the enunciation of the principle that property is theft meet with an enthusiastic reception The rights of commoners among themselves have a clear definition No one is allowed to use his rights so as to diminish or obstruct the right of another Neither may the lord do aught that will unlawfully interfere with the commoners' right, and *vice versâ* Applying these principles, it becomes clear that *à fortiori* a stranger can have no right to do anything which will lessen the lord's or commoners' enjoyments As a matter of right there is no difference in principle between claiming the right to build a mansion, inclose flower and kitchen gardens on a common, and of pitching wickets for a cricket match. The difference is merely in degree, not principle, and the using a portion of the surface of a common amounts to the offence known as "the disturbance of common" and the cattle of a stranger feeding thereon may be distrained by the lord or commoners It should, however, be mentioned that custom, which is said to be the soul of a manor, in some manors allows sports and pastimes to be held on a common as of right The same remark applies to village greens, these, however, are the exceptions which prove the rule But, admitting the wrongs done to the public arising either from neglect on the one hand or defective legislation on the other, the classes most affected ought not to overlook Victoria Park in the east and Battersea in the south In both these, great consideration is manifest for the gratification of the half-day holiday folk, and if the cricket grounds are not kept in faultless condition, the fact may be attributed to the greater amount of wear and tear and less regard of results than is seen where private purses are opened, and persons engaged for the express purpose of keeping them in condition At a public meeting of the Civil Service Club in May, 1864, it was stated that upwards of 400*l* had been expended by the members upon a piece of ground in Battersea Park, which had been specially allotted to them Furthermore, if it be asked whether these are the only "lungs" substituted for those of which the acknowledged area of the metropolis is alleged to have been deprived, the Regent's Park need only to be pointed to for an answer Not very long ago the First Commissioner of Works, himself the scion of a noble race of cricketers—was appealed to on account of the condition of the park appropriated to cricket more especially After due consideration of the matter, everything necessary was done to the satisfaction of the applicants The greatest poet England has yet produced delivered an awful verdict upon the man who happened to have no music in his soul Had the Bard of Avon lived at the present time to take a quiet stroll on a summer evening to the spot just mentioned, what would he say of the ascetic soul who purposely turned aside from the sight of varied groups of cricketers covering acres of a lovely spot in the pursuit of their most cherished pastime What, also, to hear music of cheerfulness from a thousand throats, and bursting shouts of joy on the result of a triumph, great or small These, too—considering the locality—in such violent contrasts with the growl of the bear, the roar of the lion, and the hollow scream of the condor, of necessity imprisoned in the "Zoo" close by

With the cricket proper, on holiday occasions at this part of the metropolis may be seen much of a mixed character, for instance—

> The youthful train,
> Who move in joy and dance along the plain,
> In scattered groups each favoured haunt pursue,
> Repeat old pastimes and discover new
> Flush'd with his rays beneath the noontide sun,
> In rival bands between the wickets run
> Drive o er the sward the ball with clever force,
> Or chase with nimble feet its rapid course *

A migratory club, entitled the Free Foresters, founded in 1856, soon attracted notice It took its rise from a series of friendly gatherings, in which the members of certain families played a prominent part At the first regular meeting in Oxford, therefore, a founder's kin qualification was instituted as one of the fundamental laws of the society The design of the Free Foresters is to play matches with county, university, college, and regimental elevens Also with recognised clubs in desirable localities Motto, "United though Untied" Upon this roving principle a great number of efficient cricketers formed themselves into clubs such as "Incognito," "Will 'o Wisps," &c These carried cricket into quarters not easily reached by ordinary means Less influential parties followed suit, though at a distance A great play of the fancy was often exercised in the appellation given to clubs. These partook largely of a spirited and defiant character, and the natural love of alliteration led to nicknames not distinguishable for mock modesty

As all systems of human device are apt to get out of order from abuse or neglect, it entered into the minds of many, and of Mr Kelly King in particular, that reforms were needed in affairs of cricket as administered by the Marylebone Club, and that a Cricket Parliament was the speediest and most efficacious remedy The main proposition was based on the fact that the club, who had so long held universal dominion, was a self-constituted body, and that from expansion of the game and a variety of conflicting matters incident thereto, the time had come for the expression of free opinions and different ranges of thought It was also urged that a tribunal

* "Hours of Idleness"—*Byron*

should be constituted for adjusting questions and disputes outside the pale of a mere handful of law makers. A great deal of oral and written testimony was brought to bear upon the subject. Difficulties both real and imaginary presented themselves at every step of the discussion. The title was not very euphonious to begin with, and it suggested the idea of such a confused order of business intellect, that the supporters of cricket would never consent to be guided by it. In the home county centres the subject was freely ventilated, with varied results.

Mr Bridger Stent, in addressing a Sussex Committee remarked, "They knew for many years past that the Marylebone Club had been looked up to as the law makers of, as well as the law breakers of, cricket. However, they must give them the credit for carrying out the office of law makers very well, and it had hitherto answered the purpose in a tolerably satisfactory manner, but he thought the time had come when other clubs should be represented in the matter, especially when they remembered that at the present time there were nearly twenty county ones. He had received a very pressing letter from the county of Kent, asking him to call a meeting to take into consideration the subject of a 'parliament,' the feeling generally being that the Marylebone Club was too exclusive, and to maintain its position it must throw open its doors, as the counties were determined to have the laws more in their own hands." Eventually the following resolution was moved by Mr George King, "that in the opinion of this meeting the formation of a cricket parliament, or some body in which all counties shall be properly represented, is most desirable, and that this meeting will cordially co-operate with those seeking to carry out the plan." He remarked that formerly the Hambledon Club were the arbiters of cricket, but though for some time the Marylebone Club had held that position, he fully agreed with Mr Stent that the time had now arrived when the various clubs which had sprung up all over England should have a voice in the making of rules. The Marylebone Club was too exclusive and restricted, and was not calculated to meet the views of the cricketers of England."

A very different view of the subject was taken by the county of Wilts, as may be seen from the following resolution:—"That in the opinion of this committee it is not advisable to interfere with the present authorised rules as framed by the Marylebone Cricket Club, which rules are invariably adopted and complied with in every part of the globe wherever the noble game is played, and this committee, believing that every cricketing county in England is represented by gentlemen who are members of the Marylebone Cricket Club, deem it inexpedient to elect a cricket parliament. F. H. Bathurst, Bart (president), Lieut.-Col. Bathurst (vice-president), Messrs G. E. Townsend, C. S. Bracher, R. Cobb, and F. Wells (hon. sec. *pro tem.*)"

The foregoing may be taken as fair examples of the views and feelings entertained by committees and county clubs. With regard to individual opinion, there was even less unity. Those who took a comprehensive view of cricket thought it better to bear a little ill than risk a great one, and to compare closely the real merits of a new monarchy with that which it might shake to its overthrow. Some years have elapsed since the "parliament" was proposed, and if the scheme has not been matured, it has not been without benefit in acting as a rod for chastisement, and may do so again if necessary.

The migratory spirit manifested—before alluded to—was more fully developed by the visit of an "English Twelve" to Canada in the year 1859. This number comprised a very choice pick of professional players—so choice, in fact, that they bore down all opposition, notwithstanding numerical odds. Two years later a great desire was expressed on the part of Australia to see the same team in that vast colony. After several attempts to achieve the object had failed, an arrangement was effected under the auspices of Messrs. Spiers and Pond, of Melbourne. The chief difficulty experienced was the dread of a long voyage—especially after the taste of the Canadian trip—which seemed to have inspired some of the men (Grundy in particular) with an amusing horror of the sea. Domestic ties and other engagements operated against leaving England. Eventually a very formidable team for a young colony to cope with was got together, and on the 12th of October they left the shores of Britain for Melbourne. The terms were, a first class passage out and home, with 150*l* clear of all expenses to each player, of which 50*l*. to be paid down and the balance to be received in Melbourne, the return to England by the overland route. The experiment proved a great success to the promoters, and the party returned laden with something more than empty honours. Cricket, it should be observed, had been practised in Australia for many years previous to the visit in question. Inter-colonial matches "between New South Wales and Victoria, played annually, created quite as much interest and speculation as the Derby or St Leger. To be admitted into the eleven was esteemed a high honour, the merits of the fortunate individuals were rigidly canvassed, and during the match there was intense excitement. The state of the game was every five minutes telegraphed from Sydney or Melbourne, as the case might be, to all parts of the colonies. On one occasion so great was the interest taken in this particular match at Melbourne, that both branches of the Legislature actually suspended their sittings during its continuance. Why, in the palmiest days of their renowned and superb city, the Corinthians never gave a prouder ovation to the Athenians who had sailed across the Saronic Gulf in the sacred ship for the purpose of competing in the games of the Isthmus, than that awarded to Stephenson and his companions in their Melbourne match. Nor was the enthusiasm less o'ermastering than it used to be among the Greeks during the celebration of their manly games. Everything and everybody gave place to the one supreme interest, and the result of the match during its progress occupied the thoughts, and had more absorbing interest to the mass of lookers-on than the failure of a Bill or the fall of a Ministry.

The marked success which attended this speculation soon suggested another, and Mr Marshall, of Melbourne, put himself in communication with Parr, the leading cricketer of Notts. The conditions were more favourable than those obtained by Stephenson. Altogether it was expected that each man would be able to realise nearly 500*l*. In a cricket sense, the second team were quite as successful as the party which preceded them. They were feted, honoured, and be-glorified as if beings of another sphere, and they returned laden with spoil and tokens of respect. Nearly ten years elapsed, when a third team appeared at Melbourne, under the captaincy of Mr. W. G. Grace. During this long interval the colonists had turned the instructions received from the former visitations to good account, and the hero of Europe found himself surrounded frequently by individuals scarcely inferior to the majority of the men under his own command. Another very remarkable feature of the periods in question was the formation of a band of Aboriginals, dark, but not "black as a coal." These men, gathered from widely scattered districts, and previously unknown to each other, made so much progress in the game, that they were brought to England and played a variety of matches in the summer of 1868. Soon after the terrible strife in the United States came to a close, a second visit was paid by an eleven, under the captaincy of Willsher, and still more recently by a party of gentlemen. Fuller mention of these migratory bands will be found in a chapter specially devoted to them, from which may be seen how hearty was the reception of English cricketers, professional as well as amateur, and how glorious their success. But there is an element contributing hereto which must not be overlooked. No one can for a moment imagine that all this work, carried on at such great distances, and carried on so well, was the result of mere chance. The necessary machinery could not be set in motion without wise forethought. The wires which stretch on poles from one end of England to another, and in some places lie in bunches under foot, were not unused, protocols and other agencies left unemployed. Many of the soundest thinkers on subjects of this kind consulted how best the welfare of the missionaries could be promoted, and the dignity of cricket maintained. Viewed in all their bearings, these matches justly deserve to be enrolled on the page of "famous events" during the period in which they transpired.

A glance at the progress of the game in places more inaccessible, affords another striking proof of the hold it gains upon all classes when and where it is but partially understood. Wherever an Englishman makes but a temporary stay, no matter in what part of the habitable globe, the seeds of cricket are sure to be sown, and at times spring up in a way rather difficult to perceive. Not many years ago a gentleman travelling in Jutland, was surprised by the merry shoutings of school boys playing at cricket in a somewhat rough fashion, certainly, but genuine cricket. On inquiry he found they were all Danes. They had old fashioned English bats. The traveller had no idea that the game had become naturalised among the Slesvickers and Jutlanders. No doubt it sprang from a seed by the wayside, dropped by some Danish officer after a visit to England. Pretty certain is it that the country whence it is said the conquering Anglo-Saxons came did not bring it with them to England. One remarkable feature in the case is its "naturalisation," as the peninsula of Jutland is not the most favourable climate for the game, and more remarkable still, when the whole continent of Europe is taken in connection with it. At Gibraltar cricket is as much cultivated in proportion to the capacities of the place as it is in the parent country, and it is occasionally heard of in Portugal among English residents, but not "naturalised." In fact the Portuguese entertain very ridiculous notions of cricket even now. A leading Lisbon journal gives the following picture of a match "about to take place" "To-morrow there is to come off an interesting game of cricket match between the cricket clubs of Lisbon and Oporto The object of the formation of these societies is its playing of the game of cricket match; some active running, jumping, during game, which can only be played by a person having a good pair of lungs, and in a climate where warmed punch is found insufficient to keep up the animal heat Does the reader wish to know how to play at cricket match? Two posts are placed at a great distance from one another The player close to one of these posts throws a large ball toward the other party who awaits the ball to send it far with a small stick with which he is armed; the other players then run to look for the ball, and while this search is going on, the party who struck it runs incessantly from post to post marking one for each run Sometimes it tumbles into a thicket, and the player does not cease running from post to post, and making points, when those who find the ball arrive exhausted at the field of battle, and the one who has been running falls down half dead At other times the projectile, sent with a vigorous arm, cannot be stopped, and breaks the legs of the party who awaits it The arrangements of the cricket match include a sumptuous dinner in the marquees for fifty persons, an indispensable accompaniment to every cricket match We may, perhaps, assist at this great battle, and hope the committee will place us at a safe distance from the combatants, where the principles of the game may be seen with the help of an opera glass" The public are far less enlightened by Spanish journalists Their reticence has to be accounted for not on the ground of ignorance, for it is well known that while the British army was in Spain both officers and men frequently amused themselves at cricket, and one writer testified to having seen it on the plains of Waterloo Great efforts have from time to time been made to establish the game in France but to little purpose, score sheets have certainly been filled up near the Bois de Boulogne, and eleven of Lyons on one occasion were conquerors by four and twenty runs Geneva, too, has donned pads and gloves The cry of "over" has reverberated under the shadow of Mont Blanc, but what of it after all, the grand principle of it is lacking—vitality Trace its condition up to the capital of the Czar, and the same deficiency is apparent The instincts of the nations and peoples are not in accord with those of the cricket public in the land whence the noble game had its origin, and according to present appearances it will require at least a new generation before its principles can be indoctrinated and admired Remoter still, in some countries, when it is remembered that the noble game is purely democratic.

A French journalist, M Sherer, one of the leading contributors of the *Temps*, at the time of the second International Exhibition in London, wrote a very elaborate article concerning the athletic sports of the English, with the following close "We have often thought that the noblest present our own France could receive, the most efficacious means to regenerate and strengthen our youth, would be the introduction among us of some national sport like that of the English cricket It is an exercise that excites emulation, requires force and address, calls into play every physical aptitude, invites to wholesome fatigue and to the open air, and prepares vigorous bodies for vigorous souls" 'Without frankness," said Sir Walter Scott, "there is no virtue, and without courage there is no frankness" He might have added, and "without force there is no courage" We affirm, in the most positive manner, "the Englishman is a magnificent specimen of human kind, and it is cricket which has made the Englishman what he is" Notwithstanding this magnificent compliment to cricket, and the strong recommendation to adopt it, the game is about as much "naturalized" in France now as it was a dozen years ago

Hardly true is the statement that Ireland has only recently appeared in the domain of cricket, though of late it has struck deep roots A book about a century old, under the authorship of "Philogamus," says "hurling the goals was frequently played by Irishmen in the fields at the back of the British Museum They used a kind of bat flat on both sides, broad and curving at the lower end, the bat for hurling was known and used in the time of Elizabeth, and was called a 'clubbe, or hurl batte'" Another writer a few years later, says 'After prayers (Ireland) both sexes (and of all ages) generally adjourn to the fields to witness a hurling match, or some of those manly sports to which the Irish are passionately addicted Sometimes a barony, or even a county, will hurl against another The respective parties are drawn up like two little armies, and distinguished from each other by their colours The address, spirit, and dexterity displayed during the game is truly wonderful Nor are these amusements confined to the peasantry. Young gentlemen from neighbouring counties frequently engage in them As in the gymnastic festivals of ancient Greece, men of the highest rank and most refined education appeared as candidates for the prize of personal strength and activity"* Although the writer proceeds to notice other sports of a kindred character with a certain degree of minuteness, no mention whatever is made of cricket This silence, however, is no proof of its non-existence, for in the year 1810 mention is made of "a grand match of cricket, played on the 4th of August, in the Phœnix Park, Dublin, between his Grace the Lord Lieutenant and the Officers of the 7th Light Dragoons on one side, and the Officers and Privates of the 7th, or Paget's Hussars, on the other The vice-regal party consisted of the Lord Lieutenant, Lord Frankfort, Colonel Rogas, Mr Korcet, and seven of his Grace's servants After a good deal of sport, the day was won by the latter The concourse of spectators was immense."† From this statement it may be fairly assumed that the game was previously known, and to some extent understood, else why the immense concourse of spectators? Putting conjecture aside, the present condition of cricket in Ireland, when compared with the advantages of England, is startling, and agreeably so Scarcely any journal of influence omits the notice of cricket and its advancements, not unfrequently with a flow of fervid language showing how the heart of the writer is in unison with his theme The annual visits of I Zingari to the Vice-regal Lodge have contributed much to the furtherance of the game, and the patronage of almost every 'Excellency," from the commencement of the present century till now has not proved barren of good results A few months

* Miss Owenson's "Patriotic Sketches," 1807 † *Sporting Magazine*

since it was contemplated to organise a team to visit Philadelphia, and it is quite likely that the project will be matured before the present year expires If it be asked why not play England, the answer is, "wait awhile," for the time will assuredly come, and thus, in a cricket as well as a political sense, will England and Ireland be—

> Like to a double cherry, seeming parted,
> But yet a union in partition
>
> *Midsummer Night's Dream*, iii, 2

Scotland has not made such rapid strides, but, if slow, none the less sure Though not the national game, it found its way many years since into unlooked for and unexpected places * Many believe that the game did not get beyond the Tweed before the second quarter of the present century Yet mention is made of a match on Glasgow-green in 1817, in which Colonel Cadogan took part, and was accredited with being the first to introduce the game into the West of Scotland. Not long after Greenock figured in the historic page Here it may not be amiss to remind the reader that Scotland has no lack of enthusiastic writers upon the subject of cricket Almost every club has its advocate, and some of these mount "Olympus high" in praise either of individuals or bodies corporate, while others wield the weapon with the accustomed soberness of deep thinkers—*e g*, "It is true our distinctive characteristics are not so marked as they once were, but love of country remains with us still, and whatever helps to bring the country into greater repute with strangers, or affords an additional opportunity to Scots abroad of maintaining their connection with the fatherland, must ever be dear to us A Royal Caledonian Club would do all that, for it would be a step in advance of England and Ireland, and would show to them that the old vaunted principle, "Hielanders shouther to shouther" was still active among us, and year by year the young men who went out from us would carry with them the story of the club into many lands, where they would anticipate and accept the issues of its matches with the energetic enthusiasm which glows only in the breasts of Caledonians"

Until recently, so little has been heard of cricket in the "Principality," that few believed it had ever had an existence there Such, however, is not the case, as instances might be cited to prove The Right Honourable Lord Kenyon many years ago established an annual match, to be played by the two hundreds adjoining his Lordship's estate at Gredington (in Wales) The match was fixed to take place on His Majesty's (George III) birthday As the first happened on a Sunday, the match began on the Friday previous It proved to be a grand affair for such a period in such a locality Ten handsome tents were pitched on the field, in which a picnic *dejeuner à la fourchette* was given to the visitors.† To show how the game has progressed from that time it may be sufficient to say, not more than three years ago Wales had "a week," and played four matches in the meantime

Returning from this erratic visit to far off places, it may be well to notice a few important movements carried on at home, and among these the necessity for defining

* In 1859 a match of cricket was played in Cantire, "the Land's End (Can-tire) of Scotland"

† *Sporting Magazine*, Vol 53, O S

the position of county players. The great demand upon the services and time of professionals often turned into confusion the principles upon which most important matches were based. Considerable discussion ensued upon discordant propositions, but reason triumphed. It was resolved, (1) that "no cricketer, whether amateur or professional, shall play for more than one county during the same season; (2) Every cricketer, born in one county and residing in another, shall be free to choose, at the commencement of each season, for which of these counties he will play, and shall, during that season, play only for the county chosen; (3) A cricketer shall be qualified to play for any county in which he is residing and has resided for the previous two years, or he may elect to play for the county in which his family home is, so long as it remain open to him as an occasional residence." These regulations have worked with general satisfaction. They have, at all events, set at rest the disagreeable and exciting controversies which often attended the arrangements, and sometimes protruded themselves in an ugly form at later stages, to the great regret of the genuine lover of the game and patron also. It is not a waste of words to repeat the statement that matches between county and county, when properly weighed, have ever been considered by judicious players—and, no doubt, always will be—first in importance. It may be well to state here that all county clubs have not, at the present time, county grounds; but this does not affect the qualification question. The want of a "home," or centre, tends to make the duties of management far more heavy and responsible upon the shoulders of those who undertake office. Years ago, when cricket was, comparatively speaking, in its boyhood, matches were frequently arranged after an understood fashion, whereas now, from their multiplicity and more elaborate methods of working they require to be expressed. Large and wealthy clubs employ a secretary especially qualified for the duties of such an office, and for the discharge of which he is, or ought to be, amply remunerated. Private gentlemen who act in this capacity hold an important post. Few, so to speak, estimate their services properly. In many instances they not only come short of the gratitude they merit, even when success attends their efforts, but are often blamed for failures on their part undeserved. Generally speaking, the person appointed as honorary secretary is proud of his election. The choice suggests fitness for the office and a confidence in the due discharge thereof. Nor are these qualifications unnoticed or disregarded by the editors of cricket in the height of a season. A score-sheet and the notes thereon often reveal the real fitness of the sender for the office he assumes. To evolve symmetry from chaos is not quite so easy a thing as a careless honorary secretary may imagine, and it often happens that a communication is hurled to the paper basket through the temporary and pardonable deficiency of that virtue in the editor ascribed so frequently to the ill-fated Penelope, but with more propriety to the long-suffering Job. Altogether different is the reception of "copy" from a careful and painstaking secretary. This well-established fact ought to have weight with all who desire "to see themselves in print."

Wisdom in the council requires to be supplemented by firm and cautious action in the field; consequently the captain has a very important duty to perform.

It is not necessary that the person appointed to this post should be the best practical cricketer—certainly not the best bowler,—but one of sufficient tact and experience to seize every advantage that a powerful opponent may offer in the way of defence—a weak one in an attack, or *vice versâ*. As a title of distinction, the term "captain" in cricket boasts of no antiquity, but the duties which centre in him are by no means modern. Many a match has been won by an inferior force through the tact and management possessed by this officer, and as many lost by a contrariwise defect.

The formation of Prince's Club, in 1870, was the crowning event of the period. From its locality—Hans Place, Chelsea—every convenience afforded itself for speedy access by the purely aristocratic body who promoted it. "Prince's Court" had for years previously been the resort of gentlemen well up in rackets, and as existing cricket clubs hardly met the requirements of the time, measures were taken to supply them. About twelve acres of ground adjoining, and previously in the occupation of a market gardener, were surveyed and laid out under the best available management, and in the following year flagstaffs, stumps, and all the paraphernalia of cricket were in use thereon. Whether it was politic to commence thus early, seeing how slender a foothold the turf had in the soil, was a matter of debate. Such, however, was the fervour of the promoters generally, that a match between Lords and Commons on one side, and the Household Brigade on the other, took place on the 3rd of June. A few days later the Brigade played the Christ Church Cardinals. One season sufficed to acquire a great name for the ground, which it well deserved. H.R.H. the Prince of Wales, and others of the Royal Family, were soon enrolled among its members, which in three years amounted to upwards of 900. In the height of the season such an outdoor gathering of the aristocracy is rarely, if ever witnessed, and if the cricket is not always of the first class, the company is never deficient in rank or quality. Every gentleman desirous of becoming a member must be proposed and seconded by two members of the club. The name and address of each candidate, with that of his proposer and seconder, are entered in the Candidates' Book. Each member, on election, pays two guineas entrance fee, and three guineas as an annual subscription. It is well to be reminded that the Lords and Commons matches did not originate in Belgravia. Legislators addicted to cricket might have been counted on the fingers of the hand in the early part of the present century, whereas now they may be reckoned by fifties. In this wonderfully increased number will be found gentlemen profoundly learned in almost every branch of science, and who have largely advanced the growth and influence of cricket in general by their patronage and support. A glance at the composition of the two Houses will reveal names frequently brought under the public eye either for their past or present efficiency in the cricket field. Speaking at hazard, full one hundred matches were played a year ago in which members of the Legislature took part, not unfrequently a prominent one. Nearly a score of names might be cited of those having filled the presidential chair at Marylebone—men of the finest shades of political opinion, all embued with one and the same feeling in respect to the noble pastime—a feeling known to have much to do in elevating the condition of the classes below them in the social scale. Were the matured players of two or three generations back to re-visit—not "the glimpses of the moon"—the scenes of former exploits, how changed in their eyes would be the surroundings. The men with the notched stick, squatting on the ground, would be seen elevated to a neat compartment with all the paraphernalia of important scribes, watching every movement of the game, and preparing a digest of it with the skill and cunning of experts. How wonderfully changed the general aspect also. Shepherd-looking huts brushed away by the hand of designers for large, convenient, and costly structures. In fact, advance and the consequent train of changes apparent everywhere, proclaiming as with one voice that the institution of cricket has an intense hold on the British mind.

From what has been said, the reader will see that the noble game claims not the antiquity of many others indulged in by the English nation. Its early growth was slow and silent. Even after it had taken firm root, generation after generation passed away before it assumed anything like form and comeliness. Society of the kind necessary for its development only exhibited itself here and there. Brighter days came, and people saw in cricket a noble pastime, one in which the youth of daring might become the man of enterprise, either for his individual sake or his country's good—one in which the severer student might find relaxation not incompatible with his condition—one in which none need suffer, but by which all might profit. Who can estimate the effect of these youthful agencies? The cricket of the English playground was the same which in after life revealed itself in the lonely island of the South Pacific, at the "stormy Cape," and on the slopes of the Himalayas. Its spread is now immense. The sun never goes down upon cricket; for while the north is quiet, the south is astir. From one end of the globe to the other tidings of the game come so frequently that its universality ought to be pronounced. If so, the reign of our beloved Sovereign, among its many attributes of glory and greatness, deserves in a cricket sense to be called the AUGUSTAN or GOLDEN AGE.

CHAPTER VI.

THE MORAL, SOCIAL, AND PHYSICAL ATTRIBUTES OF CRICKET SPECIALLY CONSIDERED.

To exercise their limbs, and try their art,
Forth to the verdant fields the swains depart;
The buxom air and cheerful sport unite
To make Hulse* useless by their rough delight.
Britons, whom Nature has for war designed,
In the soft charms of ease no joy can find;
Averse to waste in rest the inviting day,
Toil forms their games, and labour is their play.—*Anonymous.*

Health-preserving Exercises Natural to Englishmen—Their most favourite Pastimes and Sports—Necessity for preserving them—Mr. Combe's Theory of the Human System—The Gymnasium of the Greeks—Baron Alderson's Letter to his Son recommending Cricket—Also his Address to a Grand Jury at Huntingdon on the same subject—Baron Platt's Address to a Grand Jury at Lincoln—Sir R. Baggallay's Testimony to the Value of Cricket—The "Village Curate," a Poem—Lord Lennox on the Charms of the Game—Cambridge Lyric—Dr. Farrar's Address to the Students of Cambridge University—Archbishop of York on Sports and Pastimes—Professor Humphrey, M.D., on Cricket and Rowing—Philosophy of Sport—Cricketers of the Olden Time—Legislators and Cricketers—A Frenchman's Notion of the National Game—Vive le Cricket.

MUCH less than any other nation do the English need to be taught the art of preserving health. They are admitted to be the strongest of races—proof enough that they are the healthiest. Their rural and aquatic sports, athletic games, tastes for country life, travelling habits, stupendous and undaunted enterprises even where Mammon tempts them not—as shown in their past and present explorations in the interior of Africa, as well as in the silent and lonely pursuit o the North Pole—nourish in them that muscular pith and animal impetuosity which crush down all obstacles. The colossal character of English industrialism also stimulates an energy no less colossal. It is almost only in the cutlers' and weavers' shops, or the cotton factory, that the shrinking of the national sinew is perceptible. But for this there are antidotes. The mode of restoring health is not—as abroad—confined to gymnastics, excellent as they in many instances are. Racing, riding, rowing, skating, curling, and among field sports cricket, with the like hygienic

* A famous physician.

agencies, must, and do in a great measure, quicken Englishmen, and make them to a great extent what they physically and morally are Yet on this picture a dark spot obtrudes, the product of ignorance, neglect, or depraved habit—all tending to undo health or work in the opposite direction Crabbe inquires

> "Where are the swains who daily labour done,
> With rural games played down the setting sun,
> Who struck with matchless force the bounding ball
> Or made the ponderous quoit obliquely fall."

Let any one walk in a graveyard and read the ages on the tombstones, then ask himself why so many young fathers lie among the old men there One idea will probably be suggested, that if they have to live natural lives under artificial circumstances they ought to have some distinct knowledge of the structure of their bodies, and of those physical wants of their system which they absolutely must supply if they would lead vigorous lives and long ones The preservation of robust health is not inconsistent with the enjoyment of the most refined happiness that civilization brings Hence, as Mr Combe says, "people should be taught to understand clearly how their bodies are affected by daily habits, and what is apt to produce healthy and unhealthy action in each vital organ, how to economise the force of the machine they are for ever working, and to hinder it under all sorts of social accidents from getting out of gear" Lessons upon the nature and requirements of the human body are now forming—as they properly ought—a material feature in the education of the rising race, and it is not difficult to forecast its social and national advantages The necessity of bodily education ought to be to any man possessed of common sense, and an ordinary amount of physiological knowledge, at least as apparent as that of moral and intellectual training Independently of bodily health for its own sake, no mind can be healthy or happy without it It has been often remarked that the gymnasium was quite as essential a portion of Greek education as the school-room, and the limbs of youths and men were as vigorously trained in athletic exercises as their brains in arithmetic, rhetoric, and philosophy Even in these days of severe strife for honour and emoluments, labour and play may be made fitting helpmates to each other if carried on by healthy and judicious regulations

Richard Cobden, in answer to a request for his patronage, says "I have no hesitation in allowing my name to be used as one of the patrons of your Club [North of England, 1846] It is a game with which I have been familiar from my childhood It is a healthful, manly recreation, and if the game be played under judicious rules, such as you have adopted, it is, in my opinion, the most innocent of all outdoor amusements"

In a letter to his son, the late Baron Alderson says, "I have sent you to Eton that you may be taught your duties as an English young gentleman The first duty of such a person is to be a good and religious Christian, the next is to be a good scholar, and the third is to be accomplished in all manly exercises and games, such as rowing, swimming, jumping, cricket, and the like Most boys, I fear, begin at the wrong end, and take the last first, and what is still worse, never arrive at the other two at all I hope, however better things of you, and to hear first that you are one of the hardest workers in your class, and after that I confess I shall be by no means sorry that you can show the idle boys that an industrious one can be a good cricketer, jump as wide a ditch, or clear as high a hedge as any of them" In addressing a grand jury at Huntingdon Assizes, the same learned and philanthropic Baron said, "He could not help expressing the gratification he had that day derived from seeing the noble Lord-Lieutenant of the county (the Earl of Sandwich) mixing with his tenantry and his humbler neighbours in one of the manly sports of England (cricket) Such a proceeding was calculated to revive the good old feeling which had subsisted in days gone by between the nobles of the land and those by whom their lordships and their property were surrounded and occupied Conduct like this was far more likely to lead to a sound understanding of the best interests of each class than the demeanour which he lamented to say was but too general on the part of the highly born and wealthy towards those who did not possess equal advantages of birth and fortune The scene, which he had been a delighted observer of that morning, was calculated not simply to win but to ensure the best feelings and respect of the middle and lower classes of society for those who by the will of Providence were placed above them The respectful feelings of the lower classes for those to whom they had a right to look for support and consideration would be found to be the very best source of protection for the property of the landlord, while, on the other hand, the parties themselves felt raised in their own estimation by the occasional association with their superiors in one of the common and healthy sports of the country"

Not long after these grand utterances from the Bench Mr Baron Platt followed in a similar—though much briefer—strain In his address to the grand jury at Lincoln Summer Assizes, he referred to the iniquities concocted in beer-houses, and asked "whether it would not be worthy the consideration of country gentlemen to forward by every means in their power the establishing of the good old English game of cricket—a game which, while it served to amuse, tended also to aid the moral and social condition of the people"

A few days previous to the elevation of Sir R Baggallay to the judicial bench, the then Attorney-General, in proposing at a banquet "The Richmond Club," of which he was a staunch patron, said "He would yield to no one in enthusiasm for the game although a long period of absence as a player had made him a stranger to many of those principles with which younger men were so familiar There was no greater enjoyment for him than to watch a game of cricket One of their guests had aptly described it as a game of attack and defence It conduced, he was sure, to the health and strength of those who played, whilst it added materially to the improvement of the mind No club in the neighbourhood of the metropolis stood higher in public estimation than theirs did In fact, it was regarded as first-rate in every respect The quality of a club was not to be estimated by its success in the number of matches won, but rather by the harmony and goodwill which it infused amongst the young and middle-aged men of the neighbourhood, who derived so much pleasure from its practice"

> Another moment pause, and to the vale
> From the calm precipice we tread, look back!
> See where the schoolboy, once again dismissed,
> Feels all the bliss of liberty, and drives
> The speedy hour away at the brisk game
> Of social cricket It delights me much
> To see him run, and hear the cheerful shout
> Sent up for victory I cannot tell
> What rare effect the mingled sound may yield
> Of huntsmen, horns, and hounds to firmer hearts
> Which never feel a pain for flying puss
> To me it gives a pleasure far more sweet
> To hear the cry of infant jubilee
> Exulting thus Here all is innocent,
> And free from pain, which the surrounding chase
> With its gigantic clamours cannot drown,
> E'en though it pour along a thundering peal
> Strong as the deep artillery of heaven
>
> ("*The Village Curate*," *by M Drayton*)

Lord William Lennox, in 1840, said "The national game of cricket has a peculiar claim to the people generally, and is one of those games open alike to all It is free from selfishness, cruelty, or oppression it encourages activity, it binds gentlemen to country life, it preserves the manly character of the Briton, and has been truly characterized as a healthful, manly recreation, giving strength to the body and cheerfulness to the mind, and is one of the few sports that has not been made the subject of some invidious anathema It is calculated to promote a good understanding between parties at other times separated Nothing tends more powerfully to conciliate the affections of the humbler classes than a similarity of tastes and pursuits, all must have something to do in the interval of their toils, and as the educated can find recreation for themselves, it behoves the higher orders to be especially careful in furnishing amusements for their less fortunate brethren who are less fitted to choose their own pleasures well"

> "Beatus ille," so old Horace singeth,
> "Qui procul negotiis," all his life spends,
> Happier he to whom the spring bringeth
> Life in the cricket field, blest with old friends
>
> *Cambridge Lyrics*

At Cambridge (November, 1874), the select preacher, Rev. F W Farrar, Master of Marlborough, in addressing the students, who collected in large numbers, referred to the popular sports of the University, and classified them under the term athleticism He wished to turn the thoughts of his audience to the stern facts of that inexorable law in which believer and unbeliever alike were concerned, and in doing so he did not think he could do anything more practically useful than to take the lives of those two youths Esau and Jacob, and what came of their lives These youths were the types of thousands of other youths Whilst dwelling on the character of the former, he said, "Let the student sympathise with the athlete, while the one does not forget that his soul is the breath of eternity, and the other that his body is the temple of the Holy Ghost He that excels in athletic exercises has God's work to do in the world, and, if thoughtful and diligent, his bodily gifts may help him to do it He could bear his testimony that the public schools and universities had gained something from athleticism which was an innocent counteraction to low amusements"

The Archbishop of York, in a series of sermons preached at St James's, Westminster—same year—selected "Sports and Pastimes" as the fourth His Grace said "the subject of sports and pastimes is a difficult one to treat in a religious point of view, for the world's pleasures seem at first to be outside the sphere of the Bible, which is our law Now every creature of God is good, and "unto the pure all things are pure" The child, the aged, and the sick have their special recreations, but they may be harmless pursuits outside the range of binding duty, and they must be judged by the personal needs and capacities of those who use them That sport which the schoolboy may pursue with energy, would be accounted frivolous in the statesman In dealing with amusements the first proposition that one must lay down is, that a life wholly spent in them is quite unknown to Christianity, and must not be The very name implies that we pursue the muses or studies when we are set free Relaxation is the unbending of the muscles from their state of exertion, sports presents the limbs tossing themselves wildly in free play, diversion is the turning aside of the mind for a time from its serious aims, play means exercise Recreation is the restoration of the weary mind by pleasure, and pastime is a temporary relief from the solid pursuit of the time Many a life, however, is passed wholly in amusement, and in one common round of enjoyments. What can you say to such a life as that which knows nothing but amusement? It cannot do anything to advance the mighty purposes that go through all this meaning world Proper amusements are resting places in your life of duty It is not difficult to see that amusements which educate and strengthen have a different footing from those passive recreations which only tickle and amuse the mind, and make the day pass idly by Games of chance can never be played on equal terms, for the loss is greater than the gain can be The motions of the stars in the heavens is not more certain than the ruin such games bring at last If the chances at the table, or the bookmaker's superior skill are put as an advantage on one side, ruin comes to the other with perhaps slow, but sure feet Religion cannot regulate these forms of amusement, but to those who are pursuing it, the only advice to give is, abandon it altogether"

I love to see the man of care take pleasure in a toy,
I love to see him row or ride and tread the grass with joy,
Or hunt the flying cricket ball as lusty as a boy
All sports that spare the humblest pain—that neither maim nor kill,
That lead us to the quiet field, or to the wholesome hill,
Are duties which the pure of heart religiously fulfill

Philosophy of Sport

In a lecture on the "Early Britons," by Professor Humphrey, M.D, at Cambridge (1875), he pointed out that in none of the "barrows" in this country had there been found any bone indicating a progress or regress in the descending series towards the lower animals He had no objection to the theory of evolution, for he thought it was as great an effort of creative power to make a man out of a monkey as out of the dust of the earth But he, nevertheless, thought that it was not quite philosophical to assume too readily that such had been the case Whilst alluding to the advantages of good physical proportion, the professor avowed himself a strong supporter of the athletic element of the University He thought the playground was the proper complement of the schoolroom, and the boating on the Cam and the cricket on Parker's Piece the proper complement of the tripos

In no country but England would the attack and defence of three stumps be witnessed by enormous crowds of fashionable people with unflagging zest, and there are not many foreigners as yet who would care to face a swift bowler with no other protection than a bat The boys at French gymnasiums and lyceums are much too genteel to play at cricket, and a taste for bodily exercises must be acquired, if at all, in boyhood This remark may also be applied to the slow development of the game in other countries on the continent of Europe In all ages the instinctive pugnacity of man has shown itself in burlesques and parodies of actual warfare The Olympian games, the sports of the Roman amphitheatre, the mediæval tournament, the Spanish bull ring, and even the prize fights of our grandfathers were attempts more or less barbarous to gratify this craving Cricket, too, as well as most other manly games, depends for its interest on the same combative propensity, but its cultivation as a national pastime is productive of benefits far higher and far more widely diffused. It is eminently healthy and sociable Unlike most trials of strength and dexterity, it requires no special qualifications, and may be practised, with more or less success, by everyone who chooses Boat racing taxes some constitutions most injuriously, and rivers broad and deep enough to admit of it are scarce in this country, but a patch of level ground for cricket is easily obtainable, and the feeblest of all ages may safely indulge in it It possesses also the rare merit of promoting a friendly intercourse of classes There can be no doubt that social life in the olden times was less exclusive than it is now In the battle-field and in the foray, in the chase and before the archery butts, at fairs and merry-makings, and even in the hospitalities of the castle hall, our feudal ancestors lived much in public, mingling freely with the people A different—and in most respects a better—relation between rich and poor has been brought about by the growth of towns, and the rising sense of independence among the working classes There is a great respect for "the dignity of labour," but the upper and lower strata of society are, for this very reason, less jumbled than before Now everything which counteracts this tendency, and brings Englishmen of various ranks face to face with each other on terms of genuine equality is of the highest service to the nation A match between Gentlemen and Players might probably shock a Frenchman, but in this country the thing is far from uncommon. The amateurs meet the professionals on the field as equals and playfellows, but they do not necessarily merge all differences of breeding and education The professionals meet the amateurs on this footing without any sense of humiliation, and thus a scene is presented the like of which may be sought after in vain in any neighbouring state or kingdom

A writer in the *Sporting Review* (vol vii, p 173), observes "Among the first of our manly, healthful, and invigorating sports, is that of the fine old English game of cricket It is one that may be called purely national There is no other country in which the bat, ball, and wicket are applied so as to entrench upon our originality in the smallest way Its very associations are English Who could, for instance, picture to the imagination the phlegmatic Dutchman, with his capacious round stern, chasing or sending the ball whizzing through the air like a cannon shot, and getting a run with the speed of a roebuck The idea even appears beyond the pale of conception The effeminate inhabitants of cloudless Italy, Spain, and Portugal would sooner face a solid square of British infantry than an approaching ball from the sinewy arm of a first class bowler Instead of the bat, their backs would be turned for the purpose of stopping it Getting further to the North, skating and sledging are the amusements In Russia the winters are long enough to rot both bats and wickets This may account for cricket being unknown there Foreigners, as a rule, are likewise slow in attempting to unravel the mysteries of the game Well did the English-hearted Queen Charlotte judge that cricket was worthy a place in the festivities at Frogmore, and wisely did the government of her day appropriate sums of money to make cricket grounds at the different barracks of the kingdom for the use of private soldiers This has indeed proved to be a wise measure, not only as a valuable boon to the soldiers in the way of relaxation and amusement, but because it tended to keep the men from the public-house sinks of iniquity and mischief, and thereby to raise the character of the service A cricket club is the great bond of union between those whom the author of 'Sibyl' is pleased to distinguish as the two nations—the rich and the poor Be the peer ever so rich and the labourer ever so poor, still the field is neutral ground, where both meet in fellowship without the one compromising his dignity, and the other reduced by undue subserviency or adulation It is another of the great excellences of cricket that it has never been, and cannot now be made, a gambling game, not that a game of so much uncertainty—an uncertainty often lasting till the very last run is got, or the last wicket bowled down—is never the subject of bets—that of course cannot be said, but it is not a game in which heavy betting, comparatively speaking, takes place Blacklegs, even if they understood it enough to judge of its varying chances, would have nothing to do with it, as there is no field to enable them to 'make a book,' and there are too many players on each side to admit of the possibility of making either side 'safe'"

One great qualification for successful cricketing is courage Many a severely contested and close match has been lost through a defect of this at some critical turning point Even in these days of enlightenment reference is often made to the ancient order of chivalry, as if it were a model worthy of being preserved. Feeble indeed must have been that courage which required a coat of steel to keep it up to the sticking point when brought to bear oftentimes against unarmed and undisciplined forces. The cricketer contends with his equal, and with but slender materials for defence and attack. A cricket ball certainly is not so deadly as a cannon ball, nevertheless a flush hit from one of these missiles on the shin or ankle, when the projectile is impelled by a fast bowler or a slashing hitter, is somewhat more than a joke. It comes home to every man's feelings, and abides, it may be some time, in his memory.

These ideas are strengthened by a Scotch writer under the head of "Cricket and Cricketers of the Olden Time"—"Englishmen, from the highest to the lowest, have in all ages evinced a most ardent predilection for athletic sports. The chace, tilting and archery, along with quarter staff, were the sports and recreations of youth and manhood in the middle ages, and thus were trained the valour, hardihood, and pluck that triumphed at Cressy and Agincourt, and have carried the proud banner of St. George victorious over many famous battle fields. In these latter days have not cricket and other contemporaneous sports had something to do in forming the physique and muscle of the men who fought in the Crimea and India, or who stamped out the embers of mutiny? Surely it is believable that many a young warrior, at the first entry on active service, has reason to thank the training he received in the cricket field. Indeed, the game is one which, by giving health, vigour, and energy to the frame, has also a good sound moral tendency. It demands the exercise both of the physical and intellectual powers, requiring at once a cool head, a steady hand, a sharp eye, as well as sound judgment. What the cultured brain wills to be done, the trained arm must strive to execute. The game is, in short, beneficial in a double sense, conferring on the body health, and on the mind that calm, deliberate judgment which is so admirable a preparation for the sterner duties of the world. As a rule, cricketing is not given up with youth, but in many instances its devotees continue to practise it until well on in middle life, when activity of locomotion is by no means the easy and pleasant thing it once was. Lord Kinnaird recently ascertained that of the eleven members of the Rossie Cricket Club, who played a match in which he took part forty years ago, ten, including himself, are still alive. Rarely, indeed, can it be said that ten persons who met forty years since could still meet again."

As a rule, foreigners who occasionally look at the game see nothing in it, but the fact that one of the most accomplished scholars a few years since should write on cricket in the best review existing, viz., the *Revue des Deux Mondes*, deserves notice. That he should do so, not only intelligibly but skilfully, is not a little surprising. Alphonse Esquiros was a total stranger to a cricket match until he visited England in the year 1861. He wrote a lengthy essay on the game, which opens with a very picturesque description of a match on Goodwin Sands. He painted very lively pictures of Lords and the Oval, which he followed up by a recapitulation of the great clubs at that time existing. Like other foreigners, he failed to possess himself of any personal interest in the pastime. This coldness, so unnatural to the French disposition, was accounted for as a consequence that none but the English could understand a game in which the contenders were perpetually shifting. The story of an eleven going to Australia, and the fortunes dependent upon the enterprise, is told with a vividness and circumstantiality which very few English writers on cricket can or do parallel M Esquiros is a little inclined to sneer at the moral effect which cricket is supposed to have upon the population He insinuates that the predilection for it as an instrument for education and improvement is partly due to agreeable reminiscences in the teachers, and that this especially applies to the clergy When, he says, "the philosophers of cricket (as they call themselves) talk of civilizing and refining the people by means of the *bat*, they involuntarily remind me of the dancing master and the music in the 'Bourgeois Gentilhomme.'" It is easy to find all kinds of good qualities in what we love After all it is gratifying to know that the worth of cricket has been tested in a strange crucible, ably chronicled and dispassionately weighed by an alien thinker

A writer in *Temple Bar* is quite jubilant, as may be seen from one example "Long may cricketing nourish Great Britain! It is truly an Anglo-Saxon game, thriving best on malt and hops Its home is in the land of beer Its great ally is John Barleycorn Witness Kent and Surrey, the nursery of our best players Neither your Rhine wines nor your Clarets nor your Burgundies nourish it, they make the blood too thin. Spirits are as bad, they make the blood too hot No, cricket relies on a cool head, a quick eye, a supple wrist a swift foot, all the nobler attributes of the man, mental and physical, are brought into play by it It admits of no Dundrearys or Gautiers It is a healthy and a manly sport, it trains and disciplines the noblest faculties of the body, and tends to make Englishmen what they are—the masters of the world We should not overlook the pleasures of boating and yachting, and we admire the Volunteer movement as a noble and important institution But neither of these should be allowed to interfere with the natural development of cricket, which is the sport *sui generis*, and has its own characteristics, its own sources of gratification, its own causes of excitement There must be something in a game which creates for itself such intense devotion and attachment Whilst then the French exclaim 'Vive la Bagatelle!' let every Englishman cry 'Vive le Cricket!'"

Were it necessary to give further examples of this kind they could be produced to a four-fold extent Example, however, is one thing, and precept another Well, then, the precept of English legislators in both Houses of Parliament may here be fittingly let in For many years past there has been a meeting at Lord's, and how fierce soever may be the debating within the walls of St Stephen's, all provoking strife melts away upon the platform at St John's Wood Government and Opposition—certainly a kind of hostile array, and the ins and outs—fight their battles again and again on the ground sacred to cricketers of two generations This friendly meeting always commands attention, and deservedly so Time was when such a contest would have been impossible Here is the first representative assembly in the world so free from political passion as to devote a day annually to cricket. Yet scarcely a nation around us but is, perhaps, at this moment, discussing some tremendous political or social problem Here is a dynasty striving to reconcile the idea of popular sovereignty with irresponsible despotism, there monarchy busy in asserting for itself a higher origin than the popular will Here an ancient house boldly grappling with the spirit of disunion and revolution, there a young and giant republic convulsed with anarchy and bleeding with internecine strife In this country alone the murmurs of discontent and cry of faction are unheard The broad common sense of the nation is satisfied with the institutions which give it this repose and security, and revolts at the efforts of a few demagogues to mingle their petty jealousies with the even current of public opinion In the long run both ins and outs obey the impulse of the country, and the Houses of Parliament are a pretty true reflex of the national tendencies

There are some, however, by whom all that has been advanced is regarded as a fanciful imagination—in whose eyes man is a machine, destined only for work, and consequently physical recreation is so much wasted time. Such are to be pitied. Others, possessing no soul for the varied enjoyments of life, would so narrow and confine their limits as to rob them of their actual value These are not deserving of panegyric Then there are the moody unsocial, and ascetic, who live for themselves alone, and have no more affinity with the instincts of their own species than the oyster has with the ostrich, and whose music, if any, is that of the raven when the whole vale is resounding with the lay of merriment

CHAPTER VII.

GLANCES AT THE PAST AND PRESENT STATE OF COUNTY CRICKET.

MIDDLESEX.

Our little world, the image of the great,
Like that amidst the boundless ocean set,
Of her own growth hath all that nature craves,
And all that's rare as tribute from the waves.
To dig for wealth we weary not our limbs,
Gold though the heaviest metal hither swims;
Ours is the harvest where the Indians mow,
We plough the deep and reap what others sow.—*Waller.*

Area of the County of Middlesex—London and its Vastness—Early Notice of Cricket in the Neighbourhood of Finsbury—Unpopularity of the Game—Change of Locality—The White Conduit Club—Progress thereof—Gradual Extension of the Game—Formation of the Marylebone Club in Dorset-square—First Match played—Results of important Middlesex Matches from the Year 1790—Meeting at the London Tavern to revive County Cricket—A Ground engaged at Islington—Great Matches played thereon—Poem referring to the Conquest of Middlesex over Bucks—Notice to Quit—Lillie Bridge——Last Match with Marylebone Club and Ground—Last Middlesex Match Played—Anomalous Position of Middlesex—Duty of the County towards the Promotion of the Game.

APART from the metropolis, Middlesex—with the exception of Rutland—is the least considerable of all English counties. Its total area is less than two hundred thousand acres—or nearly equal to two hundred and eighty-two square miles, or a square of seventeen miles. Although there are no towns of any note within this area, the capital of Middlesex is the "heart of the universe." Its throbbings are felt from the centre to the pole. No such place has ever taken hold of the imagination of the most fanciful of idealists. No traveller that ever trod this globe ever set foot in a city crowded with temples and palaces, costly as they are colossal. No historian has fastened its like on the pages of "backward time." In short, the wealth of this city "set on a hill" is boundless, and its power in the arrangement of moral and political forces as vast as it is mighty. Not only does the choicest metal of the mine find its way hither—there are, too, the myrrh of the forest, the gem of the mountain, the pearl of the ocean, and, in fact, the treasures of all nations borne daily upon the breast of its river, a fact easily demonstrated by the vessels which crowd every nook and inlet capable of discharging or receiving a cargo. Facts of this kind, however, are so well known, that a reference to them is not necessary. But as the amount of care and fret incident to vast enterprise entails no inconsiderable strain upon the mental and physical capacities of the human frame, the merchants and citizens in bygone times always kept their eyes open to the necessity of a counteraction in the way of sport and pastime. Some of these are obsolete, and it is quite as well that so it should be, as they were more in keeping with the feudal ages than in these days of enlightenment. Attempts have been made from time to time for the restoration of many a defunct sport, but to no purpose.

Burton* recapitulates as the common pastimes both of town and country "bull baitings and bear baitings, in which our citizens and countrymen greatly delight and frequently use; dancers on ropes, cock fighting, shovel-board dancing, mumming, May games, wakes, Whitsun ales, &c. Plays, masks, jesters, tumblers, and jugglers are to be winked at, lest the people should do worse than attend them. Hunting and hawking are honest recreations, and fit for some great men, but not for every base inferior person, who, while they maintain their falconer and dogs and hunting nags, their wealth runs away with their hounds and their fortunes fly away with their hawks."

The human mind and the human machinery brought to bear in the successful pursuit of fame and opulence are now more than ever the object of solicitude, not only by the wisdom of a city but of a legislative assembly. There are physical laws which cannot be long transgressed with impunity, and this truth the citizens of London have recognised for ages; their history mentions bold ventures in defence of cherished pastimes even when assailed from the highest magisterial quarter.

Without further reference to the sports of the Londoners at a period when education among apprentice boys was of a very low type, it will be found necessary to make a starting from some fixed and notable point of history when cricket was an object of some curiosity and a great deal of criticism. So far back as the commencement of the last century, Middlesex figures on the historic page as a pioneer of cricket. Matches were then played on the Artillery Ground, Bunhill Fields—better known now as Finsbury Square. Considerable care and expense attended the keeping of this spot in proper order, and the public also, as the "roughs" formed no trifling ingredient in the mixture. Of the matches played only one has been transmitted to posterity giving anything like a correct notion of the manner in which it came off. Love, the poet, was present on an occasion when Kent played All England in 1746, the result of a challenge from Lord Sackville on the part of Kent. Two of the best elevens that could be procured were engaged. So severely was the match contested, and so well balanced were the sides, that Kent, after two narrow escapes, won with a wicket to spare.

Here it may be necessary again to remind the reader that not this score only, but every other relating to important matches—chiefly county ones—are faithful

* "Anatomy of Melancholy." † See Engraving.

transcripts of the documents themselves They are valuable in one sense—they reflect to a large extent the character of the period.

ENGLAND

	1st inn		2nd inn
Harris, b Hadswell	0	b Mills	4
Dingate, b Hadswell	3	b Hadswell	11
Newland, b Mills	0	b Hadswell	3
Cuddy, b Hadswell	0	c Danes	2
Green, b Mills	0	b Mills	5
Waymark, b Mills	7	b Hadswell	9
Bryan, st Kips	12	c Kips	7
Newland, not out	18	c Lord J F Sackville	15
Harris, b Hadswell	0	b Hadswell	1
Smith, c Bartrum	0	b Mills	8
Newland, b Mills	0	not out	5
Byes	0		
Total	40	Total	70

KENT

	1st inn		2nd inn.
Lord J F Sackville, c Waymark	5	b Harris	3
Long Robin, b Newland	7	b Newland	9
Mills b Harris	0	c Newland	6
Hadswell, b Harris	0	not out	5
Cutbush, c Green	3	not out	7
Bartram, b Newland	2	b Newland	0
Danes, b Newland	6	c Smith	0
Sawyer, c Waymark	0	b Newland	5
Kips b Harris	12	b Harris	10
Mills, not out	7	b Newland	2
Romney, b Harris	11	c Harris	8
		Byes ...	3
Total	53	Total	58

In the course of a few years the Artillery Ground emitted so bad an odour that the *British Champion* thundered against the game of cricket in consequence of its "immoral results" Several other publications followed with stinging rebukes These induced the noblemen and gentlemen who were the chief supporters of cricket to withdraw from the neighbourhood, and fix upon a more quiet and respectable locality in the White Conduit Fields Here they formed themselves into a club for the exercise of cricket, and from this association sprang the Marylebone Club* The vicinity was, as far back as 1720, noted for its cricket matches* The historian of Islington says, "The White Conduit House (Club?) is improving into a state of skilful play, the chief performers being Lord Winchelsea and the Hon Mr Lennox, nephew to his Grace of Richmond (1784) Thursday a grand match was played at the White Conduit Field Among the players were the Duke of Dorset, Lord Winchelsea, Lord Talbot, Col Tarleton, Mr Howe, Mr Darner,

* See "Nelson's History of Islington"

Cricket in the Second Half of the Eighteenth Century—White Conduit Fields.

Hon. Mr. Lennox, and the Rev. Mr. Williams. A pavilion was erected for refreshments, and a great number of ladies attended."* Two years later a match between Married and Single ladies occurred. This attracted so much notice that Rowlandson made a drawing of it, which a short time since realised a considerable sum of money. The only match played in the White Conduit fields worthy of mention was between the White Conduit Club and a party of noblemen and gentlemen. It is now an admitted fact that this club—of short-lived date—was the acorn from which sprung the gigantic oak known as the Marylebone Club, of which a full description is given further on. But Middlesex as a cricket county was not extinguished in consequence of this event, for about four years later a match between the Players of Middlesex and the Marylebone Club occurred on the new ground opened by Thomas Lord, in Dorset Square, and apparently got up to test the "professional" and amateur strength of the county—the former, after a close struggle were pronounced winners by thirty runs. As this match forms an important epoch in the history of Middlesex players, the score is given in full. It occupied three days, commencing on the 16th of May, 1791.

MIDDLESEX.

	1st inn.		2nd inn.
W. White, not out	39	c Fitzroy	7
S. Grange, c Bligh	4	c Beldham	30
W. Fennex, b Beldham	1	b Bligh	41
T. Shackle, b Beldham	0	run out	17
T. Lord, run out	21	c Winchilsea	21
G. Wells, c Bligh	7	c Bligh	0
W. Bedster, b Beldham	6	b Purchase	27
R. Cantrell, b Beldham	3	c Bligh	6
— Dale, c Hussey	0	not out	3
Jacob White, b Beldham	8	c Wyatt	2
— Turner, c Hussey	11	b Beldham	1
Byes	10	Byes	11
Total	110	Total	166

M.C.C. WITH BELDHAM AND PURCHASE.

	1st inn.		2nd inn.
Earl of Winchilsea, b Fennex	4	c Cantrell	10
A. Smith, Esq., b Fennex	1	not out	8
Hon. H. Fitzroy, b Fennex	6	run out	1
C. A. Wyatt, Esq., b Fennex	9	b Fennex	7
G. Louch, Esq., b Turner	36	b Turner	1
Hon. E. Bligh, b Fennex	1	b Fennex	4
G. Anguish, Esq., c Bedster	13	b Turner	0
E. T. Hussey, Esq., c Lord	0	run out	16
L. Kaye, Esq., b Grange	4	b Grange	4
Beldham, not out	44	b Fennex	1
Purchase, b Turner	10	c Cantrell	44
Byes	17	Byes	5
Total	145	Total	101

* A view of the ground is contained in Carrington Bowles's set of prints of "Manly Recreations."

From the paucity of information respecting the countenance given to the game by the middle classes of society, it may be inferred that it had not taken a very deep root in their esteem In fact, the people needed to be educated Probably they saw nothing attractive in the hard ball, the bats, or the stumps, which make up the artillery of cricket They perceived neither uniformity nor elegance in the regulation of costume, although it adapted itself in all probability to the particular occasion, and was homely and suitable for that hard work, just as a carpenter's in his shop or a soldier's in the middle of a campaign * Supposing Bunhill Fields were the point on which to place one leg of a compass in order to describe a circle, forty miles would be the extent wherein cricket was practised to any appreciable degree

Within a week of the conclusion of the above, another, bearing the same title and composed chiefly of the same players, occurred at the same place In this contest Middlesex appeared to still greater advantage Marylebone, with their two given men Purchase and Beldham, went in first, and scored 190 runs, towards which the latter contributed 62 and the former 15 Middlesex completed their first innings for 284. Marylebone put together 150 in their second innings, and thus left Middlesex 57 to get to win. This number was accomplished with only four wickets down

On the 7th of May in the following year Marylebone, strengthened by T Walker, met Middlesex again at Lord's Ground, and on this occasion Middlesex were defeated by 274 runs, nor can this result be much wondered at when Beldham scored 144 in one innings and Walker 102 The respective results were—M C C, 193 and 306—total 499, Middlesex, 111 and 114—total 225

A week later the same teams were again confronted, and the match extended from May 14th to the 18th, and although Beldham and Walker, the most formidable men of the time, were on the Marylebone side, Middlesex won the match by 5 runs

The composition of the elevens in the following year underwent a material change. The Marylebone side had in it Walker, Robinson, and Boxall The match did not occupy two days, and Marylebone won it by 54 runs, the scores being Marylebone, 80 and 98—total 178, Middlesex—61 and 63, total 124

It required nearly four long spring days to play the match in the following year Marylebone won by 100 runs Walker was the chief scorer, having marked 32 runs in the first innings and 44 in the second Fennex, on the Middlesex side, got 65 in his first innings and 62 in the second Results M.C C, 169 and 127—total 296, Middlesex, 84 and 112—total 196

On the 25th of May, 1795, Marylebone met their old opponents with the professional help of Beldham only. At the conclusion of an innings each, Middlesex were nearly 100 runs ahead, but lost the match eventually by 96 runs This result was brought about mainly by the successful batting of the Hon H Tufton, who scored 16 and 71 On the Middlesex side Mr. Boult equally

* See Engraving

distinguished himself by a score of 76 and 11 Gross results. M.C C, 80 and 249 —total 329, Middlesex, 176 and 59—total 235

A three-day match was commenced on the 26th of June in the same year Marylebone played Hammond and Purchase, but the various contributions were unusually small The largest scorer on the Marylebone side was Capt Cumberland, 37 (not out) and 3 The totals of Marylebone were 124 and 28 The largest scorer on the Middlesex side was Ray, viz 33 Totals 68 and 85, for seven wickets

Both sides left the fray in the following year with small scores The match commenced on the 19th of May, and continued up to the 11th Marylebone lost all their wickets in the first innings for 30 runs, and Middlesex stopped at 52 In the second innings of the former 83 were totalled, towards which the Earl of Winchilsea contributed 24 Middlesex required 62 runs to win, and this number cost them seven wickets Only four "extras" were recorded during the match * In the following year a great disparity in the teams existed, Marylebone were either very strong in batting or the other side deficient in the field This was not so strikingly apparent in the early part of the contest as in its later stages At this remote period of time, and with the slender materials at hand for forming an approach to the actual merits or demerits of the contenders on the occasion in question, it may be most prudent to abstain from analysing them, and let the score carry its own comment

MARYLEBONE

	1st inn		2nd inn
Hon H Tufton, c Dale	3	c Ray	12
Hon A. Upton, b Lord	10	run out .	1
Hon E Bligh, b Lord	6	c Sheppard	105
Lord F Beauclerk c Briden . ..	14	run out .	66
Hon J Tufton, not out	36	c W Beeston .	67
Hon Col Lennox b Lord ...	3	b W. Beeston	10
Hon C Douglas, b Ray	11	b Lord	. 29
T Mellish, Esq, c Barton	0	b Ray	0
Sir H Marten, c Ray	17	b Lord	0
Capt Lambert, l b w .	1	b Lord	22
Sylvester, b Ray . . .	17	not out	6
Byes	3	Byes	10
Total	121	Total	328

* On this occasion Lord Frederick Beauclerk is credited with capturing just one-half of the Middlesex wickets by his fielding and bowling As a cricketer, this nobleman (fourth son of Aubrey, fifth Duke of St. Albans) was the most remarkable during the time in which he lived He played his first match of note when eighteen years of age and continued to score well for thirty years afterwards A head bowler, superb field, and an accomplished batsman, his judgment upon critical subjects always carried great weight with it, and his decisions were rarely disputed For more than half a century he was a constant frequenter of Lord's He adopted the Church as his profession was a D D and a Vicar of St Alban's for upwards of twenty years He died in 1850, aged seventy-six

MIDDLESEX

	1st inn		2nd inn
Barton, c Lennox	27	c Beauclerk	10
Dale, c J Tufton	1	c Sylvester	0
Sheopard, st H Tufton	1	not out	8
Briden, c Lambert	11	b Beauclerk	2
Ray, b Beauclerk	6	b Sylvester	1
W Beeston, b Beauclerk	10	c Beauclerk	6
Wheeler, st H Tufton	1	c Lennox	2
J Beeston, b Beauclerk	12	c Bligh	12
Lord, c Upton	13	st H Tufton	19
Rice, b Silvester	1	b J Tufton	4
T Burgoyne Esq, not out	6	c H Tufton	0
Byes	5	Byes	3
Total	94	Total	67

To show what an uncertain game cricket is, few examples more forcible can be adduced than that given by the next match between Marylebone and Middlesex in the month of June, 1798 On this occasion the latter had the assistance of Boxall Strange to say, that Marylebone made but three double figures in both innings, the highest of which was 25 The totals of Marylebone were 25 and 85 Middlesex obtained 95 and 16 (without loss of wicket) In the month of September immediately following, Middlesex played a match with Hertfordshire Only an innings each was completed, with 30 runs for the former and 28 the latter Scarcely anything more is recorded of Middlesex up to the close of the eighteenth century

Little appears to have been done by Middlesex in the way of great matches until the year 1807, when they met once more at Lord's to play Marylebone After a contest of two days duration, Middlesex were declared winners by 48 runs Just twelve months afterwards another match at Lord's, bearing the same title, was played, when Marylebone won by six wickets, the scores being, Middlesex 91 and 75—total, 166 Marylebone 107 and 60 (four wickets)—total, 167 This match was chiefly noteworthy for the first appearance of Mr George Osbaldeston at Lord's In the sporting world generally, the name of Osbaldeston, or "The Squire" stood prominently forth during the first and second quarter of the present century His career as a cricketer was far less extensive, and his play chiefly notable for the tremendous force used in repelling a ball, and pace in delivering one At the period in question—or, to speak more correctly, within ten years of it—he had but one rival as regards pace, and that was Brown of Brighton Both required two long stops Mr Osbaldeston's fame rested chiefly on single wicket Few dared challenge, and fewer still could boast of beating him It is said that some of his single wicket matches involved the loss and gain of considerable sums of money

On the 30th of May in the same year another match occurred, which Middlesex won by 86 runs, although Marylebone had the assistance of Howard, a bowler of

LORD'S GROUND IN THE EARLY PART OF THE PRESENT CENTURY.

considerable skill and success Yet against him was arrayed a batsman of no ordinary acquirements in the person of Mr Edward Hayward Budd *

MIDDLESEX

	1st inn		2nd inn
— Pontifex, Esq , c Kinnaird	0	c Upton	5
Shackle, b Howard	9	b Howard	30
H Bentley, run out	5	c Smith	0
W Sparks, b Howard	5	b Howard	14
E H Budd, Esq , h w	76	c Upton	23
Ray, b Howard	3	b Smith	7
J Bentley, b Howard	3	st Howard	1
Goddard, b Howard	0	not out	5
Jenner, b Smith	26	c Kinnaird	3
J Batt, Esq , c Howard	0	b Howard	4
P Beeston, not out	1	b Smith	0
Byes	2	Byes	2
Total	130	Total	94

MARYLEBONE

	1st inn		2nd inn
G Leicester, Esq , c Ray	22	b Jenner ...	14
J Tanner, Esq , c J Bentley	10	b Budd	4
Col Maitland, b J Bentley	1	b Jenner	0
T A Smith, Esq , b J Bentley	3	st Ray	14
Hon E Bligh, c Pontifex	0	c Ray	0
Hon A Upton, b Ray	32	b Budd	0
Howard, c Jenner	7	b Jenner	3
Hon D Kinnaird, l b w	24	run out	0
T Mellish, Esq , c Budd	0	not out	0
H Aislabie, Esq , b Budd	1	st Ray	0
G Osbaldeston, Esq , not out	0	absent	0
Byes	3		
Total ..	103	Total	35

A long lapse of time again occurs before another match of importance is recorded for Middlesex This was in 1815, when Middlesex, opposed to Marylebone at Lord's, scored 89 and 24 against 31 and 66 Middlesex, though considered by far the weaker side, won the match by 16 runs

In the following year the tables were turned, and Marylebone won by 225 runs, although Middlesex had the assistance of Robinson, for whom the match was played as a benefit The batting of Mr Osbaldeston and Lord Frederick Beauclerk were the only features. The former scored 112 and 68, and the latter 96 and 6 Marylebone realised 260 and 112—total, 372 Middlesex, 50 and 97—total, 147

* This gentleman made a successful *debut* at Lord's when only seventeen years of age, and continued playing for fifty years afterwards As an all-round amateur cricketer, when in his prime, he had no superior Scorning the idea of danger, he would face the fastest bowler without other protection than an extra pair of hose Some of his feats with the bat, if told to an unpractised ear, would be regarded as fables Mr Budd was a man of extraordinary physical strength and endurance, for even up to three-score years and ten he would occasionally indulge in his favourite pastime Born at Missenden, Bucks, in 1785, died at Wroughton, near Swindon, in 1875

Another great void has to be filled up, but no match of importance intervenes between the last-mentioned and that of the 30th of May, 1825, when both Middlesex and Marylebone played thirteen aside In this list many fresh names were included. It was a batsman's match, no less than 671 runs were recorded, although five absentees figured on the score-sheet. It is not easy to reconcile the statements in the varied accounts given at the time The proper principles of scoring were not then understood, or if they were, it is quite certain they were not carried out

MARYLEBONE

	1st inn		2nd inn
H Herbert, Esq, b Jenner	5	c Dark	0
G T Vigne, Esq, run out	19	b Tanner	1
H Kingcote, Esq, st Jones	12	absent	—
H Lloyd, Esq, b Tanner	8	b Tanner	1
W Ward, Esq, b Tanner	18	not out	171
Lord F Beauclerk, c J Rice	39	b Mann	8
T Vigne, Esq b Jenner	3	b Dark	4
Lord Burford b Mann	8	absent	—
C Barnett, Esq, b Mann	0	b Dark	43
Hon F Gordon, b Mann	5	c Brooke	37
J Willan, Esq, b Tanner	0	st Jones	0
— Ponsonby, Esq, not out	2	c Jenner	2
Colonel Story, c Mann	0	st Jones	4
Byes	1	Byes	7
Total	120	Total	278

MIDDLESEX

	1st inn		2nd inn
E Rice, Esq, b Ward	0	b Ward	14
B Dark, c Lloyd	27	c Herbert	30
W Brooke, Esq, b Beauclerk	1	b Beauclerk	14
Mayor Cowell c Gordon	8	absent	—
Jenner, c Ward	16	c Beauclerk	2
H Bentley, st T Vigne	19	not out	13
Noah Mann jun, b Beauclerk	4	c Barnett	0
W Jones, Esq, b Ward	4	b Gordon	67
J Tanner, Esq b Ward	0	absent	—
J Rice, Esq c Gordon	1	b Beauclerk	0
T Northam, Esq, b Ward	2	c Barnett	17
W Tyler, Esq, st T Vigne	3	b Barnett	0
R Selway, Esq, not out	1	absent	—
Byes	2	Byes	25
Total	91	Total	182

Second Quarter of the Century

Middlesex met Marylebone on the 26th of June, 1826, at Lord's Marylebone scored 107 and 104—total 211, Middlesex 31 and 182 (for nine wickets)—total 213 In this match Cobbett made his first appearance at Lord's, and played on behalf of the county in which he for many years resided, and carried on a successful business in bat making

On the 17th of May, 1830, a match (twelve a side) was played at Lords, and was chiefly remarkable for the scores of Cobbett, viz, 29 and 60, who on this occasion played for Marylebone, he being then one of the ground bowlers Marylebone made 103 and 111—total 214, Middlesex 134 and 75 (with two absentees)—total 209

What the causes were that led to a seeming extinction of Middlesex as a cricket county it is not intended here to discuss The reader's fancy on this point has a large scope for display. One thing is tolerably certain, that nearly twenty years elapsed before Middlesex again "turns up" True, Marylebone frequently met the St John's Wood Club, with which a few members of Middlesex were mixed, but not till the year 1850 is there any match of importance at Lords where the county as such confront another county The lapse of time introduces almost, if not quite, a fresh catalogue of names During the long holiday, Middlesex appears to have become so enfeebled that the chances against success with surrounding counties were small indeed, even though Lillywhite, the crack bowler of Sussex had localised in Middlesex As the score on this occasion will be a fair commentary on the whole case, it is given in full

MIDDLESEX

	1st inn		2nd inn
Hon R Grimston, c Cæsar, b Lee	10	b Martingell	11
Paul, b Sherman	0	b Sherman	1
J Walker, Esq, c Brockwell, b Sherman	20	b Martingell	4
W Nicholson Esq, c Martingell, b Lee	10	c Cæsar, b Sherman	4
A Haygarth, Esq, run out	1	c White, b Martingell	10
Rogers, run out	26	c and b Sherman	11
Royston, l b w, b Martingell	18	b Sherman	0
R Kynaston, Esq, b Sherman	0	c Lee, b Sherman	18
T Craven, Esq, c Cæsar, b Martingell	1	b Martingell	3
Figg, not out	0	run out	0
Lillywhite, run out	0	not out	1
Byes 6, l-b 2, w 1, n b 4	13	Byes 2, l-b 5, n b 2	9
Total	99	Total	72

SURREY

	1st inn		2nd inn
J M Lee, Esq, c Nicholson, b Lillywhite	22	not out	1
Cæsar, c Haygarth, b Paul	13	not out	22
C H Hoare, Esq, b Royston	15		
Martingell, l b w b Royston	5		
Chester, b Royston	25		
Brockwell, not out	29	run out	26
Sherman, c Rogers, b Royston	0		
E Reeves, Esq, b Craven	3		
Lockyer, c Nicholson, b Royston	0		
Capt White, run out	0		
J Davis Esq, c Lillywhite, b Royston	0		
Byes 4, l-b 1, w 1, n b 1	7	L-b 1, w 2, n b 2	5
Total	119		54

In the following year, in the opening of the third quarter of the century, the old contest was revived, but it was found before the first day's play ended that

Middlesex were no match for Marylebone, who scored 214 in their first innings, although six Middlesex bowlers were brought against them. Chatterton alone more than doubled the runs from eleven Middlesex batsmen, who had to follow their innings. In this match Mr. Nicholson came out as wicket keeper for Middlesex. At the close of the play on the 27th of May, Marylebone were declared winners by an innings and 40 runs.

A few years after this decisive defeat an effort was made to form a county club and ground upon the Eton estate at Haverstock Hill, but it came to nothing. Undaunted, however, and urged by the sporting papers, a more successful result was at hand. In 1868 a meeting at the London Tavern, presided over by the Hon. R. Grimston, and supported by a few influential patrons of the game, took place, which resulted in the formation of a Middlesex County Club, and in less than a year the names of 250 persons were enrolled as members. A ground was set out at the rear of the Lamb Tavern, at the north-east corner of Islington Market. The first county match played on this ground was with Sussex, who were beaten by an innings. Still more significant of the condition of the newly-formed club was the "return" match, played on the 1st and 2nd of August, against Marylebone, when Middlesex came off victors by an innings and 232 runs, the scores being M.C.C. and Ground 93 and 86—total 179. As the Middlesex score introduces a new generation of cricketers, it is worth a reprint.

MIDDLESEX.

Thomas Hearne, b Wootton	125
R. D. Walker, Esq., c Biddulph, b Wootton	11
J. Frederick, Esq., b Wootton	9
Pooley, b Grundy	0
T. Case, Esq., b Grundy	116
I. D. Walker, Esq., run out	3
R. A. Fitzgerald, Esq., c Masham, b Grundy	0
V. E. Walker, Esq., b Grundy	8
George Hearne, c Randolph, b Grundy	72
Catlin, not out	24
D. Moffatt, Esq., c Randolph, b Wootton,	25
Byes 10, l-b 3, w 5	18
Total	411

This great conquest was eclipsed by another in the same year on the same ground between Middlesex and Bucks, when the latter, after being more than 200 runs ahead at the close of an innings each, were defeated by 138 runs. One William Wilson, a professor of music, invoked the Muse on this occasion, and produced the following verses, giving a "full, true, and particular account" of the progress of the match and the result.

My song is of a cricket match, as great as e'er was seen,
Twixt Buckingham and Middlesex, two right good teams I ween,
On August fourth and fifth and sixth, on wickets short and green,
The year was eighteen-sixty-four, the weather was serene—
When this famous cricket match was played,
These counties good between.

Now Buckingham did win the toss, and Leigh did quick begin,
With Golby opposite, to try a noble score to win,
But Golby sent a ball direct into Ned Pooley's fin,
Next Dupuis, bowled by V. E Walker, left with ghastly grin—
When this famous, &c

Tom Hearne show'd next that his'n was the proper style of play,
With fours, and threes, and right good hits, he featly led the way,
When he resigned for twenty nine, for four the next did stay,
Twas Bull, who got his *coup* (*cow*) *d'etat*—oh, what a glorious day!—
When this famous, &c

An obbligato duet Messrs Leigh and Markham tried,
And for two hours fully they the bowling good defied,
Till Leigh, by I D Walker, caught the ball, who quickly shied
High in the air, and 1, 0, 9, his figures were descried—
When this famous, &c

Fitzgerald in a dashing way made fifteen, but, alas!
A second Daniel caught him, and then it came to pass
That Markham, after seventy four, was bowled upon the grass!
Soon after Fletcher came in Sutton played well by the mass—
When this famous, &c

Then Barrington took Sutton's place when Sutton rick'd his knee,
And Fletcher was run out for ten, then Blinko came, d'ye see,
And Barrington was stumpt for one by Cooper, bold and free,
And Blinko gracefully withdrew,—no chance to score had he,
When this famous, &c

Two-ninety-four the jolly Bucks did for their innings take,
Then Middlesex to bat began, and feeble scores did make
Dyne went for two, and much I'm sure his honest heart did ache,
Then Cooper he was caught by Leigh, who was so wide awake,
When this famous, &c

And Daniel after scoring six was bowled by Thomas Hearne,
A famous cricketer, though rather heavy in the stern,
Then Pooley scored fifteen right well, and he applause did earn—
L B W his fate, then to leave it was his turn,
When this famous, &c

I D Walker next, who laid a duck's egg to the score,
By G Hearne he was quickly followed, who fell after two and four
The stumps were drawn till August fifth, when Frederick gave o'er,
Then V E Walker fell for five and Sewell dropt for four—
When this famous &c

A two by Catlin, then the innings ended What a lot!
R D Walker twenty-five, the largest score they got,
And seventy-six the total, the Cockneys got it hot,
But "ne'er say die" their motto was—they went in like a shot—
When this famous, &c

The second innings Catlin, faced by Pooley, did begin,
The latter eight did get, when Frederick went in,
A blow upon the cheek, poor Pooley sent the tent within,
And everybody thought that Buckingham was sure to win—
When the famous, &c

When Frederick was bowled by Hearne his score was seventy-eight,
Then R D Walker followed him, he had not long to wait
Ere Catlin fell for thirty—permit me here to state,
He played right well and carefully, assisting each good mate—
When this famous, &c

Pooley then resumed his bat, and quickly he let fly,
His score ran up to forty-three, despite his bruised eye,
And twice that number might have been, but for this reason why,
He was run out by R D. W, that batsman sly—
When this famous, &c

Then R D W run out, too, through nimble Mr Leigh
And Fitzgerald, fielding Lockyer-like, but twenty-nine made he,
Then Cooper, he made fifty-six—such scores you'll scarcely see—
And being run out, he cut his stick, all through the good Dupuis—
When this famous, &c.

George Hearne scored twenty-two right well, and by his brother bowled
And caught, came smiling o'er the green, though looking rather old
Three-forty-six six wickets down, the time to leave was told
This closed the day, the Bucks did look as if they all were sold—
When this famous, &c

Next day at twelve, or thereabouts, the sport did recommence
With Daniel, Sewell opposite, and without much pretence
The former seventy eight did score, and made a great defence,
Then I D Walker Sewell faced, and kept us in suspense—
When this famous, &c

Fletcher Frederick bowled when seventy-eight he made,
And Sewell he was bowled by Hearne, who like a hero played,
I D Walker scored forty-three ere from the field he strayed,
V E Walker not out for thirty eight, until the last he stayed—
When this famous &c

The second innings of the Bucks I now will shortly tell
Round O's for Fletcher Fitzgerald, and Barrington as well,
And after getting twenty-six Dupuis to V E fell,
Then thirty-seven were got by Leigh Oh, what a tip top swell!—
When this famous, &c

Then Bull and Marsham each got ten, and then were both run out,
And Golby seven did obtain, and was bowled by Catlin stout,
Too late bold Blinko went in, scoring two and not being out,
T Hearne was caught by Daniel well Oh, how the field did shout!—
When this famous, &c

The umpires, Thoms and Caldecourt, are both well known to fame
And fairly they their post maintained, the scorers did the same
The latter, Inwood, Howitt named—poor Inwood he fell lame
Through dotting down that lengthy score, rheumatics we did blame—
When this famous, &c

When young men of the present time grow grey and pass away,
Right well will be remembered the great and glorious day,
When Middlesex and Buckingham, with colours bright and gay,
Together near a thousand made, with first rate cricket play
When this famous, &c

During this season Middlesex played ten county matches, of which they won seven lost two, and one was "drawn" In the following year Middlesex beat Hampshire by an innings and 14 runs, and Lancashire by ten wickets, and in 1866 they were remarkably successful They beat the Yorkshire Club by an innings and 110 runs, and Surrey by an innings and 117 runs In the summary of Middlesex County averages of batting Mr V E Walker recorded 52 runs per innings, Mr J J Sewell 50, Marshall 41, Hearne 35, Mr C F Buller 33, Mr Winter 31, Mr R D Walker 28, and Mr. Daniel 19 This last-named gentleman accomplished an extraordinary feat in a match the following year against the Anomalies He made 20 runs in one over of five balls, and during an incompleted innings of 75 he struck the ball completely out of the ground—*i e*, over the boundary—five times In 1868 Middlesex confronted Kent, Sussex, Surrey, and Yorkshire They lost Sussex by nine wickets, Kent by 43 runs, Yorkshire by an innings and 24 runs, Surrey was a tie They won all the return matches But a fatal stop was soon after put to any further advances by Middlesex The warning note given out by the rod and tape of the surveyor was soon followed by a surrender of the estate, and Middlesex had to go in quest of "fresh fields and pastures new" These were not easy to find Homeless and houseless, they, notwithstanding, were able to keep the stone rolling in a match with Surrey at Marylebone This they won by 43 runs. In the return a few weeks later, Surrey were victors by two wickets.

After a search here and there for a spot on which to pitch a residence as well as a wicket, the Athletic Club running ground at Lillie Bridge, West Brompton, presented itself, but one season sufficed to show that the choice would not long answer Only two matches were played during the year 1870—both with Surrey, one of which was lost and the other won—Surrey by four wickets and Middlesex by three In the following year only three county matches came off Of these Middlesex beat Marylebone by an innings and 55 runs. Surrey by six wickets, and the third was left "drawn."

A more comfortable home opened up at Prince's Ground, on which Middlesex played county matches in 1872 without success They could lay claim to one at Lord's—viz, against Marylebone, whose score they topped by nine runs This, probably, would not have been the case if all the parties concerned in the match on the Marylebone side had been present when required to go in The absentees provoked a resolution on the part of the committee, expressive of regret and surprise that the members of the club should have kept themselves from the ground on the third day of the match and that the secretary be requested to call their attention to the general rule that all matches at Lord's, unless otherwise specified are continued on the third day

Nothing during the next season occurred to call for special mention saving the successful batting of Mr I D Walker, who in the five matches played by Middlesex put together 392 runs.

The last matches of importance played by Middlesex were with Yorkshire, Notts, and Surrey—three formidable counties The run of luck was against them, for they lost four, and two were drawn As the first Middlesex match is given *in extenso*, it may be as well to act similarly with the last It was a "return" played at the Oval on the 19th of August and two following days

SURREY

Jupp, c (sub) b Hadow	8
Mr A E Lucas, c Rose, b Henderson	50
Mr W W Read, c Henderson, b I D Walker	98
Mr S W Gore, c Thornton, b Henderson	0
Mr A Chandler, run out	12
Elliott, b Henderson	0
Mr C Tillard, c Webbe, b I D Walker	20
Mr W H Game c and b I D Walker	47
Pooley, st Turner, b I D Walker	16
Southerton, b I D Walker	26
Street, not out	9
Byes 5, l-b 1, w 1	7
Total	293

MIDDLESEX

	1st inn		2nd inn
Mr A J Webbe, b Southerton	21	c Pooley, b Southerton	12
Mr H R Webbe b Street	11	b Tillard	10
Mr C E Green, c Pooley, b Street	0	c Pooley, b Southerton	54
Mr C F Buller, b Street	14	c Chandler b Tillard	12
Mr I D Walker, l b w, b Southerton	15	st Pooley, b Southerton	19
Mr W H Hadow, not out	45	c Pooley, b Southerton	38
Mr C I Thornton, st Pooley, b Street	3	c Gore b Southerton	15
Mr C. H A Ross, c Pooley, b Street	0	b Southerton	1
Mr M Turner, c Gore, b Street	5	b Southerton	18
Mr H Henderson, c Game, b Southerton	0	c Game, b Southerton	8
Baston, c Pooley, b Southerton	2	not out	6
Byes 1, l-b 1	2	Byes 5, l-b 4	9
Total	118	Total	202

From this rapid glance of Middlesex, one thing cannot fail to strike the observant reader, viz, the anomalous condition of the county In the first place it was the earliest to foster the game and yet has been from time to time without a home or shelter for its offspring By far, too, the most rich, stable, and populous in the kingdom, and the forefront of the world yet unable to maintain for any length of time unbroken a band of cricketers capable of meeting the scattered forces of infinitely less favoured and cultured districts There must be reason for this, and that reason is probably to be found in the engrossing character of the all-absorbing city The management of a county cricket club makes large demands upon the time of persons which cannot always be spared, hence a continual change in the administration of its affairs, and everybody knows that a frequency of change in matters of this character is far more likely to retard than advance It is no answer that the Marylebone Club is included in the county of Middlesex It is quite a distinct institution, and is conducted upon a different principle Under any circumstances, it is highly desirable that Middlesex should possess a good county ground, and all the necessary adjuncts for carrying on the noble game—carrying it on in accordance with the surrounding material grandeur, intellectual opulence, and political power the like of which is without mention in past ages, and ought now to be recorded with gratitude as well as pride

When a few years since Messrs Prince opened their ground in Hans Place, Chelsea, great hopes were entertained that these desires and needs would be realised to the full How stands the case now? These gentlemen hold two pieces of land under two distinct instruments First, there is the ground on which stand the Tennis and Racquet Courts and a covered-in skating rink, all of which are held under a lease which expires on the 25th December, 1885 Secondly, there is the ground comprising the cricket field and the slip of skating ground between the trees and the wall of the racquet courts, which is held under an agreement which expires at Michaelmas, 1880 By a recent Act of Parliament for the construction of new thoroughfares and improvements in the neighbourhood of Cadogan and Hans Place, a space of 700 feet in length and 300 in breadth, is to be left undisturbed until 1880 for the purpose of cricket If these statements are incontestable, the shortness of its present occupancy is much to be deplored Middlesex, as a county, were so unfortunate in 1874, that of six matches played out and home they could only claim one Nor did they "show up" any better in the following year, for in their six matches with Yorkshire, Notts, and Surrey, they lost four, and two remained unfinished

ANALYSIS OF THE BATTING IN 1875

Name	No of Matches	No of Innings	Most Runs in a Match	Most Runs in an Innings	How often Bowled	Caught	Stumped	Run out	Not out	Total	Average of Innings Over
Mr G Bird	3	4	34	34	2	2	0	0	0	45	11 1
Mr C F Buller	4	7	58	51	1	5	0	1	0	155	22-1
Mr J W Dale	2	4	24	21	1	2	1	0	0	40	10
Flanagan	2	3	4	4	1	1	1	0	0	8	2-2
Mr C K Francis	3	4	18	17	2	1	0	0	1	32	8
Mr C E Green	4	6	54	54	3	2	0	1	0	85	14-1
Hearne	3	4	8	8	0	3	1	0	0	19	4-3
Mr W H Hadow	6	10	83	58	4	5	0	0	1	242	24-2
Mr E Rutter	2	3	6	6	2	0	0	1	0	6	2
Mr A P Snow	2	4	2	2	0	2	0	0	2	4	1
Mr A F Smith	3	5	21	21	2	3	0	0	0	22	4-2
Mr C I Thornton	6	10	39	39	4	4	2	0	0	112	11-2
Mr M Turner	6	10	23	18	4	3	0	0	3	57	5-7
Mr I D Walker	6	10	56	56	6	3	1	0	0	146	14-6
Mr A J Webbe	5	9	97	96	2	4	1	1	1	192	21-3
Mr H R Webbe	3	6	27	19	5	1	0	0	0	57	9-3

NOTE—In the construction of this table, and of all others, "hit wicket" and "leg before" are classed with those bowled The total number of runs is divided by the number of innings commenced, whether concluded or not, but the number of incompleted innings is placed to the credit of the batsman in the "not out" column

LORD'S GROUND AND THE MARYLEBONE CLUB.

The cynosure of neighbouring eyes —*Milton*

First Match of importance—Lord's wish to Retire—Purchase of the Lease by Mr Ward—Transfer of the same to James Henry Dark—Description of the Ground by "L E L"—Destruction of the Pavilion by Fire—List of Presidents from that time—Notice of Mr Aislabie, Hon Sec—Also Mr Kynaston—Visit to Lord's with a Daughter of Erin, a Sketch—Professional Cricketers and their Perverseness—Mr Bass's Address to the Rising Generation of Players—Another important Transfer of the Ground through Danger of Extinction as a Cricket Ground—Its subsequent Enlargement—Present Capacities, from an Original Survey—Renewed Levelling—Results of chief Annual Matches played at Lord's—Analysis of the Marylebone Batting in 1875—Rules of the Club

If, as a figure of speech, the philologist will allow the quotation of this line, the task of proving an appropriate fitness will not be a very difficult one, although it is not quite so easy at the present day to say much that comes within the scope of information Every tyro aiming for a place in the school of cricket literature dates his early practice from Lord's Ground, and debates upon the fortunes of the Marylebone Club—probably from the time it elected itself to the throne of cricket with about half-a-dozen members until now, an admitted representative body in form colossal, and in number "an exceeding great army" In treating of a subject beset with so much temptation to young aspirants, the best features have been often impaired or hidden, without any corresponding recompense, just as parasites cling to the stem and branches of trees, and pay for the intrusion by sickly and decaying flowers Take away the fiction, and the few facts connected with this wonderful institution abound with lasting interest As truth is eternal, every generation may sip at the same fountain with equal benefit and gratification Lord's Ground has, in fact, a history within a history when taken in connection with the county of Middlesex Nine-tenths of a century cannot be expected to pass away barren of "events," many of a curious and startling character for in all probability there is not a game adopted by Englishmen so redundant with anecdotes as cricket nor a place in which they are narrated with greater humour and effect than at Marylebone Bulk, however, defies quotation, for once begun there is no knowing at what stage to stop; and one of the objects of this book would be frustrated by ponderousness Now the foundation of Lord's and the Marylebone Club may be told in a few pages On the dissolution of the White Conduit Club in 1787 a few of its influential members assisted one Thomas Lord to seek another locality for playing matches, and in a short time Dorset-square—then "an open space" in the parish of Marylebone—was secured Hence the compound title of Lord's Ground and the Marylebone Club * The arena was about ten acres, and the first match played thereon occurred in the

* An engraving of this ground and a match being played upon it may be seen in the *Sporting Magazine*, Vol 2 The picture, however, is faulty in detail, as only two stumps form the wicket

same year It was between five of the White Conduit Club with six picked men against All England According to the magazines of the period, the match was "to be played for 1000 guineas" It is stated that Lord held possession of this ground for about a quarter of a century, and then went to the North Bank, Regent's Park Here he was disturbed after a very short occupancy, and then settled down in the St John's Wood Road, and the present Marylebone Ground was baptised with a name likely to endure from generation to generation

The first match of any importance played on the present ground occurred in the month of June, 1814 It was between the Marylebone Club and Hertfordshire. As the latter were known to be weak in bowling, Bentley was transferred to them Even with this, Marylebone were found too much for Herts, for they were beaten by an innings and 27 runs Bentley kept a book of scores, from which the following is taken

HERTFORDSHIRE

	1st inn		2nd inn
W Mowbray, c Ward	4	b Beauclerk	1
H Bentley, not out	33	run out	0
T Burton, b Budd	7	b Osbaldeston	17
S Carter, b Budd	0	st Vigne	0
W Sibley, c Beauclerk	6	c Budd	1
Taylor, b Beauclerk	6	run out	2
Denham, b Budd	10	st Vigne	21
T Carter, b Budd	1	b Osbaldeston	0
J Sibley, b Beauclerk	6	not out	3
Freeman, c Beauclerk	2	run out	5
Crew, b Beauclerk	0	st Vigne	0
Byes	4	Byes	5
Total	79	Total	55

MARYLEBONE

A Schabner, Esq, c J Sibley	55
Hon D Kinnaird, b S Carter	1
C Warren, Esq, b Taylor	25
E H Budd, Esq c T Carter	36
Hon E Bligh, b Bentley	6
T Burgoyne, Esq, run out	0
Lord F Beauclerk, b Taylor	3
G Osbaldeston, Esq, c Mowbray	18
W Ward, Esq, run out	10
T Vigne, Esq b Bentley	2
J Poulet, Esq, not out	1
Byes	4
Total	161

As a cricketer Lord never ranked very high How and why he shifted from Diss to London when a youth it is not particularly interesting to inquire His general character has frequently been penned, but not in strict accord That he was a Jacobite his son frequently denied Upon his retirement from the ground came the first note of a Marylebone unsettlement The situation was commanding for builders, and but for the prompt action taken by Mr Ward, who purchased the lease, the ground would have speedily been spotted with villas A few years subsequently Mr James Dark became possessor of the lease This he held till within about four years of his death, which occurred in the month of October, 1871.

It may be well to remark that, during the occupancy of Mr Dark, the Tennis Court and necessary accompaniments thereto were erected. Other buildings also reduced the original area of eight acres and a quarter very considerably The description of Lord's with a grand match "on," though "done to death," will not suffer much by one, two, say three reproductions

"I patronize" says a celebrated writer under the signature "L E L," "all cricketers, and delight in all cricket grounds, and look with pleasure even at two urchins with a fragment of a hat for a wicket, a bit of paling for a bat, and a raw potato for a ball But most of all my spirit is wont to delight in that fine ground where rules the monarch Dark, in name,—albeit not too swarthy in countenance, and in his actions fair to the most transparent degree of candour King James is as absolute and as energetic as he is active and bustling The locomotive spirit of the age seems to possess him wholly The air of Lord's seems always to my nostrils the purest within the same distance of Bow Church, the turf the most elastic, and although houses have almost encircled it they are neat and cheerful in aspect, and placed at a reasonable distance In themselves they must be agreeable summer residences, save and except when a smashed window and a sudden irruption from a fiery-looking ball scares the fair inmates, and pursues a course destructive as that of the bull in the china shop among the ornaments of the boudoir Yes, to the metropolitan lovers of the manly and noble game it affords in due season a convenient and endless resource of gratification At its more important matches the rising skill from all parts of the land may be found summoned to stand the ordeal of approval by the admitted critics of its mysteries"

"What a world of delight is contained in that miniature globe—a cricket ball! Well hit, it flies from the bat like a thunderbolt—far, far eclipsing in speed the swiftest coach—steam coach—on a railway, that admirable invention of modern times by which the people of this age enjoy the privilege of being able to journey from Pole to Pole (barring their necks are not broken by the way) without the slightest possible advantage either to mind or body! Repair to Lord's—repair to Lord's all you that can, to play and those who cannot play, to learn, and those who could once do the trick, but whose joints are now stiff with age, to wake reminiscences of past delights—to Lord's, where the finest air within the same distance of St Paul's is, perhaps, to be enjoyed Whilst but too many of the fields and green spots around our Babylon, erst the retreat of shepherds and shepherdesses, are now the haunts of blackguards and blackguardesses, here still meet the *élite* of town and country! This far-famed ground, as well as the noble game to which it is dedicated, seems, however, destined to perpetual changes, which are not always improvements The present season has brought more transformations The tavern, dining room, stables, &c, have been new fronted and enlarged, but they encroach somewhat on the ground, never too spacious for its main purpose. In the rear of the pavilion there has been made a thoroughfare for the spectators. This improvement enables equestrians to pass behind instead of before the watchers of the game, although it is a question whether these centaurs might not be advantageously excluded altogether from cricket grounds. There are still too many benches allowed, which, with a little shed, apparently the habitation of some deer lately added to the 'ground,' frequently obstruct the fieldsmen and stop runs, being thus disadvantageous alike to in and out sides. A ground sacred to the noble game should not be profaned by ordinary cockney assemblages—ballooning and other work of the like nature which can be carried on quite as well elsewhere. Sheep, moreover, are the only quadrupeds fit for cricket fields; horses and pony racing are better away. A cricket ground should be flat as *table* beer—a name our brewers most appropriately employ when they would describe the produce of the *ne plus ultra* of their art, as shown in removing from malt liquors any harmful inequalities tending to any corresponding elevation of the animal spirits. The game itself might be compared to other more generous liquors: exhilarating and exciting is it, like champagne; beneficial, cordial, and fortifying to the system even as port; or it may be better likened for its infinite variety to that nectarious compound of all that is exquisite in beverage—the old fashioned punch, as graphically described by John Nyren in his 'Cricketer's Guide.'"

The original pavilion was destroyed by fire on the 28th of July, 1825, after one of the public school matches, viz., Winchester *v.* Harrow, and in the conflagration nearly all the records of the club and many cricket implements were consumed. An engraving here given is said to be a correct view of the ground previous to the fire. It was rebuilt in time for holding the annual dinner of the Marylebone Club in 1826. No matches of any importance were played during the year, saving two public school matches.

In consequence of the fire before referred to, many valuable documents were lost. Such documents, for instance, as scores and notes of matches, which at the present day would be of great use to the historian. Many of the traditions handed down orally have gathered no inconsiderable amount of absurdity. Mr. James Henry Dark—frequently interrogated on the subject of documents and valuable relics destroyed by the fire—would either accompany a smile or a frown with the expressive, or, perhaps, non-expressive word, "Bosh." It would be wiser, therefore, to let them die out altogether than perpetuate them by citation. Even the names of the officers have perished from memory—at least are not sufficiently to be relied upon till about the year 1826. From that date to the present the list of Presidents is given in unbroken continuity.

1826.—Charles Barnett, Esq.
1827.—Henry Kingscote, Esq.
1828.—A. F. Greville, Esq.
1829.—John Barnard, Esq.
1830.—Hon. G. Ponsonby.
1831.—William Deedes, Esq.
1832.—Henry Howard, Esq.
1833.—Herbert Jenner, Esq.
1834.—Hon. H. Ashley.
1835.—Lord Charles Russell.

1836—Lord Suffield
1837—Viscount Grimston
1838—Marquis of Exeter
1839—Earl of Chesterfield
1840—Earl of Verulam
1841—Earl Craven
1842—Earl of March
1843—Earl of Ducie
1844—Sir John Bayley, Bart
1845—Thomas Chamberlayne, Esq
1846—Earl of Winterton
1847—Earl of Strathmore
1848—Earl of Leicester
1849—Earl of Darnley
1850—Earl Guernsey
1851.—Earl Stamford and Warrington
1852—Viscount Dupplin
1853—Marquis of Worcester
1854—Earl Vane
1855—Earl of Uxbridge
1856—Viscount Milton
1857—Sir Frederick Bathurst, Bart
1858—Lord Garlies
1859—Earl of Coventry
1860—Lord Skelmersdale
1861—Earl Spencer
1862—Earl of Sefton
1863—Lord Suffield
1864—Earl of Dudley
1865—Lord Ebury.
1866—Earl of Sandwich
1867—Earl of Verulam
1868—Lord Methuen
1869—Marquis of Lansdowne
1870—J H Scourfield, Esq, M P
1871—Earl of Clarendon
1872—Viscount Downe
1873—Earl of Cadogan
1874—Marquis of Hamilton
1875—Sir Charles Legard, Bart, M P
1876—
1877—
1878—
1879—
1880—

Previous to the dates here given, Mr Aislabie acted as hon sec to the club and down to 1842, when he died. At the first annual meeting afterwards allusions were made to his long and eminent services. The committee said "they were perfectly aware that no panegyric was wanting to induce members to do justice to the manner in which deceased had performed the duties of his office for 20 years. He was not more distinguished for his unwearied zeal and assiduity in promoting the game of cricket than for the many amiable points in his character. By his affable demeanour and general popularity he became the rallying point to all cricketers, and his loss will be severely felt." His bust remains in the Pavilion as a memorial of his worth and the esteem in which he was held.

Mr Roger Kynaston succeeded to the vacancy caused by Mr Aislabie's death. Previously thereto this gentleman was well known in cricket circles. He joined the Marylebone Club in the year 1829, and rendered very important service to it as a practical member. Few matches came off in which his club had a direct interest without active participation in them. Though not a mighty man at the wicket, he was a host in himself when behind it. As a long stop very few amateurs equalled him, and fewer still surpassed. He held the post of hon sec till the year 1858, and then resigned it to Mr Alfred Baillie. Mr Kynaston died on the 21st of June, 1874, in the 68th year of his age.

Notwithstanding the many and varied changes in the game during Mr Kynaston's long connection with the Marylebone Club, nearly all tended in the direction of improvements. Very few genuine lovers of cricket in visiting London during the season failed to take advantage of a good match The following story is amusing

"VISIT TO LORD'S WITH A DAUGHTER OF ERIN (A SKETCH) —'Here are our sixpences How goes the match, Dark?' 'Just as cricket will go sometimes, sir, all one way, they did not get fifty first innings, and don't seem likely to do better this, there are five wickets down for next to nothing' 'Well, then, let us hasten to the other side behind the scorers, and see what remains to be seen We are in luck, at all events so far, for the men in are Pilch and Mr Taylor, than whom there are no finer players in England' 'Yet there is a good deal of difference in their size, and as much in their style of playing, though both are perfect masters of the game Look! there is a hit beyond the green house' 'Yes, indeed, there is one of Pilch's peculiar *drives*, as they are called, and that green house, as you call the Pavilion, where the club dine and keep all their paraphernalia, is often hit against and beyond, and has been hit over before now, for London is not like the country, where generally ample room may be easily obtained—and this ground, though the head quarters of the chief club in the kingdom, is not more than half as large as it ought to be, and as many grounds are' 'There is another hit! and there again Mr Taylor has hit a ball right against the pales.' 'Yes, and hits in that direction, which are called square hits or *cuts*, are by far the most scientific of all' 'Why, they seem to hit every ball, they will win the match after all, will they not?' 'Hardly that; it has gone too far, but players like those are seldom idle while they remain in, and they certainly are getting runs very fast now' 'Then why do they not have better bowlers to bowl?' 'Because there are none in the kingdom This tall stout man at the end nearest the Pavilion is Mynn, and the other who bowls from the other wicket is Hillyer They, too, are very different in size and style, but both are equally good, they are going to try a change, Sir F Bathurst is the best gentleman bowler in England' 'There is another hit, but what a jump forward that man made!' 'Indeed he did, and to some purpose, for he has caught Taylor out That is Mr W Pickering, he is standing at what is called *cover point*, it is the most important place in the field except that of wicket keeper, and, except that stout man in a coat close to the wicket, the umpire, he is the best man that ever did stand there, even Caldecourt in his prime was not better than he is' 'Why, there is the man who has just come out of the Pavilion going back again' 'Yes, Mr Anson has stumped him out, the man whom you see standing behind the wicket which is bowled at, he is a very dangerous man to play tricks with There is another of Pilch's hits, and another; if it were possible to save the game, he would do it' 'And it is quite hopeless?' 'Why it is true that the law itself has not more glorious uncertainties than cricket, and this very uncertainty is not one of its least attractions, and there is no game of which it is so well proved, that it is never lost till it is won A whole eleven has been got out before now for nine runs, and that fine looking old gentleman whom you see close to us looking on with so much interest, once got 278 himself' 'Do the men ever get hurt stopping the ball?

That gentleman behind Mr Anson has such numbers come to him, and yet he never misses them' 'He is what is called the *long stop*, Mr Kynaston, the secretary of the club, and a very important place he is now filling, but accidents very seldom occur, it is true a very fine player a little while ago had his hand split down at Dorchester, but such mishaps are very rare Ah! there is the last man out, let us go and find out what is the score—57! lost in one innings Such is cricket, for I should have thought that the losing side had been the strongest However, the return match may tell a different story'"

The professional element was now becoming a very prominent feature, and few matches of importance were attempted at Marylebone without a good sprinkling of players in the programme As a matter of course, the dispositions of some required a certain amount of discipline, for at times a well planned arrangement was thrown into disorder through the wrongheadedness of perhaps but one influential member of the party They had become pet children, and consequently partook in some degree of the waywardness and self-will of the child They not only regarded cricket as an institution but that they were the most important personages belonging thereto, and it would have been a task of some difficulty to persuade many of them that greatness in cricketing was not synonymous with greatness in the abstract, or that eminence in the game was not an equivalent in the eyes of the world to eminence in the fine arts, in law, medicine, literature, politics, engineering, or any other of the grand pursuits to which men devote themselves. Mr Bass endeavoured to dissipate these notions in an address to the rising generation in the year 1849 He tells them the essentials of a true cricketer are that he should "bear and forbear He must often lose his wicket, but never his good humour, and if it should slip away just for a moment it must be recovered as soon as possible If he wishes to excel he must be bold and active—temperate to small things In dealing with a ball, as with a neighbour, he should eschew all crooked ways and cross practices and keep to the upright and straightforward course, never overreach, and always on the square He must remember *medio tutissimus*, and guard his *middle stump*, not too backward in coming forward, not too forward in going back He must 'hold his head up, yet fight low,' look well at his man, and keep his eyes open If he play too uppishly, and exalt either himself or the ball to the skies, he will certainly be *caught in the act*, and laughed at for his folly, should remember that if he stops a straight ball he must hit a crooked one, but if he misses it all his pent-up energies and dormant capacities for action will go for nothing When bowling he must use his head as well as his hands, and suiting himself to his company find out first his man and then his wicket He must try him high and low, on and off, far and near, fast and slow, and confuse his ideas both of time and space The fielder must watch the batter and work the equation, giving the dodges of the bowler and pitch of the ball and style of the batsman to find whereabouts the ball will come He must be the living and lively representative of amiability and good humour, remembering that cricket is a game of play, whereas sour, sulky or passionate ebullitions are too much like earnest He must leave his books in his study and his ledger in the counting-house and not go in for his innings with all the solemnity of a great go or insolvent's examination The cricketer must obey the laws, and never question the judgment of the captain or the umpire, a revolutionary spirit being not more subversive of kingdoms than of cricket clubs "

MATCH REGULATIONS

All persons visiting Lord's Ground are admitted subject to the observance of the Marylebone Cricket Club, and of the Marylebone Cricket Club Committee, and the Club reserve to themselves the right to require and enforce the withdrawal of any person who shall refuse or fail to comply with them

I—In all Matches played at Lord's Ground, the Umpires shall be guided by the Laws of Cricket, as laid down by the Marylebone Cricket Club

II—In the absence of special agreement to the contrary, Matches shall commences at 12 o'clock on the first day, and at 11 o'clock on the following days One day's Matches shall commence at 11 a m. The Stumps shall be drawn at 7 p m on the first day, and at 7 30 on the following days

III—The Umpires shall pitch the Wickets, and shall clear the ground on the ringing of the first bell, five minutes before the appointed hour of play, and on the ringing of the second bell, five minutes afterwards, play shall commence

IV—Dinner shall be announced at 3 o'clock, and at the expiration of half an hour, the first bell shall be rung for the clearance of the ground, the second bell being rung in five minutes afterwards, when play shall be resumed

V—On the fall of a Wicket, or termination of an Innings, within five minutes of dinner, or time being called play may be suspended at the option of the In side The bell for clearing the ground shall be rung seven minutes after the close of an Innings, the second bell two minutes afterwards

VI—Players engaged in Matches at Lord's shall not leave the Ground in a body, during play, for the purpose of refreshment

VII—In cases of noise or disorder, the Umpires shall have the power to stop the Game till order is restored, and they shall be responsible for the proper observance of the Match Regulations, and all cases of proved neglect of the same shall be reported to the Committee

VIII—All Matches made by the consent, and with the approval of the Committee, shall be entered in the Marylebone Cricket Club List, and all Members desirous of playing in Club Matches, shall apply to the Secretary, who shall submit each Monday to the Committee a list of Sides engaged in Matches during the week

IX—After Play has commenced, and during its continuance, no one, except the Players engaged in the Game, or other persons specially authorised, shall be allowed within the Ground reserved for play, and no Public Betting, or unnecessary noise or confusion of any kind, shall be permitted in the space occupied by visitors

By Order of the Committee

The condition of the M C C in 1867—a very important epoch in its history—may be to some extent ascertained by the number of matches played with the results

MARYLEBONE GENERAL LIST

Lord's, May 6—M C C v Ground Players M C C scored 102 and 91—total, 193 Players, 111 and 83—total, 194 The players won by five wickets

Lord's, May 9—Royal Artillery v Household Brigade R A, 78 and 205—total, 283 H B, 69 and 47—total, 116 Royal Artillery won by 167 runs

Lord's, May 13—M C C and Ground v Colts of England Marylebone, 134 and 125—total 259 Colts, 108 and 81—total, 189 Marylebone won by 70 runs

Lord's, May 16—Knickerbockers v M C C and Ground Knickerbockers, 86 and 40—total, 126 Marylebone, 100 and 28—total, 128 M C C won by nine wickets

Cambridge, May 16 —University v M C C and Ground University, 164 and 161—total, 325 M C C and Ground, 107 and 105—total, 212 Drawn M C C lost four wickets in second innings

Lord's, May 20 —Gentlemen of Ireland v M C C Ireland, 10 Drawn in consequence of rain No wicket down

Lord's, May 23 —Military Academy, Woolwich, v Military Academy, Sandhurst Woolwich, 67 and 66 (eight wickets)—total, 133 Sandhurst 167 Drawn

Lord's, May 27 —M C C and Ground v County of Surrey Marylebone, 129 Surrey, 38 and 79—total, 117 Marylebone won by an innings and 12 runs

Winchester, May 28 —M C C and Ground v Winchester College Marylebone, 155 Winchester, 49 and 93 (three wickets)—total, 142

Winchester, May 29 —M C C and Ground v Winchester Garrison Marylebone, 126 Winchester, 212 Drawn

Oxford, May 30 —University v M C C and Ground University, 74 and 112—total, 186 Marylebone 195 Won by an innings and 9 runs

Lord's, June 3 —M C C and Ground v Lancashire Marylebone, 139 and 56—total, 195 Lancashire, 79 and 66—total, 145 Marylebone won by 50 runs

Lord's, June 6 —M C C and Ground v. Civil Service Marylebone, 81 and 74 (four wickets) —total, 155 Civil Service, 60 Drawn

Lord's, June 10 —England v Middlesex England, 261 Middlesex, 101 and 135—total, 236 England won by an innings and 25 runs

Lord's, June 13 —M C C v Royal Artillery M C C 85 and 123—total, 208 R A 140 and 185—total, 325 Royal Artillery won by 117 runs

Oval, June 13 —M C C and Ground v Surrey M C C and Ground, 231 and 314—total, 545 Surrey, 216 and 124—total, 340 Marylebone won by 205 runs

Lord's, June 17 —South of the Thames v North of the Thames South 32 and 102—total 134 North, 61 and 46—total 107 South won by 27 runs

Lord's, June 20 —I Zingari v Household Brigade I Z, 175 H B, 97 and 43—total, 140 Unfinished

Eton June 20 —M C C and Ground v Eton College Marylebone, 106 Eton, 226 Unfinished

Lord's, June 21 —Cheltenham College v M C C and Ground College, 126 and 187—total, 313 Marylebone, 56 and 129—total, 185 Cheltenham won by 128 runs

Lord's, June 24 —Cambridge University v M C C and Ground University, 167 and 205—total, 372 Marylebone, 154 and 190—total, 344 University won by 28 runs

Lord's, June 27 —Oxford University v M C C and Ground Oxford, 102 and 32—total, 134 Marylebone, 163 Won by an innings and 29 runs

Lord's, July 1 —Oxford v Cambridge Oxford, 112 and 147—total, 259 Cambridge, 150 and 112—total, 262 Cambridge won by five wickets

Lord's, July 4 —M C C and Ground v County of Norfolk Marylebone, 103 and 127—total, 230 Norfolk, 33 and 101—total, 134 Marylebone, won by 96 runs

Lord's, July 8 —Players v Gentlemen Players, 79 and 61—total, 140 Gentlemen, 87 and 55—total, 142 Gentlemen won by eight wickets

Woolwich July 9 —M C C and Ground v Royal Artillery Marylebone, 139 and 102—total, 241 Royal Artillery, 91 and 132—total, 223 Marylebone won by 18 runs

Lord's, July 12 —Eton v Harrow Eton, 208 and 221—total, 429 Harrow, 173 and 78—total, 251 Drawn Harrow lost one wicket in second innings

Lord's, July 15 —M C C and Ground v. County of Warwick Marylebone, 194 Warwick, 41 for five wickets Discontinued

Lord's, July 18 —M C C v Gentlemen of Northumberland Marylebone, 105 and 43—total, 148 Northumberland, 90 and 59—total 149 Won by two wickets

Lord's, July 22 —M C C and Ground v County of Devon Marylebone, 66 and 82—total, 148 Devon, 59 and 39—total, 98 Marylebone won by 50 runs

Lord's, July 25 —Free Foresters v M C C and Ground Free Foresters, 242 Marylebone, 90 (six wickets) Drawn

Lord's, July 29.—M.C.C. and Ground *v.* County of Suffolk. Marylebone, 199 and 69—total, 268. Suffolk, 150 and 120—total, 270. Marylebone won by four wickets.

Lord's, July 31.—M.C.C. and Ground *v.* Charterhouse. Marylebone, 242. Charterhouse 112 and 39—total, 151. Unfinished. Charterhouse lost two wickets in second innings.

Lord's, Aug. 1.—M.C.C. and Ground *v.* Rugby School. Marylebone, 75 and 275—total, 350. Rugby, 109 and 150—total, 259. Marylebone won by 91 runs.

Lord's, Aug. 3.—Charterhouse *v.* Westminster School. Charterhouse, 86 and 145—total, 231. Westminster, 145 and 14—total, 159. Unfinished. Westminster lost one wicket.

Canterbury, Aug. 5.—North of the Thames *v.* South of the Thames. North, 169 and 141—total, 310. South, 122 and 71—total, 193. North won by 117 runs.

Canterbury, Aug. 7.—M.C.C. *v.* County of Kent. Marylebone, 230. Kent, 76 and 105—total, 181. Marylebone won by an innings and 49 runs.

Canterbury, Aug. 9.—Gentlemen of Kent *v.* I Zingari. Kent, 109 and 332—total, 441. I Zingari, 99. Unfinished.

Brighton, Aug. 12.—County of Sussex *v.* M.C.C. and Ground. Sussex, 111 and 413—total, 524. Marylebone, 164 and 118—total, 282. Sussex won by 242 runs.

Dereham, Aug. 27.—M.C.C. and Ground *v.* County of Norfolk. Marylebone, 97 and 87—total, 184. Norfolk, 176 and 9—total, 185. Norfolk won by ten wickets.

Bury St. Edmund's, Aug. 29.—M.C.C. and Ground *v.* County of Suffolk. Marylebone, 156 and 99—total, 255. Suffolk, 104 and 84—total, 188. Marylebone won by 67 runs.

BATTING AVERAGES.

NAME.	No. of Matches.	No. of Innings.	Most Runs in a Match.	Most Runs in an Innings.	How often Bowled.	Caught.	Stumped.	Run out.	Not out.	Total.	Average per Innings.	Over.
Mr. C. Absolom	3	5	96	94	3	2	0	0	0	100	20	
Mr. R. D. Balfour	6	8	95	82	3	4	0	0	1	185	23	1
Bennett	3	5	14	10	2	3	0	0	0	19	3	4
Biddulph	9	14	79	70	6	6	0	0	2	220	15	10
Mr. C. S. Boyle	5	9	38	22	5	3	0	1	0	95	10	5
Mr. T. Brindley	6	11	36	28	5	3	0	1	2	132	12	
Mr. E. Brune	4	7	61	53	2	4	0	1	0	72	10	2
Mr. F. C. Buller	4	5	23	23	5	0	0	0	0	48	9	3
Mr. H. E. Bull	3	4	78	74	1	2	0	1	0	80	20	
Mr. F. Campbell	5	7	43	43	6	0	0	1	0	71	10	1
Mr. T. Case	3	6	43	24	3	2	0	0	1	67	11	1
Chatterton	4	6	35	19	2	4	0	0	0	61	10	1
Hon. C. Carnegie	4	6	37	33	3	2	0	0	1	82	13	4
Mr. C. Cholmondeley	4	7	6	6	2	3	0	0	2	14	2	
Mr. B. B. Cooper	3	4	109	86	4	0	0	0	0	122	31	
Earl Coventry	3	4	14	14	2	1	0	1	0	24	6	
Mr. G. A. Duntze	3	5	20	20	3	2	0	0	0	35	7	
Mr. W. H. Dyke	4	5	16	13	3	2	0	0	0	20	4	
Mr. H. W. Fellows	7	9	23	23	7	1	0	0	1	72	8	
Mr. R. Wynne Finche	3	5	3	3	4	1	0	0	0	6	1	1
Mr. R. A. Fitzgerald	7	10	54	54	6	4	0	0	0	120	12	
Mr. M. P. Fitzgerald	5	9	26	14	1	4	0	2	2	57	6	3
Mr. J. J. Frederick	4	6	38	36	2	4	0	0	0	111	18	3
Mr. R. Forster	9	16	25	18	11	1	0	0	4	151	9	7
Mr. T. F. Fowler	4	7	40	40	4	3	0	0	0	67	9	4
Capt. Fyfe	4	6	21	21	5	0	0	0	1	46	7	4
Hon. T. De Grey	3	4	19	13	4	0	0	0	0	19	4	3
Mr. E. M. Grace	6	10	31	31	6	4	0	0	0	86	8	6
Mr. W. G. Grace	3	5	75	37	2	2	0	0	1	142	28	2

BATTING AVERAGES—*continued*

NAME	No of Matches	No of Innings	Most Runs in a Match	Most Runs in an Innings	How often Bowled	Caught	Stumped	Run out	Not out	Total	Average per Innings Over
Grundy . .	17	28	60	57	12	15	0	1	0	308	11
Hearne . . .	13	20	69	56	7	11	0	1	1	272	13–12
Mr W Hone	3	4	76	76	2	2	0	0	0	118	29– 2
Jordan	5	9	27	25	4	3	0	1	1	47	5– 2
Mr E M Kenney .	3	6	48	47	6	0	0	0	0	94	15– 4
Mr R L Key	4	6	21	21	5	0	0	0	1	46	7– 4
Mr A Lubbock	4	5	129	129	3	1	0	0	1	156	31– 1
Martin	3	6	17	17	4	0	0	0	2	43	7– 1
Mumford .	10	17	49	49	7	4	0	2	4	191	11– 4
Mr R A Mitchell	3	5	87	68	5	0	0	0	0	166	33– 1
Rev J M'Cormick	3	5	47	47	1	3	0	0	1	81	16– 1
Nixon	5	7	8	7	2	4	0	0	1	19	2 5
Capt Parnell	5	9	71	48	6	3	0	0	0	163	18– 1
Rev S A Pepys	3	5	43	43	5	0	0	0	0	83	16– 3
Mr W W Rose	5	7	12	11	1	5	0	0	1	19	2– 5
Mr I D Round	5	8	18	18	3	5	0	0	0	40	5
Scothern	3	5	5	4	1	1	0	1	2	6	1– 1
A Shaw	11	19	46	46	10	8	0	0	1	262	13–15
Mr C J Smith	3	5	20	13	4	0	0	0	1	22	4– 2
Mr E C Sutton	6	10	59	36	4	5	0	1	0	173	17– 3
Mr R I Ward	9	15	7	6	6	2	0	3	4	32	2– 2
Mr R D Walker	10	15	80	58	8	6	0	1	0	266	17–11
Mr V E Walker	5	8	77	62	4	1	0	0	3	151	19– 6
Mr I A Wilkinson .	7	13	105	75	4	6	0	2	1	118	9– 1
Mr A H Winter	5	9	53	34	6	3	0	0	0	142	15– 7
Wootton . .	15	25	46	32	13	2	0	3	7	192	7–17

The following played in two matches Sir John Blois, Major Milman, Capt Kenney, Lord Skelmersdale, Messrs Appleby, W B Barrington, Bisset, Carter, Drake, Kingcote, W H Maitland, Mordaunt, W M'Cormick, &c

One match Hon J Amherst, Hon E Boscawen, Capt Brand, Messrs A C Arkwright H C Arkwright, I Alexander, P E Barrow, F Baker, C L E Bell E Bourdillon, T E Bramwall, W S Baldock, I D Browne, F A Birley Brooks, W Burrows, R D Cleasby, M Churchill, E Chetwynd, W Chisholm, W F Corran, R I Cross, W C Colver, E Cooke, W F Crawley, A Bateman, E J Bateman, W Tuck, E Reid, I I Sewell &c

DANGER OF EXTINCTION—A great deal of excitement was produced in 1868 when the near expiration of the lease was everywhere talked about, for it was pretty well known that on its expiry the difficulties attending the purchase or rental of a new and convenient place would be very great Not only a large amount of money, but considerable tact and ingenuity were necessary in order to purchase the freehold Eventually a lease of 99 years was accomplished The £11,000 necessary for the performance of this feat was with very little difficulty subscribed, upon the guarantee that Lord's Ground should be spared during this long interval from the surveyor's rod, the staff of "navvies," and mountains of brick and timber Lord's Ground will therefore continue to be—for a few generations at least—what it has been to many past cricketers, the pole to the needle, or Mecca to the Mahomedan.

A very considerable alteration took place in the year 1870 by the addition of Guy's nursery ground at the west end. When Mr. Allom, the architect, ran the chain over the whole inclosure the following results were obtained: Area of ground and buildings 8 acres, 1 rood, 18½ poles. Area of sward 6¼ acres, length of road round the sward 710 yards. Geometrically considered, the ground assumes the form of an unequal-sided oblong, the greatest side running from east to west, with new entrance gates at the south-east corner. A year or two later nearly the whole of the sward was disturbed, and a considerable portion of it lifted and relaid, so that it has now the appearance of a hanging level. At the south-west corner of the pavilion earth works are thrown up in the form of an elongated quadrant, from which rise four terraces of seats, capable of accommodating 500 persons—a great convenience when important matches attract unusual gatherings. The pavilion itself, after being turned almost inside out and recased, is vastly improved in convenience, but still is a very ugly piece of architecture.

To give anything like a fair idea of the matches, great and small, that have been played at Lord's from the first year of its dedication to cricket up to the present would be a task as dull and prosaic as its results would prove valueless. Taken as a whole, for a series of years those matches between Oxford and Cambridge and the Gentleman and Players retain still a very firm hold in public estimation. The inter-university meeting is regarded as the finest in which the amateur proficiency is witnessed. It is scarcely possible to meet with two such elevens elsewhere. The contenders are usually culled from a large number of proficients, trained up to the highest point of efficiency, and though here as elsewhere the vicissitudes of the game creep in and often produce the most unlooked-for results, still there is sure to be seen in form, to a greater or less extent, a skill and finish in this, that, and the other department of the game, which justifies the opinion oft loudly expressed that the Oxford and Cambridge match is the best of the Marylebone season. Here it may be well to give a *resumé* of results from the institution of the Dark and Light Blue meeting. The first record of this match at Lords is in the year 1827, but, owing to unfavourable weather, it was not played out. In 1829 the parties met at Oxford when the residents won by 115. Then followed an interregnum of seven years, when at Lord's Oxford won by 121 runs. Two years subsequently Oxford won by 98 runs. Then the tide set in strongly towards Cambridge, who won six matches in succession. In 1846 Oxford won by three wickets. The next year placed Cambridge on the winning list by 138 runs. In 1848 Oxford won by 23 runs—(match played at Oxford). In 1849 Cambridge won by three wickets, and in the succeeding year (at Oxford) the Dark Blues won by 127 runs. From that time to the present all the matches have taken place at Lord's.

1851.—Cambridge won by an innings and 4 runs
1852.—Oxford won by an innings and 77 runs
1853.—Oxford won by an innings and 19 runs
1854.—Oxford won by an innings and 8 runs
1855.—Oxford won by three wickets
1856.—Cambridge won by three wickets
1857.—Oxford won by 81 runs
1858.—Cambridge won by an innings and 38 runs

1859.—Cambridge won by 28 runs.
1860.—Cambridge won by three wickets.
1861.—Cambridge won by 133 runs.
1862.—Cambridge won by eight wickets.
1863.—Oxford won by eight wickets.
1864.—Oxford won by four wickets.
1865.—Oxford won by 114 runs.
1866.—Oxford won by 12 runs.
1867.—Cambridge won by five wickets.
1868.—Cambridge won by 168 runs.
1869.—Cambridge won by 58 runs.
1870.—Cambridge won by 2 runs.
1871.—Oxford won by eight wickets.
1872.—Cambridge won by an innings and 166 runs.
1873.—Oxford won by three wickets.
1874.—Oxford won by an innings and 92 runs.
1875.—Oxford won by 6 runs.*

As the 1875 match was one of the closest of the series above enumerated, the full score and analysis of the bowling are appended:—

OXFORD.

	1st inn.		2nd inn.
Mr. A. J. Webbe, c Smith, b Sharpe	55	c Blacker, b Sharpe	21
Mr. T. W. Lang, b Sims	45	c and b Sharpe	2
Mr. D. Campbell, c Smith, b Sharpe	1	b Sharpe	0
Mr. A. W. Ridley, b Paterson	21	c Smith, b Paterson	2
Mr. W. W. Pulman, c Blacker, b Sharpe	25	st Hamilton, b Sharpe	30
Mr. R. Briggs, c Smith, b Sharpe	2	b Greenfield	12
Mr. V. Royle, b Paterson	1	st Hamilton, b Sharpe	21
Mr. F. M. Buckland, b Sims	22	b Paterson	0
Mr. W. H. Game, st Hamilton, b Paterson	5	c Lucas, b Paterson	22
Mr. H. G. Tylecote, c Greenfield, b Sharpe	1	not out	12
Mr. W. Foord-Kelcey, not out	2	c Paterson, b Sharpe	11
Byes 15, l-b 3, w 2	20	Byes	4
Total	200	Total	137

CAMBRIDGE.

	1st inn.		2nd inn.
Mr. F. J. Greenfield, c Ridley, b Kelcey	12	c Campbell, b Royle	14
Mr. A. P. Lucas, c Buckland, b Ridley	19	b Buckland	5
Mr. G. H. Longman, c Ridley, b Buckland	40	b Royle	23
Mr. W. Blacker, b Buckland	19	b Royle	1
Hon. E. Lyttleton, c and b Lang	23	c Webbe, b Buckland	20
Mr. H. M. Sims, l w, b Lang	5	c Pulman, b Lang	39
Mr. G. Macan, b Lang	2	not out	1
Mr. W. S. Paterson, c Ridley, b Buckland	12	b Ridley	18
Mr. A. F. Smith, c Royle, b Lang	3	b Ridley	0
Mr. C. M. Sharpe, not out	6	b Royle	29
Mr. H. A. Hamilton, st Tylecote, b Lang	5	l b w, b Lang	11
Byes 10, l-b 7	17	Byes 1, l-b 4, n-b 2	7
Total	163	Total	168

OXFORD BOWLING THROUGHOUT THE MATCH.

	Overs.	Maidens.	Runs.	Wickets.	No Balls.
Mr. Lang	52	17	68	7	2
Mr. Foord-Kelcey	45	21	71	1	0
Mr. Ridley	24-3	10	37	3	0
Mr. Buckland	50	20	72	5	0
Mr. Royle	35	10	59	4	0

* It will be seen that thirty-nine matches have been played; out of these Cambridge won nineteen and Oxford twenty.

CAMBRIDGE BOWLING THROUGHOUT THE MATCH

	Overs	Maidens	Runs	Wickets	Wides
Mr Sharpe	105-2	43	155	11	0
Mr Sims ..	30	11	44	2	2
Mr Paterson	85	33	95	6	0
Mr Greenfield	14	5	19	1	0

At the close of the second day's play Oxford had completed their double innings, and Cambridge required 174 runs to win On Wednesday morning play began at the accustomed hour of twelve The bowling was started by Mr Buckland A faulty return of the ball from mid-wicket gave Mr. Hamilton two runs Mr Lucas made four in one over, and then Mr Buckland prostrated his wicket Messrs Longman and Sharpe brought up the total to 38, when Mr Ridley tried three overs of lobs without the effect intended The ball was then transferred to Mr Royle A variety of changes ensued up to 59, when Mr Sharpe's middle and leg were prostrated At 67 Mr Blacker played "on," and Mr Greenfield joined Mr Longman A stand for a considerable time was made and 76 runs were recorded for the fifth wicket, when a "shooter" from Mr Royle set all speculation at rest about the Light Blue captain ' pulling the match out of the fire" He notwithstanding played his part well Another staunch supporter was found in Mr Lyttleton At the 42nd over the 100 appeared on the telegraph, to the consternation of some and the delight of others Mr Greenfield soon damped the ardour of the joyous party by putting up a ball in the locality of mid-off A great deal of excitement was, however, kept up when Mr Sims began to "let out," as it was just within the bounds of likelihood that the two men now in would make long scores Mr Lyttleton, after being twice missed at mid-on, struck the ball to square leg, where Mr Webbe was stationed A finer running catch under difficulties was never witnessed, and this great achievement turned the scale in favour of Oxford, as another hit or two from Mr Lyttleton would in all probability have placed Cambridge in the position of winners Rain came on just after, and necessitated a suspension of play for nearly an hour On resumption the bowling underwent frequent changes At 143 Mr Royle went over to his old wicket The scoring on the part of Mr Sims was now very rapid When Mr Paterson left, Cambridge were within 14 runs of the winning post Mr Macan then joined Mr Sims Five runs were soon added A leg-bye and a no-ball followed, and then a splendid catch at long-on, which disposed of Mr Sims When the last man (Mr Smith) appeared six runs only were wanting, but as these were not forthcoming, Oxford were declared winners The applause "all round" was of the heartiest kind, and Mr Webbe was called for, and "chaired" in a manner which showed that the old University "form" had not died out, nor was it likely to do so while two such superlative teams can be brought together at Lord's

The Gentlemen and Players' match was instituted in the year 1806, and two matches were played at Lord's in the month of July. As the first of a long series claims special interest, the full score is given It will be seen that the Gentlemen won by an innings and 14 runs Only four wickets were bowled throughout the match, twenty were lost from catches The second match was won by the Gentlemen with 82 runs to spare, the scores being Gentlemen (with Lambert), 96 and 132—total, 228, Players, 65 and 81—total, 146.

PLAYERS

	1st inn		2nd inn
T Walker c Upton	14	c Upton	24
J Hampton, st Lambert	18	c Upton	4
R Robinson, c Bligh	13	b Beauclerk	15
John Bennett, c Beldham	1	c Upton	13
J Hammond, c Lambert	0	c Beldham	2
C Howard, c Smith	2	c Upton	13
J Small, jun, c Beldham	0	not out	21
W Ayling, b Willes	1	c Bligh	8
J A Freemantle, not out	14	st Lambert	1
W Fennex b Beldham	5	c Upton	0
H Bentley, c Bligh	0	l b w	8
Bye	1	Byes	3
Total	69	Total	112

GENTLEMEN (WITH BELDHAM AND LAMBERT)

Hon E Bligh, c Hammond	22
E Pontifex, Esq, b Howard	14
W Lambert, st Hammond	57
W Beldham, c Howard	16
Lord Frederick Beauclerk, c Bennett	1
John Willes Esq, c Hampton	1
G Leicester, Esq, c Walker	14
T A Smith, Esq, run out	48
Hon A Upton, run out	11
John Nyren, c Ayling	4
C. Warren, Esq, not out	2
Byes	5
Total	195

1819—Players won by six wickets
1820—Gentlemen (with Howard) won by 70 runs
1821—Coronation Match Given up
1822—Gentlemen won by six wickets
1823—Players won by 345 runs
1824—Gentlemen (fourteen) Players won by 101 runs
1825—Gentlemen (sixteen, with Mathews) won by 72 runs
1827—Gentlemen (seventeen) won by 29 runs
,, —Gentlemen (seventeen) Players won by an innings and 42 runs
1829—Gentlemen (with Lillywhite and Broadbrige) won by 193 runs
1830—Given up in consequence of bad weather
1831—Gentlemen v nine Players Players won by five wickets
1832—Players won by an innings and 34 runs *
1833—Gentlemen (sixteen) Players won by nine wickets
1834—Players won by an innings and 21 runs
1835—Players won by six wickets
1836—Gentlemen (eighteen) won by 35 runs
1837—Players won by an innings and 10 runs †

* In this match the Gentlemen's wickets were reduced to 22in by 6in, the Players were of the size now in use—viz, 27in by 8in

† This was called the 'Barndoor Match' by some, and by others "Ward's Folly," the Gentlemen defended wickets 27in by 8in, while those of the Players were enlarged to 36in by 12in

1837 —Gentlemen (sixteen) A second match, Players won by an innings and 38 runs
1838 —Players won by 40 runs
1839 —Drawn in consequence of bad weather
1840 —Players won by nine wickets
1841 —Players won by three wickets
1842 —Gentlemen won by 96 runs
1843 —Gentlemen won by an innings and 20 runs
1844 —Players won by 38 runs
1845 —Players won by 67 runs
1846 —Gentlemen won by one wicket
1847 —Players won by 147 runs
1848 —Gentlemen won by 27 runs
1849 —Gentlemen won by an innings and 40 runs
1850 —Players won by an innings and 48 runs
1851 —Players won by an innings and 14 runs
1852 —Players won by five wickets
1853 —Gentlemen won by 60 runs
1854 —Players won by nine wickets
1855 —Players won by seven wickets
1856 —Players won by two wickets.
1857 —Players won by ten wickets
, (Second match) —Players won by 13 runs
1858 —Players won by 285 runs
1859 —Players won by 169 runs
1860 —Players won by an innings and 181 runs
1861 —Players won by an innings and 60 runs
1862 (All under thirty years of age) —Players won by 157 runs
1863 —Players won by eight wickets
1864 — Players won by an innings and 68 runs
1865 —Gentlemen won by eight wickets
1866 —Players won by 38 runs
1867 —Gentlemen won by eight wickets
1868 —Gentlemen won by eight wickets
1869 — Gentlemen won by three wickets
1870 —Gentlemen won by 4 runs
1871 —Drawn
1872 —Gentlemen won by seven wickets
1873 —Gentlemen won by an innings and 55 runs
1874 —Players won by two wickets
1875 —Gentlemen won by 262 runs

Full score and bowling analysis

GENTLEMEN

	1st inn		2nd inn
Mr A J Webbe, b Morley	0	c Pooley b Morley	65
Mr W G Grace b Shaw	7	run out	152
Mr G H Longman, c Greenwood, b Shaw	70	b Morley	41
Mr A N Hornby, b Hill .	17	b Morley ...	58
Mr A W Ridley not out	45	b Morley	6
Mr G F Grace, b Morley	0	b Morley . . .	12
Mr I D Walker, b Morley	0	b Hill	0
Lord Harris, b Morley . .	1	not out	39
Mr C E Green, b Morley .	0	b Hill .	25
Mr C K Francis, c Hill, b Morley .	5	c Greenwood, b Lockwood	18
Mr J A Bush, run out	0	b Hill	7
Byes 4 l b 3	7	Byes 10, l b 7, w 1, n-b 3	21
Total	152	Total .	444

PLAYERS

	1st inn		2nd inn
Jupp, b Francis ...	25	b W G Grace .	18
Lockwood, c and b W G Grace	7	b Francis	67
Greenwood, c and b W G Grace	51	c Green, b Ridley	16
Daft, l b w, b G F Grace	28	c Bush, b Ridley	0
Oscroft, c and b W G Grace	28	c Ridley, b W G Grace	27
Charlwood, c Harris, b W G Grace	6	c Webbe, b W G Grace	7
M M'Intyre, l b w, b W G Grace	1	not out	26
Shaw c Hornby, b W G Grace .	0	(hurt)	—
Pooley, not out	11	c and b W G Grace	0
Hill, c Harris, b W G Grace .	2	b Francis	0
Morley, b Francis	0	b W G Grace	2
Bye 1, l-b 4, w 5	10	Bye 1, l-b 1	2
Total	169	Total	165

Bowling of the Players throughout the Match

	Overs	Maidens	Runs	Wickets	Wide	No Balls
Shaw	69-3	41	65	2	0	0
Morley	105	41	171	11	0	0
Lockwood	40	6	95	1	0	0
Hill	71-2	18	148	4	1	2
M M'Intyre	21	3	62	0	0	1
Oscroft	13	3	27	0	0	0

Bowling of the Gentlemen throughout the Match

	Overs	Maidens	Runs	Wickets	Wides
Mr W G Grace	82-1	27	125	12	0
Mr Francis	80-2	54	83	4	0
Mr G F Grace	39	20	49	1	1
Mr Ridley	43	16	68	2	0
Mr Longman	3	0	7	0	4

From the foregoing list 58 matches may be counted Of these 43 were played by eleven on each side The Players claimed 26, and the Gentlemen 14

The last and most important match in which Marylebone had concern with Kent, occurred at Canterbury in the month of August Full score

MARYLEBONE.

	1st inn		2nd inn
Mr W. G Grace, c Yardley, b Foord-Kelcey	0	c and b A Penn	35
Mr A J Webbe, b Hearne	10	c Palmer, b Shaw	8
Mr G N Wyatt, c Harris, b Foord Kelcey	13	st Palmer, b A. Penn	17
Mr A W Ridley, c Shaw, b Foord-Kelcey	9	b Shaw	15
Mr I D Walker, not out	31	c Hearne, b A Penn	21
Mr F E R Fryer, c Shaw, b Hearne	18	c F Penn b George	47
Mr G Bird, run out	1	c Willis, b George	75
Mr. E O H Wilkinson, c Palmer, b George	4	st Palmer, b A Penn	3
Mr J H Ponsonby, c Palmer, b Hearne	3	b A Penn	10
Capt Meares, b Foord-Kelcey	1	st Palmer, b A. Penn	23
Capt Wood, c Hearne, b Foord-Kelcey	8	not out	0
Mr E Mitchell (absent)		c Harris, b A Penn	1
Byes 4, w 1	5	Byes 6, l-b 3, w 2, n b 1	12
Total	103	Total	267

KENT.

	1st inn		2nd inn
Mr W Penn, h w, b Grace	39	b Grace	0
Willis, c Meares, b Grace	14		
Mr W Yardley, c Fryer, b Grace	28	c sub, b Meares	46
Lord Harris, b Ponsonby	53	not out	16
Mr F Penn, b Wyatt	101	not out	10
Mr H Renny-Tailyour, b Ponsonby	5	b Meares	22
Palmer, l b w, b Ponsonby	0	c Mitchell, b Meares	6
Hearne, c Ponsonby, b Grace	8	b Meares	7
Mr W Foord-Kelcey, b Ponsonby	4		
Mr. V K Shaw, b Fryer	4		
Mr A Penn, c Wood, b Grace	1		
George, not out	0		
Bye 1, l-b 3, w 1	5	Bye 1, l-b 1	2
Total	262	Total	109

ANALYSIS OF THE KENT BOWLING THROUGHOUT THE MATCH.

	Overs.	Maidens.	Runs.	Wickets.	Wides.
Mr. Foord-Kelcey	73-2	25	121	5	2
Hearne	33	17	47	3	0
George	24-2	7	50	3	1
Mr. A. Penn	74	28	99	7	0
Mr. V. K. Shaw	12	4	36	2	0

ANALYSIS OF THE MARYLEBONE BOWLING THROUGHOUT THE MATCH.

	Overs.	Maidens.	Runs.	Wickets.	Wides.
Mr. Grace	93	38	158	6	0
Mr. Fryer	36	16	71	1	1
Mr. Ponsonby	36	10	54	4	0
Capt. Meares	26	9	55	0	0
Mr. Ridley	11	3	18	4	0
Mr. Wyatt	2	0	8	1	0

More than 200 members of the Marylebone Club took part in the matches of 1875. Of this number the names and achievements at the wicket of all who played two matches and upwards will be found in the subjoined

ANALYSIS OF THE BATTING.

NAME.	No. of Matches.	No. of Innings.	Most Runs in a Match.	Most Runs in an Innings.	How often Bowled.	Caught.	Run out.	Stumped.	Not out.	Total.	Average per Innings. Over.
Mr. F. Baker	4	6	59	31	3	3	0	0	0	110	18- 2
Col. Bathurst	5	8	34	27	5	1	0	1	1	70	8- 6
Hon. C. W. Beauclerk	3	4	7	6	3	0	0	0	1	13	3- 1
Major Battye	6	8	15	15	4	3	0	0	1	31	3- 7
Mr. G. Bird	3	4	76	75	1	1	2	0	0	118	29- 2
Mr. W. Bird	2	2	61	61	1	0	0	0	1	105	52- 1
Mr. E. Bird	4	5	37	37	2	2	0	0	1	85	17- 0
Biddulph	6	10	18	15	6	2	0	0	2	29	2- 9
Mr. C. Booth	3	5	70	70	8	1	1	0	0	123	24- 3
Mr. W. D. Bovill	5	9	27	26	3	2	2	2	0	75	8- 3
Mr. H. Bradshaw	2	2	10	10	2	0	0	0	0	15	7- 1
Mr. C. J. Brune	2	3	10	3	0	1	1	0	1	17	5- 2
Mr. C. F. Buller	2	4	71	54	2	1	1	0	0	118	29- 2
Mr. J. E. Byass	3	5	56	56	3	1	0	0	1	133	26- 3
Clayton	5	9	44	44	5	3	0	0	1	107	11- 8
Mr. J. D. Cochrane	3	4	3	3	2	0	2	0	0	5	1- 1
Mr. C. Colthurst	2	3	29	18	3	0	0	0	0	41	13- 2
Mr. T. A. Crooke	7	12	43	43	4	8	0	0	0	163	13- 7
Davey	9	13	11	11	5	2	2	2	2	40	3- 1
Mr. H. B. Dickinson	5	7	31	31	5	1	1	0	0	62	8- 6
Mr. H. Dowding	3	4	2	2	2	2	0	0	0	2	2
Mr. A. S. Duncan	2	3	18	18	2	1	0	0	0	19	6- 1
Farrands	11	17	29	22	4	7	2	0	4	109	6- 7
Mr. H. W. Fellows	2	2	6	6	2	0	0	0	0	7	3- 1
Mr. A. Fitzgerald	2	2	8	8	1	1	0	0	0	8	4
Mr. E. H. Fishbourne	4	5	9	9	4	1	0	0	0	15	3
Mr. W. H. Fletcher	2	2	4	4	1	0	0	0	1	4	2
Mr. A. Fraser	2	2	5	5	0	1	1	0	0	9	4- 1
Mr. G. Fraser	2	2	7	7	2	0	0	0	0	8	4

ANALYSIS OF THE BATTING—*continued.*

NAME.	No. of Matches.	No. of Innings.	Most Runs in a Match.	Most Runs in an Innings.	How often bowled.	Caught.	Run out.	Stumped.	Not out.	Total.	Average per Innings. Over.
Mr. C. K. Francis	2	2	31	34	0	2	0	0	0	52	26
Flanagan	11	14	29	29	6	3	0	0	5	75	5– 5
Mr. W. H. Gardiner.........	2	3	42	42	2	1	0	0	0	59	19– 2
Mr. R. E. Gaye..............	4	6	34	33	3	2	1	0	0	40	6- 4
Mr. W. Garth	6	7	34	34	2	4	1	0	0	70	10
Mr. W. G. Grace	5	10	107	83	5	5	0	0	0	306	30– 6
Mr. H. Gilbert	2	2	10	10	1	1	0	0	0	15	7– 1
Mr. C. E. Green	2	3	80	53	1	1	0	0	1	80	26– 2
Mr. W. Greenwood	3	4	35	35	2	1	0	1	0	61	15– 1
Mr. H. T. Griffiths	2	2	25	25	0	1	0	0	1	43	21– 1
Mr. A. A. Hadow	3	6	27	24	1	2	1	0	2	65	10– 5
Mr. W. H. Hadow	3	5	33	33	3	2	0	0	0	73	14– 3
Mr. W. H. Hay	3	5	47	47	3	1	0	1	0	88	17– 3
Mr. A. W. H. Herbert......	4	7	100	100	4	0	0	1	2	148	21– 1
Mr. C. A. R. Hoare	4	6	48	34	3	3	0	0	0	75	12– 3
Lord Harris	3	5	29	29	4	0	0	0	1	38	7– 3
Hon. A. B. Hamilton	3	6	10	7	3	0	1	2	0	19	3- 1
Mr. O. C. Hannay	3	6	19	10	3	2	1	0	0	42	7
Hearne, T......................	10	14	135	118	4	8	0	0	2	384	27– 6
Hearne, G. F.	4	4	34	34	1	2	0	0	1	66	16– 2
Mr. A. W. L. Hemming ...	2	4	21	16	1	2	1	0	0	32	8
Mr. B. Howell	2	3	21	20	2	1	0	0	0	21	7
Hon. W. N. Hood...........	3	5	29	29	3	2	0	0	0	30	6
Mr. W. H. Higgins	3	5	112	112	1	3	0	0	1	150	30
Mr. G. Hasler	2	2	4	4	1	1	0	0	0	7	3– 1
Mr. A. F. Jeffreys	4	7	43	26	1	1	2	2	1	71	10– 1
Mr. Kenyon-Slaney	3	4	14	9	2	2	0	0	0	29	7– 1
Earl of Lanesborough......	2	3	10	10	2	1	0	0	0	20	6– 2
Lord Lewisham	4	5	29	29	1	1	0	0	3	55	11
Mr. C. Marriott	5	8	31	28	5	3	0	0	0	113	14– 1
Capt. Meares	3	5	24	23	2	1	0	2	0	38	7– 3
Mr. W. H. Miller	2	3	61	50	2	0	0	0	1	69	23
Mr. F. S. Miller	3	5	50	50	4	1	0	0	0	83	16– 3
Capt. Middleton	3	5	49	40	2	1	0	0	2	76	15– 1
Morley	6	10	31	22	1	3	3	0	3	69	6– 9
Nixon...........................	6	9	16	16	7	1	0	0	1	41	4- 5
Mr. W. S. Patterson	2	3	40	38	1	2	0	0	0	46	15– 1
Mr. W. B. Pearce...........	2	2	18	18	1	1	0	0	0	35	17– 1
Mr. T. S. Pearson...........	2	4	20	12	2	1	1	0	0	30	7– 2
Capt. Pennycuick...........	2	3	6	6	1	1	1	0	0	9	3
Capt. G. Pilleau	3	4	11	11	4	0	0	0	0	13	3– 1
Mr. F. R. Price..............	5	7	71	60	2	3	2	0	0	153	21– 6
Price	7	10	71	71	3	5	0	0	2	221	22– 1
Randon	10	13	23	23	5	1	1	2	4	66	5– 1
Mr. W. C. Rawlinson	2	3	17	9	3	0	0	0	0	24	8
Mr. A. W. Ridley...........	2	4	24	15	3	1	0	0	0	47	11– 3
Capt. Rowley	2	4	39	31	1	3	0	0	0	70	17– 2
Rylott	14	21	27	27	12	6	0	0	3	128	6– 2
Mr. L. K. Scott..............	2	2	16	16	2	0	0	0	0	26	13
Shaw	7	12	62	50	3	5	0	1	3	155	12–11
Capt. Slade	2	2	2	2	1	1	0	0	0	3	1– 1
Capt. R. W. Smith	4	6	66	46	6	0	0	0	0	97	16– 1
Scotton	3	6	40	29	2	1	1	0	2	49	8– 1
Major Sandys	2	3	14	7	1	0	0	1	1	16	5– 1

ANALYSIS OF THE BATTING—*continued.*

Name.	No. of Matches.	No. of Innings.	Most Runs in a Match.	Most Runs in an Innings.	How often bowled.	Caught.	Run out.	Stumped.	Not out.	Total.	Average per Innings. Over.
Capt. Stephens	2	2	13	13	0	2	0	0	0	25	12– 1
Mr. E. G. G. Sutton	6	10	97	85	5	4	1	0	0	283	28– 3
Capt. J. Sutton	2	3	1	1	2	1	0	0	0	1	1
Mr. H. T. Smith	2	2	19	10	1	0	1	0	0	29	14– 1
Mr. R. T. Thornton	4	6	54	41	5	1	0	0	0	68	11– 2
Mr. C. I. Thornton	3	5	69	69	2	1	1	1	0	98	19– 3
Mr. E. W. Tritton	2	4	9	9	2	1	1	0	0	16	4
Mr. H. Tubb	2	4	10	6	1	1	1	1	0	18	4– 2
Mr. E. C. Turnbull	2	3	64	64	1	2	0	0	0	101	33– 2
Mr. W. A. Turnbull	2	2	7	7	1	1	0	0	0	7	3– 1
Mr. J. Turner	7	13	95	72	3	5	1	2	2	382	29– 5
Mr. E. F. S. Tylecote	4	7	64	64	2	3	0	0	2	160	22– 6
Mr. J. S. Udall	4	7	68	61	5	1	0	0	1	135	19– 2
Mr. I. D. Walker	3	5	64	64	1	1	0	1	2	141	28– 1
Mr. A. J. Webbe	2	4	18	10	2	1	1	0	0	28	7
West	9	14	76	51	5	3	1	1	4	213	15– 3
Mr. G. F. Wills	10	15	30	30	5	5	1	0	4	184	12– 4
Mr. J. H. Willson	2	2	2	2	1	0	0	1	0	2	1
Mr. F. S. Willett	5	7	25	25	4	2	1	0	0	75	10– 5
Lord Willoughby de Broke	2	3	11	11	3	0	0	0	0	17	5– 2
Mr. L. Winslow	5	9	37	33	4	5	0	0	0	146	16– 2
Mr. L. F. Winslow	3	4	0	0	3	1	0	0	0	0	
Mr. A. H. Wood	2	2	6	6	0	2	0	0	0	11	5– 1
Mr. G. H. Wood	6	9	26	18	3	4	1	1	0	77	8– 5
Mr. W. H. Wylde	4	8	27	27	2	5	1	0	0	77	9– 5
Mr. G. N. Wyatt	7	13	92	74	6	4	2	1	0	354	27– 3
Mr. A. P. Vansittart	5	8	31	31	5	1	1	1	0	77	9– 5
Mr. G. F. Vernon	11	18	79	74	8	8	1	0	1	285	15–15
Mr. R. G. Venables	4	5	46	32	2	3	0	0	0	65	13

The following played in one match only: Lord Anson, Lord Clifton, Hon. S. Herbert, Hon. E. Lyttelton, Hon. O. Montagu, Capt. Creagh, Capt. Follett, Major Hartopp, Capt. Hutchinson, Capt. Kington, Capt. Maltby, Capt. Winthorpe, Capt. Wood, Messrs. Allen, Alberger, Baker, Balfour, Blacket, Borthwick, Boville, Blundell, Bowen, Bramwell, Berrington, Brand, Crawford, Crowder, H. Curteis, R. M. Curteis, Dale, Doyle, Ede, Evetts, Farnham, Ford, L. Garnett, R. Garnett, W. Greenwood, Hall, Hastings, Henderson, Hewlett, Holder, Horner, Howell, Horne, Hornby, Hull, Kingby, Lawson, Lowe, W. C. Lucas, Mason, Malkin, Matthison, Maclean, Mitchell, Montgomery, Moffatt, Nepean, Philpott, Pickering, J. Ponsonby, Ratliff, Renny-Tailyour, Reid, Round, Russell, Riddle, Skinner, Soames, Sand, Smith-Barry, A. F. Smith, Shepherd, A. Smith, G. C. Smith, P. H. Smith, Stanhope, Thomas, Toynbee, C. B. L. Tylecote, Verelst, Watson, R. D. Walker, Wetherall, Wingford, Whittaker, F. Winslow, Wilkinson, and Wright.

RULES OF THE MARYLEBONE CRICKET CLUB.

I.—The Annual General Meeting and Anniversary Dinner shall take place on the first Wednesday in May.

II.—The Annual Subscription shall be 3*l.*, payable on the first day of May in each year; every new member shall pay, in addition, an entrance fee of 1*l.*

III.—Any member whose subscription shall be unpaid on the 1st of June shall receive notice thereof from the Secretary; and the name of any member whose subscription shall remain unpaid on the 1st July shall be posted up in the Pavilion, but in case the subscription shall not have been paid on or before the 31st of December, the committee shall have power to erase his name from the list of members

IV —If it shall appear to the Committee that any member whose name has been so erased has been abroad since the 1st of January preceding, he shall be re-admitted on his return, without ballot, after payment of his subscription for the current year

V —Any Member desirous of resigning shall signify his intention to the Secretary, by letter, addressed to LORD'S CRICKET GROUND, before the 1st of May in any year, otherwise he shall be liable for that season's subscription and arrear

VI —All elections of candidates shall be vested in the Committee Elections shall be held on Monday match days in the months of May, June, and July, and not more than twelve candidates shall be elected at each ballot

VI*a* —The name of every candidate, with that of his proposer and seconder (who shall both be members of the club), shall be entered in the Candidates' Book, in the order of his nomination, four weeks before coming up for ballot

VII —Ballots shall be held in the Committee Room, in the presence of one at least of the Officers of the Club, commencing at 3 and closing at 6 o'clock Not less than eight members of committee shall constitute a ballot, and two black balls shall exclude

VII*a* —Candidates shall come up for ballot in the order of their entry upon the list, unless it shall appear to the Committee desirable in the interest of the club that a particular candidate shall come up for ballot out of his regular order of rotation in which case a fortnight's notice of such change of rotation shall be given to each Member of Committee, and three-fourths of those present must be in favour of such change

VII*b* —The names of those elected at each ballot shall be placed on the notice board in the Pavilion before 7 p m on the day of election

VIII —The Officers of the Club shall consist of a President, a Treasurer, a Secretary, and not more than five nor less than three Trustees, and of three Auditors All these officers must be members of the club The President of each year shall nominate his successor at the Anniversary Dinner, if he omits to do so, or if the office of President be at any time vacant by death, resignation, or otherwise the Committee shall forthwith nominate a fresh President

IX —The offices of Treasurer, Secretary, and Trustees shall be vacated only by death, resignation, or a vote of two-thirds of the members present at a Special General Meeting Vacancies shall be filled up at the Annual or any Special General Meeting Any Trustee may, during his trusteeship, hold any other office in the club, except that of Auditor The Auditors shall be chosen annually at the Annual General Meeting, and shall not be Members of the Committee

X —The Committee shall consist of the President, Treasurer Secretary, and Trustees of the Club for the time being who shall be *ex officio* members, together with sixteen members, four of whom shall retire at the Annual General Meeting by rotation, and shall not be re-elected for one year The order of rotation to be decided by the Committee

XI —A list of the Committee, distinguishing the *ex-officio* from the other members, shall be exhibited in the Pavilion, and the order in which members shall retire shall be specified in such list

XII —The property of the club shall be considered as vested in the Trustees for the time being, The Committee shall have the entire management of the property, funds, and affairs of the club, the preparation of bye laws and regulations (not inconsistent with the general rules of the club), and the decision of all questions arising as to the construction of the rules, bye-laws, and regulations of the club. Three Committee-men to be a quorum But the freehold, copyhold, and leasehold property of the club shall be leased, charged, sold, settled, or otherwise disposed of, and similar property shall be acquired for the club, by purchase, lease, gift, or otherwise, on such terms, and in such manner, in all respects, as a Special General Meeting shall determine, and a special General Meeting may at any time or times revocably delegate, either generally or in any particular transaction or series of similar transactions, all or any of the powers of Special General Meetings, in respect of such property, either to the committee or to the trustees, and also ratify any acts which either the Committee or the Trustees shall have done in respect of such property without such previous delegation, and everything done in pursuance of this rule shall bind every member of the club as fully, to all intents and purposes, as if he had individually assented thereto

XIIa—The Committee may appoint members to fill up temporarily all vacancies occurring by death or resignation in any of the offices of the club (other than that of Auditor), until the next Annual General Meeting or Special General Meeting In the case of the death or resignation of two of the Auditors previous to the audit, a Special General Meeting shall be at once summoned to fill up the vacancies

XIIb—At the Anniversary Dinner, the Annual General Meeting, and Special General Meetings, the chair shall be taken by the President, if present, in his absence, by the Treasurer, in the absence of both by the Secretary, and in the absence of the three, by a member to be chosen by the meeting

XIII—The Treasurer or Secretary shall, at the Annual General Meeting in each year submit a statement of the accounts, certified by the signatures of at least two of the Auditors

XIV—The Committee shall, at the requisition of twenty members, or of their own authority, call a Special General Meeting, of which fourteen days' notice, specifying the object, time, and place of such meeting, shall be given in *The Times*, and at least one of the sporting papers

XV—The Laws of Cricket shall not at any time be changed, except at a Special General Meeting, of which, in addition to the formalities described in Rule XIV, notices shall be given in *The Times*, and at least two of the London sporting papers, one month before the day of meeting, and this notice shall state in distinct terms the change in the law to be proposed, and no change shall be declared carried unless twenty members at least shall vote in favour of it

XVI—If any circumstance which, in the opinion of the Committee, is likely to endanger the welfare or good order of the club, shall be brought under their notice, it shall be in their discretion to call a Special General Meeting, and, in the event of its being voted at that meeting by two-thirds of the members present (to be decided by ballot), that the name of any member be removed from the club, such individual shall immediately cease to be a member thereof, and shall forfeit *ipso facto* all subscriptions, whether for life or otherwise, and all right to, or claim upon, the club or its property

XVII—A copy of the rules of this club shall be sent to each new member, with the letter informing him of his election

XVIII—The Rules, or any of them, may be altered, abrogated, and added to, either generally or for the particular occasion at any Special General Meeting, by the vote of two-thirds of the members present and voting at such meeting

It would be an affront to the commonest understanding to say that these rules of the Marylebone Club have any binding influence on the community of cricketers as the Laws of Cricket have, although issuing from the same fountain, the latter are for the guidance of the world in general, the former for the government of the Marylebone Club in particular, which in itself resembles a kingdom to which states and dependencies turn their attention for the varied kinds of self-government they need A law applicable to one case may be totally inapplicable to another Even in the wider area of county clubs the differences of arrangement are often very striking—natural, nevertheless, seeing they are the outcome of a set of circumstances under which they exist Further down the scale, even to village clubs, scarcely any two in a county are governed strictly by the same code of regulations Marylebone is its own parallel. The number of members on its books in 1875 was 2080, and the income of the club during the same year amounted to 15,257*l* 10*s* 6*d*, of which 3324*l* 14*s* resulted from Oxford *v* Cambridge, Gentlemen *v* Players, and Eton *v* Harrow matches, in the months of June and July It is evident enough that a large staff of principals and supernumeraries must be associated in the management of matches on such a mammoth scale. It is equally clear that a large amount of forethought, firm resolve, and liberal outlay are indispensable, as nothing should be left, if possible, to that unspiritual god—Chance. Who that witnessed the recent turning inside out of the Pavilion can be unmindful of the necessity of a vigilant eye and a trusty overlooker during the seven months interval between the seasons. Why, the roads were so cut up, that to reach the Pavilion a pair of jack boots and a leaping pole were almost indispensable; and at the spot there were more of din and dust, chopping and clamour, than trustworthy Jewish historians affirm were heard during the seven years' building of Solomon's Temple.

CHAPTER VIII.

PUBLIC SCHOOL MATCHES—CRICKET-GROUND AT HARROW.*

Yet when confinement's lingering hour was done,
Our sports, our studies, and our souls were one;
Together we impell'd the flying ball,
Together join'd in cricket's manly toil.—*Attributed to Byron.*

CRICKET GROUND OPENED AT HARROW—OPPOSITION OF THE INHABITANTS—SHOOTING FIELDS AT ETON—SITUATION OF THE WINCHESTER GROUND—PUBLIC SCHOOL CRICKET PRIOR TO THE PRESENT CENTURY—ETON, HARROW, AND WINCHESTER MATCHES FROM 1805—THE FIRE AT LORDS—STANZA BY LORD BYRON—HOOD AND A HARROW BOY.

AMONG the early records of cricket in the archives of Harrow, mention is made of a match between the Percy Club and Harrow School. As far back as 1803 Roxteth Common was inclosed for the use of the boys, although strongly objected to by the inhabitants. About thirty years after a pavilion was erected, and twenty years subsequently it underwent the necessary process of draining. The ground is handy to the schools, and hence in the season every opportunity is seized for practice. Many improvements have taken place recently. Towards the close of the year 1866 an announcement was made by the freeholder that he required the land for building purposes. To avert this, a subscription list was at once opened for the purpose of raising 6000*l.* as the purchase money of the "Philalethic Ground." The head master headed the list with 1000*l.*, and the necessary balance was soon forthcoming. The Eton boys play their matches on the shooting ground, or, as it is sometimes designated, the shooting fields—a lovely spot, and kept in the best possible condition.

Say, Father Thames (for thou hast seen
Full many a sprightly race,
Disporting on thy margent green,
The paths of pleasure trace),
Who foremost now delight to cleave
With pliant arm thy glassy wave?
The captive linnet which enthral?
What idle progeny succeed
To chace the rolling circles speed,
Or urge the flying ball?—*Gray.*

* An engraving drawn and lithographed by W. Whittock. Published by G. Kellow, 11, High Holborn.

Winchester also keeps close to the college, so that in all these cases the time and convenience of the pupils have always been studied Although several school matches occurred before the opening of the present century, both the scores and other pieces of history connected with them are so frequently encompassed with contradictions that it would be unwise to give currency to them at this remote period The matches forming this chapter start from an interesting date, and, notwithstanding the great difficulty in harmonising scores and other statements that conflict, it is hoped that the mistakes are few, and the errors not many

Before proceeding with the matches in chronological order, it may be well to speak of one between Eton and Harrow in 1861 as more stirring and attractive than any played by the schools on Lord's Ground previously thereto. The following is the score

ETON

	1st inn		2nd inn
Hon T De Grey, c Walker, b Alexander	12	b Cator	5
Mr L Garnett, b Alexander	0	b Walker	12
Mr R A H Mitchell, b Alexander	12	b Acheson	26
Mr G H Tuck, b Cator	9	run out	0
Mr W H Hoare, b Alexander	5	b Cator	51
Mr F F Cleasby, b Walker	40	c Gillespie, b Walker	36
Mr A Lubbock, b Cator	0	b Walker	16
Mr O S Smith, b Walker	21	b Walker	44
Mr H B Sutherland, c Buller, b Walker	0	b Walker	0
Mr J Fredericks, not out	16	b Cator	21
Mr G S Smith, b Walker	8	not out	0
Byes 5, l b 1, w 5, n b 1	12	Byes, 4, l b 1, w 12, n b 1	18
Total	135	Total	229

HARROW

	1st inn		2nd inn
Mr H R Alexander, c De Grey, b Mitchell	0	not out	12
Mr C A Cator, b O S Smith	27	c Sutherland b O S Smith	13
Mr A G Meek, run out	7	b Mitchell	2
Mr C F Buller, b Mitchell	4	not out	14
Mr T W Palmer, st Tuck, b O S Smith	10		
Mr W Maitland, c Sutherland, b O S Smith	9		
Mr R W Gillespie, c and b O S Smith	10		
Mr I D Walker, c Tuck, b O S Smith	11		
Hon E Acheson, run out	1		
Mr C F Reid, not out	28		
Mr E W Burnett, b Fredericks	36		
Byes 4, l-b 5, w 9, n b 3.	21	L-b 5, w 7	12
Total	164	Total	53

A Harrow boy, who had courted the Muses before attending the match, describes the first day's play in the following well-expressed stanzas —

From Eton's hoar and antique towers, from Harrow's tree girt crown,
The chosen of the school went up to famous London town,
From east and west, and south and north, the merry cabmen flew,
And hostile met the light rosette and badge of deeper blue

Oh! joyful was the summer sun and bright the summer sky,
As we went up to London town i' the merry month July,
And every face was set to Lord's, and every heart to win,
And so we came into the ground and "drave the wickets in"

Oh, wondrous was the sight! the great, the lovely, and the wise,
Bent all upon the two elevens ten thousand pair of eyes
With laughing heart and mirthful face rode forth the highborn dame,
With various hue of either blue our noble ladies came

Last evening's belle from proud Pall Mall is charmed with livelier ball,
And sad, I ween, is Rotten Row, and lone Tyburnia's hall
Aye, twas a sight might well invite the pen of worthier bards
To mark Rubicus of the Church meet Miles of the Guards

And words there were, 'twas good to hear, from friends that met anew—
The sudden start, the glad surprise, the joyful "How d'ye do",
And you might see throughout the ground how three score years and ten
Could master time and for a while be Harrow boys again

Now in our annals we will mark the day with black and white
When Chatterton and Brampton stood as umpires of the fight
The whispered doubt and fear went out through all our school away,
Old men declared that Harrow boys had long forgot to play,
But Harrow told another tale before the close of day

Not every deed may I declare in these my feeble lines,
Is it not printed in the "Post" and written in the "Times",
I may not sing, how shout aloud the youth of all our land,
When fell the light blue champion before our captain's hand

I may not sing on what high wing another armed his way—
Pride comes before a fall—and so degraded fell De Grey
Lo, here's my theme, and still hereon my willing pen shall dwell,
When scarce above a hundred runs our first nine wickets fell

When loud rang out the Eton shout, till all our hearts were fear,
When died the laugh and hushed the chaff and fainter grew the cheer,
When down the steps their trustful hearts on high emprise intent,
And hopeful still against all hope our gallant batsmen went

Oh! for a bard of better fame to tune melodious lays,
For ne'er may this my feeble verse enough record their praise,
Not if I had a hundred tongues, with iron voice and will,
Who did so well uphold the name of dear old Harrow's Hill

Methought of old, in Nygian shades, I heard the father say,
Whene'er my son on your eleven shall burst the troublous day,
Know this, that Burnett's good right hand your low estate shall stay,
The Fabian spirit lives in Reid to stave defeat away

Aye, mournful sad had been my theme, sad this exultant song,
Had not the *reed* whereon we leaned been stable, sure, and strong
Oh, 'twas a goodly thing to hear our Harrow voices all,
When far across the wide expanse they drave the sounding ball

So firm they stood, nor Eton's sons against them might prevail,
Nor swift, nor slow, might overthrow the well defended bail,
And still they cross with flying feet, and steal the doubtful run,
"A tie!" "A tie!"—a moment more and the first day is won

Oh! ever rich through after years may our last wickets be,
And when they next do hold the ground may I be there to see

Eton v. Harrow.—Played August 2nd, 1805, on the first of the three grounds known as Lord's, situate where Dorset-square now is. From the full score—which is a faithful transcript of an early copy—it will be seen that Eton won by an innings and two runs. It is said that after the match the captain of the Eton Eleven sent to the Harrow captain the following lines:—

Adventurous Boys of Harrow School,
Of cricket you've no knowledge,
You play, not cricket, but the fool,
With Men of Eton College.

The reply, supposed to be written by Byron, was—

Ye Eton wags! to play the fool
Is not the boast of Harrow School;
What wonder, then, at our defeat?
Folly like yours could not be beat.

HARROW.

	1st inn.		2nd inn
Lord Ipswich, b Carter	10	b Heaton	21
T Farrer, Esq., b Carter	7	c Bradley	3
T Drury, Esq., b Carter	0	st Heaton	6
— Bolton, Esq., run out	2	b Heaton	0
C Lloyd, Esq., b Carter	0	b Carter	0
A Shakespeare, Esq., st Heaton	8	run out	5
Lord Byron, c Barnard	7	b Carter	2
Hon T Erskine, b Carter	4	b Heaton	8
W Brockman, Esq., b Heaton	9	b Heaton	10
E Stanley, Esq., not out	3	c Canning	7
— Asheton, Esq., b Carter	3	not out	0
Byes	2	Byes	3
Total	55	Total	65

ETON

Heaton, Esq., b Lloyd	0
Slingsby, Esq., b Shakespeare	29
Carter, Esq., b Shakespeare	3
Farhill, Esq., c Lloyd	6
Canning, Esq. c Farrer	12
Caplin, Esq., b Ipswich	42
Bradley, Esq., b Lloyd	16
Barnard, Esq., b Shakespeare	0
Barnard, Esq., not out	3
Kaye, Esq., b Byron	7
Dover, Esq., c Bolton	4
Total	122

A leap of thirteen years is made before the second contest worthy of note is recorded. This took place on the present Marylebone ground, when Harrow won the match by 13 runs, the scores being—Harrow, 53 and 114—total 167; Eton, 74 and 80—total 154.

The next took place in 1822 at Lord's, when Harrow won by 87 runs Thus Harrow, 99 and 105—total 204, Eton, 65 and 52—total 117

On the last day of July, 1823, the same schools were again confronted at Lord's The match was limited to one day, that being sufficient for Eton to win by an innings and 33 runs. Harrow scored 24 and 91—total 115; Eton, 148

In 1824 two days were occupied at Lord's in determining the match Harrow, 103 and 71—total 174; Eton, 123 and 52 (one wicket)—total 175 Won by nine wickets

Four days in the last week of July, 1825, were devoted to school cricket at Lord's The first match was between Winchester and Harrow, of which the full score is given

WINCHESTER

	1st inn		2nd inns
H E Knatchbull, Esq, b Wordsworth	14	l b w	60
— M'Lean, Esq, b Wordsworth	0	b Manning	8
F B Wright, Esq b Holden	14	c Barclay	8
— Elliott, Esq, c Gambier	17	c Wordsworth	14
— Bayley, Esq, b Wordsworth	34	hit w	10
Chris Wordsworth, Esq, b Wordsworth	3	b Holden	35
W Meyrick, Esq, run out	16	hit w	13
— Templeton Esq, b Wordsworth	1	b Holden	38
— Papillon, Esq, b Wordsworth	1	not out	10
R Price, Esq, run out	7	c Manning	6
— Cooke, Esq, not out	5	b Wordsworth	2
Byes	2	Byes	7
Total	114	Total	211

HARROW

	1st inn		2nd inns
Lord Grimston, b Price	4	b Price	18
F L Popham, Esq, b Price	13	run out	0
H Deffell, Esq, b Wright	33	b Price	6
— Holden, Esq, b Price	2	c Elliott	8
Chas Wordsworth, Esq, b Bayley	17	b Price	5
E Manning, Esq, b Templeton	6	b Price	0
— Barclay, Esq, b Bayley	17	c Wordsworth	4
W Davidson, Esq, b Price	4	b Price	11
T Brand, Esq, b Price	0	not out	0
J S Gambier, Esq, not out	5	c Templeton	13
E Lewis, Esq, b Bayley	5	b Price	4
Byes	6	Byes	4
Total	112	Total	73

The second, between Eton and Harrow, resulted in favour of Eton by seven wickets, the scores being—Harrow, 90 and 91—total 181, Eton, 76 and 106 (three wickets)—total 182 The Pavilion at Lord's took fire on the same evening that the match terminated

In the month of August, 1826, Winchester played both Harrow and Eton with success at Lord's They defeated Harrow by 384 runs, and Eton by 53 Thus

Winchester, 174 and 380 (of this latter number Mr Meyrick scored 146 not out)—total 554, Harrow, 29 and 141—total 170 In the Eton affair Winchester made 102 and 132—total 234, Eton, 110 and 71 (two absentees)—total 181

1827—At Lord's, Harrow played Eton, and scored 155 and 64—total 219, Eton, 166 and 50 (four wickets) The match was awarded to Eton in consequence, it is said, of some error on the part of the scorers.

1828—At Harrow, Eton beat Harrow by six wickets. Thus Harrow, 68 and 63—total 131, Eton, 78 and 55 (four wickets)—total 133

1829—At Winchester, Eton beat Winchester by four wickets Winchester scored 71 and 84—total 155, Eton, 50 and 106 (six wickets)—total 156

'Twas in the prime of summer time,
An evening calm and cool,
And five-and-twenty happy boys
Came bounding out of school
Away they sped with gladsome minds,
And souls untouched with sin,
To a level mead they came, and there
They drove the wickets in —*Hood*

1830—At Eton, Winchester beat Eton by eight wickets. The scoring in three innings out of the four, so far as the last was proceeded with, was unusually feeble, viz Eton, 55 and 61—total 116, Winchester, 116 and 1, for two wickets At the close of this match Harrow entered the lists against Winchester, and received a sound drubbing, although their opponents played "one short." Harrow made 36 and 63—total 99, Winchester, 158 Won by an innings and 59 runs

1832—At Lord's, Winchester were beaten easily by Eton, *i e*, by an innings and 10 runs Winchester scored 83 and 60—total 143, Eton, 153 Seven of this side averaged but two runs each

Harrow and Eton played on the two following days at Lord's, when Eton triumphed gloriously Harrow, 49 and 44—total 93; Eton, 249, of which nearly one-seventh were "extras" Won by an innings and 156 runs The *Sporting Magazine* of the time gives a somewhat different account, but on comparing other records therewith, the above results may be taken as substantially correct

1833—A close match between Eton and Winchester on the 1st and 2nd of August Eton, 86 and 124—total 210, Winchester, 47 and 149—total 196 Eton won by 14 runs

A match between Eton and Harrow followed Eton scored 86 and 57—total 143; Harrow, 118 and 27 (two wickets)—total 145 Harrow won by eight wickets

1834—Harrow and Winchester met at Lord's on the 30th of July, and made quick work of the match Harrow scored 48 and 40—total 88, Winchester, 46 and 43 (nine wickets)—total 89 Won by a wicket

1834—Harrow *v* Eton, at Lord's The former won by 13 runs. Thus Harrow, 69 and 97—total 166, Eton, 103 and 50—total 153 On one of the same days Eton and Winchester commenced their annual match The scoring was light on both sides, but Eton won by 13 runs Thus: Eton, 55 and 61—total 116, Winchester, 32 and 71—total 103

1835—Winchester *v* Harrow, at Lord's—A great deal of unprofitable bustle in the field characterised this match from beginning to end. No less than 604 runs were accumulated on the last Thursday and Friday of July when it was played. Winchester headed their opponents "from the hill" by 88 runs (See the full score)

WINCHESTER

	1st inn		2nd inn
W Wetherell, Esq, b Barton	26	c Brewer	7
S Bathurst, Esq, b Broughton	0	leg b w	0
F H Bennett, Esq, b Broughton	6	b Broughton	10
A Lowth, Esq, b Broughton	23	b Broughton	23
H J Rich, Esq, leg b w	10	b Barton	21
M Ward, Esq, hit w	86	b Barton	5
R Walmesley, Esq, b Barton	30	b Barton	4
R Longder, Esq, b Nethercote	15	not out	11
W H Coulston, Esq, leg b w	6	run out	12
E K Bunny, Esq, not out	11	b Broughton	1
R Gaffard, Esq, b Barton	6	b Broughton	0
Byes 16, w 8	24	Byes 5, w 4	9
Total	213	Total	103

HARROW

	1st inn.		2nd inn
W Massey, Esq, b Lowth	23	b Walmesley	30
C W A Napier, Esq, b Lowth	2	leg b w	2
T Brewer, Esq, b Lowth	0	run out	0
R H Smith, Esq, run out	14	b Lowth	2
R Broughton, Esq, c Walmesley	27	b Walmesley	26
A Talbot, Esq, b Lowth	6	b Lowth	0
H O Nethercote, Esq, c Walmesley	1	b Lowth	3
F Prothero, Esq, b Walmesley	3	b Lowth	0
H Barclay, Esq, b Lowth	10	not out	6
S Barton, Esq, not out	14	hit w	14
— Paterson, Esq, c Bennett	4	b Lowth	0
Byes 26, w 14	40	Byes 19, w 12	31
Total	144		114

Immediately on the finishing of the foregoing at Lord's, fresh wickets were pitched for Eton and Harrow, which the former won by 165 runs, the scores being Eton 111 and 149—total 260, Harrow 48 and 47—total 95 Of this latter number there were 14 byes in each innings On the Eton side 27 wide balls formed part of their total. A third match, between Eton and Winchester, succeeded, which Eton won by five wickets Thus Winchester, 97 and 60—total 157, Eton, 88 and 70 (five wickets)—total 158 Although 315 runs were totalled, the preponderance of "extras" excited surprise, viz, 71, or more than a fifth

1836—Harrow *v* Winchester, at Lord's—The latter played "one short," and beat, notwithstanding, by an innings and 8 runs Harrow totalled 29 and 24—

total 53, of which 27 were "extras;" Winchester, 69, and of these 39 were extras. The highest score from the bat was 11, made by Mr. Yatman; this was in fact the only double figure attained during the match.

Eton *v.* Harrow.—This took place upon the close of the last match. Here again the runs from the bat were few, while "extras" were in excess, viz., 89. Eton 49 and 68—total 117; Harrow, 97 and 21 (one wicket)—total 118. Harrow won by nine wickets.

1836.—Winchester *v.* Eton, at Lord's.—A match unprecedented for its disproportion of runs obtained from the bat to the total. Winchester, 95 and 128—total 223; Eton, 138 and 86 (eight wickets)—total 224. Of these 447 runs no less than 148 were extras, or very nearly one-third.

1837.—Harrow *v.* Winchester.—Played at Harrow on the 18th July. Harrow, 128 and 127—total 255; Winchester, 65 and 51—total 116. Harrow won by 139 runs.

Harrow *v.* Eton.—A two-day match at Lord's, which Eton won by eight wickets. Harrow, 89 and 62—total 151; Eton, 104 and 49 (two wickets)—total 153.

1838.—Harrow *v.* Winchester, at Lord's.—The former won by an innings and 54 runs. Winchester scored 66 and 86—total 152; Harrow, 206. It is somewhat singular that Winchester contributed just as many runs to the Harrow score as they were able to claim for their first innings, viz., 66.

Eton *v.* Harrow.—This followed upon the close of the last match, when Eton won by an innings and 30 runs. Thus: Eton, 157; Harrow, 56 and 71—total 127.

Eton *v.* Winchester, at Lord's.—In this Winchester righted itself by winning by one innings and 34 runs. Eton, 53 and 70—total 123; Winchester, 157.

1839.—Harrow *v.* Eton, at Lord's.—The latter won by eight wickets. Thus: Harrow, 59 and 65—total 124; Eton, 104 and 22 (two wickets)—total 126.

Harrow *v.* Winchester, at Lord's.—Another match, with a disproportionate share of extras, viz., 61. Harrow, 81 and 71—total 152; Winchester, 52 and 77—total 129. Harrow won by 23 runs.

Eton *v.* Winchester, at Lord's.—Played on Saturday and Monday, August 3rd and 5th. Eton scored 102 and 103—total 205; Winchester, 69 and 28 (one man short)—total 97. Eton won by 108 runs.

1840.—Winchester *v.* Harrow, at Lord's.—Although there was but a trifling difference in the amount of party results taken as a whole, such was hardly the case as regards the fielding of the two sides. Winchester obtained 118 and 86—total 204, of which 43 were contributed by 14 byes, 26 wides, and 3 no balls. Harrow, 54 and 139—total 193. In this were lumped 55 byes, 30 wides, and 2 no balls. Winchester won by 11 runs.

Eton *v.* Harrow, at Lord's.—The former won by 31 runs. Eton 122 and 86—total 208; Harrow 58 and 119—total 177. No less than 58 byes and 49 wides resulted from the two days' play.

Winchester *v.* Eton, at Lord's.—A difference of 43 runs resulted in favour of the Wykehamists, the scores being: For Winchester, 58 and 186—total 244; Eton, 122 and 79—total 201.

1841.—Harrow *v.* Winchester, at Lord's.—In this Harrow made the easy conquest of an innings and 18 runs. Thus: Harrow, 197; Winchester, 73 and 106—total 179.

Winchester *v.* Eton, at Lord's.—A match in which Winchester gained a victory of 109 runs thus wise: Winchester, 121 and 195—total 316; Eton, 94 and 113—total 207.

Eton *v.* Harrow, at Lord's.—Played on Friday, Saturday, and Monday, commencing July the 30th, and was remarkable for the long innings of Mr. E. Bayley, captain of the Eton eleven, viz., 152, the liberal contribution of 41 wide balls and 21 byes to the Eton score, and a total of 308 runs, as against 98 and 35 of Harrow, who were in consequence defeated by an innings and 175 runs.

1842.—Harrow *v.* Winchester, at Lord's.—The former won by 28 runs. Thus: Harrow, 69 and 152—total 221; Winchester, 125 and 68—total 193.

Harrow *v.* Eton.—Played at the conclusion of the former match. Harrow scored 141 and 121—total 262; Eton, 79 and 118—total 197. Eton gave their opponents 66 runs in byes and 19 in wides. Harrow, in return, 9 byes and 18 wides. Harrow won by 65 runs.

Winchester *v.* Eton.—Ball kept rolling. Eton won by seven wickets. Winchester, 106 and 177—total 283; Eton, 212 and 74 (three wickets)—total 286. The gross number of "extras" was 133.

1843.—Harrow *v.* Winchester, at Lord's.—A match of four days duration, commencing on the 2nd of August. Harrow, 96 and 135—total 231; Winchester, 86 and 131—total 217. Harrow won by 14 runs. Wet weather throughout.

Harrow *v.* Eton.—Commenced at the close of the previous match. Harrow won by 20 runs. Harrow, 99 and 52—total 151; Eton, 36 and 95—total 131.

Eton *v.* Winchester.—Further continuation. Eton, 138 and 147—total 285; Winchester, 261 and 25 (two wickets). Winchester won by eight wickets.

1844.—Winchester *v.* Harrow, at Lord's.—In this Winchester were victors by three wickets. Harrow had to follow their innings. Winchester, 169 and 30 (seven wickets)—total 199; Harrow, 63 and 135—total 198.

Harrow *v.* Eton.—The pupils on "the hill" mustered unusually weak during this quarter. The score stood thus at the finish of the match: Harrow, 60 and 91—total 151; Eton, 220. Won by an innings and 69 runs.

Eton *v.* Winchester.—This began on Saturday, the 3rd of August, and finished on the following Tuesday, when Eton won by 27 runs, the scores being—Eton, 76 and 115—total 191; Winchester, 47 and 117—total 164.

1845.—Winchester *v.* Harrow, at Lord's.—A close match, which Winchester won by 12 runs, although the fielding of Harrow was superior. Winchester, 96 and 156—total 252; Harrow, 62 and 178—total 240.

Eton *v.* Harrow.—Called the child's match from the great number of mere children selected by Harrow. But there was no help for it. Eton scored 261; Harrow, 32 and 56—total 88. Eton won by an innings and 173 runs.

Winchester v Eton—A tie match Full score given

WINCHESTER

	1st inn		2nd inn
R J Bateman, Esq, c Hornby, b Holland	44	c F Coleridge, b McNiven	9
F Bathurst, Esq, c C Coleridge, b Blore	9	b Blore	14
E Twopenny, Esq, b Blore	22	b Blore .	3
E Attfield, Esq, c Hornby, b Holland .	1	b McNiven	3
A Ridding, Esq, c F Coleridge, b Blore .	5	b McNiven . .	0
E Barchard, Esq, b Blore .	7	c C Coleridge, b McNiven .	8
W Piggatt, Esq, c Holland, b McNiven .	0	not out .	4
C E Kendall, Esq, c James, b Blore	10	b McNiven ..	1
W J Dewar, Esq, st Chitty, b Blore	6	b Blore	4
R J Baker, Esq, not out	3	c and b Blore .	1
R E Morris, Esq, run out .	0	b Blore	0
Wides .	1	Wides .	5
Total	111	Total .	52

ETON

	1st inn		2nd inn.
J J Hornby, Esq, b Dewar .	0	b Dewar .	5
C Coleridge, Esq, b Dewar ...	4	b Dewar	9
W S Deacon, Esq, b Dewar	10	run out .	39
E McNiven Esq, not out . . .	29	c and b Attfield	15
W James, Esq, b Dewar	4	c Dewar, b Attfield	4
E N Streatfield, Esq, b Dewar .	2	run out	2
J W Chitty, Esq, b Dewar	2	c Piggatt, b Dewar	7
F Coleridge, Esq, b Attfield	0	b Attfield ..	0
A F. Holland, Esq, b Attfield .	0	not out .	1
F S Wolferstan Esq, b Dewar	8	b Attfield	0
E W Blore, Esq, b Dewar	0	run out	0
Wides 3, n b 5 .	7	Byes 2, wides 9, n b 4	15
Total	66	Total .	97

1846—Harrow v Winchester, at Lord's—A well contested match Harrow won by 14 runs Thus · Harrow, 102 and 107—total 209, Winchester, 110 and 85—total 195

Harrow v Eton—In this the contenders were badly matched Harrow scored only 62 runs in their first innings and 82 in their second—total 144, Eton, 279, and consequently won by an innings and 135 runs

Eton v Winchester—This occupied three days, commencing on Saturday, August 1st, and ending on Tuesday Winchester scored 47 and 69—total 116, Eton, 171 Won by an innings and 55 runs

1847—Winchester v Harrow, at Lord's—A very tame affair. Harrow won by an innings and 24 runs Thus Winchester, 54 and 49—total 103, Harrow, 127

Winchester v Eton.—Defeat upon defeat Winchester, 65 and 71—total 136; Eton, 214 Won by an innings and 78 runs

Harrow *v.* Eton.—Eight of the Harrow side left their wickets without scoring in the first innings. Only 27 runs were totalled. The second innings produced 103, making 130 altogether. Eton, 119 and 12 (one wicket)—total 131. Won by nine wickets.

1848.—Harrow *v.* Winchester, at Lord's.—A three-day match, which Harrow won by 18 runs. Thus: Harrow, 79 and 76—total 155; Winchester, 36 and 101—total 137.

Harrow *v.* Eton.—A three-day match, which Harrow won by 41 runs. Harrow, 100 and 66—total 166; Eton, 68 and 57—total 125.

Eton *v.* Winchester.—Three days. Eton won by 65 runs, the score being: Eton, 55 and 168—total 223. Winchester, 109 and 49—total 158.

1849.—Harrow *v.* Winchester, at Lord's.—Won easily by Harrow, viz., 56 runs. Thus: Harrow, 155 and 126—total 281; Winchester, 82 and 143—total 225.

Harrow *v.* Eton.—The Dark Blues won by 77 runs. Thus: Harrow, 157 and 111—total 268; Eton, 112 and 79—total 191.

Eton *v.* Winchester.—Played on Saturday, the 4th of August, and Monday the 6th. Eton won by an innings and 27 runs. Thus: Eton, 189; Winchester, 80 and 82—total 162.

1850.—Harrow *v.* Winchester, at Lord's.—The Dark Blues effected an easy conquest. Thus: Harrow, 207; Winchester, 99 and 103—total 202. Harrow won by an innings and 5 runs.

Harrow *v.* Eton.—The Dark Blues scored 100 and 108—total 208; the Light, 105 and 104 (three wickets)—total 209. Won by seven wickets.

Winchester *v.* Eton.—The latter won by five wickets. Thus: Winchester, 108 and 74—total 182; Eton, 119 and 64 (five wickets)—total 183.

1851.—Harrow *v.* Winchester, at Lord's.—A small scoring match, which Winchester won by two wickets. Thus: Harrow, 78 and 62—total 140; Winchester, 77 and 64 (eight wickets)—total 141.

Harrow *v.* Eton.—Dark Blues won by eight wickets. Eton, 126 and 92—total 218; Harrow, 184 and 35 (two wickets)—total 219.

Eton *v.* Winchester.—A well contested match, which Winchester won by 26 runs. Score: Winchester, 80 and 140—total 220; Eton, 74 and 120—total 194.

1852.—Harrow *v.* Winchester, at Lord's.—Upwards of 600 runs were scored in this match of three days continuance. Harrow, 167 and 112—total 279; Winchester, 111 and 236—total 347. Winchester won by 68 runs.

Harrow *v.* Eton.—A three-day match. Harrow won by 71 runs by scoring 215 and 108—total 323, against 142 and 110 of Eton—total 252.

Eton *v.* Winchester.—A three-day match, which Winchester won by 30 runs. Mr. Trevilian scored 126 towards 232 for Winchester's first innings, second of Winchester 88—total 320; Eton, 158 and 132—total 290.

1853.—Harrow *v.* Winchester, at Lord's.—Harrow won by 70 runs, having scored 92 and 134—total 226; Winchester, 82 and 74—total 156.

Harrow *v* Eton —A small scoring match Eton, 58 and 79—total 137, Harrow, 53 and 85 (seven wickets)—total 138 Won by three wickets

Eton *v* Winchester —A three-day match, commencing on Saturday, July 30, and ending on Tuesday Winchester, 126 and 146—total 272, Eton, 66 and 171—total 237, Winchester won by 35 runs

1854 —Harrow *v* Winchester, at Lord's —This extended over four days, owing chiefly to unfavourable weather Harrow scored 119 and 134—total 253, Winchester, 81 and 55—total 136 Harrow won by 117 runs

Harrow *v* Eton —A three-day match, which Harrow won by 98 runs, scoring 130 and 128—total 258, against 71 and 89 of Eton—total 160

Eton *v*. Winchester —Eton, 100 and 99—total 199, Winchester, 110 and 90 (seven wickets)—total 200 Won by three wickets

1855 —Eton *v* Winchester —Played at Eton The first of a series to come off "alternately" on their own school grounds Eton, 94 and 95—total 189; Winchester, 103 and 40—total 143. Eton won by 46 runs.

Eton *v* Harrow —Played at Lord's Eton, 35 and 90—total 125, Harrow, 191 Won by an innings and 66 runs

1856 —Eton *v* Winchester —Played at Winchester, when Eton won by an innings and 4 runs Thus Winchester, 82 and 34—total 116, Eton, 120

1857 —Eton *v* Winchester —Played at Eton, when the residents won by an innings and 31 runs Winchester scored 62 and 114—total 176, Eton, 207

Eton *v* Harrow —A disputed match, with the following scores Eton, 70 and 59—total 129, Harrow, 118 and 12—total 130 Won by ten wickets

1858 —Eton *v* Winchester —Played at Winchester, when the residents won by a wicket Eton, 71 and 84—total 155, Winchester, 74 and 82 (nine wickets)—total 156

Eton *v* Harrow —Played at Lord's Eton, 44 and 97—total 141, Harrow, 148 Won by an innings and 7 runs.

Eton *v* Winchester —Played at Eton, the scores being 122 and 97 for Eton—total 219, Winchester, 121 and 99 (seven wickets)—total 220 Won by three wickets

Eton *v* Harrow —Played at Lord's Harrow, 242, Eton, 91 and 103—total 194 Harrow won by an innings and 48 runs

1860 —Winchester *v* Eton —Played at Winchester After a sharp contest of three days' duration, Eton won by 19 runs. Score. Eton, 96 and 115—total 211, Winchester, 91 and 101—total 192

Harrow *v* Eton —Played at Lord's Harrow, 83 and 274—total 357, Eton, 98 and 221 (eight wickets)—total 319 Unfinished

1861 —Eton *v* Winchester.—Played at Eton The residents won by nine wickets Winchester scored 78 and 98—total 176, Eton, 112 and 66 (one wicket)—total 178

Eton *v* Harrow —Played at Lord's Eton, 135 and 229—total 364, Harrow, 164 and 53 (for two wickets)—217. Drawn

1862 —Winchester *v*. Eton —Played on the College Ground, Winchester A close match. Eton won by one wicket. Winchester, 153 and 213—total 366; Eton, 270 and 97 (nine wickets)—total 367.

Eton *v.* Harrow.—Played at Lord's. Eton, 97 and 155—total 252; Harrow, 56 and 142—total 198. Eton won by 54 runs.

1863.—Eton *v.* Winchester.—Played at Eton. The residents made the tremendous score of 444, towards which Mr. Tritton contributed 130. Winchester made 97 and 153—total 250. Eton won by an innings and 194 runs.

Eton *v.* Harrow.—Played at Lord's. Eton, 184 and 285—total 469; Harrow, 268. Unfinished. On this occasion upwards of 20,000 persons attended, among whom were equestrians—not admitted now—numbering at the least 500. The match excited some curiosity from the fact that Mr. Buller (no bowler) took six wickets in the second innings of Eton.

1864.—Winchester *v.* Eton.—Played at Winchester. Eton won by nine wickets. Thus: Winchester, 76 and 210—total 286; Eton, 116 and 171 (one wicket)—total 287.

Harrow *v.* Eton.—Played at Lord's. Harrow, 242; Eton, 63 and 113—total 176. Harrow won by an innings and 66 runs.

1865.—Winchester *v.* Eton.—Played at Eton, and was left unfinished on account of weather. Winchester, 242; Eton, 110 (six wickets).

Harrow *v.* Eton.—Played at Lord's. Harrow, 248; Eton, 86 and 111—total 197. Harrow won by an innings and 51 runs.

1866.—Eton *v.* Winchester.—Only two batsmen had ciphers to their names throughout the match. Winchester scored 188 and 119—total 307; Eton, 291 and 17 (without loss of wicket)—total 308.

Harrow *v.* Eton.—Played at Lord's. Harrow, 302. Ten out of the eleven got into double figures. Eton, 124 and 42—total 166. Harrow won by an innings and 136 runs.

1867.—Winchester *v.* Eton.—Played at Eton. The residents won by an innings and 10 runs. Winchester scored 136 and 50—total 186; Eton, 196.

Eton *v.* Harrow.—Played at Lord's. Eton, 208 and 221—total 429; Harrow, 173 and 78 (one wicket)—total 251. Unfinished.

1868.—Eton *v.* Harrow.—Played at Lord's. Eton, 116 and 123—total 239; Harrow, 179 and 62 (three wickets)—total 241. Won by seven wickets.

Eton *v.* Winchester.—Played at Winchester. Winchester, 72 and 94—total 166; Eton, 120 and 49 (two wickets)—total 169. Eton won by eight wickets.

1869.—Eton *v.* Winchester.—Played at Eton. Eton, 169; Winchester, 24 and 59—total 133. Eton won by an innings and 36 runs.

Eton *v.* Harrow.—Played at Lord's. Eton, 237; Harrow, 91 and 127—total 218. Eton won by an innings and 19 runs.

1870.—Eton *v.* Winchester.—Played at Winchester. Eton, 46 and 121—total 167; Winchester, 92 and 76 (nine wickets)—total 168. For ten years the luck had been all one way, but the tide now turned in favour of the Wykehamists, who won by a wicket.

Eton *v* Harrow.—Played at Lord's One of the closest matches occurring for many a year The score in full is consequently given

ETON

	1st inn		2nd inn.
Mr G H Longman, b Law	8	b Openshaw	37
Mr A S Tabor, c Parbury, b Macan	10	st Baily, b Carnac	50
Mr F W Rhodes, run out	31	b Carnac	18
Mr J P Rodger, b Parbury	41	c and b Openshaw	14
Hon G Harris, b Law	12	c Baily, b Macan	7
Lord Clifton, b Crake	19	b Macan	3
Mr F Pickering, c Lucas, b Macan	35	c Lucas, b Carnac	0
Mr A W Ridley, not out	10	b Macan	1
Mr G H Cammell, b Macan	5	c Baily, b Macan	0
Hon A F Lyttelton, c Baily, b Macan	2	not out	5
Mr M A Tollemache, c Baily, b Macan	1	b Macan	2
Byes 6, l-b 6, w 3	15	Byes 7, l-b 5, w 2	14
Total	189	Total	151

HARROW

	1st inn.		2nd inn
Mr Law, b Clifton	6	c Longman, b Tollemache	9
Mr A C Lucas b Clifton	4	c and b Tollemache	13
Mr E C Baily, b Tollemache	76	c Tabor, b Clifton	16
Mr W P Crake, c Tollemache, b Clifton	1	b Tollemache	0
Mr C W Walker, b Tollemache	34	b Tollemache	16
Mr C A Wallroth, run out	30	run out	0
Mr W E Openshaw, b Ridley	7	c and b Ridley	26
Mr G Macan, not out	25	b Tollemache	17
Mr T S Dury, c Pickering, b Clifton	0	c and b Ridley	3
Mr E P Parbury, b Tollemache	12	run out	0
Mr G R Carnac, b Tollemache	0	c Harris, b Clifton	5
Byes 2 l-b 3, w 5	10	Byes 2, l-b 3, w 4	9
Total	205	Total	114

1871.—Eton *v* Winchester —Played at Eton A close match Winchester, 60 and 102—total 162, Eton, 82 and 72—total 154 Winchester won by 8 runs

Eton *v* Harrow —Played at Lord's Eton, 308, towards which Mr Ridley contributed 117; Harrow, 133 and 98—total 231 Eton won by an innings and 77 runs

1872 —Eton *v* Winchester —Played at Winchester A heavy defeat for the residents Thus Winchester, 78 and 93—total 171, Eton, 296 Won by an innings and 125 runs

Eton *v* Harrow —Played at Lord's. Harrow, 125 and 111—total 236, Eton, 110 and 127 (four wickets) Won by six wickets.

1873 —Eton *v* Harrow —Played at Lord's Eton, 145 and 166—total 311, Harrow, 146 and 167 (five wickets)—total 313 Won by five wickets

Eton *v.* Winchester —Played at Eton Winchester, 144 and 146—total 290, Eton, 226 and 65 (five wickets)—total 291 Won by five wickets

1874.—Eton *v.* Harrow.—Played at Lord's. Harrow, 155 and 145—total 300 (Mr A J Webbe claimed 157 of this number), Eton, 143 and 159 (five wickets)—total 302. Won by five wickets.

Eton *v* Winchester.—Played at Winchester. Eton, 381, Winchester, 105 and 74—total 179. Eton won by an innings and 202 runs.

1875.—Eton *v* Winchester.—Played at Eton. Eton, 230 and 46 (five wickets)—total 276, Winchester, 136 and 139—total 275. Eton won by five wickets.

Eton *v* Harrow.—Played at Lord's. Unfinished owing to weather. Score in full:

ETON

Hon A Lyttleton, b Meek	59
Mr S Harding, c Wilkinson, b Cochrane	26
Mr A Haskett Smith, b Cochrane	3
Mr W F Forbes, b Kemp .	47
Mr E W B Denison, c Banbury, b Meek	8
Mr E Ruggles Brice, b Kemp	0
Mr I Wakefield, c and b Kemp . .	22
Hon A D Grey, thrown out by Clough-Taylor .	0
Mr J M Post, c and b Meek	1
Mr H Whitfield, not out .	6
Mr C Haig-Brown, b Meek	9
Byes 7, l-b 5, w 9	21
	202

HARROW

	1st inn		2nd inn
Mr A C Tyssen, c Lyttleton, b Denison	2	not out . . .	39
Mr M G Wilkinson, b Denison	6	b Haig-Brown ...	11
Mr A H Cochrane, b Haig-Brown	19	b Wakefield .	1
Mr C W M Kemp, c Forbes, b Haig-Brown	3	b Wakefield	33
Mr A Banbury, b Denison .	0	b Wakefield	0
Mr H E Meek, b Denison . .	0	b Denison	16
Mr L Chater, not out	30	not out	35
Mr L Clough Taylor, c Forbes, b Wakefield	10	b Wakefield . ..	7
Mr G G Grundy, c Wakefield, b Forbes . .	22		
Mr S F Charles, c Lyttleton, b Denison	4		
Mr A F Stewart, c Denison, b Forbes ..	6		
Byes 6, w 2 .	8	Byes 5, l-b 2, w 5, n b 1	13
Total	110	Total	155

Of the fifty-one matches between Eton and Harrow here enumerated, Eton claims twenty-four and Harrow twenty-two, the remainder were unfinished. It is well also to say that they have not been carried on from the date of commencement with unbroken continuity. But the most striking feature connected with the match as an "annual" for nearly twenty years past is the increased and increasing hold it has upon the middle and upper classes of society. Nor them alone, for it commands the attention of the press generally more than any other event of the kind in London or away therefrom. It has, in fact, been so frequently and graphically described, that an effort of the mind is needed to say anything fresh which contains interest, for, as a rule the most ardent enthusiast is affected by the insipidity of an oft repeated tale The match of 1875 possessed a few features of a somewhat unusual character Seldom does it happen that the executive in matters appertaining to a public cricket match devise how best they can keep the public from witnessing one of their own fostering It seems scarcely credible that nearly 20,000 could have been attracted to Lord's to behold a schoolboys match, and this, too, under circumstances otherwise than favourable, True enough is it that the forces of fashion may be exhibited in a variety of forms, but those relating to cricket were never demonstrated more signally than on this occasion at Lord's "Everybody" was there, or intended to be there, as every seat was occupied either by person or ticket long before the match began, and the slightest gaze on the surroundings suggested to the mind's eye a picnic on a colossal scale So, indeed, it was All the arrangements for really examining the play—to say nothing of comfort or convenience—were subordinated to the dense wall of carriages and their aristocratic occupants, so thick and impassable that the pedestrian had to strain his eye-balls and often endure the fatigue consequent upon the frequent process of tiptoeing Great, indeed, were the arrangements for this occasion, and equally great the disappointments Shortly before the time announced for play, an uninvited visitor in the guise of a rain cloud came stealing over the ground, and quickly the beautiful and most enchanting scene of its kind underwent a wretched transformation What was an unbroken line of happy faces soon became a dark, deep wall of umbrellas For two long hours the pluvial Jupiter had his own way, the solid looking clouds then gave signs of departing, as blue rents were discoverable Thus cheered, play began as soon as the ground would permit of a foothold Some sage has said that "disappointment sinks the heart of man, but the renewal of hope gives consolation" Well, these tests were applied, and in neither case proved exactly correct, in the first instance, there was no sinking of the "heart," as those who had the appliances for making themselves jolly did so, and as to the consolation, a second cloud, thicker and heavier laden than the first, let fall its contents so lavishly that, before a wicket was taken, the stumps were pulled up and the company hasted to their homes in the best way they could The weather on the following day was all that could be desired and the ground presented such an array of beauty, rank, and fashion, the like of which is nowhere else witnessed The match was proceeded with vigorously, and the interest in it never flagged, although the chances against playing it out were as everything to nothing Shortly before five o'clock an innings by each party was completed, but as Harrow were 92 in a minority, they had to follow on When the time arrived for drawing stumps, 155 runs were scored for six wickets, and the match, in consequence, was relegated to the drawn or unfinished list 13,522 persons passed the turnstile, and paid half a crown each in so doing, and nearly 500 carriages were stationed on the ground, 1500 persons, chiefly of rank and distinction occupied the permanent and temporary stands dignified with the epithet "Grand"

CHAPTER IX.

GLANCES AT THE PAST AND PRESENT STATE OF COUNTY CRICKET—*continued.*

KENT.

LORD SAY You men of Kent
DICK What say you of Kent, —
LORD SAY Nothing but this,—'Tis *bona terra mala gens*
CADE Away with him! away with him! he speaks *Latin*
LORD SAY Hear me but speak, and bear me where you will.
Kent, in the Commentaries Cæsar writ,
Is term'd the civil'st place of all this isle
Sweet is the country because full of riches,
The people liberal, valiant, active, wealthy
Which makes me hope you are not void of pity

2nd part Henry VI, Act IV, Scene 7

GEOGRAPHICAL DEFINITION—FRAGMENTS OF ITS EARLY HISTORY—TRIAL AT LAW ON A BETTING CASE—HAMPSHIRE *v* KENT AT BISHOPSBOURNE—A GAUNT SCORE—POEM—SERIES OF MATCHES—SONG OF THE KENTISH CRICKETER—REVIVAL OF COUNTY CRICKET UNDER PILCH AT MALLING—DESCRIPTION OF THE TOWN—WINDSOR'S PRINTING PRESS—EXTRAORDINARY MATCH PLAYED THERE—SUBSEQUENT DECLINE OF KENT—RETIREMENT OF PILCH FROM MALLING—POPULARITY OF CLARKE'S ITINERANT ELEVEN—DIFFICULTIES ATTENDANT UPON NEW GROUNDS—GENTLEMEN OF KENT MATCHES—BATTING AVERAGES OF 1869—MOTE PARK—ELECTION OF LORD HARRIS AS PRESIDENT OF THE CLUB—LIST OF MATCHES IN 1875 ALSO BATTING AVERAGES FOR THE SAME YEAR, ETC, ETC

KENT, the county of the Cantii, has been honoured with more commentators than perhaps any other since Cæsar's time It was the first established kingdom of the Saxon Heptarchy, and has an area of 1624 square miles, or 1,039,419 acres If the old song about the invasion of Harold be true, and the heroism of the men of Kent not to be questioned, it is easy enough to see the reason why the white horse of Hengist is rampant on the county flag, with its appropriate motto "Invicta" accompanying The same spirit which actuated the residents of this corner of England to defend their national rights and privileges, still lives in their sports and pastimes True, the iron hoof of the invader proved at times mighty and downtreading, but by the varying changes incident to war, Kent foremost to repel, was the last to surrender So, too in the peaceful strife of cricket, Kent was early in the vindication of a game destined to stamp out many of the relics of a barbarous age. This was done by fostering the discovery of a better mode of mock warfare, while it brought out feelings more in unison with the advance of improvement and moral culture. For generations Kent has stood in the foreground of the group of patrons and performers too. Meagre as the information respecting early cricket is, Kent appears to have cultivated the game from its infancy, and to have practised it also without regarding time or circumstance. The mention of *cricketts* played in the county town in the first part of the 17th century is evidence enough of the advance made in the game, wide though it undoubtedly was. The pious rector of Otham, though far from being a Puritan, properly so called, felt serious stirrings within him when preaching in the open street of Maidstone, or he would not have called it "a profane town," insomuch as his biographer adds, "I have seen morris dancing, cudgel playing, stool ball, *cricketts*, and many other sports openly and publickly on the Lord's Day."* How long this state of things continued, the same author does not say, and 'tis hardly worth while to quote others who like to dwell upon the dark side of every picture.

From the period of this incident, history takes a deal of time to breathe. There are few, if any, signs of the pen of a ready writer. But that the men of Kent were idle while the historian slumbered is by no means to be inferred. Here and there a faint streak of light breaks out from unexpected quarters. A very curious document, recently drawn from the pigeon holes of the archæologist, will to some extent illustrate this proposition. In an action at law a defendant pleaded non-liability to the payment of an annuity on a bond, because after the 1st day of May, 1711, certain parties who styled themselves of the "County of Kent" played against certain other parties who styled themselves "All England" at a certain game called cricket, and that the plaintiff won 25 guineas upon a "bet upon tick" upon the said game within the meaning of the statute of 9 Anne against betting. The Court remarked, "It is to be sure a manly game, and not bad in itself, but it is the ill use that is made of it by betting above 10*l.* upon it, that is bad, and against the laws, which ought to be construed largely to prevent the great mischief of excessive gaming." The Court inclined to give judgment for the defendant that cricket is a game, and that the bond is void. Thus much for the advance of Kent to create all this ado. How the county progressed afterwards can best be inferred from the first recorded match committed to paper by James Love. Between this and the next quarter of a century the information is very scant and often unreliable. It developes itself chiefly on fly leaves of old books, having no relation to, or sympathy with, cricket. Moreover, judging from dingy and ill-drawn pictures, proofs abundant are given of the presence of the notched stick as the only method of scoring. An extravagant amount of ridiculous bounce was a characteristic of the age. Occasionally an old well thumbed bill comes again into daylight, setting forth the stakes to be played for, varying from 50*l.* to 500*l.*

Take the next match recorded for Kent, and here is a document by no means to

* See "Life of Thomas Wilson," 1672.

be considered a reflex of the play The object of reproducing it, however, is two-fold It exhibits the slow manumission from the stick, and gives the second stage of scoring and the status of Kent, the latter shown in a poem, which for years was allowed to pass unchallenged as to its correctness The match bears the date of August 19th, 1772, and was between Hambledon and Kent, the former apparently having a little assistance from England The scene of the play was Bishopsbourne paddock, near Canterbury. The score is a faithful transcript of the only one that has come down to the present generation from which any idea of the character of the play can be given As neither Miller nor Boorman was out, and May did not go in a second time, the match was awarded to Kent by two wickets

HAMBLEDON (WITH YALDEN AND EDMEADS)

	1st inn	2nd inn
T Brett	11	11
T Sneter	26	0
G Leer	29	7
J Small sen	22	48
Peter Stewart	13	12
T Ridge, Esq	4	8
William Barber	0	2
W Hogsflesh	0	1
W Yalden	4	1
John Edmeads	7	4
Edward Aburrow	0	6
Byes	7	13
Total	123	113

KENT.

	1st inn	2nd inn
Lumpy	14	12
R May	3	
John Wood	0	20
Pattenden	20	4
Minshull	21	9
Simmons	3	1
Fuggles	0	1
J Miller	14	17
T. White	8	5
Palmer	29	14
J Boorman	0	2
Byes	21	16
Total	136	101

Such a conquest as this, kindled the poetic fire of Kent, which in a string of verses has not been extinguished at this day In fact, these stanzas were so pointed and effective that a clergyman of Winchester appropriated them to a victory by the Hambledon Club some years afterwards These, with a few necessary alterations in names, and a trifling change in the refrain, passed muster as an original composition by the Rev. Mr Cotton for full half a century without being denounced.

Assist all ye Muses, and join to rehearse
An old English sport never praised yet in verse,
'Tis cricket I sing, of illustrious fame,
No nation e'er boasted so noble a game—
Derry Down

Great Pindar has bragg'd of his heroes of old—
Some were swift in the race, some in battle were bold,
The brows of the victor with olive were crowned.
Hark! they shout, and Olympia returns the glad sound—
Derry Down

What boasting of Castor and Pollux his brother,
The one famed for riding, for bruising the other
Their lustre's eclipsed by the lads in the field,
To Minshull and Miller these brothers must yield—
Derry Down

Here's guarding and catching, and throwing and tossing,
And bowling and striking, and running and crossing,
Each mate must excel in some principal part,
The Pentathlon of Greece could not show so much art—
Derry Down

The parties are met and arrayed all in white,
Fam'd Elis ne'er boasted so pleasing a sight,
Each nymph looks askew at her favourite swain,
And views him half stript both with pleasure and pain—
Derry Down

The wickets are pitch'd now, and measured the ground,
Then they form a large ring and stand gazing around,
Since Ajax fought Hector in sight of all Troy,
No contest was seen with such fear and such joy—
Derry Down

Ye bowlers take heed, on my precepts attend,
On you the whole state of the game must depend,
Spare your vigour at first, nor exert all your strength,
But measure your step, and be sure pitch at length—
Derry Down

Ye strikers observe, when the foe shall draw nigh,
Mark the bowler's advance with a vigilant eye,
Your skill all depends upon distance and sight,
Stand firm to your scratch, let your bat be upright—
Derry Down

Ye fieldsmen look sharp, lest your pains ye beguile,
Move close like an army in rank and in file,
When the ball is returned, back it sure, for I trow
Whole states have been ruined by one overthrow—
Derry Down

The sport is now o'er, I. O victory rings,
Echo doubles the chorus, and Fame spreads her wings,
Let us now hail our champions, all steady and true,
Such as Homer ne'er sung nor Pindar e'er knew—
Derry Down

Minshull, Miller and Palmer, with Lumpy and May,
Fresh laurels have gained by their conquest to-day,
Wood, Pattenden, Simmons, with Fuggles and White,
With Boorman will join and will toast them to-night—
Derry Down

With heroes like these even Hampshire we'll drub,
And bring down the pride of the Hambledon Club,
The Duke,* with Sir Horace,† are men of true merit,
And nobly support such brave fellows with spirit—
Derry Down

Then fill up the glass—he's the best that drinks most,—
The Duke and Sir Horace in bumpers we'll toast,
Let us join in the praise of the bat and the wicket,
And sing in full chorus the patrons of cricket—
Derry Down

And when the game's o'er, and our fate shall draw nigh—
For the heroes of cricket like others must die,—
Our bats we'll resign neither troubled nor vexed,
And give up our wickets to those who come next—
Derry Down

* The third Duke of Dorset, born in 1745, succeeded to the title in 1769 He possessed great muscular strength, and though an energetic cricketer, his fame as a patron exceeded his playing abilities He gave to the town of Sevenoaks a piece of land, known as "The Vine," to be "a cricket-ground for ever" This spot at the present day scarcely harmonizes with the intentions of the donor, or is in keeping with Knole the ducal palace and domain of the Dorsets approximate thereto This mansion, with its outbuildings, covers five acres of ground Its state rooms are adorned with many of the finest productions of the portraying art, while the hills, dales, and groves of its stately park render Knole one of the most magnificent abodes in Europe The house is in the antiquated style of English architecture

† Almost every record of "Sir Horace" gives evidence either of his great wealth or profuse liberality, especially in matters appertaining to cricket Among his "retainers" were some of the best players of the time He represented Sandwich in five successive Parliaments, extending over a period of thirty-three years "This is the only Cinque Porte, except Dover, which has the least claim to independence, and that arises from the extensive number of electors Sandwich, which has for many years ranked as an Admiralty borough from the influence of innumerable places and the douceurs which the voters hold under the patronage of that Board, has been generally represented by two members of their nomination, but Sir Horace Mann, who resides in the neighbourhood, having the largest Kentish estates of any man in the county, and being so much respected for his hospitality and convivial talents, put up for representative of that place in his own interest, which he obtained in opposition to Lord Parker, Comptroller of the Household, who was supported by Government in conjunction with Mr Stephens, secretary to the Admiralty Thus the independent interest succeeded for the first time in the election of one of their members" (See Russell's "Ancient Liberties and Privileges of the Cinque Ports," 1809) It is lamentable to think that all this material wealth should have been frittered away long before his death, which occurred in 1814, just when he had attained his seventieth year Leaving no male issue, the title became extinct

It is pretty generally admitted that the severest test of plagiarism is the transferring or adopting an author's errors The poem just quoted opens with a broad mistake, so does the copy Both the real author of it and the plagiarist are therefore wrong Surely John Nyren knew, or ought to have known, that cricket had been "praised in verse" if Mr. Cotton's acquaintance with the game had been from unadvoidable circumstances limited to the antique city of Winchester "Never praised yet in verse!—then what does James Love mean by such lines as the following, written, probably, when both these patrons of the Hambledon Club were boys?—

> Hail, cricket! hail, thou manly British game,
> First of all sports, be first alike in fame,
> To my fir'd soul thy busy transports bring
> That I may feel thy raptures while I sing,
> And thou kind patron of the mirthful play,
> SANDWICH, thy country's friend, accept the lay
> Though mean my verse, my subject yet approve,
> And look propitious on the game you love *

A second triumph awaited Kent when opposed to the Hambledon Club, on the Vine, at Sevenoaks, in the month of August, 1774 Hambledon scored 46 and 150 total 196 Kent, with some bowling assistance, totalled 240 in their first and only innings, and consequently won the match by an innings and 35 runs The Duke of Dorset scored 77, and J Miller 95

Less than a fortnight intervened when the experiment of retrieving lost laurels was made on Broad Halfpenny Down, with but a slight change in the list of contenders. Kent, as before, had foreign help chiefly in the bowling department. At the close of an innings each there was the slight difference of six runs in favour of the visiting team, although in the end Kent won the match with four wickets to spare As if there were no other elevens of equal strength, or that could be managed for a well contested match, Kent and Hampshire again met on the Vine (1775), Kent had the assistance of two bowlers, and to them in a great degree the success of the residents may be ascribed Pattenden scored more than double the amount of runs in his second innings for Kent than were procured by the whole eleven of Hambledon in their second The Duke of Dorset also signalised himself by scoring the exact number of runs in his double innings as the whole eleven of Hambledon in their second The match in question deserves notice in another respect, viz, the addition of a third stump Some doubt hovers about the "experiment,' so called In all probability the match came off under certain protests and objection to any change in the then existing state of things, as in other and far more recent times introductions with improvements have Generally speaking, invention and its reward do not belong to the same age, seeing that a period must elapse to bring up and enlighten the mind of the multitude for the reception of an advanced standard of thought

Full ten years elapsed before Kent achieved another important victory against

* See poem in full

Hambledon, and as several fresh names appear, the score of the match is given *in extenso* It was played on Sevenoaks Vine, in the month of June, 1786

HAMBLEDON CLUB (WITH LUMPY)

	1st inn		2nd inn
Earl of Winchilsea run out	6	b Boorman	5
— Lumpy, not out	1	not out	1
J Small, sen , c Brown	11	b Boorman	12
Taylor, b Clifford	2	c Bullen	19
Mann, run out	0	run out	0
Purchase, b Bullen	25	c Boorman	3
T Walker, b Bowra	43	b Clifford	10
H Walker, b Clifford	39	b Bullen	24
Sueter, b Bullen	3	b Bullen	10
Nyren, b Bullen	10	b Bullen	2
Hawkins, b Clifford	0	b Clifford	3
Byes	3		
Total	143	Total	89

KENT

	1st inn		2nd inn
Bullen, b Lumpy	27	c H Walker	4
Aylward, c H Walker	22	b Lumpy	27
Ring, b Purchase	1	not out	61
Clifford, run out	4		
Townsend, c Small	22	c Taylor	8
Bowra, c Hawkins	28	not out	3
Brazier, b Lumpy	8	c Small	4
Boorman, run out	2		
Newman, b Purchase	1	b Lumpy	1
Couchman, b Lumpy	1	b Lumpy	2
Booker, not out	5		
Byes	2		
Total	123	Total	110

From the above document it will readily be seen that Kent won by four wickets

The next match with Hambledon took place at Coxheath, in 1787, when Kent were defeated by two wickets, the scores being Kent, 140 and 194—total 334, Hambledon, 256 and 79 (eight wickets)—total 335 Only one man during the match left his wicket without a score In the first innings of Hambledon there were eight double figures,—a circumstance in those days, as now, of unfrequent occurrence The most significant fact in the following year is in relation to a match with England at Coxheath, when Kent were defeated by an innings and 80 runs, and again in 1789 by an innings and 10 runs A run of ill-luck pursued them up to 1791, for in a contest with Marylebone the latter were victors by an innings and 113 runs, the scores of Beldham and Finney (two given men to Marylebone) being nearly equal to all the runs of the Kentish batsmen in their double innings Thus: Kent, 39 and 88—total 127, Marylebone, 240 The last match of importance in which Kent as a county arrayed itself against another county before the close of the century occurred at Lord's in 1796, of which the full score is given

KENT

	2nd inn		2nd inn
Hon J Tufton, hit w	16	b Walker	0
J Hammond, b Walker	1	c Wells	39
J Pilcher, c Shackle	8	c Wells	11
Ring, c Ray	1	c Graham	14
Hon E Bligh, b Beauclerk	6	c Walker	3
Hon V Tufton, c Wells	10	run out	10
W Barton, b Walker	9	c Ray	5
T Boxall, c Ray	0	c Shackle	1
E Hussey, Esq c Ray	0	b Walker	0
— Ayling, b Walker	11	not out	6
W Bullen, not out	0	c Graham	0
		Byes	2
Total	62	Total	91

MIDDLESEX (WITH WELLS)

	1st inn		2nd inn
Earl of Winchilsea, b Boxall	0	b Boxall	6
Lord F Beauclerk, b Bullen	10	b Pilcher	14
Hon A Upton, b Boxall	0	b Boxall	0
G Leach Esq, run out	0	c Pilcher	0
T Mellish, Esq, b Boxall	2	b Boxall	1
J Wells, c Hammond	2	b Bullen	0
T Graham, c Ring	5	Ring	0
T Lert, c Pilcher	6	b Boxall	2
F Shackle, run out	2	c Hammond	24
W Ray, c Boxall	2	not out	9
T Walker, not out	13	b Boxall	3
		Bye	1
Total	42	Total	60

A period of nearly twenty years elapsed before Kent came again to the front, and during that time a fresh list of cricketers altogether, appear to have been trained Many reasons might be assigned for the long trance, and among them the volunteer movement, which was kept up to the highest pitch of tension from the alarms and dangers, both real and imaginary, which possessed the Kentish mind on the subject of an invasion by the Hannibal of the age Coxheath, a minor Aldershot, was spotted over with tents of a very different nature to those attached to the cricket field, and until the disturbing tyrant was completely overthrown the more peaceful system of warfare was not carried on with the spirit becoming a county of such pretensions as that of Kent The town of Wrotham was unknown to fame for cricket till the year 1815, when England met Kent on "The Napps" It may be said here that Wrotham is about twenty-four miles from London by the road It is seated on the banks of a stream falling into the Thames near Northfleet.

From the hills west of the town the eye embraces one of those enchanting prospects with which England, and the county of Kent in particular, so numerously abound It will be seen from the full score of the match referred to, that the England eleven possessed a strong admixture of experienced players, while on the other side the reverse was the case. Kent came off second best Little else could have been expected previous to the encounter, and the chief wonder afterwards was, that England won by no more than 51 runs Particulars —

ENGLAND

	1st inn		2nd inn
J Bennett, st Leney	10	b J Willes	10
H Bentley, b Ashby	0	run out ...	0
W Beldham, c — Willes	2	b J Willes	3
J Sherman, st Leney	3	b Ashby	0
W Lambert, c Ashby	34	c — Willes	10
Lord F Beauclerk, b Ashby	2	c Ashby	4
E H Budd, Esq , st Leney	4	b J Willes	11
G Wills, c — Willes	13	c H Barnard	0
G Osbaldeston, Esq , c Nordish	12	not out	14
T C Howard, c Nordish	1	st Leney	7
J Sparks, not out	3	c Razzell	0
Byes	1	Byes	1
Total	85	Total	60

KENT

	1st inn		2nd inn
Winter, b Bentley	0	b Bentley	4
Nordish, b Howard	9	b Bentley	7
Masters, c Osbaldeston	12	b Bentley	9
Razzell, b Howard	12	c Sherman	3
Town, b Howard	2	c Howard	8
J Willes, Esq , c Budd	0	run out	0
Ashby, b Beauclerk	0	c Howard	3
J Barnard, not out	3	not out	12
H Barnard, b Howard	0	c Sparks	2
Leney, c Sherman	2	b Bentley	2
— Willes, Esq , c Beldham	1	b Bentley	0
Byes	3	Byes	0
Total	44	Total	50

About this time a very curious song attracted notice, but by whom written it would be unsafe to speculate for want of a few important particulars The peculiarity of its diction makes it only tolerable to hear when attempted by a vocalist capable of bringing out humour without ridiculous extravagance, and as such are rarely to be found, the lay of "The Kentish Cricketer" is seldom heard It is affirmed that the writer dealt with facts As a literary production, it possesses no merit whatever, and is merely introduced here as a document, tending in some degree to elucidate the manners and actions of the uneducated classes, from which rough and ready cricketers are upon a pinch drafted.

I

My feyther and mother be boath dead and gone,
  An' ha' left only me an' our Mary,
So I go es up tu Lunnon leaves sister at whoam
  Tu take care o' de hog an' de dairy,
Cos Lunnon I heerd was a wunnerful place,
So ses I tu myself, I'll goo up for a race,
An' how I got 'onner'd I'll tell ye de case
    Tol-de-rol, lol-de-rol laddy, ri-tol-de-rol lol-de-rol lay

II

Now de fust thing I heerd on, which made my 'art glad,
  Wos a wunnerful gurt match o' cricket,
Fur in Kent ye must know, dare is many a lad
  Dat is famous for bat, ball, an' wicket
An' den as I heerd, an' arterwards foun',
It was tu be played on my Lord's cricket groun'
Deng it, I foun' 'em out, an' de stumps dey come down
                                        Tol-de-rol, &c

III.

Dey stood hankerin' about for wot I cudden't tell,
  Till my Lord sings out tu de bystanders,
Be dere ary chap here as can play pretty well,
  For I du now run short of a hand, sirs
So den I stept in, dear heart how dey did grin!
Tu be grinned at, however, ses I, is no sin

Spoken —Well, sir, my Lord he cum up tu me and axed if I cud play "Well, sir, my lord," ses I, I ses, "I beant no gurt spaiks of a player I've got one queer sort of a hit, an' dat's a switcher into round de field" 'Well, my man," ses he, "can ye boul?' "Aha, my lord, sir," I ses, "I jest can, I always het de man or de wicket tu a dead sartinty."

Sung —"Well," my Lord, then ses he, "yu're de man for me"
                                        Tol-de-rol, &c

IV

So den we went in, and de geam did begin,
  An' at fust it went on pretty rightish,
Till we'd been in once an' it looked rääther queer,
  For they knocked her about pretty tightish
'Bout losin' de geam, we thought one an' all,
When my Lord ses to me, "Cannot you take de ball"

Spoken —Well I did take de ball, an' a teejuss good boul I made on it, for I broke all dere heads, arms, legs, bats, an' wickets, an' pretty soon made de game ourn

Sung —An' de other chaps den, we made hospital men,
                                        Tol-de-rol, &c

V

Now the people all round dey seemed plaguedly queered,
  An' struck with a nashional wonder,
Tu think, as dey sed, sich a bumpkin as I
  Shud come up for to make 'em knock under,

An' de winners dey lääft, an' de losers dey swoor,
An' both on 'em called I a gurt Kentish boor,

Spoken—Well, my Lord, he lääft tu, and axed me wot my neam was "Well, sir," ses I, "my neam's Giles" "Well Giles" ses he, 'I hope no defence, but here's a fipern-note for ye" "My Lord, sir," ses I "you will defend me ef ye du I doant want none o' yer money I cum up here tu see de sites Newgate, and Cripplegate, and Billingsgate, an' all the gates fur wot I know, but ef ye like tu ask me whoam tu dinner wid ye, dat's quite anudder matter

Sung—So we went one an' tother like sister an' brother
Tol-de rol, &c

VI

Now wen I got there I was teejously scared
Tu see everythink heart and month wishes—
I was plaguedly queered wot iver tu begin fust,
Sich a huge nation sight o' Frinch dishes
An dey axed me sich questions, sich plaguey hard words

* * * * * *

Spoken—"Deng it all, my Lord," ses I "your talk beant nothin' like wot ourn is down in de country," I did'nt know nothin' wot to make on it But wen I'd got one or tu bottles o' Sham Abram—no it beant Abraham—but dat sham fizzin sort o' butiful stuff wot de ladies an genelmun drink, ye know, I 'gun to talk to my Lord den, and titter to de ladies tu.

Sung—And de ladies ye see, got and tittered at me
Tol-de-rol, &c

VII

After dinner my Lord, in a wunnerful speech,
Gits up and thanks I for my trubble
But I bows to de pason insted o my Lord,
Fur my eyes dey begun to see double
And de ladies dey lääfed, an' on titterin seemed bent,
And into de drääin' room all on 'em went

Spoken—An' I gets up, an', ses I, "Here's arter ye, I beant agween to lose my sweetheart 'recly minit arter dinner" An' den wun o' dem dandy butterfly chaps asks me how long I'd been out o' de complexion o' wild beastes? 'I'll worry soon let ye know, muster dandy," ses I, "dat I beant a wild beast, nor yet a monkey an if dese be your cockneyfied fashions, I've had enuf on 'em, an' I'll be off to de country agen, where I can have a cheek by jowl for my life"

Sung—So widout biddin 'em good bye, to de country cum I
Tol-de-rol, &c

After a slumber of nearly seven years Kent, like a giant refreshed, awoke for deeds of "high emprize" The battle ground now chosen for a combat with England was Lord's As in the match previously mentioned, the changed list of names on the part of Kent is not undeserving of notice Another important feature not to be overlooked is the stir incident to the new style of bowling, which Mr Wills tried on at Marylebone, but which the authorities would not permit This excited the wrath of Mr Wills to such a degree, that he left the ground, and his place, by agreement, had to be filled up The loss of such a man at such a time caused a considerable amount of ill expression by the backers of his party, although in the end Kent defeated Marylebone signally As this match forms an epoch in the general history of cricket, and of that in Kent more particularly, the score in full is given

MARYLEBONE

	1st inn		2nd inn
R Lane, Esq , run out	66	b Sparks	8
F Nicholas, Esq , c Barnard	22	b Sparks	12
W Ward, Esq , b Ashby	38	c Jordan	4
E H Budd, Esq , not out	40	c Evans	0
C Barnett, Esq , c Sparks	4	st Barnard	1
Lord F Beauclerk, c Jordan	7	b Ashby	14
T Nicholl, Esq , st Barnard	4	c Barton	4
H Lloyd, Esq , c Knight	7	b Sparks	3
T Bache, Esq c Barnard	1	c Evans	1
T Vigne, Esq c Barnard	16	c Knight	0
B Aislabie, Esq , run out	0	not out	0
Byes	2	Byes	1
Total	207	Total	48

KENT

Jordan, st Vigne	86
Evans, st Vigne	8
Sparks run out	36
Hopper, b Budd	15
Ashby, c Ward	7
J Barnard, Esq , b Budd	28
E Knight, Esq c Vigne	11
W Deedes, Esq , b Beauclerk	30
W Barton, Esq , run out	21
J Deedes, Esq , c Nicholl	1
Buttersby, not out	13
Byes	3
Total	259

Ten days afterwards a "return" took place at Chislehurst, when Kent were declared victors by 149 runs In the month of June these parties were again confronted at Chislehurst, but the match was left unfinished more in favour of Kent than otherwise. From this period up to 1834, the best cricket was that cultivated by parish elevens, and many matches played between them exceeded by far some that assumed a higher position in the scale

Another and a very effectual organization of Kent may be recorded among the marvels of the period Something or somebody was wanting to concentrate the forces of the county Many of the matches called Kent *v* England, or *v* this, that, or another club or county, partook so largely of the composite order, that the time had now arrived to play after the good old fashion of county against county The residence of Fuller Pilch, at Town Malling, was opportune His functions were not those of a Glendower No He had but to plant the Kent standard in his new settlement to command a troop Aye, and what a troop soon flocked to it' Let the reader imagine six men all 6ft high Nor was the quality of the remainder less, although a few inches decreased in stature Let him fancy, too, an entire team of good bats, half-a-dozen bowlers, four wicket-keepers, and all good in the field, with an ample reserve when necessary, and he will then form some idea of the united strength of Kent, gathered merely from districts between the "Lathe of Scray" and the Weald The first match with Sussex, on Pilch's Ground, at Malling, proved adverse to Kent, as the choice of the team was not left entirely in the hands of parties best adapted for such a business Sussex won by 32 runs The revival, however, of first class cricket was an epoch in the history of Kent, and more particularly in this part of the county Now, to a passing traveller, the every-day life of West Malling would convey a very imperfect idea, if any, of the place when a great match was "on" The parish itself is limited to about 1300 acres, and the population at the time of this revival was little more than 1500 This number included a large admixture of the labouring classes The "town" has but one main street, of irregular breadth, without examples of colossal or ornate architecture If, however, a visitor to cricket happened to possess a taste for archæology, and wanted to stroll, he would find gratification in the inspection of the west front of the abbey—founded in 1099 by Gundulph, the then Bishop of Rochester,—which still remains an emblem of wanton spoliation and an object of grave reflection On ordinary occasions the business of the town partook, then as now, of a steady, sedate, if not slow character , the "early" adage was practised as a night and morning study Rarely, indeed, were the slumbers of the toiler disturbed by the freaks of the reveller, who

Wakes with mirth the drowsy ear of night

The scene changed wonderfully when cricket was the "go," for important matches absorbed every other thought—the town was astir from end to end Generally speaking, the visitors on foot would "trudge it nimbly" in order to get a sight of the great players before the match began There was nothing aristocratic about the carriage company, as most of the vehicular transit betokened the well-to-do tradesman or agriculturalist Then varied machines for conveying over rough as well as smooth roads were wheeled in rank and file by the side of a narrow pavement, while their horses occupied stalls provided by the "Bear," "Bull," "Swan," &c (incongruous animals). Those country cousins and others blessed with friends in the town fared well, for an ample stock of creature comforts was furnished, and on the greatest match of the year there was often much ado in their administration Departing time presented another stirring scene—everybody wanted to see the last ball bowled, and the same everybody wanted his horse out of the stable first Hence the unwonted stir and amusement incident thereto 'More haste, less speed" Sometimes the narrow outlets became half choked, and patience was found to be a great virtue Quiet, however, was not fully restored after the din and bustle of departure The green curtain rarely fell on the carnival at head-quarters till the church clock (the only public clock in the town) notified the expiration of another day Such were the customs at Malling, extending in unbroken succession for a period of seven years, and great were the sorrows and disappointments expressed by the cricket-loving public in and about this locality when the knell of dissolution sounded by the departure of Pilch to Canterbury.

It would far exceed the limits apportioned to this chapter to give even a fair sketch of the doings of Kent in the field during the time that Pilch and his powerful band were in their glory, and when Malling was the scene of great exploits. It was probably here that the first representative of Caxton appeared. The visit of Windsor from Gravesend was hailed as a necessity. In those days telegraph plates with bold figures were not in use at Malling, and people not caring to keep a score for themselves were again and again inquiring the state of the game. Windsor's press was therefore opportune. True, the type was thick and the paper thin, the names upon it often wrongly spelt, and the order of going in confused; the arithmetic puzzling, and the ink muddy, showing clearly that Windsor had no claims to the dignity of a "comp." of the first order. Yet, with all faults, these score papers were readily purchased, and doubtlessly many may be found at this day pasted in old books in commemoration of some important circumstance. It saved the scorers a great deal of trouble, and "Old Topper" especially much annoyance, for although uniformly very communicative on matters appertaining to cricket, it required considerable skill in the arts of persuasion to get at him during business hours on great occasions, for, figuratively speaking, on an approach, he would throw out his quills like a porcupine.

The influence of Pilch in matters appertaining to cricket may be easily conceived: his quiet, unpretending manners, and his well earned reputation, made him exceedingly popular. Neighbouring clubs profited largely by connection with him. Malling considered itself strong enough at one time to challenge the rest of Kent. Here its haughty spirit went before a fall. In parish matches the run of success was remarkably striking, and this was largely due to the care of foresight exercised in the arrangement. On this point some of the managing committee were extremely sensitive. Hence a comparatively quiet contest with Benenden, for instance, involved as much curiosity and interest to the real lover and judge of the game as one on a scale accompanied with "pomp and circumstance."

One match may be cited as very remarkable. Kent had not played England for three years, and it was resolved by the Marylebone Club to give Pilch a benefit. This occurred in the month of August, 1839. On account of the popularity of Pilch, and the quality of the match, the attendance to witness it was in proportion. The ground had not a foot to spare, being crowded to its utmost capacity. Previous to commencement of play the *savans* were perplexed in their choice for sides, so well were they balanced. At the close of an innings each fifteen runs marked the difference. Much surprise, however, accompanied the second innings of Kent. No less than three wickets fell in one over from the bowling of Redgate, and such wickets! Thus: Stearman from the first ball of the over, Alfred Mynn from the second; Pilch came and played the third ball, but the next bowled him. Redgate was half mad with ecstacy, and to the general mind Kent appeared to be in a hopeless condition. Clifford pulled up a little, though the total for such a team was regarded as ludicrously small. England's turn came, and so did Hillyer's. Only

79 runs were wanting to win; nothing for such batsmen commissioned to get them. The bowling of Hillyer proved quite equal to that of the Nottingham chief. In 26 overs and two balls (nine maidens) he got five wickets for 40 runs. As the match neared its close the interest became excessive, and when the tenth England wicket fell, and three runs were wanting to win, no shouting could possibly have been more hearty by the spectators generally; even the losers—those who "dropped their coin" —joined in, seeing, as cricketers, that Kent were entitled to honour for thus pulling the match "out of the fire."

KENT.

	1st inn.		2nd inn.
Hillyer, st Box, b Lillywhite	9	b Lillywhite	0
Stearman, c Grey, b Lillywhite	12	b Redgate	15
W. Mynn, Esq., c Cobbett, b Lillywhite	10	c and b Lillywhite	1
A. Mynn, Esq., b Lillywhite	11	b Redgate	0
Pilch, c Ponsonby, b Lillywhite	35	b Redgate	0
Wenman, c Box, b Lillywhite	37	b Lillywhite	8
C. G. Whittaker, Esq., b Cobbett	1	not out	0
Mills, c Box, b Lillywhite	9	b Lillywhite	12
Dorrinton, b Lillywhite	0	b Redgate	0
Clifford, not out	0	l b w, b Lillywhite	18
Adams, c and b Cobbett	10	b Redgate	6
Byes 3, w 4, n-b 4	11	Byes 2, w 2	4
Total	145	Total	64

ENGLAND.

	1st inn.		2nd inn.
Ganatt, b A. Mynn	5	c Dorrinton, b Hillyer	3
Guy, c Wenman, b A. Mynn	30	run out	10
Hon. E. H. Grimston, c Wenman, b A. Mynn	46	c Wenman, b Hillyer	0
Sewell, c Hillyer, b A. Mynn	4	b A. Mynn	1
Cobbett, c Hillyer, b A. Mynn	10	b A. Mynn	5
Jarvis, b Hillyer	9	b A. Mynn	7
Box, c Wenman, b Hillyer	3	c Stearman, b Hillyer	12
C. G. Taylor, c Hillyer, b A. Mynn	1	b Hillyer	3
Hon. F. Ponsonby, run out	1	run out	2
Redgate, b A. Mynn	5	not out	20
Lillywhite, not out	0	b Hillyer	0
Byes 12, w 4	16	Byes 12, w 2	14
Total	130	Total	77

On the 22nd of July, 1841, Sussex confronted Kent at Malling. A meeting of two supposed equal forces was by no means unattractive to the neighbourhood, although it was "a return" match to one played at Brighton early in the season, when Kent were winners by an innings and 16 runs. This triumph arose in a great measure from the successful batting of Pilch and Wenman, who scored 53 and 52 runs respectively. The totals of Sussex were 141 and 47 in their completed innings. Kent made 204 in one innings. The choice of innings fell to the lot of Sussex, who at once proceeded to the wickets, opposed to Mr. A. Mynn and Hillyer. The former bowled throughout, but the latter made way for Martingell in his twenty-eighth over This was the first appearance of Martingell in Kent On the other side seven bowlers were pressed into service, and during the match no less than twenty-one wide balls were called Kent won the match by six wickets, the scores being—Sussex, 129 and 69—total 198, Kent, 188 and 12 (four wickets)—total 200

A few days afterwards Kent fulfilled an engagement at Lord's to play England, a match noteworthy for the character of the bowling throughout In fact it has often been referred to as one of the best in this particular, that ever occurred On the part of England, Lillywhite bowled throughout, and on that of Kent, Mr Mynn and Hillyer did the like The score is worth preserving

KENT

	1st inn		2nd inn
Hillyer, run out	1	c Guy, b Littlewhite	0
Mills, b Redgate	9	b Lillywhite	0
Dorrinton, b Lillywhite	13	c and b Lillywhite	0
Pilch, b Lillywhite	10	not out	33
Wenman, b Redgate	5	c and b Cobbett	2
A Mynn, Esq, st Box, b Lillywhite	1	b Lillywhite	3
Adams, b Redgate	1	b Cobbett	15
W Mynn, Esq, c Sewell, b Lillywhite	6	b Lillywhite	2
C G Whittaker, Esq, c Guy, b Lillywhite	0	b Redgate	12
W de C Baker, Esq, c Sewell, b Lillywhite	3	l b w, b Lillywhite	20
Martingell, not out	0	st Box, b Lillywhite	2
Wide	5	Bye 1, l b 1	2
Total	54	Total	91

ENGLAND

	1st inn		2nd inn
Bayley, b A Mynn	4	b Hillyer	1
Sampson, c Baker, b Hillyer	0	not out	2
Sewell, c Mills, b A Mynn	0	b A Mynn	3
Guy, b Hillyer	4	run out	1
Hawkins, c and b Hillyer	7	b A Mynn	8
Good, b A Mynn	0	c and b Hillyer	2
C G Taylor, Esq, not out	4	b Hillyer	17
Redgate, c A Mynn, b Hillyer	2	b A Mynn	1
Box, b A Mynn	1	c and b A Mynn	3
Lillywhite c Pilch b Hillyer	2	run out	0
Cobbett, c Whittaker, b Hillyer	3	b A Mynn	4
Byes 3, w 1	4	Bye 1, n b 1	2
Total	31	Total	44

In the month of August following a kind of return match occurred on the Beverley Ground—now the county—at Canterbury The best eleven of Kent were not brought forward, and England won by 74 runs

Another feature of the period claims notice In the month of July, 1842, the Gentlemen of England met the Gentlemen of Kent at Lord's On each side was found some of the best amateur talent of the day The match was well contested, and England won by 45 runs Sir F Bathurst bowled 24 overs, and got six wickets in one innings of Kent On the other side Mr A Mynn bowled 26 overs and 2 balls, and obtained nine wickets The match was played annually for at least a dozen years

In the same month Kent were again found at Lord's to fight another battle with England. Both sides were very strong, but there were no extravagant scores, the highest being 35 Altogether 492 runs resulted from the match—Kent beat England by 50

Three scores of this match got into circulation at the time, but they did not agree strictly in some important particulars If the subjoined may be accredited with correctness now as then, it is sufficiently curious to deserves a reprint

KENT

	1st inn		2nd inn
Hillyer b Lillywhite	11	l b w, b Lillywhite	0
Cocker, b Fenner	11	b Lillywhite	5
N Felix, Esq , c Anson, b Lillywhite	13	b Lillywhite	12
Pilch, b Redgate	10	c Anson, b Redgate	21
C G Whittaker, Esq , b Lillywhite	13	not out	13
Wenman, b Lillywhite	14	b Lillywhite	6
A Mynn, Esq , b Fenner	11	b Lillywhite	33
Dorrinton, c Sewell, b Lillywhite	10	c Box, b Barker	14
W de C Baker, Esq , not out	11	c Good, b Barker	7
W Mynn, Esq , l b w, b Lillywhite	5	b Taylor	28
Adams, not out	1	b Lillywhite	2
Byes, 6, w 4	10	Byes 9, w 1	10
Total	120	Total	151

A still more remarkable victory awaited Kent on Harvey's Royal Grounds, Brighton, against Sussex, also in the month of July In each innings of Sussex the total stopped at 93, whereas Kent scored 185 in the first innings, and 2 without loss of wicket in the second Less than a month afterwards they sustained a marked defeat at Canterbury in their annual match with England, although they started well, no less than 278 runs being scored as the result of their first innings, towards which Mr Felix contributed 74, and Pilch 98 England's first innings was likewise wealthy in runs Total, 266, of which 80 were claimed by Guy, and 58 by Barker In the second innings of Kent there was but one double figure, viz , 17, and the total reached 44 only England won by nine wickets The Gentlemen of Kent started their annual match on the same ground on the following day This was chiefly remarkable for the immense number of extras, viz., 159, springing out of it Kent, as a county, were easily beaten by England a fortnight afterwards at Bromley This defeat was, however, fully avenged in the year 1843 at Lord's, when two strong teams were arrayed At the close of a first innings there was merely a difference of six runs, but so effective was the bowling of Mr Mynn in the second innings of England, that in 24 overs and two balls he obtained eight wickets, at an average of little more than five runs per wicket On the other side Dean got four wickets in 20 overs, though at a more costly average of runs Kent won by three wickets The next notable encounter was with Sussex, at Canterbury, about the middle of July in the same year, and as this introduces several names hitherto unnoticed, the full score is given

KENT.

	1st inn		2nd inn.
Adams, b Taylor	56	c Hawkins, b Lillywhite	12
Martingell, c Bushby, b Taylor	13	c Hawkins, b Dean	40
Dorrinton, c Dean, b Lillywhite	24	c G Picknell, b Dean	8
Pilch, c Box, b Lillywhite	2	b Lillywhite	27
Wenman, b Lillywhite	34	c Box, b Dean	4
A Mynn, Esq , c and b Lillywhite	24	k Dean	8
Hillyer, c Taylor, b Lillywhite	0	c Hawkins, b Lillywhite	6
W Mynn, Esq , b Lillywhite	8	b Lillywhite	2
E Bayley, Esq , c Sopp, b Dean	19	b Dean	23
J F Fagge, Esq , c Taylor, b Lillywhite	1	run out	7
C G Whittaker, Esq , not out	1	not out	24
Byes 4, w 1	5	Byes 9, w 5, n b 1	15
Total	187	Total	176

SUSSEX

	1st inn		2nd inn
R Picknell, c Hillyer, b Mynn	0	h w, b Mynn	13
G Picknell, c Bayley b Mynn	0	b Martingell	9
Dean, c Fagge, b Hillyer	9	b Hillyer	17
Box b Mynn	11	c Hillyer b Mynn	2
Hawkins, c Dorrinton, b Mynn	0	run out	3
Bushby, not out	38	c Bayley, b Minn	1
E Napper, Esq , l b w, b Mynn	3	c and b Mynn	20
Hammond, c Martingell, b Mynn	28	b Mynn	23
C G Taylor Esq , run out	7	c and b Mynn	0
Sopp, b Fagge	23	run out	9
Lillywhite, run out	4	not out	0
Byes 16, w 2	18	Byes	9
Total	141	Total	106

In the following year the foregoing was repeated at Canterbury, when Sussex won by a wicket, and within a fortnight Kent met Sussex at Box's Ground, Brighton, when another close result occurred, this time in favour of Kent by nine runs

The next match was of a hybrid character, for, although called Kent *v* England, it might with more propriety have been called Sussex, seeing that seven out of the eleven belonged to that county The scoring throughout the four days' play was not of the modern mammoth cast. Thus England, 98 and 87—total 185, Kent, 94 and 37—total 131

By this time the reader has lost sight of Malling, as all the matches of consequence in which Kent had concern took place at Canterbury, now the chosen future residence of Pilch Four years had elapsed since Notts and Kent met at Malling, when and where the home county were signally defeated A better fate awaited them in 1845, for, though Notts had in their team such redoubtables as Barker, Butler, Clarke, Guy, Parr, and Redgate—Kent, without the aid of Alfred Mynn, beat them by an innings and 20 runs. Thus: Notts, 47 and 67—total 114; Kent, 134. The match against England at Lord's shortly after ended in favour of England by 80 runs; and they were beaten, too, at Nottingham in July of the same year by eight wickets, as well as by Sussex a few days later at Tunbridge Wells. For a set-off mention must be made of another trial between these pet counties at Box's Ground in 1846, when Kent claimed the victory by 144 runs: this, too, despite the bowling of Wisden and Dean, now in the full blaze of their glory. Another curiosity demands attention. Just 100 years had elapsed since Kent first met England—at least sufficiently strong to attract the notice of any historian. On that occasion Kent won by a wicket.* A slight turn of the table at Lord's in July, 1846, made England winners by a wicket.

KENT.

	1st inn.		2nd inn.
Hillyer, c Guy, b Dean	3	c Guy, b Lillywhite	0
C. G. Whittaker, Esq., c Martingell, b Clarke	4	c and b Lillywhite	4
A. Mynn, Esq., b Dean	21	b Lillywhite	17
N. Felix, Esq., b Clarke	3	b Lillywhite	1
F. Pilch, run out	1	b Lillywhite	27
Adams, b Clarke	1	b Dean	2
Dorrinton, st Box, b Clarke	9	b Dean	2
E. Banks, Esq., c Lillywhite, b Clarke	10	l b w, b Dean	2
Martin, c Dean, b Lillywhite	21	c Guy, b Dean	2
L. H. Bayley, Esq., not out	11	not out	2
W. Pilch, b Lillywhite	0	b Lillywhite	1
Byes 5, w 2	7	Byes	6
Total	91	Total	66

ENGLAND.

	1st inn.		2nd inn.
Martingell, c Dorrinton, b Hillyer	1	b Mynn	2
Dean, b Mynn	3	not out	5
Box, b Mynn	7	run out	7
Parr, b Hillyer	0	b Adams	16
C. S. Taylor, Esq., c W. Pilch, b Mynn	16	c Bayley, b Hillyer	43
Guy, b Hillyer	5	c Bayley, b Hillyer	2
R. P. Long, Esq., c Whittaker, b Mynn	0	b Hillyer	1
Sewell, b Mynn	2	not out	2
Lillywhite, b Hillyer	8	c Hillyer, b Mynn	0
Cornell, run out	5	b Mynn	3
Clarke, not out	10	b Mynn	0
Byes 11, w 3	14	Byes 5, w 1	6
Total	71	Total	87

In 1847 Kent and Surrey met at Preston Hall, Aylesford, a village within three miles of Malling. In this match Willsher made his first appearance as a Kent county player, and although Mr. Felix arrayed himself on the Surrey side (being born at Camberwell), Kent won by 100 runs. The average number of runs per innings from the bat was about 73.

* See "Middlesex."

The year 1847 was on two accounts eventful Kent beat England at Lord's by seven wickets The match was promoted for the benefit of Mr Alfred Mynn, who had been before the public nearly twenty years, and during that time had gathered a host of admirers and friends too, and was just forty years old Those who really knew anything of the man went to work heart and soul to make the benefit a substantial rather than a nominal one Success followed

Two days after the close of the match just mentioned Kent met Sussex at Tunbridge Wells During the match 326 runs were scored, of which 206 were claimed by Kent, who were declared winners in consequence by 80 runs Another triumph followed a week later at Canterbury The chief incident connected with the proceedings of Kent in 1848 was the bowling of Hinkly against England at Lord's. He got sixteen wickets out of the twenty, viz, six in the first innings and *all* in the second England won the match by 55 runs

It should be mentioned that, on the occasion in question, Hinkly, nearly thirty years of age, made his first appearance at Lord's. He was a left-hand bowler, straight, but not very fast, and great things were expected of him Either from blighted circumstances or blighted hopes, Hinkly's career as a first-class man was prematurely checked Score of the England innings subjoined —

	1st inn		2nd inn
Clarke, b Hinkly	3	st Dorrinton, b Hinkly	10
Dean, c Dorrinton, b Hillyer	21	b Hinkly	2
Box, c Pilch b Hinkly	36	c Hillyer, b Hinkly	18
Guy, b Hinkly	2	not out	28
Parr, c Dorrinton, b Hinkly	24	b Hinkly	4
Sewell, c Adams, b Hinkly	3	b Hinkly	6
Wisden, c Hinkly, b Hillyer	5	c Adams, b Hinkly	0
O C Pell, Esq b Hillyer	10	c Hillyer, b Hinkly	2
R Kynaston, Esq b Hillyer	2	b Hinkly	0
Lillywhite, not out	3	st Dorrinton b Hinkly	0
Sir F Bathurst, b Hinkly	0	b Hinkly	0
Byes 6, w 5	11	Byes	4
Total	120	Total	74

The popularity of the peripatetic eleven under Clarke, and the corresponding financial benefit accruing to the parties concerned in making it so, had an effect upon the real talent of Kent. As a matter of course every man wished to make the best of his opportunities, and hence Kent was chiefly affected as regards matches at home But if this were an evil, a counteraction might be traced in the formation of good parish elevens Man is naturally an imitative being, and it was barely possible that all the fine play of the Kentish chieftains witnessed, with so much interest and anxiety, would prove a barren, profitless lesson In the absence of first-rate encounters, others of less pretence filled up the void Kent, like so many wandering stars, seemed to have no astronomer sufficiently gifted to constellate them

No doubt the hon sec (Mr Norton) had quite enough to do to keep them from being "snufted out" altogether Difficult indeed is the task of pleasing everybody All history proves this Woe is it, too, when "all men speak well of thee" The inference deducible from these facts is that the hon secretaryship of a county in the condition of Kent at this period was no sinecure What about a ground? That at Canterbury is "a screwed up corner of the county" The Crystal Palace? too many attractions to draw a paying company Tonbridge? a sleepy town, without a ground fit to play upon The "Wells?" a lawn little bigger than will serve for a forecourt Gravesend? much too confined for a grand match, and never abounding with "accommodation for travellers," who, if they by mistake fail to order a basket to be sent, may suffer grievously from want of food These interrogatories prove to some extent the unsettled condition of meeting places, and such being the case, it will be as well to take a long leap from the notice of the last important Kent match and give a *résumé* of the cricket played in 1869

KENT COUNTY MATCHES

In this list are included the Gentleman's county matches, being of quite as much importance as the others The "County," so called, played seven matches, won four, lost two, drawn one The Gentlemen's achievements claim attention

Gravesend, June 2 —Gentleman of Kent *v* Knickerbockers Two days Knickerbockers, 100 and 203 (six wickets), Kent, 219 Discontinued

Crystal Palace, June 10 —County of Kent *v* County of Surrey Surrey, 80 and 134—total 214, Kent, 204 and 11 (one wicket)—total 215. Kent won by nine wickets

Brighton, June 19 —County of Kent *v* County of Sussex Two days Sussex, 159 and 89—total 248, Kent, 204 and 45 (two wickets)—total 249 Kent won by eight wickets

Gravesend, July 1 —Gentlemen of Kent *v* Gentlemen of Buckinghamshire Two days Buckinghamshire, 327, Kent, 142 and 119—total 261 Buckinghamshire won by an innings and 66 runs

Crystal Palace, July 5 —County of Kent *v* County of Sussex (return) Two days Sussex, 121 and 96—total 217, Kent, 115 and 103 (three wickets)—total 218 Kent won by seven wickets

Tonbridge Wells, July 12 —County of Kent *v* County of Sussex Two days This was an "extra" match Kent, 116 and 304—total 420, Sussex, 152 and 118—total 270 Mr Thornton scored 124 in his second innings, among which were nine sixes

Tonbridge, July 22 —County of Kent *v* Nottinghamshire Three days Kent, 112 and 114—226, Notts, 251 The latter won by an innings and 25 runs Bignall, on the part of Notts scored 116 and was not out

Marlow, August 2 —Gentlemen of Kent *v* Gentlemen of Buckinghamshire (return) Two days Bucks, 169, Kent, 27 for three wickets Rain prevented any play on the first appointed day, and on the second the match was declared drawn

Canterbury, August 11 —M C C and Ground *v* County of Kent Three days Marylebone, 449, of which Mr W G Grace claimed 127, Kent, 203 and 158—total 361 On the third day rain fell heavily Marylebone won by an innings and 88 runs

Canterbury, August 14 —Gentlemen of Kent *v* I Zingari Last day of the "Canterbury week" Kent scored 345, towards which Lieut Scott contributed 126 I Z did not go in, as the day was far advanced

Nottingham, August 19 —County of Kent *v* Nottinghamshire (return) Three days Notts, 446, Kent, 52 and 113—total 165 (a man short throughout the match, as Willsher was too ill to play) Notts won by an innings and 281 runs

Brighton, August 26 —Gentlemen of Kent *v* Gentleman of Sussex Three days Sussex, 128 and 213—total 341, Kent, 102 and 240 for three wickets—total 342 Mr Thornton scored 156 and not out in the second innings of Kent, and Mr. Cotterell 76 and not out in the second innings of Sussex. Kent won by seven wickets.

Oval, August 26.—County of Kent *v.* County of Surrey. Three days. Kent, 152 and 284—total 436; Surrey, 224 and 77 (one wicket)—total 301. Drawn.

BATTING AVERAGES.

Name.	No. of Matches.	No. of Innings.	Most Runs in a Match.	Most Runs in an Innings.	How often Bowled.	Caught.	Run out.	Not out.	Stumped.	Total.	Average of Innings. Over.
Mr. C. R. Alexander.........	2	3	19	17	1	0	1	1	0	20	6-2
Bennett	8	15	51	50	5	6	1	2	1	217	14-7
Carroll	3	4	17	17	0	2	1	1	0	27	6-3
Mr. B. B. Cooper	5	8	83	83	1	4	2	1	0	183	22-7
Henty	8	14	37	37	2	6	2	4	0	98	7
Fryer	2	3	33	19	2	1	0	0	0	36	12
Mr. P. Hilton	2	3	11	11	0	3	0	0	0	20	6-2
Mr. Kelson	4	6	37	23	3	1	0	1	1	61	10-1
Mr. R. Lipscombe............	3	5	3	3	2	3	0	0	0	5	1
Marten	7	12	36	27	2	4	1	5	0	48	4
Mr. W. S. Norton............	4	8	47	45	3	4	0	1	0	140	17-4
Mr. C. J. Ottaway	2	3	62	62	3	0	0	0	0	113	37-2
Palmer	3	4	34	34	2	1	1	0	0	49	12-1
Payne............................	3	5	29	29	3	2	0	0	0	61	12-1
Mr. F. Penn	2	3	9	9	2	0	0	1	0	16	5-1
Mr. W. Penn	3	5	33	30	2	1	2	0	0	54	10-4
Rev. J. Pepys	2	3	77	77	1	1	0	0	1	131	43-2
Remnant	2	3	25	25	0	3	0	0	0	44	14-2
Mr. W. W. Rodger	5	9	23	23	4	4	0	0	1	73	8-1
Mr. C. I. Thornton	8	13	170	156	6	5	1	1	0	586	45-1
Mr. M. A. Troughton	6	9	44	27	4	3	0	1	1	118	13-1
Mr. E. A. White	7	12	45	34	4	7	0	1	0	223	18-7
Mr. L. A. White	5	9	33	24	3	3	3	0	0	86	9-5
Mr. J. T. Welldon	2	4	58	52	2	2	0	0	0	62	15-2
Willsher.........................	7	11	70	70	3	6	0	1	1	118	10-8
Mr. W. Yardley	3	6	44	39	3	2	0	1	0	96	16

The following played in one match: Lieut. Scott, Messrs. Booth, Crawford, Hynes, A. Lubbock, Musgrave, Noakes, J. P. Rodger, Trollope, Stokes, Tomson, &c.

A simple glance at this table reveals the fact that only one name mentioned hitherto among the Kentish celebrities appears—viz., Willsher, who had but just come out. Dorrinton died in 1848, Mr. A. Mynn and Hillyer in 1861. Mr. Felix had become a paralytic, Pilch and Wenman both grown old (born in 1803), Adams stiff jointed, and Hinkly worn out. In 1871 a match was promoted for the benefit of Willsher; but though many good names were arrayed on each side, it was not a county one. In the following year Kent and Surrey met at the Mote. This match was exceedingly well contested, and Kent won by ten wickets. The result was chiefly owing to Captains Renny-Tailyour and Fellowes, of the Royal Engineers, stationed at Chatham.

Although the "Mote" is mentioned for the first time in these pages, it demands remark, for during the long period of unsettlement, Kent, by the kindness of the Earl of Romney, were allowed the use of a piece of ground in his park. Hence arose the Mote Park Club, composed chiefly of residents at Maidstone. A more charming spot it would be difficult to select or to gaze upon in the height of the season, while the surroundings to a great extent call to mind the poet's picture of

> A lovely valley
> Crowned by high headlands, where the Druid oak
> Stands like Caractacus in act to rally
> His host, with broad arms, 'gainst the thunder stroke;
> And from beneath its boughs are seen to sally
> The dappled foresters.

Doubtlessly the cricketers of Kent feel themselves under great obligations—in fact they clearly show it in one way, that is by keeping the ground in such condition that it may challenge the severest eye and most inveterate complainer—*Esto perpetua.*

As the third quarter of the century drew towards a close, it was considered politic to elect Lord Harris as President of the County Club. He had proved himself to be a fine player, and in him was perceived a fitting person for the office, though very young. In 1875 Kent was not successful, seeing that in nine matches during the season they lost six. This, however, did not in the least degree diminish the ardour for future conflicts, which, it is hoped and believed, the "whirligigs of time" will ere long turn to better account.

The subjoined analysis of the batting applies only to matches between county and county, and does not include that between the Colts or the one at Canterbury with the Marylebone Club.

BATTING AVERAGES.

Name.	No. of Matches.	No. of Innings.	Most Runs in a Match.	Most Runs in an Innings.	How often Bowled.	Caught.	Run out.	Stumped.	Not out.	Total.	Average per Innings. Over.
Mr. C. Absolom	4	8	80	63	4	3	0	1	0	128	16
Collins	2	3	20	20	3	0	0	0	0	22	7–1
Draper	4	7	28	28	3	3	0	1	0	53	7–4
Mr. W. Foord-Kelcey	3	6	17	12	3	1	0	0	2	42	7
George	4	7	2	2	2	1	0	0	0	4	4
Lord Harris	8	14	110	92	6	7	0	0	1	454	32–6
Hearne	5	9	4	4	7	2	0	0	0	12	1–3
Henty	3	5	15	14	1	3	0	0	1	21	4–1
Hickmott	2	4	7	6	4	0	0	0	0	8	2
Mr. F. Mackinnon	2	3	66	66	2	1	0	0	0	102	34
G. McCanlis	5	9	55	42	4	5	0	0	0	90	10
Palmer	4	7	14	14	4	2	1	0	0	37	5–2
Mr. F. Penn	7	12	83	79	4	5	1	1	1	328	27–4
Mr. W. Penn	3	5	16	16	2	1	2	0	0	21	4–1
Rumsey	3	5	20	13	0	4	0	0	1	20	4
Mr. E. Stokes	2	3	12	7	1	1	0	0	1	14	4–2
Mr. F. E. Street	3	6	18	12	3	2	0	1	0	21	3–3
Mr. V. K. Shaw	2	3	54	54	2	0	0	0	1	103	34–1
Willis	5	9	28	20	5	4	0	0	0	76	8–4

THE CANTERBURY WEEK.

WHAT extraordinary ideas and marvellous associations of thought cluster around the mention of this ancient city taken merely from a political and ecclesiastical stand point What centuries of time have rolled away since—as historians say—"Canterbury was the capital of the kingdom of Kent, and the seat of its kings" The locality abounds also with evidences of spirit-stirring events and the traveller journeying from almost any point to this centre will find abundant food for contemplation on his way The conflict of Lear with his daughters, described by Shakespeare; the exploits of the Roman juvenile patrician Julius Cæsar, the phlegmatic cunning of Hengist, the installation of St Augustine, the priestcraft of Thomas à Becket, the hundred thousand devotees who, in fifteen days, came on pilgrimage to his shrine; the munificence of Ralph de Born, who, on his installation to the Priory of St Augustine, invited six thousand guests to partake of his hospitality, and the poetic fervour of entertainment with which Chaucer led, from the Tabard of Southwark (now demolished)—

> Wele nine and twenty in a cumpany
> Of sundrie folk, by aventure yfall
> In felaship, and pilgrimes wer they all,
> That toward Canterbury wouldin ride,
> The holy blisful martyr for to seke

Pilgrims in groups quite as large, flock hither in the bright reign of Victoria as in the gloomy times of the Tudors. But how widely different the principle of actuation! One was to bow down to carved images, hear cowled monks chaunt solemn requiems, and seek heaven by the renunciation of all earthly enjoyments, the other to enjoy a grand exercise both of mind and body—to gaze upon the glorious outspread of the fruitful hill and valley, and sing a hymn of gratitude and cheerfulness which, according to the poet Addison, is "the best offered to the Divinity'

As a rule, few cities keep pace with the on-growth of commercial towns; and it has been frequently said that a guide-book printed ages ago would in a great measure serve the purposes of a pilgrim of the present day. To some extent such is true with respect to the metropolitan see of England This is somewhat strange when the facilities of travel have of late years served the purposes of change and improvement Most of the streets are narrow and sinuous, but the majority of them possess some rare relic of great architectural antiquity, unheeded by the ordinary traveller in consequence of defacement through the accumulated grime and soot of ages, to say nothing of form and feature gradually eaten out by the tooth of time To antiquarians of the severe school, abundant interest is nevertheless afforded, and their occasional visits create a passing notice, but the Canterbury

Week awakens a feeling of a very different kind The ordinary silence and dulness vanish at the approach of the deities of cricket The streets, very composite in their architectural order, all give signs of uniformity in their ideas of welcome to their Thespian and athletic visitors No wand of the magician could change the aspect of things more effectually than such a visit The cricket ground is situated about a mile—perhaps less—from the centre of the city, and the going thereto is charming and picturesque In the city itself the usual silence and dulness give way for one week in the year to bustle in the day time and revelry at night, when

> Rigour now is gone to bed
> And Advice with scrupulous head,
> Strict Age and sour Seventy,
> With their grave saws, in slumber lie
> We that are of purer fire,
> Imitate the starry quire,
> Who in their nightly watchful spheres
> Lead in swift round the months and years
> By dimpled brook and fountain brim,
> The Wood-Nymphs, deck'd with daisies trim,
> Their merry wakes and pastimes keep
> What hath night to do with sleep?—*Milton*

This theme, though a very tempting one, must here, for a while at least, give way to a few facts connected with the origin of the Canterbury Week In the year 1839 Messrs Felix and Mynn, two really great representatives of the game for Kent, appeared for the first time at Canterbury in a match between the Beverley and Chilston Clubs Being confined by arrangement to a day's play, it was left unfinished The "return" also shared the same fate, although Beverley, which had Mr Felix for its given man, seemed on the occasion to be much the stronger side These and other contests were continued up to 1842, when the first "Grand Cricket Week" was proclaimed with two matches, viz—Kent *v* England, and the Gentlemen of Kent *v* Gentlemen of England The first commenced on Monday, the 1st of August, and lasted three days, the second continued until Saturday The scores were as follows —

KENT.

	1st inn.		2nd inn
Adams, c Ponsonby	12	c Lillywhite	7
W Mynn, Esq, c Box	21	b Dean	0
Hillyer, st Box	3	c Fenner	8
Pilch, c Dean	98	c Box	0
N Felix, Esq, c Box	74	c Dean	0
A Mynn, Esq, c Fenner	27	c Hawkins	3
Wenman, c Fenner	0	c Fenner	0
Dorrinton, b Lillywhite	15	c Lillywhite	0
G Whittaker, Esq, c Dean	3	c Fenner	2
E Bayley, Esq not out	5	not out	17
W Barker, Esq, b Lillywhite	3	c Ponsonby	3
Byes	17	Byes	4
Total	278	Total	44

ENGLAND

	1st inn		2nd inn
Barker, st Wenman	58	not out	29
Fenner, b Hillyer	1	not out	19
Box, c A Mynn	22		
Guy, b Hillyer	80		
Good, b Mynn	17	b Hillyer	0
Butler, b Mynn	5		
Hawkins, c Baker	15		
Sewell, c Dorrinton	19		
Hon F. Ponsonby, b Hillyer	26		
Lillywhite, run out	1		
Dean, not out	0		
Byes, &c	22	Byes 9, w 1	10
Total	266	Total	58

From the above it will be seen that Kent lost by nine wickets, and from the following that the Kent side were winners by 173 runs The scores are very deficient in details, but they are here faithfully transcribed from the secretary's books —

GENTLEMEN OF KENT

	1st inn		2nd inn
W Mynn, Esq , c Boudier	9	run out	1
A Mynn, Esq , b Craven	24	b Craven	39
N Felix, Esq , b Mundy	48	b Craven	61
E Bayley, Esq , b Craven	2	b Mundy	12
J Parker, Esq , c F Ponsonby	12	run out	14
C G Whittaker, Esq , run out	0	run out	23
W de C Baker, Esq , c Kirwan	10	leg before wicket	20
F. Fagge, Esq , not out	21	run out	17
C Harenc, Esq , b Craven	5	st Anson	6
H Jenner, Esq , b Thackeray	1	not out	9
W Baldock, Esq , b Craven	6	c Mundy	10
Byes, &c	47	Byes, &c	42
Total	185	Total	254

GENTLEMEN OF ENGLAND

	1st inn		2nd inn
Captain Mundy, b Harenc	8	b Mynn	13
W Kirwan, Esq , c Fagge	18	run out	8
Hon R Grimston, run out	2	b Harenc	5
C Boudier, Esq , b Harenc	16	not out	13
Hon F Ponsonby, b Harenc	11	b Mynn	19
R Kynaston, Esq , b Mynn	1	b Mynn	16
T A Anson Esq , b Mynn	8	b Fagge	9
T Craven, Esq , run out	9	b Mynn	0
F Thackeray, Esq , run out	9	b Whittaker	3
R W Keate, Esq , b Harenc	1	b Harenc	11
Hon S Ponsonby, not out	3	b Mynn	13
Byes, &c	26	Byes &c	44
Total	112	Total	154

"It was," says Mr Davey, "on the occasion in question that the first of a series of amateur performances was given in the old and time-honoured temple of the drama in Orange-street Various objections were raised at first to this kind of entertainment, but the matter was taken in hand vigorously by the Hon F. Ponsonby, Mr Charles Taylor and other gentlemen of histrionic as well as cricketing talent, and the evening performances soon became as popular as those during the day The patronage given to both by the leading and influential families of East Kent gave such a tone to their characters and stability to their foundations that they soon became incorporated with the notable facts of the county For several years in unbroken succession the same matches were continued with but so little variation in the composition of the teams that it is scarcely necessary to go into detail. In the year 1850, however, several fresh faces appear on the scene, and the contests are sufficiently close to render a few particulars in the way of a score worthy of being reproduced. The first match was played at Lord's, in July, and the return formed the chief feature in the Canterbury Week" Score

KENT

	1st inn		2nd inn
Adams, c Chatterton, b Day	11	b Day	8
W Pilch, c Chatterton, b Day	10	c Bathurst, b Day	11
E Marten, b Wisden	4	st Box, b Clarke	20
F Pilch, b Wisden	49	b Wisden	0
Martingell, b Wisden	4	c and b Wisden	8
A Mynn, Esq, b Bathurst	7	b Wisden	5
N Felix, Esq, c Box, b Day	12	c Bathurst, b Day	1
W de C Baker, Esq, b Wisden	20	c Box, b Clarke	15
Clifford, b Clarke	2	b Clarke	0
Hillyer, b Clarke	1	b Wisden	1
Hinkly not out	2	not out	1
Bye 1, l-b 4, w 1, n-b 1	7	Byes 3, l-b 4, n-b 1	8
Total	129	Total	78

ENGLAND

	1st inn		1st inn
Chatterton, st Clifford, b Hillyer	5	c Adams, b Hillyer	11
J M Lee, Esq, c Martingell, b Hinkly	2	b Martingell	3
W Nicholson, Esq, c Adams, b Hillyer	4	st Clifford, b Hillyer	7
Box, b Hinkly	0	b Mynn	33
Parr, not out	53	not out	14
Guy, b Martingell	16	not out	6
Wisden, b Martingell	8		
J Lillywhite, run out	21		
Clarke, c and b Martingell	7		
Day, b Martingell	0		
Sir F Bathurst, c W Pilch, b Hillyer	4		
Bye 1, l b 6 ...	7	Byes 4, l b 3	7
Total	127	Total	81

On reference to the above it will be seen that a marked improvement had taken place in the style of scoring, and also that the difference between the respective totals was very small, although England won eventually by six wickets. In the return match England were the winners by 15 runs. Particulars as understated:—

ENGLAND.

	1st inn.		2nd inn.
Wisden, c Martingell, b Hillyer	6	c Adams, b Martingell	24
Clarke, run out	28	b Hillyer	6
Guy, b Martingell	18	c Hillyer, b Hollands	0
Box, b Adams	16	b Adams	12
Parr, st Wenman, b Adams	57	c Felix, b Adams	5
C. Hoare, Esq., run out	2	b Adams	5
Caffyn, c Martingell, b Hollands	13	b Hillyer	31
W. Nicholson, Esq., c Adams, b Hollands	3	c and b Hollands	5
J. Walker, Esq., c Hollands, b Adams	0	run out	5
H. Fellows, Esq., not out	6	c Mynn, b Hollands	15
Day, b Holland	3	not out	1
Byes 3, l-b 1	4	Byes 1, l-b 4, w 2	7
Total	156	Total	116

KENT.

	1st inn.		2nd inn.
Martin, b Wisden	0	b Fellows	1
Adams, b Clarke	0	c Walker, b Wisden	20
W. Pilch, b Clarke	5	b Fellows	1
Hollands, c Caffyn, b Clarke	0	b Fellows	0
F. Pilch, b Fellows	29	b Fellows	51
W. de C. Baker, Esq., b Clarke	0	b Fellows	0
Wenman, run out	30	b Fellows	29
N. Felix, Esq., b Wisden	5	b Fellows	3
Martingell, not out	8	b Clarke	5
A. Mynn, Esq., b Fellows	1	not out	16
Hillyer, c Nicholson, b Clarke	7	c Wisden, b Clarke	16
Byes 8, l-b 3, w 3	14	Byes 3, l b 4, w 5	12
Total	94	Total	163

The Gentlemen's match lasted until Saturday, when the county won with one wicket to spare. "This victory was mainly due to the spirited and, at the same time, clever batting of the Hon. E. V. Bligh, who carried out his bat, having seen four wickets down. Mr. Bligh's last few hits were hailed with great cheers; and at the finish, when the hon. gentleman threw his bat spinning in the air, the welkin rung." * "In the following year," says the same author, "the grand week commenced with brilliant weather; and although the Great Exhibition excursion trains took away many who would otherwise have assembled at the favourite August trysting-place for Kentish lasses and lads, the Canterbury ground was honoured with large assemblages of the county families and country visitors. The Kent and England match terminated early enough to admit of an innings each between I Z. and Eleven Gentlemen of East Kent. The Wanderers scored 204 runs in three

* "Record of the Old Stagers," p. 66.

hours, but the Kentish horse "came down" woefully. Nine wickets fell for six runs. Only 44 were totalled, of which Capt. Dickens claimed 30, and Mr. Crosse 7.

So slight was the variation in the cast of the programme for 1852, that little can be said except the feebleness of Kent exhibited throughout the match. Willsher scored 33 in his double innings, Fuller Pilch 26, Wenman 25, Adams 19, Martingell 12, and Mr. Alfred Mynn 10. The totals were 112 and 52. On the England side Guy made 49, Box 47, and Parr 42 in a single innings, and England won the match by an innings and 2 runs.

At this period it was evident that Kent were no match for England. On the 15th of August the latter commenced an innings which resulted in 324 runs. No less than nine bowlers were tried. On the other side Clarke and Wisden went through the double innings without being changed. The former claimed seven of the Kent wickets, the latter eight. England won by an innings and 179 runs. Years elapsed before these elevens even-handed were again brought together, and the interest in local cricket was to a considerable extent diminished in consequence. The Gentlemen's Match, before referred to, which had formed a feature of the week, was for some time discontinued, owing to the general decline of talent in the county. Here, perhaps, it may be well to give a list of the leading match of the week up to last year, from which it will be seen that many devices were resorted to for the purpose of keeping the business agoing. Great men figured in the foundation of this so called institution, and considering the lapse of three and thirty years the wonder is that it has survived so well. There must have been some influence at work, unseen, yet powerful: the pulse of last year beat with the strength of youth—at least, so said the exchequer. It is to be hoped, however, that this was not the result of unhealthy stimulants. Men, aye heroes, decay by their warrings with time, and it is not easy to replace the man for the situation. Where, it may be asked, is to be found the counterpart of the hon. sec., who guided the destinies of the week by his skill, judgment, and foresight, and who promises to tread the stage as some of the members of the foundation did, and still can do. These are matters deserving deep thought, for upon such aids and such men depend the future popularity, permanence, and prosperity of the institution. Two days out of the six are always considered "great," the first affords the bulk of the community an opportunity of real out-of-door enjoyment. There cannot be a sweeter atmosphere than that which pervades the St. Lawrence Ground, nor a prettier piece of scenery. On cricket days it is usually marked out by flagstaffs bearing bright-coloured pennants, interspersed with booths, tents, and marquees. On Thursday, usually termed the Ladies' Day, a spectacle of a somewhat different character presents itself—one altogether unique. Brilliant assemblages of the fair sex, resplendent in costumes of marvellous chromatic combinations, occupy the mossy declivity, and give to it the appearance of beds of tulips or parterres of flowers. An air of solid comfort is also imparted to the double row of carriages which betoken the presence of the wealth and rank of the neighbourhood. In fact the scene is a reflex of the olden and golden period when all social grades were not distinguished by so broad a line that contact becomes the thing next to impossible. Although there may occasionally be heard the boisterous laugh and the chat of merriment, there is a total absence of the ribald jest and the practical joke The humblest visitor, in fact, seems to study how best to cultivate that spirit of enjoyment in which the element of discord or offence has the least chance of entering The modern school of thought is in favour of an orchestra, although in times gone by, good cricketers would not have felt themselves flattered by the squeak of the wrynecked fife and the gruntings of a contrabasso

SUMMARY OF THE MATCHES FROM THE COMMENCEMENT

1842.—Kent *v* England England won by nine wickets
1843—Kent *v* England Kent won by nine wickets
1844—Kent *v* England England won by 52 runs
1845—Kent *v* England. England won by 31 runs
1846.—Kent *v* England Kent won by an innings and 3 runs
1847—Kent *v*. England. Kent won by three wickets
1848—Kent *v*. England Kent won by ten wickets
1849—Kent *v* England Kent won by 206 runs.
1850—Kent *v* England. England won by 15 runs.
1851—Kent *v* England. England won by three wickets.
1852—Kent *v* England England won by an innings and two runs.
1853—Kent *v* England England won by an innings and 179 runs
1854.—Kent *v* England England won by seven wickets
1855.—Kent and Surrey *v*. England Kent and Surrey won by 8 runs
1856—Kent and Sussex *v* England Kent and Sussex won by six wickets
1857—Kent *v*. Marylebone Club and Ground Marylebone won by 30 runs
1858—Kent *v* England. England won by five wickets
1859—North of England *v* The South South won by 90 runs
1860.—England *v* Sixteen of Kent Kent won by an innings and 48 runs.
1861.—Fourteen of Kent *v* England Kent won by 54 runs
1862.—Fourteen of Kent *v* England Kent won by 170 runs *
1863—Thirteen of Kent *v* England England won by 25 runs
1864—Thirteen of Kent *v* England England won by an innings and 83 runs

* One circumstance connected with "this" week claims notice, it was the brilliant success of Mr E M Grace in the match, M C C *v* Gentlemen of Kent, when he played as an "emergency," and upon which occasion he could hardly have been accused of egotism had he used Cæsar's quotation—"Veni, vidi, vici"—for, after playing one of the finest innings on record, 192 (not out), his prowess as a bowler was equally tested, by his taking the whole ten wickets of his opponents in their second innings For his batting exploit he was rewarded on the spot by Lord Sefton, on the part of the M C C. Mr Grace has now become the recipient, at the hands of the Hon Spencer Ponsonby, of the identical "leathern sphere" with which he did such good service, handsomely mounted on an ebony stand The ball bears an inscription on a silver plate to this effect—"With this ball, presented by the M C C to E M Grace, he got every wicket in the second innings in the match played at Canterbury, August 14 and 15, 1862 Gentlemen of Kent *v* M C C, for whom he played as an 'emergency,' and in which, going in first, he scored 192, not out"

1865.—North of England *v.* The South. South won by 27 runs.
1866.—South of the Thames *v.* North of the Thames. North won by ten wickets.
1867.—South of the Thames *v.* North of the Thames. North won by 117 runs.
1868.—South of the Thames *v.* North of the Thames. North won by 58 runs.
1869.—North *v.* South. South won by eight wickets.
1870.—North *v.* South. Unfinished. South had four wickets to fall.
1871.—North *v.* South. South won by 100 runs.
1872.—North *v.* South. North by an innings and 46 runs.
1873.—North *v.* South. South won by seven wickets.
1874.—Kent and Gloucestershire *v.* England. Kent and Gloucestershire won by 54 runs.
1875.—Kent and Gloucestershire *v.* England. Kent and Gloucestershire won by six wickets.
1876.—
1877.—
1878.—
1879.—
1880.—

Another fact is worthy of remark. At the last match there were among the spectators some who were present and took part in the early ones, and, though unable to display their cunning either behind or before the wickets, had vivid recollections of bygone times, and could "babble of green fields" to the delight and edification of many a listening group.

A few epilogues spoken in the Theatre have been selected—not perhaps the best specimens—merely to give an idea of their general characters. Were the whole series produced they would make a book with "something" in it.

On Monday, Aug. 1, and on Thursday, Aug. 4, 1842,
COLMAN'S COMEDY
OF
THE POOR GENTLEMAN,
WAS PLAYED WITH THE FOLLOWING CASTE:

Sir Charles Cropland	C. Ellison, Esq.
Lieutenant Worthington	Tom Taylor, Esq.
Sir Robert Bramble	M. G. Bruce, Esq.
Frederick Bramble	C. G. Taylor, Esq.
Corporal Foss	C. G. Bentinck, Esq.
Doctor Ollapod	Captain W. L. Y. Baker.
Humphrey Dobbins	Hon. Spencer Ponsonby.
Farmer Harrowby	T. Anson, Esq.
Stephen Harrowby	Hon. F. Ponsonby.
Valet	F. Thackeray, Esq.
Miss Lucretia Mactab	Mrs. Nisbett.
Emily Worthington	Miss Jane Mordaunt.

On the first evening a prologue, written by Mr. Tom Taylor, was spoken by that gentlemen, dressed in cricketing costume, with a bat in his hand:—

[*The speaker is carried on, struggling, by three men, who disappear, leaving him in astonishment.*]

Hearing they played to-night in the cause of cricket,
I thought I'd come and see 'um—that's the ticket!
[*Producing a ticket for the play.*]
But scarcely had I reached the play-house door,
When three chaps rushed upon me with a roar.
"We've found a Prologue! Here, you sir," says one,
"Just clear your throat, shoulder your bat, and on!"
"On! where?" says I. "Why, on the stage at once!"
And here they've left me, looking like a dunce,
To speak a Prologue—Heaven knows what upon.
[*After a pause.*]
Well, I suppose I must talk now I'm on:
Cricket's the only thing I know a bit about.
Ten years my shins and knuckles have been hit about!
But, hollo! who are those I see down there?
[*Recognising the Players in the pit.*]
Pilch, Lillywhite, and Fenner—I declare!
How are ye all? Where men like you assemble
It's not a little that shall make me tremble.
While I stand here as champion of cricket,
You mind your fielding—I'll keep up my wicket.
You will stand by me? Never mind my county;
Cricketers are all brothers; such I count ye.
Your cricketer no cogging practice knows,
No trick to favour friends or cripple foes;
His motto still is "May the best man win."
Let Sussex boast her *Taylor*, Kent her *Mynn*.
Your cricketer, right English to the core,
Still loves the man best he has licked before;
Besides in Kent, who would a cricketer fear?
Wickets you know are *planted* and grow here;
Bats come up ready made, and *Balls* (just try 'em),
It's quite a pleasure to be *ripped up* by 'em.
Yet, 'tis a nervous task—for *Umpires* rear
On every side official brows severe,
Enthroned, of course, beyond appeal or doubt,
Whose lightest word may *put* our best man *out*.
Still, tempering duty with good humour, say
To-night at least that you *admire our play*.
We'll strive our hardest to keep up the ball,
Make a good *draw* and with no *slips* at all;
We promise you that no long stops to-night
Shall tire your patience, or your gall excite;
And, *though our best man's arm be out of joint*,*
Despite his splints he'll try and make a point.

* Alluding to C. G. Taylor, Esq., who, owing to a hurt received some weeks before whilst playing at cricket, acted with his arm in splints and a sling.

Then let one voice from boxes, gallery, pit,
Proclaim, unanimous, "A slashing hit"
And should we make to-night the *hit* we seek,
Remember that our *run* will last a week

THE CANTERBURY SETTLEMENT

An Original Prologue, written expressly by John Noakes, Esq, August, 1850

At the conclusion of the "Unfinished Gentleman," Bill Downey steps forward —

BILL DOWNEY —And now the Epilogue! We keeps a poet—
His business is to let the public know it
So serve it out—proceed—turn ahead—go it!

POET (T Taylor, Esq) —An Epilogue? Oh, no, for many reasons—
I've made eight epilogues in as many seasons,
My muse is threadbare—I'm at my wits' end

LORD TOTTERLY —You hadn't very far to go, my friend

POET (*touching his head*) —
Ah! here in coveys once ideas lay,
And now I can't flush one, beat it as I may
Dry as a chip! there's nothing can inspire me,
Grace cannot charm (*to Miss Mordaunt*), and loveliness can't fire me (*to Miss Marston*),
Archness can't make me arch (*to Mrs Wigan*)—fun, drive me funny (*to Mrs Caulfield*)

MISS MORDAUNT —Do something, please

MISS MARSTON — Oh! do for love!

MRS WIGAN (*significantly*) — Try money!

HON. S PONSONBY (*with a folded bill* in his hand*) —
Oh! here's a lark, I've (*all crowd round*)—Hands off there, don't thieve it—
I've an idea

MRS WIGAN — You? I don't believe it

HON S PONSONBY —Haven't I though? for us express 'tis sent,
Look here! (*unfolds poster*) "The Canterbury Settlement"
Don't you see?—'Settlement"—Eh?—"Canterbury"
Now isn't it a good idea?

POET — Very.

SIR CHARLES COLDSTREAM —It may be good, but then there's nothing in it

HON S PONSONBY —Pooh! 'tis an Epilogue ready made (*makes an effort to begin*)

MRS WIGAN — Begin it

HON S PONSONBY —Oh, no!—the ladies first

MRS WIGAN — Well, then, I will,
My theme's to be the heading of this bill
I have it now—yes, by your eight years' aid
Our "Canterbury Settlement" is made.
As the poor emigrant 'neath alien skies
Deplores the severance of household ties,
Faces a future dark with doubt and toil,
And strikes a timid spade in virgin soil—

* This was the poster of the promoters of "The Canterbury Settlement," to be founded in New Zealand, inviting the attention of emigrants and describing the prospects &c

So histrionic emigrants came we,
Eight years ago, to tempt our destiny,
And doubtful how you'd view the daring move,
Felt that your coldness might a settler prove
MISS MORDAUNT —But, as the emigrant—time moving on—
Finds new-formed ties replace those dear ones gone,—
Calls back the thoughts that wont o'er sea to roam,
And slowly out of strangeness made a home,—
So for our "Canterbury Settlement" have we
Found a home here—a home long may it be,—
And may next year, new faces though it bring,
Still bear the same kind welcome on its wing

An original epilogue spoken by "Members of the Smith Family" Written by Tom Taylor, Esq , 1851

MR OOM (*in the boxes, as if to himself*) —
They're coming to the tag—it's time to rise—
(*Gets up and addresses the house*)
Do, pray, allow me to apologise
MRS WIGAN (*with indignant surprise*) —
Ladies and gentlemen, 'tis not to *you*,
But *us*, that an apology is due
You (*to Oom*) might have waited till they dropped the curtain
MR OOM (*deprecatingly*) —
Pray, Ma'am—you'll own that I am right, I'm certain—
I was but going to request our friends
To keep their seats when the performance ends,
To hear the epilogue
MRS WIGAN — Epilogue ! Why ! Who ?
HON S PONSONBY —Eh ! Have you got it ? (*To Miss Cathcart*)
MISS CATHCART — No, not I—have you ? (*To F Ponsonby*)
HON F PONSONBY —Not I
MRS WIGAN — Bless me, 'tis the first time I've heard—
MR OOM —You don't say so ?
MRS WIGAN — I do, upon my word
MR OOM —I must apologise Where's Mr Noakes ?
MR BENTINCK (*from the orchestra*) —He wouldn't do it—swears he's out of jokes,
Declares that he used up in our last season
The very last dregs of his rhyme and reason
MR OOM —But this year there's so large a choice of topic
MRS WIGAN —Industrial !
MR ELLISON — Social !
HON F PONSONBY — Sporting !
HON S PONSONBY — Philosophic !
MR OOM —The Papal Tithes Bill !
MRS WIGAN — The Crystal Palace !
MR OOM —It cannot be stupidity, but malice,
Induces Noakes—I never liked the rogue—
To leave us in a fix—*sans* epilogue
What will our foreign friends—
MR BALDWIN (*from the pit as a Frenchman*) —Ne vous fachez pas
Je vais vous tirer vite du l'embarras—

Je suis Français—Je viens de l Exposition,
Permettez donc qu'avec votre bonne permission—
MR OOM —Pardon, Monsieur, but English I should say—
MR BALDWIN —Ah! c'est ici qu'on ne parle pas Français!
Den I shall improvise—
CAPTAIN DE BATHE (*as an Italian in a private box*) —Ecco, Signore!
Eccome! Anch'io son Improvvisatore,
Voglio cantar l'Epilogo—con brio (*strikes chord on the guitar*)
MR OOM —English, my dear sir
CAPTAIN DE BATHE — Basta, caro mio!
O Inghilterra!
MR TAYLOR (*as German in the slips*) —Nehmen Sie mein hut!
So will ich sprechen—
Mr. OOM — English, sir!
MR TAYLOR — Sehr gut
Lass mir speak diesen Epilog—zu hand
Hier bin ich von dem Deutschen Vaterland!
MRS WIGAN —German, Italian, French! they'll ne'er be able
To make out anything of such a Babel,
Rather than leave you with this piebald lot
To make an Epilogue in Polyglot—
Come ladies [*enter ladies*], if we boast not manly lungs,
Let's show that English women still have tongues
We need not French, Italian, German, Russ,
Chinese or Hottentot, to speak for *us*,
Although I'd rather any task should fall on us—
Rather for any other speech you'd call on us—
Than for a leave taking, which every season
Makes still more difficult, for this good reason—
That as each year your kindness grows more kind
Each parting leaves a new regret behind
MISS CATHCART —New to these boards—to these kind friends unknown,
So pleasantly with me the week has flown,
When I would say "Farewell," there's something here (*puts hand on heart*),
Insists on adding "till this time next year"
MRS WIGAN – There now—the silly girl is going to cry,
The shortest way's the best—Good bye! Good bye!

At the close of "Autumn Manœuvres" in 1872 an original epilogue by W Dalby (O S) was spoken It terminated with Victory, Genius of Kent, and Genius of O S

BRITANNIA (Mrs Stephens) —The honour of Britannia's flag will be
Safe in thy hand, brave General G C B
(*Hands flag Trumpet*)
GENIUS OF KENT (Miss M Haydon) —And gladly Kent to thee and to thy force
Confides her ancient banner, the White Horse
GENIUS OF O S (Miss F Brough)—Gladly O S to her brave sons will yield,
In trust to thy proved loyalty, cemented
By thirty years of fellowship, contented,
The colours which so oft on tented field
Have proved victorious See that ye uphold
Th' untainted honour of Red, Black, and Gold

VICTORY (Miss Addison) —'Twere hard, indeed, did victory not bless
Th' united flags—Kent, Britain, and O S

SONG—VICTORY—(Air ' Kiss Kiss" from "Genevieve de Brabant")

Whose heart does not with joy o'erflow
When meeting with a trusty friend ?
Who has not felt with grief and woe
That meeting drawing to an end ?
Each cricket week grows dearer, dearer
At Canterbury to O S ,
And as the hour grows nearer, nearer
For parting, griefs our hearts oppress
Then, sad to say,
We must away !
Till next happy meeting
Take our hearty greeting ,
And thus to you
We bid adieu
Our full hearts and souls combined in this—one kiss

FINALE—GOD SAVE THE QUEEN

In 1874 the Epilogue "Woman's Rights" terminated thus —

GENIUS OF KENT (Miss Cooper) —

Before the curtain falls upon our play,
Let Kent one little word of tribute pay,
One word of praise to all who yearly seek
To swell the pleasures of our Cricket Week
As snowball rolling grows, so year by year
Our Cricket Week grows dearer and more dear,
Till, gaining strength by union wins the race,
With Kentish fire combined with Gloucester's Grace

GENIUS OF O S (*addressing the Woman's Rights Deputation*) —

And ye who advocate your Woman's Rights—
The cause of these dissensions of to-night's—
Strive not to stand without a husband's arm
That we *are* women is our greatest charm !
Men should be generals, ministers , but ye
Should rather ministering angels be ,
Your homes to bless, your children's lives to school—
Woman's best government is called Home Rule

(*To the Audience*)—And we who now your kindly verdict seek,
When the long year brings back the Cricket Week,
Will once again on Canterbury nights
Demand your smiles alone as Woman's Rights

GOD SAVE THE QUEEN

CHANGE OF WEATHER

The last ' original epilogue" bore this title, and was spoken on the 6th of August, 1875

MANAGER —Ladies and gentleman, a tag to speak
Is the fit closing for the cricket week
But, strange to say, our author none has sent,
Which leaves me in a sad predicament ,
None has arrived by post, or train, or tram

[*Enter Telegraph Boy with telegram*]
Hollo! what's this? (*Opens telegram*) It's here by telegram!
Come! I must read it to you but the fact is
At public readings I have had no practice
Well may some pangs of fear and doubt go through me,
With such an audience to listen to me
(*Reads*)—"To open the champagne"—pooh, that's absurd!
It must mean 'close the campaign" What's this word?
Did ever mortal man see people write so?
The devil take the telegram!
PLUTO (*as Mephistopheles, rises and takes it up*)—Yes, quite so
A word or two with you I am—attention!—
The party which it's not polite to mention—
In classic language, Pluto You must go
With me
MANAGER— What there? (*Pointing below*)
PLUTO— Exactly, down below
Although my happy home may fail to charm you,
At any rate I'll promise that I'll warm you
MANAGER—Thank'ye, I'd rather not I'll here remain,
Spite of hail thunder, hurricane, or rain,
In hope of change to sun and weather fair,
Than risk your very warm reception there
[*Knock at the door*]
But who comes here? I hazard a suggestion—
Live they, or are they aught that I may question?
[*Enter* JUPITER, MARS, BACCHUS, MERCURY, *and* VENUS, *all with colds in their heads*]
PLUTO—This is an honour that—perhaps you'll inform—
JUPITER—Fact is, we've only come here to get warm
The waterworks are out of gear above
I think the turncock must have fall'n in love
A day or two's repose, and we'll decamp
The clouds this weather are so precious damp
That, to avoid their teeming wet, each Planet
Seeks here a refuge in the Isle of Thanet
* * * * * *
PLUTO—Well, my good friends, since we have met together
Let's have a little chat about the weather
What caused the deluge—is it universal?
A last performance or a first rehearsal?
ALL (*shivering*)—I hope not
PLUTO—Is it that Chaos has come back again,
Or some one "shaking dewdrops from his mane?"
* * * * * *
APOLLO—Hence things of Darkness, Light, and Joy appear!
I'll have no clouds, no storms this time of year
Let gods and men alike their pleasure seek
In the warm sunshine of the Cricket Week
MANAGER—If we're to talk of cricket, let there be
Room for Old Stagers—Kent and Zingari
GENIUS OF KENT—Welcome, bright planet, whatsoe'er your name—
Phœbus, the Sun Apollo—all the same—
Thy cheery beams of warmth to all are sent
Alike to England, Gloucestershire, and Kent

MRS. LEIGH MURRAY, as *Mrs. Eventide.*—If anybody comes to me to say,
"D'ye think that we shall have a rainy day?"
I say "No! Do you think so?" And if he
Says "Yes, I do," I say, "I can't agree."
And then if he says, "Why?" I say "I'm right,
'Cause Canterbury skies are always bright."

GENIUS OF O.S.—Once more the months have sped, and in their places
Are found Old Friends, Old Stagers, and Old Faces.
Once more the old green curtain has unfurled
The bright horizon of our mimic world;
With sky serene, you meet us as erewhiles—
Warmth in your greeting—sunshine in your smiles;
No showers can damp, no clouds can dim our cause—
Our only storms, your thunders of applause.

GOD SAVE THE QUEEN.

CHAPTER X

GLANCES AT THE PAST AND PRESENT STATE OF COUNTY CRICKET—*continued.*

HAMPSHIRE*

* * * In ages past
A dreary desert and a gloomy waste
To savage beasts and savage laws a prey,
And kings more furious and severe than they —*Pope*

HAMPSHIRE AND ITS COLLOQUIAL NAMES—THE HAMBLEDON CLUB—WINCHESTER, ITS EARLY HISTORY—SCHOOLS FOUNDED BY WILLIAM OF WYKEHAM—DECLINE OF HAMBLEDON CLUB—EFFORTS TO RESUSCITATE CRICKET IN HAMPSHIRE (1863)—PICTURE OF CRICKET IN THE ISLE OF WIGHT, PAINTED IN 1761—THE MOST MARVELLOUS INNINGS ON RECORD, 1871—PRESENT CONDITION OF HANTS AS A CRICKET COUNTY, &c

THIS the colloquial contracted name of Southamptonshire is still further abbreviated into the monosyllable Hants Including the Isle of Wight, it has an area of 1625 square miles, or 1,079,216 acres A century ago it was one of the most attractive spots for cricket in the whole kingdom, and was the centre to which young talent gravitated long before the Marylebone Club existed The interesting accounts of the Hambledon Club by the press of that time—chiefly local—gave a wonderful impetus to cricket as a national pastime Nyren, many years after the dissolution of the club, speaks of the Hambledon players in very glowing terms "No eleven in England could compare with the Hambledon Club So renowned a set were the men of Hambledon, that the whole county round would flock to see one of their trial matches" He then goes on to describe the various merits of the ' knights of his round table" The principal bowlers were Richard Nyren and Thomas Brett the latter was the fastest and straightest ever known neither a *thrower*, nor a *jerker*, but a legitimate downright *bowler*—delivering his ball fairly high and very quickly, quite as strongly

* William the Conqueror had such a passion for hunting that he depopulated the country in Hampshire for an extent of thirty miles, driving away inhabitants, destroying the villages, houses, and plantations, and stocking it with deer To this desolated spot he gave the name which it still bears, The New Forest

as the jerkers, and with the force of a point-blank shot. Nyren had a high delivery, always to the length, and his balls were provokingly deceitful He had an immense advantage over Brett, for, independently of his general knowledge of the game, he was practically a better cricketer, being a safe batsman and an excellent hitter Barber and Hogsflesh were both good hands They had a high delivery and a good length; not very strong, however, at least, for those days of playing when the bowling was all fast

Among the batters the name of John Small the elder shines in all the lustre of a star of the first magnitude He was the best short runner of his day, his decision was as prompt as his eye was accurate in calculating a short run, an admirable fieldsman, always playing middle wicket, and as active as a hare What a handful of steel-hearted soldiers are in an important pass Tom Sueter was in keeping wicket He let nothing go by him; and for coolness and nerve in this trying position he had few equals He was one of the manliest and most graceful of hitters Few could cut a ball harder at the point of the bat He had an eye like an eagle—rapid and comprehensive He was the first who departed from the custom of the old players, who deemed it a heresy to leave the crease for the ball, he would go in at it and hit it straight off and straight on, and it went as if it had been fired Lear was a fine long-stop, the ball seemed to go into him, and he was as sure of it as if he had been a sand bank. His activity was so great, and his judgment so good in running to cover a ball, that he would stop many that were hit in the slip, and this from the swiftest bowling ever known What he did not bring to the stock from his bat he amply made up by his perfect fielding Curry was a splendid long field, being a sure and strong thrower, and able to cover a great space in the field He was also a good change bowler Buck, too, played long field, and was a steady man at his post He could also cut the balls very hard at the point of the bat Lambert, sometimes called the "Little Farmer," was a right-hand bowler with an extraordinary delivery, quite low, and with a twist, not like that of the generality of bowlers, but just the reverse way—that is, if bowling to a right-hand hitter, his ball would twist from the off-stump into the leg This, however, was the only virtue he possessed he was no batter, and had no judgment of the game Taylor was an admirable field. His station was between the point of the bat and mid-wicket, to save the two runs He had a general knowledge of the game, but of fielding in particular he was perfect, both in judgment and in practice. He was also a most brilliant hitter, but his great fault lay in not sufficiently guarding his wicket, he was too fond of cutting at the point of the bat balls that were delivered straight Although he would frequently get many runs, yet from this habit he could not be securely depended upon, and, indeed, it was commonly the cause of his being out Lord Frederick Beauclerc (certainly the finest batter of his day) has often thrown away the chance of a capital innings by the same incaution—that of cutting at *straight* balls One of the early matches concerning which any particulars are given in the shape of a score took place on the Artillery Ground in Bunhill Fields, July, 1773 It was entitled the Hambledon Club with Yalden against England, when England won by five wickets

HAMBLEDON.

	1st inn.	2nd inn.
T. Brett	1	14
R. Nyren	0	14
T. Sueter	29	32
J. Small, sen.	58	25
J. Aylward	8	1
W. Hogsflesh	2	14
P. Stewart	10	5
W. Yalden	4	2
Curry	0	3
W. Barber	15	25
G. Lear	0	3
Byes	5	Byes 16
Total	132	Total 154

ENGLAND.

	1st inn.	2nd inn.
— Lumpy	5	
J. Fraine	11	
T. Wood, of Surrey	15	
Childs	38	
T. White	24	1
— Colchin	1	9
J. Boorman	5	55
John Wood, of Seal	5	
William Bullen	1	1
Read	13	
Palmer, not out	52	not out 30
Byes	17	Byes 4
Total	187	Total 100

Another, played in the same year, on Sevenoaks Vine, against England, was far more adverse to the Hambledon Club, for on this occasion England won the match by an innings and 51 runs. A third match against England, played on Broad-Halfpenny Down, in Hampshire, soon followed, and ended in a victory of nine wickets by England; and shortly after the Hambledon were beaten by Surrey, who got beyond their total of 154 with six wickets to spare. Thus far it would seem that the superlative merits of the Hambledon players existed merely in the eye of the narrator of their events. It ought, however, to be stated that in nearly every match cited some fatality accompanied Hambledon by the absence of one, two, or even three of their chief players when most wanted.

The following year enabled them to retrieve their lost laurels with England in a match on Sevenoaks Vine, and another at Chertsey, but 1775 placed them twice on the defeated list in matches with Kent, and once with Surrey. On the 4th of July in the following year England beat them by four wickets, but this defeat was soon atoned for by a victory of six wickets in a kind of return match played about a fortnight afterwards. A week later and nearly the same two elevens were at work, and at the close of the contest England were declared victors by five wickets.

A match with Surrey ended in favour of Hambledon by 198 runs, the scores being Hambledon, 273 and 155—total 428, Surrey, 82 and 148—total 230.

1777 Hambledon, in another contest with England, came off victors by an innings and 168 runs Score England, 166 and 69—total 235, Hambledon, 403, towards which Aylward contributed 167 The "return" effected a reverse, England won by 25 runs A sort of third match occurred about a month after near Chertsey, when the Duke of Dorset played on the Hambledon side His Grace was one of the chief causes of the Hambledon Club winning by 30 runs Another close victory was obtained about a fortnight subsequently over England at Guildford Basin It appears that a great deal of betting accompanied the game, which terminated in favour of Hambledon by one wicket The great advance made in the style of scoring will justify giving the one in question from the *Hampshire Chronicle*, a journal to whom the public are much indebted for the events of the period to which this article refers

ENGLAND

	1st inn		2nd inn
W Bullen, b Nyren	0	b Mann	20
— Minshull, not out	33	b Mann	0
Earl of Tankerville, b Brett	1	b Nyren	46
J Miller, run out	2	b Mann	64
W Yalden, c Taylor	6	b Nyren	12
W Bowra, b Nyren	3	run out	12
J Edmeads, b Brett	1	c Francis	7
C Phillips, b Nyren	0	c Veck	18
Lumpy, run out	1	not out	6
Wood, b Brett	0	thrown out by Brett	17
Lamborne, b Nyren	0	c Aylward	9
Byes	3	Byes	8
Total	50	Total	249

HAMBLEDON

	1st inn		2nd inn
R Veck, c Yalden	1	c Bullen	16
R Francis, c Tankerville	15	b Lamborn	0
J Aylward, c Bowra	30	b Lumpy	0
J Small, sen, c Minshull	14	c Wood	35
T Sueter b Wood	14	not out	19
Noah Mann, c Bullen	23	c Edmeads	11
T Taylor, c Edmeads	20	c Wood	62
E Aburrow (Curry), b Lumpy	6	b Lumpy	8
R Nyren, b Lumpy	4	not out	4
T Brett, not out	3	b Bullen	4
W Barber, b Lumpy	0	b Lumpy	0
Byes	3	Byes	8
Total	133	Total	167

In the same year England beat Hambledon by 54 runs, and quickly after a "return" match took place on the Artillery Ground, Bunhill Fields, when Hambledon won by 131 runs.

In 1778 England and Hambledon confronted each other on the Vine, Sevenoaks, when Hambledon won by three wickets, and, after a few days' rest, they met at Stoke Down, in Hampshire, when England proved victors by 45 runs. The match was repeated in June of the following year at the same place, when Hambledon won by six wickets This was followed up by a victory of still greater moment, viz, that of an innings and 89 runs Hambledon may now be said to have reached the pinnacle of its fame. In the year 1779 England was again compelled to own Hambledon victor by 134 runs In 1781 England were defeated by eight wickets, although their victors were twice humbled by other clubs in the same year In 1782 Hambledon stands recorded as conqueror of the England team at Bishops-Bourne by 9 runs, but as conquered by the same party at Windmill Down by 147 runs shortly after The next year the Kent score is in a minority of 85 runs, but in 1784 England beat the Hambledonians by seven wickets In 1786 Kent won by four wickets, on the Vine, but lost on Windmill Downs by one wicket, and at Moulsey Hurst by 35 runs A year afterwards Kent and Hambledon met at Coxheath, when Hambledon won by two wickets, and in the same year Hambledon beat England by 266 runs England returned the compliment a few weeks afterwards by an excess of 65 runs The wreath was, however, torn from the brow of England in 1788, the scores being 63 and 81 for England—total 144, against a single innings of 220 on the part of Hambledon This was followed up by a conquest of 53 runs a few days subsequently From this period the Hambledon Club began to sink its individuality into the county of Hants The last match was against twenty-two of Middlesex, which the latter won by three wickets The scores were—127 and 90 for Hambledon, 122 and 96 for Middlesex. It would seem that the spirit of former times still lived in some of the Hambledon veterans, notwithstanding the wear and tear of a busy life, *e g* —

HAMBLEDON.

	1st inn		2nd inn
J Small, jun, c Bedster	12	b Fennex	0
W Beldham, run out	19	b Fennex	15
T Walker, c Fennex	0	b Fennex	0
J Wells, b Fennex	2	b Fennex	25
R Purchase, b Grange	0	b Fennex	1
H Walker, c Knowles	8	c J White	0
J Small sen, b Lord	14	c Cantrell	5
A Freemantle, c J White	10	b Turner	12
T Taylor, b Fennex	1	not out	2
D Hains, run out	0	b Fennex	0
T Scott, not out	49	run out	23
Byes	12	Byes	7
Total	127	Total	90

The Middlesex full score is not worth reproducing, for in those days, as at the present time, all true lovers of cricket regarded uneven sides as little better than "playing with"—and not playing—the game. Probably the hard worn plea of necessity was set up, still, the fact remains

The antiquity of a cricket club, like that of a nation or a family, is often a theme for boasting Unfortunately for the advocate who aimed to prove Hambledon, or even Hampshire, the spot whence cricket originated, he is altogether unsupported by documentary evidence of any substantial degree. Before the art of writing accommodated itself to the humbler classes of society, history must have been oral in matters appertaining to cricket especially so. Now a man may give currency to a half-truth so frequently that he himself believes his utterances to be all gospel No one gives credit to the statement that "the Hambledon Club was formed at the beginning of the 17th century," or that "the game was played with one stump 18in high, to which the club added one more stump and a bail" No doubt whatever exists respecting the Herculean look of the bats, seeing there are specimens of such weapons existing at the present day, nor has it ever been denied that "the Hambledonians were a jolly set of fellows—had plenty of wine on a wet day, and were well backed up by the sporting aristocracy of the neighbourhood" This is all very likely—in fact, nothing more likely—it is in accordance with the genius of cricket, but to claim for Hampshire an antiquity out of all keeping with the records of conterminous counties is a weak invention, to say the least of it, and will not endure the torch of investigation, or come harmlessly out of a conflict with the trenchant blade of truth

As before observed, the Hambledon Club by degrees was absorbed into the county One of the early matches played thus was on Perriam Downs, near Luggershall, in Wiltshire, when Hampshire won by four wickets, the scores being—for Surrey, 203 and 44—total 247, against 110 and 138 (six wickets)—total 249, for Hampshire In 1789 Hampshire played and beat Kent at Bishops Bourne by 29 runs, and England, in less than a month after, by 15 runs In the following year Hampshire met England on the Vine, and beat them by 44 runs Six weeks later they confronted England at Lord's, and returned winners by ten wickets Then came a run of ill-luck until 1792, when Hampshire beat England in Burghley Park by 75 runs Surrey, also, had to own themselves defeated in a somewhat singular manner, Small, the younger, and Freemantle, got more runs than the eleven of Surrey in both innings Hampshire won by 127 runs Towards the close of the same season Hampshire beat Kent by an innings and 23 runs This occurred at Dartford In 1794 Kent and Surrey combined were arrayed against Hampshire on Stoke Downs the residents won by six wickets Not liking to part with an old opponent, they were allowed three men against England, and they won the match by four wickets, the scores being—England, 226 and 85—total 311, Hampshire, 172 and 141 (six wickets)—total 313 Hampshire had a contest with Marylebone on Stoke Down in 1797, but were defeated by 113 runs, and another on the same spot, with the same party, in the year following, when they were beaten by 78 runs. On the return match a few days later, Hampshire were victors by 102 runs Up to the close of the 18th century little more is heard of this famous county than has been thus far briefly narrated In 1804 Hampshire is again represented at Lord's against the Marylebone Club, whom they beat by six wickets, and in the following year, assisted by Lord Frederick Beauclerk and Beldham, they played England, and beat them by one wicket; 677 runs were scored It was mainly owing to the "noble" given that Hampshire won the match, as the full score attached will testify —

ENGLAND

	1st inn		2nd inn
J Hammond, b Bennett	3	b Bennett	10
W Lambert, b Bennett	17	b Beauclerk	16
R Robinson, b Beauclerk	3	run out	92
T Walker, c Beldham	13	c Beauclerk	32
John Wells, b Pointer	15	c Small	1
G. Leicester, b Bennett	1	b Bennett	11
H Bentley, c Beauclerk	2	not out	20
Hon A Upton, not out	14	c Beauclerk	4
G Laurell, b Bennett	2	run out	0
J Ward, b Beauclerk	36	b Pointer	0
W Ray, st Beauclerk	2	b Bennett	2
Byes	9	Byes	3
Total	147	Total	...191

HAMPSHIRE.

	1st inn		2nd inn.
J Small, jun, c Hammond	4	st Hammond.	3
A Freemantle, run out	8	c Wells	5
Lord F Beauclerk, c Robinson	68	not out	129
J Bennett, st Hammond	10	st Hammond	0
W Beldham, b Lambert	22	c Robinson	18
R Pointer, c Walker	13	c Walker	27
B Goddard, c Lambert	6	not out	5
Col Maitland, c Wells	2	c Ray	0
J Parker, b Wells	0	run out	8
T C Howard, not out	2	c Walker	0
— Richardson, c Bennett	0	c Lambert	0
Byes	5	Byes	4
Total	140	Total	199

Another match similarly constructed took place at Lord's a fortnight afterwards, which England won by five wickets In the first match every innings totalled three figures, in the second they ran thus Hampshire, 63 and 89—total, 152 England, 67 and 86 (five wickets)—total, 153 Lord Frederick was again the chief scorer, with 37 and 32 The highest on the England side was Robinson, viz, 2 and 35, not out In 1806 the same parties met again at Lord's, when England won by 87 runs. Beldham was top scorer with 56; next Lambert, 52; Mr T Smith, 47, and Lord Frederick, 41 In August of the same year a third match was played—with a slight variation in the composition of the sides—at Stoke Down, and although Lord Frederick played on the England side, the good fortune of Hampshire prevailed, and sent England to their respective homes defeated by nine wickets In 1807 came a slight reverse, England won by 47 runs match played at Lord's

This was returned within a month. Hampshire won by 24 runs. Little is heard of this famed shire till 1816, when at Lord's the following scores were recorded:—Hampshire, 99 and 180—total, 279. Marylebone (with Lambert), 221 and 59—total, 280, without loss of wicket; but in the following week the tables were turned, and Hampshire won by six wickets. As great changes took place during the silent ten years, it may be well to give the full score of the match in question.

MARYLEBONE (WITH BELDHAM.)

	1st inn.		2nd inn.
J. Brand, Esq., c Martin	6	b Howard	17
Hon. D. Kinnaird, b Mitchell	0	b Beagley	0
J. Tanner, Esq., b Mitchell	9	h w	0
G. Osbaldeston, Esq., c Holloway	10	c Holloway	0
E. H. Budd, Esq., b Howard	4	run out	9
Lord F. Beauclerk, c Holloway	12	c Holloway	2
W. Beldham, b Beagley	36	b Carter	16
F. Ladbrooke, Esq., b Mitchell	12	b Holloway	0
H. Lloyd, Esq., l b w	1	c Carter	7
T. Vigne, Esq., b Howard	2	c Howard	1
A. Greville, Esq., not out	0	not out	23
Byes	8	Byes	7
Total	100	Total	82

HAMPSHIRE.

	1st inn.		2nd inn.
T. Beagley, c Osbaldeston	6	not out	10
C. Holloway, c Beldham	13	c Tanner	3
T. C. Howard, st Vigne	25	c Beldham	21
W. Ward, Esq., c Tanner	5	not out	36
John Thumwood, c Beldham	18	b Beauclerk	2
C. Warren, c Beldham	10		
J. Dark, c Tanner	9		
James Thumwood, b Budd	0		
F. Carter, not out	3	b Budd	9
W. Mitchell, st Vigne	0		
R. Martin, st Vigne	0		
Byes	5	Byes	8
Total	94	Total	89

Towards the close of August in the same year Epsom beat Hampshire by eight wickets. In the following year, at Lord's, the scores were: Hampshire, 181 and 162—total, 343. Marylebone (with Robinson), 155 and 113—total, 268, thus giving to Hampshire the glory of winning by 75 runs. With pretty nearly the same balance of teams, Hampshire beat Marylebone in the year 1818 by five wickets. They lost two matches with Marylebone in the following year, but gained one with Epsom. In a twelve a-side match with England soon after, they were sadly worsted by England, the scores being: Hampshire, 113 and 127; England, 245, and in another match a fortnight after England proved victors by seven wickets. Better luck attended a match with Epsom about two months subsequently; Hampshire won by 135 runs.

In 1820 another meeting of Hampshire and England occurred at Lord's, when England won by 82 runs; and in the year following England were again declared winners with, however, a much larger balance of runs in their favour—viz., 191. A more memorable match took place at Bramshill Park in 1823, which Hampshire won by five wickets. Full score given:

ENGLAND.

	1st inn.		2nd inn.
J. Sparks, c Beagley	3	c Cumble	13
J. Bowyer, l b w	5	c Cumble	42
J. Broadbridge, st Howard	0	c Cumble	40
J. Saunders, st Howard	23	b Budd	52
W. Searle, b Budd	1	b Howard	25
Lord F. Beauclerk, b Howard	70	absent	—
W. Keen, Esq., c Willan	0	c Budd	3
W. Grinham, Esq., b Budd	5	b Budd	10
T. Flavel, not out	29	b Howard	21
W. Ashby, b Brown	2	not out	3
J. W. Ladbroke, Esq., c Beagley	2	b Howard	0
Byes	4	Byes	4
Total	144	Total	213

HAMPSHIRE.

	1st inn.		2nd inn.
T. C. Howard, b Ashby	10	not out	13
T. Cumble, b Flavel	52	c Flavel	1
T. Beagley, st Flavel	18	c Gunham	1
E. H. Budd, Esq., c Keen	67		
W. Ward, Esq., c Flavel	120	not out	7
T. Price, Esq., b Sparks	17		
J. Beagley, run out	5	st Flavel	4
G. Brown, b Ashby	0	b Ashby	2
J. Willan, Esq., c Saunders	6		
H. Holland, c Ashby	11	run out	10
W. Maynard, not out	7		
Byes	6	Bye	1
Total	319	Total	39

In 1825 another match at Bramshill Park is recorded between Hampshire and Sussex. Just 300 runs were totalled. Hampshire won by 72 runs.

Hitherto no reference has been made to the time-honoured city belonging to this shire, although in its chief school the game of cricket existed long before the historian of the Hambledon Club existed—that is to say, if the hitherto uncontradicted story about Bishop Ken, who, "when a boy wielded a bat there," be correct. Be this as it may, the renown obtained by the Wykehamists in the cricket field during the past century is deserving of notice. "A person of quality" in the year 1688 speaks in the following glowing terms of Winchester school:

But now my Muse—nay, rather all the nine,
In a full chorus of applauses join
Of your great Wykeham!
Wykeham, whose name can mighty thoughts infuse,
But nought can ease the travail of my Muse;
Press'd with her load, her feeble strength decays,
And she's delivered of abortive praise.
Here he for youth erects a nursery,
The great coheiress of his piety.*
Oh, may they never vex the quiet nation,
And turn apostates to their education!

Were it within the scope and design of this book to speak of Winchester, how tempting and rich would be the subject! How rich its associations, even when, under the name of *Caer-Gwent,* it was an important city of the ancient Britons and a Roman station. How, too, when taken by Cerdic, it remained the capital of the kingdom of Wessex,—aye, and of England, throughout all the Saxon, Danish, and early Norman dynasties, till it reached the climax of its greatness in the time of the first Henry. The appearance of William of Wykeham, who, though born of poor parents, ultimately obtained some of the very high offices both in Church and State, and whose name is still identified among the most liberal of benefactors to his native county, if not to the world. He started on the road to honour and advancement as surveyor of the works at Windsor at a shilling a day. By his persuasion Edward was induced to pull down a great part of the Royal Castle, and reconstruct it in that style of magnificence to which it still owes its imposing grandeur. But the bent of Wykeham was towards the Church, and in 1357 he was ordained priest by Edyngdon, Bishop of Winchester. His rise in the Church was unusually rapid, and his liberality exhibited itself at every stage of advancement.† In 1364 he was appointed Keeper of the Privy Seal, and two years after Secretary to the King and chief of the Privy Council. Such, indeed, was his influence, that Froissart says, "Everything was done by the priest, and nothing without him." In 1366, upon the king's earnest recommendation, Wykeham was selected Bishop of Winchester. His advancement to the bishopric was followed by an appointment to the Chancellorship of England. This he held for four years, and then yielded to the request of Parliament on the ground that secular persons ought to be appointed to high offices of State. After being settled down in his bishopric, he began to gratify his architectural taste in the repairs of the cathedral, the whole expense of

* The first stone was laid March 26th, in the year 1387, near a school in which Wykeham when a boy was educated, and the building was completed March 28th, 1393. By the first charter, a Warden and seventy scholars were established; by a second, ten Fellows and the officers of the choir. (See Warton, p. 68.)

† Dr. Lowth says he only received the revenues of the Church with one hand to dispense them with the other.

which was defrayed by himself The foundation of a college was another object of consideration Lands were purchased at Oxford and Winchester, the latter for the building of colleges to act as nurseries for the former—one for the foundation of learning, the other for the superstructure The plan he conceived, as stated by Lowth, "was no less than to provide for the perpetual maintenance and instruction of 200 scholars, to afford them a liberal support, and to lead them by an entire course of education, from the first elements of letters through the whole circle of the sciences—from the lowest class of grammatical learning to the highest degrees in the several faculties" The regulations by which the new institution at Oxford was to be governed afford some useful information on the studies of the University and the mode in which they were classed The establishment consisted of a warden, seventy clerical scholars, ten chaplains, three clerks, and sixteen choristers Ten of the scholars were to study the civil, and ten the canon law, while the remaining fifty were to study divinity, general philosophy, and the arts, two of the number being allowed to study medicine, and two astronomy In the year 1391 he retired from political life, and devoted the whole of his attention to the institutions at Oxford and Winchester referred to He died in 1404, and was buried in his own beautiful chauntry in Winchester Cathedral

Although it is not difficult to prove how the youthful Wykehamists devoted their leisure hours, it is not quite so easy to determine when cricket first made its appearance among them, or by what stages it advanced The simple mention of Ken's bat is but a poor peg on which to suspend even a thread of dependable information, and it is somewhat strange that the local journals, so eloquent about Hampshire cricket, should be so reticent concerning Winchester—so reticent that one is forced to the conclusion that the game claimed but little, if any, attention in the locality. There is no doubt whatever of its existence towards the close of the last century, while proofs abundant and incontestable exist of its flourishing condition at the opening of the present, and, moreover, of the public schools of which Great Britain can boast, Winchester, if not first in position, is hardly to be surpassed.

Nor is it a little surprising that no mention is made of the most finished picture of a cricket match painted by a native of this ancient city John Plott, it is well known, was born at Winchester in 1732, and was bred to the profession of the law, which, on the expiration of his articles, he quitted, and in 1756 became a pupil of Richard Wilson, the celebrated landscape artist Having, however, more genius for portraits, he left Wilson, and became a pupil of Nathaniel Horne He afterwards turned his attention to miniature in enamel and water-colours He also studied natural history, and his drawings in that line are said to possess great merit Among other curious facts, it is stated that he scraped in mezzotints his own portrait from a picture by himself He died at Winchester in 1803 A somewhat detailed account of the picture referred to will be found in a neighbouring page

Reverting to Hants as a cricket county, a marked decline manifested itself from the date of the last mentioned match The Hambledon Club had long ceased to exist, except as a name and reference The Broad Halfpenny Down, like other famed spots, both in ancient and modern history, had been turned topsy turvey by the ploughshare, and little else remained but the old inn to mark the place where Nyren and his formidable army sallied forth to meet in mimic battle the invading hosts The historian himself was also at this time gathered to his fathers He lived, however, in his "Guide," and but for this, Hants would never have attained the eminence it so long possessed, Nyren's pencil drew pictures of cricket life in its early growth—which no other artist attempted—in the "Cricketers of my Time" It would, however, be absurd to suppose that there were not other players distributed within a hundred miles of the metropolis quite equal to his heroes if similarly petted and organized No doubt the Hambledon Club consisted of a picked team, but it is far from likely that while they were going ahead all the surrounding counties were standing by, agape In fact, little pieces of stray information crop occasionally above the surface, showing that not far from the spot so frequently mentioned might be found men who, if rightly placed, were but little, if at all, inferior

Scarcely any matches but those hitherto noticed stand on the records of cricket in which Hampshire displayed anything resembling its old form—and such being the case, if speech be silver, silence is gold

A strong effort at resuscitation was made in 1863, and a new county club, with its acknowledged head quarters at Southampton, resulted. Eleven matches were played during the first year of its existence, with credit The next year presented the dismal return of nine county matches, in which Hampshire won two and lost seven For three years an unaccountable supineness appeared to have come over the patrons of cricket, and the movements, if anything, were retrograde Not one county match occurred during the season of 1869, and only two in the following year, both of which they lost Perhaps one of the best glimpses of the condition of Hants may be obtained from an analysis of the batting in the following year —

Southampton, June 3 —Gentlemen of Hants *v* Gentlemen of Sussex Two days —Hants, 103 and 167—total, 270 , Sussex, 73 and 87—total, 160 Hants won by 110 runs

Lords June 7 —County of Hants *v* M C C and Ground Marylebone won by an innings and 83 runs

Southampton, July 15 —County of Hants *v* M C C and Ground, return Marylebone won by two runs

Brighton, July 22 —Gentlemen of Hants *v* Gentlemen of Sussex, return Hants, 321 and 54 (for five wickets)—total 375 , Sussex, 126 and 247—total 373 The chief feature of this match consisted in the free hitting of Mr Lucas for Hants, who in one instance sent the ball a long way over the boundary wall Mr Weighell scored 101 in his second innings for Sussex

Plymouth, August 2 —Gentlemen of Hants *v* Gentlemen of Devon Two days Devon, 121 and and 293—total 414 , Hants, 175 and 242 (for six wickets)—total 417 According to these totals 813 runs were scored in the match Mr Scobell claimed 125 runs in his second innings for Devon, and Mr Lucas, 115 (not out) in his second innings for Hants

Southampton, Aug 9, Gentlemen of Hants *v* Gentlemen of Berkshire Two days —Berks, 191 and 398 total 589 , Hants 158 and 126—total 281 Berks won by 305 runs In the second innings of Berks Mr J G Crowdy scored 138, and Mr A G Lee 188 A gross total of 873 runs was recorded for this active encounter

BATTING AVERAGES.

NAME.	No. of Matches.	No. of Innings.	Most Runs in a Match.	Most Runs in an Innings.	How often Bowled.	Caught.	Run out.	Not out.	Stumped.	Total.	Average per Innings. Over.
Capt. Austin	3	5	32	32	2	3	0	0	0	59	11– 4
Carter	2	4	23	15	1	3	0	0	0	41	10– 1
Mr. G. M. Ede	6	12	34	28	6	5	0	1	0	120	10
Mr. E. L. Ede	4	8	35	32	4	2	1	1	0	72	9
Capt. Eccles	2	4	29	16	1	0	2	1	0	39	9– 3
Mr. C. V. Eccles	2	4	46	35	0	1	1	1	1	66	16– 2
Mr. J. Frederick	2	4	41	25	2	1	0	1	0	63	15– 3
Mr. E. Hemsted	3	5	37	37	4	1	0	0	0	50	10
Mr. G. R. Kendle	2	4	21	21	2	2	0	0	0	21	5– 1
Mr. C. B. Longcroft	3	6	38	20	4	2	0	0	0	95	15– 5
Mr. C. F. Lucas	6	11	168	115	7	3	0	1	0	452	41– 1
Martin	2	4	5	3	2	1	0	1	0	9	2– 1
Tate	2	4	4	2	1	1	1	1	0	4	1
Mr. P. Thresher	2	4	47	47	3	0	0	1	0	50	12– 2
Mr. A. H. Wood	3	6	94	89	4	2	0	0	0	158	26– 2

The following played in one match:—Messrs. Bathurst, Butler, Edmunds, Hall, Jarvis, W. J. Kendle, Misselbrook, H. A. Peake, W. A. Stewart, Saulez, Wyndham, and Wilson; also Holmes and Ubsdell.

Hitherto, scarce any mention has been made of the Isle of Wight, and yet it is quite likely that cricket was popular and well practised there long before the formation of the Hambledon Club. At least, abundant evidence exists of such being the case before John Nyren was born. Evidences of a similar kind often reach posterity from unexpected quarters and in unlooked-for ways. A case in point:—Not many years ago a gentleman, living in the neighbourhood of Brighton, found it necessary to have his house put into thorough order, and during the process a "lot of lumber" which had been stowed away and left undisturbed for—figuratively speaking—an age, got disturbed. Among other things, a piece of canvas, on a somewhat ricketty frame, and which had suffered from the Vandalism of a coarse whitewash brush and other barbarities, was brought into prominence. By a judicious experiment of cleansing, a beautiful picture of a cricket match, dating 1761, revealed itself. Yes, a real picture, painted more than 100 years ago, and painted so well that all else of the kind that has yet come to light are trifles in comparison. It contains more than 200 figures, admirably grouped and artistically finished, which, with the landscape, present a perfect cricket idyl on canvas. The scene is said to represent Bembridge Down, near Brading;* the booths, spectators, and the general surroundings are just what may be seen at the present day. The figures will bear any amount of examination, and many of them appear as fresh as when they left the easel. The disposition of the fielders and the width between wickets may be open to adverse criticism; nevertheless, as a whole, the picture affords striking evidence

* Bembridge is a village and watering-place situated at the eastern extremity of Brading, a parish of about 10,000 acres. Brading is seven miles E.S.E. of Newport.

of care in the choice of rich and desirable pigments, deep thought in their application, and great skill in the elaboration of every particular, however minute

Nor is this picture the only incident calculated to give the Isle of Wight a place in future history In the month of August, 1874, a match was played at Cowes between the Freshwater and Northwood Clubs On the occasion Mr Collins —formerly captain of the Radley Eleven—scored 338 runs in little more than three hours, and was not out His gigantic score comprised one nine, two sevens, six sixes, twelve fives, twenty-five fours, seventeen threes, eighteen twos, and thirty-three singles, all run out! This is the most marvellous innings on record, and indisputable evidences of its truth can be at this time readily ascertained. Score attached —

FRESHWATER

Mr W H Blake, b Collins .	35
Private Jervis, run out	0
Mr F Synge, c A J Damant, b H C Damant	12
Mr W Ward, run out . . .	3
Mr. H Farnall, b Collins .	0
Mr B Ward, b Collins . . .	1
Private Stephens, run out .	6
Mr J Westbrooke, c Watson, b Collins	12
Mr J Sargent, b Watson .	2
Mr P Headdey, b Collins ..	0
Private Evans, not out . .	0
Byes 24, l-b 6, w 1, n-b 1 . . .	32
Total	103

NORTHWOOD

Rev A Watson, b W Ward	27
Mr M White, b W Ward	10
Mr W M Venning, run out .	0
Mr W B Hepburn, b Stevens .	26
Mr. E W Collins, not out	338
Mr J Jones b W Ward . .	0
Mr Temple Cooke, b Blake .	62
Mr H C Damant, b W Ward	0
Capt A W Gillett, b Blake	0
Mr F R Ransome, not out	25
Mr A J Damant, to go in	—
Byes 39, l b 2, w 4, n-b 2 ..	47
Total	535

Hampshire, when put side by side with other counties at this period, and even compared with itself in the golden age when its representatives donned the velvet cap, presents a lamentable picture of decay. How great was the influence exercised by this county over the entire domain of cricket for more than half a century! Such, however, was the state of affairs in the year 1870, that an announcement proceeded from official quarters to sell the tents and other properties of the club, and hand over the proceeds to some benevolent institution of the county *Sic transit gloria*, &c This resolve, however, does not appear to have been carried out, for up to the close of the third quarter of the present century Hampshire still showed signs of fight, and, like the noble hero famed in Scottish story, though struggling in the throes of dissolution, was seen "shaking the remnant of his blade" Better, perhaps, have died right out earlier than exhibit the pitiable condition to which it had arrived True it won one match out of four, but how disgraceful were the three defeats 'Tis said "when things are at the worst they sometimes mend" Here, then, is a wide field for Hants All well-wishers to cricket will, no doubt, heartily cooperate in raising this once famed county to the pinnacle it ages ago attained, and from which a surrounding district received the rudimentary principles of the game, afterwards turned to honour and profit

As the earliest matches of Hants are recorded in the former part of this chapter, it may not be amiss to produce the last (in the year 1875), and while they afford a lesson of the fall of a once famed county, they present also a picture of the advance in the art of scoring

The first represents the condition of Hampshire in a match against Kent at Catford Bridge in the month of June Kent occupied the wickets nearly five hours for an innings, Hants scarcely two. In the end the latter were beaten by an innings and three runs Score —

KENT

W. McCanlis, b Tate	11
Draper, b Galpin	6
Mr E F S Tylecote, b Tate	33
Lord Harris, b Tate	92
Mr E Penn, c Booth, b Paris	39
G McCanlis, c Fox, b Paris	7
Boyes, b Paris	8
Collins, b Galpin	20
Willsher, b Galpin	5
Rumsey, not out	0
George, b Galpin	0
Byes 2, l-b 1, w 3	6
Total	227

HAMPSHIRE

	1st inn		2nd inns
Mr F L Bathurst, c Harris, b Willsher	14	b Rumsey	10
Holmes, st Tylecote, b Willsher	10	c Penn, b Draper	8
Mr C Booth, c Tylecote, b George	13	b George	11
Capt Eccles, b George	0	b Rumsey	7
Mr T C Fox, b Willsher	7	b Rumsey	0
Tate, b George	3	c Harris	25
Mr R G Hargreaves, c Willsher, b George	9	b Rumsey	1
Mr E Cecil, b Willsher	4	absent	—
Jackman, not out	4	c Boys, b George	16
Paris, b George	0	not out	51
Galpin, b George	0	c G McCanlis, b Willsher	27
		Byes, 2, l b 1, w 1	4
Total	64	Total	160

About a fortnight afterwards, Hampshire were confronted by Sussex at St. Cross, Winchester, and in this instance the defeat was even greater than that at Catford Bridge. Score—

SUSSEX.

Mr. W. A. Soames, c Wood, b Hargreaves	17
Humphreys, c Galpin, b Tate	10
Mr. L. Winslow, c and b Hargreaves	44
Charlwood, c Wood, b Hargreaves	13
Fillery, b Galpin	71
Lillywhite, b Galpin	6
Hammond, b Galpin	5
H. Phillips, b Holmes	3
Kellick, run out	22
Pattenden, not out	3
Mr. A. Smith, b Galpin	0
Byes 7, l-b 3, w 2	12
Total	206

HAMPSHIRE.

	1st inn.		2nd inn.
Holmes, b Fillery	7	run out	19
Paris, run out	0	b Lillywhite	0
Rev. J. G. Crowdy, b Fillery	21	c Soames, b Fillery	0
Mr. E. B. Haygarth, b Fillery	6	b Fillery	4
Mr. C. Booth, b Lillywhite	1	c Killick, b Fillery	0
Tate, c Humphreys, b Lillywhite	0	b Lillywhite	21
Mr. R. G. Hargreaves, b Fillery	1	c and b Lillywhite	31
Galpin, b Fillery	0	not out	3
Mr. A. H. Wood, c Fillery, b Lillywhite	21	c Charlwood, b Smith	7
Mr. E. R. Prothero, not out	1	c Phillips, b Fillery	24
Mr. D. Duncan (absent)	—	st Phillips, b Smith	2
Byes	2	Byes 7, l-b 1	8
Total	60	Total	119

It ought, however, to be remarked that Sussex were unquestionably the stronger team, quite as strong, in fact, as that brought against Hants at Catford Bridge. Everybody acquainted with practical cricket is aware that no ordinary amount of confidence and courage is needed to grapple with any chance of success forces vastly superior. In the professional department two to one are great odds, and that this was the case a glance at the score will easily show. The batting of Fillery resulted in more runs than all the ten of Hants at the close of a first innings. Even among the amateurs the score accomplished by Mr. Winslow more than equalled any two of the opposite side.

In the return match at Brighton, a little change in favour of Hants occurred, and they came off winners by 30 runs; but it should be stated that some of the best Sussex players were absent on the occasion. The return match with Kent was a truly lamentable exhibition of county cricket. Kent won by an innings and 217 runs. Score as understated :—

HAMPSHIRE.

	1st inn.		2nd inn.
Mr. L. Bathurst, b Hearne	3	run out	3
Holmes, c Foord-Kelcey, b Remnant	11	c Shaw, b Hearne	7
Galpin, l b w, b Remnant	2	c Remnant, b Shaw	13
Mr. C. Booth, b Remnant	9	c F. Penn, b Hearne	0
Rev. Mr. Crowdy, c Shaw, b Remnant	6	c Mackinnon, b Shaw	18
Mr. A. H. Wood, b Hearne	1	b Hearne	9
Tate, b Hearne	0	c Mackinnon, b Remnant	0
Mr. G. Greenfield, c W. Penn, b Remnant	0	absent	—
Mr. H. Dutton, not out	0	not out	7
Greenwood, c Remnant, b Hearne	1	b Stokes	1
Mr. H. Henley, absent	—	b Remnant	14
Byes	1	Byes 7, l-b 1, w 1, n-b 1	10
Total	34	Total	82

KENT.

Mr. V. K. Shaw, b Tate	54
Mr. W. Penn, c Booth, b Tate	16
Mr. F. Mackinnon, c Holmes, b Galpin	66
Mr. W. Foord-Kelcey, c Tate, b Galpin	18
Remnant, c and b Galpin	25
Lord Harris, b Galpin	75
Mr. F. Penn, st Bathurst, b Crowdy	47
Mr. W. Smith-Masters, c Bathurst, b Tate	7
Mr. F. Stokes, not out	2
G. Hearne, jun., c Greenwood, b Galpin	0
Palmer, c Galpin, b Tate	5
Byes 8, l-b 6, w 4	18
Total	333

Although twenty-four persons took part in these four encounters, not half of this number proceeded beyond one match. The following analysis is a faithful summary of the batting of those who appeared twice and upwards.

Name.	No. of Matches.	No. of Innings.	Most Runs in a Match.	Most Runs in an Innings.	How often Bowled.	Caught.	Run out.	Stumped.	Not out.	Total.	Average per Innings. Over.
Mr. L. Bathurst	2	4	24	14	2	1	1	0	0	30	7— 2
Mr. C. Booth	4	8	24	13	4	4	0	0	0	39	4— 7
Rev. J. C. Crowdy	3	6	24	18	3	2	0	0	1	57	9— 3
Mr. T. C. Fox	2	4	7	7	3	1	0	0	0	10	2— 2
Galpin	3	6	27	27	3	2	0	0	1	45	7— 3
Mr. R. G. Hargreaves	3	6	33	31	4	2	0	0	0	75	12— 3
Holmes	4	8	30	20	0	6	1	1	0	92	11— 4
Tate	4	8	28	25	4	4	0	0	0	40	5
Paris	2	4	57	57	2	0	1	0	1	57	14— 1
Mr. A. H. Wood	3	6	28	21	3	2	0	0	1	48	8

Another strenuous effort was made to resuscitate cricket in this county in the month of June, 1876. The Mayor of Southampton, Mr. E. Jones, proclaimed a banquet to be given by him at the South-Western Hotel. Two hundred guests were invited, and many of the leading men of the town were present. It seemed the earnest of a success, for a match at that time in course of play on the Antelope Ground ended in a decided triumph over Kent; at the close of the contest Hampshire were pronounced winners by 236 runs, and out of the four county matches during the season they won three.

CHAPTER XI

GLANCES AT THE PAST AND PRESENT STATE OF COUNTY CRICKET—*continued*

SURREY

As leaves on trees the life of man is found
Now green in youth, now withering on the ground,
Another race the following spring supplies—
They fall successive, and successive rise
So generations in their course decay,
So flourish these when those have passed away —* * *

Area of the County—Mr Venn's Resolve—Early Score—Surrey v England—Beehive and Montpelier Grounds—Formation of the County Club—Apprehended Dissolution Avoided—Rules of the Club—Great Success—Erection of Pavilion—Strength of Membership—Batting Averages of 1868—Change of Secretary—Analysis of the Batting in 1875—Concluding Remarks

DID the impossible ever come to pass? Never, and never will The gentleman who engaged to get himself into a quart bottle it is said failed signally, and was ridiculed for his attempt A similar fate would accompany the writer or compiler of a book silly enough to venture upon the fearful task of condensing the cricket of a county like Surrey into a few pages—a task requiring far greater ingenuity than falls to the lot of ordinary mortals

Surrey (Saxon, *Suthrie*, the South Kingdom) possesses an advantage beyond some counties bordering upon the Metropolis in respect to extent and beauty It has an area of 485,760 acres, or 759 square miles The North Downs, of which the Hog's Back and Boxhill form portions, intersect the county from west to east An expanse of wild heath land covers a very considerable tract The west and south-west hill chain is most prominent at Leith, where it rises nearly 1000 feet above sea level, and commands a view over parts of fourteen counties Considering the many advantages for cricket Surrey is supposed to have possessed early, much surprise has been often expressed that greater advances were not made than current history gives them credit for There is no reason for doubting their capacities for meeting Kent on an equal footing as far back as the opening of the 18th century Light often breaks upon the student's page from unexpected quarters, to show, probably, that "great men lived before the time of Agamemnon." Here and there the story of a village hero is found in books apparently alien to the subject on which they pretend to treat; at other times the merest scintillation leads up to a flood of light. Many curious incidents might be related of Surrey and its standing in the world of cricket full a century and a half ago, did not compression forbid. One, however, must not be passed by. In the year 1747 a match took place between Surrey and All England, in which Mr Henry Venn—born at Barnes on the 2nd of March, 1724—played. His biographer says: "He was extremely fond of cricket, and was reckoned one of the best players in the University of Cambridge. He studied for the Church, and in the week before he was ordained the match alluded to came off. It excited considerable interest, and was attended by a very numerous body of spectators. When the game terminated in favour of the side on which he played, he threw down his bat, saying, 'Whoever wants a bat that has done me good service may take that, as I have no further occasion for it.' His friends inquiring the reason, he replied, 'Because I am to be ordained on Sunday, and I will never have it said of me "Well struck, parson!"' To this resolution, notwithstanding the remonstrances of his friends and even of the Tutor and Fellows of his College (Jesus), he strictly adhered. Though his health suffered by a sudden transition from a course of most violent exercises to a life of comparative inactivity, he could never be persuaded to play any more. He died at Clapham in 1797."*

Nor is the Rev. Mr Venn the only hero which Surrey, in the unripe stages of cricket, produced. Duncombe, the poet, has not overlooked the merits of Surrey in his imitation of Chevy-Chase—given in another chapter—when they confronted Kent at Bishopsbourne, in 1773, and won by 153 runs. As the score may receive additional light and interest when read side by side with the poem, it is here introduced:

SURREY

	1st inn		2nd inn
Earl of Tankerville, b T. May	0	c Davis	3
Bartholomew, Esq., c Simmons	3	b Miller	10
Lewis, Esq., b Dorset	0	not out	21
Stone, Esq., b Dorset	12	b Miller	24
Lumpy, b Miller	6	b Miller	8
T. Wood, c Mann	6	c R. May	6
Palmer, c Davis	22	c Dorset	38
T. White, b Dorset	5	b Hussey	60
W. Yalden, not out	17	b Dorset	1
Child, b T. May	0	b Dorset	3
R. Frances, b Dorset	5	c Wood	36
Bye	1	Byes	7
Total	77	Total	217

* Appointed first as Vicar of Huddersfield, and afterwards Rector of Yelling, Huntingdonshire.—*Grote.*

KENT

	1st inn		2nd inn
Duke of Dorset, b Wood	25	b Wood	1
Sir Horace Mann, b Wood	3	c Tankerville	22
Davis, Esq , b Wood	4	c Lewis	0
Hussey, Esq , not out	0	b Wood	0
J Miller, c Yalden	13	run out	10
Simmons, b Lumpy	5	c Yalden	4
R May, b Wood	0	not out	3
T May, b Lumpy	4	c Child	5
G Louch, Esq , c Stone	5	b Lumpy	23
Pattenden, c Lewis	0	b Lumpy	1
J Wood, c Wood	1	c Bartholomew	9
Byes	3		
Total	63	Total	78

Before two years elapsed, Surrey suffered a sharp defeat at the hands of Hambledon The figures subscribed by the victors were 168 and 357—total 525 Surrey made 151 and 78—total 229, and were thus 296 runs in arrear On the side of the winning party, as "a given man," was the Duke of Dorset The losing team had the assistance of two redoubtables, in the persons of Minshull and Miller The chief contributor was J Small sen (Hambledon), viz , 174 In the following year another match with Hambledon ended in favour of Surrey by 138 runs Kent renewed their acquaintance with Surrey after a silence of nine years Surrey were then strong enough to win by an innings and 65 runs Kent totalled 132 runs only Within a month the return took place at Bishopsbourne, when Kent were beaten by 37 runs, but twelve months afterwards Surrey effected the more significant defeat of nine wickets this, too, on the Kent ground near Canterbury (1789) For some time afterwards Surrey and Hampshire were the pet contenders, with varied victories and defeats In 1792, Surrey met Hants on Perriam Downs, and left the scene of conflict with 109 runs in their favour In order that the reader may be able to keep in memory who "belonged" to Surrey at the time, or rather who took part in the encounter against Hants on the occasion in question, the list is given—a fresh generation —

SURREY

	1st inn		2nd inn
Earl of Winchilsea, c Fennex	7	c Taylor	22
Hon E Bligh, c Harris	9	b Harris	10
Hon H Fitzroy, run out	0	run out	0
Hon G Monson, not out	10	b Fennex	20
T Walker, c Harris	58	run out	48
H. Walker, b Harris	10	b Purchase	9
John Wells, b Purchase	9	b Harris	4
W Beldham, b Taylor	15	b Purchase	11
W Bedster, b Harris	0	c Fennex	11
T Boxall, b Harris	17	not out	3
T Ingram, b Harris	0	b Harris	2
Byes	4	Byes	0
Total	169	Total	140

A match in the following year with England, on Windmill Downs, Hambledon, was highly estimated at the time by Surrey, independently of the 1000 guineas for which nominally it was to be played On examination of the names, it will occur to the reader that Surrey, who won the match by a narrow majority of runs, had some assistance This may have been the case, though not to any material extent

SURREY

	1st inn		2nd inn
T Walker, b Harris	16	c Hammond	26
Crawte, b Hammond	2	b Littler	33
J Walker run out	25	b Boxall	8
Earl Winchilsea, b Hammond	14	b Hammond	1
H Walker, c Scott	3	not out	3
Beldham, b Harris	0	c Small, sen	9
Ayleward, c Scott	9	c Scott	2
J Wells, c Hammond	8	c Harris	14
H H Fitzroy, c Hammond	1	c Hammond	3
G Louch, Esq , c Newman	15	c Littler	0
Hampton, not out	5	b Boxall	1
Byes	1	Byes	1
Total	99	Total	101

ENGLAND

	1st inn		2nd inn
Ring, b Ayleward	5	run out	27
Small, jun , hit wicket	2	c Beldham	9
Hammond c T Walker	11	b H Walker	22
Scott, b J Walker	13	c H H Fitzroy	5
Small, sen , st J Wells	2	c H Walker	21
Freemantle, c Beldham	17	c J Wells	11
Newman, Esq , b T Walker	0	b Hampton	16
Brudenell, Esq , b Hampton	3	c J Wells	0
Boxall, b Hampton	7	not out	4
Harris, c Beldham	1	c Crawte	6
Littler, not out	0	b T Walker	2
Byes	1	Byes	0
Total	62	Total	123

A match at Lord's in the same year enforces attention Surrey went in first and scored 171 runs, of which 106 belonged to Beldham (not out), second innings Lord Winchilsea contributed 19 (not out) towards a total of 83 On the part of Hampshire the chief scorer was Ring, who made 34 runs in each innings. Surrey won by 53 runs

A still more marked success attended Surrey in their match with England in June, 1794 The proceedings were somewhat irregular Beldham, on the part of Surrey, scored 72 in the first innings, and 102 in the second, H Walker 23 in the first, and 115 in the second (not out) England totalled 285 out of the 767 runs scored in the three days' play So strong were Surrey at this period that they frequently had to contend against thirteen of England The most important match with which to close the cricket business of the 18th century will always be referred to by Surrey, who met England at Lord's, and on the 1st of August were declared winners by eight wickets See score

ENGLAND

	1st inn		2nd inn
Small jun, c H Walker	25	b T Walker	1
Boxall, hit w	19	c Wells	6
Hammond, c T Walker	40	c Beldham	28
Burton, c Wells	21	b Wells	5
Freemantle, b Beldham	11	c T Walker	0
Fennex, not out	37	c Wells	10
Booth c Wells	1	c Robinson	5
Lord, c Leicester	7	b T Walker	5
J Beeston, c Whitehead	0	not out	0
Hockley, run out	3	st Leicester	2
W Beeston, c Gibbons	0	c Wells	8
Bye	1	Bye	1
Total	165	Total	71

SURREY

	1st inn		2nd inn
G Leicester, Esq, not out	9	st Hammond	2
H Walker, b Boxall	5		
T Walker, b Boxall	10		
Robinson, b Lord	74	not out	44
Beldham c Hammond	1		
Wells, c Booth	9	not out	44
Captain Maitland, b Lord	2		
R Whitehead, Esq, b Lord	32	b Boxall	1
J Gibbons, Esq, c Fennex	1		
W Lushington, Esq, b Lord	3		
Sir H Martin, hit w	0		
Total	146	Total	91

For nearly a quarter of a century Surrey sustained a prominent position among counties In 1807 they beat England at Lord's by 70 runs, and in the following year by three wickets Whether from whim or weakness no one at the present day exactly knows, they played sixteen against England with Lambert, and beat them by fourteen wickets, although at the conclusion of an innings each there were but three runs difference, but in 1809 England avenged themselves by a victory of five wickets with equal sides at Dartford, in Kent, and a fortnight afterwards at Lord's by ten wickets In the month of July, 1810, another trial of strength between the aforesaid elevens took place, when Surrey's turn came again, although on the side of England were arrayed Lord Frederick Beauclerk, Mr Ward, and other first class batsmen and bowlers too Surrey won by eight wickets Another match of the same kind in 1815 was more closely contested England won by a wicket Little is heard of these elevens for nearly seven years, when they turn up again at Lord's with lists materially changed England won by five wickets

The deficiency in county fixtures was made up in a great degree by vigorous contests among parish elevens In nearly all the home counties these elevens supplied a want. Cricket had at this time so strong a hold on the rustic population, that it was not to be extinguished for want of "grand" matches Kent could boast of its Benenden, Marden, Leeds, Malling, Hadlow, &c ; Sussex would point to Midhurst, Storrington, Petworth, Brighton, &c , while Surrey, not to be outdone either by number or strength, could as easily descant upon the dwellers round about Mitcham, Croydon, Ripley, Richmond, and Godalming A match at the latter place in 1827 clearly showed that a well chosen parish eleven from Sussex were compelled to return to Midhurst perfectly convinced that Godalming had the best of the encounter, the scores being Midhurst, 83 and 94—total 177, Godalming, 90 and 89 (four wickets)—total 179. As the "return" match was unfinished, no estimate could be formed of the approximate results The Harrow Town Club made a poor fight against Richmond in the same year The defeat of Surrey, when attempting to play Kent with such a bowler as Broadbridge given, excited no other surprise than that it ended adversely to Surrey They seemed to know nothing of the strength of the foe. In all probability not one of the contenders saw the last match between their respective counties played nearly forty years before

Nearly a dozen years elapsed before Surrey met England again at Lord's On this occasion Surrey had the assistance of Lillywhite and Broadbridge, and were enabled by the superiority of their bowling to claim a victory of 83 runs, this was not inconsiderable, seeing that 381 comprised the total scored throughout the match Respecting the character of the fielding it may suffice to say there were only eight wides in the column of extras, and not a single bye England "mended their list" at the return match played shortly after at Godalming, but were beaten nevertheless. It is somewhat singular that only one double figure occurred in the first innings of either side, and both under 20 At the close of the match the respective scores were England, 42 and 98—total 140, of which Mr Ward claimed more than a third, Surrey, 59 and 84 (six wickets)—total 143

The reader will naturally ask himself where the Surrey cricketers came from, and where their centre of action. Well, for many years the Beehive and Montpelier Clubs, Walworth served as such, independently of Hall's ground, near the "Canal Church," at Camberwell Long and romantic stories might be told of what occurred at the Montpelier, almost as far back as a hundred years But what of them now? Aye, not a patch of green is left to mark out where once stood the wickets and the tents around which were gathered senators, lordlings, and men of social distinction, but on which at times they conferred no honour If there were giants on the earth in those days, there were gamblers too Hence some of the matches belonging to the archives of Surrey had better perhaps be allowed to crumble and rot out of existence than be disturbed for the non-edification of the present generation

A real curiosity now arrests attention Surrey for the first time arranged a match with Sussex, and the parties chiefly concerned in the play met at Godalming on the 8th of July, 1830 Surrey, awed perhaps by the bowling of Lillywhite and J Broadbridge, enlisted Pilch and Ashby into their ranks The Surrey fielding was far superior to that of Sussex, and the batting too, for the latter made but two double figures throughout the match, and those of minor importance The full score, which runs thus, makes Surrey winners by 197 runs

SURREY

	2nd inn		2nd inn
Cæsar, b J Broadbridge	1	b Lillywhite	4
Woods, run out	4	not out	25
Searle, c Hooker	59	st Blake	21
Pilch, c Daniels	24	c Lillywhite	26
Saunders, b Duff	7	h w	20
H Kingscote, Esq , run out	13	l b w	8
W Keene, Esq , c Brown	8	c Daniels	0
T Potter Esq , b Lillywhite	1	b Etherington	1
J Roker, Esq , b J Broadbridge	2	b J Broadbridge	6
Richards, b Lillywhite	4	l b w	14
Ashby, not out	0	b Lillywhite	0
Byes 4, w 6, n-b 4	14	Byes 4, w 5	9
Total	137	Total	134

SUSSEX

	1st inn		2nd inn
Hooker, b Pilch	2	not out	8
Warner, b Ashby	4	c Cæsar	4
W Broadbridge, c Saunders	4	b Pilch	0
J Broadbridge, st Saunders	16	c Roker	0
Brown, b Pilch	2	st Saunders	2
Daniels, b Ashby	12	b Ashby	2
T Blake, Esq , b Pilch	0	b Pilch	1
Duff, st Saunders	0	b Ashby	0
Lillywhite, c Richards	9	c Saunders	1
W Barnard, Esq , not out	0	b Ashby	0
Etherington, b Ashby	4	b Ashby	0
Wides ..	2	Bye	1
Total	55	Total	19

A few years of breathing time now came, and Surrey wisely directed its chief attention to parish matches For a long time such clubs as Mitcham, Richmond, Putney, and other localities handy to London were recognised as nurseries for county players, and the time was anxiously waited for when the distributed talent might be effectively organised. Mitcham alone could bring a team into the field that would require a great deal of beating Evidence of this was abundant To pursue a long chain of events appertaining to parish matches would occupy far too much time and space necessary for the proper treatment of so interesting a subject

It was long a matter of surprise and remark that a county like Surrey, with its vast acreage and numerous townships—a county famed for being the first that gave tongue to cricket—should have been for a period of nearly two centuries without sufficient centralising power and influence to claim for itself really and truly proper head-quarters and a home. In the year 1845, steps were taken to effect these objects, and a general meeting of supporters to a propounded scheme was convened at the Horns, Kennington, on the 18th of October, at which the Hon. F. Ponsonby presided. About forty gentlemen, belonging to various clubs in the county, attended; and as they meant business, a great deal was got through in a short time. The chairman, in proposing success to the undertaking, said "he could not but express his gratification at seeing so many gentlemen, who had a high standing in the county and elsewhere as cricketers, muster on that occasion, which evinced the manner and spirit in which they intended to rally round the new club, established with the view of bringing out the cricketing strength of the county. The club was now established, and Mr. Denison (hon. sec.) would read the rules drawn up." In the course of his observation, Mr. Denison said, "the cricketing world in general were perfectly ignorant of the strength Surrey contained; but at the opening of the next season the cricketers of the county would be found in strong force in the field, and ready to contend with any eleven that could be brought against them." Another very enthusiastic supporter of cricket (Mr. Napper, of Dorking) said, "from his knowledge of what the play was in the lower parts of Surrey, it was his opinion that a good fight could be made against all England." The latter prediction was soon fulfilled, and the views of the previous speakers were proved in a very short time to be neither dim nor shadowy. In fact, many concurrent circumstances hastened what both prophets and good men desired to see. Close by the place of meeting was the Montpelier Club, who foresaw the necessity of shifting their quarters and obtaining a more permanent and commodious position; and close by, too, was the old market garden known as the Oval to be let, and in such condition that a trifling outlay would put the centre of it into condition for play in a very short time. No situation more favourable could by possibility have presented itself. From the first project to the completion of conditions, only a few months elapsed; and in about four years Surrey could boast of a county settlement equal to any in the kingdom, and surpassed by none. As a matter of course, all the existing and rising talent of the county gravitated to Kennington; and, for at least ten years, the sunny side of fortune accompanied the forces of the treasury and the field—great in numbers, powerful in talent, and signally favoured by the public.

The first match on the Oval, worthy of note, was between the Gentlemen of Surrey and the Players. In all probability the latter would have had the best of the encounter had it been pursued to a definite issue. The Gentlemen scored 127 and 82—total 209; Players, 150 and 16 (two wickets)—total 166. Early in the next season, Marylebone appeared for the first time at the Oval, and though not with a very strong team, they beat the newly-formed club by 48 runs. On both sides the scoring was unusually feeble. Surrey were unable to mount the region of double figures more than once during the match. A slight look at the score will reveal some improvement in the style of putting such documents together, and this is in a great measure to be attributed to the hon sec —

MARYLEBONE

	1st inn		2nd inn
A K George, Esq, c Strahan, b Brockwell	0	l b w, b Lewis	12
A Haygarth, Esq, b Martingell	4	b Martingell	0
W Hillyer, c H Brockwell	12	c Baker, b Lewis	0
R Kynaston, Esq, b Martingell	0	b Martingell	6
W Lillywhite, b Martingell	5	run out	6
W Nicholson, Esq, b Martingell	4	not out	13
F L Currie, Esq, b Martingell	13	c Denison, b Lewis	2
W B Trevelyan, Esq, c Strahan, b Brockwell	11	b Martingell	4
L H Bayley, Esq, not out	2	b Lewis	13
E Bunbury, Esq, b Martingell	4	b Brockwell	0
W Franks, Esq, absent	—	b Brockwell	0
Byes 2, w 0 n-b 1	3	Byes 4, w 1, n-b 2	7
Total	58	Total	63

SURREY

	1st inn		2nd inn
J Spenceley, Esq, l b w, b Hillyer	5	c Nicholson, b Lillywhite	3
T C Lewis, Esq, st Nicholson b Hillyer	4	b Hillyer	0
W Baker, Esq, b Hillyer	0	c George, b Hillyer	11
N Felix, Esq, c and b Hillyer	9	b Lillywhite	6
C Coltson, Esq, not out	9	b Hillyer	1
W Martingell, c Currie, b Hillyer	1	st Nicholson, b Hillyer	1
G Brockwell, b Hillyer	5	b Hillyer	0
C H Hoare, Esq, b Lillywhite	1	c Lillywhite, b Hillyer	5
C Meymott, Esq, c and b Hillyer	0	not out	4
W Strahan, Esq, b Lillywhite	0	b Lillywhite	0
W Denison, Esq, c Nicholson, b Lillywhite	2	c Currie, b Hillyer	1
Bye	1	Byes	4
Total	37	Total	36

About a month after this, Kent appeared against Surrey Considering the lapse of time—eighteen years—since they last met, it was not expected to find many on either side who were engaged at the previous county meeting Kent had several capital players among them Surrey, nevertheless, made the easy conquest of ten wickets Mr C H Hoare got more runs from his own bat than the whole eleven of Kent in a completed innings A match with Marylebone in the same year is noteworthy from the smallness of the four totals and the success of Surrey by 42 runs Surrey 53 and 88—total 143, M C C and G, 37 and 64—total 101 On the Marylebone side were Dean, Hillyer, Lillywhite, Royston, and Sir F Bathurst, as bowlers Mr Charles Taylor was the most successful bat on the Marylebone side with 0 and 20

After a few years these bright prospects were overshadowed, and to such an extent that Mr C Hoare expressed an opinion that if something were not immediately done the club would soon be at an end Great efforts were made to avert this A public meeting took place in 1855, at which one of the speakers said, "Matters had arrived at this point, that one of the two courses must be followed either the club must become lessees of the Oval, or the club must dissolve, seeing that, deprived of the Oval, the club would be without a ground even for practice The chairman remarked that for many years Surrey stood first as cricketers, it then fell off in its power, and other counties rose But why did Surrey decline? Not because it was deficient in talent, but because there was no central ground to which it could be gathered, nor any great club to seek out and draw it to one point Nor was there a sufficient amount of patronage extended by individuals to accomplish that desirable, and, indeed, necessary, object The club had now to enter a new era with effective officers and a combination of powers which he conceived would enable them to look every difficulty in the face He hoped to see in the course of a year or two a pavilion on the ground, but previous to that period their first object would be to make the ground the most perfect that could be found" A subscription list was opened, and in a short time the threatened difficulties and danger of extinction were surmounted, and Surrey started afresh, with brighter prospects than heretofore The following set of rules acted upon by the club in question will furnish the reader with some idea of the manner in which county clubs conduct their business —

RULES OF THE SURREY CLUB

I —That the Surrey Club shall hold its Meetings upon the Surrey Ground, Kennington Oval

II —That the Officers of the Club shall consist of a President, Vice-President, Treasurer, and Secretary, who must be members of the Club, and shall be *ex officio* members of the Committee

III —That the Committee shall consist of the *ex officio* members, and not less than sixteen, and not more than twenty-four Members of the Club, one-third of whom shall retire at the Annual Meeting, by rotation, and shall be eligible for re election

IV —That the President, Vice-President, and Treasurer shall not be removed, except by death or resignation, or by a Special General Meeting called for that purpose

V —That the Committee shall have the power of appointing a Sub-committee of Members resident in any part of the country to assist them in carrying out the objects of the Club

VI —That an Annual Subscription of One Guinea, without entrance fee, shall entitle a member to every privilege except that of practice from the Club Bowlers That an Annual Subscription of Two Pounds, and an Entrance Fee of One Pound, shall entitle a Member to every privilege the Club affords

VII —That the Season shall commence on the first day of May, and all Subscriptions shall become due on that day, and any member not having previously sent in his resignation to the Secretary in writing, shall be liable for that Season's subscription

VIII —That any member whose subscription shall be unpaid on the 1st of June shall receive notice thereof in writing from the Secretary, and the name of any member whose subscription shall remain unpaid on the 1st of July shall be entered in a book kept in the Pavilion for that purpose, but in case the subscription shall not have been paid by the 31st December, the Committee shall have the power to erase his name from the list of members

IX —That the name and address of every candidate for admission to the Club, with the names of his proposer and seconder (who must both be members of the Club) shall be exhibited in the Pavilion for *four* days before ballot

X —That a ballot for new members shall be held at the annual meeting, and also at the Pavilion, on Mondays or Thursdays during the months of May, June, July, and August Pavilion ballots shall be held in the presence of one member of the committee, commencing at half-past three and closing at four o'clock, not less than ten shall constitute a ballot, and two black balls shall exclude

XI —That the practice days of the Club shall be upon Mondays, Tuesdays, Wednesdays, Thursdays, Fridays, and Saturdays (except when the ground is closed for public matches), commencing on the first Club day in May, and continuing to the end of August in each year

XII —That no member shall be permitted to play a second time on the ground unless he shall have paid his subscription for the then season

XIII —That the committee shall have the power to engage as many practice bowlers and boys to be in attendance upon the ground as they shall think fit

XIV —That each member shall have the privilege of introducing one friend into the Pavilion, on his entering his own and his friend's name in a book provided for that purpose

XV —That the property of the Club, other than that legally vested in the Trustees shall be considered as vested in the Committee for the time being That the Committee shall have the entire management of the property, funds, and affairs of the Club, and shall make all byelaws and regulations A quorum shall consist of three committee men, without or in addition to, the *ex officio* members

XVI —That the Committee may appoint members to fill up temporarily all vacancies until the next General or Special Meeting of the Club

XVII —That the Committee shall have the power to appoint a Secretary at a salary the amount of which shall be fixed at the Annual General Meeting of each year The office of Secretary shall be vacated only by death resignation or a vote of two-thirds of the Committee present at a Special Meeting of that body, called for the purpose

XVIII —That the Annual General Meeting shall be held in the months of April or May in each year Ten days notice at least shall be given in writing to each member, stating the object, time, and place of the meeting

XIX —That the Committee shall appoint a professional accountant to audit the accounts of the Club That at the Annual Meeting in each year a statement of the accounts certified by the signature of the Auditor, shall be submitted to the members

XX —That the Committee of Management shall, at the requisition of fifteen members of the Club, or of their own authority, call a Special General Meeting, of which ten days notice, stating the object, time, and place of such meeting, shall be given

XXI —That if any circumstance which, in the opinion of the Committee shall be likely to endanger the welfare or good order of the Club be brought under their notice, it shall be in their discretion to call a Special General Meeting, and in the event of its being voted at that meeting by two-thirds of the members present (to be decided by ballot) that the name of any member be removed from the Club, such individual shall immediately cease to be a member thereof, and shall forfeit *ipso facto* all subscriptions, whether for life or otherwise, and all right to or claim upon the Club or its property

XXII —That a copy of the rules of this Club shall be sent to each new member, with the letter informing him of his election

XXIII —That the rules, or any of them, may be altered, abrogated, and added to, either generally, or for the particular occasion, at any Special General Meeting, by the vote of two-thirds of the members present, and voting at such meeting

Two years after the fresh era, Surrey won all their county matches, but, singular to state, they were beaten by the Manchester Club at Eccles The scoring throughout the match was unusually small, viz, about 75 runs per innings Griffith got nine wickets for 65 runs, Caffyn, three wickets for 53 runs, and Martingell, five wickets for 23 runs On the other side Wisden got twelve wickets for 70 runs, John Lillywhite, three wickets for 23 runs, Mr Rowley, two wickets for 37 runs, and Mr Makinson, one wicket for 3 runs

From the enormous amount of business Surrey had to transact, it is impossible even to present a fair account of good matches in a paragraph, and only one or two in the space of a decade can be given in full in consequence of the space they would occupy. In the year 1860 Surrey took a strong team to the Hove Ground, Brighton, and beat Sussex by an innings and 43 runs. How this was accomplished, the following transcript from the score-sheet will demonstrate:—

SURREY.

F. P. Miller, Esq., c Napper, b Wells	105
Sewell, st Knight, b Wells	62
Caffyn, c Hall, b Wells	2
C. G. Lane, Esq., b Wells	11
Griffith, c Ellis, b Wells	2
Mortlock, not out	49
E. Dawson, Esq., c Hale, b Wells	19
Lockyer, b Fawcett	10
Stephenson, b Wells	8
Mudie, c Fawcett, b Wells	3
Heartfield, st Knight, b Wells	2
Byes 4, l-b 2, w 5	11
Total	284

SUSSEX.

	1st inn.		2nd inn.
J. H. Hall, Esq., c Lane, b Heartfield	30	c and b Mudie	30
Jas. Lillywhite, run out	1	run out	0
Knight, b Caffyn	2	not out	3
Wells, h w, b Caffyn	10	c Dawson, b Mudie	3
Ellis, b Heartfield	5	b Heartfield	26
D. R. Onslow, Esq., b Caffyn	16	c Lockyer, b Mudie	4
E. Napper, Esq., b Heartfield	2	c Miller, b Heartfield	52
E. B. Fawcett, Esq., b Heartfield	7	c Sewell, b Miller	1
Reed, b Heartfield	6	c Lane, b Caffyn	4
F. F. Thomas, Esq., b Heartfield	7	b Miller	0
Stubberfield, not out	5	b Miller	16
L-b 7, n-b 1	8	L-b 2, w 1	3
Total	99	Total	142

Here is a fitting place to proclaim the complete realisation of the chairman's wishes at the general meeting previously mentioned. The Surrey club could now boast of a pavilion, with a dining-room 44ft. by 22ft., and a dressing-room 22ft. square, erected at a cost of 1200*l*; a membership of 1000, and an income of 3000*l*.—wonderful apparent strength with much real weakness. Caffyn—a host in himself—had taken up his abode at the Antipodes, and other signs of adversity were perceptible. Possessed of a surprising amount of self-confidence the county pursued the "tenor of its way," though not with "even" success.

The year 1868 was remarkable for many events relating to cricket. One incident enforces itself. In a contest with the University of Cambridge, at the Oval, Mr Absolom—a powerful hitter—made a splendid drive, for which six runs were fully made, but venturing upon the seventh, the ball was returned so sharply that it came in contact with the striker's bat before the popping-crease was reached. An appeal to the constituted authority proved adverse to Mr Absolom. He of course retired. On reaching the pavilion he was told to return. This silly mandate received the contempt it deserved. Without doubt the ignorance of the umpire sadly marred the prospects of the Light Blues, inasmuch as Mr H A Richardson, a most successful batsman in the first innings, was unable to do anything in the second in consequence of an injured hand. Furthermore, it may be said that the complexity hanging about trial matches, such as those between a county or a club, was strikingly apparent during the season in question. Hence Oxford beat Surrey in a single innings, while Surrey obtained but a trifling victory over Cambridge, and the Light Blues beat the Dark, at Lord's, by 168 runs. Trial matches of this nature afford little, if any, criterion whereby even the most calculating may judge of after acts. Little imagination or research is needed to establish such a postulate. Abundant evidence might be furnished. One grain of experimental knowledge upon the subject is therefore worth a full ounce of conjecture, and one fact more than a thousand arguments. Respecting the weather, scarcely a wet day interposed to prevent playing out an unprecedented string of matches arranged to come off here, there, and everywhere. Long scores abounded, and drawn matches there were not a few. Up to September the heat was great. In the first week it equalled in intensity any period of the spring and summer months preceding. Thus the mean maximum for the week was 106 3, the mean shade maximum 88 303, the mean minimum 50 7 degrees. There was no rain for the first eighteen days, afterwards it fell copiously. Surrey came in for a full share of these events, but is still more noticeable in the fact of two "tie" matches—a circumstance seldom recorded. The summary of the season places this county in a not unfavourable position, notwithstanding the "tall talk" and wild prophecies about a speedy dissolution.

COUNTY OF SURREY

Lord's May 25.—Surrey v M C C and Ground. Surrey, 117 and 132—total 249, M C C, 71 and 179 with six wickets down. M C C won by four wickets.

Oval, June 4.—Surrey v M C C and Ground (return). Surrey, 204 and 93—total 297, M C C 175 and 122—total 297. A tie.

Manchester, June 11.—Surrey v Lancashire. Surrey, 252 and 42—total 294, Lancashire, 204 and 93, with two wickets down—total 297. Lancashire won by eight wickets.

Oval, June 18.—Surrey v Cambridge University. Surrey, 179 and 334—total 513, Cambridge, 339 and 160—total 499. Surrey won by 14 runs.

Sheffield, June 22.—Surrey v Yorkshire. Surrey, 222, Yorkshire, 71 and 145—total 216. Surrey won by an innings and 6 runs.

Oval, June 25.—Surrey v Oxford University. Surrey, 211 and 99—total 310, Oxford, 396, winning by an innings and 86 runs.

Oval, July 6.—Surrey v Sussex. Surrey, 126 and 102, with three wickets down—total 228, Sussex, 98 and 128—total 226. Surrey won by seven wickets.

Gravesend, July 9 —Surrey v Kent Surrey, 64 and 101—total 165, Kent, 203 and 73—total 276 Kent won by 111 runs

Oval, July 13 — Surrey v Notts Surrey, 114 and 184—total 298, Notts, 58 and 166—total 224, Surrey won by 74 runs

Oval, July 16 —Surrey v Lancashire (return) Surrey, 351, Lancashire, 120 and 89—total 209 Surrey won by an innings and 142 runs

Brighton, July 20 —Surrey v Sussex (return) Surrey, 297 and 17, with one wicket down—total 314, Sussex, 166 and 145—total 311 Surrey won by nine wickets

Oval, July 30 —Surrey v Middlesex Surrey, 93 and 186—total 279, Middlesex, 112 and 167—total 279 A tie

Oval, August 10 —Surrey v Kent (return) Surrey, 136 and 136—total 272, Kent, 224 and 49, with five wickets down—total 273 Kent won by five wickets

Islington, August 20 —Surrey v Middlesex (return) Surrey, 89 and 35—total 124, Middlesex, 139 and 156—total 295 Middlesex won by 171 runs

Oval, August 24 —Surrey v Yorkshire (return) Surrey, 195 and 52—total 247, Yorkshire, 389 Yorkshire won by an innings and 142 runs

Nottingham August 27 —Surrey v Notts (return) Surrey, 69 and 78—total 147, Notts, 129 and 202—total 331. Notts won by 184 runs

BATTING AVERAGES

NAME	No of Matches	No of Innings	Most Runs in a Match	Most Runs in an Innings	How often bowled	Caught	Run out	Stumped	Not out	Total	Average per Innings Over
Buckle	2	3	10	6	1	1	0	1	0	11	3- 2
Bristow	16	29	79	79	10	11	3	5	0	275	9–14
Mr C Calvert	14	23	67	67	19	0	1	2	1	266	11–13
Griffith	13	24	80	60	6	15	2	0	1	395	16–11
Humphrey	16	29	120	103	5	21	0	1	2	654	22–16
Jupp	16	30	159	134	14	11	1	3	1	780	26
Mortlock	9	17	76	66	9	4	1	2	1	296	17– 7
Mr H Mayo	2	3	4	4	1	1	0	1	0	4	1– 1
Pooley	16	29	60	51	16	9	2	0	2	417	14–11
Stephenson	16	29	55	44	8	16	2	1	2	418	14–12
Sewell	16	28	50	50	6	10	2	7	3	157	5–17
Street	10	17	16	16	7	4	1	4	1	69	4– 1
Southerton	10	18	28	24	8	6	1	2	1	118	6–10
Mr C Noble	4	7	24	17	4	3	0	0	0	53	7– 4
Mr J W W Noble	6	10	30	24	6	2	2	0	0	98	9- 8

The following played in one match only —Messrs Brown, Bagallay, Bush, Hall, W W Lane, J Nightingale, Roberts, Pratt, Farmer, and Willis

Perhaps, with some of the many vaticinators, "the wish was father to the thought," and though in too many instances their foreshadowings were nearly true, Surrey resolved not to be awed by a run of adverse luck, but to persevere in their path illumined by the lamp of hope The executive must have been men of strong faith, seeing they lost thirteen matches before they gained one, and, in fact, won but one in sixteen At this time, there were nearly 1200 members with an income of 3500*l* A new secretary (Mr Alcock) displaced Mr Burrup, and another incident may be mentioned, that of Caffyn's return to his native country from Australia—not the man that he left it, and the fallacious hopes entertained by some that Surrey would revive again were not realised Surrey managed to beat Middlesex by six wickets, Gloucestershire by one wicket, and Kent by 129 runs

In 1872, Surrey were very successful, for, out of fifteen matches, they won eight, and two were left drawn Nor was the financial balance sheet at all discouraging in the following year, although 250*l* were required for the first time in payment for the services of the newly appointed secretary A wind from nearly all quarters blew against Surrey in 1874, notwithstanding a favourable start in June, when opposed to Gloucestershire The overthrow of Mr W G Grace for the trifling scores of 6 and 35, was doubtless very encouraging, so also the result of the match declared in favour of Surrey by four wickets How different the aspect of matters ten weeks afterwards, when the return took place at Cheltenham, and only 27 runs resulted from the first innings the top score 6 Briefly, then, be it stated that Surrey played ten matches, of which they lost six and won three Every effort was made to recover the losses thus sustained when the campaign of 1875 began As in the previous year, the season commenced with Gloucestershire against them. Surrey realised a full total of 267 Of this number the adversary came short by 26 The second, played at the Oval August 5, was left drawn, the scores being, Surrey, 241 and 54 (eight wickets)—total 295, Sussex, 169 and 158—total 327 A few days later Sussex defeated them by an innings and 37 runs, the scores being, Surrey, 180 and 71—total 251, Sussex, 288 At Cheltenham, on the 26th, Gloucestershire were winners by an innings and 84 runs On the 16th, at the Oval, in a contest with Yorkshire, the latter won by eight wickets

ANALYSIS OF THE BATTING IN 1875

NAME	No of Matches	No of Innings	Most Runs in a Match	Most Runs in an Innings	How often bowled	Caught	Run out	Stumped	Not out	Total	Average per Innings Over
Clifford	4	8	22	12	0	7	0	0	1	43	5- 3
Chandler	6	11	64	64	3	7	1	0	0	127	11- 6
Game	5	9	47	47	3	4	0	1	1	180	20
Humphrey	9	18	53	43	7	8	2	0	1	197	10-17
Elliott	10	19	63	53	8	8	1	0	2	343	18- 1
Freeman	3	6	24	17	5	1	0	0	0	29	4- 5
Jupp	10	18	90	60	5	11	0	1	1	292	16- 4
Lucas	5	10	56	50	4	4	1	0	1	145	14- 5
Pooley	10	19	57	32	8	8	0	2	1	208	14- 2
Potter	4	8	20	18	6	1	0	1	0	52	6- 4
Reed	5	10	120	98	2	5	1	0	2	247	24- 7
Strachan	5	10	41	34	5	5	0	0	0	173	17- 3
Southerton	10	18	35	33	5	5	1	0	7	160	8-16
Swann	5	10	28	28	3	6	0	1	0	91	9- 1
Street	10	17	29	21	9	2	0	0	6	74	4- 6
Wheeler	4	8	13	13	2	3	1	1	1	25	3- 1

From this slight glance—slight as respects the standing and position of Surrey—it will be seen that the acorn was first dropt or planted in this county. How, and by what mode of cultivation the sapling grew, to what extent it ramified, and for what reason it attracted so little attention are matters not easily to be ascertained. A century is a wide gap in its history; but when brought again into notice, its growth, apparently silent as the processes of Nature in life not sentient, was amply manifest. In the last cycle, the proportions assumed have indeed been vast, and every well-wisher to Surrey and to cricket will swell the "Old Oak" chorus of

> "And still flourish he, a hale green tree,
> When a hundred years are gone."

But stay; this is an age of rapid growths and equally rapid decay—rapid even to revolution. "All things are full of change; man cannot utter it." Who can tell how soon the legs of the theodolite may be straddling about the Oval, and the present beautiful sward be encompassed by the engineer taking out "quantities"? Few places, nowadays, can withstand the fierce temptations attendant upon the colour of gold, and the blandishments of speculators. Far distant, however, be the day when the buzz of approbation and the shout of applause, attending the gazers on cricket, shall be exchanged for the hum of new-made streets, and the rattle of a captured wicket for the postman's knock.

The Oval has a strong hold upon the non-aristocratic class. Its associations are adapted to their means in general, and its position to their time and convenience in particular. Their conditions of enjoyment are not trammelled, and their native instincts are allowed fuller play than would be considered quite in keeping at some loftier institutions. Here, a boisterous shout with its echo is not regarded as a breach of etiquette, and a little homely badinage is not construed into vulgarity. As a rule, the visitors to this locality know something of the game, and can, therefore, applaud the right men and the right act at the right time. Here, too, may be heard disquisitions on the deeds of the departed great; how modern bowling has revolutionised the game of cricket altogether, and subjected the wicket-keeper to perils scarcely less appalling than those which await the leader of a forlorn hope in a hot assault; how it strains the nerves of a batsman to an almost unbearable tension, and how it gives the field twice as much to do as was its share of a match when lobs and slow twists were the fashion, and when the old form was more fatal to "wood" than the new. Such theorists, who cling to one set of thoughts, fail to consider that Esop's tortoise and the doddering motto "*Festina lente*" belong to the past in matters appertaining to cricket. If the bowling is faster, say its advocates, it is merely in keeping with an age which travels fast, makes and loses money fast, and spends its vitality fast. Nor is the Oval the platform for discussions; such things creep in as commentaries upon the active scene before the eye of the visitor; and who can force back the current of thought or stay the expression thereof? Nowhere in or near the Metropolis is the power of numbers more sensibly felt, and this is a great element of success. Let the executive announce a good match, let the weather be genial, and although the place of action be two miles from the heart of the busiest and most crowded city in the universe with all the attractions thereunto belonging, the stream sets toward Kennington; and, as if by the wand of a magician, the scene is changed into a crowded amphitheatre in lieu of an ideal *Rus in urbe.*

CHAPTER XII.

GLANCES AT THE PAST AND PRESENT STATE OF COUNTY CRICKET—*continued.*

SUSSEX.

. . . . . that pale, that white-faced shore,
Whose foot spurns back the ocean's roaring tide,
And coops from other lands her islanders.
King John, Act ii., Scene 1.

CHARACTER AND EXTENT OF THE COUNTY—SILENCE WITH RESPECT TO EARLY CRICKET—NEWLAND, NOAH MANN, AND OTHERS—SUSSEX *v.* HAMBLEDON IN 1791—PRINCE OF WALES'S PATRONAGE—MATCH WITH KENT IN 1809—DIVIDED CRICKET IN THE COUNTY—LEWES *v.* HASTINGS, AN ODD ENCOUNTER—THE STORRINGTON CLUB—BRIGHTON GROUND—NOVEL AND ROMANTIC COUNTY MATCH—CLOSE MATCH WITH ENGLAND—ALSO NOTTS—LAST MATCH ON IRELAND'S GARDENS—NOVEL AND SUCCESSFUL BOWLING OF BOX—FORMATION OF COUNTY CLUB—DEMISE OF MR. BRIDGER STENT—SURRENDER OF THE OLD BRUNSWICK GROUND—A NEW ONE—BATTING ANALYSIS IN 1875—OFFICE BEARERS OF THE CLUB.

BEFORE giving utterance to this expression, the immortal Bard of Avon was no doubt pretty well "up" in the history of the South Coast in general, and this portion of it in particular. Sussex—the *Sutheaxe* of the South Saxons—can point to the bruises and scars of centuries ago, in testimony of many a hard struggle to coop out invaders. It is not so densely populated, perhaps, as some other counties in the home district, seeing that in an area of 936,911 acres, or 1464 square miles, the number of souls at a recent census did not exceed 420,000, and the increase up to this number was very rapid upon the introduction of the railway to Brighton. If peculiar gifts "run in families," that applying to cricket may be said with equal force to run in counties, of which cluster around the metropolis, Sussex has an unquestionable right to claim membership. The precise date of its coming to the front as a county club cannot be determined with sufficient certainty to form a foundation on which to build a solid superstructure. Learning necessary for the poorer classes obtrudes itself occasionally in such an awkward guise, that little can be made out of it. That the county possessed cricketers of note in the middle of the last century there is not the shadow of a doubt. Newland, for instance, of Slendon, born 1734 (the teacher of Nyren), Noah Mann, of Petworth, born 1756, and others; but no documents have hitherto been handed down to show conclusively that Sussex, in a concrete character, approached the standard of neighbouring counties, although abundant evidence is given of contests between parish and parish, or an individual club against others even out of the county Their recital would afford no interest to cricketers of the present day, even if the start occurred from 1783, when Brighthing met Netherfield It is known that Sussex (so called), with a few given men, played the town of Hambledon in 1791, and won by eleven runs, and also that, in conjunction with Surrey, they beat England by an innings and 299 runs before two years had fully expired. As this is the first appearance of Sussex in a contest of note at Lord's or elsewhere, the score is given, from which the reader will be able to see how much of so singular a success is due to the Sussex contingent

ENGLAND

	1st inn		1st inn
Captain C Cumberland, b Hammond	0	c Tufton	1
G Louch, Esq , c Beldham	0	b Beldham	1
J. Welsh, Esq , c H Walker	4	b Hammond	1
Scott c Hammond	3	run out	35
Purchase, c Wells	24	c Hammond	19
Fennex, c Beldham	8	b Beldham	12
Freemantle, b T Walker	8	not out	13
Ring, b Wells	1	c Hammond	0
Fielder, c Wells	8	b T Walker	3
Taylor, c Hammond	6	b Beldham	2
Boxall, not out	1	c H Walker	1
Byes	3		
Total	66	Total	88

SUSSEX

Earl of Winchilsea, b Fennex	56
Hon H Tufton, b Fennex	0
G Dehancy, Esq , b Boxall	1
T Nichol, Esq , b Boxall	2
T Walker, b Boxall	138
Wells, b Purchase	51
John Walker, b Purchase	24
Crawte, b Purchase	11
Beldham, b Purchase	77
H Walker, b Cumberland	51
Hammond, not out	37
Byes	5
Total	453

A great impetus was given to cricket in Sussex when the Prince of Wales, afterwards George the Fourth, resided at Brighton Whether his Royal Highness was a player or not matters little, but his promotion of the game at the time in question had a great effect upon the cricket of Brighton and its surroundings, and for many years after he came to the throne the Level was the chief place of resort for matches claiming any importance One not of county "form" may not be uninteresting even at this remote distance of time It occurred in the year 1793 between the Left Wing Officers of the Camp and the Right The Royal ground was chosen for the encounter Compared with the military achievements of the present day, the scores look very gaunt Here they are, faithfully transcribed The Left won by 35 runs

LEFT.

	1st inn		2nd inn
Captain Cranston, b Austen	9	b Blagrave	9
Whicher, b Blagrave	0	b Blagrave	17
Drew b Austen	55	c Austen	1
Philby, b Austen	5	c Child	0
Gilham, c Vellee	14	b Blagrave	1
Allee c Austen	0	c Child	0
Mitchell, c Bowes	2	b Austen	0
Whistler, b Austen	0	c Bullock	1
Boycott, run out	2	not out	6
Munro, c Austen	1	b Austen	2
J Munro, not out	0	c Austen	1
Byes	7	Byes	3
Total	95	Total	41

RIGHT

	1st inn		2nd inn.
Captain Blagrave, c Cranston	13	b Cranston	13
Austen, hit down	3	b Drew	14
Vellee, c Drew	4	c Philby	1
J Bowes b Drew	1	c Boycott	3
Child, c Cranston	6	c Cranston	16
Bullock, b Allee	10	thrown out by Cranston	0
Waring b Drew	1	not out	0
Lord Ashbrook, not out	1	b Cranston	4
Pulk, b Drew	0	b Whistler	3
Salmon, c Drew	0	b Cranston	0
T Bowes, b Drew	0	c Whicher	2
Byes	4	Byes	2
Total	43	Total	58

Mention is made of a very curious encounter between Sussex and Kent in the autumn of 1809 As the match was confined to one day, and that day very limited for sunlight, it was agreed to decide the winnership by the result of the first innings provided the game could not be played out Sussex won by three runs Kent had to pay for a fat sheep roasted whole

One of the local papers speaking of cricket played on the Level, at Brighton, says —"A match between the cricketers of this place and those of Cowfold took place on the 11th of June (1811), when the latter were the victors, and 6 runs to spare Formerly, when the Prince countenanced them, the Brighton eleven were a match for All England, and the Marylebone Club were more than once beaten by them, and reluctantly compelled to acknowledge the superiority of their skill But as nothing flourishes in this part of the world, but in the renovating rays of the patronage of the Heir Apparent, our cricketers had no sooner lost that fostering influence which could alone inspirit them to action and give new energies to every effort, than supineness succeeded, and they at last, in the gymnastic sports, dwindled and degenerated into their original insignificance"

On the opening of the 19th century, a somewhat novel feature presents itself, that of a parish club (Storrington) against its own county The club had certainly the assistance of three men, and what is little less singular, two years after Sussex divided itself into East and West If this device originated in a desire to test the relative capabilities of the county so split, neither could boast of either strength or skill, the scoring throughout was indeed feeble, averaging about 50 runs per innings As East and West did not come up to much, another experiment was tried between North and South, and, although fate forbad the match to be brought to a decisive issue, the former "looked" the stronger side, one man scored nearly twice as many runs from his own bat as the whole of the "warmer" side. In another similarly constructed affair, the North won by eight wickets In both cases there were given men on each side, so that the actual native strength must be viewed as conjectural.

While these and a few other vagaries were indulged in by sections of cricketers in order to obtain county honours, the mimicry of cricket found a time and place for its development Lewes challenged Hastings with an odd lot On a given day the challengers took their departure together for the field of action from before the Swan Inn, amid the huzzas of the surrounding multitude, in a waggon arched over with green boughs, and drawn by four oxen ornamented with ribbons, one of the party operated as charioteer with white reins fastened to the horns of the animals They were preceded by a car of a minor description (a donkey vehicle) and two Egyptian ponies, which exhibited four musicians with their faces elegantly besmeared with common rouge, and variegated with soot, to the no small diversion of a great number of spectators After the game (in which two men with wooden legs played with great alertness) the party returned in the same manner to the Swan tap, where a dinner was provided for them *

As yet, Storrington held the most prominent position as a club, and in the year 1811 confronted Sussex at High Down Hill Each side had four given men Storrington won by 14 runs, the scores being—for the Club, 117 and 107—total 224, County, 140 and 70—total 210 At the same place a year later, the Weald played the Coast, with four men given to each, when the former won by 23 runs After this fashion Sussex appears to plod on till the first quarter of the century fast tapers away Storrington played at Brighton in June, 1819, when the residents defeated them by 20 runs, and a few weeks later they were still more significantly worsted, viz, by six wickets Brighton now 'comes to the fore" Among its members were seen "men of the future"—men who have left their mark for posterity to look upon

Brighton has had many cricket-grounds in its day, but one after another disappeared in consequence of the incessant enlargement of streets and houses In

* *Sporting Magazine*, vol xlvi, p 234

the early days of the present century, the aborigines of the place, aided by occasional help from neighbouring parishes, contended against elevens of England or the Marylebone Club—not in vain either. Then matches came off on what is called the Level, a piece of ground to the north of St. Peter's Church, now surrounded by trees, and nearly denuded of turf by the many footpaths made across it and the incessant gambols of boys and men. The piece of ground before referred to as that on which the Prince of Wales used to practise and play also with the Brighton men, was afterwards known as Ireland's Gardens. When the Level became totally unfit to play upon, many county matches took place on the side of the Racecourse Hill, about half way between the town and the Course. About the year 1824, Ireland's Gardens became the recognised county ground. Here was played the famous match between Sussex and England, on which occasion 112*l* were taken in sixpences the first day. The match was lost to Sussex, owing to the freak by J. Broadbridge of throwing his bat to an off-ball, which was caught by Mr. Ward. In other respects the match possessed singular features; thus, in the first innings of England five of the number went out without a run, and the total did not average three runs, extras included. On the Sussex side there were but two double figures. See score:—

ENGLAND

	1st inn		2nd inn
Searle, b Lillywhite	7	b J. Broadbridge	7
Pilch, run out	3	b Brown	9
J. Saunders, st Slater	0	c Dale	14
W. Ward, Esq., b J. Broadbridge	2	b Lillywhite	5
E. H. Budd, Esq., b Lillywhite	8	c Dale	14
Marsden, c Dale	0	st Slater	9
Beagley, c J. Broadbridge	5	c Dale	26
R. Mills, c Lillywhite	0	not out	4
G. T. Knight, Esq., b Lillywhite	0	c Dale	3
H. Kingscote, Esq., b J. Broadbridge	0	c Brown	31
G. Osbaldeston, Esq., not out	0	c W. Broadbridge	7
Byes	2	Byes	11
Total	27	Total	170

SUSSEX

	1st inn		2nd inn
Morley, c Budd	3	c Osbaldeston	0
Lillywhite, b Mills	8	not out	0
Thwaites, st Saunders	7	h w	20
J. Broadbridge, b Knight	0	c Ward	0
Brown, c Pilch	24	b Knight	17
W. Broadbridge, st Saunders	18	h w	4
Dale, c Saunders	4	run out	20
Lanaway, b Pilch	0	b Knight	0
Baker, st Saunders	4	c Ward	7
R. Cheslyn, Esq., run out	4	run out	10
Slater, not out	0	b Budd	4
Byes	5	Byes	13
Total	77	Total	95

The names of Lee, Pierrepont, Brown, Lillywhite, Box &c, were frequently attached to grounds, but, independently of these, many highly interesting matches, in which Sussex had no concern, were played in the county One of the number is of so peculiar and romantic a character that it deserves attention An eye witness, under the signature of "N N," has thus spoken of it —

"A COUNTY CRICKET MATCH"

In wrestling nimble, and in running swift,
In shooting steady, and in swimming strong,
Well made to strike to throw, to leap, to lift,
* * * * * *
He vanquished all and vanquished was of none —*Spenser*

"These lines applied to Sir Philip Sydney, and many more by the same great bard might also fitly apply to the hero of the match about to be described A hero indeed, who was a gymnast among millions, possessed of admirable skill and power, he favoured the 'ring,' and yet did not outrage good sense by unreasonable patronage to its professors With respect to the sword, he was like Sir Piercy Shafton, the first scholar of the first master of the age With the foil, he was admirable, his *ripostes* were given with the speed of light, his time thrusts never failing, yet, he was still more formidable at singlestick These accomplishments, as will hereafter be seen, were of essential service to him, but in nothing more was he so perfect as in his country's glorious sport—cricket Here he was good, very good, at every point of the game, but as a hitter or long field, his match was not to be found, and it was on a day marked in the annals of "the noble game" by one of his most admirable displays of skill, vigour, and activity, that an incident occurred which, however slight in itself, had some influence on his future destinies

"A great county match—a real county match between *bonâ fide* neighbours—was made by the first *amateurs* of the day—Kent *v* Hampshire—and the neutral ground of Sussex was fixed on as the seat of action Could there be conceived anything more exhilarating, more exciting to a true lover of the game, than such a match—a combination of three glorious counties, the delightful scenery of Sussex and its salubrious breezes, its population, well fitted to judge of cricketing excellence, and last, not least, the bright eyes of its lasses—the prettiest in all England according to competent judges, William Cobbett for one—to 'rain influence and judge the prize!' Nor were the people of Sussex the only spectators Kent sent forth in throngs its bold yeomen and independent burgesses, and not a few of the wild foresters of Hampshire came from their remotest woods to witness a scene so interesting It was altogether a sight gratifying to an Englishman, for the rapid degeneracy of all kinds which political economy and other causes have of late produced among our peasantry, had, as yet, scarcely commenced, and in appearance and bearing they were worthy of the soil which produced them Add to all these favourable circumstances the loveliest weather of the lovely month of June, and what more could player or beholder desire

'The scene of friendly strife was nearly midway between the contending counties, in the park of a nobleman whose hospitable halls sent forth a bevy of ladies, and these were recruited from the neighbouring seats, and, indeed, from those full many a mile distant. At an early hour the wickets were pitched. Hampshire won the toss and put Kent in; but where is Evelyn at this anxious moment? He was not wont to be slack on occasions of inferior interest. 'Never fear, he will be here presently,' said the men of Kent. The play commenced. Two steady bats were together; but scarcely had the first prepared to meet the coming ball, when tric-trac, the well-known and peculiar fatal sound, so difficult to describe and yet so familiar to the ear of every player, gave token that his wicket had fallen before the sons of Ham and Bacon. A shout which rent the skies from one half of the multitude, and a deep groan of surprise and disappointment on the part of the other, arose simultaneously; but, notwithstanding these discouraging circumstances at starting, and mindful of ancient fame,

"Bold Kent made no submission.

"Their best hitter but one succeeded his fallen comrade, the impatient ball was soon again in action, and another sound peculiar quickly ensued—the joyous echo of a well-struck ball. The Men of Kent cheered, but alas! the joy was premature. The batsman, too intent upon mischief, had indeed hit the ball hard and home, but her disposition was unfortunately too 'heavenward,' and transformed into a sky-lark 'soaring sings.' Her upward flight once over, she descended with headlong speed, and, lest she should be injured by a rough contact with Mother Earth, she was clutched fast in the brawny hands of a broad-shouldered New Forester. Hampshire grew exultant, Kent gloomy, and the betting part of the ring became noisy. The protracted absence of Evelyn began to excite curiosity, but those who knew him best were convinced that stern fate alone could detain him from a sport he loved so well. The match proceeded. The wickets of Kent were lowered with more or less ease, and 126 runs were registered. The absence of Evelyn bordered upon mystery; even to his parents, who had come to see the match, and who not only regarded his absence with surprise, but alarm. Hampshire went in, and whether from superior skill or fortune, or both united, their runs came fast—faster—exceeding fast; and when the last two men quitted their wickets they had more than doubled the innings of Kent, scoring 260. In the interval of rest the multitude talked over the events of the morning. Sad, sulky, and almost fierce were the Men of Kent, but to their honour, far as they were from home, they would not even talk of a surrender. The play had commenced early, and was to be continued late, in order that the game might be concluded in as short a time as possible, and 'play the match out' was the general cry. No substitute for Evelyn had been proposed, for such was the confidence placed in his skill, that his party would not have taken any other player, or even two, whilst even the forlorn hope of his arriving before the close of the second innings remained to them. His veteran sire, though not without unpleasant misgivings that some accident had befallen his son, cheered his countrymen by recalling to their minds the infinite variety of the game, and that a match is never won till it is lost. Once more Kent sent in two champions Both played with caution, but not with timidity, and when the ninth man had succumbed to the adverse bowler, they had only two to tie The game, though so gallantly contested was, however, lost—at least so thought both the out and in-side, but in gloomy despair Kent awaited the allotted ten minutes for the absent player When just five of these had been numbered with the times gone by the rapid clang of a horse's hoofs when at its utmost speed attracted the crowd, and while yet two minutes of grace remained, the absentee appeared at a racing pace In an instant his eagle eye and quick ear perceived the peril of his county and, leaping to the ground, he threw off his coat, seized a bat, and rushed to the wicket His partner was a safe and steady player, and of good judgment Evelyn had the ball, played it, and in another minute Kent are *tye* and *four* on Hope began to revive, but formidable odds presented themselves Jack Styles played well up to him, but the force, confidence, and skill of the young squire surpassed description The red-hot balls of Elliot at Gibraltar were scarcely more terrible to his foes, and certainly not more cheering to his friends, than the red and not cool ball of this great match, urged by the vigorous arm of this astonishing cricketer. At last, when Sykes was out, he quitted his post with honour with 45 runs from his own bat, gained in marvellously quick time, and the whole day's play stood thus Kent's second innings, 182—total 308, being 48 ahead of the rival county Play now ceased for the night Kent were still sensible that they had an uphill fight to win, but they, too, felt that Evelyn was a host in himself, and despaired not Hampshire was still confident, but Evelyn was now surrounded by inquiring friends anxious to know the cause of his strange absence It was, of course, unintentional and unavoidable, but he had been made the victim of a base and ingenious hoax, doubtless by some who had heavy bets against Kent A letter, most plausibly composed, led him to believe the scene of action changed to a distance of sixty miles off across country He had only discovered his error in time to arrive at the eleventh hour

"The following day was equally brilliant, and the spectators equally interesting and numerous. Evelyn appeared in the field in the regulation cricket costume of his day—silk stockings &c—which displayed his fine athletic proportion to admiration His whole appearance was such as might have attracted a lady's eye, and possibly, if the truth could have been ascertained, it might have had such an effect He played in the field on the second day in a manner worthy of his previous evening's display at the popping-crease He was *hic et ubique*, and the hitters opposed to him declared they could not get a ball past him The first man he caught out at the first ball, close to the ground Few and far between were now the runs of Hampshire Sometimes he relieved the bowlers, and in this way also lowered a wicket But at length the crack hitter of his county, an Ajax of a fellow, Harry Hodges by name, appeared bat in hand Not long after one fieldsman retired with two of his fingers broken, another lad had his leg severely hurt, and in spite of all the exertions of his opponents he got his runs very fast

'Amongst the spectators on this memorable day were a party of ladies conspicuous above the assembled crowd for elegance of demeanour, and one of whom in particular was of surpassing beauty It happened that the open carriage in which they were seated stood within some fifty yards to the right of our hero's post in the long-field and as he passed and repassed he was thus fully given to the view of its occupants, who might in their turn have been sufficiently conspicuous to him, had he given them much of his attention, but, sooth to say, he was so intent upon the game—his duty for the time—that he scarcely perceived Louisa Wilmot, the reigning beauty of Sussex, was a pretty girl On a sudden one of the terrible hits of Hodges is heard, the stumper and leg-man play at it in vain, the ball speeds on its way, and,

"As when the bolt red hissing from above
Darts on the consecrated plant of Jove,

so flies the impetuous missive point blank for the carriage—which was much too thronged to move—directly on a level with the lovely head of Louisa Our hero was far off—so far, indeed, that an attempt to stop the ball would never have occurred to most players; but whether excited beyond himself by the danger of the ladies or the dangers of defeat, or both at once, he sprang forward with unutterable speed, and, as the ball rushed among the affrighted groups, by one astonishing leap he grasped the projectile—then close to Miss Wilmot's head—and secured it In another instant it is launched into air amidst the eager applauses of the whole Kentish party With a graceful bow to the ladies he advanced again to renew his labours in the field, nor had he even yet perceived all the exquisite beauty of the rescued maiden, for the action occupied but an instant and she had naturally averted her face from the coming ball But he had seen enough to raise some interest in his mind though now intent on conquest. On the other hand, the elder ladies who had before remarked—for play like his required not a profound knowledge of the game to win admiration—his matchless prowess in the contest, now unanimously agreed they had never seen so fine nor so gentlemanlike a young man, and Louisa, though she said little, could not avoid thinking so too The remainder of the game is soon told The rest of the Hampshire men tumbled out one after the other—as very excellent players will sometimes do—with very few runs to be recorded Evelyn himself disposed of two men in the field, and levelled one wicket with the ball The whole eleven were got out for 36, and were thus in a deficit of 12 runs There was no difference of opinion respecting the match Everyone allowed that Evelyn had run away with it The beaten men themselves almost forgot their disappointment in generous admiration of the excellence of their brother player"

The first time that Sussex played without foreign assistance was in Bramshill Park (Sir John Cope's), Hampshire It was the return match to one played in Petworth Park (the Earl of Egremont's), when Saunders assisted Sussex, and when the latter were winners by 177 runs Hampshire had the best of the encounter when both counties stood alone How it came to pass that Sussex left some of their best men at home then it would be hazardous to say now

In 1826 East Sussex were opposed to the West on Ireland's ground. The scoring throughout the match was small, very small in comparison with modern achievements, viz. East Sussex, 76 and 79—total 155; West Sussex, 57 and 62—total 119; thus yielding to the East by a difference of 36 runs. There is a dim as well as a bright side in the composition of every picture; the dark reveals the bright, and *vice versâ*. Sussex, in 1832, had lifted up their heads sufficiently high to challenge England at Lord's; and although the team of the latter were certainly not the best that could have been produced, they managed to send Sussex to their respective quarters beaten by five wickets. Score:

SUSSEX.

	1st inn.		2nd inn.
Brown, b Cobbett	0	b Wenman	10
Lillywhite, c sub	3	b Cobbett	3
James Broadbridge, run out	0	b Cobbett	21
Hooker, b Cobbett	0	c Caldecourt	2
H. Kingscote, Esq., b Pilch	1	b Cobbett	36
Meads, b Cobbett	0	b Caldecourt	7
Box, b Cobbett	3	c Ward	2
Wells, b Cobbett	6	c Ward	6
Sir St. Vincent Cotton, c Ward	15	hit wicket	1
Lanaway, run out	0	c Pilch	3
H. Howard, Esq., not out	1	not out	2
Byes 1, w 2	3	Byes 5, w 4, n b 1	10
Total	32	Total	103

ENGLAND.

	1st inn.		2nd inn.
Captain Cheslyn, b Broadbridge	1	c Brown	2
H. B. Caldwell, Esq., run out	0	b Lillywhite	0
Wenman, c Hooker	0	c Wells	20
Pilch, run out	11	not out	40
Cobbett, b Lillywhite	0	not out	4
Caldecourt, b Broadbridge	0		
W. Ward, Esq., not out	41		
H. E. Knatchbull, Esq., b Lillywhite	1	b Lillywhite	0
Sir F. Bathurst, b Lillywhite	10	b Lillywhite	0
Lord Clonbrock, c Hooker	0		
W. A. Bennett, Esq., b Lillywhite	0		
Wides	2	Byes 2, w 2	4
Total	66	Total	70

East and West Sussex exhibited cricket of a very one-sided character in 1837. The East were, so to speak, "nowhere," except in a wretched minority, viz., 78 and 32—total 110, against the single innings of the West with 172. Of this number, J. Taylor scored 86 and W. Broadbridge 22—8 at one hit. The West won by an innings and 62 runs.

A match against England at Lord's, in 1840, is noteworthy for the great strength of the respective teams and the feebleness of the scoring. Several of the most reputed batsmen in their double innings contributed, so to speak, "next to nothing." Thus, Guy, 5; Clifford, 7; Hawkins, 8; Mr. A. Mynn, 9; Wenman, 11; Pilch, 16. Sussex won by 22 runs.

In the month of July next succeeding, a very important meeting took place on the Trent Bridge Grounds, Notts. Five years previously, Sussex were defeated by Notts with three wickets to spare. It was now the turn for Sussex to carry off the palm; not, however, without a sharp struggle, as the subjoined score will to some extent show:—

SUSSEX.

	1st inn.		2nd inn.
Lillywhite, run out	23	b Clarke	3
Millyard, c B. Parr, b Clarke	10	st B. Parr, b Clarke	9
Hawkins, c and b Clarke	18	c S. Redgate, b Clarke	21
Box, c Guy, b S. Redgate	7	b Clarke	27
C. G. Taylor, Esq., c Guy, b Barker	26	c and b Clarke	1
J. Broadbridge, c Clarke, b Barker	1	b S. Redgate	0
G. Barton, Esq., b Clarke	9	b Clarke	0
D. Geare, Esq., c S. Redgate, b Barker	0	not out	3
Dean, not out	10	b S. Redgate	1
W. Crofts, Esq., b Barker	0	b S. Redgate	0
E. Sayres, Esq., st B. Parr, b Barker	0	run out	0
Byes 6, w 2, n b 3	11	Byes 6, w 1, n b 1	8
Total	115	Total	73

NOTTS.

	1st inn.		2nd inn.
Clarke, run out	17	c Box, b Taylor	13
Butler Parr, c Dean, b Sayres	16	c Hawkins, b Millyard	5
C. Creswell, Esq., c Geare, b Taylor	9	c Crofts, b Lillywhite	0
Guy, b Lillywhite	8	b Lillywhite	1
J. B. Charlton, Esq., b Lillywhite	8	b Lillywhite	0
Garratt, c Box, b Lillywhite	0	b Lillywhite	16
S. Redgate, b Taylor	3	c Millyard, b Dean	0
Barker, not out	11	c Hawkins, b Dean	25
W. Patchitt, Esq., run out	3	b Taylor	9
Samuel Parr, b Taylor	6	b Lillywhite	18
T. B. Redgate, Esq., b Taylor	0	not out	1
Byes 2, w 2	4	No ball	1
Total	85	Total	89

A fortnight afterwards, Sussex, with the aid of Pilch, played England on Harvey's (or Brown's) ground. All the journals of the time, who cared to give prominence to cricket, spoke of this match as singular and wonderful. The highest individual score at the close of an innings each was 11, and the totals—Sussex, 50;

England, 40. In the second venture, Pilch got 24 and Mr Taylor 17 (not out), all the rest were single figures—total 65. England required 76 to win, and this number they effected at the cost of six wickets.

Many and curious changes occur before another match with England, at Lord's, as here recorded, takes place. The simple fact is, Sussex had so much business on hand during this interval, that it almost defies the historian, bound to brevity. The meeting in 1844 was a great success on the side of Sussex. Every man contributed something to an innings not required to be followed up, and as a result, Sussex playing its own strength as a county, beat the Marylebone Club (Wenman and Lillywhite included) by an innings, and 12 runs. These matches, however, not being county ones in the strict sense of the term, are as nothing when placed by the side of a hard fought battle between elevens properly belonging to the county of which they fairly form a part. A better specimen of two such teams than that afforded by a match at Tunbridge Wells, in the year 1845, can hardly be adduced. Score without comment:—

SUSSEX

	1st inn.		2nd inn
Dean, run out	0	b A Mynn	5
Sopp, c W Mynn, b Hillyer	7	l b w, b A Mynn	0
Picknell, c Dorrinton, b A Mynn	8	c Martin, b Hillyer	0
E Napper, Esq, b Hillyer	8	b A Mynn	8
C G Taylor, Esq, c Felix, b Hillyer	5	b A Mynn	0
Box, b A Mynn	0	b Hillyer	3
W Napper, Esq, b A Mynn	4	c Pilch, b Hillyer	2
Bushby, b Hillyer	6	b Hillyer	14
Hammond, not out	31	c Harenc, b Hillyer	0
G Barton, Esq, l b w, b Hillyer	21	not out	0
G W King, Esq, c Felix, b A Mynn	25	c Harenc, b A Mynn	0
Byes 17, w 6	23	Byes	6
Total	138		38

KENT

	1st inn		2nd inn
W Mynn, Esq, c Sopp, b Dean	5	b Picknell	9
A Mynn, Esq, b Dean	9	b Picknell	10
Martin, b Picknell	5	run out	0
Pilch, c W Napper, b Picknell	10	not out	11
Adams, run out	16	c Barton, b Dean	5
N Felix, Esq, l b w, b Picknell	27	b Picknell	4
Dorrinton, c Sopp, b Dean	5	b Picknell	0
C G Whittaker, Esq, b Dean	2	c and b Picknell	0
C Harenc, Esq, b Picknell	11	b Picknell	1
Lefeaver, c Hammond, b Dean	4	c Bushby, b Dean	1
Hillyer, not out	0	run out	10
Byes 8, w 10	18	Byes 4, w 5	9
Total	112	Total	60

The next conquest of note by Sussex occurred in the same year at Brighton, when they met the Marylebone Club strengthened with Martingell and Pilch. At starting, Sussex were hardly so much in favour with the public as the party from town. They managed to beat them, however, by six wickets, the scores being: Sussex, 265 and 86 (four wickets)—total 351; Marylebone, 138 and 212—total 350, Picknell made 79 in his first and only innings for Sussex, and Royston 41 and 51 for Marylebone. Another stroke of fortune attended Sussex in a similar encounter at Lord's in 1847. Score: Sussex, 189 and 142—total 331; Marylebone, 107 and 116—total 223. A "return" occurred a few weeks after at Box's Ground, Brighton. Here again the county triumphed over the club, although the latter possessed themselves of Mr. A. Mynn's help—Sussex, 189; Marylebone, 86 and 67—total 153. By a very simple process of arithmetic, it will be seen that Sussex won by an innings and 36 runs. The last match played in Ireland's Gardens took place at the close of September of the same year. It was between Sussex and England, and was not inaptly termed "a war of giants." It lasted four days, and Sussex came out of the battle conquerors by 27 runs.

A match between Sussex and All England (Clarke's) in the year 1847 is often spoken of in cricket circles to this day among the curiosities of the game. England were strong in bowlers—essentially so—Sussex out-numbered them considerably, but were withal weak. Wisden, perhaps the best bowler of his day, was unable to assist. Sussex went in first, and lost all their wickets for 101 runs. England nearly trebled this amount. Six bowlers were tried at a great expense of runs, thus: Dean delivered 49 overs, from which 98 runs resulted; Challen, 27 overs, 57 runs; Picknell, 21 overs and two balls, 28 runs; Mr. E. Napper, 8 overs and three balls, 26 runs; Mr. W. Napper, 8 overs, 9 runs; Humphrey, 1 over, 5 runs. Box, who never pretended to handle a ball except behind the wicket, seeing how ineffectual good bowling was in getting out such men as Parr, Felix, Mynn, Martingell, and Hinkly, tried his hand at "lobs" and other "styles" not exactly definable in cricket phraseology, and got these stickers out at the cost of about 9 runs per man. This story is kept alive to show when the very best bowling is of no avail the very worst sometimes may be exercised to advantage. The second scoring of Sussex reached 131. Clarke and Hillyer bowled throughout. England won the match by an innings and 45 runs.

In these days of rapid acquirements, it seems strange to say that such a team as Sussex could boast of in 1850 should make so poor a fight with Surrey at the Oval, for, although ten out of the Sussex eleven scored something during the two days' play, 56 and 64 were the results, against 197 single innings of Surrey.

The match with Notts, played at Brighton in 1853, exhibits Sussex in a somewhat decaying position. The team provided for the occasion was certainly not the strongest that could be gathered from the county so regarded, especially when confronted by such an eleven as Notts brought to the Hove ground. At the close of two days' play the books stated the results to be—Sussex, 68 and 60—total 128; Notts, 136; thus winning by an innings and 8 runs.

A very signal victory was obtained by Sussex over Yorkshire on the New Ground, Bramhall-lane, Sheffield, on the 29th of August, 1855. See score:

SUSSEX.

Wisden, c Anderson, b Hodgson	148
Dean, b Hodgson	13
W. Napper, Esq., l b w, b Crossland	7
John Lillywhite, c Iddison, b Wright	14
Box, c Anderson, b Wright	13
Wells, c W. Kaye, b Chatterton	8
R. Tredcroft, Esq., b Chatterton	21
E. Napper, Esq., c Hodgson, b Crossland	31
Payne, c Hodgson, b Wright	14
Brown, b Crossland	10
James Lillywhite, not out	2
Byes 7, w 4	11
Total	292

YORKSHIRE.

	1st inn.	2nd inns.	
M. J. Ellison, Esq., b John Lillywhite	22	c Wisden, b James Lillywhite	6
Chatterton, c Wills, b Dean	21	not out	5
John Berry, c Wisden, b Dean	12	c Dean, b James Lillywhite	24
Crossland, c W. Napper, b Dean	21	b Wisden	7
Wright, c Wisden, b John Lillywhite	0	b Dean	0
Anderson, b Dean	3	c Brown, b John Lillywhite	5
W. Kaye, run out	9	c E. Napper, b John Lillywhite	0
Sampson, c Box, b Dean	2	run out	9
E. B. Kaye, run out	0	run out	5
Iddison, c and b Dean	8	c James Lillywhite, b Dean	2
Hodgson, not out	3	b John Lillywhite	7
Byes	2	Leg-byes	2
Total	103	Total	72

A very close match with Surrey on the Hove Ground, in August, 1855, places Sussex once more in a favourable light. John Lillywhite and Wisden were the chief professional representatives. The double innings of Sussex amounted to 197, towards which the former contributed 46, and the latter 68 (once not out). The chief scorer on the Surrey side was Caffyn—62. The "grand" total of Surrey 195. A difference of two runs only is very uncommon in a county match; hence its notice here.

From the universality of cricket at this period and the prospects of its developments in many minute particulars, old grounds, old scenes, and old associations became frequently so absorbed as to lose their individuality. Matches which a quarter of a century antecedent would have commanded attention, mixed in the common stream of everyday occurrences. Nor will a thoughtful mind be much astonished at this. The events of a village, a township, or even a county have their interest localised not merely in cricket, but the whole domain of history, of which, perhaps, it forms but a trifling integral part. The boy who looks into his atlas or gazes upon a huge map of England hung about the school walls, thinks it an enormous representative picture. So indeed it is. Let him then turn his artificial globe once or twice upon its axis, and he will find England a mere speck. It has been said that a Chinaman's map of the world was nearly all China, outside of it entangled clusters of islands barely supporting a name. The Celestials nowadays survey "the great globe itself" with mortal eyes, and find there are other peoples and nations on "the other side of the mountain," perhaps not cricketers as yet, but soon so appointed to be.

Returning to the Hove Ground, and the records of deeds done thereon in 1860, it is only intended at this place to speak with the utmost brevity concerning a match between Sussex and Surrey. It ended in the defeat of the former by an innings and 43 runs. Soon after this cheerless example the executive of the Club furbished their old armour, and several valiant heroes in the cause of cricket were seen busily at work. The effects of a good managing committee were quickly apparent, they wisely looked after the rising talent distributed among parish elevens, and there were few parishes in Sussex of any size who did not pride themselves on cricket. A deal of time was of course consumed in the organisation of colts, always apt to go ahead unless held in judiciously with bit and bridle. Now and then a match came off so well that Sussex was declared to be looking up, while at other times the reverse occurred. Still the committee pursued a determined course, even when the exchequer, for want of promptitude in the supply by registered members, had a cheerless look, and answered to its calls by a hollow sound. Mr Stent,* the hon. sec., had frequently to make an appeal, to the lovers of the "manly and noble game," for help, and very much of the chequered success claimed by Sussex was mainly due to his energy and foresight. He had to make his voice heard beyond Brighton—a place of slow support considering its population, wealth, and need for a health-seeking and rational pastime, especially cricket.

If success in this art of training was slow, the chances of endurance were tolerably sure. The stride from the lowest round of the ladder to the top is invariably deficient of the wisdom which accompanies a slower step-by-step advance. That Sussex did not make a very bold stand even against neighbouring counties, will be evident at a glance of the following summary (1868), from

* Mr Bridger Stent, born at Petworth, in 1820 was educated at Winchester School. In 1855 he resided at Brighton, and was a magistrate. He thoroughly understood cricket, and the way in which it ought to be conducted, he would allow neither trifling nor nonsense. This conduct enhanced the general respect due to him. He died suddenly on the 3rd of February, 1870. It may be readily imagined that the loss of such a man had a great effect upon the club. It was like removing the keystone of an arch, and yet not exactly so. Sussex was not composed of men who would sit with folded arms and bewail their loss. They looked about them for another champion, and they found one, if not as influential as the fallen one, quite as earnest to fill the void till a more fitting one could be found. Mr George W King was entrusted with the secretary's portfolio, and still holds it to the satisfaction of the county and all those who, in the way of real business, come in contact with him.

which it appears that only two matches were won out of six played at the undermentioned times and places:—

Brighton, June 8.—Sussex v. Kent. Sussex, 145 and 181—total 326; Kent, 94 and 99—total 193. Sussex won by 133 runs.

Islington, June 11.—Sussex v. Middlesex. Sussex, 249 and 7 (for the loss of one wicket)—total 256; Middlesex, 143 and 112—total 255. Sussex won by nine wickets.

Oval, July 6.—Sussex v. Surrey. Sussex, 98 and 128—total 226; Surrey, 106 and 102 (for the loss of three wickets). Surrey won by seven wickets.

Brighton, July 20.—Sussex v. Surrey (return). Sussex, 166 and 145—total, 311; Surrey, 297 and 17 (for the loss of one wicket)—total 314. Surrey won by nine wickets.

Brighton, August 10.—Sussex v. Middlesex (return). Sussex, 79 and 123—total 202. Middlesex, 246. Middlesex won by an innings and 44 runs.

Gravesend, August 24.—Sussex v. Kent (return). Sussex, 81 and 90—total, 171. Kent, 146 and 26 (without loss of wicket)—total 172. Kent won by ten wickets.

BATTING AVERAGES.

NAME.	No. of Matches.	No. of Innings.	Most Runs in a Match.	Most Runs in an Innings.	How often Bowled.	Caught.	Run out.	Not out.	Stumped.	Total.	Average per Innings. Over.
Mr. W. Carpenter…………	2	4	20	11	2	1	1	0	0	27	6– 3
Charlwood………………	6	11	54	54	3	6	1	0	1	127	11– 6
Ellis ………………………	6	11	41	30	4	2	1	4	0	96	8– 8
Mr. Greenhill …………	2	4	18	15	2	1	0	0	1	24	6
Killick ………………………	4	8	23	16	4	2	0	1	1	42	5– 2
Lillywhite, James…………	6	11	126	126	4	4	0	1	2	400	36– 4
Payne………………………	6	12	46	39	4	5	1	2	0	188	15– 8
Phillips ………………………	5	9	25	16	3	3	2	0	1	55	6– 1
Reed ………………………	2	3	9	9	1	2	0	0	6	27	9
Mr. C. Smith………………	6	12	52	47	4	5	1	1	1	204	17
Southerton ………………	6	11	24	20	5	2	0	1	3	61	5– 6
Stubberfield ………………	6	11	20	11	4	2	0	0	5	47	4– 3
Wells ………………………	6	9	30	30	1	4	3	0	1	77	8– 5

The famous Brunswick Ground, which for three-and-twenty years had been the scene of many glorious conflicts, closed soon after the demise of Mr. Stent. A match, before surrendering possession to its rightful owner, was promoted for the benefit of John Lillywhite. From its admirable organisation, the manner in which Players contended against Gentlemen, the extraordinary attendance, &c., the final contest worthy of note on the ground close by the sea will live long in the remembrance of many among the ten thousand who witnessed it.

Now comes a question with reference to this unsettlement. Did Sussex suffer much in consequence? Not at all. The present ground, for which the county is indebted to the liberality of Mr. Fane Bennett Stanford and the trustees of the Stanford estate, was soon covered with turf brought from the Brunswick, and it is now in many respects superior to that universally acknowledged almost perfect ground, although some think it falls too much from north to south, and that the subsoil, being a stiff brick clay, dries so fast that it requires an unusual quantity of water to keep it in order. It is curious enough that Sussex, for so many years famous as a cricket county, never enrolled itself as a county club till the year 1857. Up to that time their matches were kept up partly by the exertions of various holders of the grounds, and partly by the casual contributions of gentlemen who loved the game, and deemed it worthy of support. About the year 1842 a committee of five or six gentlemen took the matter in hand, and by a vigorous application of their interests and powers, gave the county that start which tended subsequently to place Sussex on a footing with its neighbours.

Many persons who did not take the trouble to ask themselves a few questions, thought—by the opening of a new ground with its attendant prospects—that Sussex would be able to carry all before them. Possibly the wish was father to the thought—a thing not more unnatural among sections of cricketers than other communities. How Sussex progressed in their new quarters may be seen from the subjoined epitome of contests with Kent, Surrey, Hants, Gloucestershire, and Yorkshire during the years mentioned :—

1872.—Six matches ; won three, lost two, drawn one.
1873.—Nine matches ; won two, lost six, drawn one.
1874.—Eight matches ; won one, lost five, drawn two.
1875.—Eight matches ; won five, lost two, drawn one.

In addition to the results of the last named year are appended a few particulars entitled

ANALYSIS OF THE BATTING.

NAME.	No. of Matches.	No. of Innings.	Most Runs in a Match.	Most Runs in an Innings.	How often Bowled.	Caught.	Run out.	Stumped.	Not out.	Total.	Average per Innings. Over.
Mr. A. W. Anstruther......	2	4	5	4	2	0	1	0	1	9	2– 1
Mr. J. M. Cotterill	4	6	191	191	3	2	0	1	0	369	61– 3
Charlwood....................	7	11	55	51	7	3	0	0	1	260	23– 7
Fillery	7	10	51	51	5	3	2	0	0	190	19
Mr. F. J. Greenfield.........	4	7	108	79	1	6	0	0	0	259	37
Howard........................	3	4	40	40	2	1	0	1	0	80	20
W. Humphreys..............	7	12	52	52	5	4	1	0	2	193	16– 1
Mr. C. M. Kennedy	3	6	13	11	1	3	0	0	2	32	5– 2
Lillywhite	7	10	42	42	2	4	0	0	4	142	14– 2
Newland	2	2	0	0	0	2	0	0	0	0	0– 0
H. Phillips.....................	7	11	18	16	4	3	2	0	2	56	5– 1
J. Phillips	4	6	47	27	1	5	0	0	0	104	17– 2
Mr. F. P. Pickering.........	2	2	24	24	0	2	0	0	0	37	18– 1
Mr. W. A. Soames	2	4	0	0	1	2	0	1	0	0	0– 0
Mr. A. Smith	6	8	12	12	3	3	0	0	2	33	4– 1
Mr. L. Winslow	4	5	124	124	1	3	1	0	0	214	42– 4

The following noblemen and gentlemen formed the council during the year 1875: Patron, Viscount Pevensey ; president, Mr. H. M. Curteis ; vice-president, Mr. H.

Brand; secretaries, Messrs. King and Smith; treasurer, Mr. Ashby; committee for *East Sussex*, Messrs. Burt, Beard, Champion, H. Curteis, and R. Loder; *West Sussex*, Viscount Turnour, Lieutenant-Col. Ingram, Major Wisden, Rev. H. Nicholls, and Mr. Buddulph; *Brighton*, Colonel Baines, Messrs. Cook, G. Cotterill, Cooke, Deering, and Pycroft.

CHAPTER XIII.

GLANCES AT THE PAST AND PRESENT STATE OF COUNTY CRICKET—*continued.*

NOTTINGHAMSHIRE.

When as our royall king was come home from Nottingham,
And with his nobles at Westminster lay,
Recounting the sports and pastimes they had taken
In this late progress along on the way,
Of them all, great and small, he did protest,
The miller of Mansfield's sport liked him best *

Climate of the County—Its Extent—Past Political condition—Intuitive Faculty for Cricket among the Inhabitants—No Home for Pretenders—Description of one—Condition of Cricket in the Early Part of the Century—Mortifying Dispute—Description of a Match by William Howitt—Defeats of England by Notts—Success of Parr and Daft at the Oval—Cricket Schism Condemned—Poem relating thereto—Summary of Matches from 1870 to 1875, with Analysis of the latter

GEOGRAPHICALLY speaking, this shire—often abbreviated into Notts—is one of the most important centres of England apart from the metropolis Here and there it exhibits a few remains of the ancient royal forest Its climate is somewhat remarkable for dryness, owing to the Derby hills interrupting the moist west winds Nottingham, the chief town—one especially notable for its cricketing proclivities—stands at the foot and on the declivity of a rocky eminence, and is watered by the Trent Past history is rich in story about the town and neighbourhood. Several parliaments were held there, and it does not require much search into the history of England, especially in the Wars of the Roses, to discover that in the 15th century Richard III. marched thence with his forces to Bosworth Field What the population of that period actually was, must remain a matter of conjecture, and by what means the two seats of government were compassed, it would be equally difficult to speak with correctness What the social condition of Great Britain also was, must be inferred In these days of peaceful rule and large enlightenment, everyone knows, or may know, that he can travel

* Be it observed the Miller of Mansfield's sport was not cricket The stanza here quoted forms part of a ballad written before the time of Edward IV, and for its genuine humour, diverting incidents, and faithful picture of rustic manners, is vastly superior to anything written in imitation of it

from London to Nottingham and back in one day for a guinea, although the distance between the two places is 130 miles Population nearly 90,000 The county of Notts, though not quite so early in the cricket field as some other counties, has during several generations sustained a good reputation from the spirited manner in which their matches have been conducted, and the school it may be said to have founded. Of all places in the world, Nottingham would be the worst for a pretender to cricket, and the Trent ground the severest platform for a *début*. Why, the very portraits which hang round the walls of the inn would, if they had the power of voice the individuals they represent once had, cry aloud against pretence. Very few persons who attend the Trent ground go for any other purpose than to see cricket played as it ought to be, independently of results, and not a few who watch the progress of the play, can to a greater or less extent advance an opinion and give a reason for it At times there is a seeming severity in the treatment of even old and deservedly famed men who, by misfortune, should repeat a mistake. In fact, "all business and no nonsense"—just the reverse picture of "a model cricketer" painted after the style of Sir John Oldcastle, Charles Lamb, or Thomas Hood Here it is He may be seen on every ground in England He belongs to the Lavender-water Club. He rejoices in a cap illustrated with a feather His shirt is of crimson hue and he revels in an embroidered belt of many colours A delicate fabric dangles at his side in the guise of a handkerchief His trousers, cornered at the knees, hang in jaunty relief over a couple of pedestals of pink hose, and his feet, enshrined in the whitest of leather, form the base of an altogether elaborate structure Most amusing is it to see him prepare for action His attitude has important claims to originality Possessed with guard, he imprints it on the ground in the most approved manner, and immediately afterwards proceeds to survey the geography of the field, never taking stock of the company—though impudently asserted so to do by hireling historians Agriculturally speaking, he is a fine bat, though cynical admirers are wont to observe that many of his innings bear a close affinity to the progressions of a distinguished quadruped if not direct, they are decidedly short. Rumour says he has been bowled by first ball, but this is deemed apocryphal. The Club is not unmindful of his prowess Its members, in token of their high admiration and esteem, have repeatedly acknowledged his scores by presenting him with numerous pairs of spectacles, and he can smile upon additional testimonials in the shape of sundry baskets of ducks' eggs. As a bowler he stands unrivalled. He plays a deeper game than the bystanders imagine He seldom aims at the wicket, he bowls for chances, and when a ball shoots, or happens to pass within a yard or two of the bails he holds up his hands after the fashion of a signalman upon the railway Should he bowl a wide ball, he rubs invisible grit upon the grass, and when he bowls a much wider, he picks up imaginary dirt from the spikes of his shoes Nor must his fielding pass unnoticed, if sprawling about be allowed It is his custom to make an easy chance as difficult as possible; and if he succeeds with a catch, immediate excursion is made to the tent to see if the scorers have duly enrolled the feat The sun is sure to invade his eyes, and when he misses a catch his astonishment is immense, and in the height of perplexity the ball is trundled to a ridiculous destination In council he is fond of argument, and in order to display his forensic ability, he knocks the wicket down at a crisis, and speculates upon the veracity of the umpire His opinions may be had gratis, and, to do him justice, they generally refer to Person the First Viewed from the left shoulder, they are quite in conformity with truth Often his memory may be said to be the offspring of modesty, he has such a faint recollection of his greatest number of maidens, and his finest innings is enveloped in doubt His final effort is to send a report of his matches to the newspapers In dropsical rigmarole, it may be seen that his bowling was on the spot, and remarkable for its destructiveness His batting and fielding were the theme of universal admiration, and, considering his style and demeanour in a game, the account in question is a matter of surprise to everybody but himself.

Probably to the mind's eye of many a reader this model man may seem overdrawn and exaggerated As a set-off, however, there will be discovered sufficient truth, if not wit, running through the picture to furnish a lesson for any and all whose inclinations tend rather to ape the game than take the trouble to work out the by no means disagreeable problem, viz, what constitutes genuine cricket and a genuine cricketer

The records of early matches, whatever they were, do not appear to have been transferred from the "notched stick" to paper, except in a skeleton guise In 1789, however, haziness gives place to a very clear view of the condition of cricket. A match took place between the Nottingham and Leicester Clubs, played at Loughborough, when the scores were for the former 31 and 23—total 54, against 70 for the latter in one innings Within a month the same match was repeated, when Leicester won by one notch, and it received the name of the "Odd Notch Match," and is so recognised to this day Leicester scored 63 and 32—total 95, Nottingham, 39 and 55—total 94 Two years subsequently, the Marylebone Club are found at Nottingham to compete with twenty-two The match was won by Marylebone with 13 runs to spare. A third match with Leicester in 1800 shows either the advance made by Notts or the retrogression of Leicester From the score given it will be seen that Notts won by an innings and 38 runs

LEICESTER

	1st inn		2nd inn
R Black, c Weston	0	run out	1
R Stringer, run out	4	c Hopkin	1
M Graham, c Neape	2	c Streets	3
J Clarke, c Streets	4	c Hopkin	2
J Farrand, b Chapman	1	b Chapman	0
J Watts, st Dennis	2	b Warsop	0
T Hall, c Dennis	1	b Warsop	0
E Arnold, c Hopkin	1	b Warsop	0
S Baldiste, b Chapman	0	run out	0
R Harris, b Chapman	0	not out	0
J Jackson, not out	0	b Chapman	0
		Bye	1
Total	15	Total	8

NOTTINGHAM

T. Neape, st. Graham	3
R. Smith, b. Farrand	1
J. Dennis, b. Farrand	1
W. Britain, b. Graham	2
R. Warsop, c. Black	10
W. Streets, b. Graham	19
H. Hopkin, leg before wicket	5
T. Warsop, b. Clarke	4
W. Jefferies, run out	5
J. Weston, not out	3
W. Chapman, b. Clarke	7
Bye	1
Total	61

A MORTIFYING DISPUTE.—Early in the present century disputes, even in high cricketing circles, were not unfrequent. One still lives in the pages of history between the Marylebone Club and the players of Notts, chiefly owing to the absence of Mr. Osbaldeston in a match he had himself promoted. It appears that the match had attracted attention in the Midland counties to an unprecedented extent, owing to the popularity of the parties concerned in it, as well as from the confidence in its coming off, seeing that the contractors were Mr. Osbaldeston on the part of All England, and Mr. Joseph Dennis on the part of the Nottingham Club. Agreeably to conditions stated, the players arrived at Nottingham in full expectation of meeting Mr. Osbaldeston, and that he would stake the money agreed to be played for, and, as usual on such occasions, pay them for their time and expenses. The "Squire" was looked for in vain, he could not be found, and the London players, in order that the people, who had many of them travelled a long distance (in those days), might not be disappointed, agreed to play for 25*l.* instead of 150*l.*, they not being able amongst themselves to make up the original stakes. This offer was accepted, and the stakes placed in Col. Cooper's hands, agreeably to a stipulated article. The match accordingly commenced for 50*l.*, but during the match one of the A. E. players, on the part of his friends, represented to the Nottingham Club that 25*l.* was a serious sum, and they should feel themselves greatly obliged if the club would agree to draw the stakes and play for nothing. As the Nottingham stakes were made up by a great number of gentlemen, amateurs of the game and others, whose shares did not amount to more than 3*s.* 6*d.*, and as the club felt the players had been extremely ill-used by their match-maker, this proposition was complied with, and the match was, towards the end, only played for honour. It may be proper to add that the Nottingham gentlemen made a present of 30*l.* to the London players to carry them home again. England scored 104 in their first innings and 87 in their second, making a grand total of 191; Nottingham, 135 and 37 (seven wickets)—total 192. The company was immense; at one time nearly 20,000 persons were present, and had the game been played on the terms originally proposed the number would have been vastly increased. A great deal of disputation arose about the affair afterwards, in which Mr. Osbaldeston came off "second best."

Several contests with All England followed with varying success The first is sufficiently noteworthy to claim a few passing remarks. It took place on the Forest Ground in 1817, previously to which all great matches had been played in the Meadows It excited, says a Nottingham historian, immense interest and was witnessed by twelve or fourteen thousand spectators Lord Frederick Beauclerk, whose name stands foremost in the score, was a brilliant hitter, an efficient bowler, and an excellent judge of the game The next, G Osbaldeston, Esq , had, two years previously, played Hopkins and Dennis at single wicket, and beaten them both by an innings, and 67 notches to spare! E H Budd, Esq , was an expert fieldsman at the middle wicket Never was there a safer hand at a catch, and his hitting was so extremely powerful, that Lord Frederick was accustomed to say, "Budd always wanted to win the game off a single ball" He caught out nine men in this particular match—the largest number perhaps on record Bennet, the next man in order, was one of the best professionals of his day—good at most points of the game Bentley was a player of considerable reputation Beldham, of Surrey, called "Silver Billy" from his fair complexion and light-coloured hair, was a most venomous batsman, he could propel the ball with extreme velocity in every direction Holloway was a good professional, though perhaps the least noteworthy of any of the team It will be sufficient to say of Howard that he was the best "stumper" of the southern counties Slater, the ninth, was astonishingly quick on his legs Lambert, the tenth—"the Little Farmer"—was an extraordinary bowler His delivery was quite low, with a twist, not like that of the generality of right-handed bowlers, but just the reverse way i e, if bowling to a right-handed hitter, his ball would twist from the off stump into the leg This deceitful and teasing style of delivering the ball was the means of lowering fourteen of the Nottingham wickets Shearman, the last of the eleven, though not an admirable player, had scarcely then attained his full reputation The fielding of the twenty-two was truly admirable, and to this, more than to their batting, may be attributed their success Nottingham won by 30 runs The concourse of people was very great, "these were the days of the Luddites (rioters), and the magistrates warned us," says Mr Budd, "that, unless we could stop our game at seven o clock, they could not answer for keeping the peace At seven o'clock we stopped, and, simultaneously, the thousands who lined the ground began to close in upon us Lord Frederick lost nerve, and was very much alarmed, but I said they didn't want to hurt us 'No, they simply came to look at the eleven who ventured to play two to one'" Score —Nottingham, 50 and 98—total 148 , All England, 53 and 65—total 118

The greatest contributor was G Smith, of Nottingham, viz , 30, who was given out in his second innings as "hit the ball twice" A greater victory was achieved by Nottingham against fifteen of Sheffield in 1822 Nottingham went in first, and scored 120 Sheffield received two innings for 122 Eventually, Nottingham won the match by ten wickets In the following year, another success awaited them in playing fourteen of Leicester , the scores being for Nottingham, 53 and 137—total 190, Leicester, 33 and 57—total 90 A match in 1826 is remarkable for the defeat sustained at Darnal, where Marsden opposed them as one of the Sheffield and

Leicester team, full notice of which is taken in the Yorkshire chapter For several years in unbroken succession Nottingham and Leicester tried conclusions The full score of a match on the Hyde Park Ground, Sheffield, in 1831, will give a pretty good idea of the relative strength of these two centres of cricket Several new names now appear, which afterwards became great Nottingham won the match in question by 125 runs, chiefly, however, by the arms of well-seasoned practitioners of the game

NOTTINGHAM.

	1st inn		2nd inn
Clarke, b Marsden	18	c C Dearman	17
Barker, b ditto	22	c ditto	3
Jarvis, c Wilson	49	hit wicket	3
Vincent, run out	1	b J Dearman	16
Heath, c Woolhouse	29	c Wilson	6
Kettleband, c Holdsworth	10	b Marsden	39
Day, c Shackerley	10	b ditto	0
Redgate, b Marsden	6	c Woolhouse	0
Slack, not out	18	c Wheatcroft	4
Sheraton, b J Dearman	0	not out	0
Good, b Marsden	7	c Marsden	2
Byes 7 w 7	14	Byes 3, w 5	8
Total	181	Total	98

SHEFFIELD

	1st inn		2nd inn
Woolhouse, leg before wicket	9	b Clarke	8
J Dearman b Barker	1	c Jarvis	0
Holdsworth, b ditto	3	not out	15
Smith, c Vincent	17	b Clarke	3
Rollins, b Barker	9	c Good	3
Marsden, b Good	4	st Vincent	40
Wilson, b Clarke	10	run out	1
C Dearman, run out	1	b Clarke	8
Shackerley, c Heath	9	st Vincent	0
Thompson, b Barker	0	b Clarke	3
Wheatcroft, not out	0	run out	3
Byes 2, w 2	4	Wide balls	6
Total	67	Total	90

Cowardice is altogether incompatible with cricket, but under some circumstances an overweening confidence in one or two persons is by no means to be commended The players of Sheffield often worshipped Marsden with more fervour than a sound policy would dictate, for, though a wonderful man, there were others in neighbouring counties little, if at all, inferior to him Every age, however, produces its hero

"Next Marsden may come, though here it must be stated
That his skill down at Sheffield is oft overrated,
But an out and out bat where the bowling is loose,
As a bowler and fielder of very great use"*

* Pierce Egan's "Book of Sports"

After this the counties of Kent and Sussex appear to be frequently selected and many excellent contests are recorded Scarcely any were wanting in interest, even when the defeats were signal William Howitt, a native, and withal a prose-poet of considerable eminence at the time, says "I will here describe a match of this fine sport, which was played on the 7th and 8th of September 1835, between the Sussex Club and the Nottingham Club, and the thoughts which it produced in me at the time The Nottingham Club challenged the Sussex Club to a match for fifty guineas a side, and played at Brighton, where the Sussex men were beaten, who then went to play the Nottingham men on their own ground The Nottingham men beat again, having three wickets to go down A more amazing sight of the kind was never seen On Sunday morning early we saw a crowd going up the street, and immediately perceived that in the centre of it were the Sussex cricketers just arrived by the London coach, and going to an inn kept by one of the Nottingham cricketers They looked exceedingly interesting, being a fine set of fellows, in their white hats and with all their trunks, carpet bags, and cloaks coming, as we verily believed, to be beaten Our interest was strongly excited, and on Monday morning we set off to the cricket ground, which lies about a mile from the town, on the Forest as it is called, though not a tree is left upon it—a long furzy common, crowned on the top by about twenty windmills, and descending in a steep slope to a fine level, round which the race course runs Within the race course lies the cricket ground, which was enclosed at each end with booths, and all up the Forest hill were scattered booths and tents, with flags flying, fires burning, pots boiling, ale barrels standing, and asses, carts, and people bringing still more good things There were plenty of apple and ginger beer stalls, and lads going round with nuts, and with waggish looks, crying 'Nuts, lads! nuts, lads!' In little hollows the ninepin and will-peg men had fixed themselves to occupy loiterers, in short, there was all the appearance of a fair Standing at the further side of the cricket ground, it gave me the most vivid idea possible of an amphitheatre filled with people In fact it was an amphitheatre Along each side of the ground ran a bank sloping down to it, and the booths and tents at the end were occupied with a dense mass of people, all as silent as the ground beneath them, and all up the hills were groups, and on the race stand an eager, forward-leaning throng There were said to be twenty thousand people, all hushed as death, except when some exploit of the players produced a thunder of applause Mr Ward, late member of Parliament for London, a great cricket player, came from the Isle of Wight to see the game, and declared himself highly delighted But nothing was so beautiful as the sudden shout—the rush and the breaking up of the ground when the decisive notch was gained To see the bat of Bent Good, the batsman on whom the fate of the game depended, spinning up in the air, where he had sent it in the ecstacy of the moment, and the crowd, which before was fixed and silent as the world itself, spreading all over the green space where the white figures of the players had till then been so gravely, and apparently calmly, contending—spreading with a murmur as of the sea, and over their heads, amid the deafening clamour and confusion, the carrier pigeon, with a red ribbon tied to its tail, the signal of loss, beating round and round to ascertain its precise position, and then flying off to bear the tidings to Brighton—it was a beautiful sight, and one that the most sedate person must have delighted to see "*

SUSSEX

	1st inn		2nd inn.
Morley, b Good	16	b Barker	0
Millyard, b Redgate	0	b Redgate	0
Taylor, b Barker	26	b Barker	3
Picknell, b Redgate	3	b Redgate	0
Daniels, b Good	0	b Redgate	2
Box, b Barker	3	run out	14
Broadbridge not out	19	c Woodward	1
Wells, b Redgate	11	run out	9
Brown, b Barker	5	b Barker	2
Bagent, b Redgate	0	run out	5
Dean, b Barker	0	not out	0
Byes 4, w 11	15	Bye 1, w 5	6
Total	98	Total	42

NOTTINGHAM

	1st inn		2nd inn
Barker, b Brown	4	c Daniels	3
Heath, b Brown	1	c Broadbridge	8
Rothera run out	1	c Millyard	0
Jarvis, c Wells	17	b Brown	14
Garratt, b Broadbridge	0	not out	2
B Parr, b Brown	4		
Day, run out	7	b Brown	4
Clarke, b Broadbridge	1		
Good, st Box	21	not out	20
Redgate, c Bagent	9	c Daniels	1
Woodward, not out	0	run out	0
Byes 12, w 4	16	Byes 4, w 4	8
Total	81	Total	60

The above score, copied faithfully from the Nottingham books, shows that even this county was not quite up to form in the way of particulars Another remarkable event occurred in 1842 A match between Nottingham and the Marylebone Club was arranged, but, owing to some slight misunderstanding, the latter declined to proceed with it This led to All England accepting a challenge The Nottingham team was a very strong one, but Fuller Pilch imagined he could summon a stronger So indeed he did His little army was composed of Box, Dean, Dorrinton, Hawkins, Hillyer, Lillywhite, A Mynn, Pilch Hon F Ponsonby, Sewell, and Wenman The best bowler of Kent, the best of Sussex, and the best of Marylebone, the lion of batters, the prince of stumpers, and the flower of point men were all under one banner "No wonder," says the historian previously referred to, "that against such an array our townsmen contended

* Rural Life in England

ineffectually" To resist the rival host, B Parr took to the stumps, Guy the point, Barker the slip (changing to long-stop at the other end), Butler mid wicket off, Noyes short-leg, S Parr long-leg, Good long-stop, and Chapman and Redgate long-fields But all was ineffectual, England's total was overwhelming The Southerners won with nearly an innings to spare, the scores being—Nottingham, 112 and 110—total 222, England, 218 and 5 (without loss of wicket)—total 223 Half the Nottingham men were caught out, Mr Mynn clean bowled five, Lillywhite and Hillyer one each It should be observed that this was the first really exciting match on the celebrated Trent Bridge Ground, although opened in 1839 by the famous slow bowler Clarke Yes! to Clarke may the adjective "famous" be rightly applied Not more in the character of a head bowler than the skilful manager of a match during its progress Although, like the hero of Trafalgar, he had but one useful eye, he could and did turn this single organ to wonderful purpose. Few of his young companions were able to discover the future utilitarian in cricket, keen as the men of Notts naturally are His first appearance at Lords was in a North *v* South match (1836), being then thirty-eight years of age. From the outset to the close of his career he played full forty years The All England movement owed its origin to him, and the success attending it was mainly attributable to his judgment and forethought

In the following year Marylebone beat Nottingham by 58 runs—a circumstance mainly owing to the batting of Lord Grimston, who made 52 in his double innings On the other side, Butler also scored 52 Redgate bowled eight wickets, and Clarke six Marylebone totalled 65 and 123, Nottingham, 61 and 69 In the match with Kent which followed soon after on the same ground, Nottingham came off victors, with eight wickets to spare, the gross score made by Kent being 151, against 130 and 22 (for two wickets) England figured as second best in the month of August, 1847, but the defeated team was very different from that of five years previously A large infusion of fresh names appear, and, in order to keep the chain of talent for such great exploits unbroken, it will be necessary to reproduce the score, from which it will be seen that Nottingham won the match with ten wickets to go down

ENGLAND

	1st inn		2nd inn
Martingell, c H Brown	0	b Tinley	4
Mr Clifford, c Guy, b C Brown	2	c Tinley, b Oscroft	11
Wright, c Guy b Tinley	29	b Oscroft	1
F Pilch, c Parr, b Tinley	21	st C Brown	11
Mr P Brett, b Tinley	7	b H Brown	4
Hunt, b Oscroft	2	b H Brown	9
Sampson, run out	15	c C Brown b Tinley	15
Chatterton, not out	13	c Tinley, b H Brown	2
Mr C O Eaton, b H Brown	2	b H Brown	1
R Roby, b H Brown	0	not out	9
White, run out	3	b H Brown	9
Byes 3, w 8	11	Byes	6
Total	105	Total	82

NOTTINGHAM

	1st inn		2nd inn
J Oscroft, b Martingell	9		
Mr H Brown, st Chatterton	3		
G Parr, st Chatterton	0		
Mr W Masters c Chatterton	51	not out	7
J Guy, c Chatterton	27		
C Brown, c Sampson	16		
J Chapman, not out	28		
T Heath, b Hunt	8		
F Tinley, c Pilch ..	8	not out .	6
T Nixon, run out	1		
J Bickley, b Hunt . .	1		
Byes 14, w 10	24		
Total	176	Total	13

The next remarkable triumph for Nottingham, especially against the southern counties, occurred in 1852 at the Oval. It was over in about a day and a half—cricket time. Nottingham came to the ground far stronger than Surrey, even if the latter had been aided with more than luck—there is a deal of luck attending cricket, no matter who may be the controlling genius at the time of play. The visitors chose to go in first, three of them were unable to score a run, but another three made ample amends for their feebleness. Guy was in his prime; George Parr had not completed more than twenty-five years, and Samuel Parr thirty-one. These three got 132 runs, and the eleven totalled 181. Surrey was singularly unsuccessful. Not one of their first-class batsmen could reach double figures during either innings, and as a result Nottingham won by an innings and 43 runs. In a second match with Surrey in September of the same year, at Trent Bridge, another triumph awaited them. The lists were but slightly altered on either side. Carefully examined, however, it is evident that the Nottingham eleven were too good for their opponents. The leg hitting of George Parr was "a sight to see," and in his score of 69 a considerable increment arose from his determined and well-directed use of the bat in this form. Surrey, it ought to be mentioned, went in first, and soon lost two wickets. Then came a stand, and four double-figure scores were recorded for the loss of six wickets. But the most successful hitter, who went in late, ran up his score quickly. The fielding of Nottingham proved superior to that of Surrey in both innings. The match ran into four days, and resulted thus: Surrey, first innings, 109 from the bat, byes 3—total 112; second, 133 from the bat, wide 1—total 134. Nottingham, 189 from the bat, leg-byes 16, wide 2, no balls 2—total 209, second innings, 36 from the bat, bye 1, wide 1—total 38. Nottingham won by ten wickets.

Early in the next year, a contest at Lord's against All England was won with much greater difficulty than the two immediately preceding. Nottingham was strong, and England not weak. At the first start the latter was the favourite. The bowling of Wisden was so thoroughly up to the mark, that it beat them, and the whole eleven were disposed of with an average of little more than five runs per man from the bat. All England nearly doubled this number in their first innings. The batting of George Parr in the second innings of Notts, however, completely turned the tide in favour of his party; some of the bowling got very wide of the mark, and it was punished accordingly. At the fall of the tenth wicket 129 runs were totalled. The task set for England was not great, viz., 76, but it proved too great for them, although they were full of confidence. Notts had a man in reserve, who had not as yet shown what he could accomplish with the ball, yclept Bickley. This sturdy native of Keyworth bowled seven wickets clean and quickly, and the whole representative strength of England was compelled to acknowledge the superior skill and prowess of the eleven from a single shire, who won the match by 27 runs. Here, again, it will be desirable to reproduce in detail the individual merits of the parties concerned.

NOTTS

	1st inn		2nd inn
Clark, run out	8	run out	1
B. Parr, run out	10	b Dean	0
Guy, b Wisden	12	b Martingell	17
G. Parr, b Sherman	4	b Dean	49
S. Parr, c Box, b Wisden	0	c Sherman, b Wisden	25
R. C. Tinley, b Wisden	5	b Dean	8
C. Brown, b Sherman	0	b Dean	0
Grundy, not out	14	c Box, b Wisden	1
F. Tinley, b Wisden	0	not out	13
Nixon, b Sherman	1	b Wisden	6
Bickley, run out	4	c Box, b Dean	0
Byes 1, l-b 4	5	Byes 3, w 4, n b 2	9
Total	63	Total	129

ALL ENGLAND

	1st inn		2nd inn
Mr. W. Nicholson, b Clark	20	b Bickley	5
Dean, run out	3	not out	0
J. Cæsar, b Clark	2	b Bickley	7
Hunt, st Brown, b Clark	0	b Bickley	6
Box, b Clark	5	b Bickley	10
Anderson, b F. Tinley	30	b Bickley	1
Caffyn, b Clark	35	b Clark	6
Wisden, hit wicket, b Clark	0	b Clark	3
Chatterton, b F. Tinley	2	b Bickley	1
Martingell, not out	12	c Brown, b Bickley	8
Sherman, b Nixon	6	Leg before wicket, b Bickley	0
Leg-bye 1, n b 1	2	Leg-bye	1
Total	117	Total	48

In 1854, the tables were turned on Notts in a second contest at Lord's with All England. This was unquestionably so great a change in the lists of players that the two cannot be compared so as to arrive at the just value of the conquest. Another match bearing the same title, and played on the Trent Bridge Ground in the same year placed England on the high level Notts had two innings for 110 and 91—total 201, England, 208 Towards this number, Lockyer contributed 47 and Dean 39 Wisden and Willsher were the chief bowlers in this match, the latter claimed seven wickets and the former five England won by an innings and 7 runs

A much closer contest stands recorded for the next England encounter, played at Newark, in 1856 Both teams comprised men of the right stamp It was not a match remarkable for big scoring, but the reverse It also deserves notice for the similarity of results thus, England made 84 in each innings, Notts, 82 in the first and 79 in the second, thereby leaving England the trifling and mystic number 7 to win by On the part of England the Kent bowler Hinkly, took twelve wickets On the other side, Grundy claimed seven in one innings, and Jackson five in two innings

Of the three professionals just named how differently the wear of time acted upon them Grundy scarcely showed weakness at all either in style or effect up to the last year of his life (1873) at the age of forty-nine Jackson, though much younger, has been as good as dead to the cricket world for years past, and Hinkly, though still living has for a long time been "the shadow of his former self" About this period Notts had such a team that Sheffield—anxious for the renewal of an old acquaintanceship—were allowed sixteen, but the bowling, of Jackson especially, was so severe that their additional numbers failed to secure them the much coveted victory, which Notts claimed by the narrow majority of nine runs

In 1859, their match with Surrey, at the Oval, figures boldly on the historic page for the prolific innings of 329, towards which George Parr contributed 130 Richard Daft also impressed the public with an opinion that in the young man not twenty-three years of age might be seen a hero who would long sustain a great reputation in the world of cricket Daft scored 52 in his first innings, and 22 (not out) in the second Surrey, though defeated, brought out a fine array of young players in the persons of the two Cæsars, Caffyn, Griffith, Lockyer, Mortlock Stephenson and others In his double innings, Caffyn scored 76, Lockyer, 72, Stephenson, 55 The contest lasted three days, and Notts won the match with eight wickets to go down the totals being for Surrey, 213 and 172, Notts, 329 and 58 for two wickets—those of Grundy and Brampton

Not content with this defeat, Surrey are found once more in arms against Notts in the following year at the Oval There were no large scores Daft recorded 35 in his double innings, and A Clark 33 On behalf of Surrey, Mr C G Lane, a very accomplished player claimed the top score of the match, viz 37 Jackson made great havoc among the Surrey wickets having bowled eight of them clean and had seven taken off him Notts scored 83 and 105—total 188, Surrey, 66 and 107—total 173, thus leaving Notts winners by 15 runs

But the race is not always to the swift Notts now exhibited signs of limping, and Surrey got ahead Matches, partaking less of the old county character, ensued The year 1862 is chiefly signalised by two matches with Cambridgeshire both of which Notts won, the first by three wickets, and the second by an innings and 30 runs In the following year a very weak team of Kent had the boldnesss to confront them at Cranbrook, and they gave Kent the drubbing they deserved The scores of 58 and 45 are commentary sufficient for the character of the eleven who hoisted the Kent banner Notts scored 280, towards which Jackson contributed just 100 Kent were beaten by an innings and 176 runs Not so was the result of a meeting at Bradford about a month previously, when Yorkshire sent them home defeated by eight wickets, and to which defeat Kent was the set off A contest between Yorkshire and Notts on the Trent Bridge ground, July 9th, brought face to face two elevens of which any county might be proud, although the fielding laid itself open to animadversion As the score in full is given, further remark may be dispensed with

YORKSHIRE.

	1st inn.		2nd inn
J Rowbotham run out	24	b Wootton	9
J Thewlis, st Biddulph, b Tinley	18	b Grundy	10
E Dawson, st Biddulph b Tinley	1	b Jackson	1
E Stephenson, c C Daft, b Tinley	32	b Grundy	30
R Iddison c Tinley, b Grundy	20	b Grundy	8
G Anderson, b Grundy	82	l b w, b Grundy	3
Mr A Walker, c and b Wootton	13	b Grundy	0
J Berry, b Wootton	8	b Wootton	18
J Hall, c Parr, b Wootton	3	c Parr, b Jackson	1
J Hodgson, not out	21	run out	1
W Slinn, b Wootton	1	not out	1
Byes 10, l-b 10	20	Byes 7, l-b 5	12
Total	243	Total	94

NOTTS

	1st inn		2nd inn
C Daft, c Slinn, b Berry	38	c Berry, b Slinn	1
C Brampton, c Iddison, b Hodgson	42	b Berry	26
T Bignall, c Dawson, b Slinn	16	b Iddison	28
R Daft, b Iddison	20	l b w, b Hodgson	25
G Parr, st Stephenson, b Iddison	8	c Hall, b Hodgson	7
J Grundy, c Rowbotham, b Iddison	0	b Slinn	4
A Clark, not out	21	c Hodgson, b Slinn	2
J Jackson, c Anderson, b Slinn	5	c Anderson b Slinn	18
R C Tinley, c Hodgson, b Iddison	0	not out	29
S Biddulph, c Rowbotham, b Hodgson	5	c Hall, b Slinn	11
G Wootton, b Slinn	2	c Anderson, b Iddison	20
Byes 2, l b 3	5	Byes 3, l-b 7	10
Total	162	Total	181

Hardly a word more alien to the genius of cricket can be imagined than that of "schism" Yet this offensive monosyllable found its way into the sporting journals, and held a place therein for a considerable time It is not intended to go into the merits of the case now—let bygones be bygones Doubtlessly both parties were to some extent blameable The Notts people, however, against whom some bitter shafts were directed, would not allow at least the charge of faint-heartedness to remain unchallenged, and they took the opportunity of publicly denouncing it in the theatre where the county eleven appeared on the stage in cricketing costume It may readily be supposed that the event drew a large company to the house, as indeed it did, and was long the subject of a lively consideration The following spirited lines were delivered by Miss Clara Denvil —

What means this paper warfare, and these spites
Display'd against our Northern players' rights?
This quarrel, call'd by some, "The Cricket Schism"—
Distasteful term! in fact a barbarism!
For should not cricket—noble, manly game—
Be played in friendly rivalry for fame?
And, in the field, should meet as equals all,
Or peer or peasant both the great and small
But some there be who other feelings stir up,
And one of those, I fear, is Mr Burrup,
Whose latest insult to our county's team
Is "That a chicken hearted lot they seem"
When I read that I cried out, "Well! I never
Heard it before of them"—Now did you ever?
[*Scene drawn, and Notts Eleven 'discovered'*]
But here they are, and, for a cowardly crew,
They don't so badly look, "George, how d'ye do?
The quantity you've had of Brighton dirt
I'm glad to see has caused no serious hurt'
Now let us, if we can, find out who may be,
In the Notts team, a "chicken-hearted' baby
Who can it be? I'm fairly posed Oh, lor'
It can't be Brampton, Jackson, or Alf Shaw
And how you would derisively have laughed
Had I term'd funky Oscroft here, or Daft
They generally show a good account
Of runs, well got, and *fairish* in amount
P'rhaps it's the last addition, J C Shaw,
Yet that can scarcely be, for we all saw
Him first appear 'gainst the crack bats of Surrey,
And send them back in a most precious hurry!
Is it Chris Tinley? Does he funk at point?
Time is indeed then getting "out of joint"
Is Bignall he? It did not so appear
When he, with Daft, got off *those runs last year*
And surely now (the mere thought turns me giddy)
It cannot be our active "Chick-a Biddy!"
Whom have we left? Ah! truly, there is Wootton,
Who about danger never cares one button,
And with him (*Arcades ambo*) our own Jemmy'
I thought you'd laugh well when I mentioned him—he
Never has failed to make his straight ones felt
When once he'd got his cap within his belt
No! Grundy's bitterest foe could never say
James ever thought Notts couldn't win the day

Though last not least I turn me now to Pair—
From "chicken heartedness" he's very far,
Best in defence as yet, and hitter hard—
To sing his praises puzzles much our bard
I might say more about him—only, hush!
I'm fearful if I did that George might blush
One more remark, though, may me well beseem,
He should be proud of leading such a team
And let hot Surrey bear this point in view,
If they've their Burrup, we've our Johnson too
So, to wind up, pray let us give one cheer,
For Mr Johnson and his followers here

The various "hits" were cordially taken up by the house, and when the reciter stepped forward to shake hands with Parr the cheering was immense

Results of Matches in the following Years

1870 —Notts played six, won three, lost two, drawn one
1871 — „ „ six, won four, lost one, drawn one
1872 — „ „ seven, won two, drawn five
1873 — „ „ eight, won five, lost three
1874 — „ „ eight, won five, lost three
1875 — „ „ ten, won six, lost one, drawn three.

As the last year forms an epoch in the division of the century, and as an unusual amount of business was transacted therein, it may be well to conclude—for want of further space—with the

BATTING ANALYSIS

Name	No of Matches	No of Innings	Most Runs in a Match	Most Runs in an Innings	How often Bowled	Caught	Run out	Stumped	Not out	Total	Average per Innings Over
Anthony	2	4	21	21	3	1	0	0	0	21	5- 1
Barnes	6	10	45	45	2	5	2	0	1	126	12- 6
Biddulph	2	1	9	5	2	1	0	0	1	9	2- 1
Clarke	9	13	40	40	3	1	3	1	2	94	7- 3
Daft	10	16	51	47	6	7	2	0	1	193	12- 1
McIntyre	10	17	35	35	6	9	0	1	1	187	11
Morley	9	13	4	4	5	1	1	1	5	13	1
Oscroft	10	18	84	53	5	9	2	1	1	236	13- 2
Reynolds	7	11	84	70	2	5	0	2	2	163	14- 9
Selby	10	18	81	66	7	8	1	1	1	342	19
A Shaw	8	12	61	56	1	6	1	1	3	146	12- 2
Shrewsbury	10	17	52	41	3	9	2	2	1	302	17-13
Tolley	2	3	49	49	2	0	0	1	0	77	25- 2
Williams	3	6	31	31	1	4	1	0	0	45	7- 3
Wylde	9	15	133	93	7	4	1	3	0	346	23- 1

By way of postscript mention might be made of the improvement during the last few years on the Trent Bridge Ground, by the erection of a commodious pavilion and the removal of buildings of a severely rustic character. It need not be said that the ground is rarely out of condition; such a circumstance would hardly be in accord with the constitution of a club of a standing and influence like that of Notts. The following gentlemen were the office bearers for the year 1875: President, Sir H. Bromley, Bart.; Vice-President, Mr. J. Johnson; Hon. Sec. and Treasurer, Capt. Holden; Committee, Messrs. W. L. Hussey, W. Lambert, M. Mason, W. H. Oates, C. Oscroft, E. M. H. Riddell, C. Thornton, J. Thornton, J. Wilkinson, and W. Williams.

CHAPTER XIV.

GLANCES AT THE PAST AND PRESENT STATE OF COUNTY CRICKET—*continued.*

YORKSHIRE.

Yorke, Yorke, for my monie
Of all the citties that ever I see,
For mery pastime and companie,
Except the cittie of London.*

Vast Extent of Yorkshire—Centres of Cricket—Antiquity of Ripon—Various Grounds at Sheffield—Marsden's Introduction to the Public—His Subsequent Great Score—Song Appertaining to it—Sundry Matches with Leicester and Notts—Important Match at Norwich—Great Score of Fuller Pilch—All England's Tour in Yorkshire—The Counties of Durham and Northumberland Reviewed—Discord among Professionals—Resolutions of the Marylebone Club Respecting Same—Schism and its Consequences—Return of Reason—Analysis of Batting in 1868—Triumphs of Yorkshire—Patronage—Batting Analysis for 1875.

MANY have been induced to ask upon what principle the division of England into counties was projected, seeing how unequally the land seems to be parcelled out. Yorkshire, the largest recipient, contains 5981 square miles; or 3,827,847 acres. It is 90 miles in length, and about 80 miles in breadth; but its population is not correspondingly large when compared with other counties. As an agricultural, manufacturing, and grazing county it stands in the front rank. If the ordnance surveyors have been correct in their admeasurements, and Alexander Cruden's castings up be alike true, then there can be no escaping from the fact that there are more acres in Yorkshire than letters in the Bible. Diverse as are the pursuits of the inhabitants stretching over this immense territory, there is one thing towards which they appear to have a special leaning, viz., cricket. York (Eboracum) is still regarded as the second city of England in point of size, though not in rank and commercial importance; while Sheffield, with its forest of chimneys, begrimed buildings, corkscrew streets, and choking atmosphere, is really one of the busiest hives of industry in the whole world. Farther north is Middlesborough, a town that has sprung up with the rapidity of

* "The Ballads and Songs of Yorkshire, transcribed from private manuscripts, rare broadsides, and scarce publications, with notes and glossary," by J. C. Davison Ingledew, M.A.

the prophet's gourd. It has not only got its oldest, but its first inhabitants. According to a recent estimate, Middlesborough numbers upwards of 50,000 souls, and there are persons still alive who can remember the place as one vast marsh. These three stations will serve as examples of the past and present condition of cricket in Yorkshire. Nothing is recorded of the locality of York previous to the present century, and but very little that is trustworthy or of importance till within the last sixty years. Scraps of information occasionally float down the stream of time respecting York and its cricketing proclivities. A match occurred on the Knavesmire Ground as far back as 1809, between the Gentlemen of Yorkshire and the Gentlemen of the Wetherby Club, for 100 guineas. Yorkshire won by an innings and 45 runs, the scores being: Wetherby, 39 and 36—total 75, Yorkshire, 120. The event excited considerable interest. A splendid entertainment was provided, and many of the first families in the neighbourhood attended it. In 1813, a match took place at Knavesmire between York and Ripon, when the resident eleven experienced a sharp defeat, the scores being—for York, 30 and 64—total 94; Ripon, 187. The latter, therefore, won by an innings and 93 runs. In the same year, Ripon played Harewood, and were victorious by 18 runs. Ripon made 80 in the first innings and 64 in the second—total 144; Harewood, 67 and 59—total 126. The chief scorers were Terry, of Ripon, with 30 and 32—total 62; and Coleman, of Harewood, with 30 and 15—total 45.

People born and bred in southern latitudes know but little about "Old Ripon," and yet there are but few cities or boroughs in the kingdom better entitled to call itself ancient. Its antiquity, in fact, is almost mythical. Like so many of our oldest towns, it began in a monastery. Alfred, King of Northumberland—not Alfred of Mercia—and all England gave to Eata, Abbot of Melrose and Landisfarne, a tract of land in "a fair situation, blest with a most wholesome reviving air," on the slightly elevated plain through which run the little rivers Ure and Skell. In course of time the erections were given to Wilfred, Archbishop of York, who afterwards found the position "so unspeakably attractive and inviting," that he resolved to make it his residence. What his admiring historian (Gent) calls a "stupendous edifice," even for those times, would probably be an object of ridicule now, but this point cannot be determined, because in the year 860 it was entirely destroyed by the unbounded fury of the Danes, after an existence of less than two centuries. St. Wilfred's week—the carnival of the district—is marked in true Yorkshire fashion by races and a fair. King Alfred also is kept in perpetual remembrance. Every night at nine o'clock the market watchman blows in front of the mayor's house what is believed to be the horn given by Alfred to the city, with its charter of incorporation, and its government of wakemen, elders, and assistants, long since changed into mayors, aldermen, and councillors. If any one doubts the origin of the custom, let him explain the origin of the horn, hung about, as it is, by medals bearing the arms of a long succession of mayors and wakemen. The horn, then, is the emblem of Ripon, and if the scores, in the matches here spoken of, be strictly accurate—and there is no reason whatever for doubting—then the horn of Ripon may surely boast of being exalted.

Sheffield gave a bolder start, in 1800, in a contest with Notts at Mansfield, but were beaten by 123 runs, and in a second contest with Notts at Warsop, late in the same year, they were again defeated, although they played twenty-two against eleven These signal defeats appear to have discouraged any further attempts at pursuing the game for many years In 1816, Ripon invited Notts to Knavesmire, and had the mortification of finding themselves beaten hollow Ripon scored only 50 and 38—total 88, against 196, the product of a single innings Though silent for a long time, the forces of Sheffield were in the meanwhile reviving The district denominated Hallamshire—known, however, only to strangers as the beautiful country which surrounds Sheffield, for the space of about five miles—became a cricket centre Various patches of turf lying at the feet of the gentle hills which give rise to the town, were the places where the young and healthy pursued the sport. The busy hand of industry by degrees covered these with buildings, and the players were driven to Grimesthorpe and other places at a distance The improvements which distinguished the game in the Metropolis, soon reached Sheffield, and within the last five and forty years several clubs existed in the town and neighbourhood which could put forth some pretentions to skill

The game became so decidedly a favourite, and the players so numerous, that a ground enclosed and devoted solely to the purposes of cricket was generally desired No individual, however, appeared inclined to enter into such a novel speculation until Mr George Steer, in 1821, prepared a piece of land at Darnal, and erected upon it a convenient stand for the spectators Upon this place the players rapidly improved, and began to inquire for some antagonists, whose defeat might increase their reputation. These soon offered themselves in the celebrated players of Nottingham, and the first match took place on the 26th of August, 1822 The wickets had not been long pitched before the Darnal players confessed their ignorance of the game as it ought to be played. Notts won by ten wickets. A scaffold erected for the occasion fell, two persons were killed, and upwards of fifty injured. The whole of the next year they devoted to practice, not venturing upon another match until they believed themselves strong enough for victory The public had, however, so strongly shown their admiration of the game, and their disposition to support it, that the proprietor ventured to form, at a great expense, another, and a more extensive ground, and, to afford the members of the club every chance of improving themselves, engaged Sparkes, a well known cricketer from Marylebone, to instruct them In 1824 the new ground was opened, and they challenged Bingham The principal players at this time were Dawson, Littlewood, Petty, Vincent, and Woolhouse, but their experience of Barker and Warsop's bowling in the Nottingham match made them fear that in so important a part of the game they would prove inefficient At this time Tom Marsden was first introduced as a promising aspirant for cricketing fame, who had played with a wooden ball and a home-made bat ever since he was five spans high The choice was fortunate Marsden proved himself a genius, he made the largest score of any player in the match, and bowled down eleven wickets A second match in the same year with Leicester brought Marsden's talents to another trial, and he justified the favourable opinion formed of him Sheffield won by an innings and 76 runs In the following year the proprietor of the grounds determined that the club should play Eleven of All England The records of this game show that Darnal lost the match, but it was evident that three days' contention with such accomplished players as Brown, Hooker, Saunders, Searle, &c, had proved of great advantage to every member of the club Full of confidence, at the latter end of the year they challenged their former opponents from Leicester This match was played at the gymnasium in that town, and was the first occasion of the Darnal players going from their own ground, they, however, proved victorious winning by a single innings The return match, which took place soon after, exhibited a different result, the club being beaten almost in one innings For the first time they had to complain of the influence of ill-luck A coalition with Leicester against Nottingham in 1826 resulted in one of the most remarkable matches of the period The Darnal players had learned to handle the bat somewhat differently than on the occasion when they first met Nottingham, and to them the bowling of Barker had now lost its terror Marsden's style of batting came into full exercise, and no less than 227 runs resulted from it Full score of the match

NOTTINGHAM

	1st inn		2nd inn
T Barker, b Rawlins	10	st Vincent	16
C Jarvis, b Ouston	3	c Gamble	13
W Clarke, b Marsden	5	b Marsden	8
G Jarvis, c Rawlins	20	b Shelton	14
G Smith run out	6	c Davis	0
R Warsop, b Marsden	3	c Woolhouse	4
J Dennis, b Marsden	0	b Marsden	1
J Kettleband b Marsden	6	c Vincent	3
G Goodall, b Woolhouse	11	not out	5
P Bramley, not out	20	b Shelton	4
G Thorpe, b Rawlins	12	st Vincent	2
Byes	5	Byes	7
Total	101	Total	77

SHEFFIELD AND LEICESTER

W Shelton, c Dennis	0
W Barber, b Barker	10
H Davis, b Barker	27
E Vincent, b G Jarvis	17
T Marsden, c Barker	227
T Gamble, c Bramley	61
G W Ouston, c Bramley	0
W Squires, b Clarke	0
H H Woolhouse, leg before wicket	0
Dearman, b Clarke	27
G Rawlins, not out	0
Byes	10
Total	379

A native poet "set his wits to work" in order that such an event might be handed down to posterity A song, consisting of thirteen stanzas of four lines each, held for many years a prominent place in the festive programmes of the locality

"What's the matter, my friends, at Sheffield to-day,
That most of the people are going away?"
"What's the matter, indeed! Why, don't you know, Mester,
That Nottingham's playing both Sheffield and Lester?"
So as I had heard it reported by many
That cricket was finest diversion of any,
I thought, just for once, I would join in their fun,
And to Darnall I got as the stirrings begun
When Rawlins and Marsden began to get warm,
The Nottingham batters were filled with alarm,
For down went their stumps with a terrible crash,
And soon was extinguished the Nottingham flash
Then old Father Dennis, enraged took his bat
In wonder whatever his comrades were at,
But Tom ript his stumps in double quick time,
And made the old boy with a round O to shine
Then man followed man in rapid succession,
And the score but slowly was making progression,
The knowing ones strangely were altered in looks,
And seemed very anxious to alter their books
Davis, Barber, and Vincent, with one or two more,
Soon made for the union a very good score
Then Marsden went in, in his glory and pride,
And the arts of the Nottingham players defied
Oh, Marsden at cricket is Nature's perfection
For hitting the ball in any direction
He ne'er fears his wicket, so safely he strikes,
And he does with the bat and the ball what he likes
Next Gamble came forward, aspiring for fame,
And for ever established for cricket his name
He kept up his wicket, that day and the next,
And Barker and Clarke were bothered and vext,
For Tom kept hitting the ball in the crowd,
Who in its applause grew boisterous and loud
Then in praises of Gamble grew equally mad—
"Thou'st nought but a good one, brave Gamble, my lad"
But I said twere a shame, and I don't understand
Why you don't give a shout for yon Kettleband,
For whenever a ball is struck out on the green,
There's sure to be him and his striped breeches seen
So for Kettleband quickly we made a good shout,
But Tom, turning round, said let him look out,
Then he drove the ball right over the people,
Some thought 'twere going o'er Handsworth church-steeple
Then homeward I trudg'd to our county folks
To tell 'em a few of our cricketers jokes
But that joke of Tom Marsden's will ne'er be forgot,
When two hundred and twenty-seven notches he got

For Marsden and Gamble we filled up our glasses
As brimful as when we toast favourite lasses,
And then drank success to all cricketers true,
Who with honour this noble diversion pursue.

Encouraged by the success which had attended the union, the Darnal and Leicester players shortly after challenged All England. The first match occurred at Leicester, and the second at Darnal. Both were played at odds, and the conquest of England has far less merit than in matches where both sides are equal in number. The long-continued and increasing success of cricket in the neighbourhood of Sheffield prohibits an extended notice in this chapter. In 1872 Sheffield met Nottingham on the Forest Ground, when Notts won by nine wickets, after a three day encounter, in which several disputes arose as to the decisions of the umpire engaged by Notts. In the following year Leicester beat Sheffield by two wickets, but in the return match with Notts, Fortune favoured them with a win of 160 runs, and within a month a third match with Notts placed Sheffield again in the victor's chair by seven wickets. An unusually long period is said to have been allotted for the next turn with Notts, viz., five days, although the scoring was unusually small for the men composing two such teams as were arrayed on the occasion. 228 runs only were totalled, and Notts won by 18 runs. Before two weeks elapsed the same clubs met on the Forest Ground, and Sheffield were again defeated, this time by 77 runs.

Not much liking this dark side to their picture, Sheffield challenged twenty-two of Yorkshire in 1832, and won by nine wickets, but the conquest had little glory in it, as the opposing party was composed—so to speak—of nobodies in the cricket world. York turns up again in 1833, but the match against Harewood reflects no credit upon them, if the uncontradicted story about drawing stumps before time so that Harewood should not get the winning run, with two wickets to go down, be really true. Anyhow, such an act must inculpate both umpires, as no other parties had the power to draw the stumps; and, although the story was not contradicted, it by no means follows that it was well-founded or could be sustained on examination. In all matches a strict adherence to time and specified condition ought to be an object of attention, and but one timepiece referred to as the arbiter in the case. There are plenty of clocks striking within hearing of the crowd at Lord's when an important match is on, differing, perhaps, a few minutes from the great chronometer at Greenwich, but the new and valuable timepiece, said to be the gift of Lord Ebury, which overlooks the ground decides the issue of the day if a dozen others in the neighbourhood get ahead of it or linger in their duties.

The Hyde Park Ground, Sheffield, early in September, 1833, presented a new feature in the cricket of this county. A match was promoted between Norfolk and Yorkshire, which the latter won by 120 runs. As seven years have elapsed since the last full score is noticed, it may be well to give the one in question in order to keep the chain of past celebrities before the eye, lest the introduction of new names should, as is too often the case, elbow them out of sight, although it cannot, perhaps, so easily put the extinguisher on their memory

YORKSHIRE

	1st inn		2nd inn
W H Woolhouse, run out	31	b N Pilch	13
E Vincent, b Daplyn	19	c Wilkinson	32
G Smith c F Pilch	19	c Wilkinson	0
T Marsden, b Daplyn	0	b F Pilch	53
G G Dawson, c Pile	7	c Pile	12
E Rawlings, b F Pilch	7	b N Pilch	6
W Lupton, Esq, b F Pilch	1	c Pile	0
P S Johnston, Esq, b F Pilch	6	b N Pilch	6
T R Barker, Esq c Pile	1	not out	4
J Dearman, not out	14	c Wilkinson	40
T Dakin, c Hogg	8	c W Pilch	11
Byes 17, w 8	25	Byes 14, w 3, n-b 2	19
Total	138	Total	196

NORFOLK

	1st inn		2nd inn.
Simmonds, b Marsden	3	b Marsden	0
Nat Pilch, run out	10	b Dearman	22
Daplyn, l b w	5	c Vincent	0
T Wilkinson, Esq, b Marsden	5	c Dearman	25
Fuller Pilch, c Vincent	10	c Vincent	23
A Spinks, Esq, b Marsden	1	not out	14
C Roberts, Esq, c Dakin	0	run out	21
Hogg, c Rawlings	1	run out	3
W Pilch run out	5	b Rawlings	8
Pile, b Dearman	20	b Marsden	11
Groom, not out	1	c Smith	0
Byes 3, w 2, n b 1	6	Byes 11, w 8, n b 1	20
Total	67	Total	147

In the following year Yorkshire met Norfolk on their new ground at Norwich, when the visitors were defeated by 272 runs, the scores being Norfolk, 215 and 191—total 406, Yorkshire, 37 and 97—total 134 The Hyde Park ground, Sheffield, was the scene of a four days' match, commencing on the 14th of July, 1834, against Norfolk A singular match in many respects, Yorkshire scored 191 and 296—total 487 Norfolk, 75 and 289 (for seven wickets)—total 364 It was then given up Fuller Pilch made 153 in his second innings, and not out While in the second innings of Yorkshire ten out of the eleven went into double figures, "Mr" Extras being the most liberal contributor with 56 The fielding on both sides was very queer, as no less than 128 extras resulted from the match, 75 of which were byes A marked defeat awaited Sheffield in their next encounter with Notts on the Hyde Park ground It began on the 8th of September of the same year, and lasted four days, when Notts were pronounced winners by an innings and 23 runs Within the next seven years the matches further north were chiefly between York and Ripon and York and Harewood, but they were not up to the form of county play. That, however, between York and Manchester in the year 1844 assumed greater importance. It took place at Hulme, when the residents won by five wickets. Another, with the Leeds Club a few weeks later, was more sharply contested, and Leeds won by the narrow majority of 18 runs. A marked success was obtained by Sheffield over their old opponents of Leicester in 1845, the scores being 37 and 56—total 93 for Leicester, while they obtained 82 in their first innings and 14 in their second without loss of wicket. Only a fortnight later the York Club were found opposed to Dalton, and at the close of the match were beaten by an innings and 78 runs, but in the next season Leeds were conquered easily, and York claimed the match by an innings and 66 runs. Another match with Leeds in the same year left York winners by an innings and 70 runs. Into the merits of these matches it is not intended to inquire. York, with the aid of two Crosslands, were evidently now resolved to go ahead, and match after match was claimed, sometimes by a narrow majority and sometimes by a large one. The first meeting of Yorkshire (so-called) and the English Eleven convinced them of their inefficiency to grapple with such a party, and, though they played sixteen, England won by eight wickets.

For some years Yorkshire appears to have been a favourite circuit of the All England Eleven, under Clarke. One match in 1848, at Ripon, is worth a passing remark. A. E. E. went in first, and only 82 runs resulted, of which Clarke and Dorrinton—neither first-class bats—scored 40. In the second innings, 58 from the bat, more than a fourth of which belonged to Dorrinton. Parr scored 19 in his double innings, Martingell, 13 (all singles), Mr. Alfred Mynn, 11, Dean, 9, Mr. Felix, 8, Sewell, 8, W. King, 4, Guy, 1, and Hillyer, 0. As the twenty-two scored but 110 in their double innings, A. E. E. won the match by 36 runs. Very little cricket—*i.e.*, county against county—stands prominently out in this vast shire, owing, in a great measure to the migratory team which had so powerful a sway among the Tykes. Much has certainly been written and said about Clarke and his band—its aim after lucre more than as apostles for the progress of genuine cricket. One good thing certainly resulted from their visits to Yorkshire, and that was the inspiriting of resident clubs. In so large a division of England it was scarcely possible to organise a county club. Hence many important townships acted as centres, and between these centres a great deal of good cricket was observable when brought into opposition. If a picked eleven of Leeds met an equally well selected team of Bradford on Great Horton Lane, or elsewhere, it was not often "a runaway match." One of the most singular contests of the character alluded to was between Leeds and Harrogate, at the latter place, in 1847. The residents went in first, and scored 46 runs; Leeds followed with 32 runs. The second innings of Harrogate reached 68—total 114. Leeds made but one run from the bat, but scored 11 extras—total 44, thus leaving Harrogate winners by 70 runs. York might be weaker than Knaresborough in a first encounter, and yet come out bravely in a second. Sheffield grew so bold in 1851 that they punished Knaresborough by an innings and upwards of 100 runs. Bedale about this time could challenge uneven numbers, and beat them Many instances of this kind might be cited as showing the local spirit of the times when All England were pervading not only Yorkshire but even higher latitudes of the kingdom

It may not be out of place here to say that the neighbouring counties of Northumberland and Durham, notwithstanding their extent, have not as yet kept pace with Yorkshire It was urged that the climate was less favourable, and yet the hardihood of the inhabitants had frequently shown itself quite equal to such an influence The dwellers on the "Coaly Tyne" patronise and play the game with spirit, and, relatively speaking, come up to the standard of many Yorkshire clubs Take, for instance, that at Tynemouth Few amateurs have shown a more genuine attachment to the game, and at one time—not long since—this club could turn out an eleven that would give any of the single clubs in Yorkshire plenty of work to beat them. North Shields Here the ground is a fine level piece of turf, and the usually excellent condition of the surface attests the unremitting care and attention bestowed upon it Very few clubs in fact, can boast of such excellent accommodation in the way of a stand This building is 80ft long, 22ft deep, and 25ft in height It is divided into two floors that on the ground contains a dressing-room for members, a club-room, and a bar The upper floors are reached by a staircase at the back—like that at Brighton, and is one long gallery with ranges of elevated seats, commanding the whole extent of the field, and presenting the best conceivable accommodation for witnessing the play *

In the year 1864 a great effort was made by the North Durham Club to further the cause of cricket in the locality of Gateshead A bazaar, presided over by a committee of influential ladies, was got up, and a considerable sum of money for levelling and fencing a ground was the result. Over the north end of the room was a design representing the arms of the cricketer—bat, ball, and wickets, with the name of the club inscribed in white letters on a blue ground At the south end of the hall was the Gateshead arms and the motto "*Caput inter Nubila Condit*," supported on the one side with the sentiment, "Prosperity to the North Durham Cricket Club," and on the other with a flag

The population of this rugged and most northern county is very sparse for an area of 1871 square miles. According to admeasurement, the Cheviot hills extend from Wooler in a S W direction, 2600 feet high, in shape nearly conical, and other ranges of hills throw their spurs toward the sea It seems as if Nature frowned a stern prohibition upon the game of cricket, which suggests a warm, if not a hot climate, smooth surfaces, and plenty of village population In spite of these drawbacks, or deficient necessities rather, Northumberland brought a team to Lord's in 1875, and although beaten—a foregone conclusion—they contrived to score 93 (one man short) and 160—total 253, with three professionals against them

* The entire erection cost about 600*l*, and was the gift of a resident member, Mr G H Shum-Storey

Returning to Yorkshire, it may be well to note here that a great centre for the transaction of its cricket business had long been regarded as a necessity. The committee of the Bradford Club acted chiefly in the management of county matches till about the year 1865, and, generally speaking, with as much success as might be counted upon when the ambitions and jealousies of different bodies of cricketers are considered, at times excessively keen. If a house divided against itself cannot stand, a county cannot. In all matters of management there must be a sound directorate. No one club in Yorkshire had any right to monopolise the title of county—Sheffield, no more than Dewsbury, and Leeds no more than Middlesborough. The ties that bound unity being snapped, Yorkshire soon became weak as others. Strategy succeeded, and it sometimes happened that two county matches were being played on the same day, and not always with the best men. Hence it happened that Yorkshire went down rapidly in the scale. An example of cause and effect.

"Discord, dire sister," appears also to have insinuated itself at this period among Yorkshiremen as well as among more southern tribes of cricket players. To the general supporters of the game this was very distasteful, and to the professionals especially injurious. A haughty spirit not unfrequently goes before a fall. It was hardly to be conceived that a system of dictation should awe independent clubs, especially such an one as that of Marylebone, who had nothing whatever to do with private quarrellings and an ultimate schism. To show the strength of their position and their feelings, too, a committee meeting was summoned to pass the following resolutions, the immediate cause being the refusal of the Northern players to take part in the annual match against the South, at Lord's:—"(1) That as the committee must decline to enter into the disputes among the professionals, or take the part either of Northern or Southern players, another eleven be elected to play in that match. (2) That the selection for the players in the match "Gentlemen *v* Players" having been considered in reference to the refusal of the Northern players to meet the Southern men, the players in all matches at Lord's be selected from those who are willing to play together in a friendly manner in the matches on that ground."

This state of affairs was much deplored at the time by all those who hungered after first-class cricket—such cricket, in fact, as Yorkshire could then exhibit. Nor was the disappointment limited to the frequenters of Lord's Ground. The refusal to play Surrey either out or home (1865), so exasperated the Sheffield Committee, that four of the leading recusants were expelled from the Bramhall-lane Ground, and thus for a while a severe blow was given to Yorkshire itself in the very heart of its cricket capital. Only three county matches were played during the season, and Yorkshire lost all.

Another season passed away without honour; but when reason once more mounted the throne, success began to follow, for in 1867 they played six matches and won three of them; in the following year, seven matches and won four. Of the latter a few particulars are given, showing how and by whom these results were brought about.

Sheffield, June 22 —Yorkshire v Surrey Surrey, 222, Yorkshire, 71 and 145—total, 216 Surrey won by an innings and 6 runs

Nottingham, July 2 —Yorkshire v Notts Yorkshire, 213 and 8 (for one wicket) Notts, 60 and 158—total, 218 Yorkshire won by nine wickets

Holbeck, July 4 —Yorkshire v Lancashire Yorkshire, 250, Lancashire, 80 and 84—total, 164 Yorkshire won by an innings and 86 runs

Sheffield, July 13 —Yorkshire v Middlesex Yorkshire, 162, Middlesex, 79 and 59—total, 138 Yorkshire won by an innings and 24 runs

Dewsbury, July 27 —Yorkshire v Notts (Return) Yorkshire, 85 and 76—total, 161, Notts, 162 and 107—total, 269 Notts won by 108 runs

Islington, August 13 —Yorkshire v Middlesex Yorkshire, 60 and 138—total, 198, Middlesex, 86 and 113 (for seven wickets)—total, 199 Middlesex won by three wickets

The Oval, August 24 —Yorkshire v Surrey (Return) Yorkshire, 389, Surrey, 195 and 52—total, 247 Yorkshire won by an innings and 142 runs

BATTING AVERAGES

NAME	No of Matches	No of Innings	Most Runs in a Match	Most Runs in an Innings	How often Bowled	Caught	Run out	Not out	Stumped	Total	Average of Innings Over
Atkinson	5	7	44	44	1	2	1	2	1	107	15–2
Emmett	7	11	19	17	5	2	2	1	1	55	5
Greenwood	4	7	8	8	3	2	0	1	1	21	3
Freeman	6	9	53	53	4	2	1	2	0	132	14–6
Iddison	7	10	57	37	4	3	1	2	0	231	23–1
Rowbotham	6	9	48	42	3	5	1	0	0	164	18–2
Mr A B Rawlinson	6	9	26	26	4	3	1	1	0	103	11–4
Thewlis	5	7	108	108	2	2	1	2	0	184	26–2
E Stephenson	7	11	25	25	5	2	1	2	1	104	9–5
H Webster	2	3	10	10	1	1	0	1	0	10	3–1
West	3	4	23	23	1	1	0	2	0	34	8–2
Mr Ashley Walker	3	4	15	15	2	1	0	1	0	31	7–3
C Webster	3	5	15	10	2	2	0	1	0	30	6
Ullathorne	2	3	28	28	2	1	0	0	0	47	15–2
Pinder	2	3	11	11	1	2	0	0	0	11	3–2
Mr Verelst	2	3	34	33	1	1	0	0	1	61	20–1

Success at length began to dawn once more upon Yorkshire, for out of eight matches against formidable adversaries in 1869, they won four and lost three. The bowling of Freeman and Emmett was very remarkable during the season in question In fact, such a power did these men possess in the art, that Yorkshire were induced to regard themselves at the top of the tree, and, considering also the abilities of Lockwood and Greenwood before the wicket, and Pinder behind it, even Notts had to look after its laurels Yorkshire were not wanting in supporters, soon as it became evident the professional class were made sensible that they might become the architects of their own fortune Agencies were employed for searching out talent and giving it a fair chance of success. The patronage of such a nobleman as Lord Londesborough was felt from one end of the county to the other There is no scarcity of patrons who overflow with good wishes without means of material assistance; plenty, too, who have means, but care not to further the game by opening their purses. Neither of these can be of much use to a cricket community spreading over such a space as Yorkshire. If this truth be thought out, and the unity of spirit and bond of peace cherished—wonderful elements in the government of society!—the issue cannot be a matter of secondary importance to cricketers who are ambitious of rank and respectability in the discharge of their various duties. A summary of the matches from 1870 to 1875 is appended, and in addition thereto an analysis of the batting, as a fair specimen of the defensive capabilities of this important county, when the third quarter of the present century terminated.

1870.—Seven matches; won six, drawn one.
1871.—Six matches; won three, lost two, drawn one.
1872.—Nine matches; won two, lost six, drawn one.
1873.—Thirteen matches; won seven, lost five, drawn one.
1874.—Twelve matches; won eight, lost three, drawn one.
1875.—Ten matches; won six, lost three, drawn one.

ANALYSIS OF THE BATTING.

NAMES.	No. of Matches.	No. of Innings.	Most Runs in a Match.	Most Runs in an Innings.	How often Bowled.	Caught.	Run out.	Stumped.	Not out.	Total.	Average per Innings. Over.
Armitage	9	15	95	68	3	10	0	0	2	214	14— 4
Bosomworth	2	3	5	4	0	1	1	0	1	6	2
Clayton	10	16	80	63	10	5	1	0	0	245	15— 5
Emmett	10	17	23	20	6	9	1	0	1	129	7–10
Greenwood	10	19	101	61	7	9	0	0	3	369	19— 8
Hicks	9	15	75	66	4	8	0	2	1	247	16— 7
Hill	10	17	39	39	8	4	1	0	4	113	6–11
Lockwood	10	18	113	74	7	8	2	0	1	355	19–13
Pinder	9	14	53	28	4	6	0	0	4	107	7— 9
Rowbotham	10	18	41	29	5	9	0	2	2	198	11
Rawlinson	2	3	71	40	1	1	1	0	0	86	28— 2
Mr. H. M. Sims	3	5	54	45	2	1	0	1	1	139	27— 4
Thewlis	4	8	27	25	3	4	0	0	1	84	10— 4
Ullathorne	6	9	18	14	6	3	0	0	0	47	5— 2
Ulyett	10	18	64	50	5	10	1	2	0	324	18

The allusions to Middlesborough have been very slight, although, as before observed, it had grown with extraordinary rapidity into a stalwart frame for cricket. Most of the matches which attracted notice were with All England elevens, and as these came not within the category of county matches they were not placed as such on the Yorkshire files. Visitors generally speaking awarded a fair amount of praise to the club for the order in which the ground was kept. From the growth of the neighbourhood this "fancy spot" somewhat suddenly became property, and without much ado the builder displaced wickets by houses—

and thus for a time the club had to suffer inconvenience. Eventually, through the negotiations of Mr. Hopkins, of Grey Towers, with Mr. Pease, the member for South Durham, a fresh field was secured, and, to show the spirit for cricket which actuated the inhabitants, 1000*l.* for the purposes of draining, levelling, and the erection of a pavilion was soon subscribed. For so aristocratic a locality as Scarborough the ground has not a very imposing appearance. It is entered through a gap in a very inartistic stone wall, and the visitor has to look down upon the combatants. The spot selected for wickets is confined, and the surroundings hardly accord with Scarborough itself, and the county in which it holds a prominent position.

CHAPTER XV.

GLANCES AT COUNTY CRICKET—*continued.*

WARWICKSHIRE AND DERBYSHIRE.

The young contending as the old surveyed.—*Goldsmith.*

* * * * * *

Be bowled out, or caught out, or stumped out; but never lay down your bat. Things may take a turn, as the pig said on the spit.—*Hood's Philosophical Maxims.*

Early Record of Cricket in Warwickshire—Birmingham and its Clubs—A Law Case respecting Stakes in a Match—Rugby School *v.* Marylebone Club—Tom Brown's Description of the Match, and full Score of the same—Other Matches between Rugby School and M.C.C.—Formation of the Derbyshire County Club—Its Progress—List of Matches for the first Five Years—Analysis of Batting.

WARWICKSHIRE.

CONSIDERING the extent, situation, and importance of Warwickshire, it does not appear to have kept pace with many of its neighbours, if Birmingham be left out of consideration. Such, however, cannot be, inasmuch as in the archives of this wonderful town are deposited documents clearly showing that cricket was played on the pleasant fields now covered with manufactories, while the battle of Preston was being fought; and if this be the case, Warwickshire may claim an advance even on Middlesex, for the defeat of the rebels occurred in 1715. Be it as it may, one thing is well authenticated, viz., the re-establishment of the club in 1819. Its formation was called "a sensational event." The members were numerous, and comprised the *élite* of the young men of the town. The meetings were held in a field opposite the Monument House, Edgbaston, every Tuesday at three o'clock. There were but three houses on that side of the road, between the Ivy Bush, Hagley-road, and the Dudley turnpike sandpits. On the other side of the lane there were but eleven houses in its whole length. The meetings were well attended, and the game was kept up with spirit for several years. The best player was David Hanbury, in Taylor and Lloyd's Bank (London), a very powerful young man, and good at every point of the game. In a match between his own and a neighbouring club, he scored more from his own bat in one innings than the opposing team did in both. Several matches were afterwards played with the Kenilworth and other clubs. One of these is noteworthy—Wolverhampton *v.* Hagley—from the circumstance of showing the literary propensities of Lord Lyttelton, one of the contenders, who occupied the intervals of play by reading a book while lying lengthwise on the ground. Messrs. Bass and Allsop took part in the match, and subsequently gave a grand indoor entertainment. From the journals of the time it appears that the affair excited no inconsiderable amount of interest and curiosity. The young gentlemen of the neighbourhood were charged, or rather taunted, with a want of gallantry, and a lady of some literary influence held up to view the pluck which the parties manifested in becoming the possessors of a cricket ball and of recording the struggle for it, while objects of more importance, and far more endearing, had to share the misfortunes of cold neglect. Sixty years ago the uncertainty of cricket was woven into a maxim which is in force at this day, viz., "that a match is never lost till it is won." A case in point. When the Birmingham men were to all appearance hopelessly beaten, Mr. Crosby, a neat and reliable hitter, went in and scored 57 from his own bat, and brought out his side victorious.

Another affair, equally worthy of mention, occurred in Trinity term, 1833. It appears that a case was tried at Warwickshire assizes, before Lord Denman, to recover 20*l.* on the following account: "The Birmingham Union Cricket Club agree to play at Warwick on the eighth of October a match of cricket, for 20*l.* a side, with the Warwick Club; a deposit of 5*l.* a side is placed in the hands of Mr. Terril on behalf of the Warwick Club, the same for the Birmingham Club. Wickets to be pitched at ten; to begin at half-past ten, or forfeit the deposit; wickets to be struck at half-past five, unless the game is finished before. To be allowed to change three men according to the list sent this morning.—T. Cooke, jun.; H. Terril." The rest of the stakes was deposited with Mr. Terril, the defendant in the case, and the match took place. At the close of the first day's play, Warwick was well a head, and next day Birmingham refused to go in, objecting to a Leamington man having played for their adversaries. The plaintiff (Hodson), as agent for the Birmingham Club, gave notice to the defendant to pay over their deposit to him and to no other person; but the defendant paid it over to the Warwickshire Club on receiving their indemnity. Lord Denman non-suited the plaintiff, but gave leave to move to enter a verdict for the plaintiff for 20*l.* if the court should differ from him in opinion. On the hearing before Barons Bayley, Vaughan, Bolland, and Gurney, a verdict was entered for the plaintiff for 20*l.* In giving judgment, Baron Bayley said:—"the first question was, whether, where a party has deposited a sum exceeding 10*l.* with a stakeholder to abide the event of a game at cricket, the game for that stake is illegal by 9 Anne, c. 14; and after full consideration we are of opinion that it is; and again, the stakeholder held this money in order to pay it to another, but as it was illegal for that other to receive it, the party depositing it had a right to stop it *in transitu*, by giving the stakeholder due notice not to pay it over." (3 Tyrwhitt, 929.)

From these statements the reader might naturally suppose that cricket had become one of the institutions of the shire, but a silence of eight years suggests the contrary. That the game was cultivated at Rugby is quite clear from the account of a match there in 1841, when Marylebone played the School. Being limited to one day it was left unfinished, although only thirteen runs were wanted to complete it. See score:

MARYLEBONE

	1st inn		2nd inn
T Chamberlayne, Esq., c Wrottesley	11	st Hughes, b Thompson ...	9
T M Wythe, Esq., c Currie (maj.), b Thompson	11	b Wrottesley	1
J Huddlestone, Esq., b Wrottesley	6	b Thompson	3
Lord C Russell, c Currie (mi.), b Wrottesley	3	run out	3
F Thackeray Esq., c Orlebar, b Wrottesley	30	b Wrottesley	58
F J Pigou, Esq., b Wrottesley	10	b Wrottesley	21
G A F Bentinck, Esq., c Blunt, b Currie (maj.)	27	l b w, b Wrottesley	0
R Wellesley, Esq., not out	28	b Hughes	0
H Rodwell, Esq., b Currie (maj.)	0	c Currie (maj.), b Hughes	2
B Aislabie, Esq., c Currie (maj.), b Wrottesley	1	b Hughes	0
W Bolland, Esq., h w, b Currie (maj.)	2	not out	1
Byes	7	Byes	1
Total	136	Total	99

RUGBY

	1st inn		2nd inn
T Hughes Esq., c Pigou, b Wellesley	29	c Bentinck, b Wellesley	0
W Thompson, Esq., b Thackeray	7	b Thackery	24
A Orlebar Esq., b Thackeray	12	run out	1
C Walford, Esq., c Chamberlayne, b Wellesley	11	b Thackeray	0
Hon A Wrottesley, b Thackeray	0	c Bentinck, b Thackeray	7
R Beard, Esq., run out	3	c Wythe, b Wellesley	1
W W Lindon, Esq., b Thackeray	0	run out	14
T Blunt Esq., c Wellesley, b Thackeray	5	b Wellesley	10
— Currie, Esq. (maj.) not out	9	b Thackeray	13
— Currie, Esq. (mi.), c Huddlestone b Thackeray	12	not out	4
— Thornhill, Esq., run out	1	not out	1
Byes 18, w 12, n b 1	31	Byes 24, w 3	27
Total ...	120	Total	102

As the incidents are so graphically described by the author of "Tom Brown's School Days," a Rugbeian, no attempt will here be made to "gild refined gold, paint the lily, or add perfume to the violet." In the extracts here given, Mr. Hughes says:—

"The morning had dawned bright and warm, to the intense relief of many an anxious youngster, up betimes to mark the signs of the weather. The eleven went down in a body before breakfast for a plunge in the cold bath at the corner of the close. The ground was in splendid order, and soon after ten o'clock, before the spectators had arrived, all was ready, and two of the Lord's men took their places at the wicket—the School, with the usual liberality of young hands, having put their adversaries in first. Old Bailey stept up to the wicket and called 'play,' and the match was begun.

* * * * * * *

"'Oh, well bowled! well bowled, Johnson!' cries the captain, and catching up the ball and sending it high above the rook trees, while the third Marylebone man walks away from the wicket, and old Bailey gravely sets up the middle stump again and puts the bails on.

"'How many runs?' Away scamper three boys to the scoring table, and are back again in a minute amongst the rest of the eleven, who are collected together in a knot between wickets. 'Only eighteen runs and three wickets down! Huzza for Old Rugby!' sings out Jack Raggles, the long-stop, the toughest and burliest of boys, commonly called 'Swiper Jack,' and forthwith stands on his head and brandishes his legs in the air in triumph, till the next boy catches hold of his heels and throws him over on to his back. 'Steady, there, don't be such an ass, Jack,' says the captain, 'we haven't got the best wicket yet. Ah! look out now at cover-point,' adds he, as he sees a long-armed, bare-headed, slashing-looking player coming to the wicket. 'And, Jack, mind your hits; he steals more runs than any man in England.'

"And they all find that they have their work to do now; the new comer's off-hitting is tremendous, and his running like a flash of lightning. He is never in his ground except when his wicket is down. Nothing in the whole game so trying to boys; he has stolen three byes in the first ten minutes, and Jack Raggles is furious, and begins throwing over savagely to the further wicket, until he is sternly stopped by the captain. It is all that young gentleman can do to keep his team steady, but he knows that everything depends on it, and he faces his work bravely. The score creeps up to fifty; the boys begin to look black, and the spectators, who are now mustering strong, are very silent. The ball flies off his bat to all parts of the field, and he gives no rest and no catches to anyone. But cricket is full of glorious chances, and the goddess who presides over it loves to bring down the most skilful players. Johnson, the young bowler, is getting wild, and bowls a ball almost wide to the off; the batter steps out and cuts it beautifully to where cover-point is standing, very deep, in fact, almost off the ground. The ball comes skimming and twisting along about three feet from the ground; he rushes at it, and it sticks somehow or other in the fingers of his left hand, to the utter astonishment of himself and the whole field. Such a catch hasn't been made in the close for years, and the cheering is maddening. 'Pretty cricket,' says the captain, throwing himself on the ground by the deserted wicket with a long breath; he feels that a crisis is past.

"I wish I had space to describe the whole match; how the captain stumped the next man off a leg shooter, and bowled slow cobs to old Mr. Aislabie, who came in for the last wicket. How the Lord's men were out by half-past twelve o'clock for 98 runs; how the captain of the School went in first to give his men pluck, and scored 25 in beautiful style; how Rugby was only four behind in the first innings. What a glorious dinner they had in the Fourth-Form School; and how the cover-point hitter sang the most topping comic songs, and old Mr. Aislabie made the best speeches that were ever heard afterwards.

* * * * * * *

'Jack Raggles, with his sleeves tucked up above his great brown elbows, scorning pads and gloves, has presented himself at the wicket, and having run one for a forward drive of Johnson's, is about to receive his first ball. There are only twenty-four runs to make and four wickets to go down, a winning match if they play decently steady. The ball is a very swift one, and rises fast, catching Jack on the outside of the thigh, and bounding away as if from indiarubber, while they run two for a leg-bye, amidst great applause and shouts from Jack's many admirers. The next ball is a beautifully pitched ball from the outer stump, which the reckless and unfeeling Jack catches hold of, and hits right round to leg for five, while the applause becomes deafening, only seventeen runs to get with four wickets—the game is all but ours!

"It is over now, and Jack walks swaggering about his wicket, with the bat over his shoulder, while Mr Aislabie holds a short parley with his men. Then the cover-point hitter, that cunning man, goes on to bowl slow twisters. Jack waves his hand triumphantly towards the tent, as much as to say, 'See if I don't finish it all off in three hits.'

"Alas, my son Jack! the enemy is too old for thee. The first ball of the over Jack steps out and meets, sweeping with all his force. If he had only allowed for the twist! but he hasn't, and so the ball goes spinning up straight into the air as if it would never come down again. Away runs Jack shouting, and trusting to the chapter of accidents, but the bowler runs steadily under it, judging every spin, and calling out "I have it," catches it, and playfully pitches it on to the back of the stalwart Jack, who is departing with a woful countenance.

"'I knew how it would be,' says Tom, rising. 'Come along, the game is getting serious.' So they leave the island and go to the tent, and after deep consultation, Arthur is sent in, and goes off to the wicket with a last exhortation from Tom to play steady and keep his bat straight. To the suggestion that Winter is the best bat left, Tom only replies, 'Arthur is the steadiest, and Johnson will get the runs if the wicket is only kept up.'

"The clock strikes eight, and the whole field becomes fevered with excitement. Arthur, after two narrow escapes, scores one, and Johnson gets the ball. The bowling and fielding are superb, and Johnson's batting worthy the occasion. He makes here a two and there a one, managing to keep the ball to himself, and Arthur backs up and runs perfectly; only eleven runs to make now, and the crowd scarcely breathe. At last Arthur gets the ball again, and actually drives it forward for two, and feels prouder than when he got the three best prizes, at hearing Tom's shout of joy, 'Well played, well played, young un!'

"But the next ball is too much for a young hand, and his bails fly different ways. Nine runs to make and two wickets to go down—it is too much for human nerves. Before Winter can get in, the omnibus which is to take the Lord's men to the train pulls up at the side of the close, and Mr Aislabie and Tom consult, and give out that the stumps will be drawn after the next over. And so ends the great match.'

The following score represents a match at Lord's in 1840 —

MARYLEBONE

	1st inn		2nd inn
T Tuck, Esq, c Langton, b Townsend	12	c T Hughes, b Balston	13
H Anderson, Esq, b Balston	14	l b w, b Townsend	6
Earl of Winterton, b Balston	16	b Balston	11
R Kynaston, Esq, b Townsend	13	c Attfield, b Balston	7
Hon Capt Liddell, c Attfield b Balston	46	(absent) not out	18
Hon Col Lowther, b Balston	6	b Seton Karr	1
Lord C Russell, c Seton-Karr, b Balston	0	b Balston	33
J H Bastard Esq, c and b Townsend	8	not out	0
G A F Bentinck, Esq, not out	21	b Seton Karr	69
A Lowther, Esq, b Townsend	9	b Attfield	10
Capt Price, b Townsend	1	b Balston	0
Byes 23, w 6, n-b 2	31	Byes 25, w 11	36
Total	177	Total	204

RUGBY SCHOOL

	1st inn		2nd inn
G E Hughes, Esq, b Anderson	32	st Winterton, b Bastard	13
G Langton, Esq, b Col Lowther	0	b Anderson	3
W H Townsend, Esq, b Anderson	15	b Anderson	28
J Wynne, Esq, b Anderson	0	c G P Adam (sub), b Bastard	0
T Balston, Esq, not out	30	b Bentinck	13
W S C Seton-Karr, Esq, b Anderson	4	b Bastard	10
S S Bateson, Esq, b A Lowther	5	b Bentinck	8
W Attfield, Esq, c Kynaston, b A Lowther	1	b Bentinck	6
T Hughes, Esq, st Winterton, b Col Lowther	30	not out	9
H R Neville Esq, b Col Lowther	0	b Anderson	7
C Freeman, Esq, b Anderson	8	b Bastard	0
Byes 4, w 12, n b 6	22	Byes 8, w 3, n-b 2	13
Total	147	Total	110

In the month of June, 1847, the Rugbeians played the Marylebone Club, at Lord's, with less chance of success than on the prenamed occasion. The lists were so changed that only two who took part in the first encounter were present at the second, viz, the Earl of Winterton and the Hon Colonel Lowther The Rugbeians scored 81 and 70—total 151, Marylebone just 100 in a single innings Not further proceeded with

It is needless to say that since this period a match between Rugby and Marylebone has usually had a convenient place in the programme at Lord's. Nor is it necessary to say that the Rugbeians are at the present day not disposed of very easily Abundant evidence can be afforded of their skill in all the requisites to qualify them for their encounters

DERBYSHIRE

ALTHOUGH cricket is not of so recent a date in this shire as many are given to believe, there can be no doubt that the impetus given to it by Clarke and his peripatetic troop of professional players did much towards the advancement of native talent The unfinished match on Holme's Ground, Derby, in 1859, against a very strong All England Eleven, proved incontestably that a considerable amount existed, and only required to be concentrated The first, attempt however, hardly came up to the standard of expectation, but if not a decided success, it was certainly not a positive failure Many of the reasons then assigned, especially those with regard to location and its natural condition, appeared then, as now to an observant eye, almost childish If Derby, for instance, had not a ground, surely it was not a difficult task to make one out of 658,803 acres In fact, its geographical position commends it, to say nothing about its attractions to the romantic traveller The surface on the N W is occupied by the termination of the Pennine chain of mountains, the highest of which is estimated at 1800 feet, composed of limestone, abounding in hill, dale, caverns, and other natural curiosities The varied scenery of the county is enriched by the waters of the Derwent Trent, Dove, and Wye Now, if only one acre in 30,000 were set apart and divided among the three most prominent cricketing townships, there would be an ample provision for the wants of the whole county

As before observed, the attempt to concentrate the scattered forces of the county in 1867 fell through, and in consequence a still more vigorous effort was made in 1870 for the formation of a county club A large meeting took place in the grand jury-room, Derby to consider the best mode of establishing it All parts of the county were represented either by some influential person or deputy "The Chairman (Mr W S Cox) said he had been unexpectedly called upon to preside at the present meeting, the object of which was to discuss the desirability of establishing a county cricket club He had been a cricketer in his younger days, and it had always struck him as being a manly game, and conducive to health, and brought together a number of gentlemen in social intercourse He thought it most desirable, if it could be done, to form a club that should embody the whole of the county —Mr Walter Boden said, at the request of several gentlemen who had had a preliminary meeting, he was solicited to call a meeting embracing the whole of the clubs in the county He must apologise for having taken upon himself to do so, but one reason why he was selected to do it was because he was one of the oldest cricketers in the county He had received a letter from the Duke of Rutland, saying he would give the club his support, and also one from Lord Vernon, who wrote that he would subscribe to it if it was supported by the many and not the few He had also received a letter from Colonel Wilmot, M P , expressing his deep regret at not being able to be present, as he was detained in Yorkshire In the year 1867 an attempt was made to discover the cricketing strength of the county by playing a north and south match, and although finally it did not turn out a success, it still brought out the merits of cricketers that were not before known This year Derbyshire had played the Marylebone Club and ground, and were victorious The Gentlemen of Derbyshire were also victorious against the Gentlemen of Kent He begged to move that a county cricket club be formed, which should represent the strength of the whole of the county, and that it be called 'The Derbyshire Cricket Club'—Mr E M Wass said there was no doubt it was most desirable to establish a county cricket club, and, speaking for the district in which he resided (Wirksworth), he was convinced that if they wished to aspire to any rank in England as cricketers, it was not only desirable to have such a club but a simple necessity There was no doubt the physique of the Derbyshire men was a good one, and they were proverbial for being strong in the arm without alluding to the other characteristic The present meeting would be regarded with a greater interest, especially in North Derbyshire, which would not only render pecuniary support, but contribute a fair share of good cricketers—The Rev T A Anson moved that the Earl of Chesterfield be requested to accept the office of president, and Mr G H Strutt the office of vice-president—Mr Hursh seconded the proposition, which was carried unanimously—The Rev E W Northey said he had been requested to move that a donation of not less than 10*l*, and a yearly subscription of 1*l* 1*s*, shall entitle anyone to membership The rev gentleman pointed out that cricket could not get on without good support—Mr Kingdon seconded the proposition, and congratulated the county upon having so large a meeting, the numbers attending arguing well for the future prospects of the club"

Fortune, however, seemed to frown upon these well-intentioned efforts The club was scarcely started when it received a severe blow in the death of its president In the first county match Derbyshire beat Lancashire by an innings and nine runs This excellent beginning revived the spirit of the committee In fact, there was cause for congratulation, especially when the strength and experience of the team with which they had to contend was taken into account and estimated Particulars

LANCASHIRE

	1st inn		2nd inn
Mr A N Hornby, c Gregory, b Hickton	1	run out	0
Ricketts, b Hickton	2	b Gregory	7
Coward, c Burnham, b Hickton	1	c and b Hickton	36
Mr J Hillkirk, c Sowter, b Hickton	1	b Gregory	17
Burrows, b Gregory	0	c Sowter, b Hickton	3
Mr A B Rowley, b Gregory	0	b Platts	1
Whatmough, b Gregory	5	not out	28
A Smith, not out	11	b Gregory	7
Mr E Wadsworth, b Gregory	2	b Hickton	8
Mr W Mills, b Gregory	2	b Platts	1
Reynolds, c Davidson, b Gregory	0	c Attenborough, b Platts	0
		Bye 1, l-b 2	3
Total	25	Total	111

DERBYSHIRE

Mr R P Smith, b Mills	17
Mr J Smith, c Reynolds, b Whatmough	1
Attenborough, c Smith, by Whatmough	8
Burnham, b Reynolds	31
Mr U Sowter, not out	17
Tilson, run out	8
Davidson, b Reynolds	8
Platts, c Whatmough, b Reynolds	2
Hickton, c Smith, b Mills	7
Mr S Richardson, st Smith, b Reynolds	5
Dove Gregory, st Smith, b Reynolds	5
Byes 2, l-b 4, w 2	8
Total	147

When the return took place on their own ground, in the month of August, they experienced a defeat In the following year they encountered Lancashire out and home, and lost both matches The season (1873) was not full of promise for Derbyshire One of their best bowlers, Dove Gregory, died early in the spring, and the two matches with Lancashire were lost, in the first case by eight wickets, and in the second by an innings and 82 runs Better luck attended them in the following year, as they lost nothing in contending either with their old adversary or Kent

In other words, Derbyshire alone came out of its county arrangements unbeaten The inference to be drawn herefrom is that it possessed a good average of bowling as well as batting strength, and was entitled to take rank among its neighbours The story of abandoning cricket in its county form, by some of its early promoters, in consequence of adverse fate, received but little credit Cricketers of the right stamp expect an occasional nipping by the north winds as well as genial breezes "from the warm chambers of the south"

The last match comprised in the five years mentioned was with Notts on the Derby Ground in the month of August, when the residents met with another defeat Score given

NOTTINGHAMSHIRE

	1st inn		2nd inn
Wyld, b Mycroft	93	st A Smith, b J Smith	40
Oscroft, b Mycroft	10	b Mycroft	0
Shrewsbury, c J Smith, b Platts	10	st A Smith, b Mycroft	26
Daft, b Mycroft	8	run out	3
Martin McIntyre, b Hay	19	c and b J Smith	9
Selby, c A Smith, b Mycroft	7	b Mycroft	0
Mr R Tolley, b Mycroft	3	b Mycroft	25
Barnes, c Platts, b Mycroft	11	run out	14
Alfred Shaw, c Richardson b Platts	0	b Mycroft	7
Clark, not out	11	c R P Smith, b Platts	16
Morley, b Mycroft	0	not out	1
Byes 4 l-b 3	7	Leg-byes	1
Total	179	Total	142

DERBYSHIRE

	1st inn		1st inn
Mr R P Smith, run out	31	run out	5
Mr J Smith, run out	19	l b w, b Shaw	6
Frost, c Bains, b Shaw	0	b Clark	24
Mr S Richardson, c Shrewsbury, b Shaw	22	b Shaw	5
Mr W G Curgenven, b Oscroft	11	b Shaw	0
Foster, c W Oscroft, b Shaw	1	l b w, b Shaw	23
Platts, st Wyld, b Shaw	13	c Oscroft, b Shaw	2
Hay, b Morley	16	b Shaw	0
A Smith, c Barnes, b Morley	4	not out	0
Bradley, b Morley	1	b Shaw	0
Mycroft, not out	11	b Shaw	0
Byes 7, l b 2	9	Leg-byes	1
Total	138	Total	66

Much of the success of the county during the year in question was due to the difficult bowling of Mycroft, who got sixty-three wickets at an average of less than nine runs per wicket, although he had to contend twice with Notts.

Summary

1871 —Two matches; won one, lost one.
1872 —Two matches, lost both
1873 —Two matches, lost both
1874 —Four matches, won three, drawn one
1875.—Six matches, won two, lost three, drawn one

Some idea of the relative merits of the players concerned in the last match may be gathered from the following

BATTING AVERAGES

Name	No of Matches	No of Innings	Most Runs in a Match	Most Runs in an Innings	How often bowled	Caught	Run out	Stumped	Not out	Total	Average per Innings Over
Mr W G Curgenven	3	5	71	71	2	2	0	1	0	90	18
Frost	6	10	40	36	7	3	0	0	0	141	14–1
Foster	6	10	61	36	5	3	2	0	0	181	18–1
Flint	3	6	11	9	4	0	1	0	1	29	4–5
Hay	4	6	16	16	2	3	1	0	0	62	10–2
Hickton	5	7	44	44	1	4	0	1	1	82	11–5
Mycroft	6	9	18	18	2	1	0	1	5	38	4–2
Platts	6	10	60	60	4	5	0	1	0	114	11–4
Rigley	3	5	34	30	2	1	1	1	0	46	9–1
Smith	6	9	22	22	4	2	0	0	3	41	4–5
Mr J Smith	5	8	35	35	3	4	1	0	0	103	12–7
Mr R P Smith	6	10	56	39	4	3	2	0	1	207	20–7
Mr A Shuker	2	4	9	6	1	1	1	0	1	14	3–2
Mr U Souter	2	3	39	39	1	2	0	0	0	63	21–0

All things considered, the efforts made to place Derbyshire in its right position among the Midland counties, and the results, may be regarded in the light of a success, and the executive can take credit for the same. Small as the undertaking may appear in the eyes of some people, a large amount of thought was involved, The wheels of a tiny watch are not thrown into a case at hap-hazard, any more than those which form part of the elaborate machinery of a gigantic steam engine. To set either a-going requires care, and to keep them in healthy motion a keen and watchful eye is indispensable. Rust may consume, and too much friction wear. There is a future for Derbyshire, if the sinews of war be so liberally appropriated to the cultivation of the game that the real talent can be commanded whenever necessity arises for the display thereof.

CHAPTER XVI.

GLANCES AT COUNTY CRICKET—*continued*

GLOUCESTERSHIRE.

> "I am a stranger here in Gloucestershire
> These high wild hills and rough uneven ways
> Draw out our miles and make them wearisome,
> And yet our fair discourse has been as sugar,
> Making the hard way sweet and delectable"
>
> *Richard II, Act 2 Scene 3*

A TRIO OF GOOD WISHES—CHANGED CONDITION OF TRAVELLING—NATURAL DIVISION OF GLOUCESTERSHIRE—CRICKET IN THE SHIRE FIFTY YEARS AGO—FORMATION OF COUNTY CLUB—SUCCESSFUL DARING—SCORE OF THE FIRST MATCH—EXTRAORDINARY BATTING ACHIEVEMENTS BY THE BROTHERS GRACE—SERIES OF MATCHES FROM THE FOUNDATION OF THE CLUB TO 1875—CONDENSED SUMMARY AND ANALYSIS OF THE BATTING—BIOGRAPHICAL SKETCHES OF THE 'THREE GRACES," &c

WRITERS, accredited with probity and research, say that the successor of this self same Richard expressed a hope to see the time arrive when every man should have "a fowl boiling in his pot' George III wished the day might not be distant when every child in his dominions would be able to read the Bible, and a more modern philosopher supplemented these desires that soon every parish in England may have a cricket club, and every boy in it be able to wield a bat At the time of this latter utterance, his faculty of benevolence must have far exceeded that of faith, especially in respect to Gloucestershire How changed the state of affairs now! What lover of cricket is "a stranger here" now? Who looks upon the Shire as one of "rough uneven ways" now? In these times, the 1258 square miles can be compassed in a few hours, taken in their natural divisions of the Cotswold Hills, the Valley of the Severn, and the Forest of Dean. The "high wide hills" could only relate to the Cotswold, which range from 200 feet to 1000 feet, mostly enclosed and arable Distance is almost annihilated by the facilities of the iron road, so that no such thing as miles drawn out and wearisome exists or need exist

Gloucestershire affords no materials for history when considered in the light of county cricket Not that the game was unknown or unpractised by generations back, there is plenty of evidence where, and by whom, long scores arose The idea of concentrating the scattered forces of the county in 1870, must have been the offspring of careful thought and close observation, for it soon ripened into a reality

The very suddenness of success helped materially to its popularity—a popularity not achieved through the assistance of extrinsic aid, but by the force of native talent purely of amateur standing The world never heard of a newly formed band throwing down the gauntlet to a long established county club composed of players eminent in every department of the game In no case can a full score be more acceptable to a reader, than that which represents a small force of recruits trying on its armour to do battle with an experienced army Hence the following, played on Durdham Down in 1870

GLOUCESTERSHIRE

	1st inn		2nd inn
Mr E M Grace, c Southerton, b Street	2	c and b Vince	18
Mr W G Grace, c Pooley, b Southerton	26	c Pooley, b Southerton	25
Mr T G Matthews c Street, b Southerton	5	c Mayo, b Southerton	7
Mr F Townsend, b Street	11	c Pooley b Southerton	20
Mr G F Grace, h w, b Southerton .	16	c Griffith, b Southerton	15
Mr C R Filgate, c Griffith, b Street	15	not out ,	48
Mr J Halford, l b w, b Street	6	h w, b Southerton .	2
Mr J Mills, c Pooley, b Southerton	15	c Pooley, b Southerton	2
Mr J A Bush, not out	3	c T Humphrey, b Southerton	14
Mr R F Miles, run out	0	b Southerton	8
Mr W D Macpherson, c Street, b Southerton	2	b Southerton	5
Byes 3, l b 2	5	Byes 2, l b 1	3
Total	106		167

SURREY

	1st inn		2nd inn.
T Humphrey, c Halford, b W G Grace	1	b G F Grace .	5
Jupp, c E M Grace, b W G Grace	14	not out	50
Pooley, c Filgate, b W G Grace	10	c and b G F Grace	8
Brown, c Filgate, b W. G Grace .	3	c E M Grace, b G F Grace	3
Stephenson, b G F Grace	4	b W G Grace	0
R Humphrey, c and b W G Grace	5	c E M Grace, b W G Grace	1
Griffith, not out	41	c Mills, b W G Grace	5
Street b G F Grace	4	b Miles	5
Mr H Mayo, c E M Grace, b G F Grace	15	b G F Grace	4
Vince, b G F Grace	1	c G F Grace, b Miles	0
Southerton, st Halford, b Miles	26	b Miles	0
Byes 7, l-b 2, w 1 .	10	Byes 3, l-b 1, w 3	7
Total ..	131	Total	88

A very simple process of arithmetic will accredit a surplus of 51 runs to the youthful club But there is less of wonder and curiosity in this result than in the process by which it was brought about. Southerton in 91 overs obtained fourteen wickets out of twenty for 110 runs, while on the other hand, two of the brothers Grace claimed sixteen wickets in 151 overs for 179 runs

In the return match at the Oval towards the close of the month next ensuing, the curiosity of the public was greatly excited, and the friends of Surrey looked confidently to a change in their favour On both sides the teams were changed materially but to the disadvantage of Surrey, who were beaten by an innings and 120 runs. Mr. W. G. Grace led off the batting, and kept possession of his wicket till he put together 143 runs. He had six bowlers brought against him, and fell at last to a slow ball. The scores at the close of the match were—Gloucestershire, 338; Surrey, 163 and 46—total 209.

After the lapse of two days, a match at Lord's with Marylebone Club and Ground occurred, and ended in another signal triumph. Mr. W. G. Grace commenced the batting of the day, and, notwithstanding the varied forms of attack by Shaw, Price, Farrands, and Wootton, he defied all till his score reached 172 out of 276. M.C.C. valued their first total at 76, second, 114, making together 190. Gloucestershire won by an innings and 86 runs.

From these surprising results of a first season Gloucestershire was baptised as the county of the Graces, and to some extent the name may not be inapplicable, although there were several others then, as now, entitled to rank among first class amateurs. Marylebone, not relishing their defeat, arranged a match to be played on the 5th of June in the following year (1871). The bowling in this case triumphed more than the batting. The three Graces got twelve wickets, and Marylebone were beaten by five wickets, although the close of a first innings exhibited a tie (113 runs). Surrey suffered another defeat a few days subsequently at the Oval, chiefly attributable to the bowling of E. M. Grace, who obtained nine wickets, and W. G. Grace five. Scores—Surrey, 161 (of which Jupp claimed 70) and 94 (Jupp 45)—total 255; Gloucestershire, 315. To show that the race is not always to the swift, two of the Graces on this occasion contributed only four runs. Mr. G. F., however, made up for the shortcomings of his brothers by 69. Street, the Surrey bowler, got seven wickets, but at the expense of 20 runs per wicket. At the close of the match Gloucestershire were announced winners by an innings and 60 runs. Defeat of a character little inferior attended Surrey on the visit to the Clifton College Ground to play the return match in the month of August. The home party went in first, and scored 400 runs before their tenth wicket fell. Of this number Mr. Matthews claimed 201, and Mr. G. F. Grace 89. Six bowlers were engaged but three only got wickets. Surrey completed their first innings for 215, second 176—total 391.

A contest with Notts, on the same ground, early in August, was left drawn. On this occasion the three Graces totalled 249 out of 399 (two wickets in the second innings to go down). Notts obtained 173 in their first innings and 125 in the second (four wickets)—total 298. The return on the Trent Bridge ground, about three weeks afterwards, resulted in a very unexpected defeat; unexpected, because Mr. W. G. Grace himself scored 79 and 116, and few of the most sanguine backers of Notts fancied they could compete successfully with it. But they did, and won the match by ten wickets.

This was not a good finish for the year '71, and the narrow "squeak" in favour of Surrey, who played an unusually weak team in 1872, gave the curious an opportunity of venturing on the dangerous path of prophecy. Before the moon of July had filled her horn, a return match at Cheltenham afforded such a decided proof of superiority by the men of the west over those of Surrey, that they were pronounced winners by an innings and 37 runs No estimate of relative proficiency with Sussex could be arrived at in their encounter at Brighton because of rain, but on the Clifton ground, in the month of August, against a truly splendid eleven, a test of strength, without the aid of Mr W Grace, exhibited itself On the part of Sussex, Lillywhite got eleven wickets in the double innings Gloucestershire won by 60 runs, the score being for the visitors 244 and 92—total 336, residents, 143 and 253—total 396

Both matches with Notts were left unfinished owing to rain, but the scoring on the Trent ground proved vastly superior to that of Gloucestershire, although all the Graces were parties thereto In fact, Notts seemed to outdo itself, considering the accredited efficiency of their adversaries No less than nine bowlers were tried, but Mr. W G Grace was the only one who made any impression upon the wickets worth recording He delivered 91 overs, from which 163 runs resulted Seven wickets were taken Selby, one of the Notts batsmen, scored (within seven) as many runs as were made by all the other side off the bat, and not out The "return," on the smooth Clifton ground, about three weeks later, promised well for the residents, although Mr W G Grace did not play, being absent in America The tally of his elder brother, who went in first, amounted to 108 in the first innings and 40 in the second His younger brother was more successful, thus, first innings, 115, second 72, and not out in either The bowling of Notts was taxed severely Morley delivered 73 overs at the cost of 84 runs (four wickets), Shaw, 50 overs, 103 runs (one wicket) As the latter did not pay, the lobs of Daft were tried From 22 overs 68 runs resulted (three wickets) Gloucestershire totalled 317 and 167 for four wickets Notts completed their first and only innings for 239, and the match was left drawn As a set-off to Notts, mention may here be made of a very decisive affair at Sheffield about three weeks previous Before the match commenced, Yorkshire were considered quite strong enough to meet any eleven amateurs in the kingdom Fallacious idea They had scarcely a chance with the single shire of the Graces Mr W G Grace led off the batting in conjunction with Mr Matthews, and this pair scored more in a single innings than the whole Yorkshire did in both innings Yes, 53 more! Gloucestershire had one man absent Mr W G Grace, in the double innings of Yorkshire, took fifteen wickets in 60 overs and a ball, for 79 runs To be brief, Gloucestershire won by an innings and 112 runs

The contest of 1873 began with Surrey, and as this was the fourth season of the new club, it may be well to furnish a full score, in order that the reader may obtain a glimpse of the changes, both with respect to the players and the condition of the play The match took place at the Oval in the second week of June and occupied three days Messrs E M and W G Grace gave first sign of play by emerging from the pavilion bats in hand Everything and everybody was ready for the start, and expectation stood tip-toe The easiest thing possible to go in, but to go out, and be compelled to do so, was quite a different affair. The Surrey bowlers tried their best To get rid of either in a legal and straightforward way beat both head and arm of the ejectors, until a large portion of the third hour had been consumed, and 157 runs resulted Strange enough, both left at this figure Surrey, elate with joy, imagined their greatest difficulties were overcome Probably they were, still there were small ones to be grappled with. Half-a-dozen batsmen needed the same kind of process to be applied as that which had preceded them, and this half dozen stuck to the stumps until the score promised to reach 300 Disappointment, however trod closely upon the heels of hope, and the tenth wicket fell for 290 Surrey fell so short of this number that they had to yield obedience to Law 46 Better success attended their second innings, notwithstanding this, Gloucester won the match by five wickets Score —

GLOUCESTERSHIRE

	1st inn		2nd inn
Mr W G Grace, c Jupp b Boult . .	83	not out .	8
Mr E M Grace, b Boult	70	b Street	18
Mr T G Matthews, b Street	16	c and b Strachan	11
Mr C R Filgate, c Southerton, b Street	23	not out	58
Mr G F Grace, c Akroyd, b Street	14	st Pooley, b Southerton	28
Mr F W Goodwyn, b Southerton	21		
Mr J Bryan, b Southerton	24		
Mr J Holford, c Jupp, b Street	18	c Southerton b Street	0
Mr J A Bush, b Street	2		
Mr R F Miles, not out	9	run out	0
Mr E A Brice, b Street	0		
Byes 6, l-b 4	10	Byes 8, l b 4 .	12
Total	290	Total . .	135

SURREY

	1st inn		2nd inn
Jupp, c Brice, b G F Grace	1	c Bryan, b G F Grace	83
R Humphrey st Bush, b E M Grace	19	b W G Grace	24
T Humphrey, b G F Grace	8	b E M Grace	10
Mr B N Akroyd st Bush b E M Grace	2	l b w, b G F Grace	30
Pooley, run out	19	c Matthews, b E M Grace	15
Mr F H Boult, c W G Grace, b E M Grace	35	b G F Grace	3
Mr N Morris, c E M Grace, b G F. Grace	11	c Bryan, b Miles .	64
Mr G Strachan, c Bush, b G F Grace	2	not out	20
Mr C W Burls, c Filgate, b G F Grace	16	c E M Grace, b G F Grace	11
Southerton, b G F Grace	0	b E M Grace	7
Street, not out	8	c E M Grace, b G F Grace	14
Byes 6, l b 4	10	Byes 4 l-b 3, w 5	12
	131	Total	293

The second match in the programme took place at Brighton on the 12th of the same month It afforded a contrast, as the score of Mr E M Grace was the only one of importance Gloucester, however, managed to win by nine runs In the following month at Sheffield the Yorkshiremen acknowledged themselves beaten by seven wickets The return at Clifton with Surrey, as well as that with Sussex at Cheltenham, was left drawn, the latter chiefly on account of the tremendously stiff scores on both sides, thus—Gloucestershire, 424, Surrey just half this number for half the wickets. A singularity. The last match of the season occurred on the 14th of August, at Clifton, the return to that at Sheffield played about a fortnight previously. In this Mr G F Grace was the hero, with 165 not out. Six Yorkshiremen tried their hands at bowling in the first innings. Hill, however, did the chief part of the business, though at a costly rate, thus—132 runs resulted from 67 overs, six wickets.

The season 1874 began inauspiciously as Surrey beat them by six wickets early in June. In the return, however, Gloucestershire recovered, and won by an innings and 24 runs. The entire score of the match amounted to 224 for 30 wickets, thus averaging less than eight runs per wicket. Mr W G Grace got 27, the exact total of Surrey in their first innings. Mr Grace got seven wickets in each innings. Sussex were beaten easily at Brighton, but the return at Clifton was left drawn. Just 850 runs were scored on this occasion for 24 wickets. Yorkshire were defeated both out and home. The closest match of 1875 was that at Cheltenham, with Sussex, when Mr Grace's party unexpectedly came off victors by 40 runs. Full score:—

GLOUCESTERSHIRE

	1st inn		2nd inn
Mr W G Grace, b Lillywhite	5	c and b Lillywhite	19
Mr E M Grace, c and b Lillywhite	65	st Phillips, b Greenfield	71
Mr F Townsend, c Fillery, b Smith	2	c Winslow, b Fillery	37
Mr G F Grace, b Smith	16	b Smith	22
Mr G N Wyatt, c Charlwood, b Lillywhite	1	c Kennedy, b Fillery	3
Mr A H Heath, b Lillywhite	0	c Phillips, b Lillywhite	25
Capt Kington, c Fillery, b Smith	17	c Charlwood, b Greenfield	4
Mr T G Matthews, b Greenfield	7	b Greenfield	1
Mr F G Monkland, not out	11	c Humphreys, b Smith	29
Mr J A Bush, b Greenfield	2	not out	8
Mr R F Miles, b Greenfield	0	c Phillips, b Lillywhite	3
Byes	4	Byes 2, l-b 9, w 1	12
Total	130	Total	234

SUSSEX

	1st inn		2nd inn
Mr J M Cotterill, c Bush, b E M Grace	13	b E M Grace	37
Mr F J Greenfield, c Townsend, b W G Grace	79	c W G Grace, b Miles	29
Humphreys, c Monkland, b E M Grace	2	l b w, b W G Grace	1
Charlwood, b G F Grace	41	c E M Grace, b Miles	14
Fillery, c Bush, b Miles	5	run out	0
Mr L Winslow, c and b W G Grace	20	c W G Grace, b Miles	2
Lillywhite, not out	19	c Bush, b W G Grace	8
Mr C M Kennedy, l b w, b G F Grace	6	c Miles, b E M Grace	0
Mr W A Soames, st Bush, b W G Grace	2	c W G Grace, b E M Grace	0
Phillips, run out	2	c G F Grace, b Miles	16
Mr A Smith, c Bush, b W G Grace	2	not out	6
Byes 4, l-b 4, w 5	13	Byes 5, l-b 1, w 1	7
Total	204	Total	120

The subjoined tables will afford a ready opportunity of estimating the strength and condition of the county, and the relative merits of the players who, during six years, took part in the varied contests.

Condensed Summary

1870.—Three matches, won all
1871.—Five matches, won three, lost one, drawn one
1872.—Seven matches, won three, lost one, drawn three.
1873.—Six matches, won four, drawn two.
1874.—Six matches, won four, lost one, drawn one
1875.—Eight matches, won three, lost four, drawn one

ANALYSIS OF THE BATTING

Name	No of Matches	No of Innings	Most Runs in a Match	Most Runs in an Innings	How often Bowled	Caught	Run out	Stumped	Not out	Total	Average per Innings Over
Mr R Brotherhood	3	6	2	2	4	0	0	0	2	3	3
Mr E A. Brice ..	3	5	13	13	1	3	1	0	0	15	3
Mr J A Bush ..	32	46	36	26	20	12	3	0	11	347	7-25
Mr R E Bush	5	8	32	32	5	1	2	0	0	73	9- 1
Mr E K Browne .	3	6	91	52	1	3	0	2	0	136	22- 4
Mr F J Crooke	8	11	36	36	6	5	0	0	0	165	15
Mr F A. Carter .	11	14	24	13	7	3	1	0	3	80	5-10
Mr S H Cobden	4	5	7	5	3	1	0	0	1	11	2- 1
Mr C R Filgate	7	13	81	58	3	7	1	0	2	234	18
Mr E C B Ford	4	5	32	32	4	0	0	0	1	49	9- 4
Mr F W Goodwyn	3	3	38	38	1	2	0	0	0	69	23
Mr C S Gordon .	13	19	96	96	4	11	1	3	0	361	19
Mr E M Grace ..	25	38	148	108	15	16	1	6	0	1050	27-24
Mr W G Grace .	34	51	208	179	16	29	0	2	4	2741	53-38
Mr G F Grace	35	52	187	180	19	24	1	1	7	1629	31-17
Mr G Halford	11	16	56	42	4	8	0	2	2	150	9- 6
Mr A W Heath	6	10	25	25	6	4	0	0	0	52	5- 2
Mr E M Knapp	10	14	96	90	4	6	1	1	2	197	14- 1
Mr T W Lang	8	10	44	44	4	5	0	0	1	126	12- 6
Mr T D Matthews	28	45	201	201	16	22	2	5	0	757	16-37
Mr R F Miles	31	42	79	79	20	10	3	3	6	308	7-14
Mr F G Monkland	5	6	24	24	1	4	0	0	1	80	13- 2
Mr F Townsend .	26	37	136	136	20	16	1	0	0	985	26-23
Mr G Strachan	12	16	50	50	5	7	1	0	3	243	15- 3
Mr G N Wyatt ..	9	16	47	36	8	7	0	0	1	189	11-13

The following played in two matches—Capt Wallace, Messrs Bryan, G E Browne Cross, Fewings, Fox, H Grace, Master, Morris, and Price In one match only—Messrs Brookes, Baily, R E Bush, Coates, Collings, J Mills, Pontifex, Quentin, and Tremenheere

In perusing this table the reader cannot fail to observe that all the contests during the six years referred to were carried on without any professional aid, and in order to show how vigorously the executive addressed themselves to the important task of forming a county club, an entirely new race of cricketers were enlisted under the banner of 1870 The peculiar gifts of cricket running in a family is not a thing so novel as to call for peculiar remark. Instances are recorded of a whole eleven, sons of one father "Family matches"—that is eleven a side—are not uncommon nowadays, but the world never heard of such a marvellous trio as Gloucestershire has been able to furnish With the brothers Grace cricket was innate, or, if taught them at all, their education must have been limited to their father or uncle, both certainly men of renown as sportsmen But admitting of family proclivities for cricket, none can be cited with greater force than that of the Graces Mr Edward Mills Grace, the second son of the late Mr Grace of Downend, near Bristol, exhibited the faculty of cricket in a striking degree when at Mr Kempe's academy If he were not the readiest of the class in Latin exercises, and not so well up as others in dealing with the theories of Bonnycastle or Euclid, it was no fault of his All are not alike gifted in the study of such writers Let the scene be changed, the schoolroom for the playground, and "Baily" instantly becomes master of the situation Daring with the bat and wily with the ball, all yield, and own his supremacy Thus the boy was seen to be "father to the man" His extraordinary performance at Canterbury will doubtlessly pass into the domain of great historical events *

Disdaining at times the recognised theories of scientific batting, he is not regarded as a model for imitation, but the rapidity with which he causes the score to travel never fails to arrest attention In the field, few—very few—come up to him in point of effect and usefulness

Respecting Mr William Gilbert Grace, the words that Shakespeare puts into the mouth of Comenius, when narrating the deeds of a Roman hero, may be as aptly applied to this English cricketer, notwithstanding the difference in the character of the strife:

> "The man I speak of cannot in the world
> Be singly counterpoised At sixteen years,
> When Tarquin made a head for Rome, he fought
> Beyond the mark of others His pupilage
> Man-entered thus, he waxed like a sea,
> And lurched all swords o' the garland"

What a God-send is Mr W G to the tribe of easy writers. Scarcely an incident in his life has been left unmentioned, to say nothing of the many which never occurred, except in the regions of romance and the fields of fancy Stripped of the rhodomontade about his boyish feats, which were in accord with those of all the rest of his family, the first fact worth knowing is, that he came before a criticising public at nearly the same age as Pilch, of whom Norfolk for many years proudly boasted From the first blush of greatness which accompanied his *début* at Lord's in 1861, its lustre has never been dimmed The heights he scales have never been reached by any man since cricket was culti-

* See foot note, p 166

vated, and to what elevation he may hereafter aspire is beyond the ken of the most astute and the imagination of the most profound. His runs have been tabulated over and over again, and subjected to almost every process of arithmetic in order, if possible, to squeeze out some fresh wonder. Mr. Grace is certainly a prodigy of prodigies.

Each of these gentlemen has been honoured with various pseudonymes, but the younger brother is almost invariably clipped of his fair proportion of baptismal rights, and Gilbert Frederick contents himself with "Fred." He is so essentially a Grace in all the attributes of a first-class cricketer, that further eulogy would be a waste of words.

CHAPTER XVII.

GLANCES AT THE PAST AND PRESENT STATE OF COUNTY CRICKET—*continued.*

LANCASHIRE AND LEICESTERSHIRE.

> Peace to the soil where high and low
> In ranks of stainless warfare blend,
> Of strife is pleasure born, and foe
> Becomes another name for friend.—*Reynolds.*

PAST AND PRESENT CONDITION OF CRICKET IN THE PALATINATE—EARLY MATCH WITH MIDDLESEX, ALSO A SERIES OF MATCHES IN 1868, WITH BATTING AVERAGES FOR THAT YEAR—CONTINUATION OF MATCHES WITH SURREY, KENT, AND YORKSHIRE—BATTING AVERAGES FOR 1875—PAST AND PRESENT CONDITION OF LEICESTERSHIRE.

HOW can May and December, Youth and Age, when yoked together, be made to agree? Socially, it is often a difficult task, but in matters appertaining to cricket nothing is more easy. The aged sire looks with rapture on the exploits of a generation half a century below him, and the rising talent is inspired by the stories of those whose deeds they would gladly emulate. Little can be said of Leicestershire in this chapter that will not find its counterpart in that appropriated to Notts, as these counties were for many years the chief centres for great cricket in the Midland districts. Of late years Leicestershire has fallen from its high estate, and has to bow to the necessities of circumstances and changes of time. The case of Lancashire is altogether different, whose start in life may be traced not much longer than a decade. Considering the past and present political and social standing of this shire, the wonder has often been expressed why it did not long ago come to the front in a form befitting itself, and the much-needed development of the manly and noble game. People pointed to Manchester as one of the most important, thriving, and wealthy cities in the world for its manufactories, and the port of Liverpool as second only to that of London, and yet scarcely any signs of cricket life, comparatively speaking, were manifest. Lancashire, it is known, was the seat of the *Brigantes* and *Voluntii* in the Roman *Cæsariensis*. It became a duchy and palatinate under Edward III., son of John of Gaunt, and since Edward IV., it has been held by the sovereign with a separate court. Hence, in cricket parlance, matches played in the shire are often called "County Palatine." When the county club was formed—say ten years ago—a surprising amount of talent exhibited itself; this, too, of the sturdy sort, just likely to grapple successfully, not only with Leicestershire in its apparent process of decay, but with shires and counties possessed of fresher nerve and greater vitality Among the early matches of the newly-formed club was one with Middlesex at Manchester in the month of June, 1866; from the full score given it will be seen that Middlesex won by 53 runs

MIDDLESEX.

	1st inn		2nd inn
Mr A Henry, b Reynolds	3	c Reynolds, b Leese	60
Mantle, c Holgate b Reynolds	14	run out	5
Mr R D Walker, c Holgate b A B Rowley	17	c Iddison, b Leese	19
T Hearne, b Reynolds	0	c Iddison, b Leese	87
Mr I D Walker, b A B Rowley	10	b Whittaker	13
Mr V E Walker, c Reynolds b Smith	41	b Reynolds	53
G Hearne, l b w b A B Rowley	0	c Leach, b A B Rowley	3
Mr C Calvert, c and b A B Rowley	25	b Reynolds	11
Mr C E Brune, not out	10	b Reynolds	8
Mr M Thompson, b Smith	5	not out	4
Howitt, c Iddison	4	b Reynolds	0
Byes 2 l-b 3	5	Leg-byes 4, w 2	6
Total	134	Total	269

LANCASHIRE

	1st inn		2nd inn.
Mr J Leach, b R D Walker	14	b T Hearne	34
Smith, l b w, b Howitt	0	b Howitt	12
Mr E B Rowley, run out	3	b Howitt	2
Mr J F Leese, run out	8	c Thompson, b T Hearne	0
Iddison, b I D Walker	1	c Henry, b Howitt	5
Mr A B Rowley, b Howitt	4	not out	31
C Coward, c Hearne, b I D Walker	85	c V E Walker, b T Hearne	4
Mr E Whittaker, c R D Walker, b Hearne	4	c V E Walker b T Hearne	16
Holgate, c Henry b T Hearne	25	b Howitt	26
Mr E Bousfield, c V E Walker b Hearne	30	b Brune	25
Reynolds, not out	1	b Howitt	3
Byes 2, l b 1, w 3	6	Byes 4, l-b 6, w 1	11
Total	181	Total	169

The second match took place at Islington nine days after the first terminated, when Middlesex won by six wickets The third was with Surrey at the Oval It lasted three days, but was left incomplete, the scores being Lancashire, 195 and 321 (eight wickets)—total 516. Surrey, 422

On the 23rd of August, Surrey went to Liverpool and returned victorious by three wickets, thus, Lancashire 125 and 86—total 211, Surrey, 116 and 96 (seven wickets)—total 212 So far it may appear to have been a very indifferent start, but when the strength and experience of the parties with whom they had to contend is carefully considered, little else could have been expected In the last match it ought to be mentioned that the bowling of Mr Appleby was very telling he got six wickets in fifty overs for 73 runs This, as an amateur against a strong team of bats, was a promise which subsequently ripened into fulfilment In a drawn match at the Oval in the year 1867, the following score was put together in a first and only innings —

LANCASHIRE

Coward, c Pooley, b Griffith	21
J Ricketts, not out	195
Mr E B Rowley, c Collyer, b Griffith	78
Holgate, st Pooley b Noble	29
Burrows b Griffith	11
F Coward, b Griffith	0
Mr A Appleby, l b w, b Griffith	8
Hickton, b Griffith	26
Mr E Whittaker, c Pooley, b Griffith	36
Storer, c and b Griffith	0
Smith, b Griffith	12
Bye 1 l-b 4, w 7, n-b 1	13
Total	429

The return match, played at Manchester in the same year, was also "drawn" Surrey, 171 and 261—total 432 Lancashire, 219 and 144 (eight wickets)—total 363.

A clear view of the cricket condition of the County Palatine (1868) is subjoined

Nottingham, May 28 —Lancashire v Notts Lancashire, 74 and 148—total 222 , Notts, 296 The latter won by an innings and 74 runs

Manchester, June 18 —Lancashire v Surrey Surrey, 252 and 42—total 294 , Lancashire, 204 and 93 (for two wickets)—total 297 Lancashire won by eight wickets

Holbeck, July 9 —Lancashire v Yorkshire Lancashire, 30 and 34—total 64 , Yorkshire, 250 Won by the latter in an innings, and 186 runs (Not as at page 254)

The Oval, July 16 —Lancashire v Surrey Lancashire, 120 and 89—total 209 , Surrey, 351 The latter won by an innings and 142 runs

Manchester July 31 —Lancashire v Notts (return) Lancashire, 168 and 53—total 221 , Notts, 127 and 110—total 237 Notts won by 16 runs

BATTING AVERAGES

NAMES	No of Matches	No of Innings	Most Runs in a Match	Most Runs in an Innings	How often Bowled	Caught	Run out	Not out	Stumped	Total	Average per Innings	Over
Mr E Bousfield	3	5	24	24	0	5	0	0	0	43	8	3
C Coward	5	10	50	41	4	4	2	0	0	165	16	5
F Coward	3	6	6	6	5	0	0	1	0	6	1	
Mr F S Head	2	3	24	24	1	1	0	0	1	43	14	1
Hickton	5	9	41	41	4	2	1	1	1	123	13	6
Iddison	4	8	43	36	0	5	1	2	0	94	11	6
W H Iddison	2	4	11	7	2	0	1	0	1	11	2	3
Ricketts	5	10	82	54	5	3	0	1	1	245	24	5
Reynolds	5	9	19	11	1	2	1	5	0	28	3	1
Mr E B Rowley	3	5	29	25	5	0	0	0	0	29	5	4
Mr E Whittaker	3	6	24	24	4	2	0	0	0	29	4	5

A favourable turn in the tide accompanied the season 1870 Four matches were played, of which they won three , the first, on the 8th of May, at the Oval, against Surrey, by eight wickets. One of the most noteworthy features of the match was the bowling of Mr Appleby, who, in his last eight overs (five maidens), got six wicket for eight runs

Hampshire had little chance with the Palatinate at Manchester on the 21st of July, as the visitors returned beaten by ten wickets Lancashire went in first, and totalled 262 Towards this amount Mr Hornby contributed 132 Hampshire completed their first innings for 138, and had to follow on The bowling of Hickton sadly overtaxed the defensive capabilities of Hants in their second innings, as all the wickets were placed to his account—six clean bowled Next in the programme stood a "return" with Surrey, at the Oval, in the month of August, when Lancashire were beaten by an innings and 15 runs Four days afterwards a "return" with Hampshire, at Southampton awarded the victory to Lancashire by 40 runs The scoring on neither side assumed the colossal proportions which the public in these batting days are accustomed to

Out of the four matches played in 1872, the best contested was with Yorkshire, at Old Trafford. Full score

LANCASHIRE

	1st inn		2nd inn
Mr A N Hornby, c and b Emmett	21	b Emmett	5
Coward, b Emmett	14	c Rawlinson, b Emmett	0
Mr J F Leese, b Emmett	6	b Emmett	8
Mr E B Rowley, b Iddison	26	c Clayton, b Emmett	2
Watson, b Emmett	0	c West, b Emmett	0
Roberts, b Emmett	20	c Rawlinson, b Clayton	13
Wm McIntyre, c Greenwood, b Emmett	12	b Clayton	11
Mr J Hillkirk, b Hill	0	c Lockwood, b Clayton	4
Mr R Dewhurst, st Pinder, b Hill	24	b Clayton	24
Mr A Appleby, b Iddison	14	not out	7
Reynolds, not out	11	c Emmett, b Clayton	0
Byes 3, l-b 5, n b 1	9	Byes 1, l b 4	5
Total	157	Total	79

YORKSHIRE

	1st inn		2nd inn
Rowbotham, b Appleby	6	b Appleby	3
Clayton, c Dewhurst, b Appleby	1	c Hillkirk, b Watson	3
Emmett b McIntyre	4	run out	29
Greenwood, run out	24	b McIntyre	9
Hill, b Appleby	3	c Roberts, b Appleby ...	2
Iddison, c Roberts b Appleby	6	not out	30
Lockwood, c Appleby, b McIntyre	2	c Leese, b McIntyre	3
Rawlinson, b McIntyre	2	l b w, b Watson	17
H Kaye, c Roberts, b McIntyre	13	b McIntyre	1
West, not out	22	c Watson b Appleby	1
Pinder, c Rowley, b McIntyre	4	c Hornby, b Appleby	1
Byes 4, l-b 2	6	Bye	1
Total	93	Total	100

If the Lancastrians did not play their full strength in 1873, as was frequently stated to be the case, they effected marvels in their weakness. They planned seven matches for the season, i e , an out and home with Yorkshire, same with Surrey and Derbyshire, and an out with Kent. They were defeated in both contests with Yorkshire, and in the single one by Kent, at Maidstone These defeats were atoned for by coming well out of the contests with Surrey and Derbyshire The first match of the seven took place at Old Trafford towards the close of May, when Yorkshire won by nine wickets The bowling of Emmett was remarkable He got eleven wickets in 54 overs for 82 runs Hill, his companion in attack, got eight wickets in 53 overs and a ball, for 47 runs Against such bowling Lancashire made a very feeble stand, and the first innings realised but 58 runs, the second 82—total 140

On the 19th of June a better fate awaited them at the Oval, when they beat Surrey by an innings and 117 runs This remarkable success was to a great extent due to McIntyre and Watson, two bowlers of an extremely opposite character, and yet both superlatively excellent These men bowled throughout the match McIntyre, in 47 overs and two balls claimed eleven wickets for 70 runs , Watson, in 46 overs, eight wickets, 79 runs The batting and fielding of Mr Hornby had much to do with the brilliancy of the conquest, nor was there a single extra run recorded against Lancashire in either of the Surrey innings, an event which contrasted strangely with the fielding of the other side See score :

SURREY

	1st inn		2nd inn.
Jupp, c and b McIntyre	8	run out	0
Humphrey, c Jackson, b McIntyre	11	c Barlow, b McIntyre	25
Palmer, c Reynolds, b McIntyre	3	c Hornby, b McIntyre	20
T Humphrey, c Barlow, b McIntyre	2	st Jackson, b McIntyre	7
Freeman, c McIntyre, b Watson	9	b Watson	10
Mr F H Boult c Barlow, b Watson	0	b McIntyre	0
Mr C W Burls, b Watson	0	b McIntyre	0
Swann, c Barlow, b Watson	3	b Watson	22
Bristow, c Reynolds, b Watson	3	c McIntyre, b Watson	8
Southerton, b McIntyre	4	b McIntyre	12
James Street, not out	1	not out	1
Total	44	Total	105

LANCASHIRE

Mr A N Hornby, c R Humphrey, b Street	128
Mr H B Parr, c Palmer, b Southerton	1
Mr E B Rowley, b Southerton	43
Mr R Roberts, c and b Boult	11
Mr J F Leese, b Boult	0
Watson, c T Humphrey, b Southerton	4
Barlow, b Southerton	0
Mr J Hillkirk, b Southerton	25
McIntyre, st Bristow, b Street	10
Mr E Jackson, not out	8
Reynolds, b Boult	9
Byes 13, l b 7 w 1, n-b 2	23
Total	262

The changes incident to cricket were strongly verified by the position of Lancashire in the following year Six matches were played, of which number one only resulted in a victory To account for this the Lancastrians referred to the absence of Mr Hornby—a host in himself Three were unmistakeably lost, and two drawn

"The darkest day," says the poet, "live but to-morrow, will have passed away" Just so! Nine matches were proposed for the year 1875, of which Lancashire won five, lost two, and two were drawn The most remarkable of these took place at Old Trafford about midsummer, and a great deal of interest was excited among the backers of the respective sides Nor them alone In such a locality as Manchester, with its thriving population, there is always to be found among the mixture of classes a strong display of spirit attending any event of the year, and the meeting with Yorkshire was not likely to be wanting in this particular, more especially as cricket in the Palatinate had, at the time in question, acquired considerable popularity, and every inducement was offered for the development of native talent Yorkshire brought a strong force—all professionals, while the opposing team had a large infusion of amateurs Only one man on each side failed to score in a first innings; but great strength exhibited itself in the second Lancashire were by far the best fielders, and every feat, whether of the in or out party, was watched and applauded; calling to mind Somerville, who says

> "Observe the attentive crowd, all hearts are fixed
> On this important war, and pleasing hope
> Glows in each breast The vulgar and the great,
> Equally happy now with freedom share
> The common joy'

The Lancashire bowling deserves notice Mr Appleby, in 69 overs, obtained nine wickets for 93 runs, McIntyre, 89 overs seven wickets, 126 runs; and Watson, 26 overs, three wickets, 54 runs Some food for thought and conjecture may be extracted from the full score attached

YORKSHIRE

	1st inn		2nd inn
Armitage, c Appleby, b McIntyre .. .	2	c Appleby b McIntyre	2
Ullathorne, b Appleby .	6	c Wright, b McIntyre	5
A Greenwood, c McIntyre b Appleby	4	c McIntyre, b Watson	27
Lockwood, c Wright, b Appleby	6	b Appleby	32
Ulyett, b Watson	14	c Jackson, b McIntyre	50
Emmett, b McIntyre	17	b Appleby .	3
Clayton, run out	7	c Parr, b Appleby .	39
John Thewlis, sen, not out	12	c Appleby, b McIntyre	9
Pinder c Appleby, b Watson	1	c Appleby, b McIntyre	. 5
Rowbotham, c Jackson, b Appleby	12	not out	29
Hill, b Appleby ..	0	b Appleby	6
Leg-byes .	2	Byes 3, l-b 5, n b 1	9
Total . . .	83	Total	216

LANCASHIRE

	1st inn		2nd inn
Mr A N Hornby, b Hill	29	not out	78
Barlow, b Hill	7	not out	50
Mr H B Parr, c Pinder, b Emmett	1		
Rev F W Wright, b Hill	3		
Mr W G Mills, b Hill	1		
Watson, b Clayton	31		
Mr E B Rowley, run out	26		
Mr J R Hillkirk not out	18		
W McIntyre, c Armitage, b Emmett	0		
Mr E Jackson, b Ulyett	1		
Mr A Appleby, b Ulyett	18		
Byes 7, l-b 10, w 2	19	Byes 8, l b 8, w 4	20
Total	154	Total	148

In the match with Kent at Old Trafford, in the month of August, the resident team beat Kent by 32 runs Scores Lancashire 164 and 118—total, 282, Kent, 145 and 105—total, 250 The ' return," at Catford Bridge, ended in favour of Lancashire by five wickets From the foregoing very brief sketches of the play and players, the Palatinate has up to the third quarter of the present century, by good fortune and its reverses, fully established itself as a respectable member of the county families dignified with the title of cricket The relative professional and amateur strength called into action during the year 1875 may be to some extent arrived at from the following

BATTING ANALYSIS

NAME	No of Matches	No of Innings	Most Runs in a Match	Most Runs in an Innings	How often Bowled	Caught	Run out	Stumped	Not out	Total	Average per Innings Over
Mr A Appleby	5	8	21	21	3	3	0	0	2	76	9- 4
Barlow	7	11	87	87	5	3	0	1	2	360	32- 8
Coward	3	5	29	25	1	2	2	0	0	51	10- 4
Mr R Dawhurst	3	5	59	59	3	2	0	0	0	82	16- 2
Mr A N Hornby	6	10	107	78	7	1	1	0	1	311	31- 1
Mr E Jackson	3	4	9	9	3	0	0	0	1	19	4- 3
Mr J R Hillkirk	7	10	36	36	5	3	0	0	2	153	15- 3
Mr J R Kevan	2	4	12	12	3	1	0	0	0	12	3
Mr J F Leese	2	4	13	12	0	4	0	0	0	13	3- 1
McIntyre	8	13	66	66	5	4	0	1	3	172	13- 8
Mr H B Parr	3	5	63	52	0	5	0	0	0	94	18- 4
Mr E B Rowley	6	9	37	27	6	2	1	0	0	131	14- 5
Mr V K Royle	3	5	21	18	2	2	0	0	1	42	8- 2
Watson	8	13	53	53	5	8	0	0	0	181	13-12
Rev F W Wright	5	8	36	32	3	4	0	0	1	108	13- 4
Stephenson	2	4	8	6	1	1	1	0	1	8	2

LEICESTERSHIRE.

It has been elsewhere remarked that Leicester, the chief centre of the shire, was at one time prominent in the community of cricketers. About the year 1790, an eleven were selected from the shire and played under the title against Marylebone in Burghley Park. Whether from defective organisation or sheer inability to cope with the adversary is not stated, but probably both causes led to their defeat by an innings and 41 runs; the scores being, Leicestershire, 59 and 110—total, 169; Marylebone, 210. Very few matches from this date, till near half a century onwards, partook strictly of the county form, except those acknowledged as such at varied times between Notts, Yorkshire, and perhaps Rutland. An effort was made in 1873 to consolidate a county club, and for this purpose the county town and the shire were formed into an "association." Two matches were played with the Marylebone Club, one at Lord's and the return on the Victoria Park Ground, Leicester. The latter place was in a shocking condition for cricket, and two, if not three, of the parties concerned in the match got knocked about after a fashion that will long live in their memories. Jordan, the ex-ground man at Lord's, went to Leicester early in the following spring and "put the place to rights." It would seem, however, that cricket is not much cared for now in this once leading locality. Two matches were arranged with Lancashire in the year 1875; the first, played at Leicester on the 14th of June, was left drawn; the scores being—Lancashire, 138 and 216—total, 354. Leicestershire, 99 and 20 (two wickets)—total, 119. The return at Old Trafford was delayed till the 13th of August, when Leicestershire were beaten by an innings and 25 runs. Leicester was a populous Saxon city at the time of the Norman Conquest, and known as the Roman *Ratæ*. Seeing that the shire has an extent of 800 square miles, and is traversed with great facility from end to end by commerce in lead, coal, iron, sheep, horses, &c., the marvel is that the manly and noble game does not find more favour in the eyes of those who might beneficially extend it either by social support or material aid.

Whatsoever may have been the causes which led to the supineness which threatened the extinction of county cricket, it is not the purpose here to discuss. Change and decay is the fate of all things sublunary. Kingdoms flourish, empires fall, and monarchies that once awed the world have perished leaving scarcely a trace of their locality, and are known now only by some monumental fragment or the historian's pen; States governed by less potent authorities have been engulphed by neighbours having the power to take and keep, so as to lose all identity and be blotted from the world's map; institutions, too, valuable in their day for the purposes of moral and mental progress, have been absorbed by others of greater pretensions; and—to carry the idea of change a little farther—it has affected the sports of the nation, and in many cases beneficially. Cricket has established itself in almost every village of the British Isles, and has found also a temporary home in quarters the least likely. Here then comes the anomaly. Why, amidst all this progress, does Leicestershire assume a stationary, if not a retrograde, position?—retrograde certainly in comparison with surrounding counties.

Of all places in England this should be the last to lag behind or exhibit weakness, the last, when there is plenty of "young stuff" to fill up the gaps which time has hewn in the ranks of old players; the last, when so many excellent amateurs belonging to the county are to be found, and found easily. What of Mr Mitchell, one of the best batsmen of the day? of Mr. G Marriott, a splendid fast round-arm bowler? and of Mr C Marriott good at any point? There is hope for Leicestershire yet, seeing that it is "not dead, but sleepeth," in fact, the signs of a new life are already manifesting themselves, and, in the opinion of the sanguine, the day is not far distant when this once famed county will be itself again, and take a high stand in the rapidly increasing community of cricket.

CHAPTER XVIII.

GLANCES AT THE PAST AND PRESENT STATE OF COUNTY CRICKET—*continued.*

THE EASTERN COUNTIES.

Rivers soft and slow*
Amid the verdant landscapes flow.—*Addison.*

* * * * *

And see the rivers how they run,
Through woods and meads, through shade and sun;
Sometimes swift, sometimes slow,
Wave succeeding wave, they go.—*Dyer.*

Essex in the Reign of Henry VIII. and Now—First Meeting of Essex *v.* Middlesex at Lord's Ground in Dorset-square—Condition of the Club in 1790—Matches at Navestock, Hornchurch, Dartford, &c.—Marylebone Club *v.* Hornchurch—Subsequent Inertness—Waking up—Great Score of Alfred Adams at Saffron Walden—Matches with Norfolk—I Z. and the Auderies—Effort to Establish County Quarters at Brentwood—Suffolk *v.* Marylebone in 1828—Visit of Clarke and his Team to Ipswich—Matches between the Gentlemen of Suffolk and Essex—Lord Chesterfield's Idea of Cricket—Norfolk slowness—The Three Pilches—Norwich *v.* Marylebone; Return—Norfolk *v.* Essex—Poets and Cricketers—Cambridge Town Clubs—The Universities—Parker's Piece—Matches Thereon—Fenner's Ground, afterwards the University—Its Area, the New Pavilion, etc.

MAN was not made to be miserable, and yet there is never a lack of writers who, to suit their peculiar tastes, can find material in every thing to make him so. Essex has not escaped. A great deal has been said about the desolating decrees of Henry VIII., which turned things upside down, and changed the entire constitution of the locality. Well! it might have been so, but that is a long time since. Enough, however, of beauty and prosperity remains to suggest a picture of a pleasanter kind. Essex is neither more nor less in extent than when it received its ecclesiastical shock, while the condition of the land and its inhabitants, too, is vastly improved. Unlike the neighbouring county, parted from it by the Thames, it has but few hills, and these of no very lofty pretensions. A large portion of the 1532 square miles belonging to Essex consists of marsh, undulating meadows, and beautiful woods.

* In Essex: The Brain, Blackwater, Cann, Chelmer, Crouch, Ingreburn, Lea, Roding, Stour, Stort, and Ter. Suffolk: The Blyth, Breton, Deben, Ore, Orwell, Little Ouse, Stour, and Waveney. Norfolk: The Bure, Nen, Great Ouse, Waveney, and Yare.

By the application of modern discoveries, the county is largely benefited. The same remark with regard to progress is equally applicable to other districts forming the Eastern Counties. No one can conscientiously deny that the hand of industry among agricultural populations is the precursor to the sports native or imported to the neighbourhood.

Full ninety years ago, Essex had cultivated cricket sufficiently to challenge its neighbour Middlesex to an encounter on the first ground recognised as "Lord's." Neither side seemed to have faith enough in themselves to enter the lists without professional help, but Essex, being the weaker side, "went to the wall," the scores being, Middlesex, 58 and 203—total, 261, Essex, 130 and 38—total, 168. Four years afterwards, the Marylebone Club met an eleven, collected from various parts of the county, at Hornchurch. The residents were no match for their more experienced visitors, who won by 166 runs. In 1792, a meeting with Kent, at Dartford, ended also in the defeat of Essex by 81 runs. The score is sufficiently curious to claim a reproduction. It is a faithful transcript of the "method" of a time not ripe for giving even a tolerable idea of the merits of the bowling. Who can account now for the success of Ingram or the disposal of Ring?

KENT (WITH BELDHAM)

	1st inn		2nd inn
Earl of Winchilsea, b Boorman	1	st Ingram	30
Earl of Darnley, c Boult	3	st Ingram	3
Hon E Bligh, c Ingram	30	b Boorman	3
Hon G Monson, c Littler	10	c Fennex	17
S Amherst, Esq, c Ingram	5	c Boorman	9
T Boxall, c Wyatt	0	not out	8
R Fielder, run out	6	b Littler	1
W Beldham, st Ingram	18	c Ingram	15
J Ring, hit w	26	c Scott	18
R Clifford, c Ingram	6	c Ingram	5
J Crawte, not out	13	c Wyatt	1
Byes	3	Byes	3
Total	121	Total	113

ESSEX (WITH FENNEX AND SCOTT)

	1st inn		2nd inn
— Wyatt Esq, b Clifford	4	not out	6
G Boult, Esq, c Beldham	2	b Boxall	2
— Den, Esq, c Beldham	0	run out	1
J Boorman, b Clifford	0	c Fielder	13
— Oxley, c Ring	6	c Beldham	0
W Fennex, c Ring	5	st Monson	26
T Scott, b Beldham	17	run out	0
T Ingram c Monson	20	c Clifford	7
— Goldstone, run out	4	b Boxall	9
— Littler, c Fielder	3	c Fielder	1
— Stevens, not out	8	b Darnley	18
		Bye	1
Total	69	Total	84

From a curious document, still preserved, it seems that no particular spot of the county was fixed upon as a chief centre, and hence confusion has handed itself down as to which really had claim to be entitled the head quarters This circumstance, however, is not a matter of surprise, seeing that Essex standeth not alone in matters of disputed local pre-eminence The following facsimile of "a card" points to Navestock, and that it was well supported there can be little doubt from the list of patrons

ESSEX

CRICKET CLUB,

For the YEAR 1790,

WILL BE HELD AT THE

GREEN-MAN, at NAVESTOCK,

On the following DAYS,

Monday May 3d	Monday July 12th.
——— 17th.	——— 26th.
——— 31ſt	——— Auguſt 9th.
——— June 14th	——— 23d.
——— 28th	

A LIST of MEMBERS.

R B Wyatt, eſq
John Ruſſell, eſq
Thomas Velley, eſq
Mr Walker,
Robert Denn, eſq
Mr John Boodle,
Rev Mr Berrington,
William Evans, eſq
Rev T Darby,
Rev W Lockwood,
Hon Capt Monſon.
Wm Dolby, eſq
Eliab Hervey, eſq
Rev E Conyers,
Wm Lynn, eſq
G Nicholls, eſq
P Mannington, eſq
Rev R Lockwood,
Rev Mr Abdy,
Rev Mr Dupuis,
Mr Clark,
John Convers, eſq
R Oliver, eſq
Holden Strutt, eſq
John Tyrell, eſq
John Henniker, eſq
John Rigg, eſq
Sir Robert Boyd, K B
Rev Mr Budworth,
T Tomlinſon, eſq
J Goodeare, eſq
Rt Hon Ld Winchelſea
Rt Hon Ld Petre,
C Tower, eſq
Sir W Smyth,
T B Bramſton, eſq
John Bullock, eſq
F Fane, eſq
J Mitchel, eſq
N S Parry, eſq
J Urmſton, eſq
J A Wallinger, eſq
J Wallinger, eſq
T Turner, eſq
J Pardoe, eſq
T Wright, eſq
J Barwis, eſq
F Ford, eſq
Rev Mr Johnſon

Early in the following year the Hornchurch Club—said to be at the time "Essex"—played Marylebone, but were defeated by an innings and 10 runs A few weeks later Hornchurch confronted Marylebone at Lord's, and in this return match, although the latter had the assistance of Walker, they were beaten by two wickets At the close of a first innings each a difference of two runs only existed, and the two in favour of Marylebone No individual scores of any magnitude were made, and but 239 totalled throughout the match.

Dating from the commencement of the present century, Essex seems to have fallen into a surprisingly somnolent condition, relieved only by a few scratch performances utterly unworthy of being kept in remembrance A match with Marylebone, at Langley Park, near Hornchurch, in 1831, is a striking revelation of weakness on the part of Essex Their score of 93 runs in a double innings against 196 of Marylebone shows that they were not refreshed by long sleep. After the expiration of four years, Essex again appeared at Lord's, represented by the Wanstead Club, but the match presented no features of interest, and, from some cause—said to be want of time—was left unfinished

That the county was not deficient in batting power may be assumed from the results of an encounter with Bishop Stortford in 1837—at that time no mean parish eleven The Essex side was composed chiefly of players residing in the neighbourhood of Saffron Walden, where the match came off The residents went in first, and occupied the wickets for nine hours producing in the meantime no less than 474 runs. Of this number Alfred Adams claimed 279 * The Herts eleven had no opportunity for going in at all, as the match was limited to one day This feat for many years was regarded as superior to that of Mr Ward's, seeing that the latter gave the most easy of chances at a very early stage of his innings, and, moreover, that the sides were not well balanced, whereas, in the case of Adams no fair chance occurred, and one side was supposed to be equal to the other If this piece of history be of any value, it shows that Essex, like many other counties, may trace its want of position to the lack of proper organisation of the means at disposal

Another lamentable display of weakness exhibited itself at Chelmsford in 1850, when the Essex Club, with the help of three professionals, were soundly beaten by the Anberries The peripatetic elevens, whether of the A E class or I Z, do not seem to have stirred the county to any perceptible extent A match between the Gentlemen of Essex and Cambridgeshire determined nothing, as it was left unfinished In the course of a few years Essex met Norfolk at Upton Park, and after two days' play, the match was declared drawn, the scores being Norfolk, 163 and 265—total 428, Essex, 179 and 40 (one wicket)—total 219 Essex brought several excellent batsmen forward on this occasion Mr E L Buxton scored 52 runs, Mr Spencer 24 Messrs J Round and W E Grimston 22 each On the Norfolk side Mr. Brereton claimed 99 before he was bowled by Mr Round

Better success attended Essex in their "return" at Dereham, in the month of July, 1868, when the residents were beaten by three wickets, thus—Norfolk, 73 and 84—total 157 Essex, 113 and 45 (seven wickets)—total 158 There has been no lack of effort on the part of many gentlemen having influence in the county to establish a county club, but they have not been attended with a corresponding success Nearly all the matches which attempt to represent Essex have been played at Lord's. Brentwood is now named as the spot likely to endure for some time. The ground is capacious, and the conditions upon which it is held are easy Several excellent players are located about the neighbourhood, and the things absolutely necessary for carrying on the business attached to a county club are a good working committee, a zealous co-operation of players, and activity on the part of those possessed of power and influence Good wishes are all very well, but something more substantial is required to keep the machinery in good working order It is questionable if a better place could have been chosen for county cricket than Brentwood, although the old town has to be reached by an uphill effort, on roads

* Composed of 4 fives, 25 fours, 23 threes, 15 twos, and 60 singles He went in first, and was last out

and pathways not yet made smooth by pilgrim feet. Villages very small, and others tolerably great, radiate from Brentwood, and scarcely any town of importance is of greater distance than an hour's ride on the iron road. The great encouragement given to cricket in the garrison town of Colchester is also a matter of consideration, as very few officers stationed there either for a long or short time are unacquainted with the game, but what is of still greater importance, they know how to play it.

As a county, Suffolk offers but little material for remark. Bury was for many years the chief centre, and occasionally added an atom to its small renown. All the credit for beating Marylebone (1828) who had the assistance of Saunders, could not be fairly claimed by Suffolk, as Pilch, a Norfolk man, contributed very largely to the success. For instance, Bury scored 56 from the bat, just half of which belonged to Pilch. In the second innings also Pilch was the chief contributor, viz., 43 out of 108. He also clean bowled nine Marylebone wickets. A long silence ensued, broken only by matches between Bury and Swaffham, in which the Suffolk Eleven usually proved themselves the better team. In one case they won by six wickets, but this was owing in a great measure to the help of Arnold, a Cambridge professional of no mean acquirements. The visit of I Zingari brought out the amateur talent of the county, and the Borderers had opportunities of meeting with good cricket at the Auberies. Still the Suffolk pulse beat feebly, notwithstanding the many attempts to consolidate its strength and shape into county form. Clarke and his All England Eleven exhibited the weakness of the county in 1852. Out of the twenty-two who played at Ipswich on that occasion, seven failed to score anything, and with Grundy and Nixon to pull up the total, reached 88 runs only. A trifling improvement was visible on the next occasion of Clarke's visit to Ipswich, but 88 runs only were totalled by twenty-two of Ipswich in the double innings; the largest score was 12—all the rest single figures. A match entitled "Gentlemen of Essex *v* Gentlemen of Suffolk," at Braxted Park, Essex, in 1854, clearly showed the existence of cultivated cricket in both counties. The contest was well maintained, and Suffolk won by four runs.

GENTLEMEN OF SUFFOLK (WITH ISTED)

	1st inn		2nd inn
— Isted, c and b A Du Cane	9	b A Du Cane	0
W B Long, Esq, b Gibson ..	1	not out	2
J F Gosling Esq, b A Du Cane	15	b Gibson	8
Rev E W Stanhope, b Gibson	6	c Gibson, b A Du Cane	3
G R Johnson, Esq c F Grimston, b A Du Cane	9	b Gibson	7
F D Longe, Esq, c Nash, b Gibson	4	c De Crespigny, b A Du Cane	12
G R Dupuis, Esq, b A du Cane	13	b Gibson	1
F Bosworth Esq, b Gibson	2	b Gibson	7
Rev F Gosling st F Grimston, b Gibson	23	c White, b A Du Cane	2
G R D'Eye, Esq, not out	10	b A Du Cane ..	0
Rev T L French, c C Du Cane, b Gibson	24	b Gibson	7
Byes 2, l-b 1, n-b 1	4	Bye 1, l-b 3, n b 1	5
Total	123	Total	54

GENTLEMEN OF ESSEX (WITH GIBSON)

	1st inn		2nd inn
C Du Cane, Esq, c Longe, b Isted	5	l b w, b Isted	1
— Gibson, b Isted	19	run out	19
Hon E H Grimston, b F Gosling	1	b F Gosling	0
Hon F Grimston, b Isted	5	run out	0
A Spencer, c Isted, b F Gosling	10	b Isted	8
E Walton, Esq not out	23	c Isted, b F Gosling	11
J G Nash, Esq, b J F Gosling	9	c Longe, b Isted	14
Rev F De Crespigny, b J F Gosling	8	b Isted	1
Sir W Bowyer Smyth, c F Gosling, b Bosworth	13	run out	0
A Du Cane, Esq, c and b Isted	6	run out	2
T G White, Esq, l b w, b Bosworth	0	not out	2
Leg bye 1, wides 6, n-b 1	8	Bye 1, l b 2, w 4, n-b 1	8
Total	107	Total	66

At a subsequent meeting in Gunton Park with the Gentlemen of Norfolk, the success of Suffolk was more remarkable, the scores being Suffolk, 251, Norfolk, 55 and 63—total 118 Here one might be tempted to ask himself whether the celebrated Philip Dormer Stanhope (Earl of Chesterfield) ever really saw the game of cricket played, and if so, what the gentlemen of the Eastern Counties think of him and themselves He used the curriculum of Cambridge, and must have heard at least something concerning the game, even if he never strolled about Parker's Piece in spring time What can he mean, then, when he says "a gentleman will not be seen at cricket, for he knows that such an imitation of the manners of the mob will indelibly stamp him with vulgarity"? Chesterfield called Johnson "a respectable Hottentot," and the surly Doctor retorted by saying, "I thought this man had been a lord among wits, but I find he is only a wit among lords" The fact is, Chesterfield didn't know everything, accomplished as he certainly was, or he would have seen that the playing of cricket has a much greater tendency to raise the "mob" up to the standard of gentlemen, than bring down gentlemen to the level of the mob It is not known exactly what effect this enunciation of his lordship had upon his son, or that portion of the public who regarded the "letters" as Gospel Dr Johnson said they were not devoid of immorality Be this as it may, and cricket what it was in the eyes of a courtier, certain is it that the nobles of the land now meet the humblest on the cricket sward without disdaining them, or feeling themselves disdained "Tempora mutantur, et nos mutamur in illis"

Norfolk, generally considered the most important of the East Anglian three, exhibited but few signs of cricket life in the early part of the present century, and when brought into prominence in the year 1820, a good reason may be assigned for its quietude The match at Lord's with the Marylebone Club will always be reckoned among the events of cricket history It introduced a youth of great promise—afterwards fully realised—and afforded Mr Ward an opportunity of recording a score which for half a century remained unreached by any batsman under similar circumstances Although the match was entitled the County of

Norfolk with certain helps, it was altogether unequal to the club against which they had arrayed themselves Fuller Pilch was a raw boy of seventeen, growing out of his trousers, and not so safe in the field when "brought before company," as he afterwards said, as when at Horningtoft, among his relations and friends.

MARYLEBONE

	1st inn		2nd inn
J Tanner, Esq , b Budd	0	c F Pilch	0
J Brand, Esq , b W Pilch	38	c Brunton	13
D Stacey, Esq , b W Pilch	8	not out	9
W Ward Esq , c Ladbrooke	278	c N Pilch	10
H T Lane, Esq , b Budd	27	run out	15
H Lloyd, Esq , b W Pilch	22	c Budd	19
G F Parry, Esq b Budd	10	run out	15
Lord F Beauclerk, not out	82	st Budd	11
C Barnett, Esq , b F Pilch	3	b F Pilch	0
Hon Col Lowther, b Budd	3	b F Pilch	9
T Bache, Esq , b Budd	0	b F Pilch	4
Byes	2	Byes	3
Total	473	Total	108

NORFOLK.

	1st inn		2nd inn
W Brereton, Esq , b Beauclerk	0	absent	
N Pilch, b Beauclerk	5	st Bache	52
E H Budd, Esq , b Beauclerk	2	c Parry	0
T Vigne, Esq , b Beauclerk	11	absent	
Frost, b Beauclerk	10	b Ward	3
W Pilch, b Tanner	9	b Stacey	0
F Pilch, c Stacey	0	b Ward	2
F Ladbroke, Esq , c Beauclerk	28	absent	
C Brunton, Esq , b Lowther	21	b Ward	4
W Greenwood, Esq , c Lloyd	6	b Tanner	9
W. Quarles, Esq , not out	0	b Ward	2
Total	92	Total	72

In the following year the Holt Club challenged Nottingham, but were easily beaten by the more experienced team bordering on the Trent The three Pilches played, and in the first innings scored 49 runs out of 80, the total Nottingham made 150 in their first innings, and eventually won by ten wickets The "return" (1822), in the Forest of Nottingham, proved adverse to Norfolk, who were beaten by 105 runs. Fuller Pilch clean bowled four wickets in each innings Notwithstanding these defeats, the popularity of the game increased rapidly, and the practice of it too The fame of the three tailors, residing at the obscure village of Horningtoft, inspired the latent heroism of the surrounding districts, and a few months sufficed the city of Norwich to beat Bury by six wickets

Frequently has it been said that no English game abounds so much in marvels as cricket. Almost every age and every place has contributed something to the common stock. In 1828 the city of Norwich had a club of its own, and so had—so to speak—Norfolk. A match under these titles occurred when Bentley, a professional, scored 74 and 88—total 162—for Norwich, and not out in either instance. W. Pilch played for the city, and was accredited with the disposal of nine county men in their double innings.

The progress of the Norwich Club is further remarkable. Among other things, it may be seen in the construction of the scores of a match with Marylebone in the year 1831, which Norwich won by 45 runs.*

NORWICH

	1st inn		2nd inn
T. Roberts, run out	0	c Cobbett, b Ward	10
W. Roberts, b Beagley	0	c and b Ward	17
J. Alexander, b Ward	57	c Strathaven, b Cobbett	6
F. Pilch, c Romilly, b Cobbett	29	b Knight	65
N. Pilch, b Cobbett	0	b Ward	6
A. Spinks, Esq., c and b Grinstead	1	c Grinstead, b Knight	23
G. Wright, Esq., c Vigne, b Cobbett	2	c and b Ward	1
W. Burt, Esq., c Cotton, b Cobbett	6	not out	0
W. Pilch, b Ward	7	b Ward	0
Spratt, b Cobbett	4	l b w, b Ward	3
E. Leathes, Esq., not out	0	b Ward	2
Byes 4, w 5	9	Wide	9
Total	115	Total	142

MARYLEBONE

	1st inn		2nd inn
Hon. Col. Lowther, b F. Pilch	3	st W. Roberts, b W. Pilch	2
T. Grinstead, Esq., b F. Pilch	0	c T. Roberts, b W. Pilch	12
Beagley, c Alexander, b F. Pilch	20	b W. Pilch	16
W. Ward, Esq., c F. Roberts, b Spinks	25	c Alexander, b W. Pilch	3
C. Romilly, Esq., st W. Roberts, b F. Pilch	6	b W. Pilch	2
G. T. Knight, Esq., b W. Pilch	41	b W. Pilch	5
Cobbett, h w, b W. Pilch	18	b F. Pilch	20
H. E. Knatchbull, Esq., b F. Pilch	4	b F. Pilch	3
T. Vigne, Esq., c W. Roberts, b W. Pilch	3	not out	1
Lord Strathavon, not out	6	run out	0
Sir St. V. Cotton, b F. Pilch	3	b F. Pilch	0
Byes 13, w 1, n-b 2	16	Bye 2, w 1	3
Total	145	Total	67

A match with Yorkshire in 1834 possessed several striking features. (See p. 250 footnote.) A few years of comparative silence ensued, and in the meantime the art of bowling had been much advanced. Scarcely a better proof of this could be adduced than in the match with Marylebone, at Lords, in the year 1844, when Norfolk won by 30 runs. Marylebone had four bowlers, and Norfolk four. In the

* This may have arisen from the acquaintanceship of Bentley, who had much to do with the improvements in the style of scoring.

first innings of Marylebone Mr. Raven obtained seven wickets in 30 overs, and Mr Fagge three wickets in 29 overs and three balls In the second innings Mr Rippingall claimed four wickets in 24 overs, Mr Fagge two wickets in 19 overs, and Pilch two wickets in six overs The fielding of Norfolk was adjudged at the time as superior to that of Marylebone. Score :

NORFOLK

	1st inn		2nd inn
S Campbell, Esq , b Lillywhite	10	b Hillyer	10
T R Buckworth, Esq , l b w, b Hillyer	2	b Lillywhite	1
A Spinks, Esq , c Dorrinton, b Hillyer	13	b Lillywhite	6
F Pilch, c Hillyer, b Lillywhite	6	b Lillywhite	41
J F Fagge, Esq , b Lillywhite	1	b Dean	6
J W Dolignon, Esq , c Lillywhite, b Hillyer	4	b Hillyer	22
T A Anson, Esq , c Smyth, b Lillywhite	4	l b w, b Lillywhite	1
W Stearman, c Kynaston, b Lillywhite	8	b Hillyer	7
H B Caldwell, Esq , b Hillyer	5	b Lillywhite	0
S F Rippingall, Esq , not out	11	b Lillywhite	0
T Raven, Esq , b Hillyer	0	not out	0
Byes 4, n b 1	5	Byes	17
Total	69	Total	111

MARYLEBONE

	1st inn		2nd inn
A Haygarth, Esq , c Anson, b Raven	25	b Rippingall	4
E S E Hartopp, Esq , l b w, b Raven	3	c Campbell, b Fagge	1
Dorrinton c Raven, b Fagge	13	b Rippingall	10
R Kynaston Esq , b Fagge	0	c Fagge, b Rippingall	5
Dean, c Fagge, b Raven	3	b Rippingall	39
Lord Glamis b Fagge	1	not out	0
Hillyer, st Anson, b Raven	9	b Fagge	1
Lillywhite, b Raven	5	c Rippingall, b Pilch	0
J W Hay, Esq , c Fagge, b Raven	2	b Pilch	5
H Raymond Barker, Esq , b Raven	7		
W Bowyer Smyth, Esq , not out	3	run out	0
Byes 5, wides 3	8	Byes 5, wide 1	6
Total	79	Total	71

So signal a victory was not allowed to remain above one year before Marylebone changed positions, or at least effected a change of position Norfolk went in first, and came out for 54 Their second innings stopped at 83, thereby making a total of 137. Marylebone got together 212 at the fall of their tenth wicket, and thus won the match by an innings and 75 runs The character of the fielding was just the reverse of that in the previous encounter Marylebone's extras consisted of five byes only, whereas Norfolk bowled twenty wides and eight byes A similar "run of luck" attended Norfolk in September of the same year at Swaffham, when Marylebone were winners by an innings and 37 runs The progress of the county was for some time slow, and its success chequered A tolerably correct idea of internal strength may be arrived at from a match composed entirely of amateurs, played at Dereham, in the month of August, 1868, between the West and East divisions of the county. Score

EAST

	1st inn		2nd inn
W R Collyer, Esq , b Jackson	40	c W Vyse, b Jackson	13
E Willett, Esq , b Jackson	10	b Tillard	3
C H Frost, Esq , b Jackson	0	b Jackson	15
F L Fellows, Esq , b Jackson	23	c W Vyse, b Tillard	1
Rev L A Cockerell b Dowell	12	b Jackson	33
P C D'Eye, Esq , c W Vyse, b Tillard	5	c A Digby, b Brereton	2
H Pelham, Esq , b Brereton	1	c Dowell, b Jackson	0
H Gilbert, Esq , c Digby, b Brereton	3	c A Digby, b Tillard	0
T Mack, Esq , b Jackson	6	b Tillard	0
Captain Custance, not out	10	b Jackson	5
T Garnett, Esq , st Vyse, b Brereton	2	not out	9
Extras	9	Extras	3
Total	121	Total	84

WEST

	1st inn		2nd inn
Rev E Dowell, b Mack	0	b Fellows	0
T Francis, Esq , b Fellows	11	b Fellows	6
A Vyse, Esq , b Mack	0	b Fellows	0
R Digby, Esq , b Fellows	1	b Fellows	15
Rev C Brereton, b Fellows	0	b Fellows	0
C Tillard, Esq , b Fellows	0	b Mack	0
W Vyse, Esq , b Fellows	12	b Fellows	14
A Digby Esq , run out	3	b Fellows	11
J Jackson, Esq , b Fellows	10	b Mack	7
Major Hollway, c and b Fellows	4	not out	1
Captain Bathurst, not out	0	b Mack	5
Extras	7	Extras	5
Total	48	Total	64

Two years subsequently Norfolk played Essex twice. The first meeting was at Upton Park, in the month of June, the second at Dereham, in July Both sides were composed of amateurs Norfolk won the first match by six wickets, and the second by one Scarcely anything has occurred subsequently calculated to bring the county into prominence, the annual match with the Marylebone Club helps to keep old relationship from becoming extinct, although in the majority of instances the Marylebone Club possessed so much strength that Norfolk had scarcely a chance of success This fact was strikingly exemplified in a match at Lord's in 1868 Marylebone scored 388 runs in their double innings against 145 of Norfolk, and consequently won the match by 243 runs Six wickets were clean bowled by Mr Smith, and three by Grundy, in the first innings of Norfolk The bowling against Marylebone reflected considerable credit on Mr Mack, who claimed nine wickets out of twenty Figg was the only professional engaged on the part of Norfolk, inferring thereby that among the East Anglians cricket had but a slow advance when compared with other districts easily pointed out upon a general map Of the cultivation of the manly and noble game in many parts of the county at this period, no doubt whatever can exist, but why it was not concentrated and utilized more successfully is a question belonging to the past Mention is often made of a Norfolk family by the name of Colman, eleven in number, and said to be brothers, who in 1845 played eleven gentlemen of Holt and Letheringsett, and beat them by seven wickets A few days later the same eleven played Norwich, but were defeated by five wickets Now the thought occurs, if only one of this band of brothers had but a tolerable idea of cricket, what might not be collected from a village, a township, a city a county? Norfolk can boast of two poets, who had to struggle hard before they became famous, but who have left undying names As yet Norfolk has produced but one humble cricketer of equal reputation in his walk of life These odds ought to be rectified A statistician once remarked that there is not one in ten millions worthy the name of a poet against the one in ten thousand competent to pass muster among decent versifiers This hazardous conjecture may have a few grains of truth in it, or it may not; one thing, however, may be taken for granted, and that is, the Eastern Counties cannot produce just now a genius like Pilch There are many good imitators who would benefit themselves and the cricket community to which they belong, if greater opportunities were afforded them of bringing the talents they possess into fuller exercise before perhaps an exacting, yet appreciative public

The adjoining shire claims a passing notice, seeing that in it is comprised the "Classic Cam" Apart from the county town, and the collegiate forces, the game of cricket has never been much fostered Soon after the commencement of the present century, "The Town" could play against good teams from Norfolk and Suffolk A spirit of emulation, also, among the different colleges led to improvement in, and a large extension of, cricket Many records exist of matches being thoroughly well contested by the Town with the Undergraduates as well as among clubs in places more remote In the year 1826 a match on "Parker's Piece" brought several gentlemen belonging to the Universities into prominence, and whose names have not been blotted from the memories of those who witnessed their early and later exploits Notably among such might be cited that of Mr Herbert Jenner, one of the very best amateur players England ever produced On the occasion just mentioned he came out as a bowler, and captured nearly half the Cambridge Town wickets, and to him very much of the Undergraduate success belonged, viz, 95 runs. About six years afterwards Marylebone met the Town Club, and were defeated by the residents with ease, the scores being—Marylebone, 50 and 71—total 121, Cambridge Town, 97 and 25 (five wickets)—total 122 A still more marked defeat awaited Marylebone in their encounter with the Undergraduates on their next visit to the Piece Their double innings realised 215 runs, of which 94 belonged to the Hon F Ponsonby The Undergraduates made 206 in their first innings, and 10 in the second for the loss of one wicket only

The defeat of Cambridge, when confronted by Notts on the introduction of round arm bowling, is thus described by a native poet—

Lo! by the banners of the crowded tent
Brave men have gathered, on ambition bent,
Strives burly Barker, pitted face to face
With sturdy Redgate of terrific pace,
On, on they press, for conquest or for fame,
Fort after fort succumbs to deadly aim
All stratagems are baffled, and at length
Surrenders Granta, destitute of strength

After a few years the strength of Cambridge returned, and in a match against England they bore away the palm The same writer thus describes a portion of the play—

But Granta smiles, with Fenner in the van
Her pride and boast have gathered to a man
Flanked by their general in fine array
Charge Box and Hillyer, foremost in the fray
Soon Diver, Arnold, Ringwood, Boning, Pryor,
Subdue the havoc of unerring fire,
And though each enemy is true to trust
Great England in her glory bites the dust.

As the members of various colleges took to cricket, Parker's Piece was the scene of well-contested matches for many years, and not unfrequently, in the height of the season, there might be witnessed several wickets pitched at the same time either for practice or an actual combat To passers-by and lookers-on a certain amount of danger existed On one occasion a lad was struck on the right ear with such force by the ball that he died three days after in consequence

As the clubs increased both in number and bulk, and no means existed of enlarging the Piece, a great deal of annoyance was experienced by the University Club when playing a set match Fenner remedied this by hiring a piece of land at the back of the County Prison This he levelled and prepared at considerable cost, and till recently it went by the name of Fenner's Ground For some years previous to his death it reverted to the University Club, and was called the University Ground—well worthy of the name What may be termed the ground proper is about 200 yards square out of an area of eight acres, exclusive of "the orchard corner" of nearly three acres The soil is clay loam, thoroughly well adapted for cricket purposes Professionals of a first-class character are invariably engaged and in nearly all the matches a display of amateur cricket is to be seen here unsurpassed for style by any kindred institution in the world Three or four years ago much apprehension existed that the spot would be disturbed by the mattock and the spade To counteract this contemplated vandalism a champion was found in Mr Ward, who went to work in earnest, and instead of the ground being now covered with "a lot of potty tenements," a magnificent pavilion is erected at a cost of more than 4000*l* If not the grandest specimen of architectural skill from an outside point of view, it is certainly the most complete structure as regards comfort and convenience that the cricket world can boast of Over and above the convenience of the building for the purposes intended, some expense has been incurred in the way of embellishments. The woodwork is beautifully carved and interlaced with the emblems of cricket. The chimney-piece is of stone, richly moulded, from the quarries of Bromsgrove, Worcestershire. Nearly, if not quite all the panelling is of oak, divided in the centre by a shelf whereon is mounted an elaborate clock, specially designed and constructed for the position. In the pediment above the timepiece, the arms of the University are carved in high relief, and the mouldings enriched with a running ornament. On the frieze under the shelf, the words, "Pavilion erected 1875," are engraved in raised letters; and beneath, on the centre panel, is inscribed the name of the Rev. A. R. Ward, in the now fashionable type of Queen Anne. The side panels also present features of interest, and are carved in character and keeping with the internal portion of the pavilion. Design, not patchwork; and a solidity that will long bear the strain of the elastic step and the silent gnawings of the common enemy—Time.

CHAPTER XIX.

INTERCOLONIAL MATCHES.

VISIT OF H. H. STEPHENSON AND HIS TEAM TO CANADA AND THE UNITED STATES.

"Be strong and of a good courage."—Joshua i. 9.
"Only be thou strong and very courageous."—Joshua i. 7.

First Intercolonial Experiment—Opinions respecting it—Long Voyage to Quebec, Attendant Sickness—Match between England and Canada—Departure for New York—Result of a Match with "The States"—Two Mixed Elevens under Lockyer and Stephenson—Summary of the Matches in 1858—Second Visit to America in 1868—Physical Condition of the States, and Inability to Cope with their English Visitors—Third Visit in 1871—Mr. Fitzgerald and his Band of Amateurs—Eight Matches engaged in—Summary of Results and Analysis of Bowling—Farewell Ode.

MANY and various were the speculations and epithets applied to the first venture of a band of English cricketers when they took ship at Liverpool on the 7th of September, 1859, for Quebec. To the minds of stay-at-home people the venture was too wild and unwise to be repaid by glory or gain. Different views were entertained by different people as a matter of course. The experiment was, however, made, and it eventuated in a success. The journey out was far otherwise than a pleasant one, as the passage proved to be more than ordinarily long and rough. All the men suffered from sea sickness—Stephenson so severely, that he was unable to take food for nearly a week. But just as they recovered from the effects incident to inexperienced voyagers, the wind increased to a gale, which lasted for a day and a night. During this period the tempest-tossed vessel had got 200 miles out of her proper path. When she had assumed a less boisterous demeanour, the captain found himself in White Bay instead of the Straits of Belleisle, and had, according to some statements, got nautically 800 miles wrong. Nearly three days were expended in pulling up this arrear. Eventually Quebec was reached without any serious disaster, much to the delight of the "Eleven," who never fully appreciated smiling corn fields, green swards, and *terra firma* before the fifteen days' experience of "the blue above and the blue below," combined with "the restless heaving of old Ocean from its lowest bed." A large crowd soon assembled to greet their arrival. The first match, between England and Canada, had to be deferred for a day or two in consequence of foul weather Soon as the sun broke through the thick clouds, they dispersed themselves at an agreeably rapid rate, and the parties prepared for action The Montreal ground is beautifully situated at the foot of a large mountain with a glorious outspread of luxurious scenery in every direction At the right hand of the entrance gate was erected a large stage for ladies, who mustered in great force When the usual preliminaries were arranged, Canada, who had won the toss, started the batting Lockyer kept wicket, Diver occupied the post of long stop, Parr, point, Grundy, mid-wicket, Stephenson, cover point, Hayward, slip, Lillywhite and Cæsar, long-field, Wisden, third man up, Jackson and Caffyn bowlers in chief. The Canadians proceeded with steadiness and caution, and seemed withal to entertain a considerable amount of respect for their opponents, and guarding against defeat by a Fabian kind of policy Over succeeded over with scarcely any kind of record that the play had actually commenced So true, in fact, was the bowling that little could be done with it, and the two early batsmen retired for 4 runs each, while the three next on the rota added only 2 to the number Eight wickets fell for 22 runs At this stage, Mr Pickering, captain of the team, made his appearance. This gentleman, when in England, stood high in the cricket world, as many an old score sheet will testify Much was expected of him on the occasion in question Whether out of "form" or practice, or whether unfamiliar to the bowling of Caffyn, is a matter forgotten now One thing is certain, he failed to score as in his earlier days, a shooter from Caffyn sent him to his tent for 8 runs Half the wickets fell for 34 runs Caffyn soon after handed the ball to Stephenson, and with Messrs Daly and Smith now in possession of the bat the score advanced to 61 before another wicket could be captured The subsequent play evinced no remarkable defence, and the innings concluded with a total of 85 runs, towards which Mr Daly contributed 19 The trifling average of less than 4 runs per man from the bat may be attributed chiefly to the deadness of the ground consequent upon the heavy rainfalls England shot ahead considerably, as the score given below shows The second innings of Canada exhibited greater weakness than the first, only one double figure occurred, viz, Mr J Smith 17, out of a total of 63 England won by eight wickets

ANALYSIS OF THE ENGLAND BOWLING IN BOTH INNINGS

	Overs	Maidens	Runs	Wickets	Wides
Jackson	70–1	31	42	11	1
Caffyn	37	14	45	9	1
Stephenson	3	1	5	1	0
Parr	31	24	27	15	0
Wisden	16	8	13	0	0
Grundy	4	2	4	1	0

Four bowlers were engaged on the Canadian side, viz, Hardinge, who in 17 overs (7 maidens) took one wicket for 24 runs (two wide balls), Fisher, 32 overs (11 maidens), five wickets, 58 runs, one wide ball, Napier, 16 overs (7 maidens), two wickets, 24 runs, three wide balls, Smith, 3 overs and one ball, one wicket, 5 runs Umpire for Montreal, Capt Campbell, for England, Carpenter

ENGLAND

	1st inn		2nd inn
Grundy, b Hardinge	2		
Wisden, c Hardinge, b Fisher	7		
Hayward, run out	17	c Bonner, b J Smith	17
Caffyn, b Fisher	18	not out	4
Parr, b Fisher	24		
Cæsar, b Fisher	0		
Diver c Pickering, b Napier	3	not out	1
Lillywhite, b Napier	4		
Lockyer not out	19	b J Smith	10
Stephenson, b Fisher	2		
Jackson, b J Smith	10		
Byes 5, w 6	11	Byes 2, w 5	7
Total	117	Total	39

Previous to the departure of the Eleven for New York, the members of the Montreal Club entertained them at St Lawrence Hall. In the course of the evening the chairman expressed, what he was sure every man present felt, the gratification caused by the presence of the Eleven of Old England among them —the Eleven of Old England meeting for the first time with them, and not only so but dining together for the first time on this continent He would not attempt to draw attention to the merits of the game—they were set forth in every newspaper But he might be allowed to say something which, perhaps, would have an echo farther than the walls of that room What he desired to say was, that it was to the cricket-ground where they played, to the river on which they rowed, and to the glorious country over which they hunted, that Englishmen owed the education which made them what they were Canada was one of the most glorious dependencies of the British Crown, peopled by men professing a variety of creeds and political opinions. Might not all be taught by the example of that day a lesson of moderation and good sense—that there might be differences without animosity—opposition without dissension—that men might strive and rival each other, as in cricket so in all other things, but yet be like brothers in good feeling He hoped the Eleven of England would be able to give a good account of this country, that they would be able to say they had met a race identical with their own, as indeed it was, which had not degenerated, and which, with the blessing of God, would not degenerate, that they would feel they had been received as brothers in birth and blood

On the first of October they left Montreal, and on the following Monday commenced the second match on the programme against Twenty-two of New York, on the ground at Hoboken, distant about four miles from the city on the opposite side of the river "The States" went in first Parr and Jackson had charge of the early bowling, the fielders dropped into pretty much the same places as at Montreal. The batsmen, one and all, appeared to be terribly "stuck up" by the slows, and by no means equal to the fast. Jackson, "true as a hair," got ten wickets for 12 runs, and Parr nine for 24 runs. To give an idea of the defensive capabilities of the team, suffice it to say nine of the number failed to get a single run. Six bowlers were brought against Parr and his companions, and, notwithstanding the numerical strength of the field, 156 runs were totalled, of which 25 resulted from extras. The second innings of the States realised only 54; the highest figure being seven, next a six, five fives, two fours, two threes, two singles, and ten ciphers. England consequently won by an innings and 64 runs.

The proportion of the batting success on the part of England was hardly in accord with that usually obtained. Two out of the three from Cambridge fully maintained their reputation.

ENGLAND.

Carpenter, c Sentor, b Hallis	26
Hayward, b Hallis	33
Wisden, run out	3
Parr, b Gibbes	7
Caffyn, b Gibbes	5
Lockyer, c Lang, b Hallis	12
Diver, c Hallis, b Gibbes	1
Stephenson, b Hallis	10
Cæsar, b Hallis	6
Grundy, b Hallis	20
Jackson, not out	8
Byes 10, l-b 1, w 12, n-b 2	25
Total	156

At the close of the match a second was projected between two elevens, headed by Lockyer and Stephenson. This turned out to be a good move. Many persons had come a long distance to see the eleven vanquished by the St. George's Club. Disappointed in their desires, the fresh match met with general concurrence. Each side was composed of six Englishmen and five Americans. Lockyer's side went in first with Grundy and Wisden, opposed to the bowling of Jackson and Hayward. Both got hit with great freedom, and before the two batsmen were disposed of the score had reached 50. The chief stay of the innings was Cæsar, who contributed more than a third of the total made from the bat. At the close of the day four wickets on Stephenson's side were lost for 36 runs. The most notable feature was the "not out" innings of Carpenter, with the same total as that of Cæsar. At the fall of the tenth wicket Lockyer's side were 70 runs in advance. Parr and Waller started the second innings, but the bowling of Jackson and Stephenson proved so effective that only three were able to reach double figures, and these were not of great magnitude. The match ended eventually in favour of Lockyer's side. During the course of the week's play an excellent band of musicians attended the ground, who not only enlivened the scene, but charmed the descendants of the Dane, Norman, and Saxon with soul-stirring strains both of a national and universal character. The score will illustrate the manner in which this supplementary match was begun, continued, and ended.

LOCKYER'S SIDE

	1st inn		2nd inn
Wisden, b Hayward	12	b Stephenson	0
Grundy, b Jackson	31	c Diver, b Stephenson	4
Caffyn, b Hayward	23	c Lillywhite, b Jackson	1
Parr, c Carpenter, b Jackson	6	run out	36
Lockyer, b Jackson	1	c Hayward, b Stephenson	14
Cæsar, b Stephenson	52	b Jackson	3
Waller, b Jackson	1	b Stephenson	12
Wilby, c and b Stephenson	9	c Jackson, b Stephenson	7
Wright c Gibbs b Hayward	10	b Jackson	0
Hudson, b Hayward	0	not out	0
Bashford, not out	0	b Jackson	1
Byes 13, l-b 4, w 1	18	Byes 2, l-b 3, w 7	12
Total	163	Total	90

STEPHENSON'S SIDE.

	1st inn		2nd inn
Sharp, run out	3	c and b Wisden	18
Jackson, c Lockyer, b Wisden	25	c Lockyer, b Wisden	2
Carpenter, not out	52	c Henry, b Wisden	3
Hayward, c Wilby, b Wisden	1	c Caffyn b Wisden	28
Diver, b Grundy	0	not out	18
Gibbs, b Wisden	1	c Lockyer, b Wisden	0
Stephenson, c H Grundy	1	c Wright, b Caffyn	3
Lillywhite, run out	1	c Parr, b Wisden	7
Lang, b Grundy	6	c Cæsar, b Wisden	0
Ford, b Grundy	0	b Wisden	0
George, b Grundy	1	run out	5
Leg-byes	2	Leg-byes	2
Total	93	Total	86

Soon as the last match ended the Eleven started for Philadelphia to play twenty-two On the first day the ground was in a very unfit condition for cricket owing to heavy rainfalls At the close of the day nine of the resident team were out for 41 runs. In Philadelphia, as in many an English city at that period, an election so absorbs business, and pleasure too, that neither has a chance of being pursued to advantage The second day was devoted by the Eleven to a stroll along the margin of the noble Delaware, or up and down the well-planned wide streets of the city Wednesday brought them again into action The Philadelphians completed their first innings for a total of 94 runs The Eleven, although playing a man short (Parr), obtained 126 Only 60 resulted from the second innings, and England went in for 29 to win The wickets of Hayward, Lockyer, and Carpenter were taken for 16 runs, but Caffyn and Grundy pulled up the remainder, and thus enabled their party to claim the match by seven wickets

The fourth match, viz, that against twenty-two of Canada, resulted also in favour of the Eleven

It is said, however, that the pleasant land of glory has to be reached very often by many a rugged and discouraging path To the truth of this the Eleven bore ample testimony The journey from Philadelphia to Hamilton was a long, tedious, and uninteresting one At almost every stopping-place a change of car was necessary, and, what was positively sad, at none of these places were refreshments to be obtained, while the keen air was perpetually whetting their appetites to a painful degree. Arrived at their destination it became doubtful whether they would be able after all to play, owing to the ungenial state of the weather The people of Hamilton assembled in large groups to see the "wonderful Eleven" who had so recently beaten three twenty-twos in succession England on this occasion won the toss, and chose the field At the close of the first day's play fourteen wickets were taken for 30 runs. Next morning the remainder fell for an additional 36 The Eleven were severely punished by the sharp weather, and they made but 67 runs from the bat On the third day Wisden and Jackson led off the bowling As the latter was not effective, Grundy took his place, and the Canadians soon discovered their inability to cope with two such proficients in the art of attack Wisden got fourteen wickets and Grundy five The highest figure scored was ten England required 40 runs to tie Jackson and Caffyn obtained 33, and not out Eight extras did the rest

The fifth and last match, that with America, played at Rochester, will not easily be forgotten by the Eleven on account of the severity of the weather No amount of field exercise could produce warmth The Americans so denominated were not long at the wickets in either of their innings Mr. Pickering scored 11 and 14 (not out), and Wright 13 These were the only double figures On the side of the Eleven 50 runs were contributed by Hayward, 19 by Lockyer, 18 by Carpenter, 14 by Caffyn, 12 by Jackson, and 26 by "extras" The twenty-two, it should be said, were drawn from New York, Rochester, Philadelphia, Newark, Buffalo, and different parts of Canada.

SUMMARY OF THE MATCHES

Eleven of England *v* Twenty-two of Canada, played at Montreal, Sept 24th, 26th, and 27th Canada, first innings, 85, second, 63—total 148. England, 117 and 32 (for three wickets)—total 149 Won by seven wickets

Eleven of England *v* Twenty-two of New York, played at Hoboken, Oct 3rd and two following days New York, first innings, 38, second, 54—total 92 England, 156 Won by an innings and 64 runs

Eleven of England *v* Twenty two of Philadelphia, played at Philadelphia, Oct 12th and two following days Philadelphia, first innings, 94, second, 60—total 154, England, first innings, 126, second, 29 (four wickets)—total 155 Won by six wickets

Eleven of England *v* Twenty-two of Upper Canada, played at Hamilton Oct 17th and two following days Canada, first innings, 66, second, 53—total 119 England, first innings, 79, second, 43—total 120 Won by ten wickets

Eleven of England *v* Twenty two of America, played at Rochester, Oct 21st and two following days America, first innings, 39, second, 64—total 103 England, 171 Won by an innings and 68 runs

VISIT TO AMERICA IN 1868

WITHIN the lapse of nine years the great struggle for independence had almost obliterated the quiet strifes of the cricket fields The terrible carnage incident to the battles between North and South had robbed both sections of the States of much of its pith and manhood. There were, however, a few who were anxious to see cricket further introduced as far nobler than the so-called national game of base ball, but these for a while had to contend against prejudices not easily to be overcome. It is well known that cricket has never taken root in American soil, although several attempts from time to time and in various forms have been resorted to. The game of base ball appears to be more adapted to the mind of the American than the scientific one in which Britons delight. Take Philadelphia as an example—for this city, Quaker though it be, leads all other localities in sports at all akin to cricket. Here the few who possess any scientific knowledge appear to check rather than promote the growth of the game. Accordingly they aver that cricket is too severe a study for youth, who, if they are ever to become proficient, should commence the study of the sport soon after they are able to walk alone, and devote a lifetime to its proper acquisition, and although it does not rank among the exact sciences, its laws are inexorable, its rules strictly defined, and the method for arriving at distinction absolutely laid down. On all great occasions the game is carried on regardless of gratification to the spectator, and this is the reason why a go-ahead people allow it to travel so languidly for want of support.

The first match took place on the 16th of September with twenty-two of the St George's New York Club, when the Eleven won by an innings and 26 runs. Space forbids more than an occasional score.

ALL ENGLAND ELEVEN

Jupp, b Norley	23
Humphrey, b H Wright	5
Smith, b Norley	22
Lillywhite, b Gibbes	13
Shaw, run out	16
Tarrant, l b w, b Norley	0
Pooley b Norley	18
Rowbotham b Norley	13
Freeman, c Lee, b Norley	10
Charlwood, not out	18
Willsher, c H Wright, b Lee	16
Byes 14, l b 1, w 6	21
Total	175

Twenty-two, first inning, 61, second, 88—total 149.

On the 22nd of the same month, the second match in the programme was played at Montreal, with twenty-two of Canada, and was left drawn. The dwellers in the Dominion had not the ghost of a chance against such an eleven as that from the old country. Only 28 runs resulted from the one and twenty wickets which fell to the attacks of Willsher and Freeman. Sixteen of the Canadians failed to make a run. On the All England side no less than 310 were totalled, of which 40 belonged to the "extra class." At Boston, on the 26th, All England scored 109 and 71—total 180, against 39 and 37—total 76, so that the Twenty-two Bostonians were bound to acknowledge a defeat by 104 runs. The contest with

Twenty-two of Philadelphia was a much closer one All England won by two wickets the scores being for the residents, 88 and 35—total 123, visitors, 92 and 32 (eight wickets)—total 124 Another match at Philadelphia, a few days later, with twenty-two of the United States, terminated in favour of the Eleven by 72 runs Thus All England, 117 and 64—total 181, Twenty-two, 47 and 62—total 109 On the 13th of October, at Hudson City, the Eleven were confronted by Twenty-two of America Here they came off victorious by an innings and 8 runs; the scores being, All England, 143, America, 70 and 65—total 135

From these examples it will be seen that "our cousins over the water" had not advanced in the art either of bowling or batting during the interval of the first and second visits In the majority of the matches just mentioned, half the batsmen failed to obtain a run, and the largest individual contribution was 15, so that the visit may be regarded more in the light of accomplished masters teaching classes of willing but uneducated pupils the mysteries of the bat and ball—nothing more!

THIRD VISIT.

Mr Fitzgerald and his Band of Amateurs

The third visit differs so essentially from the two preceding, that it has claim to a more extended notice than the second In the year 1871, a proposition was made to Mr Fitzgerald, the then secretary of the Marylebone Club, by Mr Patteson, of Toronto, and Captain Wallace, of the 60th Rifles, to play a series of matches in the Dominion, and as all the visitors were gentlemen, the Canadians proposed to entertain them as such, and pay all expenses out and home The invitation was limited to twelve persons, and after a few necessary home arrangements had been completed, the following team was selected —Hon G (now Lord) Harris, Messrs. Appleby, Fitzgerald, Francis, W G Grace, Hornby, E Lubbock, A Lubbock, Ottaway, Pickering, and Rose, with Farrands as umpire These left Liverpool in the "Sarmatian," on the 8th of August and landed at Quebec on the 17th, the distance travelled was 2656 miles in nine days and ninety minutes The first match began on the 22nd at Montreal against twenty-two Mr Fitzgerald, in speaking of the ground, says, "it will not require a poet to describe it—a civil engineer alone can do it justice, he would call it three cornered, but it would puzzle him to pitch a wicket square to any side, or, in fact, to find a good place for a wicket anywhere Rubbish has evidently, in times not pre-historic, been shot here Villas may owe their erection to the stone extracted from its quarries, roads, doubtless, have derived their substratum, and could do so still from its surface Very few spectators appeared on the ground, twelve carriages only could be counted—a very thin line indeed—and that only at one end of the ground—which impressed the Englishmen mournfully, and if it had not been for the Twenty-two who, in a variety of costume and colour dotted the ground, the scene would have been the reverse of gay" The Eleven elected to go in first, Messrs Grace and Ottaway taking the lead A local journal remarks —"Mr. Grace is a large framed, loose jointed man, and you would say that his gait is a trifle awkward and shambling, but when he goes into the field you see that he is quick sighted, sure handed, and light footed as the rest He always goes in first, and to see him tap the ball gently to the off for one, draw it to the on for two, pound it to the limits for four, drive it beyond the most distant long leg for six, looks as easy as rolling off a log ' Mr. Grace occupied a considerable portion of two days, and ended with a score of 82 Owing to indisposition, Mr Fitzgerald was unable to bat, and the tenth wicket fell for a total of 255, thus effected.—

Mr W G Grace, c Benjamin, b Lang	82
Mr C J Ottaway, b Hardman	24
Mr A N Hornby, l b w, b Green	39
Mr A Lubbock, b Lang	0
Hon G Harris, b Green	4
Mr C K Francis c Mackenzie, b McLean	11
Mr E Lubbock, c Jones, b McLean	18
Mr A Appleby, c Hardman, b McLean	9
Mr W M Rose, not out	15
Mr F Pickering, c Mills, b Lang	19
Byes 12, l b 8, w 8	28
Total	255

The Twenty-two scored 48 in the first innings, and 67 in the second—total, 118 The most remarkable feature in the match was the bowling of Mr Rose, who took 33 wickets in the double innings of the Canadians

Eleven of England v Twenty-two of Ottawa —August 27.—A lovely Canadian summer's day—sky of piercing brightness, and a fresh breeze tempering the heat A better pair of wickets, and a much greater company The out fielders had nothing to boast of, the grass, though long, was devoid of snakes, but the butterflies, "big enough to knock one down," proved annoying on account of numbers The Eleven started the batting, as before, with Messrs Grace and Ottaway The latter left with the total of 20, but the former "stuck in" till 142 were reached When the tenth wicket fell, 201 runs were totalled against 43 and 49 of the other side Time, three days

Twelve of England v. Twenty-two of Toronto —September 2nd —In this, the third match of the series, Mr Grace made his deepest mark Although the Canadians won the toss, they took the field. It is said that the wickets had been watched for months, well watered, and protected from the sun, a green oasis distinguished them from the outfielding, which was brown as a bird's eye, but not bad The day was hot, and cabbage leaves at a premium Messrs Grace and Ottaway led off the scoring, 30 runs resulted from the first ten overs In the 100 runs first obtained by Mr Grace were 30 from five hits He made 142 altogether, out of a total of 319 Toronto's double innings amounted to 214 In order to complete the week, the committee of the Toronto Club proposed a match in which an equality of sides would give a better insight of the game, and afford to the true lovers of it an additional amount of interest Eventually Messrs Grace and Appleby headed the sides, which were composed of six English and six Canadians. It lasted two days, and resulted thus:

MR GRACE'S TWELVE

	1st inn		2nd inn.
Mr W G Grace, st Hornby, b Rose ...	0	l b w, b A Lubbock	27
Mr C J Ottaway, b A Lubbock	17	st Hornby, b Rose	4
Mr W H Hadow, b Appleby	1	b Appleby .	3
Mr F Pickering, b A Lubbock	25	b Appleby .	4
Mr E Lubbock, b Appleby	4	b Appleby .	4
Hon G Harris, st Hornby, b Rose ...	65	b Appleby . ..	32
Mr H Furlong, b A Lubbock	0	c Rose, b A Lubbock	5
Lieut Henley, st Hornby, b Rose	22	b Lubbock .	14
Mr G Brunel, b Appleby	13	b Appleby	4
Mr J Brunel not out	15	b Rose	12
Mr B Parsons, st Hornby, b Rose	2	c Fitzgerald, b Appleby	0
Mr A Cameron, st Hornby b Rose	0	not out	2
Byes 3, w 1	4	Byes	8
Total	168	Total	119

MR APPLEBY'S TWELVE

	1st inn		2nd inn
Mr A Appleby, b Harris	39	b Grace . .	2
Mr A N Hornby, run out	22	c Furlong, b Grace	0
Mr W M Rose, c Pickering, b Grace	6	b Harris	8
Mr C K Francis, c Pickering, b Harris	45	c Brunel, b Grace	0
Mr A Lubbock, st Ottaway, b Hadow	0	c and b Grace	11
Mr R A Fitzgerald, st Ottaway, b Hadow .	8	not out .	26
Mr F J Gosling, not out	9	b Harris ...	0
Mr R G Gamble, c and b Harris .	16	c Harris, b Grace	0
Dr Sprague, h w, b Harris . ..	0	c Cameron, b Grace .	7
Bickel, b Harris	0	l b w, b Grace .	1
Mr W P R Street, b Harris	8	b Harris	0
Mr J Whelan, b Grace . .	10	c and b Harris .	0
Leg-bye 1, w 1	2	Byes 3, l-b 4, w 1	8
Total	165	Total	63

The next match in the programme necessitated a journey through the sulphur baths and the kingdom of paraffin on the way to London, the Forest City founded in 1824 by General Simcoe, although it does not show signs of such antiquity. The ground was marked out on a small plateau—the only one visible—in dangerous vicinity to a long range of wooden buildings, afterwards discovered to be "The Barracks." Rifle pits abounded on all sides. However, a fair wicket was obtained, dead from thunder showers, and evidently not a run-getting one.

The double total of the Twelve amounted to 250 runs; that of London 120, thus giving another easy victory to the visitors. Mr Rose obtained 21 wickets in 37 overs for 61 runs; Mr Appleby 13 wickets in 42 overs for 39 runs, and Mr Grace five wickets in eight overs for 14 runs. Mr Rose bowled through the first innings, and Mr Appleby through the second. Score annexed.

TWELVE OF ENGLAND

	1st inn		2nd inn
Mr W G Grace, c Hyman, b Gillean	31	c Cook, b Henley	76
Mr A N Hornby, b Gillean	14	b Whelan ...	21
Mr W Hadow, b Wright	2	b Hornby	0
Mr A Lubbock, run out	5	c Neville, b Whelan	8
Hon G Harris, b Gillean	1	c Elerts b Saunders	10
Mr C K Francis, b Elerts	12	b Gillean	3
Mr C J Ottoway, b Gillean	1	l b w, b Gillean	6
Mr E Lubbock, c Wells, b Elerts .. .	9	b Saunders	6
Mr W M Rose, b Elerts	2	c Elerts, b Saunders	0
Mr F Pickering, b Gillean	5	c Danks, b Saunders .	1
Mr A Appleby, not out	1	not out	4
Mr R A Fitzgerald, b Gillean	0	c Elerts, b Saunders	2
Byes 5, l-b 1	6	Byes 12, l-b 3, w 9	24
Total	89	Total .	161

Twelve of England v Twenty-two of Hamilton —Such was the title of the last match with the Canadians The journey from London to this place presented neither difficulties nor inconvenience, and four hours sufficed to bring the contending parties face to face A good night's rest sent the Twelve as fit as five-year-olds to the ground Messrs Grace and Ottaway were foremost at the wickets, and at the close of the first day's play (September 14) 101 runs were scored for the cost of four wickets Mr Grace was nearly "coopered" before scoring a single figure The last Hamilton wicket in the first innings fell for 86 runs, the second, 79—total 165 The Twelve had no necessity to go in more than once, as their 181 gave them an easy victory, viz, that of an innings and 16 runs Mr Rose obtained 22 wickets in 52 overs for 64 runs, Mr Grace 16 wickets in 36 overs, 67 runs; and Mr. Appleby 1 wicket, 25 overs, 14 runs Mr Harris bowled two overs for 12 runs The match extended to the 14th The next day was spent at the Falls of Niagara, and on Monday the Twelve directed their attention to New York Score of the Hamilton match as follows —

TWELVE OF ENGLAND

Mr W G Grace, b Wright . . .	17
Mr C J Ottaway, c Elerts b Kennedy .	45
Mr A N Hornby, b Wright . .	2
Mr A Lubbock, b Kennedy	13
Hon G Harris, b Wright	38
Mr W H Hadow, c Swinyard, b Kennedy	1
Mr F Lubbock, c Shaw, b Henley	10
Mr C K Francis, c Shaw, b Kennedy .	0
Mr A Appleby, c Sprague, b Henley	35
Mr W M Rose, not out .	6
Mr F Pickering, c Totten, b Swinyard	2
Mr R A Fitzgerald, c Elerts, b Henley	0
Byes 5, l b 1, w 4, n-b 2	12
Total	181

Twelve of England *v* Twenty-two of New York.—Sept. 18.—The English party were on the Hoboken ground in good time, and soon after twelve o'clock play began with the natives at the wickets, opposed to the bowling of Messrs Rose and Appleby The batsmen seemed shy of their antagonists, and only one of the whole number subscribed ten runs The innings terminated at 3h 15min for 66 runs. At the close of the day 101 runs were scored by the Twelve without loss of wicket Rain fell so heavily on Thursday soon after daybreak that it was feared the game would have to be postponed, but the clouds eventually cleared away, and play began at the fixed time The ground was, however, very heavy, Messrs Grace and Ottaway resumed their batting against Wright and Brewster—two bowlers of considerable local renown "The leviathan (says a writer in the *Spirit*) was soon disposed of, and as it never rains but it pours, Ottaway was neatly caught at slip by Jones in the next over Hornby and Francis were now partners. and the former, after making three singles, lifted one to long-leg, which was badly muffed by Eyre The play then became rather dull, till Francis infused a little life by whacking one of George Wright's out of the ground, over the ladies' tent, &c. The last man was Fitzgerald, but he made a very short stay, being caught at square-leg off the first ball bowled to him Total, 258 Time, 3 55 ' The second innings of the Twenty-Two was an extremely weak one, it averaged just two runs per man —grand total, 110 The Twelve won by an innings and 148 runs Mr Rose bowled 34 overs, and took eight wickets for 46 runs, Mr Appleby 54 overs, 21 wickets, 37 runs, Mr Grace 21 overs, 11 wickets, 27 runs. Score as understated

TWELVE OF ENGLAND

Mr W G Grace, c Brewster, b Wright	68
Mr C J Ottaway, c Jones, b Brewster	29
Mr A N Hornby, c Keller, b Jones	17
Mr C K Francis, c and b Greig	28
Mr A Lubbock, c Bowman, b Wright	51
Mr F Pickering, b Greig	3
Mr E Lubbock, run out	15
Mr W H Hadow, run out	3
Hon G Harris, c Lemond, b Hatfield	9
Mr A Appleby, c Jones, b Sorrance	5
Mr W M Rose, not out	9
Mr R A Fitzgerald, c Hatfield, b Wright	0
Byes 9, l-b 4, w 8	21
Total	258

The English Twelve *v* Twenty-two of Philadelphia.—Sept 21.—It may not be amiss to quote the *Spirit of the Times* with reference to this match *verbatim* —' Defeat of the Quaker City Twenty-two —The match between the English Twelve and Twenty-two players of the Philadelphia Cricket Clubs was played on the ground of the German Town Cricket Club, near Philadelphia, on Saturday, Monday, and Tuesday last The Twenty-two went first to the wickets, but they were all disposed of for 63—Large, with 13, and John Hargreaves, with 11, being the only men who scored double figures Grace and Ottaway began the batting for the Twelve, but the great bat had only scored fourteen when a ripping ball from Charlie Newhall shattered his wicket Hornby and Ottaway each got ten, and Hadow twenty-nine, but none of the others troubled the scorers much, and the innings closed for 105, about half what was expected The second innings of the Twenty-two was a slight improvement on the first, 74 runs being scored, of which Dan Newhall and Clay made thirteen each This left the Twelve only 34 runs to get—an easy task apparently, but it cost them seven wickets to obtain the required number, not one of the team reaching double figures Grace was disposed of for seven, while Ottaway did not score at all This was a close shave, and rather opened the eyes of the Englishmen, who probably had a very light idea of cricket in America after their New York experience" To this it is only necessary to add that Mr Grace obtained twenty-one Philadelphian wickets, Mr Appleby sixteen, and Mr Rose two The remaining three are recorded as run out The score of the Twelve is given with particulars

TWELVE OF ENGLAND

	1st inn		2nd inn
Mr W G Grace, b C Newhall	14	c Joe Hargreaves, b C Newhall	7
Mr C J Ottaway, run out	10	b C Newhall	0
Mr A N Hornby, b Meade	10	c R Newhall, b Meade	4
Mr A Lubbock, run out	9	b H C Newhall	3
Mr W H Hadow, c Joe Hargreaves, b C Newhall	29	b Meade	6
Hon G Harris, c and b H D Newhall	3	c J Hargreaves, b Meade	8
Mr G K Francis, b Meade	5	b C Newhall	0
Mr A Appleby, c Maggee, b Meade	2	not out	4
Mr E Lubbock, c J Hargreaves, b C Newhall	0	not out	0
Mr W M Rose, c Joe Hargreaves, b C Newhall	0		
Mr F Pickering, b C Newhall	7		
Mr R A Fitzgerald, not out	1		
Byes 3, l-b 7, w 5	15	Byes 1, l b 1	2
Total	105	Total	34

SUMMARY OF THE MATCHES

At Montreal, August 23rd and two following days England, 255, Montreal, 48 and 67—total 115 England won by an innings and 140 runs

At Ottawa, August 27th and 28th England, 201, Ottawa, 43 and 49—total 92 England won by an innings and 109 runs

At Toronto September 2nd and two following days England, 319 Toronto, 97 and 117—total 214 England won by an innings and 105 runs

At London, September 9th and two following days England 89 and 161—total 250, London, 55 and 65 (two men short)—total 120 England won by 130 runs

At Hamilton, September 12th and 13th England, 181, Hamilton, 86 and 79—total 165 England won by an innings and 16 runs

At New York, September 18th and 19th England, 249 New York, 66 and 44—total 110 England won by an innings and 139 runs

At Philadelphia, September 21st and two following days Philadelphia, 63 and 72—total 135, England, 105 and 34 (seven wickets)—total 139 England won by four wickets

At Boston, September 26th Boston 51 and 43—total 94, England, 51 and 22 (six wickets)—total 73 Not decided at sunset, and left drawn

A long night's journey landed the Twelve at Boston to play the eighth and last match of the series The pace at which the business proceeded may be imagined when it is stated that although the game did not in reality commence till past twelve o'clock, nearly all four innings were got through by dusk Thus the Twenty-two who went in first were disposed off in one hour and twenty minutes Nor did that of England occupy a much longer space Out of a total of 51 runs Mr Grace claimed 26 Five left their wickets without scoring at all Messrs A Lubbock and Francis made five each E Lubbock and extras four each Hon Mr Harris three Messrs Appleby and Fitzgerald two each The same rapid rate of disposal characterised the second Boston innings All single figures, at an average of two runs per man. Pretty much the same rate of progress accompanied the England team, who lost six wickets for 22 runs Here the match ended Four days later the "Prussian," with its freight of cricketers, passed Belleisle on its homeward passage, and a week later it reached Liverpool, making the journey out and home just two calendar months

ANALYSIS OF THE BATTING

Name	No of Matches	No of Innings	Most Runs in a Match	Most Runs in an Innings	How often Bowled	Caught	Run out	Not out	Stumped	Total	Average of Innings Over
Mr A Appleby	8	11	41	39	2	5	0	4	0	135	12– 3
Mr R A Fitzgerald	7	9	34	26	1	4	0	3	1	54	6–
Mr C K Francis	8	12	45	45	7	5	0	0	0	119	9–11
Mr W G Grace	8	11	112	142	6	4	0	0	1	537	48– 9
Mr W H Hadow	6	9	35	29	6	2	1	0	0	62	6– 8
Hon G Harris	7	10	97	65	4	4	0	0	2	183	18– 3
Mr A N Hornby	8	11	39	39	7	3	1	0	0	164	14–10
Mr A Lubbock	8	11	51	51	3	5	2	1	0	148	13– 5
Mr E Lubbock	8	11	21	24	3	6	1	1	0	94	8– 6
Mr C J Ottaway	8	11	45	45	6	3	1	0	1	160	14– 6
Mr F Pickering	8	10	29	26	5	5	0	0	0	93	9– 3
Mr W M Rose	8	10	22	22	3	4	0	3	0	78	7– 8

FAREWELL ODE ADDRESSED TO THE TWELVE BEFORE LEAVING CANADA

Farewell, ye sons of England's favoured land,
Where peace and plenty flourish hand in hand
Where'er you go, whatever realms to roam,
May you in safety reach your far off home
There may you guard your nation's wickets well,
By hits unerring as were those of "Tell"
And, lastly, may you win your final score,
Where "bats and balls" and "byes" are known no more —*Veteran*

CHAPTER XX.

INTERCOLONIAL MATCHES—*continued.*

VISIT OF THE FIRST ELEVEN FROM ENGLAND TO AUSTRALIA.

THE FIRST ELEVEN FROM ENGLAND TO AUSTRALIA—THE JOURNEY—OPENING MATCH—RESULT—GRIFFITH'S EXTRAORDINARY FEAT AT SINGLE WICKET—IMMENSE GATHERING AT NEW SOUTH WALES—NOT ONE OF THE ELEVEN BOWLED IN EITHER INNINGS—TEDIOUS JOURNEY TO BATHURST—HEAVY THUNDERSTORM—TRIUMPHS OF THE ELEVEN CHECKED—A SCRATCH MATCH IN THE ISLAND OF TASMANIA—COUNTY OF SURREY *v.* THE WORLD, AT MELBOURNE—PRESENTATION OF A PURSE OF MONEY TO BENNETT AND CAFFYN, THE CHIEF SCORERS—RESULTS OF SUBSEQUENT MATCHES—ANALYSES OF THE BATTING AND BOWLING—GENERAL CORDIALITY OF RECEPTION—SLOW ADVANCE OF CRICKET IN THE COLONY HITHERTO—REASONS WHY—H. H. STEPHENSON'S SPEECH AT THE THEATRE—DEPARTURE OF THE ELEVEN FOR ENGLAND—MEMORIAL TREES PLANTED.

THE party above mentioned left England on the 18th of October, 1861, and arrived at Melbourne on the 24th of December following. Nearly a week elapsed before the opening match of the proposed series was entered upon. It occupied the first four days of the new year. The Eleven of England were arrayed against Eighteen of Victoria, and the subjoined score will show what the results were. England, 305; Victoria, 118 and 91—total 209. England won by an innings and 96 runs.

January 9th.—Eleven of England *v.* Twenty-two of the Ovens Played at Beechworth, and after four days the Eleven were declared winners by an innings and 195 runs. The scores being 264 for England, against 20 and 53—total 73 for Beechworth. At the conclusion of the match Griffith, who obtained the longest score, played eleven of the Ovens at single wicket, and got them all out without a run! He scored six himself.

January 17th.—The third match possessed special interest, as the Eleven were confronted by the united strength of Victoria and New South Wales. The match took place at Melbourne, and lasted three days. Owing to engagements at Geelong, it was left unfinished. The United Twenty-two made 153 runs in the first innings, and 144 in the second—total 207, against 110 by the Eleven in the first innings, and 10 in the second, without loss of wicket.

January 21.—The Twenty-two of Geelong went in first, and totalled 111; the second innings reached only 80, giving 191. The Eleven made 128 and 64 (for one wicket)—total 192, thus winning by nine wickets. On the 24th the Eleven started for Sydney, where they arrived on the morning of the 27th. Two days after, the match against Twenty-two of New South Wales commenced. It proved to be a very exciting affair. More than 20,000 persons witnessed the proceedings. England went first to the wickets, and left them with a score of 175. In their second venture they were less successful; they realised 66 only, thus giving a total of 241. This comparatively small number the Twenty-two were unable to overreach, their scores being 127 and 65—total 192. England, of course, won by 49 runs. It was somewhat remarkable that not one of the Eleven was bowled during either innings. Pending arrangements for a second match at Sydney, the Eleven proceeded to Bathurst. This was a long and rough journey. Notwithstanding the joltings and other disagreeables arising therefrom, the Eleven ran up a first score of 211 against the double number of batsmen opposed to them. The provincials placed only 49 on the scoring paper in the first innings, and 25 in the second for the loss of six wickets. A heavy storm came on at this period, and as the match could not, in consequence, be further proceeded with, it was accordingly declared "Drawn."

February 2nd.—The second match at Sydney was, in all its main features, "a return." On this occasion, however, the Eleven met with the first check to their triumphs, viz., first innings, 60; second, 75—total 135. Twenty-two, 101, and 35 (nine wickets)—total 136, won by twelve wickets. Only one English wicket was bowled, viz., that defended by Wells. In order, it would seem, to prevent an accumulation of superfluous flesh on the bones of the Eleven, they were quickly transferred to Tasmania, and on the 21st they began a match against twenty-two of that beautiful island. After three days' play, England won, with four wickets to spare. Thus: Twenty-two, 109 and 141—total 250; Eleven, 176 and 75—total 251. A scratch match between two elevens, headed by Caffyn and Laurence, was afterwards played. This extended to the 26th of February. Laurence's team scored 100 in the first innings; Caffyn's, 86. Left unfinished.

During the sojourn in Tasmania, a few enthusiastic admirers of the Surrey men projected a special match under the title of "the County of Surrey *v.* the World," and on the arrival of the Eleven at Melbourne, the project was carried into execution. The World (under the direction of Hearne) went in first and scored 211, then 86 (four wickets); Surrey put together only 115, and had to follow on. They exhibited more determination in their second essay, and became possessors of 179. The champion scorer for the World was Bennett, viz., 72. Caffyn, in his second innings, made 75, and not out. At the termination of the match, each of these heroes was presented by the Melbourne Club with a purse containing ten guineas.

March 6th.—The Eleven were at Ballarat at this date, but pressure of engagements prevented a stay sufficiently long to play their match out, which was against twenty-two. The natives went in first, and put together 122; the Eleven approached this number within 7 Ballarat obtained 107 in their second and completed innings Left drawn

On the 9th of March the Eleven were again at Melbourne, but they started on the following day to compete with "Twenty-two of Bendigo and District" Three days were occupied in the matter, the Eleven won by an innings and 63 runs, thus 246, the Twenty-two, 81 and 102—total 183

At Castlemaine, where the Eleven next appeared against "Twenty-two Goldfielders,' a very different result awaited them One, in fact, altogether unexpected after the easy victory of the Bendigo party at Sandhurst, especially as the cricketing power possessed by the residents of these places is generally considered to be on a par The Castlemaine people relied solely on their own local talent Play began on the 14th, and two days sufficed to finish the match In this encounter, the Eleven scored only 80 and 68—total 148, Castlemaine, 54 and 96—total 150 with three wickets to spare

The last match—that which the Victorian players had contemplated with the greatest interest, was "England v Twenty-two of the Colony" It commenced on the 20th of March and finished on the 24th The Colonials went in first and scored 140 runs At the close of the second day's play, the Eleven had effected 180 for the loss of five wickets On the third day the remaining five were disposed of for 22 runs. The second innings of the Colonials began unfavourably, but towards the end runs increased with a rapidity altogether unlooked for, and at the fall of the last wicket 151 were recorded The Eleven now required 74 to win, and at six o'clock on the fourth day seven of their wickets were lowered for 63, and no further play was allowed Great dissatisfaction was manifested at the determination of the Victorians not to proceed further with the match, and it was therefore classed among the "drawn"

The following analyses of the batting and bowling of the English players are taken from the scoring books, used on the grounds, of the clubs above alluded to, respectively.

BATTING AVERAGES

Names	No of Matches	No of Innings	Most Runs in a Match	Most Runs in an Innings	Least Runs in an Innings	Not out	Total	Average per Innings Over
Bennett ..	13	17	72	72	3	1	290	17- 1
Caffyn	13	18	88	79	7	1	419	23- 5
Griffith	13	19	61	61	5	1	431	22-13
Hearne	12	14	37	37	0	2	138	9-12
Iddison	13	17	47	36	0	1	314	18- 8
Laurence ..	12	15	24	24	0	1	103	6-13
Mortlock	10	13	86	76	1	0	251	19- 4
Mudie	10	12	27	27	0	1	111	9- 3
Stephenson, H H	13	16	47	47	2	2	188	11-12
Stephenson, E	11	15	60	61	1	1	203	13- 8
Sewell	12	14	41	41	0	0	135	9- 9
Wells .	12	14	75	48	0	0	177	12- 9

ANALYSIS OF THE BOWLING.

Names.	No. of Innings.	Overs.	Maidens.	Wickets.	Wides.	Runs.	Average runs per Wicket.	Average Wickets. Over.
Bennett	16	244	150	75	1	426	5—31	4—11
Caffyn	20	439	213	80	2	495	6—15	4
Griffith	15	337	170	74	10	364	4—68	4—14
Iddison	21	477	183	103	3	681	6—33	4—12
Lawrence	12	175	72	46	0	243	5—13	3—10
Mortlock	1	5	0	0	0	12		
Mudie	2	9	1	0	0	24		
Sewell	14	206	140	49	3	529	4—33	3— 7
Stephenson, H. H.	5	71	31	6	4	100	6— 4	3— 1
Wells	6	65	46	9	1	33	3— 6	1— 3

From the foregoing statements it will be seen that the Eleven won six matches, lost two, and four were drawn.

It is worthy of notice, in spite of so much adverse luck, how creditably the Old Country was everywhere welcomed by the New; the defeats occasioned little or no surprise. A vast deal more experience was attached to the one side than to the other, and the "tight little island" is, after all that can be said or done, a larger place, and has a larger pick of men devoted to athletic sports than the "fifth quarter" of the globe at present possesses. During many years the Australian colonists absorbed themselves almost exclusively in commercial, industrial, and speculative pursuits, varied by little else than fishing and hunting. It was long before they renewed the traditions of English joviality. They had a desert to people, and barrenness to reclaim; but now they are formed, developed, adult. Victoria possesses almost a nation within her own frontiers; her manners, thoughts, and feelings are essentially English. No wonder, then, that the eleven should have been warmly greeted by those who might have been their colleagues at school, but whose lot has been fortuitously cast across the remotest waters of the globe. It was perceptible enough to the dullest observer who attended any of the matches that the ties of blood are not broken, and that the ancient loyalty survives, and that England is not yet separated, or likely to be so, either in heart or mind from the colonies she has multiplied throughout the world. In confirmation of these statements, an extract from a stage speech, delivered by H. H. Stephenson, the captain, may be here reproduced: "I am no orator, and on occasions like these I am easily bowled out. I had rather play three games of cricket than make one speech; but I should be wanting in gratitude to you, in duty towards my gallant comrades, if I omitted to thank you, however imperfectly, for this gratifying mark of your kindness. The farther we travel from home the more perfectly at home do we feel. The more we see of the colonies and their inhabitants the better we like them. Our tour has been a succession of fêtes and a succession of astonishments. We expected to find Ballarat a great encampment, but it turns out to be a great city. We expected to find every thing rough and primitive, but it proves to be far advanced, and comfortable as Europe As to the treatment we have experienced, and the gallant competitors we have had to contend with, how can we signify our admiration of them, and our gratitude to them? I know but of one way, and that is by speaking the honest truth about you when we return, and by telling the people in the old country how much we were delighted with all that we saw in the new one"

Previous to their departure for England each man planted a tree on the Melbourne Ground as a memorial, and, to use the language of the Jewish historian respecting the twelve stones in Jordan, "they are there unto this day" (Joshua iv. 5—9)

THE MELBOURNE GROUND—For so important an event as a first visit the M C C had given their best attention to the ground—neither time nor money had been withheld in order to arrive at perfection as near as possible—about nine acres in extent An elegant pavilion, with gable roof, stood on the northern side, and in front of it a pretty garden, full of geraniums and flowering shrubs A verandah with seats ran the whole extent of the pavilion At one end was a stand of an octagonal form for a band Water from the Yan Yean reservoir was laid on, from which 40,000 gallons an hour could have been drawn if required The importance of this in a country where occasionally hot winds blow with the thermometer varying from 110° to 120° in the shade, can scarcely be appreciated by those who have never quitted the more temperate climate of England In addition to the pavilion mentioned, there was erected on the occasion in question a "grand stand" of colossal proportions, semi-circular in form, encompassing nearly a third of the ground, and capable of seating comfortably from 5000 to 6000 people The seats were raised as in a theatre, so that all had a good view of the play Underneath were compartments let off for the sale of refreshments In the centre of this "stand" was a private box, elegantly fitted up for the use of His Excellency Sir H. Barkly and suite An immense marquee, capable of holding 500 persons, was erected near the pavilion for the special use of the players, committee, and friends The centre piece of the turf, nearly fifty yards square, was intensely green, and as level as a billiard table Ornamental iron posts, connected by chains, and each post surmounted by a small red flag, completely hemmed in the playing portion of the ground, within which the crowd were not allowed, but additional wooden fences were put up in places where the pressure was severe On the arrival of the Governor the band struck up the National Anthem, whereupon the crowd in the grand stand—the greater portion ladies—rose *en masse*, the gentlemen lifted their hats, an example followed immediately by the great gathering below, cricketers included The effect was imposing, for it not only evinced a mark of respect to the "Governor" but it proved how deep and fervent was the loyalty existing in the breasts of the colonists towards a Queen at the other extremity of the globe, and an attachment that defies space to enfeeble

VISIT OF THE SECOND ELEVEN TO AUSTRALIA

THE SECOND VISIT OF AN ALL ENGLAND ELEVEN—CONDITIONS BEFORE LEAVING ENGLAND—TIME CONSUMED ON THE JOURNEY—NAMES OF THE PARTIES—LIST OF MATCHES PLAYED AND RESULTS OF SAME—ANALYSIS OF THE BATTING

Two years afterwards another visit was projected, under the captaincy of Parr The parties forming the team were to leave England in September Primarily the conditions before starting were to be a remittance of 600*l*, and a sum of 50*l* per man as a provision for those dependent upon him during his absence, also a first class passage Doubtlessly the speculation of Messrs Spiers and Pond proved a success—one that seemed to fan the flame of enterprize among the colonists In the matter of cricket there were growing demands to witness first-class play This evinced itself unmistakably in the number of applications—a number far too great to be entertained during the limited stay of the English visitors Spreading over so great an extent of territory, the utmost wisdom was needed in order to carry out a plan that would serve the purposes of the promoters, players, and public After considerable time and discussion had been expended on making what was considered fair and equitable arrangements, the following left England on the 14th of October and arrived at Melbourne on the 17th of December, viz, Anderson, Carpenter, Cæsar, Clarke, E M Grace, Hayward, Jackson, Lockyer, Parr, Tarrant, and Tinley Caffyn, who remained in the colony, again joined the English team. As a great deal of the ground traversed by Stephenson was retrod by Parr, and as the treatment of the colonists was uniformly of the same genial and generous character, it will be sufficient to furnish a *résumé* of the matches played.

Melbourne, January 1, 1864—Four days The England Eleven *v* Twenty two of Victoria Twenty-two of Victoria, 146 and 143—total 289, E E, 176 and 105 (four wickets)—total 281 Drawn England required 9 runs to win, and six wickets to fall

Bendigo, January 7—Three days The England Eleven *v* Twenty-two of Bendigo E E, 85 and 178—total 263 Twenty-two of Bendigo, 74 and 45—total 119 E E won by 144 runs

Sandhurst, January 11—Three days England Eleven *v* Twenty-two of Ballarat E E, 188, Twenty two of Ballarat, 82 and 94—total 176 E E won by an innings and 12 runs

Ararat January 14—Three days England Eleven *v* Twenty two of Ararat E E, 137, Twenty-two of Ararat 35 and 34—total 69 E E won by an innings and 68 runs

Maryboro', January 19—Three days England Eleven *v* Twenty two of Maryboro' E E, 223 Twenty-two of Maryboro', 72 and 74—total 146 E E won by an innings and 77 runs

Otago, February 2—Three days England Eleven *v* Twenty-two of Otago Twenty-two of Otago, 71 and 83—total 154, E E, 99 and 58 (one wicket)—total 157 E E. won by nine wickets

Canterbury, February 4—Two days England Eleven *v* Twenty-two of Canterbury and Otago C and O, 91 and 66—total 157, E E, 73 Drawn

Christchurch, February 8—Two days England Eleven *v* Twenty two of Christchurch E E, 137 Twenty-two of Christchurch, 30 and 105—total 135 E E won by an innings and 2 runs

Christchurch, February 10—Three days Parr's Eleven *v* Anderson's Eleven Parr, 64 and 89—total 153, Anderson, 71 and 75—total 146 Parr won by 7 runs

Dunedin, February 16—Three days England Eleven *v* Twenty two of Otago E E, 190, Twenty-two of Otago, 98 and 49—total 147 E E won by an innings and 51 runs

Castlemaine, March 1—Three days England Eleven *v* Twenty-two of Castlemaine E E, 137, Twenty-two of Castlemaine, 54 and 46—total 100 E E won by an innings and 37 runs

Melbourne, March 5—Three days Parr's Eleven *v* Anderson's Eleven Parr, 153 and 129—282, Anderson, 168 and 115 (six wickets)—total 283 Anderson won by four wickets

Sydney, March 16 to 24—England Eleven *v* Twenty-two of New South Wales Twenty-two of New South Wales, 137 and 50—total 187, E E, 128 and 60 (six wickets)—total 188 E E won by four wickets

Sydney, March 26—Three days England Eleven *v* Twenty-two of New South Wales E E, 114, Twenty-two of New South Wales, 102 and 3 Drawn, owing to wet

Sydney, April 2—Three days England Eleven *v* Twenty-two of New South Wales Twenty-two of New South Wales, 68 and 83—total 151, E E, 75 and 77 (nine wickets)—total 152 E E. won by one wicket

Geelong, April 12—Two days England Eleven *v* Twenty two of Geelong E E, 135, Twenty two of Geelong, 106 and 64 (nine wickets)—total 170 Drawn

Maryboro', April 14—Two days Tarrant's Eleven *v* Parr's Eleven Tarrant, 164 and 74—total 238, Parr, 112 and 70—total 182 Tarrant won by 56 runs P S—On the winning side were Anderson, Cæsar, Carpenter, E M Grace, and Tinley On the losing side Caffyn, Clarke, Hayward, Lockyer, and Jackson

Ballarat, April 18—Two days England Eleven *v* Twenty-two of Ballarat E E 310, Twenty-two of Ballarat, 127 and 48 (fifteen wickets)—total 175 Drawn

Melbourne April 21—Three days England Eleven *v* Twenty-two of Victoria Twenty-two of Victoria, 150 and 83 (seventeen wickets) total 233, E E, 131 Drawn

From the foregoing it will be seen that the Eleven played sixteen matches against twenty-two, of which they won ten and six were drawn

ANALYSIS OF THE BATTING

NAME	No of Matches	No of Innings	Most Runs in a Match	Most Runs in an Innings	How often Bowled	Caught	Run out	Stumped	Not out	Total	Average per Innings Over
Carpenter	16	20	121	121	4	12	2	0	2	396	19–16
Caffyn	16	20	45	43	3	11	2	0	1	318	17– 8
Cæsar	14	16	40	40	4	10	1	0	1	178	11– 2
Clarke	13	16	18	18	3	12	1	0	0	85	5– 5
Mr E M Grace	16	21	50	44	7	13	0	0	1	274	13– 1
Hayward	15	19	65	65	11	6	1	0	1	326	17– 3
Jackson	16	19	24	24	5	6	2	0	6	154	8– 2
Lockyer	16	19	31	31	8	8	0	0	3	213	11– 4
Parr	11	12	65	65	6	5	0	0	1	194	16– 2
Tarrant	16	21	41	41	5	13	1	0	2	246	11–15
Tinley	16	18	21	21	6	5	0	0	7	98	5– 8
Anderson	10	13	47	26	6	6	0	0	1	118	9– 1

Before dismissing the brief events of the second visit, one or two incidents enforce notice A short time previous to the departure of the team, a deputation from the Maories resident at the Heads, waited upon George Parr, and in the name of their chief, presented him with a handsome piece of matting made from native flax, by members of the tribe, in return for the many acts of kindness shown by the famous Englishmen to the Maories during the cricketers' sojourn in the country This was the highest honour which the Maories could confer upon the famous "captain," one that elevated him to the rank of a chief After the ceremony, Parr had to go through the ordeal of kissing the Maorie women who made the presentation, and, much to the amusement of his companions, he went through the ceremony as if "to the manner born" A few days afterwards a farewell dinner on an extensive scale, was arranged On this occasion each member of the Eleven received a handsome shield-pin made of New Zealand gold Each pin bore the date of presentation and the name of the donor In return for this, Parr and his little yet mighty band presented a beautiful silver cup bearing the names of the Eleven and the date of their visit To the colonists the Eleven appear to have been like a hand stretched from the old country, which they could never shake warmly enough, and which they were loth to let go for a moment Their reception throughout was a magnificent example of colonial warmth, suggesting a home feeling impossible to convey in any other form

VISIT OF THE THIRD ELEVEN IN 1873, UNDER THE CAPTAINCY OF Mr W G GRACE.

Messrs Boult, Bush, Gilbert, and G. F Grace with A Greenwood, R Humphrey, Jupp, Lillywhite, M. M'Intyre, W Oscroft, and Southerton.

The Third Eleven under the Captaincy of Mr W G Grace—Their Departure from Southampton and Arrival at Melbourne—Matches Played—Analysis of the Batting, etc —The Character and Early Condition of the Melbourne Ground

All these left Southampton in the "Mirzapore" on the 23rd of October, and anchored in Galle Harbour on the 23rd of November They soon transferred their baggage to the "Nubia," bound for Sydney On the 8th of December they anchored at King George's Sound, and five days afterwards Hobson's Bay, about forty miles from Melbourne, was reached Here the mail for Geelong was dropped, and on the following morning the twelve were safely landed at their appointed destination

The first match was played on the Melbourne Ground, December 26, and two following days, under the title of All England Eleven *v* Eighteen of Victoria At starting the odds were three to one in favour of A E E, but the colonials found many confident backers when it was seen that there were two or three weak members in the Eleven, and too much would of necessity depend on the scores of the Graces It is stated that 16,000 persons attended the first day, 14,000 the second, and 10,000 the third The Victorians won the toss and went in Their batting took the visitors by surprise, for at the close of the match they were proclaimed winners by an innings and 21 runs See score —

EIGHTEEN OF VICTORIA

L Goldsmith, st Bush, b Lillywhite	17
G Gibson, c Oscroft, b Lillywhite	9
B B Cooper, h w, b G F Grace	84
H Boyle, c Lillywhite, b W G Grace	30
J Coates, c Jupp, b W G Grace	3
T J D Kelly, c and b Southerton	26
J Conway, b W G Grace	32
G. P Robertson, b G F Grace	11
W W Gaggin, c G F Grace, b W G Grace	0
B M'Gan, b W G Grace	7
W Midwinter c Bush, b G F Grace	7
C Carr, b G F Grace	8
S Cosstick, c Humphrey, b W G Grace	0
H Bishop, not out	5
Hedley, c Oscroft, b W G Grace	1
F Allan, c and b W G Grace	0
T Horan, st Bush b W G Grace	1
Wyndham, c G F Grace, b W G Grace	6
Byes 9, l-b 5, w 1, n-b 1	16
Total	266

ALL ENGLAND ELEVEN

	1st inn		2nd inn
Mr W G Grace, b Boyle	33	not out	51
Jupp b Allan	22	c and b Cosstick	0
Mr Gilbert, c and b Cosstick	13	c M'Gan, b Allan	6
Greenwood, c and b Allan	5	c M'Gan, b Allan	16
Mr G F Grace, b Allan	6	c Cooper, b Conway	28
Oscroft, b Allan	12	b Conway	0
Humphrey, c Allan, b Cosstick	4	b Cosstick	6
Lillywhite, b Cosstick	4	b Boyle	19
M Intire, c Cosstick, b Allan	9	run out	4
Bush, b Allan	0	c Conway, b Boyle	2
Southerton, not out	0	b Boyle	0
Leg-byes	2	Byes	3
Total	110	Total	135

BOWLING ANALYSIS

EIGHTEEN OF VICTORIA

	Overs	Maidens	Runs	Wickets	Wides
M M'Intyre	38	16	47	0	0
Southerton	41	22	41	1	0
Lillywhite	34	17	49	2	0
Mr W G Grace	43-1	18	58	10	0
Mr G F Grace	26	9	35	4	1
Mr Gilbert	4	0	20	0	0

M'Intyre bowled one no-ball

ALL ENGLAND—FIRST INNINGS

	Overs	Maidens	Runs	Wickets	Wides
Allan	54-1	33	44	6	0
Cosstick	47	31	53	3	0
Boyle	7	3	11	1	0

SECOND INNINGS

	Overs	Maidens	Runs	Wickets	Wides
Cosstick	26-3	20	60	2	0
Allan	52	36	40	2	0
Conway	21	11	18	2	0
Boyle	5	2	14	3	0

As the ground travelled by the third party so much resembled that of the two preceding, and the results of the contests engaged vary so little in their general character and results, it is hardly necessary to recapitulate them If not quite so satisfactory to the team who left England as the first and second venture—as many affirm it was not—there can be no doubt that the visit afforded the colonists a great deal of pleasure, and at the same time gave them an idea of the prodigious feats of the greatest cricketer England ever produced and the world ever saw Such visits as the three named in this chapter must have a beneficial effect upon the mighty future of Australia, destined as it is to play so important a part in the world's history Some one has said, ' Happy the nation that has no annals " Victoria has had annals in her time In the early digging days she had annals of a rather Newgate-Calenderish celebrity (although the crimes were committed by convict emigrants), and she once got up a rebellion on a small scale But since she has left off bowling out ministers and taken to cricket, her annals have become as dull as those of any thriving community ought to be It is said that the climate makes the people as fond of pleasure as were the Athenian youth If this be so future generations of colonial born lads are likely to maintain their fathers' prestige At present the enthusiastic cricketers of whom the world hears so much are nearly all—in Victoria, at least—of European birth Stout old Captain Cook, when surveying that desolate and unexplored land with such painstaking accuracy, would have rubbed his eyes if he had heard that within a hundred years men would have coolly crossed those seas, which he had traversed at such risk, merely to see how skilfully they could knock a red ball about with bits of wood Yet after all it is not more absurd and far less reprehensible than that men should cross the seas to cut each others throats, and it is well known voyages were made for such a purpose in the time of Agamemnon

GENERAL ANALYSIS OF THE BOWLING

NAMES	No of Matches	No of Innings	Overs	Maidens	Runs	Wickets	Wides	No Balls	Average Wickets per Innings	Average Runs per Wicket Over
Mr F H Boult	2	2	38	18	25	8	0	4	4	3— 1
Mr W R Gilbert	2	2	33	10	67	8	0	0	4	8— 3
Mr W G Grace	8	11	351	146	501	72	0	0	6— 6	6—69
Mr G F Grace	7	7	147	59	170	19	1	1	2— 5	8—18
Lillywhite	15	25	889	486	881	170	0	0	6—20	5—31
M'Intyre	11	15	305	177	253	59	1	6	3—14	4—16
Southerton	13	24	739	345	819	115	0	2	6— 1	5—94

ANALYSIS OF THE BATTING

Names	No of Matches	No of Innings	Most Runs in a Match	Most Runs in an Innings	Total	Average per Innings	Over
Mr F H Boult	10	12	10	10	50	4	2
Mr J A Bush	15	21	23	23	65	3	2
Mr W R Gilbert	15	24	44	38	202	8	10
Mr W G Grace	15	24	126	126	711	29	15
Mr G F Grace	12	19	154	154	598	31	9
Greenwood	15	25	62	62	378	15	3
Humphrey	11	17	37	36	131	7	12
Jupp	15	21	58	58	333	15	18
Lillywhite	15	21	40	40	170	8	2
M'Intyre	15	23	56	55	207	9	
Oscroft	15	23	69	69	349	15	4
Southerton	13	18	15	15	62	3	8

THE BLACK TEAM

The shadowed livery of the burnished sun —*Merchant of Venice*, act ii, scene 1

Arrival of the Black Team in England—Reception—Their History—A Match Played by them in Australia—The Return of Same in Presence of the Duke of Edinburgh—Description of their Physical Condition—Physiognomy—First Match Played and the Entire Series with Scores and Analyses of Batting and Bowling—Throwing the Boomerang and the Ball—Acrobatic and other Sports—Failure as a Commercial Speculation

In the year 1868, a party of black men twelve in number, accompanied by an European captain and three gentlemen, arrived in this country for the purpose of playing a series of matches A great deal of curiosity was, as a matter of course, excited thereby The idea of such an invasion upon the legitimate domain of cricket created amusement, and the possibility of the faintest chance of success was, by the great bulk of the English community, hard to be conceived Their history as cricketers may be briefly told. About two years previous to the time in question, a young club, formed in Victoria, was frequently visited on practice days by black boys, who hunted the leather upon the consideration that they might have an occasional use of the bat This soon led to a camp of natives amusing themselves with a piece of board for a bat, and a shea oak cob for a ball A rapid proficiency in the elementary principles of the game soon excited attention, and they were taken in hand by Mr Hayman, a squatter in the Wimmera district on the Glenelg river. In less than a year a team was got together strong and proficient enough to justify an attempt to play a match at Lake Wallace. A large number of settlers for miles around were attracted to the match The sable troop were defeated, though not with ignominy having been only 7 runs in arrear Being neither satisfied with defeat, nor with the idea that the winners were the best men, a return was proposed to take place in the following year, and on this occasion they came off victors by an innings and 156 runs. Soon afterwards they were taken to Hamilton, one of the largest inland towns, to compete with a much stronger club, and here they proved victors by an innings and 82 runs. These successes were soon trumpeted over the colony, and the black team were found playing all through Victoria and New South Wales, and in one season they claimed nineteen matches out of twenty. Four of these were "Sixteen Europeans *v.* The Eleven." This suggested the idea of bringing them to Europe. The last match played, prior to their departure, was on the 23rd of January and following day, against the crew of the *Galatea*. The Duke of Edinburgh was present. They arrived in England on the 13th of May, 1868, and for a few days they were quietly located at Malling, in order to "shake off their sea legs," and get a bit of practice.

In stature they differed as much as a like number of Englishmen, taken at random, might be expected to differ; the range of height being from five feet four inches to five feet ten inches. The colour of skin was certainly not black, but rather a sooty brown; the hair a jet black, in every instance, and curly, but not so harsh or stiff in the curl as the African negro; in form, straight and upright, rather slight limbed, with small hands and feet, tolerably broad shoulders, and a sinking in of the chest indicative of weak lungs. Their faces varied considerably in formation, especially in the nose, with higher foreheads than the negro; and, notwithstanding an evident training of the whiskers and moustache, thereby conveying a fierce military aspect, there was, generally speaking, an amount of docility somewhat prepossessing; eyes large and full with a soft expression, and a physiognomy, taken altogether, by no means unintellectual. Gathered, as they were, from wide distances in the colony, it was observed that in all of them there was a manly and dignified bearing. Within five weeks of their arrival one of the number, King Cole, was seized with a violent attack of pneumonia. He was taken to Guy's Hospital, where he died on the 24th of June.

The first match took place at the Oval on the 25th of May, from the full score of which it will be seen that Surrey won by an innings and 7 runs.

SURREY.

Mr. G. H. Jupp, st Bullocky, b Lawrence	24
Mr. C. Noble, c and b Lawrence	9
Mr. W. Baggallay, st Bullocky, b Lawrence	68
Mr. I. D. Walker, c King Cole, b Mullagh	1
Mr. G. Greenfield, c Bullocky, b Lawrence	16
Mr. C. Calvert, b Mullagh	25
Mr. J. St. Boultbee, b Lawrence	37
Mr. R. Barton, not out	16
Mr. H. Frere, b Mullagh	4
Mr. F. P. Miller, c Redcap, b Lawrence	7
Mr. H. Hibberd, c King Cole, b Lawrence	11
Bye	1
Total	222

BLACKS

	1st inn		2nd inns
Bullocky (maroon), c Walker, b Frere	6	b Miller	19
Tiger (pink), b Walker	3	b Boultbee	3
Mullagh (dark blue), st Hibberd, b Walker	33	b Frere	73
Redcap (black), b Frere	1	run out	0
Lawrence, c Calvert, b Walker	3	b Miller	22
King Cole (magenta), b Walker	14	c Walker, b Miller	0
Dick a-Dick (yellow), b Frere	0	b Boultbee	5
Twopenny (drab), c Miller, b Frere	1	b Frere	0
Peter (green), b Frere	0	b Frere	4
Jim Crow (brown), b Walker	10	not out	2
Charley, or Dumas (light blue), not out	5	b Walker	0
Byes 5 w 2	7	Byes	4
Total	83	Total	132

May 30 —Blacks v Maidstone, at Mote Park Maidstone, 150, Blacks, 122 (four wickets) Drawn

June 2 —Blacks v Kent Club, at Gravesend Blacks, 126 and 103—total 229, Kent Club, 298 Kent won by an innings and 69 runs

June 5 —Blacks v Richmond, at Richmond Richmond, 71 and 236—total 310, Blacks 97 and 82 (four wickets)—total 179 Drawn

June 8 —Blacks v Sussex Club, at Brighton Blacks, 171 and 89—total 260 Sussex Club, 151 and 112 (one wicket)—total 263 Sussex won by nine wickets

June 10 —Blacks v Lewisham, at Ladywell Lewisham, 60 and 53—total 113, Blacks 42 and 72 (four wickets)—total 114 Blacks won by six wickets

June 12 —Blacks v Marylebone Club, at Lord's Marylebone, 164 and 120—total 284, Blacks, 185 and 45—total 230 Marylebone won by 54 runs

June 15 —Blacks v East Hants, at Southsea Blacks, 120 and 80—total 200, East Hants, 209 Hants won by an innings and 9 runs

June 17 —Blacks v Bishop's Stortford, at Stortford Blacks, 58 and 99—total 157 Stortford, 126 and 23 (two wickets)—total 159 Bishop's Stortford won by eight wickets

June 25 —Blacks v Hastings, at Hastings Blacks, 119 and 185—total 304, Hastings, 152 and 113 (four wickets)—total 265 Drawn

June 26 —Blacks v Halifax, at Halifax Halifax, 64 and 130—total 194, Blacks, 166 and 29 (three wickets)—total 195 Blacks won by seven wickets

June 29 —Blacks v East Lancashire, at Blackburn. Blacks, 144 and 97—total 241, Lancashire, 234 and 6 (one wicket)—total 240 Drawn

July 2 —Blacks v Rochdale, at Rochdale Rochdale, 105 and 91—total 196, Blacks, 27 and 92—total 119 Rochdale won by 77 runs

July 6 —Blacks v Swansea, at Swansea Blacks, 193 Swansea, 68 and 92—total 160 Blacks won by an innings and 33 runs

July 9 —Blacks v Bradford, at Bradford Blacks, 40 and 171—total 211, Bradford, 164 and 16 (one wicket)—total 180 Drawn

July 11 —Blacks v Yorkshire, at York Yorkshire, 201, Blacks, 92 and 58—total 150 Yorkshire won by an innings and 51 runs

July 16 —Blacks v Longsight, at Longsight Longsight, 78 and 117—total 195 Blacks, 53 and 123—total 176 Longsight won by 19 runs

July 20 —Blacks v Bury, at Bury Bury, 99 and 93—total 192 Blacks, 53 and 128 (five wickets)—total 181 Drawn

July 23 —Blacks v Carrow, at Norwich Blacks, 235, Carrow, 82 and 101—total 183 Blacks won by an innings and 52 runs

July 27 —Blacks v Keighley, at Keighley Keighley, 118 and 146—total 264, Blacks, 101 and 142 (eight wickets)—total 243 Drawn

July 30 —Blacks *v* Bootle, at Bootle Bootle, 110 and 90—total 200, Blacks 115 and 87 (one wicket)—total 202 Blacks won by nine wickets

August 3 —Blacks *v* Commercial, at Nottingham Commercial, 91 and 372—total 463 Blacks, 76 and 57 (four wickets)—total 133 Drawn

August 7 —Blacks *v* Longsight, at Longsight Blacks 76 and 151—total 227, Longsight, 48 and 72—total 120 Blacks won by 107 runs

August 10 —Blacks *v* Sheffield, at Brammall Lane Blacks, 185, Sheffield, 133 Drawn

August 13 —Blacks *v* Dewsbury, at Saville Town Blacks, 73 and 86—total 159, Dewsbury, 217 Won by an innings and 58 runs

August 17 —Blacks *v* North Shields, at Tynemouth Blacks, 35 and 166—total 201, North Shields, 54 and 144—total 198 Blacks won by 3 runs

August 21 —Blacks *v* Northumberland, at Newcastle Blacks, 32 and 75 (three wickets)—total 107, Northumberland, 162 Drawn

August 24 —Blacks *v* Middlesborough, at Middlesborough Middlesborough, 151 and 80—total 231, Blacks, 74 and 79 (eight wickets)—total 153 Drawn

August 27 —Blacks *v* Scarborough Scarborough, 90 and 109—total 199, Blacks, 143 and 58 (one wicket)—total 201 Blacks won by ten wickets

August 31 —Blacks *v* Hunslet, at Hunslet Hunslet, 71 and 18—total 89, Blacks, 64 and 26 (three wickets)—total 90 Blacks won by seven wickets

September 2 —Blacks *v* South Derbyshire, at Derby Derbyshire, 121 and 125—total 246, Blacks, 76 and 81—total 157 Derbyshire won by 139 runs

September 4 —Blacks *v* Lincoln, at Lincoln Lincoln, 44 and 100—total 144, Blacks, 78 and 56—total 134 Lincoln won by 10 runs

September 7 —Blacks *v* Burton, at Burton Blacks, 139 and 101—total 240, Burton, 72 and 99—total 171 Blacks won by 69 runs

September 10 —Blacks *v* Bootle, at Liverpool Blacks, 148 and 156—total 304, Bootle, 91 and 59—total 150 Blacks won by 154 runs

September 14 —Blacks *v* Witham, at Witham Blacks, 184, Witham, 82 and 59—total 141 Blacks won by an innings and 43 runs

September 17 —Blacks *v* Sussex Club, at Brighton Blacks, 96 and 113 (seven wickets)—total 209, Sussex Club, 74 Drawn

September 21 —Blacks *v* Blackheath, at Blackheath Blacks, 67 and 116—total 183, Blackheath, 121 and 75—total 196 Blackheath won by 13 runs

September 23 —Blacks *v* Middlesex Club, at Islington Middlesex, 105 and 173 (nine wickets) —total 278, Blacks, 168 Drawn

September 26 —Blacks *v* Surrey Club at the Oval Surrey Club, 174, Blacks, 24 (three wickets Drawn

September 28 —Blacks *v* Press, at Mote Park Press, 101 and 74—total 175, Blacks, 82 Drawn

September 30 —Blacks *v* Eastbourne, at Eastbourne Eastbourne, 67 and 94—total 161, Blacks, 80 Drawn

October 2 —Blacks *v* Turnham Green, at Hammersmith Blacks, 48, Turnham Green, 62 Drawn

October 5 —Blacks *v* East Hants, at Southsea Blacks, 144, East Hants, 51 and 22—total 73 Blacks won by and innings and 71 runs

October 7 —Blacks *v* Hampshire, at Southampton Hampshire, 53 and 152—total 205, Blacks, 78 and 49 (three wickets)—total 127 Drawn

October 9 —Blacks *v* Fairbrother, at Reading Blacks, 284, Fairbrother, 32 and 34—total 66 Blacks won by an innings and 218 runs

October 13 —Blacks *v* Godalming, at Broadwater Godalming, 37 and 128—total 165, Blacks 79 and 25 (five wickets)—total 104 Drawn

October 14 —Blacks *v* Surrey Club

From the full score hereto attached it will be seen that Surrey won by nine wickets The match being concluded early on the second day, the Blacks gave then final performance of native pastimes, the like of which will probably never be witnessed again in this part of the globe.

BLACKS.

	1st inn.		2nd inn.
Cuzens, b Absolon	3	b Julius	63
Twopenny, b Mayo	10	b Baggallay	0
Bullocky, st Hibberd, b Absolon	21	c Holt, b Julius	14
Mullagh, b Mayo	0	b Mayo	18
Lawrence, c Hibberd, b Mayo	0	c Absolon, b Julius	12
Tiger, c Baggallay, b Mayo	9	b Absolon	0
Redcap, b Absolon	2	b Baggallay	22
Dick-a-Dick, st Hibberd, b Mayo	2	c Gregory, b Julius	0
Peter, st Hibberd, b Mayo	2	l b w, b Julius	0
Charley or Dumas, b Mayo	1	b Julius	0
Mosquito, not out	0	not out	1
Bye 1, l-b 2	3	Byes 10, l-b 2, w 1	13
Total	56	Total	143

SURREY.

	1st inn.		2nd inn.
Mr. C. W. Baggallay, b Cuzens	0		
Mr. H. Mayo, b Cuzens	5	not out	1
Mr. J. C. Gregory, not out	121		
Mr. C. Julius, b Cuzens	7	c Bullocky, b Cuzens	9
Mr. C. H. Jupp, c Tiger, b Lawrence	4		
Mr. H. Hibberd, c Redcap, b Mullagh	0	not out	10
Mr. S. F. Onslow, b Twopenny	9		
Mr. C. Absolon, c Redcap, b Lawrence	11		
Mr. F. G. Mitcham, b Lawrence	1		
Mr. W. L. Holt, c and b Lawrence	1		
Mr. Newall, h w, b Lawrence	0		
Byes 7, l-b 4, w 3	14	Byes 5, l-b 3, w 1	9
Total	173	Total	29

The novelty of this "Black visit" afforded many a rhymester an opportunity to indulge his fancy, but not one rose to the occasion, the attempts to be witty were vile, and others, to be over-clever, failures. Among moderate effusions the following broken stanzas may be taken as a fair sample:—

Your swarthy brows and raven locks
Must gratify your tonsors;
But by the name of Dick-a-Dick,
Who are your doughty sponsors.

Arrayed in skin of kangaroo,
And deck'd with lanky feather,
How well you fling the fragile spear
Along the Surrey heather.

And though you cannot hope to beat,
The Britishers at cricket,
You have a batter bold and brave
In Mullagh at the wicket.

The following table represents the batting qualifications and results of the Blacks in the matches above specified.

BATTING AVERAGES.

NAME.	No. of Matches.	No. of Innings.	Most Runs in a Match.	Most Runs in an Innings.	How often bowled.	Caught.	Run out.	Stumped.	Not out.	Total.	Average per Innings. Over.
Bullocky	42	60	72	64	17	23	13	4	3	566	9–26
Cuzens	46	72	87	87	25	32	5	4	6	1368	19
Dick-a-Dick	47	66	30	27	23	27	8	4	4	304	4–40
Dumas, or Charley	45	77	17	17	29	27	11	4	6	238	3– 7
Jim Crow	13	14	12	10	6	4	1	0	3	37	2– 9
King Cole	8	10	21	18	4	4	1	0	1	75	7– 5
Lawrence	41	57	96	63	22	18	2	1	14	1198	21– 1
Mullagh	43	74	129	94	19	36	7	7	5	1679	22–51
Red Cap	47	73	56	56	30	26	9	3	5	628	8–44
Mosquito	35	23	8	8	13	7	2	0	1	82	3–13
Peter	44	59	31	30	39	10	1	2	7	296	5– 1
Tiger	47	69	32	12	26	29	6	4	4	421	6– 7
Twopenny	47	67	40	35	34	22	2	1	8	574	8–38

Although there were not more than three who could claim much proficiency in the art of bowling, eight of them tried their hands, and with what success the subjoined analytical table will show.

NAMES.	No. of Innings.	Overs.	Maidens.	Wickets.	Runs.	Wides.	No Balls.	Average Wickets per Innings. Over.
Lawrence	69	1579	451	250	3022	1	0	3—43
Mullagh	76	1877	831	245	2489	14	0	3—17
Cuzens	47	868	361	114	1296	8	0	2—20
Twopenny	15	176	78	35	242	2	1	2— 5
Redcap	28	366	141	54	576	16	4	1—12
Dick-a-Dick	8	25	6	5	98	1	0	0— 5
Bullocky	5	22	7	4	46	0	0	0— 4
King Cole	2	14	4	1	34	0	0	0— 1

Before parting with this black team, other sports of a native cast ought to be mentioned. Dick-a-Dick appeared to claim the largest share of individual attention by "dodging the ball." Possessed of a narrow shield and triangle, he defended himself against a shower of balls incessantly pelting him from a distance of about twenty yards. He fenced off many, that must have struck his head and other parts of the body, with wonderful adroitness by means of these primitive instruments, while others he avoided by a leap or bend. The throwing of the boomerang also excited considerable astonishment. It showed what great command practice had given them over this singular projectile. On some special occasions they introduced a native sham fight, when they were costumed in a dark closely fitting overall, a doublet of opossum skins, and a parti-coloured head dress, turned up with a broad band of cabbage-tree plant, and a crest of lyre-bird plumage. All, armed with spears, boomerangs, and throwing sticks, ranged up in a single line, and upon the word of command given, they delivered three flights of spears to distances varying from 60 to 100 yards. They then separated into opposing parties of six, and facing each other at 80 yards distance, discharged their spears from each side, sometimes using the throwing sticks. In throwing the cricket ball they were also adepts. Dick-a-Dick once claimed 120 yards from a second throw. Several others could run and leap amazingly. Lawrence, the captain, and a European, signalised himself by repeatedly catching a ball on the face of his bat when thrown high into the air from long distances. As a commercial speculation, the Black Team did not pay, but they played cricket against odds, and they often came out of the contest with honours.

CHAPTER XXI.

SCHOOL AND VILLAGE MATCHES—THEORIES OF BOWLING.

Honour and shame from no condition rise;
Act well your part, there all the honour lies.—*Pope.*

Reference to Counties not hitherto mentioned—School Cricket—Match between Town Boys and King's Scholars—Cricket Match and Fete Champetre—All Muggleton *v.* Dingley Dell—A Country Cricket Match—Principal Clubs in England—Theories of Bowling—The Catapulta—Curious Bowling Incidents.

NOTWITHSTANDING the large space appropriated to Glances at County Cricket, very much remains to be told did the limits of this work permit. A great deal might be said of Bucks and Herts, which have had annals in their time; of Beds and Hunts, young but striving; of Wilts and Devon, Berks and Dorset; and last, not least, of Worcestershire, with a host of cricketers in one family. Are they not written in the books of the chronicles? What might not be also said of many clubs equal in all the essential attributes of cricket to confront—without professional aid—not a few of the counties. Then of the migratory teams, under the abbreviated titles of I. Z., F. F., Incogs, Wanderers, Butterflies and Grasshoppers, Anomalies many, and Birds not a few. The very number of societies and clubs playing under these designations defy even the barest notice; their play so accords in point of excellence with much that has been advanced respecting counties, that an easy excuse can be found for withholding further mention. Three examples, totally different in their kind, will therefore close this department of the book.

SCHOOL CRICKET.

An anonymous writer on private schools for boys says: "It would be difficult to devise a game better fitted for half-holiday recreation than cricket." The man who invented the game as surely deserves a statue to his memory as he who won Waterloo; for the grand old warrior, in the evening of his days, confessed, with an eager eye and a trembling lip, as he watched the Eton boys scoring their innings in *their* field—the field that led to his—"It was here that Waterloo was won." It is delightful to see with what aptitude and love cricket has been adopted by our schools of all degrees in town and country. It contains just that amount of exertion, diluted by that amount of rest, which it is desirable to give to boys in a sport extending over several hours, with just sufficient vagueness in its laws and regulations to free them from irksomeness in their observance, to give justification to their semi-fulfilment, and yet to have the law "o' our side," with an ample margin for that necessary ingredient in all boys' pastimes—disputation It is pleasant to see the real skill and undoubted dexterity with which the "big fellows" knock the balls about in a cricket match, but I love still better to witness the early efforts of the little embryo cricketer—the exuberant display of unrequired resources—the prodigal expenditure of strength on acts rightly requiring the slightest effort—the uncheckable and unsubduable enthusiasm at the slenderest point gained—the redoubled resolution, heroic and defiant, to retrieve all disasters and mishaps at the next innings A man may get but little real exercise at cricket, but a boy *will* have exercise out of it in one form or another, he runs when for all purposes of the game he might be walking, jumps when he might be standing still, is practising leap-frog with the nearest fielder when he should be keeping a look-out for a catch On the slightest occasion for approval, condemnation, or applause his voice is ready In bowling it is difficult to say what he aims at—the wicket, or its keeper's legs, and as he enjoys the hitting of one as much as the other, it would be uncharitable to suppose he has any partiality either way In batting, if he does not swing himself off his legs, or throw away his bat in the uncontrolledness of his effort, he will get a good six runs for a blow But fielding is his *forte* What a slogan—what a war dance—accompanies a catch! And the throw in; let his side be well content if the ball goes no farther beyond the wicket than the distance from which he has thrown it, let them look sharp, too, about recovering it, for he issues his orders to that effect with the promptness and decision of a sea captain in a gale of wind

TOWN BOYS *v.* KING'S SCHOLARS

From the Manuscript Life of the Hon Percy Hamilton

'As the spring approached, the fine manly and honourable game of cricket commenced, and Kirkonnel and myself were chosen among the eleven of the Town Boys, who, in a few weeks, were to contest for the palm of victory with an equal number of King's Scholars The greatest excitement prevailed throughout the boarding houses and college with respect to the annual trial of skill, and the utmost *esprit de corps* filled the breast of each youthful competitor Every leisure moment was devoted to practice, and as much interest was excited among the old Westminsters as amongst those at that time on the books of the school. The morning at last arrived, and having mustered our forces on the play ground (Tothill Fields), we proceeded to toss up for the first innings We lost the toss, and a shout from the 'tugmuttons' put us on our metal, as two of our best men (?) went in The batting and fielding during the first innings were extremely good, and our scores were nearly equal, the King's Scholars being only five ahead Half an hour was allowed for refreshments, and, unfortunately for our side, a troop of old Westminsters had insisted upon standing some champagne, the question was put to the vote whether we should receive the sparkling liquid when the match was over, or quaff it on the moment. Influenced by the fatigue and heat of a morning's hard work, the proposition for immediate consumption was carried by a large majority, and Frank Alderson and the Hoaxer, who had insisted on keeping the ground from the intrusion of the 'skies,' *id est* 'blackguards,' now acted as butler and drew the well waxed and fastened corks.

> "Fill the cup and let it come,
> I'll pledge you a mile to the bottom,"

spouted the stage-struck hero as he filled our tumblers with Moet's best. The effect which it produced upon us, although we were as sober as judges, was fatal to our side which was now to go in. The juice of the grape had so exhilarated our batsmen that they hit right and left at every ball, and although in some instances they got 'swipers,' viz., three, four, and five runs, upon the whole they could not stand against the sharp bowling of their adversaries. With the fielders, the effect was different; they stopped balls which in their sober senses they must have shrunk from; their legs seemed to have attained increased celerity, and their arms renewed vigour. So wonderful was the prowess, that our eleven wickets went down—many from being run out, a few caught, and the rest bowled—for only 29 runs. The Caps and Gowns now went in, and the fumes of the champagne having entirely evaporated, their steady play soon produced them 25 runs with only one wicket down. The scores were then declared to be, Town Boys, 49 and 29—total 78; King's School, 54 and 25—total 79. Dinner was provided in a large marquee erected for the purpose. Lots of toasts and speechifying took place, some bacchanalian songs were sung, a considerable quantity of old port got 'drunk on the premises,' as were many of those who imbibed it."

CRICKET MATCH AND FÊTE CHAMPÊTRE.

BY JOHN NYREN, AND SENT TO LEIGH HUNT.

"BROMLEY, *June 26th*, 1834.

'The wise men of the East invited me to stand umpire—the Married men against the Bachelors. The day was highly interesting, and I cannot forbear giving you a short account of it. If you can take anything from the description I give you for your paper (*London Journal*), do it in any way you like; this will be only a rough sketch. I call these gentlemen 'the wise men of the East,' as they will not suffer their names in print, and they live at the East end of London. When we arrived at the place of our destination, I was much surprised and delighted at the beautiful scene which lay before me. Several elegant tents gracefully decked out with flags and festoons of flowers had been fitted up for the convenience of the ladies; and many of these, very many, were elegant and beautiful women. *I am not* seventy, and

> The power of beauty I remember yet.

(I am *only* sixty-eight.) Seats were placed beneath the wide-spreading oaks, so as to form groups in the shade Beyond these were targets for ladies *who love archery*, the cricket ground in front

"The carriages poured in rapidly, and each party as they entered the ground was received with loud cheers by such of their friends as had arrived before them At this time a band of music had entered the ground, and I could perceive the ladies' feathers gracefully waving to the music and quite ready for dancing However, the band gave us that fine old tune 'The Roast Beef of Old England'

"We entered a large booth, which accommodated all our party, and a hundred and thirty sat down to the *dejeûné* Our chairman was *Young* but old in experience Many excellent speeches were made, and ever and anon the whole place rang with applause After this the dancing commenced—quadrilles, gallopades, &c, &c It was, without exception, the most splendid sight that I ever witnessed, and reminded one far more of the description we read of fairy land than of any scene in real life The dancing was kept up with great spirit, till the dew of heaven softly descended on the bosoms of our fair countrywomen

"Not a single unfortunate occurrence happened to damp the pleasure of this delightful party Had you been with us you would have sung 'Oh! the pleasures of the plains,' &c, &c Can any party in a house compare with it? God bless you and yours. JOHN NYREN

"P S—The cricket match was well contested, the Bachelors winning by 3 runs only"

ALL MUGGLETON *v* DINGLEY DELL

(By Charles Dickens)

"All Muggleton had the first innings, and the interest became intense when Mr Dunkins and Mr Podder—two of the most renowned members of that most distinguished club—walked bat in hand to their respective wickets Mr Luffey, the highest ornament of Dingley Dell, was pitched to bowl against the redoubtable Dunkins, and Mr Struggles was selected to do the same kind office for the hitherto unconquered Podder Several players were stationed to 'look out' in different parts of the field, and each fixed himself into the proper attitude by placing one hand on each knee and stooping very much as if he were 'making a back' for some beginning at leap-frog All the regular players do this sort of thing, indeed, it is generally supposed that it is quite impossible to look out properly in any other position The umpires were stationed behind the wickets, the scorers were prepared to notch the runs, a breathless silence ensued Mr Luffey retired a few paces behind the wicket of the passive Podder, and applied the ball to his right eye for several seconds Dunkins confidently awaited its coming with his eyes fixed on the motions of Luffey 'Play,' suddenly cried the bowler The ball flew from his hand straight and swift towards the centre stump of the wicket The wary Dunkins was on the alert, it fell upon the tip of his bat and bounded far away over the heads of the scouts who had just stooped low enough to let it fly over them 'Run—run—another Now then, throw her up—up with her—stop there—another—no—yes—throw her up—throw her up!' Such were the shouts which followed the stroke, and at the conclusion of which All Muggleton had scored two. Nor was Podder behindhand in earning laurels wherewith to garnish himself and Muggleton He blocked the doubtful balls, missed the bad ones took the great ones and sent them flying to all parts of the field The scouts were hot and tired, the bowlers were changed, and bowled till their arms ached, but Dunkins and Podder remained unconquered Did an elderly gentleman try to catch the ball? it struck him on the nose and bounded pleasantly off with redoubled violence, while the slim gentleman's eyes filled with water, and his form writhed with anguish Was it thrown straight up to the wicket? Dunkins had reached it before the ball In short, when Dunkins was caught out and Podder stumped out, All Muggleton had notched some fifty-four, while the score of the Dingley Dellers was as blank as their faces The advantage was too great to be recovered

"In vain did the eager Luffey and the enthusiastic Struggles do all that skill and experience could suggest to regain the ground Dingley Dell had lost in the contest, it was of no avail, and in an early period of the winning game Dingley Dell gave in and allowed the superior prowess of All Muggleton The stranger meanwhile had been eating, drinking, and talking without cessation. At every good strike he expressed satisfaction, and approved of the player in a most condescending and patronising manner, which could not fail to have been highly gratifying to the party concerned, while at every bad attempt at a catch, and every failure to stop the ball, he launched his personal displeasure at the head of the devoted individual in such denunciations as 'Ah! ah! stupid. now butter fingers, muff, humbug,' and so forth—ejaculations which seemed to establish him in the opinions of all around as a most excellent and undeniable judge of the whole art and mystery of the noble game of cricket 'Capital game, well played, some strokes admirable,' said the stranger, as both sides crowded into the tent at the conclusion of the game 'You have played it sir,' inquired Mr Wardle, who had been much amused by his loquacity 'Played it! Think I have, thousands of times—not here—West Indies—exciting thing—hot, very'

"'It must be rather a warm pursuit in such a climate,' observed Mr Pickwick 'Warm! red hot—scorching, glowing Played a match once, single wicket—friend to Colonel Sir Thomas Blazo—who should get the greatest number of runs Won the toss—first innings seven o'clock a m—six natives to look out—went in—kept in—heat intense—natives all fainted—taken away—fresh half dozen ordered—fainted also—Blazo bowling, supported by two natives—couldn't bowl me out—fainted too—cleared away—the colonel wouldn't go in—faithful attendant Quanko Samba—last man left—sun so hot—bat in blisters—ball scorched brown—five hundred and seventy runs—rather exhausted—Quanko mustered up last remaining strength—bowled me out—had a bath and went out to dinner'

"'And what became of what's his name, sir?' inquired an old gentleman

"'Blazo?'

"'No, the other gentleman.'

"'Quanko Samba?'

"'Yes, sir'

"'Poor Quanko never recovered it, bowled on on my account, bowled off on his own—died, sir'

"Here the stranger buried his countenance in a brown jug, but whether to hide his emotion or imbibe its contents, we cannot distinctly affirm We only know that he paused suddenly, drew a long deep breath and looked anxiously on as two of the principal members of the Dingley Dell Club approached Mr Pickwick, and said, 'We are about to partake of a plain dinner at the Blue Lion, sir, we hope you and your friends will join us' '—*Pickwick Papers.*

A COUNTRY CRICKET MATCH

(Mary Russell Mitford)

"I doubt if there be any scene in the world more animating or delightful than a cricket match I don't mean a set match at Lord's for money, hard money, between a certain number of gentlemen and players, as they are called—people who make a trade of that noble sport and degrade it into an affair of bettings and hedgings and cheatings nor do I mean a pretty fête in a gentleman's park, where one club of cricketing dandies encounters another such club, and where they show off in graceful costume to a gay marquee of admiring belles who condescend so to purchase admiration and while away a long summer morning in partaking cold collations, converse occasionally, and seem to understand the game, the whole being conducted according to ball-room etiquette, so as to be exceedingly elegant and exceedingly dull No! The cricket that I mean is a real, solid, old-fashioned match between neighbouring parishes, where each attacks the other for honour and a supper, for glory and half-a-crown If there be any gentlemen among them it is well, if not, it is so much the better Elderly gentlemen are obviously good for nothing, and young beaux are for the most part hampered and trammelled by dress and habit—the stiff cravat, the pinched-in waist, the dandy walk Oh! they will never do for cricket Now our country lads, accustomed to the flail or the hammer—your blacksmiths are capital hitters—have the free use of their arms, they know how to move their shoulders, and they can move their feet, too—aye, they can run! Then they are so much better made, more athletic, and yet so much 'lissomer'—to use a Hampshire phrase, which deserves to be good English Here and there, indeed, one meets with an old Etonian who retains his English love for that game which formed so considerable a part of his education some even preserve their boyish proficiency, but in general it wears away like the Greek, quite as certainly and almost as fast A few years of Oxford or Cambridge or the Continent are sufficient to annihilate both the power and the inclination No! a village match is the thing where our highest officer, or conductor—to borrow a musical item—is but a little farmer's second son, where a day labourer is our bowler and a blacksmith our long-stop, where the spectators consist of retired cricketers, the veterans of the green, the careful mothers, the girls and all the boys of the two parishes, together with a few amateurs a little above them in rank, and not at all in pretention, where laughing and shouting and the very ecstacy of merriment and good humour prevail Such a match, in short, as I attended yesterday, at the expense of getting twice wet through, and as I would attend to-morrow at the certainty of having that ducking doubled

"The match was between the A.'s and B.'s The latter, who were the challengers, went in first, and what was the amount of their innings? Think, imagine, guess! You cannot? Well they got 22—or, rather, they got 20—for two of them were short notches, and would never have been allowed only that, seeing what they were made of, we and our umpires were not particular They should have had 20 more if they had chosen to claim them Oh, how well we fielded and how well we bowled! Our good play had quite as much to do with miserable failure as their bad Well, we went in And what our innings? Guess again guess! 169 In spite of soaking showers and wretched ground, where the ball would not run a yard, we headed them by 147, and then they gave in, as well they might The B.'s were beaten, sulky, and would not move I wanted to prolong the pleasure of success What a glorious sensation is it to be for five hours winning, winning, winning! always feeling what a whist-player feels when he takes up four honours seven trumps Who would think that a little bit of leather and two pieces of wood had such a delighting power? Among the spectators nothing remarkable occurred beyond the general calamity of two or three drenchings, except that from a form placed by the side of the hedge under a very insufficient shelter was knocked into the ditch on a sudden rush of the cricketers to escape a pelting shower, by which means all parties floundered about in the mud, making faces and attitudes as laughable as Grimaldi At length we parted, the players retired to their supper and we to our homes, all wet through, all good humoured, and all happy—except the losers"—Extracted from "Our Village"

AN EDITOR'S DESCRIPTION OF A MATCH AT BOMBAY

"We went to look on at the cricket match between Naval and Military and an eleven of the Bombay Gymkhana We arrived just as Carmichael Young (with marvellous punctuality for Bombay) had won the toss for choice of innings, and were then accommodated with a comfortable long chair inside the tent, wherein we smoked our Regalia *en prince*, with our long, and, alas! not-quite-so-strong-as-they-used-to-be legs stretched out in front of us Wyer and Gell bowled throughout the innings, both well on the spot, and succeeded in disposing of their opponents for the small total of 48 runs, Gell getting three wickets in three consecutive balls! for which feat he has been presented with a new and very expensive helmet Duration of innings, one hour twenty minutes This pair also went first to the wickets to represent Bombay. Curtis and Boothe bowling Gell hit the first ball of Curtis' first over away to long leg for 6, and the first ball of his second over Wyer crumped in the same direction for 8—a stupendous smite Commander Dacres threw his arm out, he said, and 'wait field'—long leg again in a hurry, we fear The warrior from Colaba looked chagrined, and changed ends, when the bowling got more on the spot Gell feeling tired, sat on his wicket for taking which liberty the umpire very properly gave him out The 'glorious Tennent' next appeared, and began very shakily indeed, but encouraged by the manifest disinclination of the opposition to accept the chances he offered them, he warmed to his work, and, with Wyer, hit the score up to 88, when the latter was had at point for 42 runs 'The rest is silence' The wickets went down like ninepins before Tims the destructive, and the innings lasted just long enough to admit of Tennent making his 50—a very creditable performance—total 121, or 73 runs ahead Duration of innings one hour and a half Tiffin—duration of tiffin two hours Certain young fellows retired to the Bombay Club and stayed there The time was whiled away by the other athletes—some in this way, some in that others in chatting about old times over a friendly glass of sherry Ourselves smoked another Regalia and went to sleep We were awakened by the shout which hailed the truants' return, who came swaggering gaily in, good as gold 'So sorry,' they said, and laughed Dr Arnott and Bird began well, and smacked both bowlers freely. Plumer played a careful innings of 19, and Tims a brilliant one of 64 runs without a chance that we could see, although all the bowling resources of the opposition were brought into play Gell was luckily on the spot, but Wyer and all the rest were not Commander Dacres came at the last with a useful, though, perhaps, a trifle lucky innings of 26 not out, and bringing the total up to 172 runs—exactly 100 runs ahead Only ten minutes play remained, but Bombay lost two wickets for 10 runs, and had time allowed the result would probably have been very close. The fielding on the whole was good, notably that of Tennent the fleet at long leg, Brooke at cover point was very active It was a very pleasant match altogether, and we recommend anyone with a holiday on his hands, as we had, to go and spectate on a cricket match If the gentleman who walked off by mistake with our bran new helmet will kindly reproduce it he will get his own rascally old topi back from Mr Talkajee at the Bombay Gymkhana tent"

Many wandering clubs are known by distinct and often very peculiar dresses—in some instances amounting to the grotesque Others, having a fixed locality for their matches, provide themselves with flags or bannerets, with mottoes A few are given as specimens —

Name	Place	Colours	Mottoes
Basingstoke	Basingstoke	Violet and white	
Beckenham	Beckenham	Black, blue, and white	
Beverley	Canterbury	Beverley Arms	Nulli secundus
Brasenose College	Oxford	Black and gold	
Brighton College	Kemp Town	Violet and white	
Caius College	Cambridge		Labor ipse voluntas
Cambridge University	Cambridge	Light blue	
Cardiff	Cardiff	Blue and brown	
Charterhouse School	Godalming	Pink	
Cheltenham College	Cheltenham	Red and black	
Christ Church	Oxford	Black and white	
Cirencester	Cirencester	Red and black	
Civil Service	Battersea Park	Blue and gold	
Civil Service (Dublin)	Phœnix Park	Scarlet and black	

Name	Place	Colours	Mottoes
Clapton	Hackney	White	
Clifton	Bristol	Black and yellow	
Clifton College	Bristol	White and blue	
Colchester and E Essex	Colchester	Black, French grey, and	
Cowes	Cowes	Red and white	
Derby	Derby	White	
Doncaster Grammar Sch	Doncaster	Blue, white, and gold	
Ely	Ely	Cherry and French	
Eton College	Eton	Light Blue	Floreat Etona
Felstead School	Felstead	Dark blue	
Free Foresters		Crimson and green	United though untied.
Glamorganshire	Glamorgan	Badge with County Arms	
Guildford	Guildford	Crimson, black, and salmon	
Guildford Grammar Sch	Guildford	Blue and gold cross on cap	
Hackwood Park	Basingstoke		
Hampton Wick	Hampton	Blue, white, and orange	
Harlequins		Dark blue, red and mauve	
Harlow College	Harlow	Crimson and black	
Harrow School	Harrow	Dark blue and white	Stet fortuna domus
Heversham Grammar Sch	Malnthorpe	Black and white	
Hornsey	Hornsey	Crimson and blue	Concordia crescimus
Hunts	Huntingdon		Sigillum communitatis de Huntersal
Islington Albion	Wood Green		
Jesus Coll (Cambridge)	Cambridge	Scarlet and black	
Jesus Coll (Oxford)	Oxford	White trimmed with green	
Kent County	Brighton	Dark blue and white	
Lancing College	Shoreham	Dark blue and white	
Malvern College	Great Malvern	Magenta, blue, and fawn	
Marlborough College	Marlborough	Broad blue and white stripe	Majores majora sonent
Marlow	Great Marlow	Blue and white hoops	
Marylebone	St John's Wood	Red and yellow	Monogram M C C
Military College Club			Vires acquirit eundo
Mitcham	Mitcham	Dark blue	
Moor Park	Rickmansworth	Blue and orange	
Newcastle	Newcastle	Blue and white	
Oakfield	Croydon	Violet and yellow	
Oaks	Clapham	Blue and white	
Perse School	Cambridge	Mauve, black, and white	
Private Banks	Catford Bridge	Scarlet and silver grey	
Queen's College (Oxford)	Oxford	Blue and white	
Quidnuncs		Dark blue, black and yellow stripe	
Ravenscourt Park	Turnham Green	Dark mauve and light blue	
Repton School	Willington	Magenta and white	
Royal Engineers	Chatham	Red and black	Qui fas et gloria ducunt
Rossall School	Rossall	Dark blue and white	
Rugby School	Rugby	Light blue shirts and cap	
Savernake Forest	Marlborough	Blue and white	
Stockport	Stockport	White and blue	
St John's Coll (Camb)	Cambridge		Sigillima pro oratus sanctæ legæ
St Bees, Sunderland	Sunderland	White	

Name	Place	Colours	Mottoes
Surrey County Club .	Kennington Oval		
The Vyne . .	Basingstoke	Red and gold	
Uppingham School			
Westminster School . .	Westminster	Pink . .	In patriam populumque
Winchester School	Winchester		Manners makyth man
Zingari ...	Hic et ubique	Red, black, and gold .	

THEORIES OF BOWLING

So much has been said and written from time to time upon this subject that ingenuity is at fault to discover a fresh mode of treatment Even the diagrams which usually accompany almost every essay, whether upon a large or small scale, exhibit a strong family likeness of an ancient sire. Two generations cannot, however, have come and gone without leaving some traces of improvement The bowling in the early part of the present century must have been very different to that of fifty or seventy years later In the meantime, who can tell now what theories might have been propounded and brought into exercise, more especially after the "new system" became sanctioned by law? In some cases some of the most ridiculous means were adopted to ends quite unattainable To bowl at a "lightning pace" was a great object, whether the physical condition of the man was in keeping or no "The pace that kills" was a coveted theory Others went in for "pitch," which by practice might be acquired, nearly always on a given spot, rarely on *the* spot, a third studied straightness, very commendable with other requisites, a fourth altogether deficient in this particular, but effective on account of some "crooked wisdom" in the delivery of the ball These and other matters akin to bowling have been enunciated without proving how an aspirant can by any amount of application become a proficient in the art Many have tried without possessing the natural gift, and have failed, others have found themselves almost unconsciously in the possession of it Hence the varieties of style, which cannot be the result of any particular system of teaching The underhand bowler of the present day is pretty much the same as in those of Nyren and Lambert To lay down a hard and fast line for bowlers would be one of the silliest of proceedings, seeing that scarcely two in ten are exactly alike in style, physique, and mental endowments

Although this is an age of devices, it has produced no mechanical contrivance for determining what is called "pace" with reference to the velocity of a cricket ball Hence abstract terms are used, such as slow underhand, slow round arm, medium pace, fast, very fast, &c , but often all these terms are arbitrary, for what may appear fast to one person may be mid pace to another person's thinking, and to another slow may approach to fast

A bowler can lay down no dogmas for instance, if that a ball must pitch between this line and that line, and that if it pitches here you are to hit it, and if there you are to block it, for he knows that a tall player will easily drive a ball forward, which a short one must play back The esoteric doctrine of a well-known professional at one time was, "Listen all ye bowlers who stick a feather in the ground and then try to hit it as if ye were playing at quoits, that there is really no such a thing as a good ball at all abstractedly considered, but there is one sure criterion of one, 'Did it get a wicket?' If it did, it was a good ball wherever pitched, if it failed, though it passed one half inch over the bails and no more, the less said about it the better" Another questionable piece of advice from the same quarter is, "If you have a batsman who is perpetually shifting himself before his wicket, bowl at his legs below *the knee*, and upon hitting them appeal immediately to the umpire at your end, and if the ball is pitched in a line with the wicket, the umpire will give him out"

The great evil in bowling generally is the peril resulting from pace, and, strange to say, a much higher premium is offered for the fast man with his attendant wildness than for the steadier process, which in the long run pays best It may be all very well to talk of the English pluck that will "kiss the cannon's mouth," but that pluck may be played the fool with in a comparatively civil strife like cricket The uncertain course a ball frequently takes when propelled by a strong arm and an energetic impulse, overtaxes the keenest eye and maturest judgment, and the chances are quite as often in favour of the batsman, from the erratic course the ball takes, as in that of the bowler, from the ripping style in which a wicket is occasionally torn down Straightness, with variety of pitch, pays better as a rule than the arrow's swiftness with the uncertainty of a boomerang It is a maxim laid down by the best of cricketers that a bowler, like a poet, "nascitur non fit" He may by steady practice become an average batsman, but without talent for bowling he can never be taught to excel

John Nyren says "The best method of holding the ball to bowl is between the thumb and fingers, firmly enough to steady it, yet that it may leave the hand with ease When practising, let the bowler always use a ball of the required weight, and measure the exact distance that is settled from one wicket to the other—viz, two-and-twenty yards If his pace be moderately fast, he should endeavour to pitch the ball about four yards and a-half before the wicket, if it be slow, somewhat nearer, and in swift bowling not farther off than five yards The young practitioner cannot do better than to place a mark upon the ground at the stated distance from the wicket, according to the speed at which he intends to bowl, and to aim at that mark In a match, when running to bowl, he should fix his eye upon a certain spot where he is desirous the ball should pitch; there will be no difficulty in selecting an object for the purpose of a guide, either a difference in the colour of the grass, or a slight unevenness in the ground will answer the purpose. This is a rule from which he should not deviate, all the finest bowlers I have known have pursued this plan, for, if the length be correct according to his rate of bowling he can do no better than adhere to that distance He should also habituate himself to bowl with equal ease on either side of the wicket, he will experience the advantage of such practice, for he will frequently notice that the ground on one side will prove more favourable to his play than on the other, it may happen also that upon trying the two he will

SLOW, EITHER UNDER OR OVER HAND

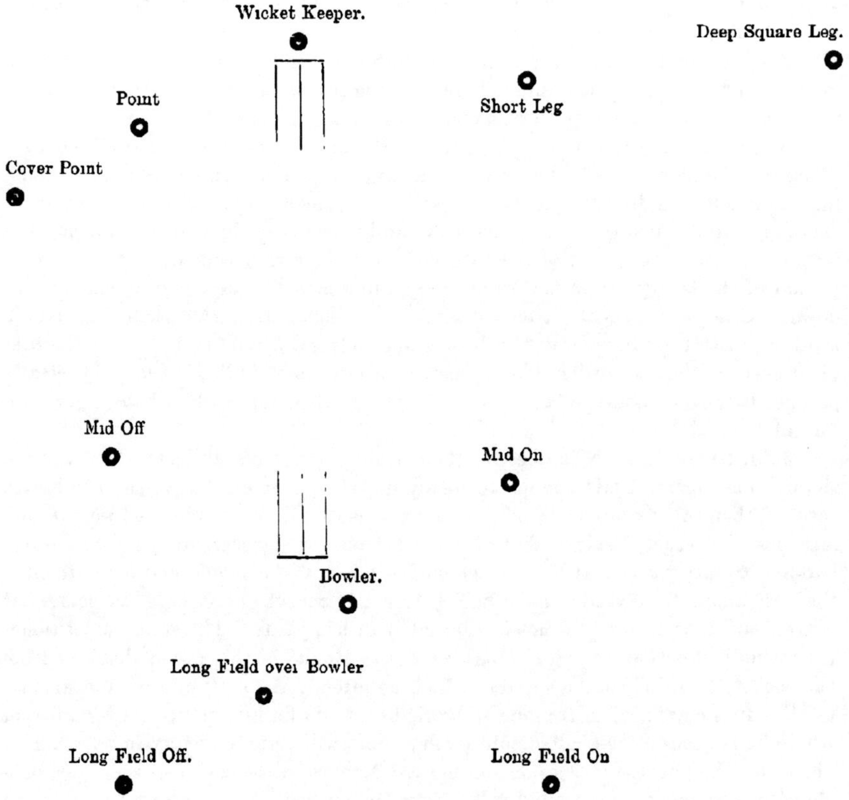

Wicket Keeper.

Deep Square Leg.

Point

Short Leg

Cover Point

Mid Off

Mid On

Bowler.

Long Field over Bowler

Long Field Off.

Long Field On

perceive the ball to rise better on one side than the other of the wicket All these things will turn to the young bowler's account if he play *with his head* as well as his hands Besides, changing the side of the wicket is never agreeable to the batsman. A quick eye, with practised observation, will induce the bowler early to detect the weak points of his adversary; let him not neglect this, and then regulate his balls accordingly A good length ball now and then pitched a little wide of the off-stump will often turn to a great advantage, for it may produce a catch when a straight one may be stopped with ease In his little book upon cricketing, Lambert has laid down some useful instructions on bowling I cannot, however, approve of his recommending the young player to give a *twist* to his balls, for, in the first place, there are a hundred chances against his accomplishing the art, and ten hundred in favour of the practice spoiling his bowling altogether I never perceived any twist in Lambert's own bowling unless, indeed, the ground was in his favour If the young practitioner have once gained a good high delivery, let him never run the risk of losing it, for in this department of the game it is the greatest gift he can possess It is not the least important objection I have to offer against the system to say that it reduces the strikers too much to an equality, since the indifferent batsman possesses as fair a chance of success as the most refined player, and the reason of this is obvious, because, from the random manner of delivering the ball, it is impossible for the fine batsman to have time for that finesse and delicate management which so particularly distinguished the elegant manœuvring of the chief players who occupied the field ten years ago If, therefore, the present system be persisted in a few years longer, the elegant and scientific game of cricket will decline into a mere exhibition of coarse horse play"—*Cricketer's Guide*, 1840

"The difficulty of playing the overhand bowling," says Mr. Denison, "consists, in the first place, that the ball is rarely overpitched, and if a little underpitched, the quickness and height of the rebound covers the error; 2, that the being delivered at a greater height the rebound is higher; 3, that it admits of more bias, and lastly, that the ball has more rotary motion round its own axis, which gives greater quickness and variety after the ball pitches"

The weak point in many young bowlers is to imitate the bowling of a giant, with but half his physical strength Seize every available opportunity for practice bowling, but let it be round and slow, and it will not long go unrewarded Still, after all, bowling is a "gift"

Reverting to the diagrams, it may be said once for all that they have little if any claim to originality, and merely represent on paper the ordinary stations appointed to fielders at the outset of the game, and previous to the estimate of the bowler's tactics or the batsman's skill Upon these points hinge the shifts of the fielders. Some matches would last for "ever and a day," were not devices of this kind resorted to In the year 1853, it was discussed whether twelve aside ought not to form the orthodox number. This arose from what was deemed the necessity for a middle wicket man on the "on side," and the equally pressing call for a third man up Many chances, 'twas said, are missed if there be only two men in the slips, and many rash "skyers" go unpunished if the whole "on" side in front of

MID PACE ROUND ARM

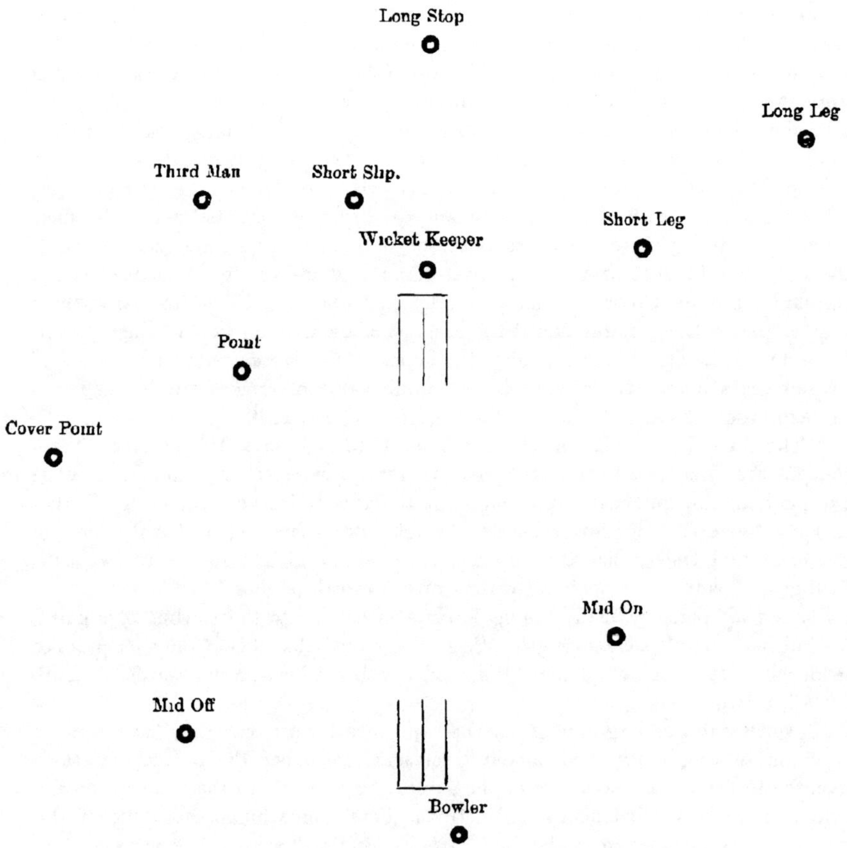

Long Stop

Long Leg

Third Man

Short Slip.

Short Leg

Wicket Keeper

Point

Cover Point

Mid On

Mid Off

Bowler

the wicket has to be defended by the bowler alone. The proposition was not adopted in words, but as will be seen in the diagrams, the suggestion is acted upon whenever circumstances demand it. Some of the best bowlers are at times extremely self willed and perverse, they don't like the idea of being taken off. They may possess so much of the gifts of pitch and straightness as to bowl five, ten, or fifteen maiden overs in succession; but while this pounding away serves to display skill, it retards the progress of the game and weakens the attacking parties without a corresponding reward.

THE CATAPULTA.

About forty years ago Mr. Felix suggested the application of the Roman catapult to the purposes of propelling the cricket ball, and a few years later Caldecourt, at that time one of the "ground" at Lord's, and a good bat maker withal, simplified the machine. The great object of the instrument was the facility it afforded for practice, and on this account it received a liberal share of patronage.

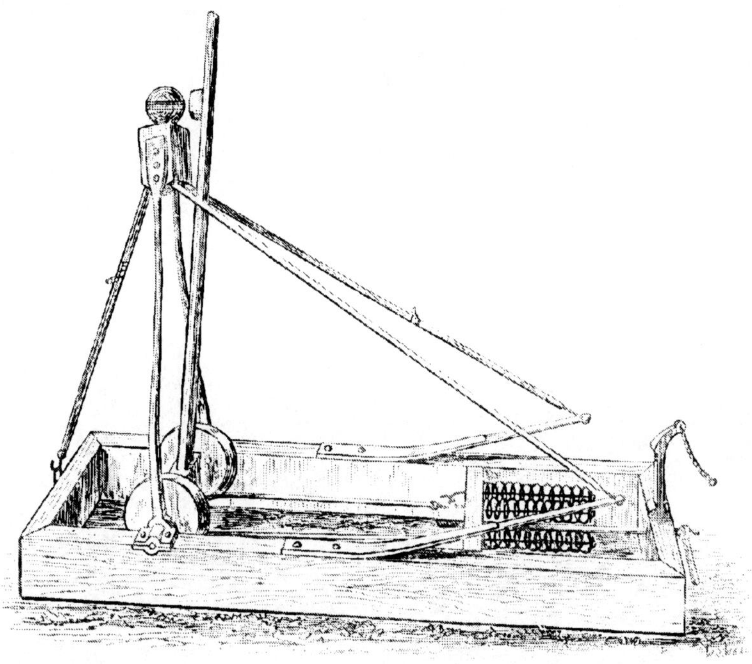

Many differences of opinion arose respecting the real merits of the catapulta as a bowling substitute. The reader will be able to draw an opinion for himself from the two extracts given. "This instrument is accredited to Mr. Felix, who, according to his own showing, borrowed the idea from the resources of the beleagured Archimedes and irresistible Marcellus for the more friendly encounter of the cricket

MID PACE LEFT HAND BOWLER

Long Stop

Third Man

Short Slip

Wicket Keeper

Point

Leg

Cover Point

Short Mid Off

Mid Off

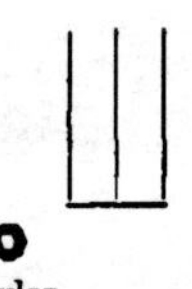

Mid On

Bowler

field, diverting the attacks from which 'tower and temple went to the ground,' to the more humble task of lowering obstinate wickets. Get it to a severe pace and a good pitch, and steady indeed must be the player who can do much execution against it. The catapult may be regarded as a most useful invention, and a benefaction to the cricketing world, valuable everywhere but doubly so to country clubs, which cannot always command the services of a good hired bowler to practice against. As there is little in it to wear out, it is in the end cheap; and though not quite as good practice as a first rate bowler because a ball does not certainly come from it in quite the same manner as it does from the hand, still it is not without some advantages over the best of them. It never tires, is never ill, it can bowl even after wet, and it can adapt its pace without spoiling its pitch to suit any degree of proficiency.' Another writer in the *Sporting Magazine*, 1838, says: "I allude to the catapulta, a convenient instrument, which will make any man with eyes in his head a bowler! Let them have a railroad for the ball to run upon, and the thing is complete. As to the invention, I doubt not the ingenuity, but I sincerely hope that it will never supersede Nature's catapulta—a free shoulder, with its proper appendages; a strong arm, and a steady hand."*

Great Bowling Feats.—On the 5th of September 1826, in a match on Uxbridge Common between the Etonian Club and Eleven Gentlemen of Uxbridge, Mr. H. Brandt bowled eight of the Uxbridge wickets in twelve balls without a single run being got.—*Sporting Magazine*, Oct., 1826, p. 444.

Ringwood, of Cambridge, in the month of August, 1840, at Saffron Walden, disposed of one innings by bowling all the wickets.

In the month of July, 1848, Hinkly got all the wickets of a single innings.

A greater feat was accomplished by Wisden, at Lord's, July, 1850, in a match North *v.* South. He clean bowled all the wickets in the second innings of the South.

1871.—In the University match at Lords, Mr. Butler got all the wickets.

Among the *mirabile dictu* of A.D. 1872 was the bowling of Armitage in a match at Keighley, between Wakefield and Keighley. Score:—

WAKEFIELD

	1st inn.		2nd inn.
H. Grist, c Smith, b Armitage	11	b Armitage	0
J. W. Bradley, b Armitage	29	b Armitage	6
W. Catley, c and b Armitage	2	c Wild, b Armitage	0
H. Whitehead, c and b Bolsover	2	c Widdop, b Armitage	14
J. E. Bradley, b Armitage	2	b Armitage	1
A. Knowles, c and b Armitage	0	c Widdop, b Armitage	2
J. F. Clegg, c Waring, b Bolsover	0	b Armitage	3
W. Bennett, b Armitage	5	not out	0
L. Jackson, c and b Armitage	14	b Armitage	6
H. Marriner, l b w, b Armitage	0	c Butterfield, b Armitage	3
J. H. Wallis, not out	4	b Armitage	1
Byes 2, l b 1	3	Leg-bye	1
Total	72	Total	37

* There is a patented catapulta altogether different in its construction, portable, and much cheaper.

FAST, TO A RIGHT-HANDED BATSMAN.

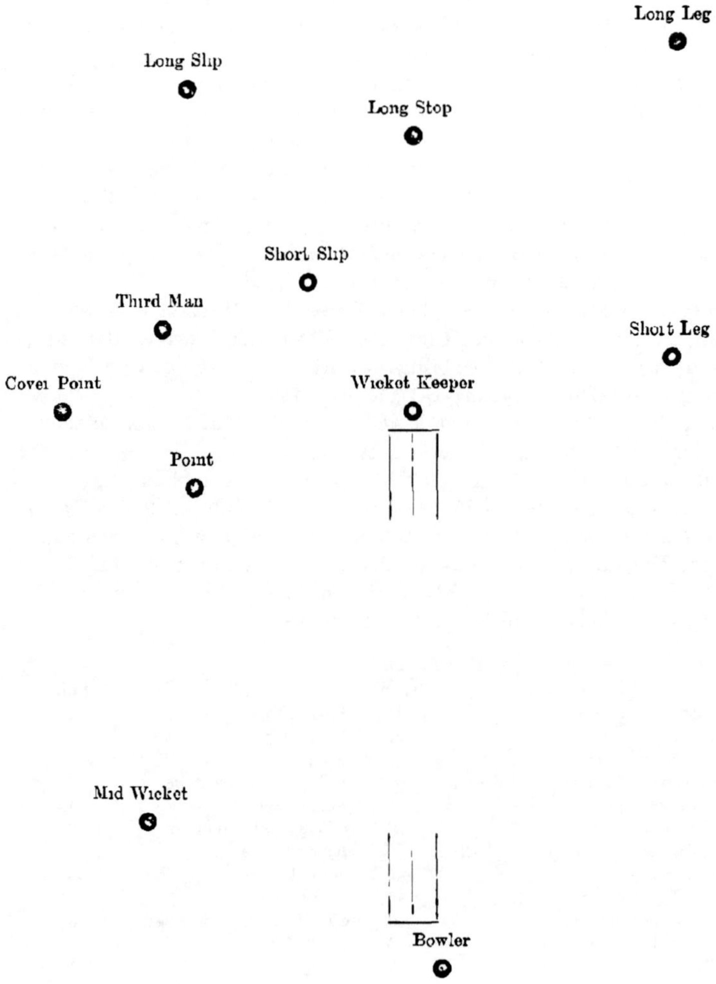

Long Leg

Long Slip

Long Stop

Short Slip

Third Man

Short Leg

Cover Point

Wicket Keeper

Point

Mid Wicket

Bowler

In 1872 (August 6), James Lillywhite got all the wickets.

Richmond Club *v.* The Owls (1873).—Mr. E. C. Bovill obtained all the Richmond wickets (six clean bowled).

In a match played at Portsmouth, May 23, 1873, between Havant and Portsmouth Port and Garrison, Private Burtsell bowled five wickets in seven balls, without a run.

On the 28th of July, 1873, M.C.C. and Ground played the Gentlemen of Worcestershire at Boughton, when Farrands obtained all the Worcestershire wickets (five clean bowled).

Eleven Players *v.* Sixteen of the Crystal Palace Club (1873).—In this affair Mr. G. H. Clote took all the wickets of the Players (seven clean bowled).

Mr. J. St. Boultbee got all the wickets in an innings when Oakfield played the St. John's Wood Club, in 1873.

As a veteran bowler, Mr. Charles Absolon distinguished himself above all others during the year 1873. In a match at Shoreham with a neighbouring parish he obtained seventeen wickets out of twenty; and in another match at Southgate he also obtained seventeen wickets. During the season in question Mr. Absolon bowled in sixty innings, with an average of more than six wickets per innings.

A short time since (1874), in a match between the Gentlemen and Players, at Lord's, Allan Hill, a very fast bowler, took three wickets in three successive balls, and obtained a new hat in consequence. This feat is chiefly notable when the three batsmen are considered, viz., Messrs. Hornby, Ridley, and I. D. Walker. It moreover turned the tide of success in the direction of the players, who had been beaten for seven years previously.

A very remarkable bowling feature characterised a match played on the 24th of June, 1874, at Aldington, near Hythe, between eleven of Smeeth and eleven of Willesborough, when Mr. E. G. Blomfield, of Trinity College, Oxford, bowled seven wickets in 8 overs (maidens) without a run.

In a match at Hong Kong, on the 31st of October, 1874, an officer attached to the 80th regiment, bowled a fast underhand and knocked the middle stump clean out of the ground, but both bails remained undisturbed.

In the match at Lords, between the M.C.C. and Ground and the County of Notts (1875), Alfred Shaw obtained seven wickets for 7 runs in 41 overs and two balls (36 maidens). Four months subsequently the same bowler obtained seventeen wickets in a match between North and South Notts. Of this number, nine were clean bowled and eight caught off him. The same bowler, in the year 1870, greatly distinguished himself in a match between the M.C.C. and Ground and Thornton Hall, when he claimed nine wickets in each innings, the latter innings at an average of 2 runs per wicket.

CHAPTER XXII.

CURIOSITIES OF CRICKET.

A thing of beauty is a joy for ever,
Its loveliness increases; it will never
Pass into nothingness.—*Keats.*

Female Matches—Cricket on the Ice—On the Sands—Long Scores and Short Scores—Long Hits, Long Innings, Long Throws—Matches for Money—Family Matches—Deaths from the Cricket Ball, &c.

In looking through this chapter, the reader may probably find a few things to smile at, many that will tax his belief to a considerable extent, and some to ponder over. Now, as faith is an act of the mind, no harm can be done by giving it a little exercise, *cum grano salis.* Some of the statements are avouched by written authority, others are traditional, and, perhaps, have gathered a trifle in their float down the stream of time. What has occurred may be repeated, and if so, doubts hitherto existing in the minds of many will perchance give way. The curiosities, such as they are, might be multiplied to a great extent were any important end to be gained thereby. The few here given, it is hoped, will suffice.

In the month of June, 1797, a match between eleven married women of the parish of Bury and eleven maidens, which was won by the former, whose notches at the conclusion of the game outnumbered those which the maidens got by 80. So famous are the Bury women at a cricket match, that they offer to play with any eleven in any village in their county, for any sum. (See also "Common Place Book," by R. Southey, Poet-Laureate.)

Amazonian Match.—A very extraordinary performance took place in the month of October, 1811, at Ball's Pond, between two female elevens selected from the county of Surrey and Hampshire. The match was promoted by two noblemen, and the stakes were stated to be no less than 500 guineas. Owing to some misunderstanding, the places and dates of the contest were shifted. The spacious ground was enlivened with marquees and booths well supplied with gin, beer, and gingerbread. The performers were of all ages and sizes—from fourteen to sixty; the young had shawls, and the old long cloaks. The Hampshire were distinguished by the colour of *true blue,* which was pinned in their bonnets in the shape of the Prince's plume. The Surrey were equally as smart; their colours were blue surmounted with orange The Surrey side consisted of Ann Baker (60 years of age, the best bowler and runner of the side), Ann Taylor, Mary Barfutt, Hannah Higgs, Elizabeth Gale, Hannah Collas, Hannah Bartlett, Maria Cooke, Charlotte Cooke, Elizabeth Stick, and Mary Fry Hampshire Sarah Luff, Charlotte Pulbain, Hannah Parker, Elizabeth Smith, Martha Smith, Mary Woodson, Nancy Porter, Ann Poulters, Mary Nevile, Mary Hislock, and Mary Jongan Very good play took place at starting, one of the Hampshire lasses made 40—one innings—before she was thrown out, at the conclusion of the day's sport, the Hampshire lasses were 81 ahead The unfavourableness of the weather prevented any more sport that day, though the ground was filled with spectators On the following day the Surrey lasses kept the field with great success, and on Monday, the 7th, being the last day to decide the contest, an unusual assemblage of vehicles of all descriptions surrounded the ground by eleven o'clock, tandems, dog carts, hackney coaches, &c, formed a complete ring, several handsome females, dressed in azure blue mantles, graced these vehicles The Earl of Barrymore, in a single horse chaise, was amongst the spectators At three o'clock the match was won by the Hampshire lasses, who, not being willing to leave at so early an hour, played a single wicket game, in which they were also successful An engraving of this extraordinary affair may be seen in the print room of the British Museum The squatters on the ground, with their notched sticks and the two stumps, indicate to some extent the condition of cricket at the period when Rowlandson sketched the play

On the 23rd of May, 1823, at Hockwood-cum-Walton, Norfolk, eleven married and eleven single females played for eleven pairs of gloves, when the former won. They were dressed in jackets and trousers, tastefully decorated with blue ribbon —*Sporting Magazine* June, 1823, p 164.

On Monday, August 4th, 1823, a match was played at Buckland, in Kent, between ten married and ten single women employed in the paper mills there It was contested with uncommon spirit on both sides, the single women beating by about 20 runs They got 113 in their second innings

In a ladies' school near Frome the pupils are allowed to play cricket They have a special dress for the purpose, and the best cricketers are said to be the best scholars —*Shepton Mallet Journal*, 1868. In another establishment a few sedate folk objected to the practice of such a "tomboy game," but was rebuked by a youngster, who said "It makes girls who play it stronger than others, and not so lackadaisical"

The *Melbourne Argus* of the 21st of April, 1874, publishes the following 'A cricket match of a novel description has been played at Sandhurst, with the object of swelling the funds of the local charities The players were ladies, who went into regular practice for the match, and the progress which they made was astonishing, for they picked up the points of the game with wonderful aptitude. At first it was expected that they should play in the Bloomer costume, as being less likely to interfere with their freedom of movement than any other, but the innovation was considered too startling for a British community, and the idea was given up in favour of an attire of the ordinary shaped dress, made of calico, with a coloured jacket to distinguish the respective sides Everything being in readiness, the ladies—the one side wearing red Garibaldi jackets and sailors' hats, and the other blue jackets and similar hats—marched in pairs—red and blue being linked together—from the tent into the field, headed by their captains Their appearance was very picturesque, and they were loudly applauded by the on-lookers The reds first handled the bat; and they secured a total of 62 runs before the last wicket fell After the lapse of half an hour the reds took the field and they put their opponents out for 83 runs One innings each only was played When the ladies had assembled in the booth, Mr Abbott, chairman of the Hospital Committee, thanked them for the successful effort which they had made on behalf of the charities Mrs Rae replied, stating that the ladies had thoroughly enjoyed the game, and had the utmost gratification of knowing that their efforts had been productive of a substantial addition to the funds of the charities"

A match was played on the ice at Harewood in Yorkshire on the 15th of February, 1838, between Harewood and Stark The former scored 486 runs in a completed innings the latter 212, with six wickets to fall A man named Barrett made 13 runs from one hit

The Sheffield Skating Club played a match on the ice on skates at Chatsworth, the seat of the Duke of Devonshire, on the 1st of March, 1848 The ice was in splendid condition and smooth as a piece of glass After the first innings, the parties retired to a tent, fixed on the edge of the dam, and partook of an excellent lunch The game was renewed, and the balls played with were made of gutta percha The frost had a tendency to make them hard, and very sharp hitting caused them to break The sides were headed by Messrs J and M Dodsworth One side totalled 150, the other, 162 —*Sporting Magazine*

Matches on the Ice —On the 15th of January, 1851, the "Long Meadow," at Oxford, being covered with a thick coat of ice, a match was got up, and headed by Messrs Bacon and Turner It lasted a whole day, when an innings by each party was concluded Mr Bacon's side totalled 126 runs, Mr. Turner's 128 Among the hits was one drive for 10 runs The match caused great excitement in the City, and hundreds of people were present to remark on its progress Notwithstanding the expertness of the players in skating, the falls were numerous, but no bones were broken

In the first week of January, 1854, the weather was so intensely cold that the large reservoir at Daventry was covered with ice of sufficient thickness to play a match of cricket upon it The game was sustained with great vigour throughout a whole day.

Within the last five years "ice matches" were frequently got up on the "spur," *i e*, in a hurry Some of these were neither devoid of incident nor attraction Mention may be made of one in Cambridgeshire, if only for the humorous description given of it by a journalist who accompanied a portion of the players to and from the scene of action —"Never were winds more boisterous than when we started from the Cambridge station for the fens of Swavesey. Vegetation was asleep except a few hard hearted cabbages in the ghost of a garden, and, saving one or two rooks, not a bird was to be seen, much less heard Certainly there were several flocks of sheep, but even they looked disconsolate over a bad breakfast Not a chimney seemed to have filled its pipe till the 'smoke so gracefully curls' Arrived at the destination, the ground looked not at all unlike so many puddles of soapsuds. The scene which presented itself was original, animated, and in some respects curious Close by the water, and protected by a little clump of bushes and trees, were what appeared to be the remains of an old cart shed 'faked up,' to use a rustic expression, with odd pieces of sacking The interior, together with the outside, was well littered with straw This 'carpet' was crowded with numerous chairs whereon sat ladies and gentlemen having their skates adjusted Viewed from a humourist point, the place seemed to be the remains of a farm-yard invaded by a troop of cordwainers bent upon driving a roaring trade, as each customer appeared to be trying on a shoe at the hands of his or her attendant 'snob' Proceeding by the ice to the wickets the winds increased in such force and sharpness that it was difficult to make any advance unless by a 'shack' At length the wickets, fixed in blocks of wood, were, by the aid of big lumps of earth, made able to stand alone *minus* the bails The match to be played was between eleven University and All England players and Sixteen of the neighbourhood of Swavesey, which included several members of the colleges The Sixteen went in first and scored 125 runs in one hour and a half Mr Baker made one hit for 12 and another for 9 Mr Graham, of Trinity Hall, was not out for 24 The ice was smooth as glass All the fielders wore skating pattens The Eleven put together 230 in less than two hours Pryor started with a 7, Hayward carried out his bat for 52, composed of five fours, four threes, five twos, and singles, Smith retired after putting together 51, by an eight, a six, five fours, &c There were only eight wickets down when the match was given up for want of daylight. Score as follows

THE SIXTEEN

J Nightingale, run out	1
M J Barker, b Pryor	5
M C Baker, c Sounders, b Masterson	77
P Coleman, b Carpenter	0
M D Long, l b w, b Carpenter	0
E Prince, b Masterson	8
W Tomkins, run out	1
R Fisher, b Carpenter	3
H B Jones, c Carpenter, b Masterson	1
G Graham, not out	24
C S Williams, run out	0
W Cox, st Carpenter, b Masterson	3
E Tompson, b Masterson	0
J Masters, run out	0
W Brown, b Carpenter	0
J Masterson, run out	1
No ball	1
Total	125

THE ELEVEN.

W. Newman, st Graham, b Masterson	0
J. Newman, b Masterson	8
F. Pryor, b Masterson	37
J. Fordham, b Masterson	11
E. Carpenter, l b w, b Masterson	1
W. Saunders, c Masterson, b Graham	11
D. Hayward, run out	10
G. Masterson, l b w, b Graham	4
J. Smith, retired	51
R. West, not out	27
T. Hayward, not out	52
Byes 11, l-b 4, w 2, n-b 1	18
Total	230

Long scores were not unknown in the early days of scientific cricket; for, in a match between Surrey and Sussex (1792), the latter put together a total of 453 in one innings, of which T. Walker claimed 138.

A match was played at Salisbury, June 6th, 1793, by ten of the neighbourhood of Tedworth against twenty-two of Milton and Pewsey, which resulted in favour of Tedworth by 88 notches. One of the ten got more notches in the last innings than the whole twenty-two.

A match very remarkable for its long score occurred at Cambridge on the 4th and 8th of August, in the year 1868, between the University Long Vacation Club and the United College Servants. The L. V. C. started the batting, and the two early wickets fell without a run; the third realised but sixteen, and the fifth 79. Then followed tremendous hitting, as no less than 287 runs were added before the sixth wicket was captured. The next advanced the score to 597; eighth, 654; ninth, 677; tenth, 689. The score is worthy of preservation.

THE UNIVERSITY.

Mr. F. J. Hall, l b w, b Mason	0
Mr. T. B. Nichols, b Newman	0
Mr. A. W. Spratt, b Mason	12
Mr. W. J. Batchelor, b Coulson	289
Mr. C. Saxton, c and b Mason	13
Mr. E. M. Tims, b Thomas	18
Mr. A. E. Tillard, b Mason	152
Mr. W. A. Prince, c Gray, b Thomas	114
Mr. E. A. Bennett, not out	46
Mr. J. Collin, c Edmunds, b Coulson	2
Mr. H. C. Winter, b Thomas	4
Byes 21, l-b 3, w 10, n b 5	39
Total	689

Ten bowlers were engaged, and 204 overs and one ball delivered. Only ten maidens occurred during the innings, which occupied the greater part of two long days.*

The average of Mr. Batchelor in the L. V. matches was rather more than 106 runs per innings during the season in question.

* Authenticated by Mr. E. A. Bennett, M.A., of Emmanuel College.

In a match at Lord's, August, 1815, Middlesex (with Robinson) *v.* Epsom (with Mann), the following results are recorded —Middlesex, 51 and 67—total 118, Epsom, 476 The latter won by an innings and 358 runs

This was the largest, till June, 1859, when an Oxford Eleven scored 546 for seven wickets

Coulston Park *v.* Harrow Blues, played July 25th, 1844 C P put together 315 runs for three wickets at the call of time and the discontinuance of the game

In a match between the two "houses" at Marlborough College, June, 1866, a boy named Mornington scored 274 runs (not out) The total of the innings was 497

Clifton College, Classical *v.* Modern, played at Clifton, on May 14th, 19th, and 26th, 1868 —For nine wickets the Classical made 630 runs, Mr E F S Tylecote contributing 404 to that number, and finally carrying out his bat Score

CLASSICAL

Mr E F S Tylecote, not out	404
Mr W C Cross, c Barstow, b Warner	30
Mr L J Stow, st Bush b Wilson	1
Mr E N P Moor, c Wilson, b Bush	8
Mr F W Goodwyn, c Wilson, b Taylor	52
Mr H S Hall, b Bush	11
Mr C Lyon, c Taylor, b Bush	9
Mr E M Goodman, not out	8
Mr Bodington, c Taylor, b Wilson	42
Mr S N Fox, c Taylor, b Bush	25
Mr G Bird, c Beattie, b Bush	10
Byes 16, l b 4, w 10	30
Total	630

MODERN

Mr W E Fox, b Hall	2
Mr J Fox, b Goodwin	0
Mr A T Taylor, run out	2
Mr A J Bush, c Moor, b Tylecote	49
Mr C R Deare, run out	0
Mr G N Wilson, b Goodwin	5
Mr C B Barstow, c Tylecote, b Goodwyn	2
Mr A Cross b Tylecote	20
Mr F G A Wiche c Boyle, b Tylecote	1
Mr Warner, c Cross, b Goodwyn	0
Mr Beattie not out	4
Byes 9, l b 1, w 5	15
Total	100

In a match played at Haileybury, terminating on the 15th of June, 1868, viz, Classical *v.* Modern, Mr E P Ash scored 40 (not out) and 228

A match between the Oxford University and Mr C D Marsham's Eleven occurred in the month of June, 1871, when the University scored 521 runs for eight wickets

In a match (July, 1871) on the King's School Ground, Sherborne, Mr W H Game scored 26 runs in two overs, and 281 during his innings against Motcomb House

On the 12th of July, 1872 (?), Kent and Sussex played a match at Tonbridge Wells, when Mr I C Thornton scored 124 runs in his second innings, among which were nine sixes.

On the 27th of September, 1873, a match between Eastbourne and Trinity College, Cambridge, took place at this favourite Sussex watering-place The so-called residents totalled 508 in their first and only innings No time was left for the Collegians to try their skill with the bat

In the year 1873 Mr M A Troughton, playing for Mid-Kent against South Northwood, at Gravesend, received the first and last ball of the day In the meantime he scored 206 runs and not out

In the same year a school match took place at Carshalton between the North Cheam first eleven and the Carshalton House second The latter completed an innings for 215. The former failed to score at all

On the 25th of July, 1874, the Harrow Blues played the Coulston Park Club The Blues were two men short, and concluded an innings for 78 runs Coulston totalled 315 for the loss of three wickets The match was not further proceeded with

About a month previously the Crystal Palace Club and the Marlborough Nomads met on the Palace ground. The resident club completed an innings of 425 runs for nine wickets The Nomads did not go in

The most marvellous innings on record is that of Mr Collins in 1874, when he scored 338 runs in little more than three hours, and was not out.*

As the truth of this statement was much questioned at the time when first published, an application was made to a gentleman of unimpeachable veracity, who witnessed the match The following reply was given

Northwood Cricket Club, Cowes,
Sept 3rd, 1874

Dear Sir,

I have received your note, and on the other side I send you full copy of the score made by Mr. W E W Collins for this club, against Freshwater, on the 27th ult You will find that the total is 338, instead of 337, as previously sent you Mr Collins was in 1867 captain of the Radley Eleven, and now plays chiefly in Northamptonshire and Hertfordshire, and is usually a heavy scorer I think, in the report of the match I sent your correspondent here, I mentioned the time in which the runs were made, viz, a little over three hours, the ground was in splendid condition for scoring, but I imagine the runs have never been made on any ground in anything like the time Mr Collins scored nineteen off one over, and fourteen and fifteen off several others I shall be glad to give you any further information you may require

Yours truly,

H C Damant

* See page 188

The year 1875 was very productive in long scores. In a match between University College, London, and Grove House, on the 12th of June, the latter kept in all day, and scored 403 runs for the loss of seven wickets.

Epsom *v.* Kensington Park.—The result of a day's play on the 19th of June, 1875, was—Epsom, 458 for eight wickets, although one of the eight contributed nothing.

South Town *v.* Browne's Eleven (Clifton College), June 23rd, 1875.—Remarkable for the score of 308 runs made by Mr. Bush in his two innings; the second "not out" for 228.

In a match at Cambridge, between Et Ceteras and Perambulators, Mr. Absolom scored just 100 runs in seventy-five minutes. He had five companions in the meantime.

An astounding circumstance connected with cricket is recorded in a match played at Chatham between the Royal Engineers and I Zingari, in the month of August, 1875. The R. E. kept possession of the wickets for two whole days, and scored 724 runs for the loss of seven wickets, although one of the number added but a single to this mammoth total. Score:

ROYAL ENGINEERS.

Hon. M. G. Talbot, run out	172
Mr. L. K. Scott, c Kemp, b Crutchley	164
Mr. H. W. Renny-Tailyour, b Fryer	26
Mr. L. B. Friend, b Crutchley	1
Mr. H. W. Stafford, c Fellowes, b Crutchley	58
Mr. F. T. Maxwell, b Fryer	64
Mr. P. G. Von Donop, run out	101
Mr. H. Mitchell, c Balfour, b Russell	62
Mr. C. W. Stratford, not out	21
Mr. E. S. E. Childers, Mr. H. E. Abbott, Capt. Fellowes } did not go in.	
Byes 21, l-b 12, w 22	55
Total	724

In the month of September, 1875, the United South of England Eleven played Eighteen of Hastings and district. Mr. W. G. Grace was five hours and a-half at the wicket, scored 210 runs, among which was one hit for six, which, being measured, was found to be 118 yards from hit to pitch.

In an annual match at Lord's between the M. C. C. and Ground and Oxford University, Hillyer bowled seven wickets in the first innings and six in the second.

Mr. Meyrick, a Wykehamist, got 146 runs three times, and remarked on the last occasion "it was very odd he never got more than 146."

A match occurred at Lingfield between Tunbridge School and Ford, on the 29th of July, 1871, when Mr. A. H. Hoare, of Edenbridge, scored 316 runs. He gave one chance, a hard one, at 221. He was finally caught at deep long on. He was six hours and ten minutes at the wicket.

THE SCHOOL.

A. Courtnay, b C. S. Hoare	0
J. C. Hoare, b A. Hoare	3
W. Pattison, b C. S. Hoare	17
F. H. Fox, c Revell, b C. S. Hoare	19
C. M. Chapman, b A. Hoare	2
S. Towers, b C. S. Hoare	10
C. S. Escreit, b A. Hoare	3
H. R. Peake, b C. S. Hoare	1
S. Luscombe, b A. Hoare	0
W. Glade, run out	15
S. Boulton, not out	1
Byes 5, l-b 2	7
Total	78

FORD.

N. Morris, sen., c Towers, b Fox	1
W. Morris, b Fox	17
N. Morris, jun., c Escreit, b Fox	7
W. Webber, run out	2
A. Hoare, c substitute, b Fox	316
C. S. Hoare, b Towers	74
A. Geere, b Fox	40
F. Bamford, c Escreit, b Towers	3
W. Revell, run out	0
A. De Christy, b Towers	6
A. Stamford, not out	38
Byes 18, l b 12, w 6	36
Total	540

EXTRAORDINARY SCORE.—Gentlemen of the South *v.* Players of the South (1869).—After a fierce struggle of three days at the Oval, the above match was brought to a conclusion. No less than 1136 runs were recorded for twenty-one wickets. Both parties seemed to have had quite enough of the encounter. Every batsman scored something; fifteen went into double figures and three into treble. The Gentlemen's innings lasted eight hours and ten minutes. Final results:

PLAYERS.

	1st inn.		2nd inn.
Jupp, c and b V. E. Walker	76	not out	43
Pooley, c Richardson, b W. Grace	78	c Richardson, b Fryer	50
Silcock, c Fryer, b W. Grace	11	not out	12
James Lillywhite, l b w, b G. F. Grace	27		
Humphrey, c W. Grace, b I. Walker	40		
Griffith, c V. Walker, b G. Grace	7		
Charlwood, b G. F. Grace	155		
T. A. Mantle, st Richardson, b I. Walker	2		
Willsher, not out	57		
Bennett, st Richardson, b I. Walker	3		
Southerton, c W. Grace, b I. Walker	5		
Byes 3, l-b 9, w 2	14	Byes 1, l-b 1, w 1	3
Total	475	Total	108

GENTLEMEN

Mr W G Grace, c and b Mantle	180
Mr B B Cooper, c and b Mantle	101
Mr R Pauncefote, b Jas Lillywhite	31
Mr I D Walker, c Willsher, b Bennett	90
Mr W Yardley, l b w b Southerton	25
Mr F E R Fryer, c Mantle, b Bennett	49
Mr C J Thornton, b Bennett	2
Mr H A Richardson c and b Bennett	1
Mr G F Grace, c Pooley, b Silcock	6
Mr V E Walker, not out	21
Mr F Baker c Pooley b Southerton	18
Bye 16, l-b 12, w 1	29
Total	553

A Very Long Innings—St. John's v Christchurch—The following match was played at Cowley Marsh four years ago

C C C

H B. Carlyon, c Sheffield, b Henderson	2
H Seton-Karr, b Henderson	16
A G Rawstone, run out	13
H A Dalton, c Sheffield, b Henderson	0
T Thistle, c Champneys, b Henderson	32
A Nesbitt, c Pulman, b Henderson	3
J W Barry, b Briggs	9
W O Goldschmidt, b Briggs	2
B Nelson, st Pulman, b Thornton	5
R H Chambers, not out	0
H Ingleby, b Henderson	2
Byes 4, l-b 3	7
Total	91

ST JOHN'S

F R Henderson, run out	3
R T Thornton, b Carlyon	116
J A C Tanner c Dalton, b Thistle	24
R Briggs, c Goldschmidt, b Dalton	30
G P Elwes, st Thistle, b Ingleby	149
W W Pulman, not out	249
F W Champneys b Dalton	6
R W Sheffield, c Thistle, b Dalton	40
W F Lovell, c Seton Karr, b Dalton	0
E G Saye, c Ingleby, b Dalton	7
E A Wells, c and b Ingleby	24
Byes 2, l b 3, w 26, n b 2	33
Total	681

A specimen of tall scoring is worthy of mention in a match played on Woolwich Common between the Royal Artillery and the Oxford Harlequins Two days were occupied in the capture of fifteen wickets only for 859 runs, which gives the average of 57·4 per wicket. Mr Frank Crawford, of the Royal Artillery, scored 171, and Messrs Ottaway and H E Bull, of Oxford University, 123 and 122 respectively Despite the large total of the Royal Artillery (427), the Harlequins beat them, with five wickets to spare

One of the smallest scores on record for a county match occurred in 1800 between Notts and Leicestershire, when the latter obtained 15 and 8 only, against 61 of the former

In the month of August, 1855, the Second Royal Surrey Militia played the Earl of Winterton's eleven at Shillinglee The Earl's party scored 92 in their first and only innings The Militia completed their first innings without a run The most extraordinary part of this affair consisted in the fact that Challen, one of the Earl's fast bowlers, produced neither a wide, bye, nor leg ball

On the 26th of August, 1859, between the Chalcott Club and Bow H Payne played for Chalcott, went in first, and brought out his bat for 24 runs, none of the rest scored He again went in first, and got all the runs

On the 17th of September, 1866, a match took place between two elevens of Ickford and Chilton, villages situate on the borders of Oxon and Bucks Ickford were all put out for one run only This was obtained by Mr Lipping, of Ickford Chilton won by an innings and 40 runs

In a match at Lord's on the 24th of July, "Charterhouse v Westminster," 9 wickets of Westminster's second innings fell for 9 runs, and 7 of these were "extras"

Short Scores —A match (Grantham v Stamford) was played at Burghley Park in the summer of 1870, when the second innings of Grantham realised but 4 runs, although several excellent batsmen took part in it

In the year 1871 Capt Homfray's Eleven played Mumble's Visitors at Swansea Only one of the Visitors scored in their first innings, and even he failed to get more than 2 runs

Nether Stowy v Bishop's Lydiard —In a return match played at the latter place in 1875 the second innings of Nether Stowy resulted in two runs—both leg-byes.

The smallest total recorded for 1875 was in a match at Earls Heaton, on the longest day of the year, between Mr Hirst's Eleven and Mr Frances's Eleven, when the latter were all disposed of in seventeen balls without a run of any kind

Eleven of Lord Lyttelton's Family v Bromsgrove Grammar School —One of the most remarkable matches of the season (1867) occurred at Hagley Park, the seat of Lord Lyttelton Considering the great variety in the ages of the Lyttelton family—from the father and two uncles down to the youth of ten years—it was supposed that the school at Bromsgrove would have little, if any difficulty in collecting an eleven quite equal to this family, renowned as they were in cricket circles The result of the day's play, however, proved otherwise The School went to the wickets first, and made a very good score The chief incident during the innings calculated to provoke notice was a catch made by

Lord Lyttelton which involved a neat piece of tumbling and elicited hearty shouts of applause His lordship, as head of the "Family," headed the batting, but he received a summary dismissal from his honourable post. After this the hitting began in earnest, and was kept up with spirit, 170 runs were recorded for the loss of six wickets The innings culminated with 191 In the second "School" innings the scoring was feebleness itself Nine wickets realised but 24 runs, and the total reached only 51 It now remained for the "Family" to get twelve, this number was obtained without loss of wicket A full score is added

BROMSGROVE

	1st inn		2nd inn
Mr T Hills, b S G Lyttelton	23	b C G Lyttelton	4
Mr T Collis, b C G Lyttelton	0	run out	5
Mr R Stracey, c and b S G Lyttelton	3	c S G Lyttelton, b N G Lyttelton	1
Mr W T Kemp, c S G Lyttelton, b C G Lyttelton	27	run out	2
Mr C. Smith, b C G Lyttelton	16	c S G Lyttelton, b C G Lyttelton	9
Rev J Wilson, not out	23	c C G Lyttelton, b N G Lyttelton	11
Mr G G Davies, c N G Lyttelton, b A V Lyttelton	3	not out	11
Mr W L Smith, b N G Lyttelton	17	c N G Lyttelton, b C G Lyttelton	2
Mr S Cator, c A V Lyttelton, b N G Lyttelton	19	st N G Lyttelton, b C G Lyttelton	1
Mr P Rufford, run out	2	c Lord Lyttelton, b N G Lyttelton	0
Mr G Gordon, c Lord Lyttelton, b S G Lyttelton	3	run out	0
Byes 6, l-b 1, w 7	14	Bye 1, l-b 3, w 1	5
Total	150	Total	51

THE FAMILY

Lord Lyttelton, b Cator	0
Hon C Lyttelton, c Stracey, b Hill	27
Hon S G Lyttelton, b Hill	51
Hon A V Lyttelton, c Stracey, b Hill	46
Hon N G Lyttelton, b Cator	15
Hon A T Lyttelton, c Kemp, b Cator	16
Hon R H Lyttelton, b Cator	3
Hon E Lyttelton, c Hill, b Cator	0
Hon A Lyttelton, b Hill	14
Hon and Rev W H Lyttelton, b Cator	0
Hon Spencer Lyttelton, not out	0
Byes 4, w 15	19
Total	191

In the second innings of "The Family" the Hon N G Lyttelton scored (not out) 3, the Hon. E. Lyttelton (not out) 7, extras, 2—Total 12

A great curiosity in the way of "Family Matches" occurred at Bromley two years since. Score in full attached —

BLUNDELLS

	1st inn.		2nd inn
Samuel Blundell, c W Walmisley, b R Walmisley	3	b J R L Walmisley ..	3
Henry Blundell, b Percy Walmisley . .	7	c Wm Walmisley, b J R L Walmisley . .	4
Thomas Blundell, b Percy Walmisley .	7	c sub, b Richard Walmisley .	0
Wm Blundell, b Percy Walmisley ...	2	c and b J R L Walmisley	0
Thomas Blundell, jun, b Richard Walmisley	1	run out ..	1
Fred Blundell, b Percy Walmisley	9	c and b J R L Walmisley ..	3
George Blundell, b Richard Walmisley . .	0	b J R L Walmisley .	2
James Blundell, b Percy Walmisley .	2	not out	0
Frank Blundell, not out	0	b Richard Walmisley	8
Walter Blundell, b Percy Walmisley . .	0	c and b J R L Walmisley	4
George Blundell, jun, b Richard Walmisley . .	2	st Wm Walmisley, b J R L Walmisley	3
Byes 20, w 3 . .	23	Bye 1, w 1	2
Total	56	Total .	30

WALMISLEYS

Percy Walmisley, b S Blundell . .	0
Shaftesbury Walmisley, jun, c and b H Blundell	2
Walter M Walmisley, b H Blundell .	0
Richard J Walmisley, b S Blundell	2
Lieut W H Walmisley, b H Blundell . .	0
James Walmisley, c J Blundell, b H Blundell	0
Shaftesbury E Walmisley, b S Blundell .	0
John Walmisley, c J Blundell, b H Blundell	0
John R L Walmisley b H Blundell	4
Edmond Walmisley, not out	1
Phillip W G Walmisley (absent)	0
Byes 7, w 2	9
Total	18

In the second innings Percy Walmisley scored, b S Blundell, 4, Shaftesbury (not out), 15; Walter M (run out), 19, Richard J, b H Blundell, 17, James, c S Blundell, b H Blundell, 2, Shaftesbury E (not out), 0, and John R L, b Geo Blundell, jun, 1, byes 12, wides 5—Total 75

To these might be added the names of Bovill, Brotherhood, Cæsar, Cronk, Garnett, Lubbock, and many others

The Nore Sands, Sept 23rd, 1854—During the Crimean War a match was got up by a party of gentleman for the entertainment of the Russian and Finnish officers residing at Sheerness on parole. Wickets were pitched between the Nore light vessel and the Jenkin buoy, in order to keep the distance within the parole. Several yachts were engaged for the occasion, and the inhabitants of the neighbourhood vied with each other in their attention to the captives, who, though not understanding cricket, expressed their gratitude for the kindness manifested towards them on the novel occasion

Malta—A match was played at Ricasoli in 1873, and although the ground was made of asphalte, and the glare of the sun on the white limestone buildings and grounds on every side pains the eyes, still the match was contested with vigour and spirit to the very end

Rapid Scoring.—About two years since a very weak team at Eastbourne played against good bowling and a fair field, composed of Trinity College, Eastbourne, and Masters, and scored 503 runs in four hours and a-half, thus averaging nearly 112 runs per hour continuously

Political Challenge.—" In the year 1809 an announcement appeared in the public prints that a grand match for the highest stakes ever known to have been played for was about to take place The scheme originated with H R H the late commander-in-chief, the club of general officers on one side against All England It was well supported by the Secretary at War, as well as all the members present on the occasion Mr Whitbread and Mr Canning accepted the challenge on the part of All England A great deal of speculation got afloat as to the result It was broadly asserted that the military were overmatched, for though H R H was a good runner, he was anything but a good long stop, while the Secretary at War was not only a miserable fieldsman, but once at a great match near Ferrol, when he had the game in his own hands, lost it in a most unaccountable manner by never stirring from his wicket On the other side, Mr Whitbread is known to be a very hard hitter, and Mr Canning is allowed to catch a ball and throw it in with more dexterity and quickness than any man in the kingdom. The proposed match did not come off, the duel between Lord Castlereagh and Mr Canning much about this time resulted in so severe a wound in the thigh of Mr Canning that cricket with him was altogether out of the question "

The Sere and Yellow Leaf.—A match took place at Aylesford, a small village in Kent, thirty years ago, between eleven under 60 years of age and eleven over 60, all residents The latter team included one octogenarian and six who had passed 70 years. The juveniles scored 30 and 44—total 74; the "old uns," 41 and 22—total 63

A match took place in Shillinglee Park, 1843, between thirty-seven labourers on one side and the Earl of Winterton's eleven on the other, when the latter won by five wickets Three years afterwards the Earl's eleven contended with fifty-six labourers, but the match was left unfinished The labourers scored 74 and 84—total 158, the Earl's party 94 and 24, three wickets This is the largest number on one side ever recorded After all, it was said at the time to be a mere mockery of cricket, as scarcely one man of the fifty-six had really any notion of good play "

Married Men against the Bachelors.—The first match of this kind is said to have been played at Witney in Oxfordshire It was played for a considerable sum, and terminated in favour of the Bachelors The amazing skill and agility displayed by the competitors for the reward of the winged goddess both pleased and astonished the numerous and polite company assembled on the occasion As soon as the match was decided the conquerors and the conquered adjourned to the Red Lion Inn, where they sat down to an elegant repast, and concluded the day in friendship and glee

A grand veteran cricket match between the One Arm and One Leg Pensioners of Greenwich Hospital, for 1000 guineas, was finally decided at the Montpelier Gardens, Walworth, on Monday the 19th of August, 1811, in favour of the one arm side The match was the best contested ever witnessed The first and second innings were played on the 8th and 15th, and postponed from the state of the weather being so much to the disadvantage of the one-legged players, who several times lost or broke their timbers, which disaster befel three of them on the last day As soon as the umpires declared the match to be in favour of the single arm cricketers, they drove off the ground in a triumphal car to Greenwich, with all the usual trophies of rejoicing and exultation The sport created much diversion, and the company was numerous in the gardens each day —*Sporting Magazine*

In Vol 16 of the *Sporting Magazine* mention is made of a match at Lord's in 1800, between Eleven of Westminster School and Eleven of Eton College, for 500 guineas At starting, Eton were favourites at five to four Westminster scored 54 and 31—total 85, Eton 213

On Thursday, July 7, 1808, a match was played on the Montpelier Grounds, Walworth, for 300 guineas, between eleven gentlemen of the Friday's Marylebone Club and eleven of the Tuesday's Montpelier, when the latter won by 90 runs

On the 4th of July, 1808, a match took place at Lord's between eleven of the County of Surrey and All England for 1000 guineas, which the former won by 60 runs.

A grand match at Lord's between ten gentlemen of M C and Howard and Eleven of Middlesex, for 500 guineas aside, in the month of May, 1808, resulted in favour of Middlesex by 83 runs

A grand match at Lord's in June, 1808, for 1000 guineas aside, created especial interest It was between eight of the Marylebone Club, with Beldham, Robinson, and Walker, and seven of the Homerton Club, with Lambert, Hammond, Bennett, and Small Marylebone scored 264 and 141—total 405, Homerton, 84 and 165—total 249. Marylebone won by 156 runs

Money Match —Stakes Disputed —In the year 1810 a match took place between the Gentlemen of the Ripon Club and the Fleetham and Scruton players, at Kirklington, in the North Riding of Yorkshire The Fleetham party took their innings, and made 54 notches. When four of the Ripon gentlemen were out they had only run fourteen. At this time a question arose whether a gentlemen ought not to be called out who had stood before his wicket and stopped the ball Three (?) of the umpires were decidedly of opinion that he ought to go out, as were several gentlemen belonging to the Ripon Club, Afterwards, to satisfy some of the party, it was determined by lot for him to go out Notwithstanding this, two or three of the Ripon gentleman positively refused to continue the game, and immediately left the field, in consequence of which the opposite party imagined themselves entitled to the stakes, and took measures for the recovery thereof (1811)

Betting to a great extent was indulged in at one time, very much to the detriment of the game in the eyes of the general public Mention is made of a match which lasted four days, at Bramhill Park It commenced on the 14th of August, 1823, between Hants and England, when one gentleman won 145 guineas by giving sixty to receive one guinea for each run obtained by Messrs Ward, Budd, and Begley The result is not surprising when it is stated that Mr Ward scored 120 and Mr Budd 67 in a single innings.

The *Sporting Magazine* mentions a match between Lord Kennedy and Capt. Barclay for 100 guineas The latter undertook to find a man capable of throwing 100 yards, forward and backward, but he could not beyond 98 yards It took place in Hyde Park on the 24th of December, 1822

In a trial at Lord's, between George Parr and a soldier whose name has been forgotten, in the year 1846 (June 16th), the famous leg hitter of Ratcliffe, and thrower too, beat his military opponent Parr's throw, being carefully measured, was stated to be 109yds 2ft

In 1848, Mr H Fellows hit the ball 132yds. before bounding.

Mr. Gillett, in the Exeter College Sports, Oxford, threw 116yds 22in. (another account 26in) on the Bullingdon Ground, November, 1858.

Three years after, in the same month, Mr Rhodes threw 112yds 9in in the University Athletic Sports, Oxford.

At the Oxford University Athletic Sports (1873), Mr Baker threw 110yds 1ft. 10in., and gained the first prize Mr Hodges 106yds. 2ft. 2in

The Longest Throw on Record —The *Australasian* of January 16th, 1874, gives currency to the following statement "A wonderful throw was witnessed by the spectators at the Clermont cricket match on Boxing Day. The *Telegram* says that between the innings some discussion arose amongst the players as to the distance some of them could throw, and it was decided to test the powers of those who professed to excel in this line by a match Amongst several good throwers, Billy, the aboriginal, astonished everyone by sending the ball a distance of 140yds, as measured with a tape This throw surpasses the best we have ever heard of in the colonies or in England. It takes a good thrower to throw 100yds , and in athletic sports in England the man who can get beyond 110 is almost certainly the winner A 120yds is very rarely heard of, and hitherto a throw of 130 has been quite unknown "

The *Australasian* of Oct 17th, of the same year, in answer to a question, says "We believe that the Queensland aboriginal's throw (over 140yds) is the longest on record, as the distance was measured at the time, and vouched for by trustworthy persons "

As a set-off to this paragraph, it may not be amiss to say that in 1823 Lillyhett, of Havant, threw a ball 123yds before it pitched He was afterwards easily beaten by Baily, on Kingston Bottom In 1853 Mr E B Fawcett threw 126yds 6in at Brighton There could have been no possibility of mistake about this, as the spot where the ball pitched was accurately marked, and measured from the line of delivery, and the feat was moreover witnessed by many In 1861 Mr. Rhodes 112yds 9in in the Oxford University Athletic Sports, and in 1873 Mr Game 127yds 15in in the same University sports. Other kindred incidents might be adduced if necessary. But the most remarkable performance of the kind in

English history occurred at Walderton Down, about the year 1819, when George Brown, of Brighton, threw a 5¼oz ball a distance of 137yds and back

On occasion of the athletic sports at Eton College, March 11th, 1875, Mr W F. Forbes threw a cricket ball 122yds 2ft He belonged to the Eton eleven *

Martin, for several years the keeper of the Christ Church Ground at Oxford, says that Mr Walter Fellows hit a ball 173yds before it pitched, and that the distance was measured in his presence

Charles Arnold, of Cambridge, mentioned by Mr Denison as a capital field was backed to throw 110 yards on Parker's Piece. He exceeded this number by 2 yards

In a match between M C C and Ground *v* County of Herts, played at Lord's, in June, 1874, Wootton on the second day struck a bail twenty-seven paces from the wicket Distance measured.

In the same week Willsher knocked a bail four yards further than the above in a match between Kent and Surrey, played at the Crystal Palace Ground

In the year 1874 a match occurred at Bramall Lane, Sheffield, between Notts and Yorkshire, when Emmett struck Bignall's wicket so violently that one of the bails was sent flying to a distance of 46 measured paces

In the month of June, 1875, Mr E Steed, of Tonbridge School, struck an off bail with such force, that he sent it through the air the extraordinary distance of 46yds 1ft

So sharp was a throw by Mr E C Rawson (Rossall), standing short slip in a match at Liverpool in the year 1875, that a bail was knocked from the wicket to the distance of 76yds

The tremendous pace of Mr Foord-Kelcey may be imagined from the fact that, in his bowling Mr W H Hadow, in the match between the University of Oxford and the Gentlemen of England, 1875, he sent the bail 48yds from the wicket

DEATHS —A sad and fatal accident occurred on the 1st of October, 1870, to a youth named Bishop, of the Callington Grammar School, Launceston. Shortly after his arrival on the cricket ground he incautiously got close to the wicket, at which a batsman was striking with all his might at a tempting ball, but which he missed, and the bat came with such fearful force on his head that he died almost immediately

In 1872 a youth named Hamilton Plumptre Lighton, attached to Repton School, was bowling to a fellow pupil The ball was played back, and struck the bowler on the side of the head above the right ear. He was stunned for awhile, but on recovering resumed play No danger was apprehended A few hours subsequently he became insensible, and died, at the age of 17

A young man named Baker, while playing cricket at New Brighton, Liverpool, July 24th, 1865, was struck so severely on the temple by a ball that he died almost immediately

In a match at Borden, Kent, July 6th, 1868, between the cricketers of that village and Greenstreet (Sittingbourne), Mr Gillon hit a ball to bowler which was

* It is stated that the same young gentleman afterwards threw 132yds, and Mr Wakefield—another Eton boy—115yds 5in

returned with such force to the stumps that it struck the batsman on the jugular vein and killed him on the spot Deceased was only 18 years of age

A few years since a very painful incident occurred on the Meadows Cricket Ground, Nottingham A young man named Thomas Tomms was engaged with others from New Radford in a match About twelve o'clock his turn came to go in After he had obtained three runs and was engaged in running another, he came into violent collision with one of the umpires, and complained that he had hurt himself He, however, continued playing, but almost immediately after his wicket was taken He then became worse, and a surgeon (Mr Worth) was promptly in attendance, but before he arrived the poor fellow expired

In the year 1870, Platts of Derbyshire was one of the ground bowlers at Lord's A match occurred at Lord's between Notts and the Marylebone Club On the third day of play a young man named George Summers, of Nottingham—a first-class batsman—was struck so forcibly on the cheek by a ball from Platts, that he reeled and fell He died a few days after at the age of twenty-six Verdict, concussion of the brain.

A young man named Thomas Rowland Sissons, miller, of Silkstone, was killed in a field at Dodworth, near Barnsley, whilst engaged in a game at cricket As deceased was in the act of playing, a ball, bowled by a man named Goldthorpe, struck him on the temple, but without apparently doing him serious injury He continued playing for about half an hour afterwards He then complained of being in pain, and was put into a cart and removed to his residence at Silkstone, where he died about six o'clock the same evening

SERIOUS ACCIDENTS —During the progress of a match in the barrack field, Woolwich, between the Household Brigade and the Royal Artillery, Captain Stewart, of the 2nd Life Guards, in attempting to catch a short ball from the wicket, fractured and lacerated the middle finger of his left hand He received immediate attention at the Royal Artillery Infirmary, but amputation being considered requisite, he proceeded to London During the same match, Captain Taswell, R A , was struck by a ball between the eyes with considerable force, and such was the effect at the time that it was feared the result would be fatal. He, however, after a time recovered

A match was commenced at Stoke Down, in Hampshire, on the 23rd of July, 1795, and after playing three days it stood adjourned to June 28th of the following year. The sides were headed by the Earl of Winchelsea and Mr Leigh respectively

Mention is made, in the 70th vol of the *Sporting Magazine*, of a match projected by the Duke of Dorset and Sir Horace Mann between the Hambledon Club and All England On this occasion John Small, the celebrated ball maker, was in *three whole days*, although opposed to some of the best players in the kingdom, nor did he at last lose his wicket, his ten mates all having their wickets put down

On the 28th of August, 1817, a game of cricket of rather a novel nature took place at Lewes, between Mr Stuard and Mr Baxter, of that town The latter, a pupil of Lambert's, permitted his adversary (a gentleman little skilled in the profession) to bowl at a sheepwattle set up the broad way, whilst he bowled at the regular wicket The match was however decided in favour of Mr B by a single hand innings, which proves that science can guard a wattle better than many self-taught players can a common wicket —*Sporting Magazine*

A long and particular account of a match at Darnall, nearly fifty years ago, between the "best men of Leicester and Sheffield and Eleven of Nottingham Club," was published in the sporting journals of the time The play occupied three days Among the very extraordinary events occurring in the meantime were the balls that rebounded from Marsden's bat one may be remarked which may convey to the amateur some idea of his great powers At the near wickets to the tent he struck at a well-pitched ball, which rose somewhat high, clearly out of the ground It was driven over the highest part of the stone wall on the right of the entrance to the green at the height of 45 feet from the ground, and alighted at the distance of *one hundred and thirty yards* from the place where it was struck. The single innings, in which Marsden played so conspicuous a part, realised 380 runs, towards which he contributed 227 , Nottingham, double innings, 178 —*Sporting Magazine,* vol 68, p. 377)

In the year 1840 Thomas Adams, in a Kent *v* England match, hit a ball to leg with such force at Lord's, that it bounded on the roof of the Tennis Court, and made a large gap in the slating It was not repaired for some years purposely to gratify curiosity

A curious incident is recorded respecting a match played at Hong Kong on the 31st of October, 1874, between members of a club at this place and H M 80th Regiment Mr C——, a fast underhand, bowled, and although the middle stump was driven some distance away, the two bails remained in their original position undisturbed

A precisely similar case occurred at Sheerness in the previous year

A curious match occurred at Barnsley, Yorkshire, between Messrs Parker and Richardson, both of that place The bet was that R could not bowl out P in an hour After some of the best play of the kind ever witnessed in the neighbourhood, it terminated in favour of R So well was it contested, that only one minute of "time" remained when the ball struck the wicket

In a match between the Royal Engineers *v* The Establishment, played at Chatham about five years since, there were 101 extras

Double ties are not of frequent occurrence A short time since the Ifield Club played Balcombe Each side scored 44 in the first innings and 24 in the second

A match was played at Acapulco in 1876 with a temperature of 135° in the sun

Three batsmen were got out from one ball How was this done? Two were run out, a no ball affair of course, and the third bowled

CHAPTER XXIII.

LAYING OUT GROUNDS AND SUBSEQUENT MODES OF TREATMENT.

The sharpened scythe prevents the grassy height,
And reaps the scanty harvest of the night;
The rolling stone renews its morning round
To crush the springing turf and sink the knotty ground.—*Addison*, 1697.

AS spectres are said to flee at the approach of morning, so will difficulties, in nine cases out of ten, vanish by the rays of information and the appliances of art. Few things connected with cricket open up more discussion and criticism than the spots on which the game is played. A cricket ground, and how to make it, may appear to the uninformed rustic mind a task not to be accomplished very easily. In these days such an avowal would be nothing more nor less than an affront to the understanding of any gentleman's gardener, or a land steward. 'Tis true many theories are propounded, in which, however, one general idea is involved, and a few kindred principles are insisted upon. These are a level surface, a proper subsoil, that is, one through which water will easily percolate; and if not, how to adapt drain pipes, the soil on which turf is to be placed, and subsequent top dressings. Now, any one acquainted with the nature of soils knows how to supply the deficiencies of one by use of the other, provided such materials are attainable in the localities where they are required. As no man is expected to make bricks without straw, so neither can he make a cricket ground without essential materials for the purpose, and still more without a knowledge of the right method of their use. Opinions on the latter point are of course diverse. It is obvious, however, that the best method of proceeding must be regulated by the special circumstances of each case. Very many points have to be carefully considered in addition to subsoil and soil, such as the presence or absence of trees, whether the neighbourhood is dry and arid, humid and damp; and, moreover, what agriculturists sometimes call "the lay of the land." Now, as conditions vary, no fixed rule can be given. If the turf of a ground requires to be relaid, it must be attended to in the autumn. Should circumstances arise to prevent this, the earliest months of the following year, when favourable, should be devoted to the purpose. Rolling with as heavy a roller as may be practicable should be resorted to for at least twice a week. The horses employed ought to have boots to prevent their feet making indentations. Should the month of March be too dry, the earth must be made malleable by watering If the herbage is scant, a top dressing of sifted garden mould, with a sowing of proper grass seeds, will be beneficial, but with respect to "any" top dressing particular caution is necessary A good ground has been spoiled for a whole season in consequence of road dirt alone having been used, the which, when dry and the wind blowing flew about as the dust in the road whence it was taken So also the use of ashes so roughly sifted that clinkers are left, such a dressing not only lacerates the ball, but influences its direction from the pitch, and causes a false rising Bones, too, are apt to produce a similar effect Under any circumstances, rolling and watering, if necessary, early in the spring and continued is the only way to ensure a good ground Sheep feeding is generally admitted to be a great help, with proper mowing by a lawn machine

The lines selected for the motto of this chapter were applied to bowling greens, cricket was but little practised, if at all, by the accomplished poet Whether he approved the practice of such frequent mowing is not clearly deducible, but most probably he did not Mowing every morning appears to be a severe strain on the plant Vegetable physiology is, in fact, plain on this point; the root cannot grow without the leaf, or the leaf without the root If the blade or leaf is killed down the root will soon suffer, if it be not destroyed The result is large patches completely bare of verdure, mere level surfaces of mud in winter, in summer, baked clay, and in wet weather, ugly and repulsive castings up of worm-hills, &c Worms and moles are not the only enemies against which the keeper of a ground has to contend Even insects make war, and at times fierce havoc Some imagine that sheep droppings have produced a very destructive grub One thing is certain, that the *Tipulæ*, or Daddy Long-legs, are very troublesome customers, and almost defy the *ordinary* means of destruction without destroying the turf with them

On the general principles thus far enumerated, a cricket ground may be laid down with good reason for counting upon its success, and when in condition, the task of keeping it so is not a very difficult one, unless circumstances arise beyond the reach of human control It would be the height of folly to gloss over radical defects You may inclose rotten material in a substantial looking edifice, you may envelope corruption with the surface of health, but as time wears on, and the stress is applied, the hidden ill is sure to reveal itself

Lord's Ground is called a hanging level There is a dip of nearly seven feet At the top the mould, so to speak, is scarcely skin deep, and as the drain pipes—laid some years ago—tell of less regard to skill than expense, their hiding places may be easily traced on a summer evening when the sun is going down

However sound an individual opinion may be, it is well to test it by that of others, and few men are better entitled to be heard on such a subject as a cricket-ground than the thoughtful user of land in agricultural districts, where the game, as a rule, is the chief out-of-door summer sport in their varied localities A few extracts from private note-books cannot fail to give instruction to those who have not had opportunities for gaining much experimental knowledge.

A Middlesex contributor says:—In making a ground, should the surface be light or shifty, the bottom should be constituted of heavy loam or clay. *Vice versâ*, if the surface be heavy loam or clay, then there should be a dressing of three inches of chalk or gravel and coated with light soil, sand, or ashes, or anything resembling them. The ground and sand should be six inches, then level up to the nature of the ground. When the substratum has been manufactured, the turfing and keeping that in order must be by mending, rolling, watering, dressing, never forgetting ashes, road scrapings, bush harrowing, and feeding off the rank or redundant herbage by sheep. Such processes will suggest themselves, however, to an intelligent professional who has the charge of a ground. But it is your efficient gardener who generally understands the nature and manufacture of subsoils, and therefore it is that many a little field in the neighbourhood of large towns is made into a cricket ground, and kept in good order at a trifling expense. With regard to space, this depends a great deal upon circumstances and situation; 200 yards long by 150 broad must not be regarded as a makeshift.

The field should be as level as possible; a fall of one inch to the yard is not an insurmountable objection, but more than that is not good. Two hundred and forty yards long by two hundred and forty wide and square is a nice size. In the centre of this there must be at least forty-two yards by forty-two of drained or naturally dry land, laid nearly level, and if possible of poor, tough, wiry grass and sod that will stand wearing by the batters' and bowlers' feet. Before proceeding further on this matter, there is one all important point to be settled, viz., what is the subsoil of the field, and particularly that under the forty-two yards in the centre — clay, sand, gravel, peat? Is it wet or dry? or does it hold a larger quantity of water in wet weather? or in hot, dry weather does it go as hard as a brick, and full of cracks without showing deep holes? This piece should be nearly level, highest in the centre, with a fall of half an inch in the yard all round, that the ground may dry quicker after rain. The forty-two yards can be extended according to the size of the field and the condition of the funds. On a very dry situation a dead level is no objection.

Another writer says:—A cricket ground is easy to make, and at little expense, on any dry level subsoil. By dryness I mean a subsoil which allows the water to percolate through it to a sufficient depth to be out of the way of moistening the surface by the same power a sponge possesses, when placed in a wet basin, of sucking up the water; earth or soil has this power, and that is one reason why drains placed near the surface, a foot or eighteen inches deep, are of no effectual use to make a dry surface. With a dry subsoil you can at once proceed to make your cricket ground, as afterwards described, without the expense of any drainage whatever. If an open loose subsoil, sand, gravel, peat, and wet, it must be made dry; in subsoils of this kind one deep and large drain will frequently effectually cure a large field, or even a neighbourhood. If possible, and the sand, gravel, or peat be not too thick, go through them with your trench, and the extra width a deep drain will lay dry in such subsoils will save you the expense of many smaller ones of less depth, and do the work more effectually, but in this case the advice of a practical man, some one in the neighbourhood, a land agent, or anyone accustomed to the draining of land, might be of great service. Until the subsoil is dry, you cannot put soil and sod on it that will be good and safe to play cricket upon As to clay subsoil, which holds a large quantity of water in wet weather, this must be made dry before a cricket surface can be put upon it There is no other way to dry this kind of ground except by drainage Your drains must be near together, on account of the water-holding nature of the ground, and they must be deep enough to take away the water sufficiently low down to prevent the earth from sucking it up to the surface From three feet six inches to four feet deep, and four or five yards apart, three-inch tiles, and a fall of not less than half an inch to the yard, will make this subsoil dry enough to put on a cricket surface, and although the main part of the water will rise at the bottom of the trench after the tiles are placed, I think it an important point that these drains should be filled with broken stone, coarse gravel, or rough cinders to within a foot or eighteen inches of the surface of the ground The tiles of your main drain should be larger than the three-inch pipes of which your branch drains are made, and larger in proportion to the number of branches it has to receive The opposite ends of your branch drains to the main drain should be connected by an air drain, one end of which should be open to the air. This is a point of some importance, for in dry weather, when perhaps your drains are making no water, still a draught of air through and under the ground may be doing good by causing the seams in the ground to open and crack, and so prepare it for more effectual and quick drainage when wet weather comes

Now of the surface of a cricket ground The first thing to be done is to take up the sods Say that you have decided to relay forty-two yards by forty-two, the sods must be nicked out with a verge-cutter—a line and a stick eighteen inches long—to keep the sods all of a size, a spade made on purpose, with an iron hook, which cuts the sods or turf without breaking them. One inch and a half is about the thickness Wheel them to one side of the piece you intend to take up, and stack them five or six cartloads together, this presses them, and causes the old rough coarse grass to rot off When the sods are off is the best time to drain You must now examine the thickness of the soil It should be at least from nine to twelve inches thick after the sod is taken off This soil must be lightly dug and levelled to the form required, viz, highest in the centre of the forty-two yards, with a gradual fall of half an inch to the yard all round Now will be the time to cover all the ground you have to resod with four inches in thickness of sand You can then bring back the sods and commence laying them, put them close and even (pains taken and laying may give you a fair ground the first season), throw sand about a quarter of an inch thick on the new-laid sods—the weather will then assist to wash in the sand No cattle must be allowed upon it heavier than a sheep, and man for a little time must walk carefully over or keep off it

The first thing is to underdrain with 3in tiles, the depth and distance apart of the tiles to be determined according to the light or heavy nature of the subsoil

If it be clay or peat—especially the latter—it may be found necessary to remove six inches or nine inches of it, and replace it with good loamy mould. This mould should be well trodden down, and especial care should be given to levelling and to the removal of any stones before the turf is placed, as on this mainly depends the evenness of the work when finished. Drains placed near the surface are of no real use, and hence the tiles should be sunk at a depth not less than three feet.

The best time of the year to commence making new grounds, or redress old, is about the middle of October, and when necessary to introduce seeds, the ground should have a good dressing of well-sifted loamy mould. Road sand is often recommended as a winter covering for a ground, but any species of sand should be avoided, as tending to make the surface gritty and loose.

If possible, a natural level should be chosen for a match-ground, but as this is often difficult of attainment, the next best thing is to set about making as near a true level as circumstances will permit. If the slope of the ground be such as to involve any considerable amount of work, the first thing to do is to carefully remove the old fibrous or tilled surface soil, and lay it on one side, and then proceed to dig up and carefully reduce the subsoil to the required gradient, and, although anything like hard *caking* is to be avoided, care must be taken that it be done not only evenly, but firmly, or afterwards the soil will be constantly sinking in places, and thereby causing much and very difficult and delicate work. Having levelled the subsoil, proceed to restore by placing over it the richer and better surface soil, and in doing this exercise the greatest care to produce a firm and perfectly smooth surface. Too much care cannot be given to this portion of the work, for however much pains may be taken in afterwards placing on the turf, if the surface be not firmly and evenly prepared, it is certain to fail under the stress of actual cricket and the vicissitudes of weather, and cause much vexation.

The turf to be used is that of the ground operated upon, *i.e.*, if it was a pasture having a turf of its own, and therefore thoroughly acclimatised, of course labour and skilful management may reduce it to the proper condition of fineness for playing on. If the ground chosen should be part of an arable field, then, if possible, obtain turf from some field or ground near having the same natural soil. Great care must be taken not to get foreign turf, that is, turf off a totally different soil, or in all probability the consequence will be that all the better grasses that flourished luxuriantly in their natural home will perish or drag on a miserable existence that will be very disappointing. Cases are recorded in which cricket-grounds have been formed on a stiff clay soil by committees who have seen and recollected with pleasure the beautiful short close turf growing on chalk downs. Full of enthusiasm, they rush off and buy some of this turf, and place it on their carefully levelled ground, and during the following year point with pride to its luxuriant appearance, and forthwith congratulate themselves on their success. But alas! for them, in a few years—probably in two or three—they will find to their disappointment that all the finer and more delicate grasses have perished, and that they have little left but a crop of the different species of plantains, hawkweeds, daisies, &c, and the coarser and hardier grasses that can accustom themselves to the new conditions of their existence

In some cases, when the soil or subsoil is of a very tenacious clay, it may be advisable to introduce at some considerable depth beneath the surface a layer of a few inches, or even a foot, of chalk, for the purpose of uniform drainage, but a proceeding of this nature should hardly be entered on without the advice of some experienced cultivator of land in the district In other cases—such, for instance, as when it may be too sandy or peaty—it may be necessary to remove a portion of the surface soil, and replace it by some good mould or loam, but these are details which should always be referred to local experience

THE NEW SUSSEX COUNTY GROUND offers an instructive lesson As this is one of the most recently formed grounds of importance, and is generally acknowledged to be a first success, it might be most useful to give a few particulars as to the means employed to bring about so desirable a result, and also as to the size and general arrangement of the ground

In 1871 (says Mr Cooke) the committee turned their attention to this field, then covered by a splendid crop of barley To the inexperienced eye it appeared to present, when viewed from a distance, a nearly natural level, but when it was staked out it was found there was a fall from north to south of about twenty feet! This was awkward, but, as it had to be remedied, no time was lost, and plans were made, and the work commenced soon after the crop was gathered in A space, nearly in the centre, 200ft square, was set apart as a "match ground," the surface soil removed and the process of levelling commenced The subsoil having been duly dug and levelled, the surface soil was replaced, and a match ground made with only a very slight fall towards the south (the actual fall is 1ft in 100ft) Then commenced the process of levelling the outsides for fielding purposes and general practice, the surface soil was removed from the north and south ends, much of the subsoil dug from the top or north end and carted to the bottom or south end, and the surface soil returned to produce the approach to a level at present exhibited It was not allowed, even had it been expedient, to make a true level (the possible future of the ground for building purposes having to be taken into consideration), and the present state of the ground may be best described by saying that it has a rather sharp fall from north to south for about 340ft, to the edge of the match ground, then the match ground itself with its fall of 2ft in 200ft, and then again a rather sharp slope for about 195ft The width of the ground is 544ft The whole area comprised within the boundary walls (which are built of concrete) is, as near as possible, nine acres

All round the ground, and extending for five feet from the walls, a border was prepared and properly trenched, and many hundreds of young trees planted, but the depredations of hungry sheep, who appear to have a special fancy for tender bark, have effectually destroyed what would by this time have been a very pleasing feature of the ground Next comes a thoroughly well made and highly finished road twenty feet wide, which though used as a carriage drive on match days and other occasions, is primarily intended for bicycle races and practice, and pedestrian contests, and as the "turns" are good, and a complete circuit measures nearly half a mile, the road is much appreciated

On the west side, and immediately opposite the match ground, from which it is distant about 120ft, is a well appointed and most convenient pavilion for the exclusive use of members of the County Club In addition to a large central room or hall, it contains a committee room, gentlemen's dressing room, lavatories, &c, and, with a private entrance from the carriage road, a neat little ladies' cloak room Underneath the whole building, which is seventy feet long and twenty feet wide, are rooms for the storage of marquees, forms, chairs, and all the requisites of a well-managed cricket ground. Along the whole front of the building, which is about nine feet above the level of the ground, is a terrace covered by a verandah; and descending to the level of the ground is a series of fixed benches or seats, which affords accommodation to a large number of members of the club

A little to the south of the pavilion, and on the same side of the ground, is a very neat little building of two stories in height, which is generally considered to be one of the best things of its kind to be found on any cricket ground in England On the upper floor is a very comfortable room nicely finished, and furnished with seats and desks, capable of accommodating a considerable number of the gentlemen of the press On a level with this, but of course partitioned off and snugly private, is the box for the scorers of the game, and underneath the whole is the office (duly connected with the scoring box by speaking tubes) where the official cards are printed Outside, and in front of this building, is the telegraph board for announcing the state of the game; and on the opposite side of the ground is a corresponding board A little south of the press pavilion, and still on the same side of the ground, is the dressing-room for the county professional players, and under it are more store rooms, &c There are other buildings on the ground used by private clubs who practise there, and on match days marquees are erected for the use of the lady friends of members of the County Club.

The Brighton Company's water service is put on in a series of deeply laid pipes, and extends to both sides of the match ground, so that, by the use of a reasonable quantity of hose pipe, the whole can be watered when and as necessary At the entrance of the ground an excellent hotel has been erected by the county committee, where not only members and players, but also the general public, can take dinner, luncheon, or anything they require. The whole of the ground surrounding the match ground proper has been let to private clubs and schools for general practice, each club or school having its portion for wickets accurately measured off.

Protection in Winter.—Here again the mode of protection and the cost of the same must depend largely upon situation and strength of finance In some cases scarcely any outlay is necessary, while in others a great deal of care is needed to avoid damage, or in restoring a ground to its normal condition The area of the barrack field at Woolwich appropriated to cricket is twenty acres and three perches During two months in winter about two acres of this is protected by ropes The other parts are not protected at all, and the only beings to be seen straying upon it are cows. In other districts, where animals are apt to stray, a portion of the ground needs protection This is effected by various means, according to the situation of the spot and the financial condition of the clubs to whom the ground is apportioned Sheep are harmless enough, yea, beneficial, but the shoes of horses make indentations not easily rubbed out by the ordinary process of a common roller Everybody visiting the St Lawrence ground in the Canterbury week is struck with its condition for the purposes of cricket, and the question often arises, what kind of preparation was made five or six and twenty years ago, to get it into a state producing the satisfactory results? To this it may be said, that one year did not achieve the object, nor five The ground at that period was not level, but was made so by degrees at the suggestion of many a visitor, who saw with different eyes to those of the executive, and good advice was not disregarded There are about ten acres of the ground, *i.e.*, from one extremity to the other, but little more than half of this area is adapted for cricket purposes, the soil is clay, and the subsoil chalk It has a fall from S W. to N E Previous to the Week, the mowing machine is kept in exercise, and a steam roller is used, not merely in the line of wickets, but transversely, so that the ground is truly as level and compact as a billiard table—no redundancy of herbage, not greater in proportion, and scarcely less smooth, than the baize over which the billiard ball has to travel The great secret of its condition may be referred to top dressings, and their application at the right time The proverb about the broth and too many cooks furnishes, no doubt, a considerable amount of truth, but there is another proverb about which there can be little scope for cavil, *i e*, in the multitude of counsel there is wisdom and safety Moreover, while the opinions of learned theorists are valued and thought over, the ideas of the humble practitioner may, and often do, contain much real wisdom and usefulness A few scraps from the "records of a ground man" (manuscript) will, in a great degree, serve to illustrate this proposition He puts lawns and cricket grounds pretty much on the same footing as respects preparation, although one is merely regarded in the light of quietude and ornament, the other of bustle, wear and tear The ground man, evidently not ignorant of field and garden culture, shall speak for himself

Land or Lawn Drainage —In the first place, this operation should be commenced as early as possible in the winter months The drains should be cut from two to three feet in depth according to the soil, with an interval of twenty-four feet between the drains In clayey soils twelve feet will not be too near At the bottom of the drain should be placed one-inch pipes, these should be well puddled over six inches deep with clay, and then return the earth They should have an outfall at the least elevated side of the lawn, by having pipes somewhat less than an inch bore, so that moles cannot creep in this bore will be found sufficient to carry off all the water of the heaviest rain

Making New Grounds —It is, generally speaking, necessary in making a cricket ground to dig from six to nine inches A foundation of chalk is very desirable, as it keeps the turf dry in winter and cold in hot summer weather. Open the trench about two feet wide, and as deep as good soil goes down The chalk and soil then place in alternate layers. When this is done, the whole area should be levelled, raked, and made firm, if the soil should be stoney, it will be advisable to get some good mould and spread over it to the depth of from three to six inches The mould should be all of one sort, in order to make the growth of grass even and of the same colour Any trifling uneven parts of the surface can be remedied with a turf beater when the grass has got strong and the land sufficiently settled down to bear the operation without suffering All new grounds should be made in the autumn months, the earlier the better

Turf may be obtained either by sowing grass seeds or laying turf from a common or down When the latter plan is adopted, which is far better than any which can be obtained from seeds, great care is required to remove stones The surface must be raked strictly level, yet sufficiently loose for the roots of the turf to cling to The best season for laying down turf is from September to March, although it will grow at almost any time of the year not frosty Being cut with a proper turfing iron, equal length, width and thickness may be obtained. Here, again, care is necessary Roll each turf up tight, the grass side inwards, and pile them up by tens, especially if they are cut by the 100 In replacing them, join up edge to edge, making good all deficiency of broken parts as the laying proceeds This done, a turf beater, made either of elm or oak plank, should be used, and afterwards a heavy roller in moist weather Should the joints be affected by hot weather, a plentiful supply of water and the application of a little properly prepared mould will soon put the matter to rights

For grass seeds equally appropriate to lawn and cricket grounds, the following are to be commended as certain to produce a close and velvety turf.

Grass Seeds for Lawns and Cricket Grounds —After a course of careful observation of the numerous kinds suitable for the purpose which have come under my notice, I can confidently recommend the following varieties as most certain to procure a close velvety turf

	Light Soil lb	Medium Soil lb	Heavy Soil lb
Cynosurus cristatus (Crested dogstail)	5	6	7
Festuca duriuscula (Hardish fescue	3	3	4
Festuca tenuifolia (Fine leaved fescue)	2	2	1
Lolium perenne tenue (Fine rye grass)	20	20	20
Poa nemoralis (Wood meadow grass)	1½	1⅓	2
Poa nemoralis sempervirens (Evergreen ditto)	1½	1⅓	2
Poa trivialis (Rough-stalked meadow grass)	1½	1⅓	2
Medicago lupulina (Yellow trefoil)	2	2	1
Lotus corniculatus (Bird's-foot trefoil)	2	2	1

These should be mixed in their proper proportions, and sown at the rate of three bushels or sixty pounds per acre, or one gallon to six rods or perches After the sowing has been accomplished, the ground should be again rolled, and as soon as the young plants have attained the height of two or three inches, the whole plot should be carefully gone over with a sharp scythe Frequent mowing and rolling are indispensable to maintain the turf in good order By adopting these means a close green sward will be obtained in nearly as short time as a lawn produced by turf, and at much less expense It will sometimes happen that annual weeds indigenous to the soil come up, these can easily be checked, if not destroyed, by mowing them off as soon as they make their appearance Plantains, dandelions, and daisies, too, will often appear, and these must be cut up, each one singly, about an inch below the surface, and about a teaspoonful of salt dropped over the cut. Most birds are very fond of grass seeds and care should be taken to keep them off until the seeds are well up For the lawns requiring improvement it is only necessary to sow fresh seeds, either in the spring or autumn, using a small toothed rake, and rolling afterwards Moss in lawns is generally a sign of poorness in the soil or want of drainage. To effect its removal, I recommend, after raking off as much moss as possible, a top dressing with rich manure applied in the winter and a sowing of more seed in the spring, another light top dressing, by encouraging the growth of grass, destroys the moss This should be applied in the spring at the rate of about twenty bushels per acre On croquet or cricket grounds, where the turf has become bare, a light dressing of manure over the whole playing square will often be found beneficial in encouraging the growth of finer kinds of grasses, and help to produce a close-growing turf This should be done either in September or early in March The subsequent rolling and mowing will depend upon circumstances Here it may be well to mention that lawn mowing alone will not ensure a good bottom without that compression which the roller and the beater only can give

Lawn Dressing.—With artificial manure the nitrate of soda is about one-third dearer than Peruvian guano, but more powerful in its effects upon daisies and plantains Vendors of this article make up quantities as small as seven pounds of the former and fourteen of the latter, the manure should be applied at the rate of three and a half pounds to the rod in bright sunny weather if it is desired to destroy daisies, plantains, &c, as well as to strengthen the grass, but if there are no daisies to be killed, put it on in dull showery weather, to avoid the grass being browned After dressing the lawn with either nitrate of soda or guano in bright weather, the grass will assume a brownish hue, but it will soon recover and regain its proper colour, therefore you need not feel any anxiety on that score Sprinkling the nitrate over the surface of the lawn in a dry state is preferable to mixing it with water previous to using

Ashes are the remains of a substance which has undergone burning, and are as various in the proportions of their components as are the bodies capable of being burnt Whatever be the substance burnt, the process should be advanced as slowly as possible, for by such regulation more carbon or charcoal is preserved in the ashes, which is the most valuable of their constituents The simplest mode of effecting a slow combustion is to bank the burning substance over with earth, leaving only a small orifice to admit the air sufficiently to keep up a smouldering fire

Ashes have been usually recommended as a manure most useful to heavy soils, but this is a decided mistake As fertilisers they are beneficial upon all soils, and they can never be applied in sufficient quantity to alter the staple of a too tenacious soil To thirty square yards twenty-eight pounds are an average application, and they cannot be put on too fresh

Peat ashes contain

Silica (flint)	32
Sulphate of (gypsum)	12
Sulphate and muriate of soda (glauber, and common salt)	6
Carbonate of lime (chalk)	40
Oxide of iron	3
Loss	7

They are an excellent application to lawns, &c

Coal Ashes—They are very useful for forming dry walks, and sprinkling on the surface in the kitchen and flower garden department

Soap boiler's ashes contain

Silica	35	0
Lime	35	0
Magnesia	2	3
Alumina (clay)	1	5
Oxide of iron	1	7
Manganese	1	8
Potash, combined with silica	0	5
Soda, ditto	0	2
Sulphuric acid, combined with lime	0	2
Phosphoric acid ditto	3	5
Common salt	0	1
Carbonic acid, combined with lime and magnesia	18	2

They are good for all grass lawns and cricket grounds

Wood ashes are one of the best manures for close velvety turf, but they always produce clover if much used, and that is very bad for cricket grounds There is no wear in it, and it makes the ground play very uneven The ball gets up from it and punishes the batsman, breaks his finger, or knocks the finger-nail off, and then the ground is condemned and the owners as well, and after all it is the beautiful and elegant clover There is nothing like clean, pure grass turf for cricket grounds, but a little clover does not injure a croquet lawn Wood ashes generally contain silica, alumina, oxides of iron and manganese, lime, magnesia, potash (partly in the state of a silicate), soda, sulphates of potash and lime, phosphates of lime, chloride of sodium (common salt), and carbonates of lime, potash, and magnesia, with a considerable portion of charcoal

Mowing is, next to digging, the most laborious of the gardener's employment, and requires much practice, as well as an extremely sharp scythe, before he can attain to the art of shaving the lawn or grass plot smoothly and equally There have been several good mowing machines invented by Messrs Shanks, Green, and others, and they cut, collect, and roll the grass at the same time, and are much better and easier than the old scythe system, and a man can mow three times as much with a mowing machine as he can with a scythe

For all this care about grounds English cricketers ought to be very thankful.

Great benefits are seldom estimated until by force of circumstances they happen to be diminished or entirely withdrawn. Many eminent players are every year drafted to some foreign station. They carry the love of the game with them, but how inadequate are the means for practising it as they ought. Here is a ground hard as a flint; there, one soft as a bog. Here, the light of the sun is long and distressing; there, it is doubtful and deceiving. But whatever may be the change of circumstances under which they exist, those who really delight in the game subordinate all trifling inconveniences to it, and are happy withal.*

* H.M.S. CHALLENGER.—On our journey home we made a halt at Cape de Verd Island, when an opportunity presented itself of playing a match. The club boasted of only fifteen members, and if they had not met with a run of bad luck they would probably have carried off the palm. They entertained us at cricket and other amusements they got up. Their ground is young, and being based on a volcanic soil is not likely to improve.—*Extract of a Letter from Lieutenant Carpenter to the Author.*

CHAPTER XXIV.

THE LAWS OF CRICKET, AND A COMMENTARY THEREON.

For Law's the wisdom of all ages,
And managed by the ablest sages;
Who, though their business at the bar
Be but a kind of civil war,
In which th' engage with fiercer dudgeons
Than e'er the *Grecians* did and *Trojans*,
They never manage to contest
T' impair the public interest.—*Hudibras, Canto* 3.

TO the timorous, the word Law is the embodiment of terror; but the stronger-minded hail it as a necessity. Society, in its rudest forms, has a code of some sort expressed or understood, and as nations widen into form and eminence, so must their modes of government change, and their laws also. Some may be too severe as others are lax. The happy medium is the slow growth of time and interchange of thought and communication. It is said that a celebrated lawgiver of Athens, when he exercised the office of *archon*, made a code of laws for the use of the citizens, which, on account of their severity, were said to be written in letters of blood. The Athenians must surely have had a fearful existence. But as that was more than 2000 years ago, it may as well be numbered among forgotten events. Horrifying as the statement may be to civilised ears, there yet lives a barbarian under the title of King who delights to consummate his laws, whatever they may be, "in pools of gory hue." His subjects must hold their lives upon very precarious leases.

The Medes and Persians, who laid claim to much learning and culture, made their laws irrevocable—a fact that suggests want of wisdom, seeing how impossible it is to make fixed codes work well while everything in nature and among peoples is perpetually changing. Hence Medea, where is it? and Persia, what is it? Society must either be on the advance, or else it retrogrades.

The ancient Romans exhibited a great deal of wisdom in their law making. The scheme was hung up in some public place that it might be exposed to any passer by. Here it remained for three weeks, or during the space of *tres nundinæ*, including three market days, whereby the inhabitants, both of the city and country, had an opportunity of examining it. Orators and lawyers harangued upon the scheme, so that every man might be able to hear what was said for and against it. After this came a general voting, and if the law was approved by the majority, it was engraved in copper. The ceremony had such an effect, that the law so made not only remained in force to the end of the Roman Empire, but survived it. Some people would regard this mode of proceeding as tedious, and aver that it is an easy matter by a subsequent act to correct the errors or supply the deficiencies of a former one. Just so; but is it not better to ponder over the probable effects of a new proposition before it passes into a law? Even in our sports a great deal of thought is necessary to compass rightly the meaning of the laws by which they are governed, especially by those entrusted with their administration, many of whom are "ignorant and unlearned men," and against whose decision there is no appeal. Now, there are more ways of settling questions than at first sight appears on the face of the cricket code, and on this account some explanations are here offered with all deference to those having any concern in the matter. By reverting to the first published code,* and comparing it with that of a century later, a very great difference is perceptible. The various alterations and enlargements are not matters for wonder—they point rather to a necessity. Nor are these laws so perfect now as they might and ought to be. Some will bear a double interpretation; and although a few may be determined easily off hand by the least erudite of umpires, there are others which puzzle the most astute.

I.—That the Ball must weigh not less than five ounces and a half, nor more than five ounces and three quarters; it must measure not less than nine inches, nor more than nine inches and one quarter in circumference. At the beginning of each innings either party may call for a new ball.

In order to bring the ball within the scope defined the process of making it involves great care and nicety. When this leading law was first propounded, balls were so imperfectly made that the stitches frequently gave way before a match was half played out. Such is not the case now-a-days. All first class makers stamp their names, as a guarantee of quality and correctness. John Small, of Petersfield, Hants, is credited with the invention of the treble-seamed ball. Mr Robert Dark a few years previous to his death was in possession of a few tools once used by Small in manufacturing the ball. Two balls are amply sufficient, with fair usage, to carry a match through, even if a thousand runs are knocked out of them—aye, twice this number if they have nothing but a proper ground to travel over.

II.—The Bat must not exceed four inches and one quarter in the widest part; it must not be more than thirty-eight inches in length.

In the primitive stages of cricket there was neither limitation to length, nor stipulation as to the width of the bat. Several pictures extant represent it as an instrument of great length, curved as a volute at the lower extremity, fit only for hitting. The changed character of the bowling necessitated a pod or blade, which was limited to the lateral extent mentioned in the law. There were not, however, any variable restrictions as to the length of the pod, provided it did not get beyond the thirty-eight inches. It was soon found that if the shoulder of the bat was out of proportion with its general construction it would not only look clumsy, but would be unwieldy, and—without any compensating advantage—offer chances to the field.† Lambert says, in his appendix

* See page 25.

† Bats in the early part of the present century were not so elegant as now. Wisden has one in his possession of the following dimensions: 3½in. at the shoulder, and 4in. at the base, 35in. in length from end to end, and 2¾in. the pod.

DIAGRAM OF WICKETS.

This diagram does not require much to be said in the way of explanation. No. 1, with the hole in the centre, was two feet wide and one foot high. It is not known exactly when No. 2 displaced the primitive size with its more elegant proportions of twenty-two inches by six. Nor is it quite certain when the third stump made its first appearance with an increase of two inches in height and one in breadth. No. 4 is the wicket of the present day.

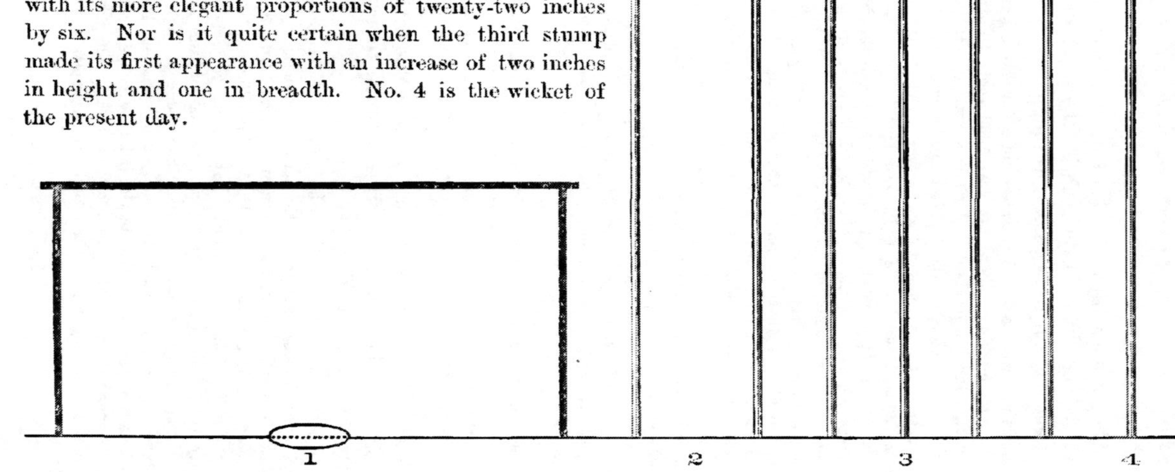

to "The Cricketer's Guide" "There is no particular height for a bat, but it is advisable not to have it higher than twenty-one inches in the pod, and as much narrower and shorter as may be thought proper" No mention is made of weight, but match bats vary from two pounds to five or six ounces beyond

III—The stumps must be three in number, twenty-seven inches out of the ground, the bails eight inches in length, the stumps of equal and sufficient thickness to prevent the ball from passing through

The stumps in their erect and complete form constitute what is termed a wicket It is stated in the MS of an old cricketer, about the year 1700, that the stumps were but two in number, and were one foot high and two feet wide A material change, both in height and width, followed before the eighteenth century closed About 1775 a third stump was introduced, making the breadth of the wicket six inches and its height twenty-two inches Other changes succeeded, until in the year 1818 the present standard of width and height was adopted, and a second bail introduced These stumps should be equal in width, not larger in circumference at the bottom than at the top, as is sometimes the case Although five detached pieces are used in ninety nine matches out of a hundred, there are other modes of forming a wicket, not forbidden by law, for instance, there is one patented by a house in the city which consists of an oblong metal plate, fixed in the ground by two long spikes, and fitted with three sunk collars of vulcanised indiarubber, which receive the ends of the stumps Each stump is held in its true position by the collars, and when down can be replaced in much less time than ordinary, and without disturbing the ground The entire wicket can be fixed in two minutes The stumps in common use can be easily adapted to the base plate, which from its construction insures invariable correctness of dimensions (Patented by Messrs Fuller and Margaret, London)

There is another which takes the name of a "Self-acting Regulation Wicket" This is so constructed that, after yielding to the blow of a ball, it instantly regains its original position, so that when once pitched for a match, or for practice, it requires no further attention throughout the time of play The entire wicket is formed by placing a frame or "shoe" into the ground, and the stumps are acted upon by means of a spiral spring

It should be observed that the bails form a very important part of the wicket, as indicators whether it was struck or not, but matches have been played without them, owing to the prevalence of wind and the agreement between umpires to dispense with them One would think that while Boreas was blowing great guns, cricket would be out of harmony with him altogether

IV—The Bowling Crease must be in a line with the stumps, six feet eight inches in length, the stumps in centre, with a return crease at each end towards the bowler at the right angles

This is the "measured tread" on which so much depends—often the line of vexation to the bowler, and of much close watching on the part of the umpire It is a "no balling" station, and a point to which the attention of the looker-on is turned with especial interest The object of the "return crease" is to prevent the bowler from indulging in erratic distances from the wicket in delivering the ball Very few umpires have much respect for the science of trigonometry, consequently their right angles are often somewhat obtuse, and not unfrequently acute It is, nevertheless, their duty to acquire sufficient knowledge of angles to prevent any unfair confusion to the batsman by allowing such as would throw him off his given guard, which is generally calculated from the spot at which the bowler is known and expected to deliver It does happen that bowlers of a somewhat elastic disposition appear to overstep the mark, when in reality such is not the case, and for this they have at times to pay an unjust penalty All umpires are not equally quick-sighted.

"Æquam memento rebus in arduis,
Servare pedem"—*Hor*

In the arduous task of bowling, therefore, preserve the "measured tread"

V.—The Popping Crease must be four feet from the wicket, and parallel to it, unlimited in length, but not shorter than the bowling crease.

Our early legislators decreed that the "popping crease" should be cut exactly three feet ten inches from the wickets. In the year 1828 two inches were added, thus extending the batsman's hitting area to the present size. The practice of cutting the creases was kept up at Marylebone till the year 1864, much to the detriment of the ground itself, as it tended to weaken, if not destroy, the fibre of the turf, already in a decaying condition. The plan now adopted is to set out the wicket with a wooden frame of the exact dimensions required by the statute, and then to describe the crease by a white line outside the frame. This can be rewhitened when obliterated by hard wear or damp weather. In the very early stages of cricket no mention is made of the popping crease. A large hole was dug between the two stumps which then constituted a wicket, and into this hole the butt end of the bat had to be placed to indicate a run effectually made. As many severe injuries arose from such a method, the popping crease was substituted. Although the term unlimited, as applied to this white line, is, or ought to be, intelligible to the meanest mental capacity, a case is recorded of a batsman being declared out because "he ran round his ground." The umpire was "taken off," but the match was lost in consequence of the stupid decision.

VI.—The Wickets must be pitched opposite each other by the Umpires, at the distance of twenty-two yards.

Like the laws of the Medes and Persians, No. 6 altereth not. Why twenty-two yards were originally resolved upon as the limits of distance, is not more mysterious than the appointment of eleven persons as the necessary number for playing the game. Imagination has taken wild flights on this topic. Although the law makes no mention of the choice of pitching, custom awards the privilege to the parties leaving home. Lambert says: "It has been the custom when two matches are played by the same parties, that the one that goes from home should have the choice of innings and pitching the first wicket, which must be within thirty yards of a centre fixed on by the adversaries, but this must be agreed on at the time of making the match; but if only one match is played, or two on the same ground, the umpires must pitch the wickets." The fitness of the ground in and about the pitch of the ball is a matter of great importance, and requires the closest scrutiny, as any inequality impairs the best bowling, baffles the best batsmen, and often gives rise to serious accidents.

VII.—It shall not be lawful for either party, during a match, without the consent of the other, to alter the ground by rolling, watering, covering, mowing, or beating, except at the commencement of each innings, when the ground may be swept and rolled, unless the side next going in object to it. This rule is not meant to prevent the striker from beating the ground with his bat near to the spot where he stands during the innings, nor to prevent the bowler from filling up holes with sawdust, &c., when the ground is wet.

Before cricket had assumed the stalwart proportions of the present day, no such law as this was needed. The bowling, though at times very fast (according to Nyren), had few of those dangers which accompany the speed of many a round-arm celebrity of the present day. Every precaution ought to be taken to prevent accidents arising from defective surfaces. Such implements as the scythe, roller, besom, and hydrants should be well and judiciously used before a match is attempted. In extreme cases, the refusal of an umpire to grant a request would subject him to a question of fitness for the proper discharge of his duty. On the other hand, an evil would ensue from the too liberal granting of a batsman to make deep holes in the ground for a footing. A few years ago the Marylebone Club instructed their umpires not to allow it. The practice, however, is not quite discontinued, although it ought to be. Sawdust was first introduced by Lord Frederick Beauclerk, in

1806 When Rule VII was first introduced, the parties were compelled to apply for the roller and broom within one minute of going in This short notice was repealed in 1859, and the law enlarged to its present dimensions

VIII —After rain the wickets may be changed, with the consent of both parties

When this rule was framed, the baneful practice of betting held sway, and as umpires frequently "stood in," every advantage was taken in adverse weather—money being the primary, cricket the secondary consideration Such is not the case now, and these important guardians of the play have their eye on fair and honourable competition, although some, perchance, may have a strong predilection, which, considering the infirmities of human nature, is by no means unnatural Matches have been pushed to such extremes that the batsmen have been besmirched and half blinded by the mud spots of their own scattering About eight years ago, a match occurred at Harrow which lasted three days in consequence of frequent pluvial interruptions A part of the field was covered with water, and fresh wickets were pitched on the third day and in the middle of an innings

IX —The Bowler shall deliver the ball with one foot on the ground behind the bowling crease, and within the return crease, and shall bowl one over before he change wickets, which he shall be permitted to do *twice* in the same innings, and no bowler shall bowl more than two overs in succession.

Until within the last seven years this law scarcely received a touch of alteration from the period of its being framed The bowler was only allowed to change wickets once in the same innings He may now do so twice, but in order to guard against any unfair use of this privilege, he must not bowl more than two overs in succession Notwithstanding the clear definition of a no-ball, an umpire in a very important match in 1863 called "no-ball" because the bowler delivered it with *both* feet *behind* the crease Much disagreement arose in consequence of this decision One party as strenuously supported the umpire as the other condemned him A remedy was found in cashiering the illiterate functionary for evermore in matches of public importance Although some clubs insist on bowling more than four balls to the over the M C C do not yet perceive the necessity for any departure from this honoured rule, except in one day matches, when five or six are agreed upon by the sides previous to commencement of play Some contend for five balls as the sub-multiple of ten, and thereby more convenient in gathering up analyses from the score sheet If the whim of every theorist were to be consulted, there is no telling what figure should be selected Any bowler kept closely to work on a blistering summer day, finds four balls quite enough at a time No bowler can deliver a ball without one foot being on the ground, although the contrary has frequently been asserted It may occasionally appear so, but 'tis an optical illusion, and a physical impossibility A little consternation was caused a year ago in a match of some local importance at Portsmouth A bowler left his wicket A and crossed over to B After bowling two overs he returned to A, but imagining wicket B suited him better, went across to it again Before completing an over the umpire was reminded that the said bowler had been there before He, however, ruled that the over must be completed, during which five runs were scored and one man caught out A dispute arose which neither party could settle, viz, were the runs of any value, or was the man out

X —The ball must be bowled If thrown or jerked the umpire shall call "No ball"

A very few years ago Law X was, for discussion, the most fruitful in the whole code, the cutting out of two vexatious passages has rendered its dispensation a very easy matter now

XI —He may require the striker at the wicket from which he is bowling to stand on that side of it which he may direct

This formed one of the early canons, and it does not appear to have been disturbed to any appreciable extent It is one purely of convenience to the bowler, and would give him a great advantage, if not kept in wholesome check Moreover, a batsman might not feel himself very well pleased at being "required" first to this side and anon to that, according to the caprice of a bowler The only difference between the original and the present law exists in the words "order" and 'require" The former certainly assumes a more imperative aspect that the latter What the effect of a refusal on the part of an obstinate batsman might lead to is not pointed out In all probability the umpire's services would be called into requisition It has been said there is nothing in the rule to prohibit the bowler from changing his side every ball, and without giving the batsman notice of his intention In such case the bowler would obtain a great advantage over the batsman, who, by taking guard from one extremity, would have to contend with an angle at which he might not be able to determine whether the ball was on the wicket or not

XII—If the bowler shall toss the ball over the striker's head, or bowl it so wide that, in the opinion of the umpire, it shall not be fairly within the reach of the batsman, he shall adjudge one run to the party receiving the innings, either with or without an appeal, which shall be put down to the score of wide balls such ball shall not be reckoned as one of the four balls, but if the batsman shall by any means bring himself within reach of the ball the run shall not be adjudged

Elsewhere the question of what is a wide ball forms the subject matter of a note, and here, too, it forces itself prominently forward A somewhat curious incident relating to a wide ball took place a few years since at the Oval, Kennington Mr E M Grace bowled a ball by no means of the ordinary kind, it reached an altitude of nearly twenty feet, and then fell at an angle altogether unlooked for by the batsman, who however, drove the awkward visitor to leg, and scored two runs The trick was repeated, but Jupp turned sulky, and did not attempt to play it, then came a third, which the same batsman disregarded altogether, and the wicket was hit The umpire declared in favour of the bowler, but the "company" hissed, and denounced the proceedings altogether How could a ball be *wide* twenty feet over head? Mr Denison frequently urged the M C C to a definition of a wide ball, but he did not live to witness one to his satisfaction The first mention of wides on the score-sheet appears to be in a match at Brighton, between Kent and Sussex Previous to this they were lumped with byes

XIII—If the bowler shall deliver a "No Ball," or a "Wide Ball" the striker shall be allowed as many runs as he can get · and he shall not be put out except by running out In the event of no run being obtained by any other means, then one run shall be added to the score of "No Balls,' or "Wide Balls," as the case may be. All runs obtained for "Wide Balls" to be scored to "Wide Balls" The names of the bowlers who bowl "Wide Balls" or "No Balls" in future to be placed on the score, to show the parties by whom either score is made If the ball shall first touch any part of the striker's dress or person (except his hands) the umpire shall call "Leg Bye"

First comes the inquiry what is to be understood by a "wide ball?" Here great confusion of ideas often prevails, as the matter is entirely in the hands or brains of umpires among whom much diversity of opinion is expressed The prevailing definition of a wide ball is one bowled beyond the reach of the striker supposing him to make a reasonable effort to hit it But then it is argued there is a material difference in the reach of batsmen when extended to the utmost limit, so that the same kind of ball—in fact the same ball—may be within and without reach, according to the physical condition of the striker The law was framed, no doubt, to check wild bowlers, not to set a premium upon short batters "The umpire shall call leg-bye," says the latter clause of this rule, but more runs may be obtained from the same ball It would, however, be useless to run a bye without there was a chance of making two runs, seeing that without attempting to run, one would be scored, and the wicket not endangered To run a bye from a wide or no ball does not add two to the score—one for the wide or no ball, and one for the bye When two or more result, they are placed to score of wides or no balls, as the case may be, not to byes It the striker hit a no ball, and he obtains runs thereby, the runs will be placed to his own score, and one for a no ball will not be reckoned In former years only one run was scored for a wide or no ball, and at the present day some bowlers complain of the injustice in punishing them for other people's transgressions The notification of a leg-bye is usually by the umpire putting his hand to his leg, or lifting the leg up The run was first suggested by Mr Denison, in 1845, to particularise the padded legs, from those which went directly to the long stop At first he was ridiculed, but at length his reasoning prevailed, and in 1856 it formed part of the law in question

XIV —At the beginning of each innings the Umpire shall call "Play," and from that time to the end of each innings no trial ball shall be allowed to any bowler

Any explanatory remarks upon such a law as this may at first sight appear altogether superfluous Of late years, however, the practice of trial balls has so increased as to make the law a nullity It is no uncommon thing to see a fresh bowler ' do" a complete over for what he is pleased to call the swing of his arm, and even to repeat this little game on changing ends Some maintain the right by long use, which in fact amounts to no right, even though lawmakers sitting so frequently in council allow the law to stand unaltered year after year, and when one dip of ink would define its meaning, limit its use or abuse, or cancel it altogether

XV —The Striker is Out if either of the bails be bowled off, or if a stump be bowled out of the ground

Clear as if written with a sunbeam. Cases have occurred concerning which the promoters of this law had never bestowed a thought They naturally supposed, if the stumps were struck with any force at all, the bails must fall Not many years since, in a match of importance, one of the bails was displaced from its socket by the ball, and fell again into it Two similar cases are also recorded In none of these cases was the least doubt entertained about the removal of the bail, but in two out of three the umpire said 'Not out' A curious case occurred about a year since in a military match at Hong Kong A ball of such tremendous pace was delivered, that the middle stump was driven clean out of the ground to a distance of five yards The bails, however, held together, and thus an old-fashioned wicket was presented to view On appealing to the startled umpire, that functionary declared ' not out," because the bails did not drop He did not vouchsafe an interpretation of the second clause of the law

Another case is mentioned by Peter Bancalari A ball so struck the wicket that a bail fell out of the groove, and stuck between the stumps within " a hair's breadth of the ground ' The batsman was declared " not out "

XVI —Or, if the ball, from the stroke of the bat, or hand, but not the wrist, be held before it touch the ground, although it be hugged to the body of the catcher

Some people regard fielding of the hugged character as clumsy It is easy enough to look on, criticise, and condemn, when it is not quite so easy to do the thing clean It often happens that the most difficult and clever fielding is altogether unappreciated, while that of the more sensational kind is applauded to the echo If the ball be caught close to the ground, even if the hand of the fielder touch it, so long as the ball itself does not, the striker would be out

XVII —Or, if in striking, or at any other time while the ball shall be in play, both his feet shall be over the popping crease, and his wicket be put down, except his bat be grounded within it

Many have been the disputes respecting the fairness of a bowler in putting down a wicket whilst pretending to deliver the ball At first glance the act has a childish look about it, and not in keeping with the character of cricket; but if a batsman starts before the ball is delivered, he takes an undue advantage, and must bear the consequences. The ground between the popping crease and wicket belongs to the batsman, and the instant he leaves it he lays himself open to the adversary. The bat must be grounded within the limits of the popping crease—that is beyond, or over the white line, not upon it, as the crease itself is a part of the measured ground between the wickets. In the event of a batsman being put out by an unfair start, it has been asked how the event should be recorded in the score sheet. Strictly speaking it cannot be run out, because the ball has not been delivered; but in the absence of any other acknowledged mode, it is so recorded, upon the principle that the wicket put down when the batsman is not in the act of striking ought to be so defined, in contradistinction to a wicket put down while in the act of striking, which is invariably marked "stumpt."

XVIII.—Or, if in striking at the ball, he hit down his wicket.

"Hit wicket" was a punishable offence more than a hundred years ago, and has continued so till the present time without any attempt at amelioration. If a batsman, in making or rather completing a run, hit the wicket either with his bat or person, he would not be out, unless it be with an intention of leaving his opponents a broken wicket to deal with, in which case the umpires would have to interfere. A singular case transpired in the year 1866, at Gravesend, in a return match between Kent and Sussex. Wells, a batsman of diminutive proportions, happened to hit his wicket while preparing to meet the ball before it was actually delivered. An appeal to the umpire resulted in giving Wells out, who was extremely indignant. Nor he alone. The decision was disputed. How could a man be "striking at the ball" which was undelivered, was the argument, to which a stronger might have been added, "Who could say whether it might not have been a "no ball?" Although the words "hit down" are used, if the wicket be hit with sufficient force to remove a bail it is enough. Another case is recorded of a similar character at King's Walden, in Hertfordshire, when Mr. Money knocked off a bail as Hughes was about to deliver the ball. An appeal to the umpire (Thoms) was immediately responded to "Not out." Winchester played Eton at Lords in 1845, when Mr. Bateman was given out "trod on his wicket."

XIX.—Or, if under pretence of running, or otherwise, either of the strikers prevent a ball from being caught, the striker of the ball is out.

"Prevent" in this instance means a design on the part of a batsman to thwart the fielder in the execution of his duty. But who, it may be asked, can penetrate or fathom the mazes of purpose? It is a matter for an umpire who has to decide off hand, and a very perplexing matter. There are many umpires too many—who have the organs for, and the capacity of, seeing, but who are often afraid to use their eyes.

XX.—Or if the Ball be struck, and he wilfully strike it again.

"Wilfully" is an adverb in legal formularies of very ugly aspect. In the matter of cricket a batsman is fully justified in wilfully striking the ball a second time if it be in defence of his wicket. The object of the law in question is to prevent a striker from baulking the field by a dangerous and unfair interference with the ball when hit away from the wicket for the purpose of obtaining runs. Moreover, the hit would be useless, as nothing could be scored from it. A case is recorded in the year 1832 of a batsman who, in attempting a run, prevented the ball from reaching the wicket-keeper's hands by the interposition of his bat. On appeal the man was given "out," and very properly so.

XXI.—Or if in running, the wicket be struck down by a throw, or by the hand or arm (with ball in hand) before his bat (in hand), or some part of his person be grounded over the popping crease. But if both the bails be off, a stump must be struck out of the ground.

"Ball in hand" means the hand which knocks down or strikes the wicket. In other words the ball must not be in hand detached from that which puts down the wicket. A case occurred not long since of a wicket-keeper prostrating all three stumps with one hand and holding up the ball with the other. On appeal to the great authority for the time being a verdict of "out" was pronounced. This was repudiated by some and acknowledged by others. But the umpire was wrong. Had even the wrist of the hand which held the ball touched any portion of that which put down the wicket, the decision would have been a good one, as contact is necessary. Over the popping crease means beyond and not upon it. Sometimes the whole wicket is in ruins. In such case the keeper must put up a stump and knock it down before the batsman can be legally declared out. If a batsman, in running, happens to drop his bat—a very common circumstance—he is not compelled to pick it up. Nor does the law say that he shall not continue to run without it, although it would be manifestly unfair to permit him to do so.

XXII.—Or, if any part of the striker's dress knocks down the wicket.

That is to say, any part of the dress while the batsman is in the act of striking. Here the opportunity is convenient for observing that if a wicket be knocked down by a ball struck from the opposite batsman, the man would not be out, even if he happened to be off his ground. The ball must be fielded. It has, however, been held that if the ball merely touches the hand, or even other parts of the fielder's person, and is in consequence directed into the wicket, the batsman, if out of his ground, loses his wicket. The only part of the striker's dress likely to imperil his wicket is his hat and this he usually guards against by testing its adherence to his head before venturing to strike. Wind is often a capricious enemy. If any part of the striker's dress impede the ball so as to retain it temporarily, the batsman may be caught from it. A few years since a batsman played a ball into the folds of his pads, where it remained until removed by the wicket-keeper. "How's that, umpire?"—"Out." A somewhat similar circumstance of older date is recorded. A few runs were wanted to win, and a dependable batsman was sent in; he played the first ball into his breeches' pocket; he then started to run, and would have continued his course up to the winning figure had not an antagonist rolled him over and thereby abstracted the ball. Another case is mentioned in which the ball ran up the handle of the bat and secreted itself in the batsman's jacket pocket. He ran round the field in order to work it out without touching it, and in the end succeeded, though pursued by a strong pack, and got back to his wicket before the ball was thrown in. This man's name was Charles Hodsoll, of Dartford, a descendant of the Hadswell mentioned by Love in his Poem of 1746. Another case still more singular and delicate, is said to have occurred with the celebrated Mr. Ward, who played a ball into the inclosure of his pantaloons, and as extraction by the field was out of question, the matter was compromised. These statements may appear to have a smack of the marvellous, but facts are stubborn things.

XXIII.—Or, if the striker touch or take up the ball while in play, unless at the request of the opposite party.

To an ordinary observer this canon might be regarded as an incumbrance to the statute book, so rarely is it brought under notice. A little inspection, however, opens up one important proposition, viz. that the bat and ball cannot be confounded in their respective times and usages, without destroying one of the primary and essential principles of cricket. No batsman has any right whatever to handle the ball while a match is in progress, and no fielder ought to make use of the bat under any circumstances till the turn arrives for him so to do. The very last law in the statute book in language not to be mistaken forbids this, although it does not punish offenders after the same fashion as it does a batsman whose fingers willingly or otherwise handle the ball.

It is rather strange that no mention is made in any law respecting the number of persons composing the 'opposite party.' Lambert in the early part of the present century, says "In a regular and full game the number of players consists of twenty-two—eleven on each side." Nyren subsequently said the same thing. As yet no one has hazarded a theory respecting this mystic number. Doubtless there was a reason for it. On the construction of double wicket a great deal of thought must have been expended before thought assumed the shape of law, whether written or understood The early promoters of "fast" in one sense were not slow in another

XXIV—Or, if with any part of his person he stop the ball, which in the opinion of the umpire at the bowler's wicket shall have been pitched in a straight line from it to the striker's wicket, and would have hit it

Notwithstanding the apparent plainness of this rule, it is the most perplexing and disagreeable with which an umpire has to deal Many ingenious theories have been propounded for simplifying it but hitherto without success With the present style of bowling, it is regarded as a nullity A ball to get a wicket will rarely be pitched as required by the law, and when it does so it will rather work to the off than to the wicket, and in some instances it will even break back Such being the case, it is almost impossible for the umpire, standing where he usually does to determine whether a ball wide pitched will obtain a right bias to hit the wicket It has been stated over and over again by those who have examined the matter critically, that a round-arm bowler, in delivering a ball outside the wicket, cannot pitch it within the line from wicket to wicket so that it would hit the stumps Nor was it ever contemplated that a batsman should be taught to calculate the peculiar spin an expert (slow) might put on the ball, or a rough ground give to a wide pitched one, and then if he failed to strike it, and it hit his leg, that he should be given out The question also of the line from wicket to wicket, or from hand to wicket ought to be determined upon Law X has ceased to distract the attention of the legislator and annoy the player, why should not XXIV be at once grappled with and its tormenting elements rooted out? So long ago as May 19 1797, Lord Frederick Beauclerk, in a match at Lords, was given out l b w Somewhere in Kent about the year 1835, a man was given out l b w, no doubt wrongly The batsman refused to leave, and laid down by the side of the wicket, protesting against the decision Nor would he leave The opposite side kept shouting for another man to come in, but no heed was taken of it They then demanded the match, and amidst much confusion it was broken off How few are the decisions on this law that give satisfaction, in fact l b w is a fruitful source of contention (contention, however, confined to cricket pavilions and tents, but which once forced itself into a court of justice) * The umpire has to decide, first, whether the ball would have taken the wicket Secondly, whether it was pitched straight Subtle diagrams have been drawn to assist in the decision, imaginary positions argued upon, rotation about an axis and the angle of incidence mentioned with appalling levity in vain, the evil is still uncured, potion and lotion have failed to eradicate the offending paragraph It may be asked if the rule could not be put thus "Out, if with any part of his person the batsman stop the ball, which, in the opinion of the umpire at the bowler's end &c" It is thought this trifling alteration would simplify the duties of the umpire The bat, and not the leg, is the recognised guard of the wicket If the ball pitches wide and turns in, it is of course much more difficult to be played, but a good batsman, i e, he who plays at the ball and not at the place where the ball is likely to be, will have so much the more scope for displaying his skill and quickness On the other hand, the bowler who can make his balls pitch in one direction and then turn in, is entitled to something for his superiority to a perfectly straight and plain bowler L b w is recorded in the annals of cricket as far back as the year 1795, in a match between England and Surrey, at Moulsey Hurst, so that the law has the stamp of antiquity upon it

XXV—If the players have crossed each other, he that runs from the wicket which is put down is out

Supposing both start to run and have not crossed, but are both at the same wicket which is put down, he that arrived last would be the victim Scarcely any position in the whole range of cricket presents a more ludicrous appearance than two batsmen at one wicket

XXVI—A ball being caught, no run shall be reckoned

In other words the batsman who is caught while attempting a run, cannot score even it he completes it before the ball is caught It has, however, been decided that the run would be good if the

* *Lane* v *Barnes* See *Times*, June 15, 1853.

ball was caught in its descent from the roof of a building, the top of a tent, from a rebound against a wall or tree: all such balls being regarded as "let," or hindered in the course they otherwise would have taken. An understanding to this effect ought to be entered into before play commences, in order to avoid disputes. A very singular thing occurred recently in a match between Kent and Sussex at Tonbridge Wells. A ball, hit rather high, and likely to fall over the boundary, *i.e.*, a "canvas wall," the fielder made a strong effort and caught the ball, and in so doing caused the canvas to yield. The umpire declared the man not out—caught beyond boundary. A question arose as to the correctness of the decision, seeing that the feet of the fielder were within the boundary.

XXVII.—The striker being run out, the run which he and his partner were attempting shall not be reckoned.

This wholesome regulation was suggested in consequence of a practice which at one time prevailed, of daring a run upon the feeblest pretence when a match was nearing its close; and when, perhaps, but two or three runs were wanting, and as many persons were provided to get them, yet not to be depended upon. It was "nip, touch, and away." Such play was regarded as childish and contemptible. To this, the law in question proved to be a salutary check.

XXVIII.—If a lost ball be called, the striker shall be allowed six runs; but if more than six have been run before lost ball shall have been called, then the striker shall have all that have been run.

Many curious and almost incredible circumstances might be narrated connected herewith. Originally the law applied to balls struck at so great a distance as to elude the fielder's observation. When such was the case, he would very properly exclaim "Lost ball," in order to stop the running, which might otherwise be continued to an indefinite extent. A case is recorded of a ball being seized by a mastiff dog before a single run was completed. The fielder, unable to coax the animal, had recourse to harsher measures; but to no purpose. He then claimed the privilege of lost ball, and the dog was whistled off. In another place a ball was struck with such force into the crevice of a tree, that the fielder used all the force at command to extricate it, but in vain. The batsmen were making the most of this singular event, until the cry of lost ball stopped further running. Again, a ball rolled into a pond, and floated to within two yards of the bank. The fielder on this occasion was not desirous of a bath, and he had no ready means of pulling the ball to shore. Failing to call lost ball, the batsmen continued running, and succeeded in effecting seven runs, the last of which won the match. Another case is worth quoting. A match was played upon a portion of Sheen Common set apart for cricketing purposes, and which reflected great credit upon the parties intrusted to keep it in order. A very hard hitter sent the ball far beyond the ordinary bounds, and it lodged in a furze bush, thoroughly armed at all points against aggressive legs and fingers (*Nemo impune me lacessit*). The fielder became confused, while the batsmen ran like antelopes, as but few runs were required. The ball was as visible in the bush as the sun was above it, yet it could not be extracted before the match was won. Query, can that be really a lost ball which can be touched and seen, and yet not handled by ordinary means?

XXIX.—After the ball shall have been finally settled in the wicket keeper's or bowler's hand, it shall be considered dead; but when the bowler is about to deliver the ball, if the striker at his wicket go outside the popping crease before such actual delivery, the said bowler may put him out, unless (with reference to Law XXI.) his bat in hand, or some part of his person be within the popping crease.

The *ruse* frequently adopted by wicket keepers of holding the ball, in order to catch an inexperienced hitter off his guard, has long been denounced as a contemptible experiment. "Finally settled" is generally understood to mean the time when the wicket keeper has taken the ball, and the batsman is within the limits of the popping crease It is the duty of the wicket keeper to return the ball immediately If, however, it be the last ball of the over, it is dead without being returned As regards the bowler, it is quite fair on his part to turn round and put down the non-striking batsman's wicket if he attempts to steal a run by ' following up," because the batsman flagrantly violates Law XVII, and he must therefore put up with the punishment due to his transgression Should the bowler miss the wicket, and a run or runs ensue, they are scored to byes. although it is as difficult to understand why, as it is to determine the class of extras to which they really belong

Happily, in England a disturbance with regard to this rule is very rare, but in the Colonies something more than lingual manifestations of disapproval occur Two years since, at Melbourne, a wicket keeper felt so annoyed at an adverse verdict, that he threw down the ball in disgust As it lay on the ground the batsman walked towards his partner to caution him against reckless running Meantime the ball was returned to the wicket keeper, who put the wicket down again The batsman refused to leave, although the umpire gave him out A row commenced, some decreed in favour of the decision, and as many denounced it, stone pelting ensued, and the match was broken off All this stir and disorder arose from a positive ignorance of what a dead ball is, and how "finally settled" is to be interpreted

XXX —The striker shall not retire from his wicket and return to it to complete his innings after another has been in, without the consent of the opposite party

No one will question the propriety of such a law as this, the injured or retiring party ought not to come in again until a wicket has fallen This little act of formality usually devolves upon the captains

XXXI —No substitute shall in any case be allowed to stand out or run between wickets for another person without the consent of the opposite party, and in case any person shall be allowed to run for another, the striker shall be out if either he or his substitute be off the ground in manner mentioned in Laws XVII and XXI. while the ball is in play

A "sub" very often appears upon the scene, and many strange events and perplexities have ensued The principal is, however, liable for any incompetence or rash act on the part of the sub A few examples by way of illustration A and B were batsmen, the latter required a sub C B struck a ball, from which A and C effected a run B seeing the certainty of A and C getting home in time walked leisurely to the wicket where his deputy was The ball was thrown in, and the wicket-keeper prostrated the stumps at which A was The umpire, on being appealed to, replied "out" C asked *who* was out He answered A, but presently changed his mind and said B

At Harpenden a batsman had a sub, and in hitting at a leg ball struck him on the back The ball was caught, and the batsman was given out

A case occurred at Gravesend in which the principal, forgetting he had a deputy made a run, but it did not count

Another case of forgetfulness is recorded, the principal ran instead of his deputy, and had his wicket put down What was the decree of the umpire? Out, according to Law XVII A few years ago in a match at Brighton, between the Royal Artillery and Gentlemen of Sussex, the "sub" ran, his principal followed him (unthinkingly) An effort was made to put down the opposite wicket, but failed, the ball was then thrown to the other end, and as neither principal nor deputy were within bounds, the former was given out, apparently astonished at the activity of the field.

XXXII —In all cases where a substitute shall be allowed, the consent of the opposite party shall also be obtained as to the person to act as substitute, and the place in the field which he shall take

A very few years ago the situations of a substitute were negatively specified, thus, he was not to bowl, stand at point, cover point nor stop behind in any case At present much greater latitude is afforded

XXXIII —If any fieldsman stop the ball with his hat the ball shall be considered dead, and the opposite party shall add five runs to their score, if any be run they shall have five in all

Very rarely does a violation here occur—so rarely, in fact, that scarcely one person in ten who habitually frequents a match is aware of such a rule being in existence In the year 1866 the wicket-keeper in a county match took off his pads and threw them down in the locality of short leg Presently a ball was impeded by them, and the party in appealed to the umpire, who awarded the five runs penalty for a hat obstruction This was stoutly objected to at the time, and became afterwards the subject of disputation not of the coolest kind, as these runs changed the character of vanquished to apparent victors The framers of the law never contemplated such an event, and the decision was bad To stop the ball with a hat is a wilful act, and for a direct purpose, viz , to prevent fair winning In the other case the agent was passive, and if placed contrary to law, the very judge who punished for what he considered an infraction could and ought to have prevented it

XXXIV —The ball having been hit, the striker may guard his wicket with his bat or any part of his body, except his hands, that the 23rd law may not be disobeyed

Originally the decree ran thus "If a striker nips a ball up just before him, he may fall before his wicket or pop down his bat before she comes in to save it" A curious case occurred at Oxford in the year 1850 Mr Randolph was at the wicket He wore a straw hat with a wide brim A ball rose and knocked off the hat while he was in the act of striking It twisted in the air, and fell perpendicularly on the wicket The umpire (Peter Bancalari) went to remove it, but the impatient batsman took it off himself, and in so doing removed the bails He was given out Had he permitted the umpire to do this he would have retained his post

XXXV—The Wicket Keeper shall not take the ball for the purpose of stumping until it have passed the wicket, he shall not move until the ball be out of the Bowler's hand, he shall not by any noise incommode the Striker, and if any part of his person be over or before the wicket, although the ball hit it, the Striker shall not be out.

Scarcely any part of an umpire's day's work taxes his vigilance more severely than the duty enforced by this rule An inexperienced one is often bamboozled by an expert behind the wicket The law itself is plain enough, and it only requires a firmness of purpose to carry it out Sometimes the bowling is of such a character that the wicket keeper prefers taking his stand at a considerable distance from the ' sticks " Stumping in such a case is a matter next to impossible Should the wicket, however, be struck down by a ball thrown from the wicket-keeper's hand, the batsman would be recorded as stumped out, and not run or thrown out

XXXVI —The Umpires are the sole judges of fair or unfair play, and all disputes shall be determined by them, each at his own wicket, but in case of a catch, which the Umpire at the wicket bowled from cannot see sufficiently to decide upon, he may apply to the other Umpire, whose opinion shall be conclusive *

A bit of bungling on the umpire's part occurred a few years since in a very important match at Cambridge, which demands notice as a warning to sleepy or inefficient persons undertaking the

* Many players cannot be made to understand how they are out, and invariably demur to the decision of the umpire It would be well to bear in mind an old coursing law (1801), by the Ashdown Park Club—viz , If any gentleman, after judgment given, arraigns the decision, or finds fault with the judge, he is to be amerced a gallon of wine at the pleasure of the subscribers —*See* Daniel's "Rural Sports"

onerous post A ball was struck, and a doubtful catch resulted therefrom—doubtful on account of its difficulty, and it became the subject of an appeal The first umpire said "He didn't see it," and the second, "He wasn't looking" The batsman, of course retained his situation, and although not worth a run, as last in he made a score sufficient to win the match Now it may be asked who is to estimate the wrong-doing in a case like this and who can tell how much good cricket has been neutralised by such inefficients? If there is an object of charity seeking an appointment, such object never ought to be paraded in the form of an umpire, on whom important decisions depend, and concerning which a large amount of time labour, and money has been expended in order to obtain a wreath worth striving for

With respect to fair or unfair play, the two do not supply adequate provision Unfairness may occur in a variety of ways, and it is next to impossible to legislate for every incident that may arise To the umpire's judgment the appeal is made, and whether his decree be sound or not when critically examined, the appellants must bow In a match at Gravesend about eight years since H H Stephenson was given out for "obstructing the ball" The umpire maintained that the ball was kicked in order to baulk the fielder H H declared most emphatically to the contrary, but yielded without a grumble to Luck's decision In a public school match a youth, labouring under the fearful apprehension of a weak defence when tested by a slow and very straight bowler, kept his bat immovable in the blocking-hole To this style of thing the wicket-keeper demurred, while the batsman shouted to the umpire 'Am I out if I don't move my bat?" to which he received the instantaneous reply, 'You are if you do"

XXXVII.—The Umpires in all cases shall pitch fair wickets, and the parties shall toss up for the choice of innings The Umpires shall change wickets after each party has had one innings

"Fair wickets" are considered to be such when all the inequalities of the ground about the usual pitch of the ball are overcome in the best available manner Care with respect to a level is a matter of great importance as few bowlers like an uphill wicket The process is simple enough When the spot is determined upon a stump is erected, which afterwards forms the centre of the wicket A wooden frame of dimensions requisite to compass the bowling and popping creases is then laid down, and an application of lime or chalk liquid is used to mark the boundaries A chain or tape serves to measure the proper distance between wickets No one would suppose that a surveyor, however humble, could mistake such a task, and yet in the year A D 1866 part of an innings had been played through in a county match when a bowler, fancying something wrong had the temerity to "step it," and found the distance a yard short As a rule, the wickets are pitched north and south if convenient so to do the object being to avoid as much as possible the sun's shadow between them The captains represent the "parties' spoken of That the umpires should change wickets at the end of an innings occurred first in the year 1845

XXXVIII —They shall allow two minutes for each striker to come in, and ten minutes between each innings When the umpire shall call "play," the party refusing to play shall lose the match

This proper disposition of time is not enforced by umpires of the present day with the strictness it deserves, unless, perhaps, when a game is running close, and they are reminded of their duty by the vociferations of lookers on How many matches might be rescued from the limbo of the "drawn,' if a prompt adherence to this rule were observed? A case in point occurred about ten years since when two clubs of considerable self importance played a match near Regent's Park, when, after repeated calls, which the batsman treated with contempt, the umpire drew the stumps and declared the game lost by the scorner's party A great deal of disputation and angry feeling resulted but the great majority of cricketers and the press also, backed up the umpire The waste of time at the present day is really monstrous, and much of the cricket indulged in by clubs with showy bannerets, aristocratic mottos, and high sounding names is not worth being registered, chiefly on account of its fragmentary nature, which might often be otherwise if the precious stuff of which life is made were turned to the best account.

XXXIX.—They are not to order a striker out unless appealed to by the adversaries.

They—meaning the umpires—would be very much "out of order" if they attempted such a thing. A case, however, occurred recently of a somewhat perplexing nature. The bowler delivered a no ball, and the batsman in endeavouring to make a run was caught by the wicket keeper, who, seeing the striker out of his ground, put down the wicket. On appeal, the umpire at the bowler's end said the ball was struck and caught, and the second umpire pronounced the batsman out of his ground, and of course "run out." But how the fact could be elicited was the difficulty. Could both umpires be appealed to, and were both bound to agree that the striker was out. As the matter seemed to be one of importance to the rustic mind, it was referred to a "higher court," who took time to consider their verdict.

XL.—But if one of the Bowler's feet be not on the ground behind the bowling-crease, and within the return crease when he shall deliver the ball, the umpire at his wicket, unasked, must call "No ball."

The word "crease" occurs no less than fifteen times in the laws of cricket, and yet the word is nowhere so defined as to render its meaning strictly intelligible. In referring to the original code of law, the phrase runs "creases shall be cut," meaning thereby an incision by some sharp instrument into the turf to the extent named. Of late years it has been found better to abandon this practice, seeing that it tended to weaken the fibre if not to destroy it altogether. The crease has given place to the white line, and there is not much likelihood of its ever coming again into vogue. It may be as well to mention that a "no ball" forms no part of the "over," any more than a wide, although a bye would. Notwithstanding a bye counts to the score, it has no effect as regards a maiden over. Maidens are understood to be such as to produce no runs from the bat. The first mention of "no ball" on the score sheet occurs in the year 1830 at Lord's, in a match between Marylebone and Middlesex.

XLI.—If either of the strikers run a short run, the umpire must call, "one short."

It is scarcely necessary to say here that the "short run" is determined by the popping crease, over which the bat in hand must be put down if the foot of the batsman does not arrive there.

XLII.—No Umpire shall be allowed to bet.

This highly beneficial rule ought also to apply to scorers, for although the latter check each other, it is not very difficult for an expert to hoodwink one less shrewd than himself. Moreover, the mistake of a scorer would not be so apparent as that of an umpire, who has all eyes upon him, while a single run, more or less, would do as much wrong to the parties concerned in the match as the most dishonest award of an umpire. There was a time when an umpire would be chosen for his known predilection to "win, tie, or wrangle"—aye, and would

"Prove his doctrine orthodox
By oft repeated blows and knocks."

Such days and such ways are among the unreviving past; it is, nevertheless, wise to put temptation out of the way, and in lieu thereof to select the fearless and the just in the discharge of a proper duty.

XLIII.—No Umpire is to be changed during a match, unless with the consent of both parties, except in case of violation of the 42nd law, then either party may dismiss the transgressor,

The only causes likely to necessitate a change are, sudden or severe illness, or positive incapacity Against the former there is no effectual guard, although, for the latter, there is How often has "a good-natured fellow" been pressed to stand, probably with a view to narrow the expenses of even a respectable club To the outside world the good fellow resembles the fly in amber, about which nobody cares, while everybody wonders how he got there When a man is found to be notoriously wanting in the elementary principles of the game, his removal from the post into which he has been thrust is a relief to both parties—ay, and to himself especially Hence, in such case there is little difficulty in carrying out the rule A habit has sprung up of late of leaving the post of umpire merely to keep another pressing appointment A notable instance of this kind occurred about ten years since in Hertfordshire in an All England match No 1 left the ground within three hours of the last day's play No 2, thinking a couple of hours would settle the match, took his place He, however, could not stay it out, and No 3 was left to settle a disputed point which belonged solely to No 1, at that time thirty miles away A great deal of dissatisfaction was the result Surely persons who affect so rigid an enforcement of one law ought not to ignore its next-door neighbour

XLIV —After the delivery of four balls the Umpire must call "over," but not until the ball shall be finally settled in the Wicket Keeper's or Bowler's hand, the ball shall then be considered dead, nevertheless, if an idea be entertained that either of the strikers is out, a question may be put previously to, but not after, the delivery of the next ball.

Sometimes in a one-day match, five or six balls constitute the over This private arrangement does not invalidate the general law in its after details Not unfrequently an umpire is at fault in calling the over agreed upon, but the batsman must take the consequences arising therefrom A bowler or a wicket keeper is not to be deprived of a wicket (supposing he has got one) from a surplus ball, any more than a batsman is the runs (if any acquired) from a similar defect in the umpire's reckoning The words "must" and "shall" are sufficiently stringent and peremptory to keep the machinery in good going order and yet in a Middlesex match some years ago, Hearne, in preparing to deliver a ball, the last of an over, observed a pigeon fly across the play, and instead of bowling at the wicket, threw at the pigeon and brought it down There are no instructions in the law how to proceed when an umpire is glaringly at fault in calling "over," and much disputation has arisen in consequence A batsman may be bowled by a forbidden ball, and the man goes out grumbling Of course this would not be the case if runs had been made from it Another is stumped, and the wicket-keeper rejoices, and in this case one umpire backs up the default of the other "Must" is a stronger word than "shall," yet in spite of it an umpire occasionally secures a wicket Again, the word "*then*" has always been read stronger in connection with the immediately preceding words "finally settled" than with the remoter ones previously quoted

XLV —The umpire must take especial care to call "No ball" instant upon delivery—"Wide ball" as soon as it shall pass the striker

If all umpires would wait just long enough to ascertain whether the ball has passed the wicket before calling "Wide," many disagreeables might be spared The "No ball" is quite another affair, and demands instant decision A case is recorded where an umpire called "Wide" which in reality was a "No ball" Instant upon delivery the ball was compassed and hit before the crease, and the man caught from it "How's that?" from half a dozen at once "Out," said the confused umpire A stormy protest ensued, and the match broke off in disorder In addition to the calls suggested by this rule, the umpire has to take notice of byes It is not a little remarkable that, with all the seeming regard for completeness in the management of the game, the term "bye" is not even hinted at, although it forms so striking a characteristic, and is, moreover, regarded as one of the best exponents of the fielding In its strict sense it means a run obtained from defective fielding of a ball not struck, and is generally chargeable to the long-stop When byes were first permitted the bowling was underhand, but when round-arm became all the go and pace regarded as the grand object to be achieved, the bowling grew so dangerous that the legs of the batsmen needed protection, and as necessity is the parent of invention, pads of various designs were brought into notice Some of these were of such huge proportions that a ball which in all probability would have been secured either by wicket keeper or long-stop, glanced off in the direction of square-leg, or at least out of a straight course, and thus the fielder was charged with a mistake quite out of his power of overruling Leg-byes were then admitted as part of a score (*See* Law XIII)

XLVI—The players who go in second shall follow their innings if they have obtained eighty runs less than their antagonists, except in all matches limited to one day's play, when the number shall be limited to sixty instead of eighty

The primary object of this rule is to save time and to bring the contest to a decisive issue This, however, is rarely accomplished, as a great deal of time is frittered away, and the uphill work of "pulling off the arrears" usually deprives the match of its chief interest The rule in practice at Lord's in the case of one day matches is, "That a match in the absence of express stipulations to the contrary must be played out or given up before one side can claim the victory agreeable to law and with respect to bets It must therefore be decided between the two sides whether they intend to stand by the first innings or not before the commencement of the game If they do not decide and the match is not played out it is of course 'drawn'"

XLVII—When one of the strikers shall have been put out, the use of the bat shall not be allowed to any person until the next striker shall come in

Nothing can be plainer, and yet it is treated with a degree of contempt quite unaccountable when the fundamental principles of the game are considered to be bound up with it The constant practice of snatching the bat from the hand of a "not out" during the short interval of two minutes is, to say the least, puerile and ridiculous Moreover, the continuity of the game is impaired A case occurred last year in a very important match at Gravesend, which interrupted the play considerably Mr G F Grace got hold of a "not out" bat, and struck a ball into an orchard near the ground, where it was lost The home parties demurred to providing another ball, and some time elapsed before the game could be proceeded with How much better would be the fielding of amateur cricketers if they would gratify their fidgety propensities by a little practice with the ball during the interim, and thereby keep their fingers in form for a catch whenever it occurs rather than subject themselves to the ridicule which attends a mistake! If the last law is worthy of the position of binding up the rest of the code, let it be respected by lawmakers as well as by others, remembering

> Example is a living law, whose sway
> Men more than all the written laws obey —*Antony and Cleopatra*

One duty imposed on the umpires at Marylebone in the "match regulations" is to see that all matches played at Lord's shall be in conformity with the laws of the Marylebone Club This functionary is, however, at times in such a fix as to let "I dare not wait upon I would" In such case every true lover of cricket and well-wisher for its furtherance may exclaim, "Heaven help him!"

"The Committee of the Marylebone Club think it desirable that, previously to the commencement of a match, one of each side should be declared the manager of it, and that the new laws, with respect to substitutes, may be carried out in a spirit of fairness and mutual concession, it is their wish that such substitutes be allowed in all reasonable cases, and that the umpire should inquire if it is done with the consent of the manager of the opposite side Complaints have been made that it is the practice of some players when at the wicket to make holes in the ground for a footing, the Committee are of opinion that the umpires should be empowered to prevent it"

SINGLE WICKET

I —When there shall be less than five players on a side, bounds shall be placed twenty-two yards each in a line from the off and leg stumps

"Lambert's Guide" (1816) says "single wicket matches are played with from one to six on each side When the striker runs to the bowler's wicket and strikes off the bail placed on two stumps with the bat and returns to his own wicket, this is counted a run When less than four are at play, if the striker moves off the ground except an agreement to the contrary, he shall be allowed no notch for such stroke" From this note it will be seen that the variation in single wicket practice has been but slight during the long interim

II —The ball must be hit before the bounds, to entitle the striker to a run, which run cannot be obtained unless he touch the bowling stump or crease in a line with his bat or some part of his person, or go beyond them, returning to the popping-crease as at double wicket, according to the 21st law

III —When the striker shall hit the ball, one of his feet must be on the ground, and behind the popping-crease, otherwise the umpire shall call "no hit,"

Suppose the batsman be caught off a "no hit" What then? Would he be out? The law is silent on this point It is, however, within the province of reason to say that he would, for it may be regarded as a case parallel to a "no ball," in which the bowler has to suffer every disadvantage without a corresponding set-off

IV —When there shall be less than five players on a side, neither byes nor overthrows shall be allowed, nor shall the striker be out if caught behind the wicket, nor stumped out

Lambert's words are "The wicket must be touched with the ball in hand, or thrown at and knocked down in front For if it be knocked down by a throw or by the ball in hand behind, it is not out, as when the ball is behind the wicket or bounds, the ball is out of play, and consequently can do no execution.

V —The fielder must return the ball so that it shall cross the play between the wicket and bowling stump, or between the bowling stump and the bounds, the striker may be run till the ball be so returned.

That is until it is in the bowler's hand dead, according to the opinion of the umpire

VI —After the striker shall have made one run, if he start again he must touch the bowling-stump and turn before the ball cross the play to entitle him to another.

VII —The striker shall be entitled to three runs for lost ball, and the same number for ball stopped with hat in reference to the 28th and 33rd laws of double wicket

In one case the forfeiture is one half, and in the other three fifths, with this fractional difference against the field

VIII —When there shall be more than four players on a side there shall be no bounds All hits, byes, and overthrows shall then be allowed

IX—The bowler is subject to the same laws as at double wicket

X—No more than one minute shall be allowed between each ball

BETS

I—No bet upon any match is payable, unless it be played out or given up

II—If the runs of one player be betted against those of another, the bet depends on the first innings, unless otherwise specified

III—If the bet be made on both innings, and one party beat the other in one innings the runs of the first innings shall determine it

IV—If the other party go in a second time, then the bet must be determined by the number on the score

In the year 1855 George Williams sued Thomas Mills, in the Woodstock County Court, for 2*l*, he (Mills) having kept the sum as holder of stakes of 1*l* each The deposit was for a single wicket match, which did not come off, owing to the non-attendance of the defendant, who still kept the stakes It was shown that the parties agreed to meet at nine in the morning, when the plaintiff attended, but the defendant did not appear His Honour (J B Parry, Esq) said he was of opinion that, as the plaintiff omitted to pitch his wicket and get some one to bowl to him, he could not claim the stake Each to pay his own costs

---

THEORY OF SCORING

In scanning these pages, or even a portion of them, the eye of the reader must have been frequently arrested by the word "score," and probably strange ideas of the mode by which it is compounded have been entertained A few words on this subject may, therefore, be fitting here Seeing that it is not easy always to obtain a person quite *au fait* in the art of scoring, the aid of the nonprofessional becomes an absolute necessity This duty is often avoided, either on the ground of diffidence or expressed incapacity Now if the former cannot be easily cured the latter can Provided with a proper score sheet, the rudimentary principles can be mastered in a single lesson, thus, if a batsman makes a hit for a single, mark the figure one against his name, if three, add that figure thereto, and so on till he completes his innings; next add these figures together, and place them against his name in the total column The same process must be adopted with every batsman till the innings is completed On every well constructed score sheet there is a line denoting the number of runs totalled at the fall of each wicket, thus .

1	2	3	4	5	6	7	8	9	10
86	*90*	*133*	*140*	*147*	*150*	*186*	*193*	*195*	*200*

What can be easier? The analysis of bowling seems at first sight a difficult operation, but it is more apparent then real Care and attention are the chief

ANALYSIS OF THE BOWLING—FIRST INNINGS.

Bowlers.	No Balls.	Wide Balls.	No. of "Overs" and Runs made from each Bowler. 1	2	3	4	5	6	7	8	9	10	11	12	13
C. M. Sharpe			....	....	..3.	....	....	3...	....	.3..	.4.2	.1..	....	12..	....
			...1	....	4...	...1	...3	....	.1..	1...	..3.	....	....	....	....
			...4	4...	.w.1	.1.w	.1.1	...1	..2.	....	4..2	...3	...3	..1.	....
			...4	....	2...	....	....	....	....	....	1...	...1	.1.w	....	1...
			...1	....	2...	..2.	....	..2.	....	3.2.	....	1..2	...1	....	1...
			....	..1.	.w..	.w									
H. M. Sims		1	..3.	..3.	1...	1...	...1	....	11..	....	....	...1	....	..21	.2..
		1	...1	1..2	11..	...1	....	.1.2	1...	....	..w.	....	....	..w.	.2..
W. S. Patterson..............			....	...1	....	....	4...	..11	....	....	....	....	....	....	....
			2...	4...	..4.	.2..	....	1...	....	....	..w.	.32.	....	...1	....
			w...	3...	1...	.3..	....	2.1.	....	..1.	4.1.	....	2...	..2w	....
			..1.	.212											
F. J. Greenfield..............			.4..	....	..13	.1..	....	....	1...						

Bowlers' Names.	Total No Balls.	Total Wide Balls.	Total Balls.	Total Maiden "Overs."	Total Runs.	Total Wickets.	Bowlers' Names—con.	Total No Balls.	Total Wide Balls.	Total Balls.	Total Maiden "Overs."	Total Runs.	Total Wickets.
1. C. M. Sharpe			274	29	89	5	6.						
2. H. M. Sims		2	104	10	30	2	7.						
3. W. S. Patterson			164	21	51	3	8.						
4. F. J. Greenfield			25	3	10		9.						
5.							10.						

ANALYSIS OF THE BOWLING—SECOND INNINGS.

Bowlers.	No Balls.	Wide Balls.	No. of "Overs" and Runs made from each Bowler. 1	2	3	4	5	6	7	8	9	10	11	12	13
C. M. Sharpe			1...	...1	1w..	..w.	...1	....	...1	....	....	4...	....	....	....
			.4..	....	w...	....	..2.	....	..12	21..	....	...4	.412	....	....
			.w.1	1.2.	5...	.411	21..	..1.	.1w.	..12	..11	..44	.1.w		
W. S. Patterson..............			....	.1.1	....	...4	1...	....	3w..	....	....	..2.	...2	..12	....
			..2.	....	1...	..1.	.21.	.4.2	...1	.11.	1...	2...	....	...2	11..
			..1.	ww..	..1.	....	...1	....	....	1...					
F. J. Greenfield..............			...2	..w.	....	..11	1...	.2..	.1.1						
H. M. Sims			...1	....	1..1	..2.	32.4								

Bowlers' Names.	Total No Balls.	Total Wide Balls.	Total Balls.	Total Maiden "Overs."	Total Runs.	Total Wickets.	Bowlers' Names—con.	Total No Balls.	Total Wide Balls.	Total Balls.	Total Maiden "Overs."	Total Runs.	Total Wickets.
1. C. M. Sharpe			148	14	66	6	6.						
2. W. S. Patterson			136	12	44	3	7.						
3. F. J. Greenfield			28	2	9	1	8.						
4. H. M. Sims			20	1	14		9.						
5.							10.						

F F F

requisites, yet some knowledge of the game is desirable. On reference to the example here given of the Cambridge bowling in the University match* (a faithful transcript from the M.C.C. books), it will be seen that Mr. Sharpe led off; the four dots represent balls and as none of them were hit, it is called a maiden over. From the third ball of Mr. Sims the batsman made a hit for three. Precisely the same thing resulted from the next over of each bowler. In the twenty-ninth over of Mr. Sharpe he got a wicket, hence the letter "w" instead of a dot; so also in the following over. In the summary at the foot Mr. Sharpe is accredited with 274 balls (which, divided by four, gives 68 overs), 20 maidens, 89 runs, and five wickets. If the same process is adopted with the bowling of the second innings, the results will be found to tally with those given at the page before referred to. Members of the sporting press enter more minutely into it, by describing the changes of bowling and the precise point at which a wide or no-ball enters into the calculation; but the foregoing may be regarded as sufficient for general purposes. On several occasions that highly accomplished nobleman, the Earl of Carlisle, occupied the scoring tent in the Castle matches when Lord Lieutenant of Ireland, and always evinced the greatest interest in the progress of the game. Who would not have felt themselves honoured in checking the noble scorer on such occasions, and what a page could he not have contributed to the glories of cricket had he put pen to paper on such a theme.

* Page 111.

CHAPTER XXV.

SONGS AND POEMS.

"The poetry of earth it ceaseth never."

ALL history is indebted largely to the rough rhymester and balladist, seeing that they precede. Probably few countries have been better supplied than England with wandering minstrels in praises of native sports. With regard to cricket, little or nothing of its early career would have been known but for the pen of the poet. In fact, nearly all that is definitely known comes not from players of the game—whatever form its early steps might have assumed—but from persons who had to tread a very different stage than the cricket field for their bread and amusement. D'Urfey wrote thirty-five plays and but one line respecting cricket; Love, a comedian, wrote one farce* and 314 lines on cricket—the former in the reign of Charles, the latter in that of the second George. Love's poem created little or no sensation at the time of its first appearance. This arose, no doubt, from the little knowledge his critics possessed of its subject. Even in a second issue many years later, the reviewer defines the poem as a very decent and classical one, and does credit to the taste, spirit, and good sense of the author. But a great deal more may be said of it than this. People in the present day can appreciate it for the light it throws upon the state and condition of the game at the time (1746) to which it refers. There has been nothing like it since for sustained interest, and the marvel is that our great cricketers of the last century should have been so slightly acquainted with the poem, or possessed so little regard for the story so well told as to allow an escape from their memory. Posterity will be glad to peruse the effusion submitted to their notice in this chapter.

It is, furthermore, necessary to bear in mind that the other compositions are not selected so much for literary merit as they are for examples which presented themselves to the minds of the varied writers. It is hoped that all possess some amount of merit, however trifling that may be. Would they were worthier.

The following poem was written in 1746, and describes a great match played between Kent and All England on the Artillery Ground, Finsbury. It was addressed to the members of the Richmond (Surrey) Cricket Club, by

* "Bucks have at ye all."

its author James Love, comedian, in the following prefatory manner, about the year 1775

"Gentlemen,

"The following little poem, which near thirty years ago was the effusion of a youthful mind, is reprinted for your amusement. The greatest circumstance in its favour is that it is founded upon fact, and may serve to entertain the true lovers of cricket by a recollection of many particulars at the time when the game was cultivated with the utmost assiduity, and patronised by the personal appearance and management of some of the most capital people in the kingdom. If the admirers of a manly *British* exercise should, in a vacant hour, receive the least entertainment from the production, it will amply satisfy the author's utmost ambition, who, as an inhabitant of Richmond, would ever be happy to contribute his mite to the pleasure of his friends and neighbours, and is then most obedient and humble servant,

"JAMES LOVE"

While others, soaring on a lofty wing,
Of dire Bellona's cruel triumphs sing,
Sound the shrill clarion, mount the rapid car,
And rush delighted through the ranks of war,
My tender muse in humbler milder strains,
Presents a bloodless conquest on the plains,
Where vigorous youth in life's fresh bloom resort
For pleasing exercise and healthful sport,
Where emulation fires, where glory draws,
And active sportsmen struggle for applause,
Expert to bowl, to run, to stop, to throw,
Each nerve collected at each mighty blow

Hail! cricket, hail! thou manly British game,
First of all sport! be first alike in fame
To my fir'd soul thy busy transports bring,
That I may feel thy raptures while I sing!
And thou, kind patron of the mirthful play—
SANDWICH, thy country's friend—accept my lay
Though mean my verse, my subject yet approve,
And look propitious on the game you love

When the returning sun begins to smile,
And sheds its glories round the sea-girt isle—
When new born nature, deck'd in vivid green,
Chases dull winter from the charming scene—
High panting with delight the jovial swain
Trips it exulting o'er the flower-strewed plain,
Thy pleasures, CRICKET, all his heart control,
Thy eager transports dwell upon his soul,
He weighs the well turned Bat's experienced force,
And guides the Ball's impetuous, rapid course,
His supple limb, with nimble labour plies,
Nor bends the grass beneath him as he flies,
The joyous conquests of the late flown year
In fancy's paint, with all their charms appear,
And now again he views the long-wished season near

O thou sublime inspirer of my song,
What matchless trophies to thy worth belong,
Look round the globe inclined to mirth, and see
What daring sport can claim the prize from thee
Not puny Billiards, where, with sluggish pace,
The dull ball trails before the feeble mace,
Where nothing can your languid spirits move,
Save when the marker bellows out, "Six, Love!"
Or when the ball, close cushioned, slides askew,
And to the opening pocket *runs a cou*,
Where no triumphant shouts, no clamours dare
Pierce through the vaulted roof, and wound the air,
Nor yet that happier game where the smooth bowl
In circling mazes wanders to the goal
Not Tennis' self, thy sister sport, can charm,*
Or with thy fierce delight our bosoms warm,
Though full of life, at ease alone dismayed,
She calls each swelling sinew to her aid,
Her echoing courts confess the sprightly sound,
While from the racket the brisk balls resound,
While, much divided between fear and glee,
The youth cries "Rub"—O flee, you lingerer, flee—
Yet, to small space confined, e'en she must yield
To nobler cricket the disputed field

O parent Britain, minion of renown,
Whose far extended fame all nations own,
Of sloth-promoting sports forewarned, beware,
Nor think thy pleasures are thy meanest care
Shun with disdain the squeaking masquerade,
Where fainting vice calls folly to her aid
Leave the dissolving song, the baby dance,
To soothe the slaves of Italy and France,
While the firm limb and strong braced nerves are thine,
Scorn eunuch sports, to manlier games incline,
Feed on the joys that health and vigour give
Where freedom reigns 'tis worth the while to live

Nursed on thy plains, first Cricket learnt to please,
And taught thy sons to slight inglorious ease,
And see where busy counties strive for fame,
Each greatly potent at this mighty game
Fierce Kent ambitious of the first applause,
Against the world combined asserts her cause
Gay Surrey sometimes triumphs o'er the field,
And fruitful Sussex cannot brook to yield,
While London, queen of cities! proudly vies,
And often grasps the well disputed prize
Thus, while Greece triumphed o'er the barbarous earth,
Seven cities struggled which gave Homer birth

* It must be confessed that tennis is nearly allied to cricket, both as to the activity, strength and skill that are necessary to be exerted on each important occasion The judicious use of Hercules and Mercury, the gods of strength and swiftness, so very peculiar to the game of cricket, cannot be questioned

And now the sons of Kent, immortal grown,
By a long series of acquired renown,
Smile at each weak attempt to shake their fame,
And thus with vaulting pride their might proclaim
"Long have we borne the palm triumphant, still
No county fit to match our wondrous skill,
But, that all tamely may confess our sway,
And own us masters of the glorious day,
Pick the best sportsmen from each several shire,
And let them, if they dare, 'gainst us appear
Soon will we prove the mightiness we boast,
And make them feel their error to their cost"
Fame quickly gave the bold defiance vent
And magnified the undaunted sons of Kent,
The boastful challenge sounded far and near,
And, spreading, reached at length famed Newland's ear,
Where, with his friend, all negligent, he laughed
And threatened future glories, as they quaff
Struck with the daring phrase, a piercing look
On Bryan first he cast, and then he spoke
"And dare the slaves this paltry message own?
What, then, is Newland's arm no better known?
Have I for this the ring's wide ramparts broke
While Rumsey shuddered at the mighty stroke?
Now, by Alcmena's sinewed arm I swear,
Whose dreadful blows no mortal strength can bear,
By Hermes, offspring too of thundering Jove,
Whose winged feet like marble lightning move,
By every portion of the pleasing war,
My chief delight, my glory, and my care,
This arm shall cease the far-driven ball to throw,
Shrink from the bat, and feebly shun the blow—
The conquering trophies from this forehead torn
By boys and women shall in scorn be worn,
Ere I neglect to let these blusterers know
There live who dare oppose and beat them too
Illustrious Bryan, now's the time to prove
To cricket's charms thy much experienced love!
Let us with care each hardy friend inspire,
And fill their souls with emulating fire
Come on! True courage never is dismayed"
He spoke—the heroes listened and obeyed,
Urged by their chiefs, the friends of cricket hear,
And joyous in the fated lists appear
The day approached To view the charming scene
Exulting thousands crowd the level green
A place there is* where City warriors meet,
Wisely determined not to fight but eat,
Where harmless thunder rattles through the skies,
While the plump *buffcoat* fires and shuts his eyes

* "A place there is"—*Est in secessu Locus* The author here has followed the example of all great poets, both ancient and modern, who never fail to prepare the reader with a pompous description of the place where any great action is to be performed

To the pleased mob the bursting cannons tell,
At every circling glass, how much they swell
Here, in the intervals of bloodless war,
The swains in milder pomp their arms prepare,
Wide o'er the extended plain, the circling string
Restrains the impatient throng and marks a ring,
But if encroaching on forbidden ground,
The heedless crowd o'erleaps the proper bound,
*Smith** plies with strenuous arm the smacking whip,
Back to the line the affrighted rebels skip
The stumps are pitched Each hero now is seen,
Springs o'er the fence, and bounds along the green,
In decent white most gracefully arrayed,
Each strong built limb in all its pride displayed
Now, Muse, exert thy vigour and describe
The mighty chieftains of each glorious tribe!
Bold Rumsey first before the Kentish band
Godlike appeared, and seized the chief command
Judicious swain! whose quick discerning soul
Observes the various seasons as they roll,
Well skilled to spread the thriving plant around
And paint with fragrant flowers the enamelled ground
Conscious of worth, with front erect he moves,
And poises in his hand the bat he loves,
Him *Dorset's* prince protects, whose youthful heir
Attends with ardent glee the mighty player,
He at *mid-wicket* disappoints the foe,
Springs at the coming ball, and mocks the blow
E'en thus the rattlesnake, as travellers say,
With stedfast eye observes its destined prey,
Till, fondly gazing on the glittering balls,
Into her mouth the unhappy victim falls
The baffled hero quits his bat with pain,
And muttering lags across the shouting plain
Brisk *Hadswell* next strides on with comely pride,
Tough as the subject of his trade—the *hide*,
In his firm palm the hard bound balls he bears,
And mixes joyous with his pleased compeers
Bromleyan *Mills* attends the Kentish throng,
And *Robin*, from his size, surnamed the *long*,
Six more, as ancient custom has thought meet,
With willing steps the intrepid band complete
On the adverse party, towering o'er the rest,
Left-handed *Newland* fires each ardnous breast,
From many a bounteous crop the foodful grain,
With swelling stores rewards his useful pain,

* "Smith, the master of the ground, has been the principal cause of the high light in which cricket at this time flourishes There would have been a fine opportunity of introducing in this place the celebrated Vinegar, who so long here triumphed without a rival, but, alas! the nobility and gentry have entirely robbed this famous spot of its favourite diversion by transplanting the heroes, who lately cut such figures here, to Tottenham Court and Broughton Amphitheatre, with a malicious intent to rob the commons of their amusement and engross the whole joy themselves"

While the glad Farmer, with delighted eyes,
Smiles to behold his close-crammed granaries rise
Next *Bryan* came, whose cautious hand could fix,
In neat disposed array, the well piled bricks
With him alone scarce any youth could dare
At *single wicket* try the doubtful war,
For few save him the exalted honour claim
To play with judgment all the various game,
Next his accomplished vigour *Cuddy* tries,
Whose sheltering hand the neat formed garb supplies
To the dread plain her *Durgate* Surrey sends,
And *Weymark* on the jovial train attends,
Equal in numbers bravely they begin
The due dispute *The foes of Kent go in*

With wary judgment scattered o'er the green
The ambitious chiefs of fruitful Kent are seen,
Some at a distance for the long ball wait,
Some nearer planted seize it with the bat,
Hodswell and Mills behind the wickets stand,
And each by turns the flying ball command
Four times from Hodswell's arm it skims the grass,
Then Mills succeeds The seekers out change place
"Observe!" cries Hadswell to the wondering throng,
"Be judges now* whose arms are better strung"
He said—then poised, and rising as he threw,†
Swift from his hand the fatal missive flew,
Not with more force the death-conveying ball
Springs from the cannon to the battered wall,
Nor swifter yet the pointed arrows go
Launched from the vigour of the *Parthian* bow
It whizzed along with unimagined force,
And bore down all, resistless in its course,
To such impetuous might compelled to yield,
The bail and mangled stumps bestrew the field
Now glows with ardent heat the unequal fray,
While Kent usurps the honours of the day,
Loud from the ring resounds the piercing shout,
"Three *notches* only gained—five *leaders* out!"
But while the drooping player invokes the gods,
The busy better calculates the odds
Swift round the plain in busy murmurs run,
"I'll hold you ten to four, Kent"—"Done, sir, done"
What numbers can with equal force describe
The increasing terrors of the losing tribe,
When, vainly striving 'gainst the conquering ball,
They see their boasted chiefs dejected fall?

* "Be judges now" "Aspice num mage sit nostrum penetrabile telum"—*Virg Æ*, bk 10, line 48
† "And rising as he threw"

"Corpore toti
Fminus intorquet Murali concita nunquam
Tormento sic saxa fremunt nec fulmine tanto
Dissultant crepitus Volat Atri, Turbinis instar
Extremi duum Hasta ferens"

Now the two mightiest of the fainting host
Pant to redeem the fame their fellows lost,
Eager for glory—for the worst prepared—
With powerful skill their threatened wickets guard
Bryan, collected for the deadly stroke,
First cast to Heaven a supplicating look,
Then prayed "Propitious powers! assist my blow,*
And grant the flying orb may shock the foe"
Thus said, he waved his bat with forceful swing,
And drove the battered pellet o'er the ring,
Then, rapid, five times crossed the shining plain
Ere the departed ball returned again
Nor was thy prowess, valiant Newman, mean
Whose strenuous arm increased the game eighteen,
While from thy stroke the ball returning flies,
Uninterrupted clamours rend the skies
But oh! what horrid interchanges oft are seen
When faithless fortune seems the most serene
Beware, unhappy Bryan! oh, beware!
Too heedless swain, when such a foe is near
Fired with success, elated with his luck,
He glowed with rage, regardless how he struck,
But, forced the fatal negligence to mourn,
Keps† crushed his stumps before the youth could turn
The rest their unavailing vigour try,
And by the power of Kent demolished die
Awakened echo speaks the innings o'er,
And forty notches deep indent the score
Now Kent prepares her better skill to show,
Loud rings the ground at each tremendous blow,
With nervous arm performing God-like deeds,
Another and another chief succeeds,
Till, tir'd with fame, the conquering hosts give way,
And head by *thirteen* strokes the toilsome fray
Fresh roused to arms the labour-loving swain
Swells with new strength and dares the field again,
Again to Heaven aspires the cheerful sound,
The strokes re echo o'er the spacious ground
The *Champion* strikes, when, scarce arriving fair,
The glancing ball mounts upward in the air,
The batsman sees it, and with mournful eyes
Fixt on the ascending pellet as it flies,
Thus, suppliant, claims the favour of the skies
"O mighty Jove! and all ye powers above,
Let my regarded prayer your pity move,
Grant me but this Whatever youth shall dare
Snatch at the prize descending through the air,
Lay him extended on the grassy plain,
And make his bold adventurous effort vain"

* "Propitious powers" "Te precor Alcide captis ingentibus adsis"—*Virg*

† "Keps is particularly remarkable for handling the ball at the wicket and knocking up the stumps instantly if the batsman is not extremely cautious"

He said. The powers, attending his request,
Granted one part, to winds consigned the rest.
And now illustrious *Sackville*, where he stood,
The approaching ball with cautious pleasure view'd;
At once he sees the chief's impending doom,
And pants for mighty honours yet to come.
Swift as the falcon, darting on its prey,
He springs elastic o'er the verdant way;
Sure of success, flies upward with a bound,
Derides the slow approach, and spurns the ground.
Prone slips the youth, yet glories in his fall;
With arm extended, shows the captive ball!
Loud acclamations every mouth employ,
And echo rings the undulating joy.
The Counties now the game triumphant lead,
And vaunt thir numbers fifty-seven ahead.
To end the immortal honours of the day,
The chiefs of Kent once more their might essay.
No trifling toil e'en yet remains untried,
Nor mean the numbers of the adverse side;
With double skill each dangerous ball they shun,
Strike with observing eye, with caution run.
At length they know the wished-for number near,
Yet wildly pant, and almost own their fear.
The two last champions even now are in,
And but three notches yet remain to win.
When, almost ready to recant its boast,
Ambitious Kent within an ace had lost,
The mounting ball, again obliquely driven,
Cuts the pure ether, soaring up to heaven.
Weymark was ready—Weymark all must own
As sure a swain to catch as e'er was known;
Yet, whether Jove and all-compelling fate
In their high will determined Kent should beat,
Or the lamenting youth too much relied
On sure success and fortune often tried,
The erring ball, amazing to behold!
Slipp'd through his outstretched hand, and mock'd his hold;
And now the sons of Kent complete the game,
And firmly fix their everlasting fame.*

THE PHILOSOPHY OF SPORT.

Bear lightly on their forehead, Time! strew roses on their way!
The young in heart, however old, that prize the present day,
And, wiser than the pompous proud, are wise enough to play.

I love to see a man forget his blood is growing cold,
And leap, or swim, or gather flowers, oblivious of his gold;
And mix with children in their sport, nor think that he is old.

* See Score, p. 84.

SURREY TRIUMPHANT, OR THE KENTISH CRICKETERS' DEFEAT *

A PARODY ON CHEVY CHACE, BY THE REV J DUNCOMBE, M A

THE reader need scarcely be reminded that the italics, with which the poem abounds, represent the same words as are to be found in the old ballad Mr Duncombe was one of the six preachers in Canterbury Cathedral, and also curate of Sundridge near Sevenoaks The match related took place in 1773, at Bishop's Bourne, the residence of Sir Horace Mann, respecting whom see footnote, page 141.

God prosper long our harvest work
  Our rakes *and* hay-carts *all* '
An ill-timed cricket-match *there did*
  At Bishopsbourne *befall* '

To bat and bowl *with* might *and* main,
  Two nobles *took* their *way* ,
The hay *may rue that is* unhoused,
  The batting *of that day*

The active *Earl of* Tankerville,
  An even bet *did make,*
That in Bourne paddock he would cause
  Kent's *chiefest* hands to quake,

To see the Surrey cricketers,
  Out bat them and out-bowl
To Dorset's Duke *the tidings came,*
  All *in* the park of Knowle ,

Who sent his Lordship *present word,*
  He would prevent his sport
The Surrey *Earl not fearing this,*
  Did to East Kent *resort,*

With ten more masters of the bat,
  All chosen men of might,
Who knew full well in time of need,
  To aim or block *a right*

[From Marsh and Weald, their hay-forks left,
  To Bourne the rustics hied,
From Romney, Cranbrook, Tenterden,
  And Darent's verdant side ,

Gentle and simple, squires and clerks,
  With many a lady fair,
Famed Thanet, Forvell's beauteous bride,
  And graceful Sondes were there]

The Surrey batsmen chose the ground
  The ball did *swiftly fly*
On Monday they began to play,
  Before the grass was dry ,

And long ere supper time *they* did
  Near fourscore notches gain ,
Then having slept, they in their turns,
  Stopt, caught, and bowled amain

The fieldsmen stationed on the lawn,
  Well able to endure,
Their loins of snow white satin vests
  That day had *guarded sure*

Full fast the Kentish wickets fell,
  While Higham house and mill,
And Benham's upland down *with* shouts
  Did make an echo shrill

Sir Horace from the dinner *went,*
  To view the tender ground ,
Quoth he, " This last untoward shower,
  Our stumps has almost drowned ,

If that I thought 'twould not be dry,
  No longer would I play "
With that a shrewd young gentleman
  Thus to the knight did say

" *Lo* ' *yonder doth* the sun appear,
  And soon 'twill shine forth *bright,*
The level lawn and slippery ground
  All drying in our sight ,

Not bating e'en the *river* banks,
  Fast by you pleasant mead "
" *Then cease* disputing," Lumpy *said,*
  And take your bats *with speed ,*

And now with me, my countrymen,
  Let all your skill be shown,
For never was there bowler *yet,*
  In Kent *or* Surrey known,

That ever did a bail dislodge,
  Since first I play'd a match,
But I durst wager hand *for* hand,
  With him to bowl or catch "

* See page 194

Young Dorset, like a baron bold,
  His jetty hair undressed,
Ran foremost in the company,
  Clad in a milk-white vest

"Show me he said, one spot that's dry,
  Where we can safely run,
Or else, with my consent, we'll wait
  To-morrow's rising sun"

The man that first did answer make,
  Was noble Tankerville
Who said, "To play, I do declare,
  There only wants the will

Move but the stumps, a spot I'll find
  As dry as Farley's board" *
'Our records," quoth the knight, 'for this
  No precedent afford

Ere thus I will out-braved be,
  All hazards I'll defy,
I know thee well, an earl art thou,
  And so not yet am I

But trust me, Charles, it pity were,
  And great offence to kill,
With cold or spasms, these harmless men,
  For they have done no ill.

Let us at single wicket play,
  And set our men aside"
Run out be he,' replied the Earl,
  "By whom this is decreed!"

Then stepped a gallant squire forth,
  Bartholomew was his name,
Who said 'I would not have it told
  On Clandon down for shame,

That Tankerville e'er play'd alone,
  And I stood looking on,
You are a Knight sir, you an Earl,
  And I a Vicar's son

I'll do the best that do I may,
  While I have power to stand,
While I have power to wield my bat,
  I'll play with heart and hand"

The Surrey bowlers bent their backs,
  Their aims were good and true,
And every ball that scap'd the bat,
  The wicket overthrew

To drive the ball beyond the booths,
  Duke Dorset had the bent,
Woods, mov'd at length with mickle pride,
  The stumps to shivers sent

They ran full fast on every side,
  No slackness there was found,
And many a ball that mounted high,
  Ne'er lighted on the ground

In truth, it was a grief to see,
  And likewise for to hear
The cries of odds that offered were,
  And slighted everywhere

At last Sir Horace took the field,
  A batter of great might,
Mov'd like a lion, he awhile
  Put Surrey in a fright,

He swung, till both his arms did ache,
  His bat of seasoned wood,
Till down his azure sleeves the sweat
  Ran trickling like a flood

"Hedge now thy bets," said Tankerville,
  "I'll then report of thee,
That thou art the most prudent Knight,
  That ever I did see"

Then to the Earl the Knight replied
  "Thy counsel I do scorn,
I with no Surrey man will hedge
  That ever yet was born"

With that there came a ball most keen,
  Out of a Surrey hand,
He struck it full, it mounted high,
  But ah! ne'er reached the land

Sir Horace spoke no words but these,
  "Play on, my merry men all,
For why? my innings at an end,
  The Earl has caught my ball"

Then by the hand his Lordship took
  This hero of the match,
And said, "Sir Horace, for thy bets,
  Would I had missed my catch!

In sooth my very heart doth bleed
  With sorrow for thy sake,
For sure a more good tempered Knight
  A match did never make"

A squire of Western Kent there was,
  Who saw his friend out-caught,
And straight did vow revenge on him
  Who this mischance had wrought

A Templar he who in his turn,
  Soon as the Earl did strike,
Ran swiftly from his stopping place,
  And gave him like for like

* Master of the Ordinary

Full sharp and rapid was the ball,
 Yet *without dread or fear,*
He caught it at arm's length, and straight
 Returned it in the air

With such vehement force and might
 It struck his callous hand,
The sound re-echoed through the ring,
 Through every booth and stand

So thus were *both these* heroes caught,
 Whose spirit *none could doubt*
A Surrey squire *who saw* with grief,
 The Earl so quickly out,

Soon as the Templar with his bat,
 Made of a trusty tree,
Gave such a stroke as had it scap'd,
 Had surely gained him three,

Against this well intended ball
 His hand *so rightly* held,
That ere the foe could ground his bat,
 His ardour Lewis quell'd

This game *did last* from Monday morn
 Till Wednesday afternoon,
For when * Bell Harry *rung* to prayers,
 The batting *scarce was done*

With good Sir Horace, *there was* beat
 Hussey of Ashford town,
Davis for stops and catches famed,
 A worthy Canon's son,

And with the Mays, *both* Tom and Dick,
 Two hands of *good account,*
Simmons was beat, and Miller too,
 Whose bowling *did surmount*

For Woods of Seal *must needs I wail,*
 As one in doleful dumps,
For if he e'er should play again
 It must be *on his stumps* †

And with the Earl the conquering bat
 Bartholomew did wield,
And slender Lewis *who,* though sick,
 Would never leave *the field*

White, Yalding, Wood, and Stevens too,
 As Lumpy better known,
Palmer, for batting *well esteemed,*
 Childs, Francis, and Squire Stone

Of byes and overthrows *but three,*
 The Kentish heroes gained,
And Surrey, victor on the score,
 Twice seventy-*five* remained

Of near three *hundred* notches made
 By Surrey, eight were byes,
The rest were balls which, boldly struck,
 Re-echoed to the skies

Their husbands' woeful case that night
 Did many wives *bewail,*
Their labour, time, and money lost,
 But all would not prevail

Their sun-burnt cheeks, though *bathed* in sweat,
 They kiss'd and wash'd them clean,
And to that fatal Paddock begg'd
 They ne'er should go again

To Sevenoak town *this news was brought,*
 Where Dorset had his seat,
That, on the Nalebourn's banks, his Grace
 Had met with a defeat

"O heavy news!" the Rector ‡ *said,*
 "The Vine *can witness be,*
We have not any cricketer
 Of such account as he"

Like tidings in a shorter *space,*
 To Barham's Rector *came,*
That in Bourne Paddock, knightly Mann
 Had fairly lost his game

* Canterbury Cathedral

† One of this poor man's legs was bound up, and it was feared must undergo amputation As the stanza here parodied has been injudiciously substituted in the later copies of Chevy Chace, printed in 1824, the sense at the same time being so burlesque that the Spectator dared not quote it the original stanza, in which that absurdity is avoided, is here added from the ' Old Ballad of Otterburn," printed in the reign of Henry VI., together with a parody, so that the reader may take his choice

ORIGINAL

"For Witherington my heart was woe,
 That ever he slain should be,
For when both his legs were hewn in two,
 Yet he kneeled and fought on his knee"

PARODY

' *For* bare-footed Wood *my heart was woe,*
 That his leg bound up *should be,*
For if *both his legs* should be cut off,
 He would kneel *and* catch *on his knee*"

‡ Rev Thomas Curteis, D D

"*Now* rest his bat," the Doctor *said*,
  "*Sith 'twill no better be*,
I trust we *have* in Bishopsbourne,
  Five hands *as good as he*

Yet Surrey men *shall never say*
  But Kent return *will* make,
And catch and bowl them out length,
  For her Lieutenant's sake"

This vow 'tis hoped will be performed
  Next year on Laleham down,
When, if the Kentish hearts of oak
  Recover their renown,

From grey-goose wing some bard, I trust,
  Will pluck a stouter quill
Thus ended the fair match of Bourne,
  Won *by Earl* Tankerville

This vow full well did Kent *perform*,
  After on Sevenoak Vine,
With six not in, the game was won,
  Though White got fifty-nine

God save the King and bless the land,
  With plenty and increase,
And grant henceforth that idle games
  In harvest time *may cease*.

WILLOW THE KING

THE following is one of a list of school songs sung in the public hall at Harrow on Thursday, June 29, 1876, at a luncheon given by the Governors of Harrow School in honour of the opening of the new school on the foundation of John Lyon *Stet Fortuna Domus*.

Willow the King is a monarch grand
Three in a row his courtiers stand,
Every day when the sun shines bright
The doors of his palace are painted white,
And all the company bow their backs
To the king with a collar of cobbler's wax
  So ho! so ho! may the courtiers sing
  Honour and life to Willow the King!

Willow, King Willow, the guard hold tight,
Trouble is coming before the night,
Hopping and galloping, short and strong,
Comes the leathery Duke along,
And down the palaces tumble fast,
When once the leathery Duke gets past
  So ho! &c

"Who is this?" King Willow he swore,
"Hops like that to a gentleman's door?
Who's afraid of a Duke like him?
Fiddle-de dee!" says the monarch slim
"What do you say, my courtiers three?"
And the courtiers all said 'Fiddle-de-dee!'"
  So ho! &c

Willow the King stept forward bold,
Three good feet from his castle hold,
Willow the King stept back so light,
Skirmished gay to the left and right
But the Duke rushed by with a leap and a fling,
"Bless my soul!" says Willow the King
  So ho! &c

Crash the palaces sad to see,
Crash and tumble the courtiers three!
Each one lays, in fear and dread,
Down on the ground his respected head,
Each one kicks, as he downward goes,
Up in the air his respected toes
  So ho! &c

But the leathery Duke he jumped so high,
Jumped till he almost touched the sky,
"A fig for King Willow,' he boastingly said,
"Carry this gentleman off to bed!'
So they carried him off with the courtiers three,
And put him to bed in the green baize tree
  So ho! &c

"What of the Duke?" you ask anon,
"Where has his leathery Highness gone?"
O, he is filled with air inside—
Either it's air, or else it is pride—
And he swells and swells as tight as a drum,
And they kick him about till Christmas come.
  So ho! &c

THE WILLOW TREE,

FROM BOUGH TO BAT

THE stanzas here given form part of a poem written expressly for this work by an enthusiastic lover of cricket, but who, from a severe malady, has been rendered unable to complete his design

I well remember, when a roving lad,
  A willow weeping by the river side,
At spring the boughs with yellow tassels clad,
  Were often pencilled in the tranquil tide

And when awoke the blue forget me not,
  And purple violets rich odour made,
The thorn and thicket round the peaceful spot
  Became to Philomel a sylvan shade

I sought the shadow of the drooping leaves
  When summer frolick'd with the fruit and flowers,
And when the autumn smiled to shocks and sheaves,
  There would I wander in the harvest hours

Blithe were the birds with song, and oftentimes
  I listened to the lark, sublime and sweet,
And ever by the bloom of balmy limes,
  The merle and mavis gladden'd my retreat

Not that the minstrel at the golden gate
  I valued more than any other bird,
To me the cuckoo, with his merry mate,
  Sang as the dearest bards I ever heard

For know they were the heralds of the spring,
  The pioneers of peace from clime to clime,
They came as vernal choristers to sing,
  And bring glad tidings of the summer time

And as the bleat of lambkins o'er the lea,
  And down the dell the clamour of the kine,
Were all in turn as lullabies to me,
  When trolling on the bank with rod and line

Oft would I throw my silken tackle out,
  To lure the lusty pike adown the stream,
Mine was a luxury to spin for trout,
  And angle for the barbel or the bream

I watched the matron moorhen, with her young,
  Sail from the swan to seek the lanky sedge,
And lov'd to loiter where the spider flung
  His flossy fabric on the haw-capp'd hedge

At length, when winter pav'd my path with snow,
  And bore upon his brow an icy crown,
And black were berries on the silver'd sloe,
  The woodman came to hew my idol down

He bared his brawny arm, and firm and free
  Around the burly bole he made his mark,
And with his hatchet high he smote my tree,
  And soon to shivers fell the wrinkled bark.

Then bending o'er his axe the edge to feel,
  He sharpen'd with a stone the burnished blade,
Till from the cleaval of the deadly steel,
  Chip after chip flew quivering to the glade.

Soon with a crash I heard my favourite fall,
  Cut down to earth with unrelenting will;
And bough and branch, and tiny twig, and all
  Were wheeled away upon the timber-gill.*

But, not to ponder o'er the past, as one
  Who mourns the exit of some dear old friend,
I wend my way beneath a smiling sun,
  To trace my treasure to a better end.

See by the bench the skilful workmen stand,
  Each mind absorbed in meditative mood;
With crafty implement and cunning hand
  To fashion into form the riven wood.

To model true in shavings ankle deep,
  How well they ply the chisel and the plane;
Fine tempered tools the narrow groove to keep,
  And leave the line of gnarled and knotted grain.

Look! set in motion by the whirl of wheels,
  See how the lathe revolves for future fame;
Turn'd is the treadle till the speed reveals
  A noble weapon for a glorious game.

BEHOLD THE BAT! allied to ash and cane,
  For pride and power, mark how it rattles round;
Destined at length the laurel leaf to gain,
  And strike for honour on the battle ground.

And see, as from a sheath men draw the sword
  In action ready for the friendly fray,
Bound is the handle with a waxen cord,
  And polished is the blade prepared for play.

Then let us take a stroll, with eager eyes
  To see the struggle on the fertile field,
Where flag and banner, under azure skies,
  Float o'er the chieftains who my willow wield.

Lo! they advance in graceful armour clad,
  Right gallantly to guard the famous fort;
Intrepid heroes, girt with glove and pad,
  Ambition seeking in a manly sport.

* This word does not appear to have attracted the notice of any philologist, although in some districts it represents a carriage as familiar to the rustic eye as a cart or a coach. The vehicle is strongly put together, and has two wheels of an unusually large diameter. Its use is to convey timber from the place where grown to some other locality. It has also the names of trolly and tug, but the one chosen above is far more euphonious than either.

And mark, from east to west, from south to north,
  Peer and plebeian strive in bold array,
E'en as the Briton from the breach breaks forth,
  To charge and keep the enemy at bay.

Muse o'er the grand precision of the ball,
  Straight as an arrow from the bended bow;
See how the foemen at the fortress fall,
  And marvel at the true and timely throw.

Hark to the martial music of the band,
  Where youth and beauty in a circle sit;
See winsome woman wave her lovely hand,
  Pleased with the mighty and majestic hit.

Hark to the shouts that echo from the rear—
  Succumbs a champion to the splendid catch.
Smile at the truthful and triumphant cheer,
  For England's noblemen have won the match.

Aye, now the strife is o'er, and bye and run
  For pure analyses are dotted down,
Know that the victory thus lost and won
  Is worthy of a wreath of rare renown.

The charm of childhood and the aim of age,
  It should be written in the book of fame;
Engraven on the fair and fervid page,
  If only for the glory of the game.

A recreation, eminent on earth,
  It has no parallel on grassy glade;
For health and happiness, it is well worth
  More favour than all other pastimes played.

Thus, while I write to venerate in verse
  Our country squires who play a princely part,
Who from their ample coffers prime the purse,
  And gold and silver give with hand and heart,

And mark the arbitrators—men who stand
  As able advocates o'er stumps and bails;
Apt umpires who, when holding up the hand,
  With truth adjust the balance of the scales—

So ends my theme, and now that I desire
  To put away in peace a homely harp,
I'm happy in the hope that o'er my lyre
  No class will cavil and no critic carp.

A few words of prose by way of elucidation. The bat is, more frequently than any other implement used in the game of cricket, the private property of the user, and is often regarded with feelings almost of affection, especially if it has aided its owner to defend wickets and obtain long scores. All match bats are made of willow—the *salix* of Linnæus. There are many species. The manufacture of the blade is commenced by cross cutting the tree into pieces a little longer than the finished blade, to allow for cracking at the ends. The saw used for this purpose is very sharp, with the teeth set wide on account of the soft-tough nature of the wood. The lengths are then cleft with wooden wedges into pieces large enough for single pods, when a man with a sharp axe chops them a little nearer into shape. They are then stacked up in the open air for about twelve months to season, and if sufficiently dry and hard, they are shaped with a drawing-knife and put into a lathe, where the shoulders are turned. After this process the faces and edges are pressed and hammered, to harden them against the force of the ball. When in this state the handle is inserted. This is the most difficult part of the operation, as there is nothing to prevent its parting company with the blade except the goodness of the work and the glue. All kinds of pegs, pins, and screws have proved worse than useless. The bat is once more put into the lathe and the handle turned. The final shaping of the blade is then performed with very sharp planes and spokeshaves, smoothed with glass paper, and polished with a piece of bone or burnished steel. It is transferred again to the lathe, and the handle bound with fine waxed twine, and finished. Even after all this it is kept some time in stock, and in order to fill up any outer pores of the wood, a little linseed oil is applied. The lines which run down what are called straight grained bats are caused by the rings showing the yearly growths of the tree. The handle of the bat is made by squaring from twenty to thirty pieces of cane and fixing them together before inserting them in the pod.

THE WHITE WILLOW TREE.

(Leno.)

They may sing of the oak, and its wide-spread renown,
And liken its shade to a stern monarch's crown;
They may crown it the king of the forest and glade,
And point to its triumphs of battle and trade—
To the years it has stood 'mid the tempest and storm—
Of its grandeur, its prestige, its age, and its form;
But its soft-hearted brother is dearer to me,
Hence the song that I sing is, the White Willow Tree.

There's no stain on the willow of worship or war,
No loud shriek of anguish to triumph or mar;
And as long as the willow's green branches expand,
The name of its heroes shall ring through the land.
Can you find me a Briton whose heart is not stirred
When the names of a Pilch, Grace, or Filer is heard?
Or a youth who has not been delighted to see
The baton well used from the White Willow Tree?

In the tent or the field, where the willow's supreme,
The peasant forgets all his cares in a dream;
And the fop and the upstart their level soon find,
Where social distinctions are thrown to the wind.
In the broad glare of noon, on the velvetted floor,
Men meet as they met in the glad days of yore;
And there, in derision of rank and degree,
New friendships are formed through the White Willow Tree.

As I sit in my slippers, or lean on my staff,
Or erst with a neighbour a bottle I quaff,
Oft gabble of giants whose triumphs are o'er,
Whose deeds still are cherished by rich and by poor,
I call back the Mynns, the Wenmans, the Wards,
Who won their renown with the white willow swords;
And so from my aches and my pains are set free,
As of cricket I chat, and the White Willow Tree.

THE SAGE'S REMEDY.

Dreaming, dreaming, and deeply disconsolate,
Sits a philosopher, cursing his race—
Cursing them early, and cursing them so late—
Really, his language is quite a disgrace.
What is the grief, then, that moves our philosopher?
Is it that Julia Jane is unkind?
Is his heart pained by that scornful toss of her
Pretty head—showing he's not to her mind?
Say, have late suppers impaired his digestion?
Few men can smile when they think of blue pill;
Has he attacked the Ozokerit question?
Was he cut out of his maiden aunt's will?
Surely no such misfortunes would cause his depression,
Neither Julia nor physic has wrung his heart's chords;
His complaint, diagnosed by the learned profession,
Is the want of some really good practice at Lord's.
From August he's dragg'd out a weary existence,
In rackets and fives has sought pleasure in vain;
Now merry May comes, and, with cricket's assistance,
Once more he can breathe and be happy again.
Then, John, call a Hansom, bring out the old bat,
The flannels and pads, with the ancient spiked shoes;
Some twisters from Royston, some bumpers from Platt,
Are the very best cure for a fit of the blues.
The Doctor, well padded, has been there two hours,
The Major is bowling his own special lobs;
Jemmy Grundy still shows that a cricketer's powers
Are not of a sort the thief "Old Time" robs.
So to Lord's with all haste on the first day of May,
That's the place to drive all one's blue devils away.

ODD THOUGHTS AND RESOLVES IN VERSE.

(Anonymous.)

When settled in heaven, which I hope will be soon,
I'll play oft at cricket, and bowl with the Moon;
A bright rainbow my *bat*, my wicket the *Sun*,
And I'll *score* with a star whenever I run.
Old Mars shall keep wicket with his iron hand,
And Neptune as *long stop* behind him shall stand;
Great Jupiter *long fag*, because he can shy
The ball, like a thunderbolt, straight through the sky.

Swift Mercury *leg*, jolly Bacchus *square nip*,
Apollo *cover point*, Vulcan *short slip*,
Pluto *long stop*, from the regions below,
Long fag to the off will make Æolus blow
Rough Boreas shall blow as hard as he can,
And I, if you please, will be mid-wicket man,
Then our opponents may search all through heaven,
And make out as they can another Eleven
Our field the blue sky, with a cloud for a tent
Which after a shower good Jupiter sent,
Twin Castor and Pollux our umpires shall be,
They may settle disputes if we can't agree,
Two bright little angels, with pens for their wings,
Shall act as our scorers, and tell us who wins,
I'll order a comet to come without fail,
With lantern and tinder box under his tail,
To light our cigars, and, to finish our cheer,
Sweet Hebe shall wait with a barrel of beer
And if, my dear Alice, you'd like to be there,
I'll get you a seat on the tail of the Bear
New stumps are wanted, to the number of six,
So, good Mr Charon, pray lend us the *sticks*

MY SIRES OF OLD WERE CRICKETERS

(G W. King)

My sires of old were cricketers—a cricketer am I,
And 'tis my boast that I can play a game I rate so high
I prize my peerless pastime for its freedom and its fun,
It revels on the grassy plain, and glows beneath the sun
I've heard of foreign pleasures that are very fair to see,
But cricket, glorious cricket, is quite fair enough for me,
And he that will not play or pay to help the manly game,
May lie forgotten in the grave—an unremembered name
We may not have th' excitement that some other sports may show,
The thrill that maddens betters when the horses form a row,
We may not boast the ardour that fills the huntsman's breast
When horse and hound sweep madly on and he's before the rest,
But we've ecstatic moments when we've hit a six or four,
And proudly walk back to the tent when blest with a long score
And we have many hard fought games that tell of strength and pluck,
And stout must be our hearts to stand against a run of luck
There's not a land that on its plains a set of stumps will bear,
But England's sons are seen to play a game of cricket there,
There's not a clime so hot or cold but echoes to the shout
Of "finely played!" "well bowled, my boy!" "now run, and run it out"
Our ancient institutions, and our good old cricket laws,
Have won from all the nations round their wonder and applause
Oh, he must be a duffer, boys and cold must be his breast,
Who won't support the noble game, or in it do his best

INVOCATION TO CRICKET.

(From the first number of the *Hedgehog and Saut Water Gazette*, a comic and satirical weekly periodical, published in Greenock, September 11th, 1865, and edited by John M. K. Brodie.)

It is the proud distinction of our isle
That, midst our race for riches or for place,
We seek the weary hours away to while
In sports where strength competes with manly grace;
A warlike folk, we love the strifes of peace,
And with our "Isthmian games" outrival ancient Greece.

* * * * * *

In all our games we show a grand fervour,—
Strive for the palm, as Jason for the fleece:
When Greek met Greek, tough was the tug of war;
When Scot meets Scot, tough is the tug of peace.
Though to our strifes, perchance, some errors fall,
Try but their spell and you'll forget them all.

Some love the noble art of self defence,
And like to box or fistic triumphs view;
Some love *le sport*, and gallant leap each fence,
And startle Reynard with a hoarse hallo!
While some with matchless steeds (but these are few)
Have yearly strifes for Epsom's "ribbon blue."

* * * * * *

They are not of a class, but from all ranks,
For cricket is like death, and levels all;
The master proud receives his servant's thanks—
All fear the scorn which on a duffer fall.
Palmam qui meruit is each man's aspiration,
The best ranks highest whatsoe'er his station.

How glad one feels when off to play a match,
By coach, or boat, or swiftly rushing train!
How large the chickens fancy loves to hatch,
How lordly rise the *Chateaux en Espagne*!
What though the castles fall, the embryo chickens die,
Waiting another day bright hope doth midst their ruins lie.

THE CRICKETERS' CLUB.

(A New Song by an Old Hand.)

We've a song for the stag, for the fox, and the hare,
We've a glee if afflictions attack us;
We have po ts by hundreds, whose voices declare
All the honours of Venus and Bacchus.
But our theme shall be cricket—to bat, ball, and wicket,
Our chorus due honours shall yield;
Put him out! put him out! who refuses to shout
Long life to our glorious field.

Leave to statesmen their game—let them scramble for swag,
Since their *ins* and their *outs* must be foes;
But our sides are friends, our contention but play,
And we pledge the same cup at the close.
Fill a bumper to cricket—to bat, ball, and wicket,
Our chorus due honours shall yield;
Put him out! &c.

With the sky for our roof, where's the palace can match,
With the lovely green turf for our throne,
With—alas! I am out—I have given a catch!
'Nother man! for my innings are done.
Yet in parting, to cricket—to bat, ball, and wicket—
Our chorus due honours shall yield;
Put him out!

THE FINE OLD ENGLISH CRICKETERS.

(Anonymous.)

Let "Bell" declaim on Hillyer's fame, and all the modern band,
I'll try a little song about the good old underhand;
So, while to present stars we give them honest all-round praise,
Just now we'll rip up ancient scores, and celebrate the ways
Of the fine old English cricketers,
Those of the olden time.

And first our voices all, I'm sure, must join with one accord
To hail the king of cricketers, the veteran William Ward;
Who, while his wicket proudly stood for two long days and more,
Two hundred runs and eighty-six displayed upon the score,
Like a fine old English cricketer, &c.

Next comes a noble patron of this truly noble game,
So fill the bumpers round and toast Lord Frederick Beauclerk's name;
Whose nervous arm so straight and true sent in the ripping ball,
That down with one terrific smash went wickets, bails, and all,
Like a fine old English cricketer, &c.

The time would fail if now we tried to sound the praise of all
The heroes of the Hambledon—of Nyren, Jenner, Small;
But first to drink "t' auld Squire's" health we can a moment spend,
Who to "the turf," in double sense, has ever been a friend,
Like a fine old English cricketer, &c.

With muttered hints of "throwing" then no bowler ever met,
And "wide balls" were a genus strange to men unknown as yet;
Leg guards and indiarubber gloves would have been "somewhere" flung,
And batsmen padded "cap-a-pied" been scarcely known among
The fine old English cricketers, &c.

And though the game, like all things else, has made a wondrous stride,
Yet in the annals of the past we still may take a pride;
And when such rare old worthies shall have bid the world adieu,
We hope that to the sport there'll be as faithful friends and true
As the fine old English cricketers,
Those of the olden time.

THE ALERT CLUB.

The following stanzas are extracted from an old manuscript poem written in the early part of the present century. Author not named:—

RECITATIVE.

Come hither, lads, let exercise excite you
To join our club, if cricket may delight you;
Depart from us, ye lazy and inert,
You must not members be of "The Alert."
That appellation brothers will support,
And not by indolence disgrace the sport.

AIR.

What club e'er formed can ours surpass for innocent amusement?
Mirth, concord, and society being the chief inducement,
Consisting of such members as would scorn to act inglorious,
Or abjectly absent themselves because the game's laborious.

CHORUS.

With bats, balls, bails, and stumps, also white dresses clean and smart,
We'll turn out in the field, my boys, where each will play his part.

The fops, we know, our sport despise, and say they really wonder
The ball don't prejudice our eyes, nay, strike our limbs asunder.
Such idle thoughts ne'er penetrate, our heart's completely steel'd,
For should a blow us overthrow, we'd scorn to quit the field.
With bats, &c.

Great benefit we all receive from this our sweet diversion,
Any pain it will relieve with circumspect exertion;
Freely circulate the blood, and free the face from blotches,
Doctors you never need consult, if you have running notches.
With bats, &c.

In our marquee you'll always see good cheer without profusion,
And should a friend enter therein, we deem it no intrusion,
But them receive, and freely give, with welcome truly hearty,
And there's no doubt, ere he goes out, he'll wish to join our party.
With bats, &c.

Come brothers all, let's drink about, and make a good beginning,
With song and punch and mirth and wine there surely is no sinning;
On Friday afternoons we'll meet, from May until September,
And drink with hearts of love replete, "Success to every member."
With bats, &c.

A CRICKET MATCH (HARROVIAN).

(Ideal.)

Oh, cricket is a grand old game,
And worthy of its world-wide fame;
All foreigners in vain essay
A game which only Britons play.

The name conveys a cheery sound,
And bears your fancy to the ground
Where, pitched upon the level green,
In triple row the stumps are seen;
The scorers' tents and white marquees
Are tipp'd with flags that catch the breeze,
The flannels gay and dresses fine,
To form a varied scene combine.
And when the actual play begins,
What loud applause each batsman wins,
Who, careless both of rope and bound,
Hits sixers clean without the ground;
And those who steal runs, one by one,
Now to the offside, now the on
('Tis thus the largest scores are raised),
By connoisseurs are warmly praised.
And now that ball, with fell intent,
The unguarded bails has spinning sent;
Now off a lob, with mischief fraught,
A slashing bat at length is caught,
And cheers enthusiastic rend
The air as both first innings end.
Then follows dinner, when is told
How each was caught, or stumpt, or bowled;
How play'd round arm or underhand,
What batsman made the longest stand;
Who sixers hit, who out for duck
Retired with curses on their luck;
Against whose name displayed the score
That ignominious "leg before;"
Or how to lend the bowler aid
Some ass his wicket level laid.
Dinner at length is o'er. Again
The friendly contest burns amain;
Spectators but one common aim
Acknowledge as they watch the game;
As batsmen one by one succumb,
And others in their places come,
A breathless interest sways the field,
Which lasts until such time as yield
One side or other. Then succeed
Congratulations, lawful meed
Of cricketers who do and dare
Such actions as entrance the fair.
For ladies with the rest combine,
And cricket think a game divine;
Not that, alas! the science they
Of cricket with delight survey;
But *they their* game pursue, while *we*
Alone the game of cricket see:
Their praises ne'ertheless inflame
All lovers of the noble game.

My muse, I fear, has wearied you,
And craving leave I'll bid adieu,
Your pardon hoping to obtain,
Harroviensis, I remain

"FLOREAT CRICKET"

(Begley)

'Tis right, as England beats the rest
  Of Europe and the world at all things,
That so her sports should be the best,
  And England first in great and small things
No German, Frenchman, or Fijee, will ever master cricket, sir,
Because they haven't got the pluck to stand before the wicket, sir

Chorus

'Tis a grand institution deny it who can,
  By the world is acknowledged its fame,
Long live each true Briton who'll play like a man
  At cricket—our national game

Though Romans "pila" played of old,
  And moderns play at "mourra,"
Could these 'ere boast a wicket bowl'd,
  Or brag they had hit a "fourer?"
I doubt if Romans old or new could ever muster pluck, sir
To field *one* swinging hit to leg, or try to save their duck, sir
Chorus

Can Greece, in all her boasted pride
  Of warrior, patriot, bard, and sages,
Show *one* who never bowled a wide
  As England can in modern ages?
Amid the ranks of heroes, all who shall be, or have been, sir,
With Kent's old hero none may cope, illustrious Alfred Mynn, Sir
Chorus

Old England shows a grand array
  Of thirty gallant names, beginning
From cricket's birth until the day
  When round-arm sent the bails a spinning
There's Box and Wenman, Felix, Pilch, who all could hold a bat, sir,
Which neither Greek nor Roman did I think you'll own that's flat, sir
Chorus

The finest scene the game affords
  Is that 'twixt Harrow School and Eton,
When thousands breast the ropes at Lord's,
  To see the latter "College" Beaten
You ne'er can name a grander game, or view a finer sight, sir,
Than when two crack elevens meet in amity to fight, sir
Chorus

A PARTING ADDRESS.

(C. Jolly, 1856.)

Fair Summer's gone, with all her beauteous flowers,
Her balmy winds, her sunlit rainbow showers ;
Her face, averted, seeks some distant shore,
And, weeping, leaves chill Winter all her store.
The forest now, with "sere and yellow leaf,"
Before Autumnal tempest bends in grief ;
While thick the foliage scattered on the earth,
Proclaims the approach of Winter's frosty birth.
No more is heard the thrilling song of morn
Warbled from throats that hailed the coming dawn,
Save Robin Redbreast, who, with plaintive lay,
Around our dwelling nearer comes each day—
Twitters and chirrups, and begs but from our store
A few stray crumbs, till Winter's morn is o'er,
And Spring again her verdant garb shall throw
O'er hill, o'er dale, where flower bank'd streamlets flow.
One season past, while *on the tented field*,
While over head old Sol his chariot wheeled,
We've met the foe, and with full hearts intent,
On victory, the fiat forth we've sent
Which scattered all their vaunted strength of play,
And gained the trophies that our toils repay.
Till Fame the thousand-tongued from out her car
Proclaimed our triumph in the manly war.
O, cricket! best of games, the noblest, manliest sport,
The merriest battle that e'er mankind fought!
The healthy recreation thou canst give,
Might kill disease and bid the weakest live ;
Might chase the chill'd blood through the clog'd up vein,
Till the cheek glows with ruddy health again ;
Might make the misanthrope unclose his heart,
Till fellow mankind claim'd the better part.
Scarce twelvemonths' since our club had not been formed,
Though many hearts the noble game had warmed.
Till in the path a hopeful few had stray'd,
'Missioned by Friendship ; they her voice obeyed—
They cleared the wilderness, they broke the ground,
They sowed the seed, tho' malice darkly frown'd.
They watched its growing, aye, and strove with might,
Till strong it grew o'erreaching envy's height.
Their voice directed, their example led,
Kind fortune smiled, and on the good work sped.
Firm was the union, for the cause was just.
No schemes ambitious, no wealth-getting lust,
But mirth and friendship led the cheerful way,
And emulation lent her vigorous ray.
Till victory at last their efforts crown'd,
And 'mid our colours, laurel wreathlets bound.
Their toil is over, nobly have they done
The appointed task ; well, too, have they won

The heartfelt thanks that mankind may bestow
On truthful, generous friendship here below
Dear to their hearts must be the thought that they,
Though but a few, have cleared the rugged way,
Where we may freely in this noble sport
Forget awhile the troubles life has brought
Soon as again old Winter shall die out,
All earth shall welcome Spring with merry shout
The bubbling springs shall burst their icy bounds,
Their music mingling with the forest sounds,
Sweet flowers shall spring up from their leafy beds,
And dance with joy when Spring with Nature weds,
And godlike Sol shall mount his radiant car,
And bid old Cricket seize the tools of war
Then with firm hearts again we'll take the field
With bat and ball, and eager hands to wield
The fate of clubs Who 'gainst us shall combine
In friendly rivalry, to conquer their design,
But let them come united in one band,
WISDOM our leader, boldly forth we'll stand
And try our skill, with merry hearts and free,
'Till fortune smiles, and conquerors we shall be
But if perchance the laurel on our brows,
By play superior, decorates our foes,
What then? at festive board we'll pledge success
To our next game nor persevere the less,
And as the sun, cloud-hidden for a while,
Oft breaketh forth with lovelier, brighter smiles,
So shall our club, though vanquished, stronger be,
And by the lesson win back victory

THE CRICKET ENTHUSIAST

(C JOLLY, 1856)

The sports of old England are many and rare,
And the hunt has been sung of the fox, stag, and hare,
Of the jovial crew met at dawn's early gleam,
But my song shall be cricket, and cricket my theme

I love the gay race course, the hunt I love too
When hunter and hound dash away through the dew,
But better I love on the green tented field
To meet hearty good friends, and the willow to wield

There pride and contempt quits the haughtiest brow,
And the lord greets the labourer fresh from the plough,
Both forget for a while all the chances of life,
And both share the joys of the soul stirring strife

Ye students that plunge in "the fountain of mind,"
Haste away to the field, leave your book lore behind,
Ye pale sons of commerce, leave mart, desk, and 'change,
And away 'mid the fresh air and wild flowers range

Old Homer hath sung of the heroes of Troy,
Whose best boast was how they did God's gift destroy,
But bloodless and guiltless, and better by far
Are the heroes that shine in the bold cricket war

If war hath its glories so peace hath its charms,
No carnage or death howl their horrid alarms,
But the hand and the heart, and the eye of a friend,
Are the fruits and the spoils that do cricket attend

Success and long life to the manly old game,
On the altar of peace 'tis a bright steady flame,
'Tis the child of content, 'tis the handmaid of health,
'Tis the link in life's chain that from toil creates wealth

Then fill high the cup, brim it o'er with rich wine,
Give a cheer for the health-giving labour divine,
Let the shadows of life for a time pass away,
And bask in the bright beams of friendship's warm ray

THE SPORTS OF MY ANCESTORS

My ancestors lov'd British sports, for cricket were renowned,
And challengers, however bold, in them acceptors found
I can't forget the tales they told, the wonders they achieved,
Which to my school-boy ears were far too great to be believed,
And busy memory paints the match that first I went to see,
Though many years have passed away, 'twas yesterday to me

Close to an oft frequented spot were raised the slender stumps,
The surface round about well searched for dubious dints and bumps
Here the contenders, fitly clad for freedom and for ease,
Did fly about, and each and all were busy as the bees
Should storm or sunshine prove severe, there was a sheltering shed,
With stores of biscuit, cheese, and beer, Schiedam and gingerbread

Oh, twas indeed a glorious sight, as close the scoring ran,
To see the strong anxiety which spurred on every man!
The bounding pulse the active limb, the head the hand, the heart,
Were all strung up to concert pitch to play the victor's part
And I can now in fancy hear that mirthful, boisterous shout,
When fate, or luck, or something else, had put the last man out

And when the game was lost and won, and all the stumps were drawn,
What jokes and puns, and laughter too, were heard across the lawn,
And memory brings those old times back with force and mixed delight,
In having such "a meet" as this around the board to night,
For 'twas the plain old fashioned plan to close a merry day
In fragrant clouds, with social glass, and mirth-inspiring lay

Then let us toast our native land, from whence the game took rise,
Our Queen and all the Royal line who cricket patronise,
Our Peers and Senators also, and Britain's hardy ones
With old John Bull who gives the pluck to all his far-famed sons
And thus shall we keep up the plan, a good one you must know
Our grandsires were delighted with so many years ago

EVENING SONG.

(WRITTEN IN 1850, AND SET TO MUSIC BY THE AUTHOR)

Uplit is seen the evening star, for down the arc of day
Phœbus has rolled his burning car, and night resumes its sway.
Now rally brothers one and all, a song brooks no control;
Ye lovers of the bat and ball, taste the inspiring bowl.
Then fill a goblet to the brim, and quaff this toast with me—
Success to every cricketer, wherever he may be.

Lo, cricketing its fame extends like ray lines from the sun;
If the round world has claim to end, thither its courses run
The stumps are raised far off and wide, the sounds from bat and ball
Are heard where runs the lava tide, and roaring waters fall.
Then fill, &c.

Here teachers of the sacred word, and those that arms adorn,
With ploughers of the soil accord, and reapers of the corn;
Old Ocean's chiefs, who dangers brave, join him with horny hand,
And statesmen, too, distinctions waive, though magnates of the land.
Then fill, &c.

Talk ye of Greek or Roman nerve, of Sparta's iron brood,
Heroes a nation's sport to serve, who shed their choicest blood;
Britannia's bulwarks 'gainst her foes, her strongest tower, I wis,
Lie in the hearts and arms of those who play a game like this.
Then fill, &c.

THE DEITY OF PEACE.

The Teuton boasts his needle gun, and talks of war and death;
The Yankee of his ironclad—its fierce destructive breath;
But we'll exalt the cricket bat in every English home,
And hail it as the deity of peaceful years to come.
Thus may we speed by word and deed wherever we may go
A mighty spirit in the land, now moving to and fro.

Let sportsmen brush and bugle laud as emblems of the chase,
And poets sing the trophies that baronial mansions grace;
Sure notes as joyous can be struck from out the willow wood,
When carved to shape that tokens peace and fosters brotherhood.
Then let us speed, &c.

Gird, then, the bat with leaves of bay and sprigs of fragrant flowers,
While deep and treble voices join in chorusing its powers,
For sire and son, both old and young, its uses know full well,
As may be seen on village green, in hamlet, town, and dell.
So shall, &c.

The cannon ball, the sword, the spear, may yet be useless things,
When o'er the world the merry shout from harmless warfare springs.
Then bumpers fill with glowing hearts, and toast in manly strains
The pleasures springing from the bat on cricket-tented plains.
Thus shall, &c.

THE HARROW ALPHABET, 1864.

A Stands for Amherst and Arkwright, who bowled all Eton out,
B Buller is our captain—now let Harrow raise a shout
C Is the catch that Evetts made, and so the match was won,
D Is the double shuffle, who could not score a run
E Stands for Evetts, pretty good at football and at cricket,
F Is the funk that Eton showed when they were at the wicket
G's For H R Grimston, who taught us how to field and catch,
H Is my hat which I threw up when Harrow won the match
I 'I will shout and I will sing' for we have won the day,
J Jump for joy Harrovians, all who came to see the play
K Knock your heads together Etonians, for you are done
L Landed all my money at 5 to 1—that's fun!
M Stands for "Monkey" Hornby, and Montgomery so tall,
N Nobody can beat him, for at point he's best of all
O Oh! that I had words to sing the praises of those twins.
P The Phippses, who on Harrow side show always how it wins.
Q Quail, ye young Etonians, when at Lord's next year ye see
R Richardson, who fields so well and bats so steadily
S Stow and Smith—my verse now sings Stow, captain for next year,
T Tremble, ye Etonians, he may well inspire fear
U Unto you, Harrovians, I dedicate this song,
V Verses which, though not too short, at least are not too long
W Which, though foolish seem, I trust at least may be
X 'Xpressive of the match at Lords, and our great victory
Y You, at least, Harrovians true, will grant this readily,
Z For Z there is no word to end my A B C —ONE OF THEM *

HARROW AND ETON MATCH, JULY 14TH AND 15TH, 1865

On London when the sun was low
All hoofless was the untrodden Row,
And straight as arrow was the throw
Of Amherst bowling rapidly

But London saw another sight
When the bell rang at fall of night
Commanding colours, dark and light,
To quit the scenes of revelry

By tent and "Parry" fast parade
Each horseman and each cockney blade,
And furious every Dobbin neighed,
To leave the noisy revelry

Then shook the air, with plaudits riven,
Rushed off the swell to dinner driven
And, darker than the blue of heaven,
Far flashed the blue millinery

* Harrow won by one innings and a large number of runs (see p 133)

But fiercer yet the steeds shall go
O'er London's side of Rotten Row,
And stronger yet the biceps throw,
Of Amherst bowling rapidly.

'Tis morn! and scarce Harrovian
Can brook the chaff of Eton "don,"
Where furious Frank and fiery John
Shout 'neath heaven's sulphurous canopy.

The combat ceases. On ye brave
And rush to triumph, or to rave;
Wave Harrow. All thy sisters wave,
And cheer with all thy energy.

Some few shall thousand voices greet;
Our arms be their triumphal seat;
And every boy that throngs their feet
Re-echo Harrow's victory.

IDYLL TO COMMEMORATE THE RETURN OF THE SECOND ELEVEN FROM AUSTRALIA (*See* p. 318.)

Hail! all hail! victorious band;
A thousand welcomes to your native land!
Old England's heart leaps forth amain,
And greets upon her strand her gallant sons again.
Not yours the gory spoils of war,
But glorious triumphs won in climes afar.
No widow's tears nor orphan's wails
Tarnish your well won laurels in Australia's vales.
And there, while history shall unroll
Of the new Southern empire her emblazoned scroll,
With brighter glory shall she gild your fame,
And stamp a general nation's love upon your manly game.
Perchance some bard of "native fire"
Shall wield with Homer's power his graceful lyre,
And in the fervour of heroic verse,
Like Greeks and Ilions, your conquering deeds rehearse;
How Tarrant's balls, with mighty force,
Like gunshot dashed the wicket on the course;
How Tinley, with strategic hand,
Slowly, but surely, displaced his adversary's stand.
How Clarke, with wizard might,
Would catch the ball, however swift its flight;
While thundering plaudits sound
To greet his dexterous skill from thronging thousands round!
Next see the *duo* stand,
Hayward and Carpenter the course command;
Surprising with unrivalled play—
Invincibles—their innings only closed with day!
And Caffyn, too, the Surrey pet,
Like lightning show'd them how the scores to get;
And on the well won field did he
At cricket show his county's old nobility!

How he and doughty Anderson
Maintained their places till Old Time said "Done"
How Jackson's matchless bowling
And Lockyer's ready skill, cut short their adversaries' polling!
How Cæsar's feat
Of *Veni vidi, vici*,
The ancient shade
Transferred his glory, when his namesake played!
Or tell how modest Grace
Though crippled sore, maintained his sturdy place!
With Tarrant's bowling straight,
The pair of lively heroes vanquished adversaries eight
Nor must we forget afar
The skill in generalship of Captain Parr,
So long did he defend his wicket,
He seemed his name's longevity at cricket
Then hail! all hail, victorious band!
A thousand welcomes to Britannia's strand,
Her peerless glory and renown!
And long may every clime your conquering prowess own

SONG OF THE CRICKETER.

(Written in 1850)

(Set to Music by J W Thirlwall, also by Herr Meyer Lutz.)

The Duke of Wellington once remarked in the house of Lords that his success in arms was owing, in a great measure, to the manly sports of Great Britain, and one sport above all—cricket

I seem not to care for hound, fox or hare—
The chase of the wild roe I relish still less
No gathering of scarlet or green can compare
With the "meet" of old friends in a cricketing dress,
So fill up a bumper, and joyously call
For success to the friends of the bat and the ball!

Here's a sport that encrimsons with roses the cheek,
Strews a garland of flowers o'er life's chequered day,
Tunes the pulse to sweet music—gives strength to the weak,
Why surely, then, cricket is worthy a lay
So fill up, &c

The vassal and peer in the pastime engage—
The hale mountain peasant—the chief in the glen,
All ages commingle—youth, warrior, and sage,
For of men it makes boys, and boys become men
So fill up, &c

Then welcome the sober enjoyment that flings
Such witchery round the spot where it lives!
The bud in the heart, to the sunlight that clings
Will bloom in the pleasure that cricketing gives
So fill up, &c.

RECITATION—KING TIME, A CRICKETER

(Written in 1850)

King Time in a whim from his throne took a stray—
Not to look at the flowers in the carpet of May,
Or breathe the sweet perfume from orchard and bush,
Hear the laugh of the rill, or the song of the thrush—
But to see how much havock in brick, wood, and stone,
Had been made by the wings of a century gone
He viewed the groined porch, he gazed on the tower,
Eyed the cracks where the mortar had lost all its power,
The high polished marbles, once mocking his sway,
Fast dwindling their beauties and records away!
While the monarch in triumph tramped over the dead,
The slab seemed to shrink at the breath of his tread,
And the spire which had latterly felt his advance
Quailed, fearfully quailed, at his withering glance!
He turned to the stream which went loitering past,
The tree of the Druid, with trunk rotting fast,
The arch of the bridge that had got all askew,
The slime and the worm, that were eating it through,
The castle and keep on the brink of the hill,
The spot and remains of the old water mill
He frowned on the daisy, which, modestly gay,
Bloomed o'er the sunk battlement gone to decay,
Scanned the moss—that soft clothing with which earth was dight,
"When first she was hatched from the great egg of Night!"
But here ceased his musing Aroused by a shout
"Ho! Ho!" says the King, "what's this racket about?"
For just in his track, on a beautiful green,
Was a grand match of cricket—a sight he'd ne'er seen
While tents were erected for shelter and ease,
And flags chaunted music to every breeze,
There Health was disporting her crimson-hued vest,
And Joy danced attendance on every guest,
The players were valiant, the company gay,
Bright Phœbus ne'er shone on a more happy day.
So rare was the contest, such wonders were done,
Time was mute as his effigy chiselled in stone!
He thought of the feats on the great Trojan plain,
When Hector, brave chief, by Achilles was slain,
Of Xerxes' vast army, disputing the pass
Of Thermopylæ, with a Leonidas,
Of England's rude prowess when Cæsar came o'er,
How Hengist and Horsa contended for power,
How York and how Lancaster's roses were shed,
And uncivil wars dyed the kingdom with red!
Then glancing awhile on the soul-cheering play,
By turns o'er his face came a frown and a ray
'These players deride me, they're so merry and blythe"
Then turning his glass he glanced at his scythe,

And said to himself, "I'll soon conquer ye all—
Yet there's much I admire with this bat and the ball!"
So at eve when the wine in its plenty did flow,
And tales were retold of things done long ago;
King Time was so pleased, said the game was so good,
That he'd spare all the players as long as he could!

THE GAME OF LIFE OR DEATH AMONG THE CRICKETERS.

When men are in a moralising strain,
And gravely talk about the brittle stuff
Of which poor *human life* is made,
'Tis ten to one
That, ere they've done,
They shake their heads and make this sage reflection,
That life is transitory, fleeting, vain—
A very bubble,
With pleasures few and brief; but as for pain,
There's more than *quantum suff.*—
Nay, quite enough
To make the stoutest heart afraid,
And cloud the merriest visage with dejection!
And then, what dismal stories are invented
About this "vale of woe;"
Zounds! 'twere enough to make one discontented
Whether one *would or no!*
Now, Life to me has always seemed a game—
Not a mere game of *chance*, but one where skill
Will often throw the chances in our way—
Just like (my favourite sport) the Game of Cricket;
Where, though the match be well contested, still
A steady player, careful of his fame,
May have a *good long innings*, with fair play,
Whoever bowls, or stops, or keeps the wicket.
"Softly my friend (methinks I hear Death cry)!
Whoever bowls, you say; sure you forget
That in Life's feverish, fitful game
I am the bowler, and friend Time keeps wicket?"
Well, be it so, old boy, is my reply;
I *know* you do; but, Master Drybones, yet
My argument remains the same,
And I can prove, *Life's like a Game of Cricket.*
Sometimes a batsman's lull'd by Bowler Death,
Who throws him off his guard with *easy balls*,
Till presently a rattler stops his breath—
He's out; Life's candle's snuff'd—his wicket falls.
In goes another *mate*. Death bowls away,
And with such art each practis'd method tries,
That now the ball winds tortively along;
Now slowly rolls, and now like lightning flies
(Sad proof that Death's as subtle as he's strong!).

But *this rare* batsman keeps a watchful eye
On every motion of the Bowler's hand,
And stops, or hits, as suits the varying play,
Though Death the ball may *ground*, or toss it high,
The steady striker keeps his self command,
And *blocks* with care, or makes it swiftly fly
Still bent on victory, Old Drybones plies
With patient skill, but every effort fails,
Till Time—that *precious* enemy—prevails
O! envious Time! to spoil so good a game!
Fear'dst thou that Death at last had met his match
And ne'er could bowl him out, or get a *catch*?
Yea, verily, old Time, thou seem'st to doubt
The bowler's skill, and so, to save *his* fame,
Didst watch the *popping* crease, with anxious eyes,
Until the wish'd for opportunity
Arrived, when thou could'st stump the batsman out!
O! what a player, how active, cheerful, gay!
His "Game of Life," how like a summer's day!
But yet in vain 'gainst Death and Time he tries
To stand his ground, they bear away the prize,
And, foil'd at last he yields his bat, and—dies!
Some are bowl'd out before they've got a notch—
But mates like these can *helpmates* scarce be reckoned—
Some knock their wickets down, while others botch
And boggle so, that when they get *a run*
It makes Time laugh—Death, too, enjoys the fun,
Shakes his spare ribs to see what they have done,
Then out he bowls the bunglers in a second!
And yet, although old Messieurs Death and Time
    Are sure to come off winners *in the end*,
There's something in the game of Life that's pleasant,
For though "to die" in verse may sound sublime
(*Blank* verse, of course, I mean—not doggrel rhyme)
    Such is the love I bear to Life and Cricket,
    Either at single or at double wicket,
I'd rather play a good long game, and spend
    My time agreeably with some kind friend,
Than throw my bat and ball up—*just at present*—*S Maunder*

THE VEXED BOWLER.

(Written in 1860—Author not named)

Oh! have you heard the news of late
About a cricket match so great?
If you have not, I'll tell you straight
About a vexed bowler

Chorus

Rippers twisters, fast and slow,
He tried them all, but still "no go,"
He could not lay the wicket low,
Alas! for vexed bowler

This prowler to the wicket goes,
And to the crease he pops his toes,
Resolved at once he would dispose
Of the opposing batsman
CHORUS (as before)

But batsman, he would not be done,
The ball he knock'd about like fun,
And everywhere the fielders run,
And loudly swears the bowler.
CHORUS.

Then every dodge the bowler tries,
But still the ball so nimbly flies,
Yet never for a catch would rise,
And busy keeps the scorers
CHORUS

The bowler finds he's got his match,
And then begins his nob to scratch,
And tripping tries his man to catch—
Poor disappointed bowler!
CHORUS

At last he says, "'Tis very strange,
Somehow I cannot get the range,"
And thinks they'd better try a change,
The bat has beat the bowler.
CHORUS

The moral draw, if you are wise,
Never opponent to despise
Until you've taken well his size,
Unlike the vexed bowler
CHORUS

ONE ARM AND ONE LEG

(WRITTEN IN 1868 FOR "THEORY AND PRACTICE")

There is a pleasure in the thought
That men who have our battles fought
Can meet in friendly feud together,
Though clash of sword and rifle aim
May be reflected in a game
Our children play upon the heather
Yea, though all strategies of arms
Are bound in fair and false alarms,
Defeat or victory at cricket,
Though bloody deeds by fortress wall
Are parodied when bat and ball
Defend and storm the stubborn wicket
Thus thought I, when with vision dim,
With feeble step and loss of limb,
Old warriors in the strife contended,
Strove as of yore, a veteran band,
That from the foe, by sea and land,
Our Queen and country had defended

May be, shouts echoed round the spot
That mingled with the musket shot
At Balaklava, great in story ,
Or mimick'd was the deadly stroke
Of sabre flashing in the smoke
On lofty Alma, shorn of glory

So grew I glad, and like a bard
That yearns to men whose fate is hard,
This simple song and toast repeated
Old England's heroes are our boast,
Long may they guard our ancient coast,
And never, never, be defeated

THE GENTLEMEN CRICKETERS' TEAM

A Song.

Respectfully dedicated to its subject (Author not named) —*Wickets in the West*

I've a toast to propose to you, so gentlemen, hand on
The Mumm and the Cliquot, the Moet and Chandon ,
The toast that I offer, with pleasure extreme,
Is the health of "The Gentlemen Cricketers' Team"

And first here's the health of their captain, Fitzgerald,
Whose time honoured name stands in need of no herald ,
All know that he manages matches as well
As a match-making mother with daughters to sell

Next, here's to the chief of the ball-driving race,
A giant in cricket as well as a Grace ,
Bat, bowler, or field, in himself he's a host,
All round the best player that Britain can boast.

Here's to Hornby who bears the cognomen of "Monkey,"
All muscle, and never—never feeble nor funky ,
For pluck, skill, and strength he is hard to be beaten
By picked men from Winchester, Harrow, or Eton !

Here's the left-handed bowler, that Lancashire swell,
Whom Ottawa batsmen remember so well,
He bowled a whole innings (and bowled like great guns)
In *apple pie* order for—only three runs !

And here's to his *confrère*, spectacular Rose—
A rather quick bowler of dangerous "slows ,"
And now to the Lubbocks, a brave pair of brothers,
Who rank with the Graces, the Walkers, and others

Now, here's to four stars of the Oxford Eleven
(With all due respect to the home-keeping seven),
Here's to Harris and Ottaway, Francis and Hadow,
May Time ne'er decrease his Herculean shadow !

Here's to Pickering, lastly—his name is enough
To prove that he's made of good cricketing stuff ,
Warm welcome, I'm sure, he will ever be shown,
For the sake of his uncle as well as his own

So here's to them singly, or taken together—
A finer set yet never hunted the leather,
Once more, then, I pledge you, with pleasure extreme,
The health of "The Gentlemen Cricketers' Team"

THE FINE OLD ENGLISH GAME

THIS song was written about the year 1830 (authorship disputed) It can be sung either to the "Highland Home" melody, or "The Fine Old English Gentleman."

No sport or pastime can compare with that which I shall name,
'Tis good for peasant and for peers—a fine old English game,
It does no harm, it breeds no strife, it hurts no honest mind,
It thrills with rapture every vein, yet leaves no sting behind.

CHORUS

Then sing a song to cricket, that fine old English game

It flushes with the glow of health each manly cheek and brow,
It bids the slow and sluggish blood in kindlier currents flow,
It knits the sinews into strength, and quickens every eye,
It nerves the hand, renews the heart, and bids all sorrows fly
Chorus—Then sing, &c

Oh, what a pleasant sight is that when in the fresh free air,
Blue sky above, green earth beneath, all nature calm and fair,
Its votaries like brothers meet, to test each other's skill,
And win or lose, conclude the game with kindness and good will.
Chorus—Then sing, &c

Array'd in seemly garb they stand upon the verdant sward,
A sight which Mitford might portray, or Blackwood's brawny bard,
Whilst pleased spectators clustering round, look wondering on the whole,
And lovely eyes look kindly on, and lovelier faces smile
Chorus—Then sing, &c

Erect, and graceful, and serene one at the wicket stands,
Grasping the ready bat with strong, as well as pliant hands,
The bowler hurls the flying ball, which seems to bound with life,
And scattered fielders wait around, to aid the noble strife.
Chorus—Then sing, &c

The contest o'er, the conquerors and conquered, each and all
Partake the festive cup, unmixed with either pain or gall,
With many tales, and jocund song, they speed the hours away,
Shake hands at parting, and agree to try some other day
Chorus—Then sing, &c

When Death at last shall bowl us out—which surely must be so—
And knock our guarded wickets down, with his unfailing blow,
May we give up the game like men prepared for such release,
Make our accounts all straight and clear, and quit the field in peace
Chorus—Then sing, &c.

IN MEMORIAM

(S Maunder)

The hero of this poem stood out prominently in the cricket world during the greater portion of his life He was born in the vicinity of Goudhurst, Kent, on the 19th of January, 1807 The family of Mr Mynn in the two preceding generations were renowned for gigantic stature, stalwart form and great proficiency in athletic pursuits These properties Mr Mynn possessed in a pre-eminent degree, his height being 6ft. 1in, and his weight for many years about nineteen stone, with a figure strictly symmetrical Long before he arrived at man's estate he had acquired great fame, and was the chief agent in Kent for developing the round-arm bowling under the tutelage of Mr Wills himself At one time his life was in danger in consequence of having his legs fiercely bowled at because his wicket could not be taken No man earned and enjoyed popularity as a thorough cricketer longer than Alfred Mynn He died in 1861, and was buried in the village churchyard of Thornham, about three miles from Maidstone

Jackson's pace is fearful, Willsher's hand is very high,
William Caffyn has good judgment, and an admirable eye
Jemmy Grundy's cool and clever, almost always on the spot,
Tinley's slows are often telling though they sometimes catch it hot
But however good their trundling—pitch, or pace, or break, or spin—
Still the monarch of all bowlers, to my mind, was Alfred Mynn

Richard Daft is cool and cautious, with his safe and graceful play,
If George Griffith gets a loose one, he can send it far away
You may bowl your best at Hayward, and whatever style you try
Will be vanquished by the master's steady hand and certain eye
But whatever fame and glory these and other bats may win,
Still the monarch of hard hitters, to my mind, was Alfred Mynn

You may praise the pluck of Burbidge, as he plays an uphill match
You may thunder cheers to Miller, for a wondrous running catch,
You may join with me in wishing that the Oval once again
Shall resound with hearty plaudits to the praise of Mr Lane,
But the gentlemen of England the match will hardly win,
Till they find another bowler, such as glorious Alfred Mynn

When the great old Kent Eleven, full of pluck and hope, began
The grand battle with All England, single handed, man to man,
How the hop-men watched their hero, massive, muscular, and tall,
As he mingled with the players, like a king among them all,
Till to some old Kent enthusiasts it would almost seem a sin
To doubt their county's triumph when led on by Alfred Mynn

Though Sir Frederick and "The Veteran" bowled straight and sure and well,
Though Box behind the wicket only Lockyer can excel,
Though Jemmy Dean, as long-stop, would but seldom grant a bye,
Though no novices in batting were George Parr and Joseph Guy—
Said the fine old Kentish farmers, with a find old Kentish grin,
"Why, there ain't a man among them as can match our Alfred Mynn"

And whatever was the issue of the frank and friendly fray,
(Aye, and often has his bowling turn'd the fortunes of the day),
Still the Kentish men fought bravely, never losing hope or heart,
Every man of the Eleven glad and proud to play his part.
And with five such mighty cricketers. 'twas but natural to win,
As Felix, Wenman, Hillyer, Fuller Pilch, and Alfred Mynn.

With his tall and stately presence, with his nobly moulded form,
His broad hand was ever open, his brave heart was ever warm;
All were proud of him, all loved him. As the changing seasons pass,
As our champion lies a sleeping underneath the Kentish grass,
Proudly, sadly, we will name him—to forget him were a sin.
Lightly lie the turf upon thee, kind and manly Alfred Mynn!

ANOTHER POEM ON THE SAME SUBJECT BY ANOTHER HAND.

Fame is oft won by Queen or King,
  Though glory's self is small:
I sing the praise of Alfred Mynn,
  His bat and cricket ball.

There was an Alfred years ago,
  To none was known to yield,
He hurl'd defiance on the foe
  And well he kept the field.

At Chevy Chace a hero fought,
  And though in "doleful dumps,"
He held for long his foes at nought,
  Until he lost his *stumps*.

Well, Death's a foe 'taint fair to play,
  The match he's sure to win,
But he alone could win the day
  Against our Alfred Mynn.

A truce to folly—he is fled;
  But memory long will trace
The bearing of the buried dead,
  His form, his noble face.—F. B. E.

CHAPTER XXVI.

GLOSSARY OF WORDS AND PHRASES.

Teach me, some Power, that happy art of speech
To dress my purpose up in gracious words.—*Rowe.*

* * * * * *

Words are but pictures of our thoughts.—*Dryden.*

* * * * * *

Good phrases are surely, and ever were, very commendable.—
2nd Henry IV., act 3, scene 2.

EVERY art has its nomenclature; every science its vocabulary. From the building of the tower in the valley of Shinar, when the lip was confounded, and speech in consequence split into mysterious divisions, this kind of erudition has been cultivated in some way. With the progress of ages and the intercommunication of peoples and nations, primitive language became in time all but obsolete, or at least submitted to a higher standard of literary appellatives. The transfer of the quarry to the pyramid could not have taken place without giving birth to ideas connected with the process, any more than the early navigation of the great globe itself. Changes of climate and scenery also would naturally produce ideas of which words and phrases were the embodiment, so that in course of time these ideas were portrayed in intelligible language, if not always strictly appropriate. At this period of the world's history there is scarcely a science from the one of lofty order down to that which has barely the pretence of ranking itself as such, but is permeated with a language peculiarly its own. There are people who object strongly to the continuance of ancient words and phrases respecting sciences to which the public devote much attention now. For instance, not only in botanical gardens, but in private collections, simple flowers are made to retain their old polysyllabic epithets; so that few persons, unless versed in botany, know what to make of them. Doubtlessly, much of it is jargon to untutored ears; still, it is the outcome of an art or science, and there is no escape from it, even were such a thing desirable. Nor does it stop here. Nearly every kind of sport has at least an idiom, if not a language of its own; some of these sports are recognised chiefly by the Shibboleth password, and others have so fair an admixture of understandable English that but little effort is necessary to arrive at a speedy comprehension of their respective meanings. To this latter class the Glossary belongs. The primary excuse for its introduction is, that no dictionary at present exists which supplies cricket with necessary words and phrases coined to represent the game in its manifold aspects antecedent to, and attendant upon the play Though not so complete as might be desired, there is probably enough—in the present condition of cricket—to meet the requirements of the general reader.

A.

ABSENT —Not present A player may not be on the ground at one period of the match, although he may be at another If he fails to appear when called on to bat, he is marked *absent* on the score sheet

ABSENTEE —One who does not turn up when wanted

ADROIT —Dexterous, skilful, active

> He is a very *adroit* player —*Colloq*

ALERT.—On the look-out

> The wary Dunkins was on the *alert* —*Charles Dickens.*
> There is a necessity for the striker to be continually on the *alert* —*Lambert*

ALL OVER THE WICKET —The whole construction of the wicket disarranged This phrase relates specially to bowling

ALL THERE.—A term often applied to an effective bowler, thus

> He was *all there* · *Sporting Magazine*

AMATEUR —A non-professional player, whether patrician or plebeian The word is also applied to the lovers of cricket

> The *amateurs* of the manly game had a great treat at Lord s on the 21st of August, 1845 the match lasted four days —*Sporting Magazine*

APPEARANCE —Object of sight, a term applied to the presence of a player, thus "He put in an *appearance*," *i e*, at the wicket or in the field.

APTITUDE —Fitness.

> He displayed an *aptitude* for the post assigned him —*Sporting Magazine*

ARTIST —Although but faintly applicable to cricket, the word is sometimes applied to a player of eminence

> No bowler can be so good that he cannot profit by the lessons of that unrivalled *artist* —*Sporting Magazine*
> Hunt and Chatterton are finished *artistes* —*Denison*

ASKEW —A term often applied to a wicket when not strictly correct as regards its geometrical construction

ASPECT.—Look of the game during its varied changes

ASPIRANT —A candidate Usually applied to young players anxious for promotion

ATTITUDE —Posture, especially of the batsman and bowler at the call of play It nevertheless refers to the fielders as well, at the same period

> The posture or position of a person or the manner in which the parts of the body are disposed —*Webster*
> It is best to observe one particular distance of running and *attitude* before delivering the ball —*Lambert's Cricketer's Guide*, 1816

Gentle Mr Clark, a portrait of the modern Tantalus in *attitude.*—*Sporting Magazine*

The best *attitude* for a cricketer in taking his stand at the wicket is exactly that adopted by the fencer —*Felix*

Which of the athletæ can vie with the *attitude* preparatory to this all powerful effort —*Idem*

His *attitude* has important claims to originality —*The Model Cricketer*

No game places the body in more graceful *attitudes* than cricket —*Thomas Miller*

> If in law he is skilful, I know not that's flat—
> He's skilful at cricket, and most with the bat,
> Yet so much to his *attitude* seems to attend,
> You might fancy 'twas all you might have to commend
>
> *Pierce Egan's Book of Sports*

Each fixed himself into the proper *attitude* by placing one hand on each knee —*Charles Dickens*

Average —A mean proportion The result of a man's batting or bowling in any given number of matches, divided by the number of innings played

B

Back Play —In this performance the batsman gets about two feet behind the popping crease if the wicket is not endangered It thus gives him a little more time to judge how the ball is coming and to act with a greater degree of certainty

Back-up — Figuratively speaking, means to support or assist, thus, when a batsman watches the chances of a run, after the ball is delivered from his wicket, and goes towards the opposite one, it is called *backing-up* The term is also appropriated to the fielders, who so dispose themselves as to prevent runs being obtained by overthrows

Bails —Two pieces of wood, four inches in length, placed transversely in a groove, on the top of the stumps, so delicately, that as a rule one falls on the wicket being struck either by the ball or bat

The top or cross piece of the wicket in a game of cricket —*Webster*

Bail Ball —A ball so pitched that it will just take the top of the stumps

Balista —A military engine for projectiles

The *Balista* was of different kinds, and sometimes discharged stones or bullets —*Fosbroke.*

The word is now applied to a machine for bowling

Ball —

Anything of a round form —*Barclay*
A round thing to play with —*Walker*
Any round thing —*Bailey*
A round thing either to play with the hand, foot, or racket —*Johnson*
A cricket *ball* is perfectly spherical —*Donald Walker's Games and Sports*

A cricket *ball* is certainly not quite so much *a round thing* as an oblate spheroid

Ball, Dead —Said so to be when finally settled in the bowler's or wicket-keeper's hand (*See* Law XXIX)

Barred.—An abbreviation of debarred, *i.e.*, a barred man is not allowed to play in a specified match.

Bat.—No dictionary makes use of the word Bat in the sense now understood till the year 1702 and subsequently, when it is defined "a club; a stick curved towards the bottom, used to strike a ball with at the play called cricket." Any large club, particularly one curved and flat on one side towards the bottom, used in the game of cricket.

> A heavy stick or club, a piece of wood with one end thicker or broader than the other, used in playing ball.—*Webster.*
>
> The sceptre of delight.—*Felix.*

For further illustration of the word, see pp. 416, 417.

Bat, Cane Handle.—This and the whalebone handle possess a spring said to defy all chance of breaking.

Bat Gauge.—An instrument for determining the exact width of the bat.

Bat, Repercussive.—

> One that does not jar and is unusually effective in driving.—*Bartlett.*

Batsman.—Any person using the bat at the time a match is being played.

Block.—To *block* a ball is merely to stop it without intending to make a run from it.

> He *blocked* the doubtful balls.—*Charles Dickens.*

Bounds.—Stumps placed in different parts of the field in single wicket matches. (*See* Law relating thereto, p. 398.)

Bowled.—When a batsman's wicket is struck by the ball he is pronounced *bowled out*. This word is, however, frequently accompanied with some qualifying phrase or adverb, such as *off his pad, clean*. The latter is synonymous with the *bowled down* of the last century.

Bowler.—The person who attacks the wicket with a ball.

Bowling Crease.—A white mark drawn in a line with the stumps.

Break Back.—A ball that suddenly turns from a direct course after it has pitched, either on or off, according to the character of the bowling, *i.e.*, right or left-handed.

Bump Ball.—A ball caught after it has bounded from the ground.

Bumptious.—Haughty and unbecoming in demeanour.

> He is a very *bumptious* fellow.—*Colloq.*

Butter Fingers.—A term of derision applied to a fielder who either misses a fair catch or fails to hold the ball when it comes to him.

> Taunting us with the agreeable appellations of milk-sop and *butter-fingers*.—*Lord W. Lennox*, 1841.
>
> I wonder the spectators did not hiss some of the *butter-fingers* off the ground.—*Australasian.*
>
> "Ah! ah! stupid—now then, *butter fingers*."—*Charles Dickens.*

Byes.—Runs obtained after the ball passes the wicket, and attributed chiefly to some defect in long-stopping.

C

CAN YOU?—A question frequently put by one batsman to his companion as to his ability to effect another run

CAPTAIN.—The manager of a match whilst in course of play

CATAPULT.—An instrument used for bowling purposes (see p 344)

CATCH.—To catch a ball is to hold it after it has been struck into the air and before it touches the ground

CAUGHT.—The preterit of catch, which is abbreviated on the score-sheet by the letter "c"

CHAFF.—

Light, idle talk by way of making fun or turning into ridicule —*Colloq*

At the end of Strand they made a stand,
Swearing that they were at a loss,
And *chaffing* say that's not the way
They must go to Charing Cross —*Old Song* (*Webster*)

CHALLENGE.—A summons to contest

In 1746 Kent challenged All England —*Love.*

CHAMPION.—A chief.

The last two *champions* even now are in,
And but three notches yet remain to win —*Love*, 1746

CHANCE.—Opportunity; accident

He seldom aims at the wicket, he bowls for *chances* —*The Model Cricketer*
He gave several *chances* —*Colloq*

CHANGE BOWLER.—When a bowler in chief gets punished, or is not "effective," he is relieved by one of the fielders The *change*, though, perhaps, inferior in the art of bowling, often works wonders

CHELTONIAN.—A pupil of Cheltenham College.

CHOICE OF INNINGS.—By this is understood the option of going in first or otherwise The choice is effected by "the cast of a piece of money," or, in more familiar language, the "toss."

CLAMOUR.—Noise

While from thy stroke the ball returning hies,
Uninterrupted *clamour* rend the skies —*Love*, 1746
A herd of boys with *clamour* bowled,
And stumpt the wicket —*Tennyson*

CLEAN BOWLED.—A batsman is said to be clean bowled when a ball goes directly into his wicket. Sometimes now, as of old, the phrase *bowled down*, or *slick*, is adopted

COACH.—The party who undertakes important preliminary arrangements of a match is frequently so denominated, but the word may be applied with greater force and significance to professionals at public schools and inexperienced clubs

Cock-a-hoop.—A phrase implying triumphant elation on some real or fancied success

> The match put the home made ones quite *cock-a-hoop*, Kent winning by an innings and three runs to spare —*Sporting Magazine*

> Miller was a beautiful player and always to be depended upon, there was no flash—no *cock-a-whoop* about him—but firm he was and steady as the pyramids —*Nyren*

> And having routed the whole troop,
> With victory was *cock-a hoop*
> *   *   *   *
> Found in few minutes to his cost
> He did but count without his host —*Hudibras, Canto* 3

Cock-sure.—Confident, certain

> Don't be too *cock-sure*, a match is never lost till won, nor won till lost —*Cricket Adage*.

Cogging —

> Cheating at dice play —*Bayley*

> Obtruding by falsehood —*Walker*

> As to dicing, I think it becometh best deboshed soldiers to play at on the heads of their drums, being only ruled by hazard, and subject to knavish *cogging* — *King James I Address to his Eldest Son*

> Your cricketer, no *cogging* practice knows,
> No trick to favour friends, or cripple foes.—*Tom Taylor*

Collared.—The preterit of *to collar*, a verb used to denote bowling brought into subjection The word is not to be found in any dictionary applied in this way To *mill*, was formerly the synonyme used, and, although it may have a pugilistic ring about it, few will deny that it is quite as suggestive and more euphonious

> Mr ——— knows how to *mill* the bowling —*Denison*

Colt —This word may be traced as far back as 1789 The *colts* of that time consisted of young noblemen, gentlemen, and plebeians Fifty years ago it was understood to mean young players aspiring to professional fame Nowadays it is difficult, from the specimens often produced, to form a correct idea of the term

Complement —The full number, complete list; proper quantity

Complexion.—*See* "Aspect"

Contest —Strife for mastery.

Cover Point —The fielder stationed on the offside of the batsmen usually between point and slip, but varying his position according to circumstances

Crafty —Artful, deceiving

> He is a *crafty* card —*Colloq*

> And would the games that Homer sung, the men of Granta please,
> Like cricket match, from morn to eve, on Parker's level piece ?
> Or who, like stern Achilles, then would sulk in canvas wall,
> But boldly guard his wicket from the swift and *crafty* ball
> *Cambridge Lyrics*, by R R F, 1857

> With a thorough knowledge of the game he had a *crafty* manner He was one of the most foxheaded fellows I ever saw —*Nyren*

CRICKET —

A kind of play with a ball —*J R*, 1702
A game with bats and balls —*Philips*, 1716
A sort of play —*Kersey* 1722
A play —*Harris*, 1724
A sort of game played with bats and a ball —*Bayley*, 1731
The name of an exercise with bats and ball —*Dyche*, 1735
A play (" Ludus baculi et pilæ ") —*Dr Littleton*
A sport at which contenders drive a ball with sticks or bats in opposition to each other —*Dr Johnson*
A sport at which the contenders drive a ball with sticks —*Walker*, 1790
A game which is played with a bat and a ball —*Barclay*, 1815
A game much played in England and America with a bat, ball, and wicket, the players being arranged in two contesting parties —*Webster*, 1850

CRICKET-BAG —An elongated, but somewhat shallow receptacle, constructed to carry a player's bat, shoes, and other articles necessary for a match, &c

CRICKETED —Played at cricket

They boated and they *cricketed* —*Tennyson*

CRICKETER —One who plays at cricket

We have not any *cricketer*
Of such account as he —*Duncomb* 1773

CRICKETICAL —An adjective sometimes applied to lovers of cricket

The poem may give pleasure to the critical as well as the *cricketical* reader —*Universal Magazine*, 1776

CRICKETING —

Playing at *cricket* —*Colloq*

Or go to Cambridge like another *gentle*,
Where folly's well deserving of the *rod*,
To see the boys that patronise cigars
Cricketing those that don't
If ye are green ye'll go of course, readers
But if ye are grey ye wont
Because I went myself and do pronounce
A fact sufficiently surprising—
That though the clouds were all day rising,
I could not see a single player once —*Byron*

On the first day of the Bantry Sessions the judges, counsellors, lawyers, jurors, clients, and process servers for want of business went *cricketing* —*Skibbereen Eagle*, 1868

CROSS OVER —To cross over is to change wickets, which a bowler is permitted to do twice in an innings (See Law IX)

CRUMP —This appears to have originated with some Sussex players in the last generation, and has maintained its hold to the present time It has no reference to the crooked back, but was, and still is, intended to signify a mastery of the bat over the ball

He soon *crumpt* the bowling —*Colloq*

Curly.—This adjective is applied to a ball which assumes a tortuous rather than a direct movement, caused chiefly by the inequalities of the ground, or design of the bowler In other words, a ball which, after pitching, works towards the inside of the line of projection.

Cut —To make this hit to perfection, the ball must be judged to bound well to the off, rather short, so that in its bound it would pass clean under the elbow

> You must throw yourself back with a sort of back-lounge close to the wicket, and whilst in this act, raise the bat well over the shoulders, and suffer the ball well to pass ere you let fly at it Welcome, thrice welcome, thou great majestic hit!—*Felix*

Cut Over —A blow received from the ball on an extremely sensitive and vital organ

> There is no fun in being *cut over* —*Echoes from Old Cricket Fields*

D

Daisy Cutter.—It is applied in cricket circles to a ball either propelled by the hand or bat sharply along, and close to the ground

> A sporting term for horses that go so near to the ground that they frequently touch it with the tip of the toe —*Topian*

Dead Beat —When a side is overpowered by superior force, or "used up" from exertion, it is said the players are "dead beat" "Beat into a cocked hat" is a phrase used to denote the same thing

Deep Field —A remote station in front of the striker, either "on" or "off"

Defence —A striker is said to possess the faculty of a good defence if he can guard his wicket well, although he obtains but few runs Sometimes called a "stiff wicket"

Delivery —The act of discharging the ball

Demoralised —This word has crept into use with cricketers of late, and is chiefly used in the past tense, especially when a side is thrown into disorder by weakness or a run of ill luck, &c

> To the *demoralisation* of the batting the defeat of the Canadians is due —*Wickets in the West*

Disposition of the Field —Arrangement of the fielders.

Ditto —The same Inserted in scores in lieu of repeating names

Do or Die —An expression denoting the resolve of a batsman to get runs or get out

> As well arrest the hurricane, as try
> To make him pause who burns to *do or die.*

Doff —To take off

> He *doffed* the gloves and took a turn at bowling —*Sporting Magazine*

Don —To put on.

Double Wicket.—Two wickets with a batsman at each, as opposed to single wicket.—(See Law VI., &c)

DRAW.—A beautiful style of batting, whereby the ball is turned between the wicket and the legs of the batsman.

DRAWN MATCH.—A match is said to be drawn when from untoward circumstances or want of time, it cannot be played out.

DRIVE.—A hard forward hit; it is designated on, off, or straight according to the course taken by the ball.

DUCK'S EGG.—This term relates to the cipher, so frequently appended to an unfortunate batsman's name; it is synonymous with the hateful "round O," and not very distantly connected with the "pair of specs" in cricket phraseology.

> And when eleven are matched against eleven,
> And wrestle hard the mastery to gain,
> Who tops the score is in the seventh heaven—
> Who lays an *egg*, in the abyss of pain.—*M. K. Brodie*, 1865.

DUFFER.—A player of very inferior, if any, merit.

> The play might indeed be greatly improved; the —— party have shown themselves little better than *duffers* in the field.—*B. L.*

E.

ELÈVE.—Pupil.

> Mr. Duff, an *élève* of the Harrow School, launched out with a degree of boldness that astonished the natives.—*Sporting Magazine.*

ELEVEN.—The mystic number requisite to play the orthodox game of cricket.

> Oh, Muse! awanting from the sacred nine,
> Goddess of cricket, lend thy aid divine;
> Leave now thy home the Grecian fabled heaven,
> Help while I sing thy game and *our Eleven*.—*M. K. Brodie*, 1865.

EMERGENCY.—Any one who is called upon to fill the place intended for another.

> Summoned to Canterbury as an *emergency*.—*Facts and Feats.*

ENTRANCE.—The important moment when a batsman emerges from his pavilion, or tent, and proceeds to the wicket.

ETONIAN.—A pupil of Eton College.

EVEN.—Level, smooth, equal in surface; free from irregularities.

> This will *even* all inequalities.—*Evelyn.*

EXIT.—The period of departure from the wicket.

EXPERT.—This adjective, when converted into a noun, applies to a player endowed with special all-round gifts of which the number is not legion. The word is also used to denote the merits of a fielder.

EXTRAS.—Runs not obtained from the bat, and placed at the foot of the score sheet. In all matches of importance, the items of which extra runs are composed are specified, seeing that they illustrate to a considerable extent the character of the fielders.

F.

FALSE OVER.—An over in which either more or less balls are delivered than the number stipulated for.

FETCH.—To *fetch* a run was formerly the verb used as synonymous with to get, make, mark, or obtain a run; for instance:

> Aylward *fetched* the extraordinary number of 167 runs from his own bat.—*Nyren*, 1775.

FIELD.—In the parable it is said "the field is the world;" in cricket the field is circumscribed to the players standing therein, during a match.

FIERY.—One of the ungenerous appellations a ground receives when it is hard, and probably not quite so verdant as a lawn or smooth as a billiard table.

FIGMENT.—A feigned idea.

> He is always proposing something that can't come off. He is full of *figments*.—*Colloq.*

FIST.—This word has crept into use as a substitute for hand. Sometimes a player is called "no bat," or "a good bat," as the case may be. *Fist* is therefore a synonym.

> As a batsman he is no *fist*.—*Colloq.*

FIXTURE.—The date on which a match is announced to take place.

FLOORED.—Prostrated. This word, once very handy in milling circles, is now transferred to a different kind of materialism, thus—

> When *floored* like the stumps may a friend break the fall,
> Be our love for each other "all round" like the ball.

FLUKE.—A bit of sheer luck.

FOLLOW ON.—An abbreviated expression for follow your innings, or go; for instance:

> They *followed* their go.—*Sporting Magazine.*

FOOTHOLD.—A good foothold is that afforded by the ground when in thorough condition. Wet weather very often counteracts it, so that for a time even spiked shoes avail but little.

FORM.—This word, derived from the Latin *forma*, is very suggestive of classical beauty; in cricket, however, it applies more to the style of the individual, in whatever department he may be stationed during a contest. *In form* and *out of form* are everyday expressions at a cricket match, and they often signify a great deal.

FORWARD PLAY is an advance by the bat to meet the ball near the place of its pitch.

FULL OF THE BAT.—An expression often evoked from bystanders when the ball has been struck forward with great force; thus, he hit with the full of the bat, or got well hold.

FULL PITCH.—A ball tossed beyond the popping crease is thus designated.

G

Genius.—A man endowed with superior faculties.—*Addison.*

> Marsden proved himself quite a *genius*, and bowled down eleven wickets.—*Sporting Magazine.*

This word, though hardly applicable to cricket, is insisted upon by some, therefore has to be recorded.

Gets up.—Under certain conditions of the ground, and of the bowling, the ball, it is said, *gets up*—*i. e.*, it obtains a greater rebound than was expected.

Gloves.—Coverings worn upon the hands to protect them from sharp and dangerous visitations of the balls.

Go.—This verb is frequently converted into a noun, to express either the character of a bowler or his performance; thus, there is *no go* in him, or in it.

Go Back.—A sort of injunction emanating from one batsman to another, when either attempts a dangerous advance.

Ground.—The place selected for play. By reference to the Laws, it will be seen that the word *ground* has also a circumscribed limit.

Ground Man.—The person in charge of the ground, whose chief duty is to keep it in order.

Grubs.—Akin to sneak (which see).

Guard.—A batsman often applies to the umpire for guard, *i. e.*, to know which stump or stumps his bat is defending.

H.

Half Volley.—When a ball is so pitched that the batsman can reach forward and hit it hard just as it rises from the ground, it is termed the *half volley*.

Hanging Guard.—Sometimes called the back block. Here the bat is made to hang in a vertical position, and to follow the ball back to within half a foot distant of the wicket.

Harrovian.—A pupil of Harrow School.

Harrow Drive.—Some persons define this phrase to mean a fluke in the slips, after an ineffectual attempt to play forward.

Head Bowler.—A head bowler differs vastly from the mere machine. He endeavours to find out the weak points of the batsman, and then by variations of pitch, pace, and style, he usually succeeds in his object.

Her.—In the early days of cricket, the neuter gender was often converted into the feminine; thus, in speaking of the ball, it was a common thing to say "he hit *her* hard," "there *she* goes" was likewise shouted by the rustics with a similar amount of appropriateness.

Hit.—A ball is said to be *hit* when a batsman strikes successfully at it for the purpose of getting runs.

Hit Wicket.—If, perchance, a batsman in playing should strike his wicket and a bail fall therefrom in consequence, it is so termed

Hold Hard.—Stand still

Hollow Match.—When the luck runs persistently on one side, and a great disparity of results ensues, it is called a *hollow match*.

> *Hold hard*, hold hard! the Harding cries,
> Hold hard, hold hard! each voice replies,
> And Lushington holds hard, nor tries
> In vain to fetch a run.—*Eton Poem*

Hollow Victory.—A victory easily won

> The *victory* was won *hollow* by the former.—*Sporting Magazine*, 1797
>
> In a great measure the *hollow victory* was due to the exaggerated opinion formed of the Englishmen's bowling.—*Wickets in the West*, p 76

Home Party.—The party residing at, or about the place where a match between two parishes, townships, or clubs comes off

Home Pitch.—A ball pitched up to the stumps is so denominated

Hostilities.—This word, so surrounded with ideas of animosity, confusion, and unfriendliness, is much used nowadays in a totally opposite sense, thus

> They commenced friendly *hostilities*.—*Colloq*
>
> We have shown ourselves generous, and have carried on our *hostilities* with humanity.—*Atterbury*

Hot 'un.—A ball that comes with greater force to the hand than usual.

> Hadow put a finger out of place in trying to catch a *hot 'un* from W G.—*Wickets in the West*

How's That?—This interrogatory is one put to the umpire generally with considerable vehemence and emphasis by the fielders, on the supposed ground that the batsman has infringed upon, or come within the clutches of some law

I

Incommode.—The wicket-keeper shall not by any noise *incommode* the striker (See Law XXXV.) No man at the present day is so ignorant as to be unable to understand the meaning of this word after reading the definitions of the celebrated American philologist

> To *incommode* is to annoy, disturb, trouble, molest, inconvenience, disquiet, or vex.—*Webster*

Innings, Double.—In a completed match one of the two parties must go in twice, and this constitutes a double innings

Innings, Single.—Each party is entitled to two innings, but if from circumstances only one can be completed, it is called an innings each, or *single innings*

J.

JERK —A ball delivered with the forearm off the elbow, in which case the hand usually comes in contact with the body

K.

KICK —The ground is said to kick when the ball, after being pitched, rises almost perpendicularly

KILLED —This harrowing verb is used in cricket merely to imply the ascendency of the bat over the ball

> The bowling was *killed* —*Sporting Magazine*

L

LAST MAN —The player who goes to the wicket last on his side

LEATHER HUNTING —A term fancifully applied to the fielders in a match who are kept in constant exercise by chasing the ball

LEG BEFORE WICKET —A batsman is said to be leg before wicket when he stops a straight pitched ball by other means than his bat or hands Contracted on the score-sheet to "l b w."

LEG BYE —A bye off the leg, cases, however, are on record in which byes from other parts of the body have been transferred to the leg

LEG-GUARDS —Leather cases fitted to the legs for protection of the same against attacks of the ball

LEG STUMP —The stump nearest to the striker

LENGTH BALL —A pitch may be of any length, but a *length ball* carries with it the idea of a good ball

LEVELLING —Used when a wicket is prostrated by a fierce assault

> No Minerva can avert an *all-levelling* ball from the aim of his Bœotian adversary —*Canning*

LISSOMER —Probably derived from "lithe," flexible, pliant

> A Hampshire phrase, which deserves to be good English —*Miss Mitford*

> On every village green and skirting park,
> Towards which the city casts its stony arms,
> You may at eve the *lissome* youth remark,
> Whom cricket hath ensnared with her charms.—*Domus Domus*, 1865

LOB.—A slow underhand ball, with a high parabola

> The artful slow bowler, with his long-pitched *lob* They chance a *lob* after the sharp-shooters they have been facing —*Sporting Magazine*

Long Field Off.—The fielder stationed behind the bowler, and at a considerable distance from his left hand.

Long Field On.—The fielder corresponding to long-off, but stationed on the bowler's right hand.

Long Hop.—A short-pitched ball, grounding some distance in front of, and going with a long hop to the batsman.

The same preconceived dread of the straight *long hop*.—*Wickets in the West*, p. 155.

Long Leg.—The fielder usually placed deep behind the striker on the "on" side.

Long Slip.—A position behind the wicket and between slip and long stop, varying according to the pace of the bowling.

Long Stop.—The fielder stationed in a direct line behind the wicket-keeper.

Loose.—This adjective is frequently applied to batting, bowling, and fielding too; either in its individual or general character. Careless play is its true definition.

Lost Ball.—Many amusing efforts have been resorted to for determining the meaning of a lost ball; the pith is, one that cannot be seen, or if seen, not conveniently got at.

M.

Maiden Over.—An over from which no runs are obtained by a batsman.

Manipulate.—Although this word has no place in the pages of Johnson, Walker, and such like philologists, it has found a home in the columns of cricket literature, and, used as a verb, is intended to signify something done by the hand—having *manipulus*, from *manus*, the hand, for its root.

Man Short.—It often happens that a team enters the field without its complement; or, by some casualty, may be deprived the use of one or more of its members during the match, in which case they are said to play a man short, &c.

Marking Frame.—A wooden machine of the exact dimensions of the ground belonging to a batsman when a match is in course of play.

Marlburian.—A pupil of Marlborough College.

Match.—A contest to try strength or skill, or to determine superiority. An emulous struggle.

A solemn *match* was made—he lost the prize.—*Dryden*.

Medium Pace.—Neither very fast, nor very slow.

Middle Stump.—The centre stump of the three which constitute a wicket.

Mid Wicket.—A station between point and bowler when off, and between bowler and batsman when on. (See Diagram.)

This term has frequently been used to abbreviate *middle of the wicket*, and in lieu of mid stump; in neither case is the application deserving.

He bowled his middle wicket.—*Colloq*.

'Tis glorious at Lord's to view the middle wicket spin,
From a ball propelled like lightning by the giant arm of Mynn.
Sporting Magazine.

MIZZLE.—To retire, or leave.

> Down went the stumps, out went the man; in came a successor; up went his wicket and he was obliged to *mizzle*.—*Sporting Magazine*, vol. lxxviii., O. S., p. 218.

MOIETY.—Half. Thus:

> Hawkins got 50, a *moiety* of the total, 100.—*Sporting Magazine*.

MOUNTEBANK.—A man who has recourse to antics when at the wicket, and ridiculous capers when in the field, damaging alike to his own common sense and the interest of the match in which he is concerned.

MUFF.—A derisive monosyllable applied to a defective fielder.

> Some good fielding on the part of   and a few *muffs* by way of contrast.—*Wickets in the West*, p. 98.
>
> In short they were *muffs*.—*Bolland's Cricket Notes*.

MUFFED.—A word derived from neither French nor Dutch roots, but coined to express a clumsy way of handling the ball.

MULL.—This is also a coined word, with a similar idea to the foregoing; thus: "He made a precious *mull* of it."

N

NATTY.—A fanciful word to express neat and elegant play.

NERVOUS.—Strong, vigorous, well strung, &c. It also means just the reverse. Few cricketers go to the wicket on great occasions, and at a critical juncture of the play, without experiencing sensations very far from agreeable.

NE SUTOR ULTRA CREPIDAM.—This old and valuable proverb is frequently quoted in the cricket field, and applied to fussy persons who understand little, very little, of the matters they have taken in hand. Bustle is not business.

NETS.—A texture of thick string woven into large meshes, and used for stopping the ball at practice.

NIX.—German, "*Nichts*," Nothing.

> Dicker went out for nix, 0. Lillywhite got nix in either innings.—*Sporting Magazine*.

NO BALL.—A ball delivered with the bowler's foot beyond the prescribed limits. (*See* Law XII.).

NOM DE GUERRE.—An assumed name adopted for the convenience of the user thereof, but attended with perplexity to parties having to provide the public with correct information.

NOTCH.—"A nick or hollow cut in anything."—*Johnson*. This word, coeval with cricket, was used to signify the progress of the game. In fact, the *notched stick* was almost the only record kept for many generations.

> Loud from the ring resounds the piercing shout—
> Three *notches* only gained, five leaders out.
> *   *   *   *   *
> Awakened echo speaks the innings o'er,
> And forty *notches* deep indent the score.—*Love*, 1746.

Nearly thirty years later, speaking of the Duke of Dorset, the poet says

He firmly stands, with bat upright,
And strikes with his athletic might,
Sends forth the ball across the mead,
And scores six *notches* for the deed
Gentleman's Magazine

Notwithstanding the antiquity of the word, and its inappropriateness to modern times, even so recently as the year 1833 the *Sporting Magazine* says "Three of their wickets fell without a *notch* " (Sussex *v* England)

NOT OUT—A self-evident phrase; but it is significant when placed against the name of the man or men in possession of the wickets when the game is discontinued, given up, or won

NOT YET—An expression used by one batsman to another in order to avoid risks in running.

O.

O.—A sign of no value when standing alone

I'm a most unlucky cricketer, and though I know the game
Extremely well, whene'er I play, it always is the same
No matter what the bowling, whether medium, fast, or slow,
The same bad luck pursues me, and my score is always O —*Punch*

OBSTRUCTING THE BALL—A man may be given out, but seldom is on such an account A ball may be obstructed in a variety of ways, for example—when the striker by motion or gesture so interferes with the field that a catch is prevented, or more particularly when in running he purposely diverts a ball from its course to the wicket.

OFF HIS FEET—A man is said to be bowled off his feet when the ball comes in contact with them and then passes into the wicket

OFF HIS PADS—A similar remark is accorded when the ball passes from the pad or pads of the striker into the wicket

OFF HIT—Sometimes confused with the *cut*, though essentially different in character This is easily demonstrated by the position of the batsman

OFF-SIDE—That side usually to the left of the bowler and to the right of a right-handed striker

OFF-STUMP—The stump farthest from the striker

ON HIS DAY—This phrase is referred to one of Spenser's Knights, who *on his day* achieved unsurpassed feats Cricketers at times are a wonder to themselves

ON THE SPOT—A phrase applied to a bowler when having great command of the ball

OUT—Retirement from the wicket A man may be out in a dozen ways at cricket (*See* Laws)

OUT OF REACH—When a fielder is unable to compass or get fairly at a ball it is said to be out of reach

Outsider —One not belonging to the original team

Over —The number of balls agreed to be delivered by one bowler before the ball is transferred to another (*See* Law IX)

Over-Matched —If there be an undue preponderance on one side either of numbers or talent the weak side is said to be over-matched

Over-Pitched —Too much up—*i e*, the ball

Over the Wicket —A change in the position of the bowler, usually from the off to the on-side in right-hand bowling

Over-Throw —When the fielders so throw the ball that their companions are not able to secure it, either from negligence or inability, and a run results, it is called an over-throw

P

Pads —Leathern protectors fitted to the legs, in order to prevent injury from a severe visit of the ball

Phase —Although this word applies to objects studied by astronomers, it is sometimes used to denote the changes or aspects of cricket during a match

Pitch Full —Akin to the home pitch

Pitch Home —A ball so delivered that it would strike the stumps before touching the ground

Pitch Short —In this the ball has a greater parabola than the half volley and long hop, and less than the home pitch

Play —When all the parties are got into position for a match the word *play* is shouted by the umpire as a signal to begin It is also used by the public in somewhat more stentorian tones when there is any indication of trifling with time

Playing the Ball —To play the ball is a very common phrase, the real meaning of which is to guard the wicket rather than attempt runs, especially when beset with danger

Plucky —Spirited

> He is a *plucky* man who can play well with a good heart against the frowns of Fortune

Poking.—A style of play characterised by no hitting powers, simply on account of the shoulders and elbows being tied

Popping Crease —The white line in front of the wicket and four feet distant therefrom

Practice —An exercise of the game unrestricted by the laws attendant upon a match

Press Gang —A half witty expression adopted by simpletons towards members of the fourth estate engaged in taking notes of matches in order to their publication.

Professional —One who devotes the whole or chief portion of his time to cricket either by playing the game or in teaching others how to play The word has the stamp of nearly a century upon it Years ago the professional graduated from the paid man, or player, into his present full blown title.

Push—This word has lately been revived It is intended still to signify such a peculiar form of delivering the ball as the word itself suggests. It is also applied to batting

> He would bring the ball by a twist from under his armpit, and with this action *push* it as it were from him—*Nyren*

Q

Quartered—Knocked about

> The terrific style of carries us back to the days of no pads, &c, when the batsman cut away at everything, with the blood streaming through his silk stockings, and his fingers cruelly *quartered*

Quatrain—This word—derived from the Latin *quatuor*, and recently added to the phraseology of cricket—is used to describe a particular number of runs on the score-sheet, thus—he obtained three twos, five threes, and a *quatrain* of fours. After all, it has a pedantic look about it

R.

Reach—Power of taking in the hand—*Johnson*

Return Ball—When a ball is played back to the bowler it is often said to be *returned* to him.

Return Crease—This is situated at the extremity of the bowling crease, and at right angles therewith Sometimes it is wilfully or ignorantly made obtuse

Return Match—In a match proper, it is usual to play one out and the other home The second match, whether at home or otherwise, is called the *return*

Roller.—A machine turning on its own axis for levelling the ground

Rot—A word much used to signify very bad play

Rotary Motion—

> Hold the ball with your thumb and finger tips on the seam to assist the *rotary motion* and the twist—*Adventures of a Cricket Ball by an Old Boy* (undated)

Round Arm—This epithet is applied to a bowler who delivers the ball with his arm on a level with his shoulder, or above it

Run—Very few philologists make use of this monosyllable as a noun. Among cricketers it is recognised as a measured distance reached by a rapid action of the legs, thus, if a batsman can leave one popping crease and reach the opposite before the ball while in play does, it is called a *run*

Run it Out.—Here is a phrase remarkable for the urgency and vociferousness of its application It is chiefly indulged in by lookers-on, who fancy themselves better able to judge of the probabilities of a safe run than the parties directly concerned in it Many a match has been won by the judicious exercise of this exclamation—aye, and quite as many lost, for the want of knowing when to be silent and when to shout

RUN SAVED —To save a run, considerable thought and judgment must be exercised, but the ways of saving a run are too dependent on circumstances to be specified here

RUN SHORT —If a batsman in running fails to reach beyond the popping crease, it is called a run short, and counts nothing on the score sheet

S.

SAWDUST —Dust from wood Introduced in 1803 for the purpose of assisting the foothold

SCIENTIFIC —Many persons repudiate the idea of applying such an adjective to cricket Mr Felix, however, says

> Though cricket is a game for boys, it is a *science* for men

In opposition to this, a learned writer remarks

> Pity that the Governors at Oxford and Cambridge cannot be brought to take this view Many a man in an agony for his *testamur* would feel greatly relieved at heart if he might only put this *science* down in his list, and pass his examination at Cowley instead of in the schools Many a senior wrangler and Fellow of Trinity on the other hand, would, it is feared, be forced to admit that there are other things in the beautiful laws of motion than are even to be found in the last edition of Whewell's " Dynamics "

SCORE —A notch cut with an edged instrument "An account kept by notches cut in wood"—*Barclay* A particular account in writing of the progress of a cricket match, and the number of runs obtained by each player concerned in it.

SCORE CARD —A printed card, with the names of the players and the results of each person's innings

SCORER —One who keeps tally, as in cricket or other games —*Webster*

> I know when
> Instead of five you *scored* me ten —*Swift*

SCORE SHEET —A large sheet of paper, with ruled lines, on which the runs obtained and the overs delivered are marked as they occur

SCORING BOX —A small enclosure, so situated as to command a full view of the play

SCRATCH MATCH —A match usually got up in a hurry, and without much regard to classification of merit

> They partook of the nature of *scratch matches* —*Chronicles of F F*

SCREW —A bias put on the ball by the thumb and second or third finger of the bowling hand

SECRETARY —An officer appointed chiefly to manage the internal arrangements of a club When acting thus, without any emolument, he is styled hon sec

SET —The number of runs required to win Used as a verb, it refers especially to the condition of a batsman when at the wicket, as, he is *well set*

> The bowling became loose after the batsmen were well *set* —*Colloq*

SHARP.—A change of position among fielders, according to the change of bowling, thus, in very fast, the point is placed behind the wicket, and the slips set *sharp* (See Diagram) The word is also used to denote punctuality, commence at twelve *sharp*, *i e*, precisely

SHIVER.—This verb and its preterit are often used in cricket with respect to the force of various bowlers, thus—he'll soon *shiver* his timbers, and, again, his timbers were soon *shivered*, somewhat allied to the phrase bowled "all over the wicket"

Sometimes used as a substantive, thus—

The stumps to *shivers* sent —*Duncombe*

SHOOTER.—A most dangerous and deceptive ball, which does not rise after the pitch.

His *shooters* (Jackson's) are the most terrific, teasing, trying sort of artillery that ever were propelled by human power —*New York Spirit of the Times*

SHORT LEG.—The fielder stationed within a few yards of the wicket behind the batsman, nearly square for medium pace, and sharper for fast bowling

SHORT SLIP.—The station betwixt point and wicket-keeper, sometimes called first slip

SHY.—To shy is synonymous with to throw

SIDES.—The divisions of the players into distinct parties

The sides were well chosen —*Sporting Magazine*

With sides so well balanced a good match may be expected —*Colloq*

SIGHT OF THE BALL.—A batsman is said to have got a sight of the ball when he has been in for a considerable time, and not without success. "Big as a balloon" is a common phrase

SINGLE WICKET.—(*See* p 398)

SKEW WICKET.—(*See* Askew.)

SKYER.—A lofty hit

He *skied* one of Greig's, &c —*Wickets in the West* p 215

SLIPPERY.—Wanting in foothold

SLOGGER.—A hard and slashing hitter Derived from an old German verb *schlagen*, preterit, *schlog*—"I oop mit mein compercella und *schlog* him ober de Kop" (Hans Breitmann)

Mr T is a rattling batsman, but very apt to *slog* —*Review*

SLOGGING.—(*See* Slogger)

There was a little *slogging*, which soon terminated the innings —*Wickets in the West*, p 153

SLOWS.—A designation given to bowling of a tardy but deceptive and alluring character

SMOTHERING THE BALL.—To smother the ball, is in other words to kill it

Come down upon it as soon as pitched —*Denison.*

This method destroys the twist, break, and other dangerous peculiarities incident to the bowling.

SNEAK.—A ball of a grovelling tendency, and admired by few.

SNICK.—This word, derived from the Prov. Eng. *snick*, a notch, and allied to the German *schnitt* (a cut) is used in cricket to denote a hit to slip or leg that was not intended, or a chance one.

SPANKER.—A word chiefly applied to a clean, hard, and long hit.

> A dashing innings, including one *spank* for 6. A *spanking* hit for 6.—*Wickets in the West*, pp. 93 and 215.

SPIKE SHOES.—Shoes with projecting pieces of iron fixed in the soles to prevent the wearer slipping.

> The flannels and pads, with the ancient *spiked shoes*,
> Are the very best cure for a fit of the blues.—*Ode.*

SPIN.—To obtain a *spin* is one of the gifts peculiar to fast bowlers.

SPOONING.—Getting under the ball. In derision, it is called "spoon victuals," especially at Cambridge.

SPLICED.—This word relates chiefly to one of the various ways in which a wounded bat may be restored.

SPRUNG.—When a bat has received a partial fracture in the handle, it is said to be sprung.

SPREAD EAGLE.—A phrase of modern application to a wicket in a sprawling condition.

SPURT PLAYER.—The verb to "spurt" has till recently been confined to the gushing of some liquid substance, or the bursting of a bud. Of late years it has been applied to sudden physical efforts, thus:

> The long steady sweep of the so-called paddle tried him almost as much as the breathless strain of the *spurt*.—*Hughes.*
> He is a *spurt* player at cricket.—*Colloq.*

Sometimes it is spelt "spirt." (*See* Johnson, Walker, and Webster.)

SQUARE LEG.—This fielder stands nearly square with the batsman, but shifts according the exigencies of the play.

STAY THERE.—An expression analogous to hold hard, stop, wait, &c. Sometimes a hand or finger is held up to denote the same thing.

STAY.—Caution, restraint of passion, steadiness.

> With prudent *stay* he long deferred
> The rough contention.—*Philips.*

STEPPING OUT.—An advance beyond the popping crease to hit a ball is said to be stepping out.

STIFF BAT.—Usually applied to a batsman who stubbornly defends his wicket. Synonymous with stiff wicket.

STING.—A word often used to express the effect of a ball with a severe impetus upon a tender hand, *i.e.*—

> His bowling had a tremendous lot of *sting* in it.—*Review.*

STRAIGHT BAT —Upright

STUCK UP —A position in which the batsman is completely nonplussed by the character of certain balls, which may hit him or his wicket anywhere

STUMPT —To stump is to strike the wicket with the ball in the same hand

> A herd of boys with clamour bowled,
> And *stumpt* the wicket —*Tennyson*

This word stands recorded as far back as 1746.

STYLE —Manner or form

> Edgar's *style* is provocative of merriment, but he generally turns the laugh to his own side —*Wickets in the West*, p 96
>
> In cricket, *style* without precision is similar to fine language without meaning—worse than useless —*Colloq*

SUBSTITUTE —A deputy Often abbreviated into "sub"

SWARD —The turf, applied usually in cricketing to the whole area of the play

SWIFT —An adjective much used in early cricket to denote speed both in bowling and running

> And rising as he threw,
> *Swift* from his hand the fatal missive flew —*Love*, 1746
> And *swift* flew the cricket ball over the lawn —*Anon* 1773

> The ball is a very *swift* one, and rises fast —*Tom Brown*, once præprector and captain of the Rugby eleven
>
> His delivery was from the shoulder, and he bowls a *swift* destructive ball —*Wickets in the West*, p 150

SWIPE —To hit fiercely and anyhow

> Mr ——— is a fine free hitter, but he is prone to *swipe* —*Sporting Magazine*

SWIPER —This inelegant noun is applied to one who goes in for hitting regardless of consequences. When thus used it is intended to convey the idea of mischief, thus—

> Before a dozen balls are delivered a *swiper*—the *pila velox*, as Horace calls it—from an Herculean tug mutton—*Anglicè* King's Scholar—"cuts us down," puts us *hors de combat*, and we are reluctantly carried off the ground —*Lord W Lennox* (1840)
>
> "Oh, do let the *swiper* go in," chorus the boys —*Tom Brown's School Days*
>
> We are not preaching the doctrine of a *swiper* —*Wickets in the West*
>
> Rosa paralysed them, the batsman at the wicket was no longer the stout lad we had seen *swiping* at practice — *Wickets in the West*, p 54

T.

TAIL.—The lower part By a figure of speech in cricket, *tail* is used to denote an inefficient portion of a team when engaged in any particular match

TEAM —The party composing either side is often metaphorically converted into a *team*.

TEASER.—A tormentor

> As we tell how they tell,
> Where Falkner's swift 'uns go,
> Or Goodrich, with his artful twist,
> Sends in the *teasers* slow —*Chronicles of the F F*

TELEGRAPH.—A machine constructed for publicly notifying the progress of a match. The word is also frequently used as an interjection when the scorers or their assistants are either nodding or sluggish in their attention to duty.

THERE OR THEREABOUTS.—An expression tending to give a correct idea on the part of the bowler where to pitch the ball.

> We Hampshire lads can bowl a *bit* or *thereabouts*.—*Morton's Speed the Plough.*

THIRD MAN UP.—Here is a fielder, deemed by some a sort of jack at a pinch, usually placed between point and slip, but deeper.

THROW.—To throw, says Johnson, is to fling; to cast; to send to a distant place by any projectile force.

> He heaved a stone, and, rising to the *throw*,
> He sent it in a whirlwind at the foe.—*Addison.*

THROWER.—One that throws.—*Shakespeare.*

THROWN OUT.—A ball thrown by a fielder into the wicket without being touched by any one on its passage.

> I think (says a writer in the *Sporting Magazine* of 1823), that when a ball is well hit away, and pursued by a good fieldsman and thrown back to the wicket from a long distance with precision, to be one of the finest features of the game, and never fails to command the approbation of the surrounding multitude.
>
> Wood, *thrown out* by Brett, August, 1777. (See Nyren.)

TICE.—Supposed to have been derived from the verb *entice*. A ball pitched up to the block hole.

TIE.—When the totals are identical the match is declared to be a tie. The first on record was between Kent and the Hambledon club in 1783. The scoring was done on the notch system. A longer and deeper indentation at every decade assisted the notchers in their casting up.

TIME.—The period fixed upon for discontinuing the day's play.

TIMING THE BALL.—On this subject a very great deal might be said; *timing the ball* is a gift intuitive rather than acquired. The hand and eye of the batsman, combined with some practical knowledge of the angles of incidence and reflection, act so completely in unison that the ball is deprived of a large share of break or twist before any dangerous quality in the bowling has time to develop itself; or, again, when the batsman strikes at the precise moment, *i.e.*, neither too soon nor too late, so that an effective hit ensues unattended by ordinary risks. Mr. Felix says:

> The forward play has much to do with well *timing* the ball, and the body, relying upon the accurate judgment of the eye, will be thrown forward with the required rapidity, in order to meet the ball in time. The half volley off cut and the half volley leg hit are both the result of well *timing the ball*, and in this fact lies the perfection of that brilliant batting which has distinguished many of the old with the modern bats; and upon a just appreciation of this fact is founded the apparent contradiction that some of the weaker men hit harder than their more muscular competitors.

TOO SOON.—Over anxious, as when a batsman plays at the pitch and not at the ball.

Too Late.—Just the reverse; without regard to pitch.

Toss.—The casting of a piece of money into the air and calling out "heads" or "tails," "man" or "woman," before it reaches the ground.

Touched the Ball.—No batsman is permitted to touch the ball with his hands during his stay at the wicket.

Trial Ball.—A ball delivered by a bowler merely as an experiment.

Tric-trac.—This word cannot be found in any English dictionary. There is a picture by D. Teniers bearing the title, but it affords not the slightest glimpse to the meaning of the word in its application to cricket.

> The well known familiar and fatal sound, difficult to describe, and yet familiar to every player.—*Sporting Magazine.*

In more familiar phraseology, it means "bowled slick."

Trimmer.—Used in cricket to denote fast and smart bowling.

> Brothers Phillips and Eddowes
> Next enlivened the meadows,
> But an inclement *trimmer* sent Eddowes away.—*Chronicles of the F. F.*

> At length a *trimmer* Dick sent down,
> Bob viewed it with a scoff,
> And turn'd to play it off the bail,
> But found his leg bail off.—*M. K. Brodie*, 1865.

Trip.—In cricket this word has no allusion to the light fantastic, but to move nimbly along, and also its opposite, to stumble or fall.

> No innate consciousness of knowledge can console him for an unforeseen *trip.*—*Canning.*

Twist.—Complication.

> His bowling has got a good deal of *twist* upon it.—*Colloq.*

> The wisest will fall to a dangerous ball,
> That *twists* like a living thing.—*Old Song.*

> For a long time they could not tell what to make of that cursed *twist* of his.—*Nyren.*

Twister.—

> Your cricketing boy, full of teasers and *twisters,*
> Of backing well up and saving a run;
> May talk till his lingual appurtenance blisters,
> Of the scores he has made, and the matches he's won.—*Weeds from the Isis.*

> The batsman now his weapon raised
> To meet a puzzling *twister,*
> And though he did not hit amiss
> By too hard-hitting missed her.—*Anon.*

Two-Leg.—This is usually an umpire's expression in answer to a batsman desirous of guarding his leg and middle stump.

U.

Umpire.—This familiar word in cricket is derived from the French *umpère* (father, an arbitrator, one chosen to decide a dispute). It occurs but once in the Bible, and there in the margin against the 33rd verse of the 9th chapter of the

Book of Job, and is chosen by the annotator in place of *daysman*, which also means a person chosen to decide a dispute Kersey says—

> A third person chosen to put a final end to a controversy left to the determination of two arbitrators in case they should not come to an agreement about the matter

According to Shakespeare, an umpire is a common friend to decide disputes

In matters of cricket an umpire is invested with much larger powers; he has to decide, off-hand, very important and ticklish questions, and against his verdict there is no appeal

> Some mark the runs upon the shaven spray,
> And others *umpires* stand whom all obey
>
> *Bavin of Bays* (1764)

> From a state of ignominious vassalage our country rose to the place of *umpire* among European nations —*Macaulay's History*, vol i, p 1

UPPISH —A word strained from its original meaning, and applied to a species of batting which tends too much to elevate the ball

UPRIGHT PLAY —This phrase is frequently adopted to characterise the play of a batsman who always looks a ball full in the face and keeps the handle of his bat in a direct line with the bowler

URGE.—To urge means to incite, to press forward, to push. In the latter sense it is used by Pope in the well known distich —

> The judge to dance his brother serjeants call,
> The senators at cricket *urge* the ball
>
> * * * * * *
>
> The ball the stout cricketer *urges*
> Cleaves a pathway of peace o'er the plain,
> The weapon he wields leaves no scourges,
> No record of carnage or pain —*Bolland*

V.

VELOCIOUS —An adverb seldom used, although not devoid of meaning

> Some their vigour lend
> To bowl *velocious*, and the wicket rend —*Perfect* (1768)

VELOCITY.—Speed, quick motion

> The ball travelled with extraordinary *velocity* —*Sporting Magazine*

VICISSITUDE —Revolution, change —*Atterbury*

> The *vicissitudes* and odd turns of success which attend all games are very conspicuous and often unaccountable in cricket —*Saturday Review*

VIS-A-VIS —Face to face Applied usually to batsmen at the wicket

W

WELL BOWLED.—
,, HIT—
,, FIELDED—
,, PLAYED—
} Expressions of approval generally speaking very audible Sometimes the adverb is omitted, thus, bowled, &c

WICKET—A small gatelike framework, composed of three stumps set vertically in the ground, with two bails lying horizontally on the top, at which the ball is bowled or thrown

WICKET KEEPER—The fielder stationed immediately behind the wicket

WRIST PLAY—If the epithet elegant may be applied to such a thing as batting, *wrist play* has a strong claim to it In fact, it is an accomplishment possessed by few

WILLOW WEAPON—One of the many names given to the bat

The ball is struck by a bat formed of *willow*—*Walker's Games and Sports*

Y.

YORKER—A ball between a tice and a full pitch

Z.

ZANY—A merry-andrew, a buffoon—*Webster*

Preacher at once and *zany* of thy age—*Pope*

In cricket it is generally applied to to a man who pretends to admire and understand, but is absolutely ignorant of the game

ZINGARI, I—The plural (with the definite article) of an Italian word signifying a gipsy, wanderer, &c. In English the definition is a race of ubiquitous cricketers, who commence play before the May fly is up and continue until the first pheasant is down.

POSTSCRIPT.

SHAKESPEARE AND CRICKET;

AN ENFORCED DISSERTATION.

By Jove himself!
It makes the consuls base; and my soul aches
To know, when two authorities are up,
Neither supreme, how soon confusion
May enter 'twixt the gap of both, and take
The one by the other.—*Coriolanus*, Act iii., Scene 1.

NONE of the early poets, who drew their images so largely from the pastimes and occupations of men, make the slightest allusion to this now national game. Even Shakespeare, whose plays abound with similes drawn from the noblest as well as the meanest diversions, never hints it.—Cricketer's Manual, Fifth Edition, 1851.

* * * * * * *

Notwithstanding the persistence of some theorists respecting the development of cricket in the time of Shakespeare, no one has yet been able to produce any evidence of his knowledge thereof, although some passages in his plays have been cruelly twisted about in order to illustrate false ideas.—Theory and Practice of Cricket, p. 9 (1868).

* * * * * * *

"Lord Campbell has vindicated Shakespeare's reputation for legal acquirements, and we commend the foregoing 'evidence' from Shakespeare's plays to Mr. Box, with the hope that he will in the next edition of his book retract his imputation on the universality of Shakespeare's genius."—Official Hand Book, Philadelphia, 1872.

ANY MAN POSSESSING A TITHE OF THE LOGICAL ABILITY *accredited to* Lord Campbell might have done the same thing as the learned Chancellor, simply because the evidence of facts touching his subject is clear to transparency; but it would require ten Lords, no matter how learned, to sustain a case without a tittle of evidence to support it. Lord Campbell's acumen would have been severely tested in proving one of the 115 instances cited by the "Official Hand Book." Many of them are so utterly beside the mark, that it would be an affront to the understanding of Englishmen, who have Shakespeare at their finger-ends and at the tip of their tongues, and by whom the universality of Shakespeare's genius has always been as much applauded as its grandeur and its opulence. Why? Because it is a universality which does not include merely an incomparable variety of subjects and ideas, but also the most wonderful diversity of illustrations. There have been, however, loud and angry debates about the extent of Shakespeare's learning; be this what it may, he excites universal astonishment by the wealth and width of his information. Nor can this be much wondered at. His sublime phantasies sought not any dainties as nutriment, but solid facts of every kind in the past as well as the present.

Though he was a diligent and discursive reader, and made whatsoever he pursued the food of his creative mind, yet it was chiefly the actualities of the world around him that afforded stimulation and suggestion. Books interested him only so far as they gave a richer colour and deeper significance to life in its manifold aspects and activities. From his youth up Shakespeare is said to have been of a robust and energetic temperament, and attracted by all human occupations and pastimes, as well as by all the forces and forms of Nature.

Nothing thoroughly human or spontaneously natural was too small for his sympathetic glance. It should be borne in mind, however, that this sublimest painter of the visible was the subtlest interpreter of the invisible; the most lofty of idealists, no less than the most masculine, most massive of realists. The Middle Ages were at an end when Shakespeare wrote. On the ruins of mediævalism industrious Europe was springing into existence. An immense impulse had been given to commerce and colonisation by the discovery of America a hundred years before. Shakespeare was far too deep and wise a philosopher not to bow to the inevitable; but, as a fact, he turned away from the new civilisation and polemic developments to surround himself with the enchantments of mediæval romance; and it is very remarkable that this acutest of observers, the sharpest of delineators, did not take the subject of his plays from contemporary works—wrote no dramas to picture contemporary manners. He dwelt in idyllic realms, and all his dramas, whether they rise to the height of the most terrible tragedy or descend to the lowest comedy, are the transcripts of his idyllic visions. This, with their instinctive insight into humour and universal Nature, gives them their place. No one incapable of sojourning as Shakespeare sojourned in idyllic regions can ever expect to read his works to much advantage,

From the predominantly idyllic character it is proper to remark that the dramas of "the immortal bard" are silent with regard to many of the incidents and customs of the period. Every ancient and foreign country was to Shakespeare a transfigured England, so that his Greeks, his Romans, his Italians, are simply Englishmen. But before making these countries English, he renders England itself the Eden of his imagination. The England of his own day interested him no farther than that it recalled the England of days long gone by; and perhaps in his inmost soul he thought Robin Hood, the bold, merry, and generous outlaw, the only amiable person either in public or private history. Unlike Cervantes, the most gifted of his contemporaries, who mocked the knight-errant and the age of chivalry, Shakespeare revered and glorified an outlaw for the deeds of his time, though not achieved by arms.

His allusions are therefore generally to things that had long since died out, or which were shortly to disappear. In the country where Shakespeare had spent his youth—trusting to tradition,—he was a true son of Nimrod, and changed the whole current of his fortunes by a poaching adventure Judging from his works, the hunting instincts ran strong in him to the last His plays swarm with illustrations drawn from the chase, especially from hawking For sports and games he had a hearty regard This is manifest in the poetical adornments he often lavished around them, but nothing can be more conclusively shown than that he nowhere makes either a direct or indirect allusion to CRICKET

From the demise of Shakespeare to the present time there have not been wanting severe reviewers of his works. The real admirers of the author care, however, little about them, and yet, to understand much of what is written, the services of the antiquary and verbal critic are not to be disregarded as worthless A short glossary, a few explanations of old usages, and a few suggestions for the restoration of a corrupted text might be accepted and consulted But these helps become hindrances when they swell to ten times the space of the text, and the author smothered by the paltry polemics of annotators and the grovelling transcribers of black letter Oft times the text is found to bear so slender a proportion to the commentary, that he who wishes to read nothing but Shakespeare must keep his forefinger constantly employed in turning over the leaves, and after all is but poorly compensated for the time employed The reason of this requires but little seeking out If examined closely, a large portion of these commentaries consists in tedious dissertations on old customs keen and solemn controversies on the comparative merit of rival readings or projects of punctuation One era after another has produced a commentator and critic, the greatest men of each successive period have considered themselves well employed, and have brought forward the fullest stores of their learning and the highest powers of their genius to elucidate both clear and mysterious passages Now, this being the case, it seems very strange that out of the 115 quotations, which the Philadelphian oracle cites as bearing upon the question of cricket, not a glimmer of light penetrated even such minds as Pope, Johnson, Coleridge, Hazlitt, Schlegel, and a host of others

This by itself would not prove that the "manly and noble game," as it is now properly called, was utterly unknown in the districts in which Shakespeare moved, but the fact serves, along with other negative evidence to demonstrate cricket had not gained any notable place among the pastimes of the English people

Pigeon matches are denounced by every true sportsman as a cruel and cowardly amusement All right descendants from Nimrod believe that sport to be ignoble that is not accompanied with a certain amount of difficulty and danger Now if these are some of the mythical elements in the history of this particular sport—if sport it deserves to be called —and if it be debated whether the sport can be traced as far back as Shakespeare's time, his silence on the matter would be as important from the broad and deep impressions of himself as a sportsman, which he has left on his productions When it is, therefore, determined to settle the antiquity of cricket, it is right that Shakespeare should be critically read and examined as to his familiarity with respect to field games, as well as to those within doors, and if nothing flashes upon his inspired pages which bears the remotest semblance to cricket it is fair to conclude that the game—even if it had its birth in the reign of Elizabeth, as seems probable,* but not before the close of Shakespeare's career—emerged from its rudest and most rudimentary state.

The simple assertion that he knew nothing about the game, or, if he did, deemed it too insignificant to be glanced at, even in the hastiest, haughtiest fashion, would not have been disturbed had not the recent attempt, half serious, half jocular, been made by an American to prove, by numerous quotations before alluded to, that cricket was exactly one of the things that Shakespeare was most in the habit of speaking about. If a joke was meant, the fun is too ponderous to be amusing, and if logic was intended, arguments and proofs are lamentably lacking. It has been stated by some theorists that "cricket was not known till a century after Shakespeare's time," but documents recently discovered in unexpected quarters prove incontestably its existence previous to the reign in England of the Stuart dynasty, although in what form no corroborative description has been forthcoming. In order to confute this statement and to show at the same time Shakespeare's knowledge of the game, the clumsy device of introducing Shakespeare as a spiritual medium has been adopted by the Philadelphia critic with a profusion of sentences requiring an immense effort of credulity to suppose. Very few of these sentences, in fact, relate to any game whatever, and but two of them, which point apparently to cricket, will be found on close examination to have nothing at all to do with it. When, in "Love's Labour Lost,"† Costard says of Nathaniel, "He is a marvellous good neighbour, in sooth, and a very good bowler," he alludes to the ancient and popular game of bowls—nothing else. In "Coriolanus,"‡ Menenius asks the citizens, "Where go ye with bats and clubs?" Here, bat means a staff, club, cudgel—a weapon for a serious conflict, not an instrument for a pastime. Menenius Agrippa, in the same scene of the same play, says to the citizens "Make you ready your stiff bats and clubs." Such words as these can have about as much reference to cricket as the previous utterances of Agrippa. In the "Merry Wives of Windsor," Anne Page protests her willingness to be "bowled to death by turnips" rather than an union she detests. It is plain that her discourse is coloured by bowls, not cricket, of which she could never have heard. The other quotations from the same humourist may be at once dismissed, seeing that no reference to cricket or even bowls is contained in them.

He might, however, have discovered additional allusions, not to cricket, but to bowls, if he purposed to indulge in more than a little banter. In "Troilus and Cressida," Pandarus, chiding the coyness of Troilus, says to him, "So, so, rub on, and kiss the mistress" the small bowl aimed at, in the game of bowls or bowling, and generally called the mistress, and sometimes the jack or the block. A curious illustration drawn from bowling is furnished by the fifth scene of the fourth act of "Troilus and Cressida." Ajax, when commanding the trumpeter to sound, exclaims, "Blow, villain, till thy sphered bias cheek outswell the colic of puffed Aquilon."

* See p. 19. † Act V, Scene 2. ‡ Act I, Scene 1.

The expression is intended to denote the swelling out of the cheek like the bias of the bowl. "Was there ever such hard luck? When I kiss'd the jack upon an upcast to be hit away! I had an hundred pound on't! and then a whoreson of jackanapes must take me up for swearing, as if I borrowed mine oaths of him, and might be taken up at his pleasure." To which the reply is, "What got he by that, you have broke his pate with your bowl." In a long speech of the Bastard, in the second scene of the second act of King John, some of the lines derive all their brilliancy and vivacity from the metaphorical introduction of the game of bowls. Few English words have such a vast variety of meanings as *jack*, both in itself and as a portion of compounds. It is often difficult to ascertain in what sense it is understood by Shakespeare; but when in "The Tempest" Stephano says to Caliban, "Monster, your fairy, which you say is a harmless fairy, has done little better than played the jack with us," it is quite reasonable to suppose that the jack in bowls is understood. In Shakespeare's time the keys of a spinet or virginal were called jacks. Richard III, in addressing Buckingham, compares him to a jack, but the language is so enigmatical that the exact sense is somewhat difficult to define. In any case, it may be seen from Shakespeare's allusions at the close of the 16th century to bowls had reference to that game alone, and to force any of his allusions in this particular in the direction of cricket is as dishonest as it is preposterous.

About twenty years after Shakespeare's death, Francis Quarles, in one of his "Emblems," wrote an elaborate treatise on Bowling, from which it is evident that the bowls were then made of what was called Brazil wood. He uses the technical phraseology of the period. From the fullness, the force, and the accuracy of the production, and from the absolute silence of Quarles in regard to cricket, which, if only beginning its scientific development, would have furnished him with an admirable illustration, cricket could not have occupied a similarly important place with bowls.

The task now becomes difficult, because it is so easy. If, instead of being comparatively unknown, cricket obtained in the time of Shakespeare the supremacy of which it now boasts, the illustrations springing from it would have enlivened many of his pages, and then there would only have been the brightest to cull from; but when there has been no growth to glean, nothing can be more wearisome to iterate and re-iterate a negation. Yet to this cricket in its relation to Shakespeare must come.

To bring honour and some life into the realms of negation a glance may be thrown at another game famous at the period chiefly referred to in the foregoing remarks, and though hinted at in other parts of this volume it will not suffer by repetition. From the remotest antiquity, the ball held a foremost place in human amusements. Strutt gives an account of the English ball games in his well-known book of "Sports and Pastimes," an account doubtlessly correct so far as it goes, but cramped rather by the dryness of the epitomizer than by the flow and glow of the historian. It is evident from the rapid delineations of this popular author, and from the chronicles or comments of other writers, that tennis once held the mastery which cricket has since acquired, though it differed from it in being a sort of monopoly for grandees and monarchs. Bowling was the game for the people, tennis for the privileged classes. Strutt endeavours to persuade that cricket sprung from club-ball,* but perchance it would be nearer the truth to believe that cricket blends into a harmonious whole, features and forces both in bowling and tennis, though it has scientific complications and varieties which neither of them possessed.

In "Pericles, Prince of Tyre" there is still a stronger use of tennis as a metaphor. Addressing the fishermen, Pericles speaks of himself as "a man whom both the water and the wind in that best tennis court both made the ball for them to play upon." It is certainly very bold, but not very rational, to call the sea a tennis court. For the sake of the boldness the lack of the naturalness may be pardoned. In the play of "Henry the Fifth" the French ambassadors present to the English monarch some tennis balls, employing the terms used in the game, such as Hazards, Rackets, Courts, &c., evidently in derision. Henry, in a fiery speech, threatens to turn the tennis balls into gunstones.* Tennis assumes but so much of the imposing character as to dispense with the necessity of further examples, and the same deductions may be drawn as in the case of bowls, viz., that the game of cricket was not familiar either to Shakespeare or contemporary writers. So far, in fact, as Shakespeare is concerned, cricket might also be kept in countenance by football; but the latter has enriched his pages by at least one illustration. In the "Comedy of Errors," Dromio of Ephesus asks Adriana, "Am I so round with you as you with me, that, like a football, you do spurn me thus?" Then he adds, "You spurn me hence, and he will spurn me hither. If I last in this service I must case me in leather." Here, then, is one of those quibbles of which the groundlings are so fond, and which, from the peculiarity of his genius, Shakespeare perhaps did not himself dislike. Dromio wishes to speak of himself as round in the sense of spherical, like a football, and as round in the sense of plain spoken. In the latter sense, Malvolio employs this word in "Twelfth Night," where he says to Sir Toby Belcher, "I must be round with you." Again, in "Henry V.," the monarch, when examining some of his soldiers who do not recognise him, says: "I am reproof in some things too round." It is not astonishing that Shakespeare never brings cricket into mention, seeing that in all probability it had never been brought under his notice. Yet there is reason for amazement at his silence in regard to football, a game as ancient as it is vigorous and healthy withal. Football, as one of the simplest of games, is, notwithstanding one to test strength and agility, but it offered Shakespeare nothing suggestive. Molière, justifying his plagiarisms, insists that he took his property wherever he found it. No doubt this is true, and that he seized eagerly the illustrations that were readiest and homeliest; yet, as a sovereign artist, he had a sympathy with universal art, and the more games had the denomination of art the more sure were they of arresting his attention. In football it is generally admitted there is neither art nor science.

Furthermore, it was not so much the attributes of a game as its popular characteristics which in the main attracted Shakespeare, for his allusions to chess,

* Act I., Scene 2.

unquestionably the most scientific of all games, are remarkably few. Chess has always been regarded as ancient as it is scientific, and among the Egyptian hieroglyphics are to be found striking resemblances of a chess board, and it was from India to Europe that the game doubtlessly travelled. The arrangement of the figures on the chess board resemble to some extent the order of battle in an ancient Indian army. The name chess is said to be derived from the Sanscrit *Tschaturanga*, signifying four-bodied, whereby is indicated the Indian army in its customary four divisions. Some of the terms in chess, it is well known, are purely of Oriental origin, for instance, "mate" for the Arabic *matt*, which means dead. From its military nature, chess was just the game to excite Shakespeare's eager and robust martial instincts. Perchance he might have viewed it as a representation too diminutive of glorious war, possibly, too, its movements were too slow for his rapid humour. In "The Taming of the Shrew," when Katharina says to Hortensio, "I pray you, sir, is it your will to make a stale use of me among these rustics." Here is supposed to be a quibbling allusion to the stalemate in chess. On the insulting speech in "King John" of Eleanor to Constance, "Out, insolent, thy bastard shall be a king, that thou mayest be a queen and check the world," Howard Staunton, equally famous as a player of chess, and a commentator on Shakespeare, remarks, "It has been doubted whether Shakespeare, who had cognisance of nearly every sport and pastime of his age, was acquainted with the ancient game of chess." Surely the passages thus far given may and ought to be taken to settle this point decisively. The allusion is obviously to the queen of the chess board, which in this country was inserted in those remarkable forms of language which characterised the 16th century.

As more exciting than chess, cards and dice seem to have interested him in a much greater degree than the more illustrious game. Furthermore, gambling prevailed, and was carried to frightful excesses at the period in question, and it is quite likely that Shakespeare occasionally indulged in what was the fashion of the age. Consequently the more gambling abounded the more was chess kept in subjection. In "Love's Labour Lost," the Princess says, "Since you can cog, I'll play no more with you." Both as a word and as a rub, it has a variety of meanings, but to cog the dice signifies to load them for the purpose of cheating. Hence a person is said to cog when he wheedles, cajoles, or defrauds another. It is one of the many slang phrases which may be found used by poets of all ages and of all time. Among other opprobrious names which, in the "Comedy of Errors," Dromio of Syracuse hurls at Dromio of Ephesus is "Mome," respecting which Staunton discourses with considerable fluency. Sir John Hawkins derives the word from "momon," which signifies the gaming at dice in masquerade, the custom and rule of which is, that a strict silence is to be observed, whatever sum and stakes there may be, but not a word must be spoken. Hence comes the English word "mum" for silence. The Spanish word "moma" has nearly the same meaning as the French "momon." Both are derived from the Greek "Momos" and the Latin "Momus," the god of laughter, who sneered at the other deities. When the Duke in "Twelfth Night" says to the clown, "You can fool no more money out of me at this throw," what suitable metaphor, it may be asked, can it suggest other than that of dice?

In the "Two Gentlemen of Verona," Proteus makes use of the word "noddy" in the double sense of a game of cards and a fool. Upon examination it will be seen noddy resembled in some particulars that now in almost universal use under the name of cribbage. To the many books on Shakespeare, one more at some future time may perhaps be added, viz., a work directed to his illustrations; not those alone suggested by the grand aspects of nature, but those also from archery, fencing, falconry, puppet shows, pyramids, and various other things. In essaying thus far to achieve a small part of such a scheme, one object has been kept steadily in view, in the frequent allusions made to games cognate to cricket and others having no relation thereto. For all those who can be satisfied with argument, enough has been said, and it would be travelling out of the projected orbit to advance farther, but from others infatuated by silly crotchets, it is hardly possible to expect conviction. It is not too much once more to repeat, although Shakespeare acquainted himself with the pastimes and diversions of his age, he had no idea of cricket, and has not in any portions of his writings exhibited even

The baby figure
Of the giant mass of things to come at large.

There were people in Pope's days who declared that Garth did not write his own "Dispensary," and there are people now who maintain that such a man as Shakespeare never lived, and that Sir Walter Scott was not the author of "Waverley." Such fatuists will probably walk the earth to the end of time, both in England and Philadelphia, and among them a few who, without a tittle of evidence, will vainly strive to prove from Shakespeare that cricket was as much known and played in the reign of Elizabeth as in that of Victoria. Not long since an American archæologist proposed a visit to Stratford-on-Avon for the purpose of opening Shakespeare's tomb in order to obtain a photograph of the poet's venerable remains, being of opinion, though dead 260 years, a portrait might be obtained which would enable the current representations of him to be rendered more nearly approximate to a correct likeness. Misguided man! Many instances are on record where, after a similar lapse of time, remains have been found in a surprising degree of preservation, but the admission of external air into their leaden coffins has invariably reduced them in a few minutes to their elemental dust. John has too great a veneration for the wishes of the immortal bard to bow to the caprices of Jonathan. The vehement enthusiasm of which this proposal is fairly illustrative may often be observed in persons whose acquaintance with Shakespeare's works is of the shallowest description.

INDEX.

A

B

C

F

G

I

Z.

PRINTED BY HORACE COX, 346, STRAND, LONDON.

Lightning Source UK Ltd.
Milton Keynes UK
UKOW021945050313

207197UK00005B/87/P